About the Writing Programs Office

Purpose

The Writing Programs Office (WPO) administers the department's undergraduate writing courses (English 104, 203, 210, and 301), supervises GATs and lecturers teaching these courses, oversees the department's computer classrooms, and coordinates a grading program for the English 104 proficiency exam. We are responsible for the quality of teaching in these courses and student access to them. In addition, we handle all matters pertaining to the courses (e.g., textbook selection, plagiarism, instruction, and classroom situations).

Our Goals are:
- To ensure the quality of undergraduate writing courses and
- To prepare departmental graduate students for professions as writers, teachers, and editors

For undergraduate English 104, 203, 210, and 301 students, we offer:
- Information (print and electronic) about writing courses, placing out of English 104, and course substitutions
- Forces for technical writing sections
- Grade appeals
- Mediation services
- Course syllabi
- Electronic resources to supplement writing courses
- Advising for the Professional Writing Certificate and the Society for Technical Communication

For graduate students and lecturers, we provide:
- an extensive professional development program, including pedagogy and technology workshops, mentoring, and videotaping
- print and electronic teaching resources, including the Handbook for Graduate Assistants Teaching English 104, 203, 210, and 301, course syllabi, and teaching resources
- Mediation services
- assistance with book orders
- a library of textbooks, teaching resources, and materials related to composition
- an annual book fair for publishers to showcase new resources
- technical assistance
- opportunities for supervisory, publishing, and grading assignments
- travel and teaching awards

Because writing courses require student participation and teacher evaluation, we do not permit audits.

Office Hours
The Writing Programs Office is open Monday through Friday from 8:00 a.m. until 5:00 p.m. (The office is closed for lunch between noon and 1:00 p.m.)

University Writing Center
If you need more information about writing, contact the University Writing Center, located in the Sterling Evans Library.

Contacting the Writing Programs Office
For additional information, you can:
- Contact us by phone during office hours at (979) 845-9936.
- Come by our office in person, second floor of the Blocker Building, room 224.
- Send us an email at info-wpo@english.tamu.edu.

Writing Programs Office Staff

Director of Writing Programs
Associate Director of Writing
Instructional Technology Coordinator
Graduate Research Assistants

Writing Programs Office Associate

Revision Symbols

ab	39a–d	Abbreviation
ac	37a, 39e	Acronym
adj	20a	Adjective
adv	20b	Adverb
agr		Agreement
	21d	pronoun-antecedent
	22e	subject-verb
APA	11c–d	APA documentation
ᐺ	33	Apostrophe
arg	7	Argument
awk		Awkward
cap	37	Capital
CMS	11e–f	CMS documentation
coh		Coherence
	20e–f	modifiers
	3c	paragraphs
:	35d	Colon
,	31	Comma
cs	19	Comma splice
con	30	Conciseness
coor	24b	Coordination
COS	11i	COS documentation
crit	1a–f	Critical reading and writing
CSE/CBE	11g–h	CSE/CBE documentation
—	35e	Dash
⸜		Delete
dev		Development
	2e	essays
	2d	paragraphs
. . .	35h	Ellipsis points
emp	26	Emphasis
ex	29	Exactness
!	35c	Exclamation point
frag	18	Fragment
fs	19	Fused sentence
hy	36f	Hyphenation
id	29c	Idiom
ital	38	Italics

log	7h–i	Logic
lc		Lowercase
mm	20e–f	Misplaced modifier
MLA	11a–b	MLA documentation
n	39f–g	Number
∧		Omission
¶		Paragraph
//	25	Parallelism
( )	35f	Parentheses
.	35a	Period
pl		Plural
pred	23d	Predication
pro	21	Pronoun
?	35b	Question mark
" "	34	Quotation marks
red	30a(1)	Redundant
ref	21e	Reference
rep	26e, 30c	Repetition
rev	3	Revision
;	32	Semicolon
sg		Singular
/	35i	Slash
sp	36a–e	Spelling
sub	24a–c	Subordination
[ ]	35g	Square brackets
t	22b	Tense
trans	3d	Transition
∿		Transpose
u		Unity
	3c	paragraph
	23	sentence
⊙		Unnecessary comma
usg	28, Glossary of Usage	Usage
var	27	Variety
vb	22	Verb
wc	28c–d, 29a–c	Word choice
w	30a–b	Wordiness
ww		Wrong word

The Aggie Writer's Harbrace Handbook

Cheryl Glenn | Robert Keith Miller | Suzanne Strobeck Webb | Loretta Gray

CENGAGE
Learning·

Australia • Brazil • Japan • Korea • Mexico • Singapore • Spain • United Kingdom • United States

CENGAGE
Learning™

The Aggie Writer's Harbrace Handbook

Cheryl Glenn | Robert Keith Miller |
Suzanne Strobeck Webb | Loretta Gray

Executive Editors:
Michele Baird

Maureen Staudt

Michael Stranz

Project Development Manager:
Linda deStefano

Senior Marketing Coordinators:
Sara Mercurio

Lindsay Shapiro

Production/Manufacturing Manager:
Donna M. Brown

PreMedia Services Supervisor:
Rebecca A. Walker

Rights & Permissions Specialist:
Kalina Hintz

Cover Image:
Getty Images*

* Unless otherwise noted, all cover images used
by Custom Solutions, a part of Cengage Learning,
have been supplied courtesy of Getty Images with
the exception of the Earthview cover image, which
has been supplied by the National Aeronautics
and Space Administration (NASA).

For product information and technology assistance, contact us at
Cengage Learning Customer & Sales Support, 1-800-354-9706

For permission to use material from this text or product,
submit all requests online at **cengage.com/permissions**
Further permissions questions can be emailed to
permissionrequest@cengage.com

ISBN-13: 978-1-413-02663-4

ISBN-10: 1-413-02663-X

Cengage Learning
5191 Natorp Boulevard
Mason, Ohio 45040
USA

Cengage Learning is a leading provider of customized learning solutions with
office locations around the globe, including Singapore, the United Kingdom,
Australia, Mexico, Brazil, and Japan. Locate your local office at:
international.cengage.com/region

Cengage Learning products are represented in Canada by Nelson Education, Ltd.

For your lifelong learning solutions, visit **custom.cengage.com**

Visit our corporate website at **cengage.com**

Printed in the United States of America

Contents

Chapter 8 — Finding Sources Online, in Print, and in the Field 223 — **find**

Chapter 9 — Evaluating Sources Online and in Print 248 — **eval**

Chapter 10 — Using Sources Responsibly 264 — **src**

G Grammar

S Effective Sentences

Chapter 24 Subordination and Coordination 612 **sub/coor**

Chapter 25 Parallelism 621 **//**

Chapter 26 Emphasis 628 **emp**

D Diction

P Punctuation

M Mechanics

Preface

What are the origins of first-year writing handbooks?

The first writing handbook of rules and conventions was Edwin A. Abbott's 1874 *How to Write Clearly.* Abbott's aim was to help his classics students at the City of London School produce more fluent English translations of their Greek and Latin lessons, and his handbook was the first college-level text to equate clear writing with the mastery of specific rules, fifty-six of them, to be precise. In the United States, *How to Write Clearly* became wildly popular—not in classics, but in English composition courses, because it provided easy-to-use error-based rules for writers.

With the 1862 Morrill Act, the federal government provided funding for the establishment of Mechanical and Agricultural Colleges (which later became the major state universities), and the university population in the United States exploded. Higher education was no longer reserved for the sons and daughters of the upper classes. College writing classes suddenly expanded from thirty to one hundred students—a flood of students who needed to learn how to write—and teachers desperately sought ways to handle the paper load of weekly themes. *How to Write Clearly,* along with a number of other popular rule-governed and exercise-based handbooks, tried to meet this need. The handbook had established itself as the *sine qua non* of writing instruction.

How did the *Harbrace Handbook* get started?

The book you have in your hands is not the first handbook, but, since 1941, it has served as the paradigm for all the successful handbooks that followed. In the 1930s, John C. Hodges obtained federal funding to support his study of the frequency of errors in college students' essays. Hodges, an English professor at the University of Tennessee, collected some twenty thousand student papers that had been marked by sixteen different professors of rhetoric from all over the United States. Then, working with a cadre of graduate students, he counted and analyzed the errors in those papers, creating a taxonomy that he used to organize the 1941 *Harbrace Handbook of English* into thirty-five sections.

A masterpiece of organized minimalism, easily accessible to teachers and students alike, the *Harbrace Handbook of English* captured the attention of both groups, as it responded to their needs in a material way. In the preface to that first edition, Hodges wrote:

> The *Harbrace Handbook of English* is a guide to the correction of student themes and also a text for use in class. It presents well-known subject matter in an easily usable form, and thus lightens the instructor's task of grading papers. The book contains only thirty-five major sections. To determine the sections actually needed (and consequently the numbers to appear in the correction chart), twenty thousand freshman themes were tabulated according to the corrections by sixteen instructors.

What makes *The Writer's Harbrace Handbook* so good?

Firmly established as the granddaddy of all handbooks, the *Harbrace Handbook of English* evolved into *The Writer's Harbrace Handbook,* Second Edition, which continues the Hodges tradition of up-to-date reliability and practicality. Like all of its predecessors, this edition of *The Writer's Harbrace Handbook* responds to the material needs of teachers and students. Still providing teachers with a simplified method for marking student papers, this handbook also gives both teachers and students the ease of reference and attention to detail that have made the Harbrace handbooks the standard of reliability. Without diminishing its longstanding commitment to helping students make the best decisions in terms of grammar, style, punctuation, and mechanics, this "writing first" handbook also guides them as they develop their abilities as writers. Therefore, *The Writer's Harbrace Handbook* provides priorities for any writing course, on any topic of composition.

What's new about this edition?

This edition differs from the previous one in two readily apparent ways: a cleaner, clearer design and a larger trim size. These physical changes are not superficial, however; together, they enhance the handbook's overall accessibility and signal substantive changes in content. So maybe you *can* tell a book by its cover!

- **Emphasis on the Rhetorical Situation** Perhaps the most significant substantive change is this edition's attention to the rhetorical situation—to the writer, the audience, the message, the context, and the exigence (the specific reason for writing). Decisions about the most effective information to include, the best arrangement of that information, and the most appropriate language to use all grow out of an understanding of the rhetorical situation.

  Chapter 1, "Reading and Writing Critically," lays a rhetorical foundation that resonates throughout all of the writing chapters and many of the grammar chapters that follow. When students are guided by the rhetorical situation, they can read and write more effectively and efficiently, whether in an English class, a science course, or the workplace.

- **Revamped Chapters** Attention to the rhetorical situation has invigorated all of the writing chapters, whether totally revamped or completely new, for the contemporary rhetorical situation includes writing with technology and writing across the disciplines. The following chapters have been thoroughly revised in light of contemporary composition pedagogy, while maintaining those aspects of traditional rhetorical theory that are still widely respected.

  Chapter 2, "Planning and Drafting Essays," guides students through the process of finding appropriate topics, writing clear thesis statements, arranging their ideas, and developing initial drafts. At every step of the way, students are encouraged to make decisions based on their audience and their purpose for writing.

  Chapter 3, "Revising and Editing Essays," helps students understand the importance of revising their written work—of seeing it again—in terms of the overall rhetorical situation. Besides emphasizing editing and proofreading, this chapter encourages students to share their work with peers (whether fellow students or colleagues) and teaches them how to respond productively to the writing of others.

Chapter 6, "E-designing," formerly titled "Document Design," has been refocused to emphasize writing for the Web. Making liberal use of visuals, this chapter helps students understand that principles of good design are rhetorical and can be applied to produce effective, attractive Web pages, easy-to-read email messages, and final copy for paper documents.

Chapter 7, "Writing Arguments," covers the basics found in any good argument chapter: establishing an arguable statement, distinguishing between fact and opinion, understanding a Toulmin argument, and recognizing rhetorical fallacies. But, in this edition, the chapter has been expanded to address different kinds of arguments: deliberative *(What is the best course of action?)* and judicial *(What happened?)*, as well as invitational *(I want to explain my point of view so that you understand—and then I'd like to understand your point of view).*

- **New Technology Chapters** Two new chapters provide a rhetorical lens students can use for composing and researching electronically, whether on the Web, through email and Listservs, or via electronic databases and cataloguing systems.

  Chapter 5, "E-writing," helps students understand how the rhetorical situation shapes electronic communication. Beginning with composing for the Web, including the effective use of hyperlinks, this chapter highlights the role of audience, purpose, and context in electronic communication while explaining netiquette, demystifying online discussion groups (both synchronous and asynchronous), and introducing online courseware and collaboration tools.

  Chapter 9, "Evaluating Sources Online and in Print," provides guidelines for assessing the credibility of a text by determining the credentials of its author(s) and publisher (or sponsoring organization). Because students regularly use the Web for research, an entire section is devoted to the process of evaluating the timeliness, content, and credibility of Web sites. Finally, this chapter explains the difference between writing that is biased and writing that is imbued with committed values.

- **New Writing-across-the-Curriculum Chapters** Because rhetorical situations exist across the disciplines and in the workplace—not just in first-year writing classes—this edition has three new chapters that serve to complement Chapter 13, "Writing to Interpret Literature."

Chapter 12, "Writing Academic Discourse," looks at how disciplinary cultures differ with respect to what they consider evidence to be, how they use evidence, their language and writing style, and their documents and formats. This chapter also introduces students to the concepts of qualitative and quantitative evidence and to thick and thin description.

Chapter 14, "Writing in the Social and Natural Sciences," discusses the scientific method and style and describes formats for observation reports, applications of theory, reviews of research, and library research reports. Empirical evidence and replicability are also explained.

Chapter 15, "Writing in Business," seeks to help students with the transition from academic writing to workplace writing by showing a model business proposal and a model grant proposal. The sample letter of application and résumé are linked to the business proposal.

- **Thoroughly Revised Grammar, Mechanics, and Punctuation Chapters** have new exercises. Nearly all of the exercises have been replaced or rewritten as continuous discourse on lively and informative topics. Many examples have been replaced with new ones germane to students and the problems they often encounter in their writing.

  Chapter 16, "Sentence Essentials," and Chapter 17, "Phrases and Clauses," introduce grammar terms and topics that help students understand the rhetorical choices they make when they write sentences. These chapters thus prepare students to craft effective sentences as well as to revise common errors.

  Chapter 22, "Verbs," provides essential information not only on the forms of verbs but also on their use. Students learn that even their choice of tense or voice affects the meaning their writing expresses.

- **Expanded Style Guides for Researched Writing** To reinforce our commitment to writing across the disciplines and in the workplace, we have expanded our style guides to include *The Chicago Manual of Style* (CMS), *Scientific Style and Format: The CBE Manual for Authors, Editors, and Publishers* (CSE/CBE), and *The Columbia Guide to Online Style* (COS). (*The Writer's Harbrace Handbook* itself is edited according to *The Chicago Manual of Style,* which is the style guide used by

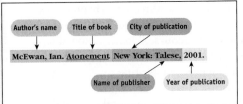

most publishers.) Of course, we maintain our thorough coverage of the style guidelines from the Modern Language Association (MLA) and the American Psychological Association (APA). MLA coverage includes updates from the latest edition (2003) of the *MLA Handbook for Writers of Research Papers.* In addition, all explanations of citations have an easy-to-use directory and color-edged pages to help students find exactly the type of citation they are looking for in the style guide they are using. And each type of citation (book, article, or computer source) is represented visually so that students may better understand its major components and how they are arranged.

■ **New Student Papers (and an emphasis on student writing)** This edition features new student papers for nearly all of the writing chapters. In chapters 2 and 3, you'll find a new student essay on balancing school and work, "Working toward a Degree." The ideas for the essay originate in brainstorming and clustering, develop through several drafts that include a peer-reviewed version, and come to fruition as a strong example of student writing. We've also included new student papers for each of the style guides (MLA, APA, CMS, and CSE/CBE). The new chapters on writing in the disciplines feature a lab report, a field report, a grant proposal, and a business plan—all written by students. And three of the student papers illuminate different angles on coffee culture, a topic we feel is relevant to students' lives: "Starbucks in Vienna: Coffee Cultures at a Crossroads" appears as the MLA paper; "Roxy's Coffee Shop," as the business plan; and "Just Coffee: A Proposal in the Classical Arrangement," as a sample argument.

■ **"Beyond the Rule" Boxes** To help all students—whether English is their native, second, or third language—we've included "Beyond the Rule" boxes, which will

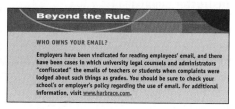

Beyond the Rule

WHO OWNS YOUR EMAIL?

Employers have been vindicated for reading employees' email, and there have been cases in which university legal counsels and administrators "confiscated" the emails of teachers or students when complaints were lodged about such things as grades. You should be sure to check your school's or employer's policy regarding the use of email. For additional information, visit www.harbrace.com.

enrich students' understanding of the rules and conventions that substantiate the effectiveness of their rhetorical choices. The boxes link directly to our new Web site, **www.harbrace.com**, and provide additional information on quirks of grammar, punctuation, and mechanics, rules, and conventions. These boxes also suggest alternative rhetorical choices for writing.

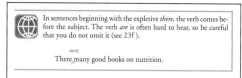

Although grammar checkers identify many comma splices and some fused sentences, they routinely miss many others. In fact, a grammar checker could not reliably identify the comma splices and fused sentences in this chapter. For example, the grammar checker failed to identify any of the comma splices in exercise 5 on page 526. See Using a Grammar Checker on page 468.

■ **Computer Boxes** To support students' facility in all kinds of electronic writing, we've included numerous computer boxes that provide useful information about working with electronic media. The use of technology in writing is integrated throughout the handbook.

■ **Globe Boxes** The number of English-as-a-global-language boxes has doubled since the last edition. These boxes identify

In sentences beginning with the expletive *there,* the verb comes before the subject. The verb *are* is often hard to hear, so be careful that you do not omit it (see 23f).

are
There~many good books on nutrition.

common areas of confusion caused by native language differences, but they also address concerns that may arise for all students as they draft, revise, and edit their work.

Supplements

Instructor Supplements

Instructor's Flex-Files

Flex-Files are designed to give you maximum flexibility in planning and customizing your course. Providing an abundance of instructor materials, the Flex-Files consist of two main sections. "Part One: Questions for Teachers" raises a variety of pedagogical questions (and gives possible solutions) for you to consider in teaching your course with this handbook. "Part Two: Sample Syllabi and Activities" offers a sample syllabus with possible assignments for a semester-long course and a sample syllabus with possible assignments for a quarter-long course. Additionally, this section contains sample in-class collaborative learning activities, technology-oriented activities, and critical thinking and writing activities. The Flex-Files also include the following supplementary materials: (1) an ESL insert aimed at helping mainstream instructors teach writing effectively to their ESL students, (2) an insert on disability issues as they relate to teaching first-year composition, (3) the Answer Key for the exercises in the handbook, and (4) the Answer Key for the College Workbook.

Diagnostic Test Package

Built into Thomson Learning's BCA (Thomson Learning's grade book), the Diagnostic Test Package includes online testing correlated to this handbook. This package contains sample TASP and CLAST tests for instructors to deliver in a lab, at home, or in the class; practice versions of the TASP and CLAST tests for students; and general diagnostic tests designed to help instructors and programs place students in the appropriate writing course.

Instructor's Correction Chart

To make marking your students' papers easier, you can prop up on your desk the oversized, laminated chart listing all of the sections of the handbook and showing the editing symbols correlated to them.

Student Supplements

The Writer's Harbrace Handbook CD-ROM

A fully interactive version of the handbook, this CD-ROM includes over 200 animated examples of the most important choices and conventions for writers. Interactive versions of all the handbook's exercises are tied into a course management system and, where appropriate, automatically graded. In addition, the CD-ROM contains several other useful resources.

Electronic "Beyond the Rule" Resources Designed to guide students as they make rhetorical choices in the context of ever-evolving rules for standardized English, the "Beyond the Rule" boxes address usage conventions that are in flux and provide additional information on points of writing and grammar. The electronic materials direct students to additional online resources as well as to electronic exercises designed to help them identify the best language choice among several options, according to their rhetorical situation.

Model Student Paper Library Animated and interactive as they move through the writing process, four student papers demonstrate proper use of MLA, APA, CMS, and CSE/CBE citation and documentation styles, respectively. The model student paper library also provides interactive examples of the research process and online research activities. In addition, this library contains student papers demonstrating each of the rhetorical methods as well as models of arguments based on Aristotelian, Rogerian, and Toulmin approaches.

The Writer's Harbrace Handbook Web Site

The free companion Web site provides links, sample syllabi, quizzing and testing, sample paper library, and other student and instructor resources.

Heinle InSite

Heinle
InSite
For Writing and Research™

Heinle InSite is an online writing resource for students, instructors, and program administrators. Within one integrated program, students can submit papers, review and respond to peers' papers, and work on writing and grammar problems by linking directly to online handbook content. As a component of InSite's paper-portfolio service, an "originality" checker enables students to check their own drafts for properly quoted and paraphrased material prior to final submission. Additionally, students can conduct online research with access to InfoTrac® College Edition, a database of more than 3,800 scholarly and popular sources with more than 10 million articles. Instructors using InSite can assign, view, and grade student papers and peer reviews and track all grades with a built-in course management system. Program administrators can view and track student progress from an individual-to a system-wide level.

InfoTrac® College Edition

Indispensable to writers of research papers, InfoTrac® College Edition offers students around-the-clock access to a database of more than 3,800 scholarly and popular sources with more than 10 million articles, providing information on almost any topic.

The Resourceful Reader, Sixth Edition

Offering a balance of classroom favorites and seldom- or never-before-reprinted pieces, *The Resourceful Reader* is a rhetorically arranged reader that has been completely reshaped in the sixth edition to be in line with current rhetorical theory. The pedagogical apparatus accompanying each reading addresses global issues of meaning, purpose, audience, and rhetorical strategy as well as local issues of language, style, grammar, punctuation, and mechanics. An instructor's manual accompanies the reader.

Writer's Resources CD-ROM, Version 2.0

This CD-ROM has more than 4,500 interactive exercises and activities, including many with animation and audio clips. A new section covers all stages of the writing process from prewriting to the final draft. Four student peers provide commentary on the writing process as they proceed through each stage. In addition, through the word-processing application being used by the student, the CD-ROM can launch over a hundred customized writing templates that guide the user though writing exercises in sentence, paragraph, and essay creation. More than an electronic exercise program, Writer's Resources helps students develop the skills necessary for choosing effective words, writing structurally balanced sentences, and developing detailed paragraphs as well as for writing a summary, an analysis, and an argumentative essay.

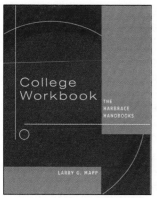

College Workbook

Twenty-seven units in five parts correspond to chapters of the handbook and cover grammar, punctuation, usage, style, and writing. This printed workbook combines exercises with clear examples and explanations that supplement the information and exercises found in the handbook.

Think About Editing: An ESL Guide

A self-editing manual for ESL writers, *Think About Editing* is designed to help intermediate to advanced students edit their writing to correct grammar, structure, and usage. The manual is prefaced with a correlation guide that links its units to corresponding sections in *The Writer's Harbrace Handbook.*

Dictionaries

The following dictionaries are available for a nominal price when bundled with the handbook: *The Merriam-Webster Dictionary; Merriam-Webster's Collegiate Dictionary,* Eleventh Edition; and *Heinle's Newbury House Dictionary of American English with Integrated Thesaurus.* The latter was created especially for ESL students.

Acknowledgments

Who wrote this handbook?

John C. Hodges carried forward his vision of a useful handbook for many editions of the *Harbrace Handbook*—and his influence continues with every edition. With the fifth edition, he was assisted by Mary E. Whitten (North Texas State University—now University of North Texas), who guided the book from the sixth through the tenth editions. Suzanne S. Webb (Texas Woman's University) joined the handbook on the tenth edition to enhance its rhetorical elements and add a section on logical thinking. In the eleventh edition, Winifred Bryan Horner (Texas Christian University) and Robert K. Miller (University of St. Thomas) joined the team, so that Win could add her rhetorical expertise and Bob could rework the research paper chapter.

The twelfth, thirteenth, and fourteenth editions profited from the three-person team of Sue, Win, and Bob, with remarkable results. Three new chapters, "Writing Arguments," "Reading and Thinking Critically," and "Writing under Pressure," were included in the handbook. By the fourteenth edition, the *Harbrace Handbook* appeared in three different versions to meet the growing diversity of handbook users: *Hodges' Harbrace Handbook* continued to emphasize grammar first, while *The Writer's Harbrace Handbook* and *The Writer's Harbrace Handbook,* Brief Edition, as their titles suggest, gave primary emphasis to writing, thereby rounding out the family of Harbrace handbooks.

With Win's retirement, rhetoric and composition specialist Cheryl Glenn (The Pennsylvania State University) and linguist Loretta Gray (Central Washington University) joined Sue and Bob to produce what we all hope is the best edition so far.

Who helped?

The fifteenth edition of this handbook and the other two versions took shape during a two-day meeting in Boston with members of the Heinle editorial staff. For their collective ideas, enthusiasm, support, and wise counsel, we remain grateful. In particular, we thank Michael Rosenberg, Publisher, whose pride in the Harbrace family of handbooks never wavered as he supported a new author team and its new ideas through many months of work. We're all grateful to Dickson Musslewhite, Acquisitions Editor, who worked tirelessly to put together our highly successful team—and then tapped his seemingly endless good humor to put up with each of us! On a number of occasions, he plied a tired author team with more ideas and, therefore, more work, but he always tempered his direction with the goodwill and good sense that characterize the best of rhetors. Stephen Marsi, Editorial Assistant, kept track of all our travels and expenses—and, most important, our reimbursements—for which we are grateful. The indispensable Katrina Byrd, Marketing Manager, advised us on ways to clarify the handbook's classic and new features; Lianne Ames, Production Editor, helped to bring this huge project to completion. Jane Hoover carried out the copyediting, typemarking, and proofreading with style and care. And Linda Beaupre gave the book its clear and aesthetically pleasing interior design and a cover that travels effortlessly into the twenty-first century. Without the help and support of these amazingly imaginative people, we simply could not have produced *The Writer's Harbrace Handbook*.

But it is Michell Phifer, Senior Development Editor Extraordinaire, to whom we each owe a special thanks. A scrupulously careful editor—and our constant intellectual companion—Michell successfully managed to herd the likes of us four academics. On a daily or often a twice- or thrice-daily basis, she prodded our thinking about each chapter and about the project as a whole, massaged our sometimes convoluted writing and thinking into accessible prose, nudged us to improve what we thought were good (but clearly not good enough) exercises, and challenged us to locate more effective examples of professional and student writing. Michell was always on our team and guided our collaboration until the very last minute, until the presses rolled.

The successful completion of our work would not have been possible without the research assistance of Keith Gibson and the clerical help of Danielle Luzzo, both at The Pennsylvania State University. At the University of St. Thomas, Andy Leet and Jo Young provided efficient and valuable technical assistance on many occasions. In addition, this project benefited from the support and encouragement of those overseeing our university schedules and workloads: Patsy Callaghan, Chair of the Department of English, and Liahna Armstrong, Dean of Arts and Humanities, both at Central Washington University; Michael Mikolajczak, Chair of the Department of English at the University of St. Thomas; and Hugh Burns, Chair of English, Speech, and Foreign Languages at Texas

Woman's University. Lou Thompson, Dene Grigar, and Rae Murphy of Texas Woman's University offered support and suggestions.

We would also like to thank the students whose indefatigable efforts went into the model student papers new to this edition: Melissa Schraeder and Nicole Hester, The Pennsylvania State University; Laura Klocke, Andy Pieper, Nikki Krzmarzick, and Geoffrey Rutledge, University of St. Thomas; Mike Demmon, University of Nevada, Reno; and Heather Jensen, Roxanne Kirkwood, and Alicia Obaldo, Texas Woman's University. Aaron Munk, Seattle University, created the student Web site. For writing and revising—and revising some more—we remain indebted to you. After all, good student writing, the kind that you have produced, is what this book is all about.

And we cannot forget our valued and amazingly imaginative colleague, Robert Yagelski at The State University of New York at Albany, who served as our technology consultant for this entire project. A consummate professional, Bob helped us envision chapter 5, "E-writing," and provided more good information than we could possibly use for each of the computer boxes.

Heartfelt appreciation is also due another consummate professional, Patrick Bizzaro, East Carolina University, who helped us realize the writing-across-the-curriculum chapters and kept us on track with them. We are the beneficiaries of his generosity, his good-humored and tireless reading and rereading, and his vast understanding of the subject.

We want to thank those colleagues who reviewed *The Writer's Harbrace Handbook* throughout the course of its development. Their astute comments, frank responses, and thoughtful suggestions helped shape what is the final version—until the next edition. We thank them for taking the time out of their already busy schedules to help us.

Specialty Reviewers

For writing across the curriculum, Patrick Bizzaro, *East Carolina University,* and Christopher Thaiss, *George Mason University*; for technology and composition, Samantha Blackmon, *Purdue University,* and Rebecca Rickley, *Texas Tech University*; for library research, Marianne Hageman, *University of St. Thomas*; for grammar, Martha Kolln, *The Pennsylvania*

State University; for argumentation, Marie Secor, *The Pennsylvania State University*; for ESL, Tony Silva, *Purdue University*; and for research, Helen Schwartz, *Indiana University–Purdue University Indianapolis*

Handbook Reviewers

Stephen Calatrello, *Calhoun Community College;* Janice Cooke, *University of New Orleans;* Cecile deRocher, *Georgia State University;* Donna Gessell, *North Georgia College and State University;* Judith Hanley, *Wilbur Wright College;* David Mulry, *Odessa College;* James Richardson, *Morehouse College;* David Rieder, *University of Texas at Arlington;* Paula Ross, *Gadsden State Community College;* and Michael Sirmons, *Austin Community College*

Focus Group Participants

Victoria Anderson and Joseph Janangelo, *Loyola University;* Vinson Burdette, *Tri-County Technical College;* Maria Clayton, *Middle Tennessee State University;* Michelle Eble and Lynée Gaillet, *Georgia State University;* Gabi Gautreaux and Kim McDonald, *University of New Orleans;* Karen Grossaint, *Regis University;* Elizabeth Howells, *Armstrong Atlantic State University;* John Hyman, *American University;* Trish Jenkins, *University of Alaska-Anchorage;* Raymonda Johnson, *Harold Washington College;* Peggy Jolly, *University of Alabama at Birmingham;* Sandee McGlaun and Linda Williams, *North Georgia College and State University;* and Patricia Webb, *Arizona State University*

Manuscript Reviewers

Sue Beebe and Michael Hennessy, *Southwest Texas State University;* Suzanne Bordelon, *San Diego State University;* Lauren Coulter, *University of Tennessee at Chattanooga*; James Crawford, *Walters State Community College;* Peter England, *Blinn College;* Cynthia Haynes, *University of Texas at Dallas;* Patricia Lonchar, *University of the Incarnate Word;* Rebecca Marez, *Del Mar College;* Cindy Moore, *St. Cloud State University;* Fiona Paton, *The State University of New York at New Paltz;* Chere Peguesse, *Valdosta State University;* Deborah Coxwell Teague, *Florida State University*; Freddy Thomas, *Virginia State University;* Donna Winchell, *Clemson University*

Finally, we are grateful to our friends and families. Although our faces toward the screen meant our backs toward you, you were never far from our thoughts. After all, without you, our work would be neither possible nor worthwhile.

To all of you reading this preface and using or considering using this handbook for the first time, know that we're grateful to you, too. In fact, if you have advice for how we might improve the next edition or if we can help you in any way, write us c/o Heinle, English Editorial Department, 25 Thomson Place, Boston, MA 02210.

Cheryl Glenn
Robert Miller
Suzanne Webb
Loretta Gray

JUNE 2003

Writing

1 Reading and Writing Critically

You read and write critically every day—even if you don't realize it. You read accounts of sporting events to analyze why one team won—or lost; you read leases to see if you can abide by the terms; you write up insurance information to save as much money as possible; you take notes from Web sites on international affairs to write a summary for your public service organization. In short, every day you employ many of the same reading and writing strategies you need to succeed in college. Reading and writing critically—whether done in or out of school—overlap in a number of important ways, all of which have to do with actively engaging a text by determining the author's credibility, purpose, intended audience, and context. In addition, reading and writing critically offer you the opportunity to evaluate key points and the amount of support each merits, what needs to be said, and what is best or purposefully left unsaid. When you *read* critically, you read more efficiently and effectively—and you can talk knowledgeably about what you've read. When you *write* critically, you improve your understanding of what you've read; you generate new ideas and communicate them clearly and concisely to your audience.

Critical writing takes many forms, some of which are discussed in this handbook:

- an essay from personal experience (**3h**),
- an argument from personal experience and research (**7j**),
- an argument based on research (**8, 11b, 13–15**),
- an interpretation of a literary text (**13g**),
- a lab report and a field report (**14b–d**),
- a Web page for an organization (**6d**),
- a résumé (**15c**), and
- a business letter, a business plan, a grant proposal (**15a–b, 15e**).

Whatever form it takes, critical writing (like critical reading) involves a process of active engagement, an ability to interact with a text, step by step, until it fulfills its purpose, transferring its meaning to its audience.

This chapter, then, explains reading and writing as processes involving a series of sometimes overlapping steps (**1a**), processes that can help you

- understand the rhetorical situation (**1b**),
- read in terms of the rhetorical situation (**1c**),
- distinguish between content and your personal response to a text (**1d**),
- write in terms of the rhetorical situation (**1e**),
- understand the rhetorical situation of each course (**1f**), and
- take advantage of academic support services (**1g**).

1a Reading and writing are best approached as processes.

It's easier to read and write if you break each of these intellectual tasks into components you can undertake one at a time. For example, when reading critically, you can begin by previewing a text, by reading the author's name and the title, then skimming the entire text to consider what you already know about the author and the subject and what you can expect from the reading itself (see **1c**); you can then read for content (**1d(1)**), noting your personal responses and experiences (**1d(2)**). You can also reread certain difficult paragraphs before continuing your first reading; then, after your first reading, you can go back and reread the entire text so that you understand it more fully.

FEATURES OF THE READING PROCESS

Previewing

Skim through the reading; get a sense of how the information is organized and what the reading consists of. Assess what the reading demands of you in terms of time, effort, and previous knowledge (see **1c**).

Reading for Content

Determine who the author is and what you already know about him or her. Then determine what the author wants to communicate—to whom and for what specific purpose. As you read, note the author's major points, underlining or highlighting them. Talk back to the text itself as though you were carrying on a conversation with the author: Write in the margins and annotate key passages whenever you have something to say or a question to pose (see **1d(1)**).

(Continued on page 4)

(Continued from page 3)

Noting Your Personal Response

Try to determine what the author thinks and why he or she holds that opinion. Then determine what *you* think and why *you* hold your opinion. In other words, what information do you agree or disagree with—and why? What passages brought to mind your own experience or expertise? What have you learned from this reading? What confuses you about this reading? What would you like to know more about (see 1d(2))?

Rereading

Check your understanding of the content. Consider why the author chose the title and how he or she presented the material to an audience; determine the specific purpose; and note how the information is organized and how supporting ideas are developed (see 1d(1), 2c–d, and 6c).

Effective readers and writers know that they cannot do everything at once. They simply cannot preview, skim, analyze, and respond simultaneously; nor can they generate and organize ideas and simultaneously develop them with clarity and precision. Reading and writing are processes that are different every time. Despite the infinite variations of the writing process, writing usually involves four basic stages.

STAGES OF THE WRITING PROCESS

Prewriting

If you are responding to a specific assignment, you need to understand what exactly your teacher or supervisor wants you to do: narrate, describe, explain, show, report, analyze, compare/contrast, or define (see 2e). You also need a sense of the audience—is it the teacher or supervisor, your classmates or colleagues, or some other person or group? Are you being asked to respond to a particular reading? If so, be sure to read critically first (see 1c–d); then determine which passage in the reading stimulated or troubled you. That passage might provide a starting place for you to think about your topic. Talk with others involved with the assignment about your initial idea for writing. Keep notes as your thinking and topic evolve. Make a list of the ways you might develop your topic. Try keeping a journal, freewriting, listing, clustering, or questioning as a way to generate more ideas (see 2a). In short, do whatever it takes to energize your thinking and jump start your writing.

Drafting

Quickly write down your ideas, writing as much as you can. If unexpected and seemingly unrelated ideas pop into your head as you draft, write those down, too. Don't worry about being perfect or staying on topic. The more ideas you get down on paper, the more options you'll have as you begin to organize, clarify your thesis and purpose for writing, and revise. You'll benefit from an extensive and very rough draft. It's progress you're after at this stage, not perfection.

Revising

Now is the time to focus your purpose for writing, establish a clear thesis statement (see 2b), and organize your ideas toward those ends (2c). You might find that a rough outline can help you here (2c(2)). On a computer, you can easily cut, paste, delete, and add in order to improve your focus and development. This is the time to start stabilizing the overall structure of your essay as well as the structure of the paragraphs (2d). It's also the time to reconsider your introduction and conclusion (3b) and ask a peer who is working on the same assignment to respond to what you've written (3e). As you work through this stage, remember that revising means producing another draft for further revision and editing.

Editing

As you prepare your piece of writing for final submission, you'll want to concentrate on its surface features: punctuation, spelling, and Standardized English (see 3g). Reading your writing aloud to yourself is one of the best ways to discover which sentence structures and word choices could be improved. Another good way to catch surface errors is to trade essays with someone working on the same assignment and read each other's work.

Chapters 2 and 3 provide detailed discussions of writing as a process; relevant additional information can be found in chapters 12 through 15.

Exercise 1

Using "Stages of the Writing Process" (above) to stimulate your thinking, compose a one-page description of the process you usually employ when approaching a piece of writing assigned by a teacher or supervisor. Be sure to consider what you already do well and what you might improve.

1b | Critical readers and effective writers understand the rhetorical situation.

Critical readers and effective writers have a clear sense of the **rhetorical situation,** that is, the context for which they are interpreting a reading or creating a piece of writing. Components of the rhetorical situation are the sender (or writer), the receiver (intended audience or reader), the message itself, and the context (see figure 1.1). The sender's purpose arises out of the particular rhetorical situation. As you read and write, then, you'll want to consider the following issues:

- The nature and the receptiveness of the intended **audience,** whoever will be reading the piece of writing
- The author's relationship with that audience, the writer's **credibility** as an author
- The particular need or situation that inspires this piece of writing, also called the **exigence**
- The author's goal, or **purpose,** what the author hopes to achieve in a piece of writing
- The **message,** the contents and delivery of the piece of writing itself
- Whatever else (opposing or supporting views) has already been said on the subject, part of the **context.** When and where (and through what medium) the exchange between writer and reader takes place are also part of the context.

Figure 1.1. The rhetorical situation.

The more you read and write—and the more you preview a written text—the more you'll see that author, purpose, audience, and context are interdependent: A writer's purpose must be appropriate for the intended audience and the context; the audience might change according to the writer's purpose or context; the context affects the audience and the writer's purpose (see 1e).

| 1c | **Critical readers preview a text to understand its rhetorical situation.** |

In order to understand a text fully, critical readers often **preview** it, determining ahead of time the features of its rhetorical situation (author, audience, exigence, purpose, and context) as well as how difficult the text will be to understand, how interesting it is, and what they are likely to learn from it. By previewing, you assess the text's difficulty, interest, and informativeness—an assessment that will improve your reading comprehension.

You preview reading all the time—when you thumb through a newspaper or a magazine looking for articles that stir your interest. Sometimes a simple preview helps you identify a topic you're interested in reading more about; sometimes, the preview leads you to an article that you decide not to finish. A systematic preview, though, can give you more reliable results, making your reading more efficient. As you preview a text, you might try using the following features.

FEATURES OF A TEXT FOR PREVIEWING

Title

Titles and subtitles can reveal the focus of a text and sometimes even its thesis (see 3b(3)). If the title provides little information, do not assume that the work itself will be useless. Looking at other parts of it will give you a clearer sense of the work as a whole, as well as how much you already know about the subject.

Author

Sometimes the author's name alone is an indication of the expertise or tone she or he brings to the topic. You'll want to consider what you already know about the author, if anything. For instance, if Dave Barry is the author, you can expect the essay to be humorous; but if Ellen Goodman is the author, you can expect the essay to be timely, political, and thought-provoking.

Directories

Books usually have features that direct readers to specific sections within them. A *table of contents* identifies the chapters and often the main sections within a book; an *index*, at the back, lists the specific topics covered. Checking these directories can help you determine whether the book will have the kind of information you are looking for and, if so, exactly where you can find it. A *bibliography* indicates how much research was involved in writing the book; it can also direct you to other useful sources. Using information from the directories, you can decide how much or what sections of a book you want to read.

Length

Considering a text's length allows you to estimate how much time you should set aside for reading. By checking length, you can also estimate whether a work is long enough to include useful content or so short that it might skim the surface of the subject it addresses.

Visual Aids

The extent to which visual aids are useful varies, but a quick check for graphs and illustrations can help you decide whether the work has the kind of information you need.

Summaries

Both books and articles often contain summaries, and reading a summary can help you decide whether the work as a whole will be helpful. Reading a summary can also help you follow a difficult text because it tells you the major points in advance. Summaries can often be found in the *preface* of a book, as well as in introductory and concluding chapters. Scholarly articles often begin with a summary identified as an *abstract* (see **8d** and **14c**). Within articles, the introductory and concluding paragraphs often include summaries (see **8d**).

In addition to looking for these features within a text you are previewing, look inside yourself as well so that you can prepare to engage the text critically. Assess how much you already know about the subject or the author. If you are unfamiliar with the subject matter, you might want to supplement your understanding by locating a less demanding treatment of the topic, either in print at the library (see 1g(3)) or online. If your values or opinions differ greatly from those of the author, you'll want to pay close attention to passages in the text that you might be tempted to skim over without stopping to understand. Without abandoning your values, you can increase your capacity for critical reading by being alert for occasions when you might dismiss new ideas without considering, let alone understanding, them.

The following questions may help you in previewing articles, essays, and books.

CHECKLIST for Previewing a Reading Selection

- How long is this work, and how long are different sections of it? Is the organization straightforward or complex? How much time will I need to read this selection until I understand it?

- What do I already know about this subject? Can I keep this knowledge in mind as I read so that I can connect with the text?

- Do I have strong feelings about this subject that could interfere with my ability to understand how it is treated in this text? (See 1d.)

- Do I know anything about this author, and, if so, can I trust what he or she writes? If the author is unfamiliar to me, is any biographical information included that will help me assess his or her credibility? (See 7c and 9a.)

- What does the title tell me? The subtitle? If there are subheadings in the text, what do they reveal about the organization or the way the subject is being handled?

- What do the table of contents and the index indicate about what is in the book? Does the article include an abstract?

- Are there graphs, figures, or other visual aids? What do they illustrate? How might they be useful to me?

- Is there a bibliography that indicates how extensive and current the research is?

- When was the book or article published?

- Where is the author's thesis? (See 2b.)

(Continued on page 10)

(Continued from page 9)

- Has the author included a summary near the introduction or conclusion of any of the chapters or subsections?
- Would it be easier for me to understand this text if I read something simpler on the same topic first?

Besides asking yourself these questions, you can also scan the first and last sentences in every paragraph. The central idea of a paragraph can, of course, occur anywhere within the paragraph (see **3c(1)**), but it often appears in one of these two sentences, which also often suggest a sense of content and overall organization.

The main outline of a text can also be determined by words that indicate sequencing, such as "There are *three* advantages to this proposal. . . . The *first* is . . . . The *second* is . . . ." In addition, you can scan for key phrases writers use to signal important points. The phrase *in other words,* for example, signals that a writer is about to paraphrase a point just made—probably because it is important. Other key phrases include *in this article* (or *chapter*), which can signal a statement of the author's focus or purpose, and *in summary, in conclusion,* and *the point I am making,* which signal that a point is being made about the information just presented.

Previewing is a way to make reading easier and more meaningful. It can also help you select appropriate material when you do research (see chapter **8**). But remember that previewing a text is not the same as reading it for understanding.

| **1d** | Critical readers distinguish between the content of what they read and their personal response to that material. |

Reading is a transaction or exchange between a writer and a reader within a particular setting, called the *rhetorical situation* (see **1b**). The writer tries to choose words that express the intended meaning and will be understood by others. The reader then tries to understand what exactly the author wanted the words to mean within the specific rhetorical situation.

Sometimes, however, communication between writers and readers breaks down. Writers may have used language carelessly, or readers may have read in haste. Moreover, even language that is well chosen can be misleading because words have different specific meanings (or *denotations*) as well as strong associations (or *connotations*) that vary from reader to reader (see 29a) and from culture to culture (chapter 28). Critical readers and writers strive to be successful and efficient communicators by developing strategies for preventing misunderstandings and for working through misunderstandings when they do occur.

To read a text critically, you need to ask at least four questions:

- What exactly is this writer trying to say? Why?
- Who is the writer's intended audience?
- How did the writer try to communicate the content?
- What does this text make me think or feel? How does the author want me to think or feel?

(1) Understanding content requires paying close attention to the words on the page or the screen.

Speakers of English use the same word to mean different things, depending on the context. For instance, you might use the word *skinny* to mean "with no-fat milk" when you're buying a latte, to mean "beyond slim" when describing how someone looks, or to mean "the truth" when using slang. In every case, *skinny* means something different—and your audience (the waiter, your sister, a friend) knows what you mean. When you read, you are the audience, the one who often determines the meanings of words and sentences from their **context**—the sentences, paragraphs, sections, and chapters surrounding them. On first reading a sentence, you might think you understand its meaning; but by the time you finish reading the entire paragraph, you might be able to enhance your understanding of that first sentence given the information provided in the following sentences. Your challenge as a reader, then, is to understand as much as you can but to keep that understanding flexible enough to accommodate what will come. If you are reading a twenty-page chapter, you probably need a preliminary understanding of the first ten pages if you are going to understand the next ten. But if you then reread the entire chapter, your understanding of all the material is likely to deepen. Accordingly, critical readers usually reread texts that are important to them.

When reading for content, make sure you understand the words on the page. When you encounter a word that is new to you, the meaning may be defined in the text itself, or you might be able to infer the meaning from the way the word has been used. But whenever a new term appears in a critically important position such as a thesis statement (see **2b**) or a conclusion (**3b(2)**), look it up in a good dictionary (**28e**).

Transitional words indicating sequencing (see **1c** and **3d**) or movement within a text also help you grasp content. Transitional expressions—especially those indicating purpose, result, summary, repetition, exemplification, and intensification (see page 90)—alert you to important points. When reading from a book or article you own, you might benefit from underlining, highlighting, or writing back to passages that interest or confuse you, or that you question. If you've borrowed a book, you can use sticky notes to highlight and annotate the text. With an electronic text, you can print out a hard copy, use your word-processing program to annotate, or respond to a downloaded file directly on the screen and then save both versions.

(2) Recognizing a personal response requires that you separate what a writer has said from the way you feel about the message.

Often what we hear or read provokes a reaction. We can become immediately prejudiced toward or against a speaker or text if we mishear, misread, or in other ways allow our personal responses to interfere with our ability to understand. Critical readers are always aware of their reactions and work hard to keep their personal responses from interfering with their ability to understand. So, in addition to reading for content (see **1d(1)**), they also keep track of what they think about or how they're reacting to this content. That's not to say that they read passively; critical readers read actively, noting where they agree or disagree, become frustrated or intrigued, sympathetic or annoyed. And they keep track of what feature of the writing (or themselves) triggered each response: Was it the writer's tone (see **3a(3)**), an example that evoked a personal memory, a lapse in the organization (**2c**), the topic itself (**2a**), a visual element such as a photo or illustration, or something altogether separate from the text, such as trying to read it late at night?

By noting personal responses and recognizing that they are independent of a work's content even if they are inspired by it, critical readers increase their understanding of the purposeful choices writers make when communicating with readers. Personal responses often serve as the basis for new pieces of writing (see **2a**). Often, good readers and writers use techniques from the following checklist.

CHECKLIST for Recording Personal Responses

- Note passages that capture your attention. Underline or highlight your own copy; highlight with a different text color when reading on a computer screen.

- Put a question mark in the margin when you do not understand a passage—or if you question its accuracy.

- Put an exclamation point in the margin when a statement or example surprises you.

- Write *yes* or *no* in the margin when you agree or disagree. When a passage reminds you of another passage (or something else you have read), note that association in the margin.

- Keep a reading journal (see **1d(3)**). Include at least one question, compliment, or reservation about something you read each day.

- Correspond by email with other people who are reading the same material (see chapter **5**).

- Talk with friends and family members about any texts you have enjoyed reading.

---

(3) Keeping a reading journal or participating in e-discussions about reading selections increases comprehension and generates ideas for writing.

Take opportunities to write daily. Like a personal journal or a writer's notebook (see **2a**), a **reading journal** (or, in some classes, an online discussion forum; see chapter **5**) provides a daily opportunity for you to write in order to understand your reading and your reactions to your reading. Because you'll be responding to your reading—listening to it, talking back to it, arguing with it, extending it, connecting it with your own experience—you'll be more likely to engage the reading, understand it, and remember it. Writing regularly about your reading, then, helps to increase your comprehension and identify responses that could be the seeds from which larger pieces of writing subsequently grow.

Your reading journal can focus on the reading you're doing for one course, for all your courses, for your job—or on all the reading you do. Whatever your focus, you'll want to design your journal in such a way that you'll benefit in terms of both comprehension and creativity. One way to do this is to keep a **double-entry notebook,** a journal in which each entry has two distinct parts: summary and response. For example, if you keep your journal in a spiral notebook, you could use the left side of each page to summarize your understanding of what you've read (see **10b**) and the right side to record your responses to it. (Or you might prefer to format computer files into columns.)

A first-year student composed a double-entry notebook for her computer science course. When she read Douglas Hofstadter's "A Coffeehouse Conversation on the Turing Test," she summarized Hofstadter's views about thinking computers on the left-hand side and responded to his thinking on the right-hand side of the notebook. The following is an excerpt from that notebook.

Summary	Response
Hofstadter explains how the Turing Test can measure a computer's intelligence. He has one of the characters explain that the Test is based on an Imitation Game in which a person tries to convince his or her interrogator that he or she is the opposite gender. Likewise, a computer that could convince a person that it was a person would be actually intelligent.	I don't know about this. Hofstadter seems to really buy into this test as a measure of intelligence, but I know some people that would have trouble passing it. Besides, just because a computer can come up with a few quick answers doesn't mean it thinks the same way I do. What about emotion, creativity, all that sort of stuff?

Try always to keep separate the entries devoted to summarizing content from those devoted to your personal response or reflection (see **1d(2)**). This separation will come in handy when you need to review what you have written. When you're preparing for a written examination (see **4d**), for example, you will be able to easily identify the entries that will help you remember content. And when you're involved in the brainstorming necessary for drafting an essay (see chapter **2**), you can turn to those entries in which you recorded your own ideas, responses, or reflections. Most of all, keep in mind that improving your reading and writing is always about progress—not perfection.

 "Don't believe everything you read" is a common saying that reflects the way most readers in the United States approach a text. Although they expect a published text to have been reviewed for accuracy, they may find factual errors, inconsistencies in logic, or weak support of claims. Many of your reading and writing assignments will require you to do the same, so be prepared to question an author's ideas and test out your own.

1e | Effective writers actively engage all elements of the rhetorical situation to achieve their purpose.

Consider, for example, how your writing varies depending on the person to whom you are writing and the circumstances. You would not convince a prospective employer to hire you if you wrote a job application letter as though you were writing to your closest friend. Nor would you use formal business language in writing to that friend, regardless of the context: Social factors and the circumstances in which written communication takes place are important parts of the context for writing. You should demonstrate flexibility when writing for any occasion. The combination of author, exigence, purpose, audience, and context is called the *rhetorical situation.* Assess your rhetorical situation when you are planning to write (see chapter 2), and remember it when you are revising your work (chapter 3).

(1) *Purpose* means your reason for writing.

The clearer your purpose, the better your writing is likely to be. To clarify your purpose, it helps to ask yourself whether you want to

- express how you feel about something,
- create a mood,
- amuse or entertain,
- report information,

- explain or evaluate the significance of information,
- analyze a situation,
- clarify a point or situation, or
- argue a point or argue for or against a course of action.

Depending on the overall purpose, writing can be described as expressive, expository, or argumentative. Any of these types of writing can be used to help you fulfill your overall purpose.

Expressive writing emphasizes the writer's feelings and reactions to people, objects, events, and ideas. Personal letters and journals are often expressive, as are many essays and short stories. The following example (paragraph 1) comes from an essay designed to convey how the author feels about the relationship he had with his father. (For ease of reference, each of the sample paragraphs in this chapter is numbered.)

1   At just about the hour when my father died, soon after dawn one February morning when ice coated the windows like cataracts, I banged my thumb with a hammer. Naturally I swore at the hammer, the reckless thing, and in the moment of swearing I thought of what my father would say: "If you'd try hitting the nail it would go in a whole lot faster. Don't you know your thumb's not as hard as that hammer?" We were both doing carpentry that day, but far apart. He was building cupboards at my brother's place in Oklahoma; I was at home in Indiana putting up a wall in the basement to make a bedroom for my daughter. By the time my mother called with the news of his death—the long distance wires whittling her voice until it seemed too thin to bear the weight of what she had to say—my thumb was swollen. A week or two later a white scar in the shape of a crescent moon began to show above the cuticle, and month by month it rose across the pink sky of my thumbnail. It took the better part of a year for the scar to disappear, and every time I noticed it I thought of my father.

                                —**SCOTT RUSSELL SANDERS**, "The Inheritance of Tools"

Expository writing focuses on objects, events, or ideas, rather than on the writer's feelings about them. Textbooks, news accounts, scientific reports, and encyclopedia articles are usually expository, as are many of the essays students are expected to write in college. When you report, explain, clarify, or evaluate, you are practicing exposition. Paragraph 2 comes from an essay that explains how paleoanthropologists—in this case, a paleoanthropologist named Mac—discover their prizes.

2   Searching only in the most promising areas isn't the key to [Mac's] success; perseverance is. He walks the same territory over and over again, changing courses around obstacles, and he tells his people to do the same. If you walked to the left around this bush yesterday, then walk to the right today. If you walked into the sun yesterday, then walk with the sun at your back today. And most of all, walk, walk, walk, and *look* while you are doing it. Don't daydream; don't scan the horizon for shade; ignore the burning sun even when the temperature reaches 135°F. Keep your eyes on the ground searching for that elusive sliver of bone or gleaming tooth that is not just any old animal, fossilized and turning to rubble, but a hominid. Those are the prizes we seek; those are the messengers from the past.

—**ALAN WALKER AND PAT SHIPMAN**, *The Wisdom of the Bones*

Argumentative writing is intended to influence the reader's attitudes and actions. Most writing is to some extent an argument; through the choice and arrangement of material, even something as apparently straightforward as a résumé can be an argument for an interview. However, writing is usually called argumentative if it clearly supports a specific position (see chapter 7). In paragraph 3, note how the author calls for students to claim their own educations.

3   The first thing I want to say to you who are students, is that you cannot afford to think of being here to *receive* an education; you will do much better to think of yourselves as being here to *claim* one. One of the dictionary definitions of the verb "to claim" is: *to take as the rightful owner; to assert in the face of possible contradiction.* "To receive" is *to come into possession of; to act as receptacle or container for; to accept as authoritarian or true.* The difference is that between acting and being acted-upon, and . . . it can literally mean the difference between life and death.

—**ADRIENNE RICH**, "Claiming an Education," *On Lies, Secrets, and Silence*

Writers need to identify their overall purpose for each piece of writing, knowing that they can tap different methods of development (such as narration, description, and cause-and-consequence analysis; see 2e), all of which have specific purposes or subpurposes, to work toward that overall goal. For example, in order to support your argument, you may find yourself reporting information or expressing your reactions to an experience. Although you may mix methods of development, you should be sure to align your method or methods with your overall purpose for writing. The following checklist may assist you.

CHECKLIST for Assessing Purpose

- If you are writing in response to a specific assignment, what does your instructor want your writing to do? Talk to your instructor or reread your assignment sheet (see 1f) to see what goals (and limits) have been set for you.

- Has your instructor provided a purpose for your writing, or can you define your own?

- Are you trying primarily to express how you feel? Are you writing to improve your self-understanding or trying to help others understand you better?

- Are you trying to be entertaining or inspiring? What do you hope to accomplish by treating your subject humorously?

- Are you writing primarily to convey information? Are you trying to teach others something they do not know or to demonstrate that you have knowledge in common?

- Are you writing primarily to argue for or against a course of action? Do you want your readers to stop a certain behavior or to undertake a specific action?

- Do you have more than one purpose in writing? Which one is primary? How can the other purposes help you achieve your primary one? Or are some of your purposes in conflict?

- Are you trying to demonstrate that you have specific writing skills and are knowledgeable about your subject?

Exercise 2

Select one of the following subjects, and write two paragraphs that begin to develop an expressive, expository, or argumentative essay on that subject.

1. your finances
2. your generation
3. your career goals
4. your computer expertise
5. your favorite musical group
6. volunteer work
7. a memorable lesson
8. music or dance performances
9. student housing

(2) *Audience* refers to those who will read your writing.

Understanding your audience—their values, concerns, and knowledge—helps you tailor your writing in terms of length, quality and quantity of details, the kind of language to use, and the examples that will be most effective. Some writers like to plan and draft essays with a clear sense of audience in mind; others like to focus on the audience primarily when they are revising. (See chapters 2 and 3.) At some point, however, you must think clearly about who will be reading what you write and ask yourself whether your choices are appropriate for that audience.

(a) Specialized audience

A **specialized audience** has a demonstrated interest in your subject. If you were writing about the harm done through alcohol abuse, members of an organization such as Alcoholics Anonymous or Mothers Against Drunk Driving would constitute a specialized audience, as would nutritionists, police officers, or social workers. These audiences would have different areas of expertise and possibly different agendas, so it would be unwise to address each of them in exactly the same way. In each case, however, you could assume that your audience had a special interest in your subject and some knowledge of it.

As you consider your relationship with a specialized audience—what audience members know that you do not, how much and what sorts of information you might provide them, and how best to develop your information—you can continue to think about your overall purpose. You'll be writing to experts, so you'll want to establish common ground with them by acknowledging that you recognize their expertise and mentioning areas of agreement, adjusting your tone and language choices as you tailor your writing to their knowledge and attitudes. (See 3a(3) and chapter 28.) You'll want to provide your audience with new information—or a new way of understanding information with which they are already familiar. The average reader would probably be confused by the language in paragraph 4 because it was written for a specialized audience of rhetoricians who are already familiar with the terminology of their discipline.

4   Rhetoric as persuasive discourse is still very much exercised among us, but modern students are not likely to have received much formal training in the art of persuasion. Frequently, the only remnant of this training in the schools is the attention paid to argumentation in a study of the four forms of discourse: Argumentation, Exposition, Description, and Narration. But this

study of argumentation usually turns out to be an accelerated course in Logic. For the classical rhetorician, logic was an ancillary but distinct discipline. Aristotle, for instance, spoke of rhetoric as being "an offshoot" or "a counterpart" of logic or, as he called it, dialectics. The speaker might employ logic to persuade the audience, but logic was only one among many "available means of persuasion." So those who study argumentation in classrooms today are not really exposed to the rich, highly systematized discipline that earlier students submitted to when they were learning the persuasive art.

—**EDWARD P. J. CORBETT**, *Classical Rhetoric for the Modern Student*

Many of the essays you will be assigned to write in college—in history, economics, and psychology, for example, as well as in English—are for a specialized audience, your instructor, who is already familiar with the material. For example, if you are writing an essay about a novel assigned by your English instructor, it is not necessary to summarize the plot unless you have been specifically asked to do so. You can assume that your specialized audience already knows what takes place. Instead of telling your instructor what he or she already knows, use your essay to communicate your interpretation of the material you both have read, an interpretation that might grow out of your personal response to that material. (See chapter **13**.)

Since no one knows everything about a subject, members of a specialized audience will usually enjoy thinking about their subject in a new way, even if they're not learning new information. So writing for a specialized audience doesn't mean you have to know more than your audience does; it may be sufficient to demonstrate that you understand the material and can discuss it appropriately.

(b) Diverse audience

A **diverse audience** consists of readers with different levels of expertise and interest in your subject. For example, if you are writing about upgrading computer software in a report that will be read by various department heads of a company or about the responsibilities of public schools for your local newspaper, you should be aware that some of your readers probably know more about software or schooling than others. When writing for a diverse audience, you can usually assume that your readers have interests different from yours. You can also assume that they share a willingness to learn about new material if it is presented clearly and respectfully by someone who is establishing common ground with them. Paragraph 5 helps a diverse audience of readers understand how critical teaching functions within U.S. schools.

5   Critical teaching aims to transform. That ambition is both subversive and entirely common, akin, that is, to the aim of any teaching. Schools, after all, accept the burden of assisting the nation's young people to become responsible and productive citizens. Hence, teaching is always a transformative act: students aren't expected to leave their classrooms thinking, knowing, judging, living in the ways they did before they entered them—fundamentalist students encounter evolution in biology class; students raised on television read literature; students from "liberal" backgrounds study growing crime rates in sociology and the cost of assistance programs in economics; "conservatives" study the women's movement in history class or Marxism in philosophy. The choices teachers make in their classrooms are always, in part, choices about what children "ought" to become, what the nation "ought" to aspire to through the productive action of succeeding generations. These are political choices: the question is, what indeed *should* students become and who should have the power to say so? What indeed *should* the nation aspire to, and who should compose the stories about that aspiration? Critical teaching differs from other sorts primarily in its answers to these questions and in its self-consciousness about the political nature of schools (including its own practices). It presumes that American citizens should understand, accept, and live amicably amidst the realities of cultural diversity—along axes of gender, race, class, and ethnicity—that are the hallmarks of American society. It presumes that people are entitled to fairness in their social and economic lives. It presumes that a critical citizenry, willing as well as able to take responsibility for the nation's future, is preferable to a passive, unengaged citizenry that lets government, business, and mass media do its thinking. Finally, it presumes that no one group is exclusively entitled to the privilege of representation, but that each has a right to tell its story, critique other stories, and participate in forming a community responsive to the needs of all its members.

—C. H. KNOBLAUCH AND LIL BRANNON, *Critical Teaching and the Idea of Literacy*

To attract the attention of a diverse audience, you'll want to establish what its members are likely to have in common despite their differences. In the previous example, you might consider whether all the readers have the same knowledge of critical teaching, the same experiences in critical literacy. Do they believe in the potential of teaching and learning to change human lives—or not? Do these readers already think, read, and write critically? Do they have the same level of education? The key to communicating successfully with diverse readers is to find some way to draw them together on common ground and to join them there. In the previous example, then, the author considered all members of the audience to be educated readers, interested in the relationship among teaching, learning, and participatory democracy. That consideration enabled the author to make appropriate choices in diction (see chapters **28**, **29**, and **30**) and detail (see **2e**).

There will be times, however, when you simply won't know much about your audience, even though your purpose for writing might be to evaluate a product or argue for a course of action. When this is the case, you can often benefit from imagining a thoughtful audience of educated adults, with whom you may even share common ground. Such an audience is likely to include people with different backgrounds and cultural values (see **7e(2)**), so be careful not to assume that you are writing for readers who are exactly like you. To a considerable extent, the language you use will determine whether diverse readers feel included in or excluded from your work. Be careful to avoid jargon or technical terms that would be understood only by a specialized audience. If you must use a specialized term, explain what you mean by it. (See **28c** and **28e**.)

(c) Multiple audiences

Writers often need to address multiple audiences. At work, for example, you might need to write a memo or a letter that will be read not only by the person to whom it is addressed but also by people who receive copies. The readers in a multiple audience can have distinctly different expectations. If, for example, you are asked to evaluate the performance of an employee you supervise and send copies to both that person and your boss, one part of your audience is probably looking for praise while the other is looking to see whether you are a competent supervisor.

The use of email for communication (see **5a–c**) has increased the likelihood of writing for multiple audiences because messages can be forwarded easily—and not always with the writer's permission. Other electronic texts, such as those generated by Listserv dialogues, MOOs, or online conversation through a Web site, can also reach multiple audiences. When writing texts for electronic submission, consider whether anyone outside your immediate audience might take an interest in your work, and whether that interest is likely to work to your advantage.

When writing essays in college, you may also find yourself writing for multiple audiences. For example, you'll write essays that you'll not only share with your writing group but submit to your instructor; you may find that you can use an English essay as the foundation for developing another essay for your psychology or history class; you may take a linked or team-taught course in which you'll submit written work for evaluation by two instructors; or you may write an essay for a diverse audience and submit it to an instructor who is a specialist on your subject. In each of these cases, you are writing for multiple audiences. This kind of writing requires that you consider a variety of attitudes and positions (see 7d–e). Doing so is helpful when planning an essay and also when reading what you have drafted from different points of view as you prepare to revise it (see chapter 3). The following checklist may also help you assess your audience.

CHECKLIST for Assessing the Audience

- Who is going to be reading what you write?
- What do you know about the members of this audience? What characteristics can you safely assume about them? What do they have in common? How are they different?
- What values do you share with them?
- How do you differ from them?
- How much do they already know about your topic?
- What kind of language is appropriate or inappropriate for this audience?
- How open are the members of this audience to views that may be different from their own? Are they likely to prefer hearing you restate what they already know, considering another point of view, or learning something new?
- What level of expertise will they expect from you?
- What do you *not* know about this audience? What assumptions would be risky?
- Are you writing with one audience in mind and then expecting a different audience to read what you have written? If so, have you clearly indicated the intended audience so that you can address that audience specifically, in the hope that your readers will imagine they are part of it?

When writing in your native language, do you expect your audience to agree with you? If so, how do you feel when your audience disagrees with you? In academic and professional journals and books in the United States, disagreement is often expected. In fact, as long as respectful language is used, disagreement can show that readers are interested in an author's ideas.

Exercise 3

Take notes during a class or at a meeting you regularly attend. Using those notes and your memories of the class or meeting, write a one-page essay in which you describe that occasion to one of the following: (1) a member of your family, (2) an instructor or supervisor, or (3) the dean of the school or a department head. Then, write a second, one-page description that is to be read by all three.

Exercise 4

Examine an introductory and an advanced textbook in a discipline of your choice, and locate a passage in each devoted to the same issue or concept. Photocopy these passages, and prepare a class presentation in which you explain how they reveal differences in audience.

Beyond the Rule

CONSIDERING AUDIENCE

There are times when considering audience can get in your way—even inhibit you—as a thinker and writer. When you're worried about being judged by an audience (your teacher, your friends from class, the scholarship committee) or trying too hard to find just the right phrasing, you may benefit by writing a draft without thinking about audience. For a discussion of when and how to delay consideration of audience, visit www.harbrace.com.

(3) *Context* means the circumstances under which writer and reader communicate.

Context includes time and place, writer and audience, and medium. An essay written outside of class may be very different from one written in the classroom, even if both are written for the same instructor and in response to the same question. What you are able to write is always influenced by time and place, and your instructor is likely to take this into account—expecting more from you when you have had advanced coursework, more time to write, and better conditions for writing. Similarly, an instructor may expect more from an essay written at the end of the course than from one written at the beginning.

Context is also influenced by social, political, religious, and other cultural factors. Your background and beliefs often shape the stance (or attitude) you take when writing. An essay written shortly before your school's winter break, for example, could be influenced by both your anticipation of a combined religious holiday and family reunion and whether or not you think your audience shares that anticipation. Or a political crisis, such as the September 2001 terrorist attacks on the United States or another massacre in the Middle East, might prompt you to reconsider the purpose of an essay you are drafting for your political science course. Writers who consider their audience as well as the context in which they are writing are more likely to communicate their ideas effectively.

The medium for which you are writing can be considered part of the context as well. Writing material for a Web page or another online medium may require you to think differently about organization and style. Writing for such media may also require more or less time than writing a traditional academic essay or business letter, depending on how familiar you are with the technology you will be using for the task. (See chapter 5.)

When you read the work of other writers, you will sometimes find that the context is specifically stated, as in the following passage.

6   In the twenty-second month of the war against Nazism we meet here in this old Palace of St. James, itself not unscarred by the fire of the enemy, in order to proclaim the high purposes and resolves of the lawful constitutional Governments of Europe whose countries have been overrun; and we meet here also to cheer the hopes of free men and free peoples throughout the world.

—**WINSTON CHURCHILL**, "Until Victory Is Won"

Often, however, the context must be inferred. Whether you choose to identify your context or not, it is essential that you consider it.

CHECKLIST for Assessing the Context

- Under what circumstances are you writing? If you are free to choose the time and place in which to write, have you set aside a time when you are likely to do good work and found a site where you can work without distractions?

- Under what circumstances will your writing probably be read? For example, if it is going to be one of many reports in a pile on a manager's desk, can you help that person quickly see the purpose and thrust of your work?

- How has your response to the assigned task been influenced by other things going on in your life? Are you satisfied with your response, or has it put your purpose or goal at risk? Can you make any changes in your schedule that will allow you to focus more attention on your writing?

- Have you been asked to write an essay of a specific length? If length has not been specified, what seems appropriate for your purpose and audience?

- What document design (see chapter 6) is appropriate for this context?

---

(4) *Exigence* means the circumstance that compels you to write.

Exigence is the particular need or situation that calls for writing. A parking ticket, a birth or marriage, a winning lottery ticket—these are all events that may compel you to write. As soon as you know that you can use words to address a particular need or situation, you can decide whether your words will solve a problem, explain a point, make a claim, or entertain. Once you determine the exigence for your writing—the reason that impels you to write—you'll be better able to gauge all the elements of your writing (from word choice to organizational pattern) in terms of your overall purpose.

Beyond the Rule

EXIGENCE

Historical events often serve as the exigence for writing. The September 2001 terrorist attacks on New York City and Washington, D.C., provided many people—from journalists to schoolchildren—with a reason to write. The collapse of the Quecreek Mine in Somerset, Pennsylvania, in July 2002 offered another occasion for many people to write. For more information, visit www.harbrace.com.

1f | Successful academic reading and writing grow out of understanding the rhetorical situation of each course.

College students who succeed at reading and writing actively engage the rhetorical situation of every class, which means that they read critically every course syllabus and assignment sheet, the written texts that establish student rights and responsibilities. Understanding these specific written texts is critical to successful completion of your coursework.

(1) A syllabus states course requirements and the plan for meeting them.

On the first day of class, an instructor usually passes out a **syllabus,** a concise statement of the main points of the course, including the readings, due dates, and sometimes the assignment sheets. Usually, the instructor goes over the syllabus during the first class meeting and revisits (to modify) the syllabus during the term. The instructor stays familiar with the syllabus, and you'll want to as well because it contains important information that students sometimes overlook. You'll need to read it carefully as you prepare for every class meeting and every assignment; otherwise, you might misunderstand a requirement or a due date.

CHECKLIST **for Reading a Syllabus**

- Note your instructor's name, office number, and office hours. See whether your instructor has included an email address (see **5a–b**) and indicated any preference for how you should get in touch outside of class.

- Note the texts required for the course. If you can only obtain a different edition of a text, consult with your instructor first to see if the difference will matter. Also check for advice about buying used copies.

- Look closely at what the syllabus says about writing assignments. How much reading and writing does the course require? When are essays and assignments due? How firm are these deadlines? Are there penalties for turning in late papers? Are there opportunities for revision?

- When are exams scheduled (see **4d**)? If there are quizzes, will they be announced in advance?

- Does the syllabus indicate that some assignments will be given more weight than others? If not, how will your final grade be determined?

- Does the syllabus indicate an attendance policy? Are there penalties for missing class or being late?

- Will there be a Web site or other online component for the course? If so, how will it be used, and how can you access it? (See **5c–d**.)

Even if all of your questions about the course are answered the first day, hold on to your syllabus so that you can review it regularly. Clearly defined policies and expectations can be overlooked when you have many demands on your time.

Many instructors post their syllabi on Web sites created for their courses. An electronic syllabus is easier for the instructor to modify once the course gains momentum. Be sure to review a course's electronic syllabus from time to time, or if your instructor is using a print syllabus, keep track of any changes. Every course Web site is different, but there are basic guidelines to follow.

> ### CHECKLIST **for Using a Course Web Site**
>
> - Be sure you can access the course Web site. Find out which Web browser properly displays the site, including its specific links and other elements. Because a slow Internet connection can also be a problem, access the Web site as soon as you can, and see your instructor if you have any problems.
> - Learn whether the course Web site contains information and resources that are not included on the syllabus. If an instructor briefly describes a writing assignment on the syllabus but includes extensive guidelines and deadlines only on the course Web site, then it's vital that you have easy access to that site.
> - Check the links on the course Web site. There may be a link to a Web-based newsgroup for the course or to a required reading. Make sure that such links work properly on your browser, especially if you need any of them to complete a course requirement.

(2) Reading a writing assignment carefully is essential to completing the task successfully.

An assignment sheet explaining what an instructor expects you to accomplish deserves your serious attention, for you need to work as efficiently as possible in college. You want to respond to each assignment exactly as directed in terms of length, focus, format, and purpose. Instructors write out assignments so that they receive the kind of writing they want to read. For example, an assignment sheet might indicate that your instructor wants you to write two paragraphs developing an idea (see **2b–c** and **2e**) that might eventually become the basis for a three-page essay. For now, your instructor specifies that you should not worry about punctuation and mechanics (see chapters **31** through **39**) or document design (chapter **6**)—only about that main idea. Don't misunderstand the assignment because you read it too quickly. Rather, read it carefully, and concentrate on fulfilling what your instructor has asked you to do. Ask questions if you are still unclear about what is expected.

Whether you are asked to submit an essay (see chapters **2** and **3**), an argument (chapter **7**), a research paper (chapters **8** through **11**), or some other form of writing (chapters 12 through 15), you have a better chance of completing your project successfully if you read the assignment sheet with the following concerns in mind.

CHECKLIST for Reading an Assignment Sheet

- What does this assignment require you to do? Are there subject, formatting, or length restrictions? Are you expected to submit all of your process writing along with the final copy?
- Have purpose, audience, context, and exigence (see **1b** and **1e(4)**) been supplied for you? Or will you choose these components of your assignment?
- How much flexibility does this assignment allow? What are your choices? Are there guidelines for making free choices?
- What strengths can you bring to this assignment?
- What do you still need to learn if you are going to complete this assignment successfully?
- How much time should you devote to this assignment? When should you get started?
- Do you have questions about the assignment for your instructor? How might a visit to the writing center help you? (See **1g**.)

1g | **Successful students take advantage of academic support opportunities.**

One of the biggest advantages to studying at a college or university is the availability of academic support services and trained personnel. All students inevitably need academic support at some point in their college careers. Too often, though, students don't get the help they need because they don't know what resources are available, where those resources are located, and—most important—how to use them for their own benefit. Students who take themselves seriously, who claim their education, are neither too shy nor too proud to seek out the multiple means of support on their campus.

(1) Your instructor can clarify course assignments and requirements.

Your instructor should be able to help you with most of the questions you have in a course, whether they concern a reading assignment, the due date for an essay, or a concept essential to your understanding. In most cases, your instructor is your grader, so you'll want to be sure that he or she has articulated the assignment (whether verbally, in print, or online) in such a way that you know what it is you are expected to do. You can get answers or clarifications for most of your questions either in class or immediately afterward. But you're likely to get more time and attention when you visit your instructor during office hours. The checklist that follows includes tips for making your office visit a productive one.

CHECKLIST for Getting Help from Your Instructor

- Learn the instructor's office hours and location.

- Make an appointment, and then appear on time. Keep in mind that most instructors want their students to come during office hours.

- Before the visit, identify the goals you have, writing out your questions and concerns. What information do you need most? What do you need to take away with you if this meeting is going to be productive?

- If you are planning to discuss a specific reading or writing assignment, bring a copy of it to the meeting.

- Tell your instructor what you need. Do not expect your instructor to read your mind.

- Once you have clearly stated your questions and concerns, pay close attention to the answers you receive, writing them down, if necessary.

- Don't hesitate to return.

In addition to conferring with instructors in their offices, you may also be able to consult with them by email (see **5b**) or through a Web site (see **5c–d**) created especially for a class. The course syllabus (see **1f(1)**) may include an electronic address as well as a policy about communicating by computer. If not, ask whether such communication is possible and under what circumstances it would be appropriate. Most instructors are happy to answer short questions via computer; questions needing longer answers probably merit an office visit.

(2) Writing centers enable you to get help from tutors.

Many successful college writers benefit from visits to their school's writing center, where they can discuss their work-in-progress with fellow students, who are trained to assist them with their writing. Because writing tutors usually represent many majors, they bring to their work a wide range of writing experiences from virtually all disciplines. (In other words, writing assistance is not limited to essays for your English courses.) Your school most likely has a writing center where this kind of student-to-student consultation takes place on a regular basis. And that writing center probably maintains a Web site where you can get information about services, hours of operation, and additional resources for writing. Some schools provide specific writing centers for specific people—for undergraduate writers, graduate student writers, and faculty writers—staffed by different groups of trained tutors. Regardless of their student or faculty status, writers who visit a writing center are demonstrating their commitment to writing well and to reaching their own writing goals. They do not expect tutors to write or correct an essay for them.

CHECKLIST **for Visiting a Writing Center**

- Learn when the center is open and how long you can expect a tutorial session to last.
- Find out whether you can get help whenever you stop by or need to make an appointment.
- If you are working on a specific assignment, bring the material with you: your assignment sheet, books or articles, and, most important, anything you have already written. Although many writing tutors will be able to help you with your prewriting, it'll be more efficient if you have something down on paper.
- Be prepared to explain your understanding of the assignment to your tutor and to indicate the specific kind of help you need. If you bring along the instructor's comments or past graded work, the tutor can use specific information from them to help you.

- Only you will know when a visit to the writing center will be most useful to you, but many writers find that they benefit from a visit early on in the writing process, after they've written an initial draft. Other writers, however, find that they benefit more toward the end of the process, during revision and before they're ready to edit and proofread.

- Recognize that tutors are ready to help you with your *writing;* rarely will they serve as proofreaders or editors. In fact, they may ask you to read aloud what you've written so that *you* can catch your own surface errors and organizational weaknesses. For this reason, you'll want to visit the center a day or two before your assignment is actually due.

- If you have a good session with a tutor, learn his or her name so that you can develop a working relationship. Many writing centers encourage weekly meetings with the same tutor so that writer and tutor can develop a collaborative learning relationship.

- If you have a frustrating experience with a tutor, ask for someone else on your next visit, and do not judge the entire staff by a single bad experience.

(3) Libraries have trained staff members who are ready to help you.

The staff of your school's library can help you find the material you need for writing from research (see chapters **8** through **11**). The reference desk is a good place to start because many instructors want your research to come from print as well as electronic sources (CD-ROMs, Web sites, or online discussion groups; see chapters **5** and **8**). The library's own Web site is often an excellent resource for your research. You can expect to find appropriate direction for your research by simply stating your needs at the reference desk; there, you can show a librarian your assignment, talk about your research question, or explain the problem you're trying to solve. The more information you provide the librarian, the more direction you'll receive.

Moreover, many libraries offer workshops and other training sessions on finding information in print sources as well as on the Web (see **8c–d**). Although librarians are unlikely to review your reading and writing assignments with you (this kind of help comes more appropriately from an instructor or writing tutor), librarians are trained to provide you with information that increases the ease and confidence with which you gather material for an assignment.

Planning and Drafting Essays

Experienced writers understand that writing is a process (see **1a**). Think of the writing you do out of school, and you'll realize how experienced you already are. When you make a gift-giving list, for example, you consider the recipients, the gift ideas, and the appropriateness of each gift for the occasion; then, while you shop, you may cross off some items, move some around, add new ones, and make annotations. Whether in or out of school, you continually consider your purpose, audience, and context (see **1e**). You revise and edit what you write (see chapter **3**).

This chapter will help you

- find good topics (**2a(1)**),
- focus your ideas (**2a(2)**),
- write a clear thesis statement (**2b**),
- organize your ideas (**2c**),
- use various strategies to develop effective paragraphs (**2d–e**), and
- write a first draft (**2f**).

Effective writers begin any writing project by focusing on these steps one at a time. As they work, they may revisit an earlier stage of the writing process at the same time as they begin working on the next stage. They know that the stages are sometimes separate and sometimes overlapping.

As you plan and draft an essay, you may need to return to a specific activity several times. For example, drafting may help you see that you need to go back and collect more ideas, modify your thesis, or even start over with a new one. Experienced writers expect the writing process to provoke new ideas and to reveal places that need improving. (See chapter **3**.) They know that effective writing takes serious effort; developing ideas helps writers gain new insights as well as a sense of accomplishment.

2a | Writers find appropriate subjects and decide how to focus them.

Whether you are assigned a subject or are free to choose one, you must consider what you already know—or would like to learn about—and what is likely to interest your audience (see 1e(2)). You must also decide how to narrow your general **subject** into a more specific **topic** so that you can develop that topic adequately within the time and page limit available to you.

When you take a writing course, you might be asked to choose your own subject. In this case, you should consider your interests and your experience. The first step toward interesting an audience in a subject is to be interested in it yourself. Often the best subject is one drawn from your own experience, which has given you specific knowledge of hobbies, sports, jobs, and places. Such subjects are important to you and could interest readers if you write with a clear purpose and well-chosen details (see 1e(1) and 2d).

More often, however, you will be asked to write essays about subjects outside your personal experience but within your academic experience. For instance, you may be assigned an essay for a course in ancient history. If you are not limited to a specific question, you will be responsible for choosing your topic—but it will have to be related to the course. Just as you do when you write about personal experience, you should make an effort to find material that interests you and begin focusing on a topic. Look in your textbook, particularly in the sections listing suggestions for further reading. Go through your lecture notes, reading journal, or marginal annotations you've made for the course (see 1f). Ask yourself if there are any details of the subject that have surprised, annoyed, or pleased you—something you feel strongly about and would like to explore further. Writing about a subject is one of the best ways to learn about it, so use a writing assignment not only to satisfy your audience but also to satisfy yourself.

(1) There are several ways to explore subjects.

If you have a hard time finding something to write about—or have so many ideas that you have trouble choosing among them—try some of the following invention exercises: **keeping a journal, freewriting, listing,**

clustering, and **questioning.** Discussing assignments with classmates, friends, or an instructor can also help you generate ideas and decide which ones are likely to yield good essays, the kind that are interesting to write. In other words, to generate ideas, use whatever methods produce results for you. Different methods may work better for different subjects and different writers; if you run out of ideas when using one method, switch to another. Sometimes, especially for an assigned subject completely removed from your own interests and knowledge, you may need to try several methods.

(a) Keeping a journal

Keeping a journal is a good way to generate subjects for essays. You will benefit from writing in a personal journal or a writer's notebook every day.

In a **personal journal,** you reflect on your experiences. Instead of simply listing activities, meals, or weather reports, you use writing to explore how you feel about what is happening in your life. You might focus on external events, such as what you think about a book or a film, or on your inner life, such as changes in your moods or attitudes. Writers who keep a personal journal usually write for their own benefit; they are their own audience and do not share what they write with others. But in the process of writing the journal—or reading it—they may discover subjects they can use for essays.

Like a personal journal, a **writer's notebook** includes responses to experiences. In this case, however, the emphasis is on recording and exploring material for future projects. You can often benefit from keeping a writer's notebook in which you list quotations and observations that invite development. When time allows, you might also draft the opening pages of an essay, outline an idea for a story, or experiment with writing a poem.

Some writers keep both a personal journal and a writer's notebook. Others use only one of these types—or create a combination of the two. Still others prefer to keep a **reading journal** (see **1d(3)**). You might find it convenient to keep your journal in a word-processing file on your computer, especially if you use a laptop. In any case, feel free to write quickly, without worrying about spelling or grammar.

Because you don't have to worry about grammatical correctness when writing journal entries, you can pay more attention to your ideas. In fact, if writing in English sometimes slows you down, try using your native language instead. You can decide later which parts of your journal entries are worth translating into English. A journal can also be a place to experiment with sentence patterns and vocabulary. You can begin learning new words and phrases by listing in your journal those that you read or hear in your classes.

(b) Freewriting

When freewriting, writers record whatever occurs to them, without stopping, for a limited period of time—often for no more than ten minutes. They do not worry about whether they are repeating themselves or getting off track; they simply write to see what comes out. Freewriting is another good way to generate ideas for a writing project because no matter what you write, it will contain ideas and information you didn't realize you had. The entries in a personal journal or a writer's notebook are often freewritten, but freewriting is not limited to journal writing. You can take out a sheet of paper and freewrite whenever you have a few minutes to spare. Some writers use colored marking pens (or change the font in their word-processing program) to identify different topics generated by this activity.

In *directed freewriting,* you begin with a general subject and record whatever occurs to you about this subject during the time available. When Melissa Schraeder's English instructor asked her to write for five minutes, assessing some of the main challenges to being a happy and successful college student, she produced the freewriting on page 38. (This freewriting represents the first step toward her essay, three different versions of which appear in chapter 3.)

As the color shading shows, Melissa's freewriting generated several possible topics for an essay about being a successful college student: managing stress, finding creative approaches to studying, and balancing work and school. Some of these topics overlap; all of them have to do with managing time and stress. Melissa could write an essay on ways to manage stress or ways to make studying more enjoyable. Or, since she mentions the necessity of working while in school, she might want to focus her essay on balancing the demands of her much-needed job with those of her schoolwork.

(c) Listing

One way to gather ideas about a writing topic is to make an informal list, a process also known as **brainstorming.** The advantage to listing is that, like outlining, it lets you see individual items at a glance rather than having to

Sometimes I feel like being successful in school and simultaneously remaining sane, much less happy, are incompatible goals. Schoolwork can be very stressful and it requires important sacrifices to stay on top of your studies. Especially when working on those classes that I don't particularly enjoy such as my math or science classes, it is often difficult for me to keep a positive attitude while studying. But I have learned that it takes both time and commitment to do well in school and that oftentimes sacrifices are well-invested and hard work usually leads to good results.

This is why I have had to be creative in my study habits and patterns, a challenge that I have come to surmount only with lots of experience and practice. An example of one of the small compromises I make with myself in order to feel more at ease when studying is to invite a friend along to study with me. Studying seems less gloomy when done in pairs since it is comforting and motivating to know that you are not the only one who is working hard.

Probably the biggest challenge I face in maintaining my success and happiness as a college student though is the balancing act between my schoolwork and my part-time job. With tuition so high and all the extra expenses such as books and technology fees that accompany a modern college education, most students find that they have to work in order to stay afloat and I am certainly not exempt from this rule. Even though I usually only work around 15 hours a week, those 15 hours can be quite crucial in the midst of exams and papers with strict deadlines. Since I always try to put my school-work first, there are definitely some weeks where I wish I didn't have to work at all!

pick them out of a block of writing. It also encourages the establishment of relationships. Jot down any ideas that come to you while you are thinking about your subject. Do not worry if the ideas lack any kind of order, and do not worry about the form in which you write them down; grammar, spelling, and word choice are not important at this stage. Devote as much time as necessary to making your list—perhaps ten minutes, perhaps an entire evening. The point is to collect as many ideas as you can—to make progress, not achieve perfection.

Melissa made the following list after she had decided to focus her essay on the challenge of balancing schoolwork with a part-time job.

Need to place schoolwork first

Part-time job can be career experience

Part-time job can also be motivating to do well in school so you don't always have
to stay at this job

You will value your education more if you have had to work hard for it

Part-time job can also remind you that your personal stress is not the only thing in
the world, nor the most important

Need to have understanding employers who value employing good students

Need to have flexibility in scheduling job hours, especially for exam and paper
weeks

Having a part-time job forces you to keep on top of schoolwork, to be consistent in
your studies

This list may appear chaotic, but earlier items suggest later ones, and a review of the whole list may indicate items that need to be rearranged, added, or deleted. As you look through the list, you will note that some ideas are closely related and can be grouped together. For instance, "Need to place schoolwork first" leads easily to "Part-time job can also be motivating to do well in school so you don't always have to stay at this job" as well as to "You will value your education more if you have had to work hard for it." Melissa has also used several words and phrases that are clearly related to balancing schoolwork and a job: "flexibility," "motivating," "keep on top of schoolwork," and "be consistent in your studies." Order and direction are beginning to emerge.

For an example of a list written and revised under pressure, see page 125.

(d) Clustering

Instead of listing ideas in a column, you can try arranging them in a kind of map that shows how they relate to one another. To try **clustering,** write your main subject in the middle of a blank sheet of paper and then draw a circle around it. Surround that circle with others containing related ideas, and draw a line between each of them and the circle containing the main subject (see figure 2.1). As you think of additional ideas or details, place them in circles and connect them with lines to the circles to which they are most closely related. Doing so will establish various ways of exploring your topic and provide a visual image of how these trains of thought connect. Although you are unlikely to pursue all the directions you have charted once you narrow your focus (see **2a(2)**), the connections you have established can help you determine how you want to organize your essay (see **2c**). Clustering is easy to do with pen and paper, but most word-processing programs enable you to create boxes, lines, and circles quickly so that you can do this activity directly on your computer.

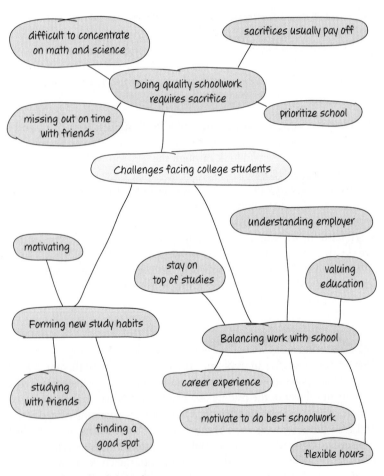

Figure 2.1. Example of clustering.

(e) Questioning

You can also explore a subject by asking yourself some questions. There are two structured questioning strategies that can help you explore a subject: journalists' questions and the pentad. **Journalists' questions**—*Who? What? When? Where? Why?* and *How?*—are easy to use and can help you discover ideas about any subject. Using journalists' questions to explore the subject of balancing schoolwork and a job could lead you to think about it in a number of ways: *Who* typically has to work part-time while in college? *What* should college students look for in a part-time job? *When* should students work? *Where* should students work? *Why* can part-time work be an important part of the college experience? And *how* can students balance part-time work with good schoolwork; *how* can a part-time job influence a student's attitude about schoolwork?

Kenneth Burke's **pentad** consists of five points of consideration; he calls it a dramatistic pentad because it uses the drama of human life as the basis for exploring any subject.

Act	What is happening?
Actor	Who is doing it?
Scene	What are the time, place, and conditions in which the act occurred?
Agency	How was the act accomplished?
Purpose	How and why did act, actor, scene, and agency come together?

This method can help you discover relationships among the various features of your general subject. For example, consider "remaining sane"—one of the ideas generated by Melissa Schraeder in the freewriting on page 38. What is the relationship between the act (remaining sane) and the actor (Melissa)? Does she sometimes feel sane because she's balancing school and a job? Because she is committed to hard work? Because she's pleased with the good results of her efforts?

 Word-processing programs can facilitate brainstorming activities, such as freewriting, listing, and clustering. Some writers like to keep files of their brainstorming activities, which they can consult later when they begin drafting. Sometimes, freewriting or listing can yield phrases, sentences, or even

(Continued on page 42)

(Continued from page 41)

paragraphs that a writer decides to use in a rough draft. If those phrases, sentences, or paragraphs are saved in a word-processing file, they can easily be copied and pasted directly into the rough draft. Most word-processing programs allow you to open several files at once, so that you can easily move from a brainstorming file to a rough draft. Computers in the labs or library at your school may even have special programs for brainstorming activities. Ask your instructor about these. In addition, you might consider brainstorming online with friends or classmates. You can use instant messaging sites, chat rooms, or MOOs (Multiuser dimension, Object-Oriented virtual spaces) to exchange ideas about a topic. In fact, your instructor may have set up a discussion board or created a forum for your class to use (see chapter 5).

(2) Writers need to focus their subject ideas into specific topics.

Exploring a subject will suggest not only productive strategies for development, but also a direction in which to focus a topic. Some ideas will seem worth pursuing; others will seem inappropriate for your purpose, audience, or context. You will find yourself discarding ideas even as you develop new ones and determine your topic.

A simple analogy helps explain focus: When you want a picture of a landscape, you cannot photograph all that your eye can take in. You must focus on just part of it. As you aim the camera, you look through the viewfinder to make sure the subject is correctly framed and in focus. At this point, you may wish to move in closer and focus on one part of the scene, or you may decide to change the angle, using light and shadow to emphasize certain features of the landscape. You can think of your writing the same way—focusing and directing your ideas just as you focus and direct the lens of a camera, moving from a general subject to a more specific topic.

For example, "balancing work and school" is too large and general a subject to make a good topic for a college essay. However, some of the ideas that emerged in the freewriting (see page 38) and the list (page 39) on this subject can be grouped to form a topic that is both interesting and manageable. Or a single idea, if well chosen, might lead to a sharply focused essay of some depth.

In addition to reviewing the ideas you have generated through strategies such as freewriting and listing, you can also achieve focus by thinking in terms of how strategies you might use for developing your ideas (see **2e**) can take you in different directions. Working with "balancing a part-time job with schoolwork" as a large subject that she needed to narrow into a topic, Melissa considered it in terms of the following development strategies:

- *Narration.* What kind of story can I tell about part-time work for college students?
- *Description.* What kind of part-time job do I have? What is my place of work like? How do my employers treat me?
- *Process.* How have I gone about balancing my own part-time job with my schoolwork?
- *Cause and consequence.* What have been the causes of my success in balancing my job with my schoolwork? Concentration? Commitment? What were some of the consequences when I have made mistakes in balancing these two in the past? Exhaustion? Frustration? What is the primary cause? What are contributory causes?
- *Comparison and contrast.* How do my study habits and academic skills compare with those of students who do not work and those of students who do? How does my work-and-school lifestyle compare to my previous school-only lifestyle?
- *Classification and division.* How can I classify the different types of jobs that college students take on? How can I divide up the desirable qualities of jobs and employers? How many jobs are listed in the classified ads each day? How many college students feel they must take a job?
- *Definition.* How do I define "success" in college? Is career experience as important as good grades? What constitutes a "good attitude" toward your education?

The following sentence suggests a focus on comparison and contrast:

Before I came to college and took on a part-time job, I spent all of my free time either studying or hanging out with friends.

This sentence focuses on cause and consequence:

Now that I'm working part-time and taking classes full-time, I have little free time to spend with my friends or relax.

Sometimes a combination of strategies leads to a focus:

When I think of how much leisure time I had before I came to college, I almost get depressed. I used to spend Saturdays hanging out with my friends at the mall and Sunday afternoons reading a novel. Now that I'm in college, working part-time and carrying a full load of classes, I have little time to hang out with my friends, and no time for pleasure reading. So instead of getting depressed, I try to concentrate on the positive consequences of working while attending school.

Although you might need to combine two or more strategies to develop your writing (see 2e), thinking initially in terms of a single strategy can help you clarify your focus.

Because writing is a form of thinking and discovering, your focus might not emerge until after you've written your first draft. When you compare the draft of Melissa's essay on working while attending school (see pages 97–101) with the final version of it (pages 111–114), you will see how drafting and revising can sharpen a writer's focus.

Whatever method you use to bring a topic into focus, your choice should be determined not only by your interests but also by your purpose, the needs of your audience, and the time and space available. The following checklist may help you assess your topic.

CHECKLIST for Assessing a Topic

- Is the topic appropriate for your writing task?
- Can you do justice to the topic in the time and space available to you? Should you narrow it?
- Do you know enough about the topic to write a paper of the length your instructor requires? If not, how will you get additional information?
- Are you willing to learn more about the topic?
- Are you interested in the topic?
- Can you interest your audience in the topic?

Exercise 1

A. Choose one experience from your earlier education that has potential as an appropriate writing topic. In one paragraph, explain why that experience is worth sharing with others. Identify the audience that would most benefit from understanding the experience, and then write a second paragraph describing how much information you would need to include to ensure that this audience understands and appreciates its significance. Set some limits for yourself in terms of your needs as well as those of your audience: What details do you wish to keep private? What details make your experience unique? What details are essential to your telling? What details are common to everyone who has shared this experience?

B. What interesting idea or concept have you learned about in a course recently? Write one paragraph about that idea or concept for your instructor, demonstrating that you understand what you have learned. Then, rewrite the paragraph for a smart ninth grader, who is interested in the general subject but doesn't know about this particular idea or concept.

Exercise 2

Explore part A or B from exercise 1 by experimenting with one of the following strategies: freewriting, listing, clustering, or questioning. Then consider how you could focus the ideas you have generated to form a topic. To illustrate the different directions you could follow, depending on your focus, ask and answer five questions about your subject—either the journalists' questions or the pentad.

2b | A clearly stated thesis conveys your main idea.

Once you have focused your subject, you've gone a long way toward developing a controlling idea for your content and your approach. By this point, you've probably also established your purpose for writing, whether to explain, teach, analyze, argue, or compare. Your subject, purpose, and focus all come together in a controlling idea, or **thesis,** which is appropriate for your audience and context (see chapter 1). In the first draft or two, your thesis may be only tentative. By your final draft, however, you'll have developed a clear thesis statement.

(1) Essays usually include a thesis statement.

Most pieces of writing benefit from a **thesis statement,** an explicit declaration (usually in one sentence) of the main idea. Your thesis statement, then, will convey a single idea, clearly focused and specifically stated, that has grown out of your exploration of a subject. A thesis statement can be thought of as a central idea phrased in the form of an assertion. It is a claim (see **7d**)—that is, it indicates what you claim to be true, interesting, or valuable about your topic.

An explicitly formulated thesis statement helps keep your writing on target. It identifies the topic, the approach, and, in some cases, the plan of development. Notice how the following thesis statements do all of these. The first is from an expressive essay.

> Dave Rahm was a stunt pilot, the air's own genius.   **—ANNIE DILLARD**

With this simple statement, the author establishes that the topic is Dave Rahm and indicates that she will discuss his genius as a stunt pilot. She conveys enthusiasm and awe about his expertise.

The following thesis statement (in two sentences) for an expository essay divides student excuses into five kinds, using humor to make a point.

> With a show of energy and creativity that would be admirable if applied to the (missing) assignments in question, my students persist, week after week, semester after semester, year after year, in offering excuses about why their work is not ready. Those reasons fall into several broad categories: the family, the best friend, the evils of dorm life, the evils of technology, and the totally bizarre.
> **—CAROLYN FOSTER SEGAL,** "The Dog Ate My Disk, and Other Tales of Woe"

The main idea in an argumentative essay usually carries a strong point of view, as in the following, which unmistakably argues for a specific course of action.

> Amnesty International opposes the death penalty in all cases without exception.   **—AMNESTY INTERNATIONAL,** "The Death Penalty: Questions and Answers"

You will probably try out several tentative thesis statements as you explore your topic. It's just as important for you to allow your thesis statement to remain tentative in the early stages of writing as it is to allow your essay to remain flexible. Rather than starting with a preconceived thesis, then, which you must struggle to support, you should let your final thesis statement grow out of your thinking and discovery process as you draft and revise. Your goal should be a statement that is neither too obvious nor too general. The following tips might help you develop a thesis statement.

TIPS FOR DEVELOPING A THESIS STATEMENT

- Decide which feature of the topic interests you most.
- Write down your point of view or assertion about that feature.
- Mark the passages in your freewriting, journal, or rough draft that support your position.
- Draft a thesis statement, and consider whether you can address the full scope of this tentative thesis in your essay or whether it's still too broad to be developed sufficiently.
- After your first or second draft, if your essay has grown beyond your thesis (or vice versa), revise your thesis to widen or narrow its scope in the direction your essay has taken.
- If you're unhappy with the results, start again with the first tip, and be even more specific.

Beyond the Rule

THESIS EVOLUTION

Usually, you'll be able to narrow down your thesis statement as you draft and revise. But on those occasions when you cannot seem to clarify your thesis statement, simply keep writing and working to shape your essay. Writing is a process of discovery, so don't be worried when you don't "discover" your thesis statement until the very last stages of the writing process. For more information about developing a thesis statement, visit www.harbrace.com.

A clear, precise thesis statement helps unify what you write; it's a promise to your readers that you'll stay with the topic you've declared. Thus, your thesis statement will guide not only your decisions about which details to keep and which to toss out, but also your search for appropriate additional information to strengthen your points or support your assertions. No matter what thesis statement you develop, you'll need enough relevant information to support it credibly and clearly. And if you have information about your subject that is interesting but does not really help you keep your promise, that information might lead you to a more purposeful focus.

As you write and revise, check your thesis statement frequently to see whether you have drifted away from it. Do not hesitate to tweak your thesis, however, if you find a more productive or attractive course to pursue. Make whatever adjustments you need to ensure a unified essay. When you revise, test everything you retain against the thesis statement you have finally decided on—your original or a new version you have developed—and scrupulously discard anything that does not help you keep your promise to your readers (see chapter 3).

A thesis is usually stated in a declarative sentence with a single main clause—that is, in either a simple or a complex sentence (see 17c). If your thesis statement announces two or more coordinate ideas, as a compound sentence does, be sure that you are not losing direction and focus. For example, the following thesis statement, composed of two sentences, coordinates and focuses two ideas, indicating a discussion that will contrast men's and women's use of language.

> Male students are more likely to be comfortable attacking the readings and might find the inclusion of personal anecdotes irrelevant and "soft." Women are more likely to resist discussion they perceive as hostile, and, indeed, it is women in my classes who are most likely to offer personal anecdotes.
>
> —**DEBORAH TANNEN,** "How Male and Female Students Use Language Differently"

If you wish to sharpen your thesis statement by adding information that qualifies or supports it, subordinate such material to the main idea:

> Many who today hear me somewhere in person, or on television, or those who read something I've said, will think I went to school far beyond the eighth grade. This impression is due entirely to my prison studies.
>
> —**MALCOLM X,** "Prison Studies"

As you clarify your thesis statement, resist using such vague qualifiers as *interesting, important,* and *unusual,* which can signal that the topic lacks interest or focus. For example, in the thesis statement "My education has been very unusual," the vague word *unusual* may indicate that the idea itself is weak and that the writer needs to find a sharper focus. However, this kind of vague thesis may disguise an idea of real interest that simply needs to be made specific: "Our family grew closer after my parents decided to teach me at home." The following examples show how vague thesis statements can be clarified and sharpened.

Vague	It is hard to choose a major.
Better	Choosing a major is difficult for me because I enjoy so many different classes, and I usually end up with more courses each semester than I can responsibly handle.
Vague	Bobby Knight is a unique individual.
Better	A successful college basketball coach with an uncontrollable temper, Bobby Knight has earned his place in the media spotlight.
Vague	Young people are too influenced by the media.
Better	The frequent use of unusually thin models in television and magazine advertisements has contributed to the rise of eating disorders among adolescent girls and boys in the United States.

Thesis statements appear most often in the first or second paragraph of an essay, although you can put yours anywhere that suits your purpose—occasionally even in the conclusion. The advantage of putting the thesis statement in the first paragraph, however, is that readers know from the beginning what you are writing about and where the essay is going. Especially appropriate in college writing, this technique helps readers who are searching for specific information to locate it easily. If the thesis statement begins the introductory paragraph, the rest of the sentences in the paragraph usually support or clarify it, as is the case in paragraph 1. (For ease of reference, each of the sample paragraphs in this chapter is numbered.)

1   America is suffering from overwork. Too many of us are too busy, trying to squeeze more into each day while having less to show for it. Although our growing time crunch is often portrayed as a personal dilemma, it is in fact a major social problem that has reached crisis proportions over the past 20 years.   —BARBARA BRANDT, "Less Is More"

If the thesis statement is the last sentence of the opening paragraph, the preceding sentences will build toward it, as is the case in paragraph 2.

2   The story of zero is an ancient one. Its roots stretch back to the dawn of mathematics, in the time thousands of years before the first civilization, long before humans could read and write. But as natural as zero seems to us today, for ancient peoples zero was a foreign—and frightening—idea. An Eastern concept, born in the Fertile Crescent a few centuries before the birth of Christ, zero not only evoked images of a primal void, it also had dangerous mathematical properties. Within zero there is the power to shatter the framework of logic.   —**CHARLES SEIFE,** *Zero: The Biography of a Dangerous Idea*

(2) A main idea is necessary even when a thesis statement is not required.

Some kinds of writing do not require an explicit thesis statement, but they still have a main, or controlling, idea. Writing without a thesis statement is sometimes acceptable when the work is narrative or descriptive. A memoir or a journal, for example, is unlikely to have a thesis statement. And reports of information, such as news stories or business memos, frequently do not require a thesis statement. Yet, even in cases such as these, readers should be able to sense a clear direction and focus. You can help your readers understand your main idea by staying focused on it as you draft and revise.

Most of the writing done for college courses contains an obvious thesis statement. The following checklist may help you assess the thesis of an essay.

> **CHECKLIST for Assessing a Thesis**
>
> - Is your thesis clear? In other words, what is your topic? What comment are you making about that topic? What promise are you making to your readers?
> - If your thesis is vague or too broad, how can you make it more specific? (See pages 47–49.)
> - How does your thesis relate to or interest your audience?
> - Is your thesis an accurate reflection of what you believe to be true about your topic?
> - Where is your thesis located in your essay? Would your readers benefit from having it stated earlier or later?
> - Does your thesis make a claim that is not obvious or too general to support in the length of your essay?

- What two assertions can you make to support your thesis?
- What specific support (examples, illustrations, or experiences) can you think of to support your assertions?

 In some cultures, the type of thesis statement described in this chapter may seem overly direct, even rude. In the United States, however, directness is expected. If you do not state your thesis or main idea clearly, readers may think that you are unprepared or unqualified to write about your subject.

2c | Arranging ideas requires choosing an appropriate method or combination of methods.

Many writers need a working plan to direct their ideas and keep their writing on course. Some use informal written lists; others use formal outlines. Such methods are especially helpful when writing lengthy papers (see chapters 7 and 8) and when writing under pressure (chapter 4). Whatever method you choose for organizing your writing, remember that you can always change your plan to suit any new direction your writing takes. The point is to have a way to direct your effort toward fulfilling your purpose.

(1) Informal working plans can be composed quickly.

An informal working plan need be little more than an ordered list that grows out of a collection of ideas. Melissa Schraeder made such an informal working plan as she prepared to write on balancing work and school. Before she started to write her first draft, Melissa reexamined her freewriting (see page 38) and her first list of ideas (page 39). She decided to focus on the value of learning to balance work and school. Some of the other things she wrote about, being stressed and sometimes feeling gloomy, seemed to fit in with the value she places on a careful balance. She formulated a tentative thesis statement and made an ordered list to chart one possible direction for her essay.

TENTATIVE THESIS STATEMENT: Balancing a part-time job with success in school-work is not only a manageable task, but also a valuable experience contributing to growth as a student and as a growing individual.

1. account of my own experiences with balancing work and school
2. describe how I am able to work and maintain success in my studies
3. the importance of having understanding employers who allow for flexible scheduling
4. stress need to make schoolwork top priority
5. part-time work can offer career experience or motivate you to do well in school in an effort to move beyond the work you do part-time
6. working to fund your education means that you will value it more and stay on top of your studies

When you make such a list, ideas might overlap. For example, it may not be possible for Melissa to separate "maintain success in studies" from "flexible scheduling." Some ideas may be discarded, and others may occur to you as you draft. But a list can be the beginning of an overall plan.

As Melissa continued to work on her essay, she made several changes in her original plan. For example, she decided to discuss the consequences of balancing work and school right at the start of her essay, before concentrating on her reasons for working. She also decided to write a conclusion that included recommendations for incoming students: reasons why working is a valuable experience and ways to balance work and school. Because writing is a process, changes of this sort are natural.

(2) Rough outlines can help writers develop ideas.

Writers sometimes find themselves required to follow a plan of organization that has been determined for them, either by their instructor or by the discipline in which they are writing. The ancient Greeks referred to an organizational pattern that was familiar to both speakers and audiences of that time as "the arrangement." In fact, that **classical arrangement** proved to be so successful, especially in posing an argument, that many writers still use it today (see 7g(1)). The simplest way, however, to consider arrangement is to think of Aristotle's claim that every speech needs a "beginning, a middle, and an end." Your essays need those features as well.

Often, however, your arrangement grows out of your early drafts. An outline may, too, for it's much easier to arrange information you have in front of you than to spin an outline out of nothing in particular. Some writers develop excellent plans early in the writing process, turning a working list into a formal outline; others discover after they have done some writing that they need to rethink their original plan. But whether it is written before the first draft or after it, a rough outline is often helpful for analyzing a draft and preparing to revise it. For example, if an outline shows only one subentry under a heading, that section of the draft might need rethinking. The material could be either unnecessary or inadequately developed, or it might belong under a different heading.

Although rough, an outline offers an essay a structure, much like the basic framework of a house. And, like the framework of a house, a rough outline can quickly become more elaborate and detailed. As you work and think, you might introduce indentations, letters, and numbers into your rough outline to indicate various levels of subordination and coordination in your material. Thus, an outline becomes a visual image of your thinking. The main points form the major headings, and the supporting ideas form the subheadings. An outline of Melissa's essay might look something like the following.

TENTATIVE THESIS STATEMENT: Balancing a part-time job with success in schoolwork is not only a manageable task, but also a valuable experience contributing to growth as a student and as an individual.

I. Balancing work with school is manageable
   A. Your own sacrifices will determine success
      1. Time with friends
      2. Use breaks at work wisely
      3. Get a good handle on your school schedule and determine how far ahead you need to start assignments
   B. Best if you have an understanding employer
      1. An employer who puts school first and values scholarship
      2. Take advantage of university-run work programs
   C. Flexibility in scheduling hours
      1. Plan ahead around exam and paper weeks
      2. Often need to sacrifice weekend time in order to get in hours

II. Balancing work with school is valuable experience for students

   A. Provides discipline

      1. In prioritizing schoolwork, those students who work part-time jobs often have a good handle on their academic schedules and stay on top of their studies

      2. Working students learn the importance of time management and set realistic goals and timelines for themselves

   B. Working to pay for education leads students to place more respect and value on their education

      1. More serious about schoolwork

      2. Realize the importance of timely completion of degree

         a. Sleep becomes a priority

         b. Exercise seems less important

   C. Part-time work can offer career experience

      1. Internships

      2. Career-related work

   D. Part-time work can motivate students to achieve excellence in school as a means of moving beyond the scope of part-time work

      1. Face boredom or monotony in job

      2. Face low wages

      3. Constructive use of potential negativity

The types of outlines most commonly used are topic and sentence outlines. The headings and subheadings in a topic outline are expressed in grammatically parallel phrases; a sentence outline contains headings and subheadings that are complete and usually parallel sentences. A topic outline has the advantage of brevity and highlights the logical flow of your paper; a sentence outline forces you to think through your ideas more thoroughly. In fact, the headings in a sentence outline can often serve as tentative topic sentences in a first draft. Here is a sentence outline Melissa might create from her rough outline.

TENTATIVE THESIS STATEMENT: Balancing a part-time job with success in schoolwork is not only a manageable task, but also a valuable experience contributing to growth as a student and as an individual. Since so many students need to work while going to school, I hope to show them that while holding a part-time job and doing well in school may seem difficult at first, in many ways these two undertakings are quite compatible.

I. Balancing work with school is a manageable task.

    A. As with most things in life, your own individual sacrifices in this balancing act will determine your success.

        1. You will often need to limit or carefully schedule the time that you spend with friends.

        2. Bringing along your books to work, you can get a heads up on nightly work by using your work breaks as study time.

    B. You can minimize the pressure put on yourself by choosing a job where you work for an understanding employer.

        1. You should look for an employer who understands the need to put schoolwork first and who values scholarship in employees.

        2. A good place to look for such an employer is in university-run businesses where supervisors are advised to view employees as students first and foremost.

II. The challenge of balancing work with school can be a valuable learning and growing experience for college students.

    A. This challenge provides students with a degree of self-discipline as working students need to prioritize their schoolwork carefully, thus learning the importance of realistic goal setting and time management.

    B. Students who work to support their own education often develop a heightened sense of respect, value, and responsibility for it.

    C. Certain types of part-time work such as internships or major-area work programs can give students valuable career experience.

    D. Other types of part-time work, such as factory, food service, or maintenance work, while less directly valuable to the education process, often have positive motivating effects on students' academic attitudes.

Regardless of the type of outline you use, you need enough headings to develop your topic fully within the boundaries promised in your thesis.

You can create an outline quickly and easily with a word-processing program; some programs even have functions to help you work with outlines. These functions can be especially useful if your instructor has asked you to submit an outline with your first draft. If you are using a newer word-processing program, consult the Help feature for instructions on how to use the outline functions.

2d | Draft your essay by writing well-developed paragraphs.

You compose a draft by developing the paragraphs that will constitute the essay as a whole. If you are working from an outline, especially a topic or sentence outline (see **2c(2)**), you can anticipate the number of paragraphs you will probably write and what you hope to accomplish in each paragraph. If you are working from an informal working plan (see **2c(1)**), you will have a sense of where you want to take your ideas but may be uncertain about the number and nature of the paragraphs you will need. In one case, you enjoy the security of a clear direction; in the other, you enjoy the freedom to pursue new ideas that occur as you draft. In both cases, however, you need to develop each paragraph fully and then ask yourself whether any additional paragraphs (or additional supporting information within any paragraph) would help your audience understand the main idea of your essay.

Paragraphs have no set length. Typically, they range from 50 to 250 words, and paragraphs in books are usually longer than those in newspapers and magazines. There are certainly times when a long paragraph makes for rich reading, as well as times when a long paragraph exhausts a single minor point, combines too many points, or becomes repetitive. On the other hand, short, one-sentence paragraphs can be effectively used for emphasis (see chapter **26**) or to establish transition (see **3d**). Short paragraphs can also, however, indicate inadequate development. There will be times when you can combine two short paragraphs as you revise (see chapter **3**), but there will be many more occasions when you need to lengthen a short paragraph by developing it with specific details or examples.

Inexperienced writers are often unsure about paragraph length, so they may fall into the habit of writing short paragraphs for fear of going overlong or long paragraphs for fear of not adequately developing their ideas. Experienced writers don't worry so much about paragraph length; rather, they concentrate on getting words on the paper or on the screen, knowing that all paragraphs can be shortened, lengthened, merged, or otherwise improved later in the writing process. So think of revising and developing your paragraphs as a luxury, an opportunity to articulate exactly what you want to say without anyone interrupting you—or changing the subject.

(1) You can develop a paragraph with details.

A good paragraph gives readers something to think about. You will disappoint them if you end a paragraph too soon. Consider paragraph 3.

3   My liberated hair made me happy. No longer was I addicted to the beauty
     shop; I was charmed by my own creativity with my own hair—no Korean-
     hair extensions, no relaxers, no dyes.

This paragraph is short, and it promises details that remain unmentioned: How exactly did her hair make the writer happy? What had happened at the beauty shop? How exactly did the writer's hair show off her creativity?

Now consider a well-developed paragraph by Alice Walker.

4   *I stood in front of the mirror and looked at myself and laughed.* My hair was
     one of those odd, amazing, unbelievable, stop-you-in-your-tracks creations—
     not unlike a zebra's stripes, an armadillo's ears, or the feet of the electric-blue-
     footed boobie—that the Universe makes for no reason other than to express
     its own limitless imagination. I realized I had never been given the opportu-
     nity to appreciate hair for its true self. That it did, in fact, have one. I re-
     membered years of enduring hairdressers—from my mother onward—doing
     missionary work on my hair. They dominated, suppressed, controlled. Now,
     more or less free, it stood this way and that. I would call up my friends around
     the country to report on its antics. It never thought of lying down. Flatness,
     the missionary position, did not interest it. It grew. Being short, cropped off
     near the root, another missionary "solution," did not interest it either. It
     sought more and more space, more light, more of itself. It loved to be washed;
     but that was it.   —**ALICE WALKER,** "Oppressed Hair Puts a Ceiling on the Brain"

Notice how the series of details in paragraph 4 support the main idea (italicized), the topic sentence (see 3c(1)). Readers can easily see how one sentence leads into the next, creating a clear picture of the hair being described.

(2) You can develop a paragraph by providing examples.

Like details, examples contribute to paragraph development by making specific what otherwise might seem general and hard to grasp. Details describe a person, place, or thing; examples illustrate an idea with information that can come from different times and places. Both details and examples support your ideas in terms of the rhetorical situation. (See 7e.)

The author of paragraph 5 uses several closely related examples (as well as details) to support the main idea with which he begins.

5   *Illiterates live, in more than literal ways, an uninsured existence.* They cannot understand the written details on a health insurance form. They cannot read the waivers that they sign preceding surgical procedures. Several women I have known in Boston have entered a slum hospital with the intention of obtaining a tubal ligation and have emerged a few days later after having been subjected to a hysterectomy. Unaware of their rights, incognizant of jargon, intimidated by the unfamiliar air of fear and atmosphere of ether that so many of us find oppressive in the confines even of the most attractive and expensive medical facilities, they have signed their names to documents they could not read and which nobody, in the hectic situation that prevails so often in those overcrowded hospitals that serve the urban poor, had even bothered to explain.   —**JONATHAN KOZOL**, "The Human Cost of an Illiterate Society"

You can also use one striking example, as in paragraph 6, to illustrate your main idea.

6   Glamour's lethal effect on the psyche is also caught in the language that commonly describes its impact: "dressed to kill," "devastating," "shattering," "stunning," "knockout," "to die for." Perhaps it's not surprising that Rita Hayworth's famous pinup pose in which she's kneeling in a silk negligee on satin sheets was taped to the bomb that was dropped on Hiroshima.

—**JOHN LAHR**, "The Voodoo of Glamour"

Exercise 3

Examine some of your own writing—such as an essay you have recently drafted, email messages that are still on file, or entries in your journal—and select one paragraph that holds potential interest. Write out the original paragraph, and then rewrite it, developing it with additional details or examples.

2e | **Experimenting with different strategies can help you develop your ideas.**

When drafting essays, you can benefit from techniques that help writers develop their ideas. Certain strategies can be used to frame entire essays by providing a way to organize ideas. Often referred to as **rhetorical meth-**

ods, these strategies for developing paragraphs (and essays) are already second nature to you. Every day you use one or more of them to define a concept, narrate a significant incident, supply examples for an assertion, classify or divide information into specific parts, compare two or more things, analyze a process, or identify a cause or consequence. You use rhetorical methods to generate ideas, to focus your topic (see **2a(2)**), and to clarify your meaning for your audience. When drafting an essay, you may discover that you need to define a term or explain a process before you can take your readers further into your topic. Writers have the option of tapping one, two, or several of these rhetorical methods to fulfill their overall purpose.

These rhetorical methods reflect the human thinking process, the ways we naturally make decisions, teach or explain, entertain, argue a point, or evaluate. But thinking is rarely simple or straightforward; hence, writers often use the rhetorical methods in combinations. For example, a formal definition can be developed through both comparison and contrast, and narration can be developed through description. One rhetorical method is not inherently superior to another. What matters is that you choose one of these methods—or some combination of them—that helps you develop your paragraph (or essay) and eventually fulfill the needs of your rhetorical situation (see **1b**): your purpose, the expectations of your audience, and the specific context in which you are writing. Experienced writers know that attending to all the features of the rhetorical situation helps them determine which points to develop and decide which rhetorical method or methods can best support that development.

(1) Narrating a series of events tells readers what happened.

A narrative discusses a sequence of events, normally in **chronological order** (the order in which they occur), to develop a particular point or set a mood. This rhetorical method, which often uses a setting, characters, dialogue, and description, usually uses transition words or phrases such as *then, later, that evening,* or *the following week* to help guide readers from one incident to the next. Whatever its length, a narrative must remain focused on the controlling idea. Drawn from Charles Darwin's journal, written during his voyage on the *Beagle,* paragraph 7 uses narrative to convey a sense of wonder at the power of nature.

7   The day has been memorable in the annals of Valdivia, for the most severe earthquake experienced by the oldest inhabitant. I happened to be on

shore, and was lying down in the wood to rest myself. It came on suddenly, and lasted two minutes, but the time appeared much longer. The rocking of the ground was very sensible. The undulations appeared to my companion and myself to come from due east, whilst others thought they proceeded from the southwest. This shows how difficult it sometimes is to perceive the direction of vibrations. There was no difficulty in standing upright, but the motion made me almost giddy; it was something like the movement of a vessel in a little cross-ripple, or still more like that felt by a person skating over thin ice, which bends under the weight of his body.

—**CHARLES DARWIN**, "Great Earthquake"

(2) Describing something to show how it looks, sounds, smells, or feels adds useful detail.

By describing a person, place, object, or sensation, you can make your material come alive. Often descriptions are predominantly visual, but even visual descriptions can include the details of what you hear, smell, taste, touch, or sense in some less physical way. In short, descriptions appeal to the senses.

Description should suit your purpose and audience. In describing your car, for example, you would emphasize certain features to a potential buyer, others to a mechanic who is going to repair it, and still others to a friend who wants to borrow it. In paragraph 8, Kathleen Murphy makes her description of Clint Eastwood vivid by blending visual and auditory images and suggesting tactile sensations. Writing for movie fans, Murphy seeks to convey to that audience what is attractive about the kind of masculinity Eastwood embodies in one of his early films.

8   His gait is that of a ghost or a predator, his poncho'd torso remaining strangely still, propelled ahead by the long legs, as though swimming upright in slow motion. Paradoxically, the hands of the remorseless gunfighter are those of a musician or a painter: elegant, long-fingered, with graceful wrists. In these formative stages of the Eastwood persona, his often nearly whispered vocal tones seem too pressured for ordinary speech. The silky, then increasingly abrasive sibilance of his drawl, like sand or gravel shifting in water, works best for epigrams, cryptic ripostes, up-close seduction.

—**KATHLEEN MURPHY**, "The Good, the Bad, and the Ugly"

(3) Explaining a process shows readers how something happens.

Process paragraphs, in explaining how something is done or made, often use both description and narration. You might describe the items used in a process and then narrate the steps chronologically. Add an explanation of a process to a draft if doing so can illustrate a concept that might otherwise be hard for your audience to grasp. In paragraph 9, Garrison Keillor explains how to get started on a letter.

9   The first step in writing letters is to get over the guilt of *not* writing. You don't "owe" anybody a letter. Letters are a gift. The burning shame you feel when you see unanswered mail makes it harder to pick up a pen and makes for a cheerless letter when you finally do. *I feel bad about not writing, but I've been so busy,* etc. Skip this. Few letters are obligatory, and they are *Thanks for the wonderful gift* and *I am terribly sorry to hear about George's death* and *Yes, you're welcome to stay with us next month,* and not many more than that. Write those promptly if you want to keep your friends. Don't worry about the others, except love letters, of course. When your true love writes *Dear Light of My Life, Joy of My Heart, O Lovely Pulsating Core of My Sensate Being,* some response is called for.   —**GARRISON KEILLOR,** "How to Write a Personal Letter"

(4) Analyzing cause or consequence establishes why something happens or predicts results.

Writers who analyze cause or consequence raise the question *Why?* and must answer it to the satisfaction of their audience, differentiating the **primary cause** (the most important one) from **contributory causes** (which contribute to but do not directly cause a situation) or the **primary consequence** (the most important one) from **secondary consequences** (which occur because of an event but are less important than the primary consequence). Writers who analyze cause or consequence usually link events along a time line, just as you would to a police officer if you were describing a traffic accident. Always keep in mind, though, that just because one event occurs before—or after—another event, doesn't necessarily make it a cause—or a consequence—of that event (see **7i(9)**). In paragraph 10, humorist Dave Barry uncovers a historical cause for the male tendency "to do extremely little in the way of useful housework."

10   Somewhere during the growth process, a hormonal secretion takes place in women that enables them to see dirt that men cannot see, dirt at the level of *molecules,* whereas men generally don't notice it until it forms clumps large enough to support agriculture. This can lead to tragedy, as it did in the ill-fated ancient city of Pompeii, where the residents all got killed when the local volcano erupted and covered them with a layer of ash twenty feet deep. Modern people often ask, "How come, when the ashes started falling, the

Pompeii people didn't just *leave?*" The answer is that in Pompeii, it was the custom for the men to do the housework. They never even *noticed* the ash until it had for the most part covered the children. "Hey!" the men said (in Latin). "It's mighty quiet around here!" This is one major historical reason why, to this very day, men tend to do extremely little in the way of useful housework.   —**DAVE BARRY**, "Batting Clean-up and Striking Out"

Writers can also demonstrate effects, as in paragraph 11, which explores the effects automobiles have had on our society by asking us to imagine life without them.

11   Let us imagine what life would be like in a carless nation. People would have to live very close together so they could walk, or, for healthy people living in sunny climes, bicycle to mass transit stops. Living in close quarters would mean life as it is now lived in Manhattan. There would be few freestanding homes, many row houses, and lots of apartment buildings. There would be few private gardens except for flowerpots on balconies. The streets would be congested by pedestrians, trucks, and buses, as they were at the turn of the century before automobiles were common.
—**JAMES Q. WILSON**, "Cars and Their Enemies"

(5) Comparing or contrasting helps readers see similarities or differences.

A **comparison** points out similarities, and a **contrast** points out differences—to reveal information. When drafting, consider whether a comparison might help your readers see a relationship they might otherwise miss or whether a contrast might help them establish useful distinctions. When writing a definition, for example, you might help readers by demonstrating how the right word makes a difference; after all, as Mark Twain wrote, "The difference between the right word and the almost right word is the difference between lightning and a lightning bug."

In paragraph 12, Jane Tompkins uses descriptive details in her revealing comparison of her two kindergarten teachers.

12   The teachers, Miss Morget (pronounced *mor-zhay*) and Miss Hunt, were tall and thin but unalike in every other way. Miss Hunt was young and attractive. She had chestnut brown hair, stylishly rolled, hazel eyes, and a prominent chin. At first, her smart outfits and polished good looks fooled me into thinking she was the nice one. But there was a twist to her mouth sometimes and a troubled look in her eyes that frightened me, and when she spoke to the children, there was iron in her voice. Miss Morget was old and kind. Her frizzled white hair stuck out, softening her sharp nose; and her pale

eyes, which held a twinkle, made me pretty sure she wasn't going to do or say anything mean. She spoke in a gentle, cracked voice that was never angry; but the children knew when she meant business, and they minded.

—JANE TOMPKINS, *A Life in School*

Two valuable kinds of comparisons are metaphors and analogies. A **metaphor** is a figure of speech that makes an indirect comparison of one thing to another, as in "He was a lion in uniform." (See **29a(4)**.) An **analogy,** on the other hand, makes a direct comparison of the similarities between two things. Try to remember that just because two things are alike in some ways, they are rarely alike in all ways. (See **7i(7)** on false analogy.) In paragraph 13, Nelson Mandela draws an analogy between leadership and gardening.

13   In some ways, I saw the garden as a metaphor for certain aspects of my life. A leader must also tend his garden; he, too, plants seed, and then watches, cultivates, and harvests the result. Like the gardener, a leader must take responsibility for what he cultivates; he must mind his work, try to repel enemies, preserve what can be preserved, and eliminate what cannot succeed.   —NELSON MANDELA, "Raising Tomatoes and Leading People"

(6) Classifying or dividing material can give order to it.

To classify is to categorize things into groups based on certain common characteristics. **Classification** is a way to understand or explain something by establishing how it fits within a category or group. For example, a book reviewer might classify a new novel as a mystery—leading readers to expect a plot based on suspense. **Division,** in contrast, separates an object or group into smaller parts and examines the relationships among them. Divided into chapters, a novel can also be discussed according to components such as plot, setting, and theme (see chapter **13**).

Classification and division represent two different perspectives: Ideas can be put into groups (classification) or split into subclasses (division) on the basis of a dividing principle. Classification and division often work together. In paragraph 14, for example, classification and division work together to help clarify the differences among the kinds of pressures college students endure. Like most paragraphs, this one mixes rhetorical methods; the writer uses definition as well as classification to make his point.

14   I see four kinds of pressure working on college students today: economic pressure, parental pressure, peer pressure, and self-induced pressure. It is

easy to look around for villains—to blame the college for charging too much money, the professors for assigning too much work, the parents for pushing their children too far, the students for driving themselves too hard. But there are no villains, only victims.

—**WILLIAM ZINSSER,** "College Pressures"

(7) Defining an important concept or term clarifies meaning.

By defining a concept or a term, writers efficiently clarify their meaning and develop their ideas. By defining a word for your readers, you can immediately connect with them; they know what you are and aren't talking about. Definitions are usually constructed in a two-step process: The first step locates a term by placing it in a class; the second step differentiates this particular term from other terms in the same class. For instance, "A concerto [the term] is a symphonic piece [the class] consisting of three movements performed by one or more solo instruments accompanied at times by an orchestra [the difference]." A symphony belongs to the same basic class as a concerto; it too is a symphonic piece. However, a symphony is differentiated from a concerto in two specific ways: A symphony consists of four movements, and its performance involves the entire orchestra. Paragraph 15 defines volcanos by putting them into a class ("landforms") and by distinguishing them ("built of molten material") from other members of that class. The definition is then clarified by examples.

15   Volcanos are landforms built of molten material that has spewed out onto the earth's surface. Such molten rock is called lava. Volcanos may be no larger than small hills, or thousands of feet high. All have a characteristic cone shape. Some well-known mountains are actually volcanos. Examples are Mt. Fuji (Japan), Mt. Lassen (California), Mt. Hood (Oregon), Mt. Etna and Mt. Vesuvius (Italy), and Paricutín (Mexico). The Hawaiian Islands are all immense volcanos whose summits rise above the ocean, and these volcanos are still quite active.   —**JOEL AREM,** "Rocks and Minerals"

A definition can be clarified and extended by details and examples, as in paragraph 15, or by synonyms and etymology (the history of the word). Synonyms are often only one or two words immediately following the term and set off by commas:

Sophomores, **second-year students,** derive their name from two Greek words meaning "wise fool."

Use the rhetorical methods just described to make your essay as a whole more understandable to your audience. Make sure, however, that you are using them to support your thesis and fulfill your overall purpose. If a paragraph or two developed with one of the methods is contributing to the main idea of your draft, then it is contributing to your purpose. If the development of a paragraph doesn't support the thesis, then you need to revise or delete it (see chapter 3). Revision is both a luxury and a necessity—and gives proof of progress.

2f	Your first draft allows you to continue exploring your topic and to clarify what you think.

When writing a first draft, get your ideas down quickly. Spelling, punctuation, and correctness are not important in the first draft; ideas are. Experienced writers know that the most important thing about a first draft is to have done it, for it gives you something to work on—and against. If you're not sure how to begin, look over some of the journal writing, clustering, listing, or rough outlining you've already done, and try to state a tentative thesis. Then write out some main points you'd like to develop, along with some of the supporting information for that development. Keep your overall plan in mind as you draft. If you find yourself losing track of where you want to go, stop writing and reread what you have already done. Talk with someone working on the same assignment. Write in your journal, or do some more clustering. You may find that you need to revise your plan—or you may need to rethink your topic. Experienced writers expect a change in plan as they write and revise.

If you feel stuck, move to another spot and draft paragraphs that might appear later (see 4c). Doing so may help you restart your engine, for when you're actually writing, you think more efficiently. You can then move on to another part that's easier to write—another supporting idea, an introduction, a conclusion. But don't worry about writing a provocative introduction or a sensible conclusion at this point. Later, when you're revising, you can experiment with ways of introducing and concluding an essay (see 3b). What's important at this stage is to begin writing, and then keep writing as quickly as you can. Save this early work so that you can refer to it as you revise (see chapter 3).

Although some writers like to draft in longhand, using a word-processing program when drafting offers distinct advantages: You can easily move from one part of a piece to another. Knowing that you can scroll up or down easily allows ideas to flow. And when you save a draft in an electronic file, you are well positioned for making revisions later.

Finally, remember that writing is a form of discovering, understanding, and thinking. As you draft, you're likely to discover that you have more to say than you ever thought you would. If you have confidence in your plan, you may choose to suppress any idea that is not directly related to what you had intended to cover. You may, however, often benefit from the development of unexpected ideas. So, whenever drafting leads you to a place you did not intend to visit, give yourself permission to explore that place if you sense that it may hold a useful discovery. You can consider whether to integrate this new material into your plan when you prepare to revise.

Revising and Editing Essays

Revising, which literally means "seeing again," lies at the heart of all successful writing. When you see again, you see with a different set of eyes—those of the reader instead of the writer. **Revising** entails rethinking what you've already written in terms of your overall purpose: how successfully you've addressed your audience, how clearly you've stated your thesis, how effectively you've arranged your information, how thoroughly you've developed your assertions. **Editing,** on the other hand, focuses on issues that are smaller in scale. When you're editing, you're polishing your writing: You choose words more precisely (see chapter 29), shape prose more distinctly (chapter 30), and structure sentences more effectively (chapters 23–27). While you're editing, you're also **proofreading,** focusing even more sharply to eliminate surface errors in grammar, punctuation, and mechanics. Revising and editing often overlap (just as drafting and revising do), but they are distinct activities that concentrate on large-scale and small-scale issues, respectively. Experienced writers know the difference—even when they're doing both at the same time. Usually revising occurs before editing, but not always. Edited passages are redrafted, rearranged, and even cut as writers revise further.

As you revise and edit your essays, this chapter will help you

- consider your work as a whole (3a(1)–(2)),
- evaluate your tone (3a(3)),
- compose an effective introduction and conclusion (3b),
- choose an appropriate title (3b(3)),
- strengthen the unity and coherence of paragraphs (3c),
- improve transitions (3d),
- benefit from reviewers' comments (3e),
- edit to improve style (3f),
- proofread to eliminate surface errors (3g), and
- submit a final draft (3h).

3a | Revision is essential to good writing.

In truth, you're revising throughout the writing process. Even in the earliest planning stages, you're revising when you consider possible subjects and discard them in favor of more appropriate ones. You're also revising after you've chosen a subject, when you decide to change your focus or emphasize some new feature of the subject. And of course, you're revising when you realize that the sentence or paragraph you've just written doesn't work there and decide to move or delete it.

Even though revision occurs throughout the writing process, you will do most of your revising after you've completed a draft—no matter how much you may have revised while planning and drafting. You may rewrite specific sentences and paragraphs as well as reconsider the draft as a whole. A few writers prefer to start revision immediately after drafting, while their minds are still fully engaged by their topic. But most writers like to let a draft "cool off," so that when they return to it, they can assess it more objectively, with fresh eyes.

How long should you wait, then, before revising? Generally, the more time and distance you can put between writing the draft and revising it, the better. But time constraints often mean that the best you can do is let a draft cool off overnight. Even twenty-four hours will provide you more objectivity as a reader and will reveal more options to you as a writer.

Using word-processing software, writers sometimes print each draft as they complete it, labeling and dating the drafts to keep track of their progress. However, most newer word-processing programs enable you to track your revisions easily without printing, a feature that is especially useful if your instructor requires you to submit all drafts or if a peer group is reviewing your drafts. If your word-processing program does not have this feature, you can save each new version of your work in a separate file. By opening two or more of those files on your computer screen, you can easily compare the different versions. You may find that the ease with which you can return to a draft and change it on your computer may encourage you to revise more frequently.

(1) Anything and everything on the page can be revised.

As you reread your essay as a whole, you will want to recall your purpose, restate your thesis, and reconsider your audience. Does your main point come through clearly in every paragraph, or do some paragraphs digress, repeat information, or contradict what has come before (see **2d**)? Sometimes writers realize that they are getting off track as they generate new ideas; they're also willing to eliminate such digressions, repetitions, and contradictions.

In addition to taking care of your main idea, you'll also want to revise in terms of audience expectations. In other words, you'll want to criticize your work not only as a writer but also as a reader. Revising demands that you gauge what you've written to the audience you're addressing (see **1e(2)**). How does your overall purpose connect with the expectations of your audience? How will your audience respond to your thesis statement? Which of your assertions will your audience immediately understand or accept? Which examples or details will interest your audience? Which of your language choices were aimed expressly at this audience? In other words, revising successfully requires that you examine your work both as a writer and as a reader. As a writer, you must ask yourself whether your words accurately reflect your intention and meaning. As a reader, you must ask yourself whether what is clear and logical to you will also be clear to your audience.

As you read and revise for your overall purpose, you'll also be reading and revising paragraph by paragraph, making sure each paragraph is well developed (see **2d**), as well as unified and coherent (**3c**). You'll be assessing whether each paragraph leads smoothly to the next, whether you need to rearrange any, and whether your transitions are effective (see **3d**). It's especially important to recheck the transitions after you've deleted, added, or rearranged paragraphs; you'll want to make sure that the text flows logically, from one paragraph to the next.

(2) What is not on the page can be more important than what is on the page.

Writers are always on the lookout for what they've put on the page—and what they may have left out. What information might the audience be expecting? What information might strengthen this essay? Your best ideas will not always surface in your first draft; you will sometimes have an important new idea only after you have finished that draft and taken a good look at it. No matter how complete a draft seems, ask yourself whether something is missing. You might use listing and questioning strategies to discover what's missing (see **2a(1)**). Or you might share your draft with a classmate or colleague who is working on the same assignment, asking that person to mark confusing or unclear passages (see **3e**).

(3) Your tone helps you fulfill your purpose.

Tone reflects a writer's attitude toward a subject, so you'll want to make sure that your tone is appropriate to your purpose, audience, and context (see **1e**). When revising, consider how your writing sounds. If you want to present yourself as confident, well informed, and fair-minded, then you'll want all of your words and sentences to convey that tone. If some passages sound defensive, self-centered, or apologetic, you should revise them, keeping in mind that those tones rarely sustain a reader's interest, let alone goodwill. Your challenge is to make sure that your tone contributes to eliciting from your readers the desired response—to you as well as to the information you're presenting.

Consider the difference in tone between the following two writers, both of whom grew up in the American South and are describing the expectations for women in their family. Paragraph 1 is by a black woman who is a celebrated anthropologist and writer; paragraph 2 is by a white woman who is a prize-winning novelist and essayist. (For ease of reference, each of the sample paragraphs in this chapter is numbered.)

1   Mama exhorted her children at every opportunity to "jump at de sun." We might not land on the sun, but at least we would get off the ground. Papa did not feel so hopeful. Let well enough alone. It did not do for Negroes to have too much spirit. He was always threatening to break mine or kill me in the attempt. My mother was always standing between us. She conceded that I was impudent and given to talking back, but she didn't want to "squinch my spirit" too much for fear that I would turn out to be a mealy-mouthed rag doll by the time I got grown. Papa always flew hot when Mama said that. I do not know whether he feared for my future, with the tendency I had to stand and give battle, or that he felt a personal reference in Mama's observation. He predicted dire things for me. The white folks were not going to stand for it. I was going to be hung before I got grown. Somebody was going to blow me down for my sassy tongue. Mama was going to suck sorrow for not beating my temper out of me before it was too late. Posses with ropes and guns were going to drag me out sooner or later on account of that stiff neck I toted. I was going to tote a hungry belly by reason of my forward ways. My older sister was meek and mild. She would always get along. Why couldn't I be like her? Mama would keep

right on with whatever she was doing and remark, "Zora is my young'un, and Sarah is yours. I'll be bound mine will come out more than conquer. You leave her alone. I'll tend to her when I figger she needs it." She meant by that that Sarah had a disposition like Papa's, while mine was like hers.

—ZORA NEALE HURSTON, "Dust Tracks on a Road"

2   The women of my family were measured, manlike, sexless, bearers of babies, burdens, and contempt. My family? The women of my family? We are the ones in all those photos taken at mining disasters, floods, fires. We are the ones in the background with our mouths open, in print dresses or drawstring pants and collarless smocks, ugly and old and exhausted. Solid, stolid, wide-hipped baby machines. We were all wide-hipped and predestined. Wide-faced meant stupid. Wide hands marked workhorses with dull hair and tired eyes, thumbing through magazines full of women so different from us they could have been another species.

—DOROTHY ALLISON, *Two or Three Things I Know for Sure*

Exercise 1

A. Reread paragraphs 1 and 2 by Zora Neale Hurston and Dorothy Allison, and then write a short analysis of how each of these women sounds. Be sure to identify specific words and phrases that led you to attribute this tone to each of them.

B. Reread the paragraphs by Hurston and Allison, and then rewrite each paragraph in your own words, trying hard to maintain the author's tone. Or you might want to create your own paragraph about the expectations for women or men in your family and establish your own tone. Identify specific words and phrases from the originals that helped you with your version(s). Be prepared to read your paragraph(s) aloud and share your findings with the rest of the class.

Exercise 2

Study the first draft of Melissa Schraeder's essay (see pages 97–101) and then study her final version (pages 111–114). Write a paragraph that compares the tone of these two versions, listing specific words and phrases that support your comments.

When Melissa Schraeder revised the first draft reprinted later in this chapter (see pages 97–101), she decided to change her tone after one of her readers commented that she sounded too confident about her ability to balance work and school. Although she didn't want to sound as though balancing work and school was impossible, Melissa surely didn't mean to imply that doing so could be easy. A consistently easygoing tone wasn't appropriate for her rhetorical situation (see **1e**).

The thesaurus and grammar checker in your word-processing program may give you advice that can affect the tone of your writing. However, it's up to you to make choices that maintain or enhance the tone you wish to create. For example, a grammar checker may suggest that you change a word you have intentionally repeated in order to achieve a specific effect and create a certain tone. If you are using these features of your word-processing program as you revise your writing, give careful consideration to the suggestions they make.

3b | Introductions, conclusions, and titles guide readers in responding to your entire essay.

Your introduction, conclusion, and title play a special role in helping readers understand your essay as a whole. In fact, readers look for and read these parts of an essay carefully, expecting guidance and clarification from them.

(1) An effective introduction arouses the reader's interest and establishes your topic and tone.

Experienced writers know that the opening paragraph is important; it is their best chance to "hook" their readers with tantalizing information that establishes the topic as worthy of their time and the writer as worthy of their trust. Effective introductions make readers want to read on. Mark Twain built on the success of *Tom Sawyer* when he wrote the introduction for *Huckleberry Finn,* using Huck to speak directly to the readers:

> You don't know about me without you have read a book by the name of *The Adventures of Tom Sawyer;* but that ain't no matter. That book was made by

Mr. Mark Twain, and he told the truth, mainly. There was things which he stretched, but mainly he told the truth.

Twain's lively introduction connects with the audience and establishes that the story is being told by an uneducated boy. And for a novel—or for any piece of writing that is long and complex—an especially good introduction orients the reader as to the direction the work will take. Readers of *Huckleberry Finn,* for example, can expect another story like *Tom Sawyer,* in which the author tells the truth, mainly.

Introductions have no set length; they can be as brief as a couple of sentences or as long as a couple of paragraphs or more. The only feature of introductions that remains the same, regardless of their tone or length, is their location. Introductions always appear first—but they are often drafted and revised much later in the writing process, for introductions and the thesis statements they so often contain (see **2b**) evolve naturally as writers revise their material, sharpening its focus and developing it to fulfill the overall purpose. You may wish to try several different introductions as you revise, to determine which is most effective. Using a word-processing program, you can easily change the introduction in your draft to compare the effects of different versions.

You can arouse the interest of your audience by writing introductions in a number of ways.

(a) Opening with an unusual fact or statistic

3   The most recent statistics from the U.S. Substance Abuse and Mental Health Services Administration's National Household Survey on Drug Abuse indicate that nearly 7 million youths between the ages of 12 and 20 binge-drink at least once a month. And despite the fact that many colleges have cracked down on drinking, Henry Wechsler of the Harvard School of Public Health says that two of every five college students still binge-drink regularly. For a male that means downing five or more drinks in a row; for a female it means consuming four drinks in one session at least once in a two-week period.   **—BERNICE WUETHRICH,** "Getting Stupid"

(b) Opening with an intriguing statement

4   After smiling brilliantly for nearly four decades, I now find myself trying to quit. Or, at the very least, seeking to lower the wattage a bit.

—AMY CUNNINGHAM, "Why Women Smile"

(c) Opening with an anecdote

5   10:00 P.M. Time for the nightly lockdown and head count. The heavy metal door to my cell lets out an ominous grinding sound, then slides abruptly shut with a loud clang. I hear other doors clanging almost simultaneously down the cellblock. The walls reverberate, as do my nerves. Even though I know it's about to happen, at the sudden noise my skin jumps. I'm always on edge in here, always nervous, always apprehensive. I'd be a fool not to be. You never let your guard down when you live in hell. Every sudden sound has its own terror. Every silence, too. One of the sounds—or one of those silences—could well be my last, I know. But which one? My body twitches slightly at each unexpected footfall, each slamming metal door.

—**LEONARD PELTIER**, *Prison Writings*

(d) Opening with a question your essay will answer

6   You ask me what is poverty? Listen to me. Here I am, dirty, smelly, and with no "proper" underwear on and with the stench of my rotting teeth near you. I will tell you. Listen to me. Listen without pity. I cannot use your pity. Listen with understanding. Put yourself in my dirty, worn out, ill-fitting shoes, and hear me.   —**JO GOODWIN PARKER**, "What Is Poverty?"

(e) Opening with an appropriate quotation

7   Wordsworth said we "half perceive and half create" the beauty we find in nature, and I guess that's what I'm saying, too. On the one hand I see the forest differently now because of the ideas and knowledge I bring to it. I accept it because I know more and am more confused about notions I used to take for granted. On the other hand my sense of this landscape, my pleasure in it, seems to come from outside, too, unbidden and uncontrolled, surprising. I didn't expect to feel the way I do and even resisted it. Satisfaction is the feeling actually produced in me when I walk here over time. Enjoyment is what I experience in the presence of these trees and these openings, just empirically, prior to thoughts and theories.   —**CHRIS ANDERSON**, "Life on the Edge"

(f) Opening with an example

8   Libby Smith knows what it is like to be a victim of gay bashing. First, there were the harassing telephone calls to her home. Then, one evening last March as she went to get her book bag out of a locker at the University of Wisconsin at Eau Claire, she was attacked by two men.

—**MARY CRYSTAL CAGE**, "Gay Bashing on Campus"

(g) Opening with general information about the topic or with background on how you came to choose it

9   I fell in love with it—college basketball, that is—at a drafty old barn in Lincoln Square in Worcester, Massachusetts, not far from where one of my great-uncles once owned a saloon. This Worcester Memorial Auditorium was square and huge, and it had towering murals depicting men loading shells into the big guns of a dreadnought and firing artillery along the banks of the Somme. You had to walk up broad staircases to see the murals in their entirety, and I didn't have the courage for that until I was nearly ten. I continued to love it—the whole raucous, tumbling parade of it—through my undergraduate days at Marquette University, where Al McGuire put together a delightfully rambunctious program. I even loved it when I covered it for five years, more or less full-time, for the *Boston Herald*. I have missed one Final Four since 1982, and I can tell you exactly where and when I stopped loving college basketball: I stopped loving it in a hotel in Indianapolis in 1999, on a Saturday afternoon, before the national semifinals.

—**CHARLES P. PIERCE,** "ConMen"

(h) Opening with a thesis, simply stated

10   Complaining was great when I was a kid. Well, maybe not great, just better than now. When you are a kid, your sense of entitlement is more intact. At least that's how it seems from this distance. Things are supposed to be a certain way—*yours.* Oh sure, things are supposed to go your way as an adult, but it's not always appropriate to mention this.

—**CARRIE FISHER,** "The Art of Complaining"

Whatever type of introduction you choose to write, use your opening paragraph to indicate your topic, engage your readers' attention, and establish your credibility (see 9a).

(2) An effective conclusion helps readers recognize the most important points of your essay and understand why those points are significant.

Just as a good introduction tantalizes readers, a good conclusion satisfies them. It wraps up the essay in a meaningful, often thought-provoking way. As you draft and revise, you may want to keep a list of ideas for your conclusion that move beyond a simple restatement of the thesis (see 2a(2)). Some suggestions for writing effective conclusions follow, beginning with the technique of restating the thesis and main points.

(a) Concluding by rephrasing the thesis and summarizing the main points

11   The Endangered Species Act should not take into account economic considerations. Economics doesn't know how to value a species or a forest. Its logic drives people to exploit resources to the point of extinction. The Endangered Species Act tells us that extinction is morally unacceptable. It was enacted by a Congress and president in a wise mood, to express a higher value than a bottom line.

—**DONELLA MEADOWS,** "Not Seeing the Forest for the Dollar Bills"

(b) Concluding by calling attention to larger issues

12   Nonetheless, the greatest growth industry in this country is the one dedicated to the mirage of good grooming as the road to immortality. Immigrants past built bridges and schools, gilded the cherubim in the corners of churches. Today an entire immigrant class makes a living painting toenails and opening pores. Advances in science and medicine have combined to offer this: the tattooing of permanent eyeliner, the bleaching of teeth, the lasering of sun spots. The waning days of a great nation can be charted only in hindsight. But surely it is a danger sign of some sort when a country is no longer able to care for its own cuticles.

—**ANNA QUINDLEN,** "Leg Waxing and Life Everlasting"

(c) Concluding with a call for a change in action or attitude

13   Our medical care system is in trouble and getting worse. While the experts try to figure out how to achieve utopian goals at affordable prices, let's do something practical about the suffering on our doorsteps. Primary care is the most affordable safety net we can offer our citizens. By all means, let's continue the debate about universal, comprehensive insurance to cover all medical costs, but, in the meantime, let's provide primary health care to all uninsured Americans—now!

—**GORDON T. MOORE,** "Caring for the Uninsured and Underinsured"

(d) Concluding with a vivid image

14   At just past 10 A.M., farm workers and scrap-yard laborers in Somerset County looked up to see a large commercial airliner dipping and lunging as it swooped low over the hill country of southern Pennsylvania, near the town of Shanksville. A man driving a coal truck on Route 30 said he saw the jet tilt violently from side to side, then suddenly plummet "straight down." It hit nose first on the grassy face of a reclaimed strip mine at approximately

10:05 Eastern Daylight Time and exploded into a fireball, shattering windowpanes a half-mile away. The seventy-two-year-old man who was closest to the point of impact saw what looked to him like the yellow mushroom cloud of an atomic blast. Twenty-eight-year-old Eric Peterson was one of the first on the scene. He arrived to discover a flaming crater fifty feet deep. Shredded clothing hung from the trees, and smoldering airplane parts littered the ground. It did not look much like the site of a great American victory, but it was.

—**RANDALL SULLIVAN**, "September 11th, 2001 Somewhere over Pennsylvania"

(e) Concluding by connecting with the introduction

Introduction

15   In the Prelude to *Middlemarch*, George Eliot lamented the unfulfilled lives of talented women: "Some have felt that these blundering lives are due to the inconvenient indefiniteness with which the Supreme Power has fashioned the natures of women: if there were one level of feminine incompetence as strict as the ability to count three and no more, the social lot of women might be treated with scientific certitude." Eliot goes on to discount the idea of innate limitation, but while she wrote in 1872, the leaders of European anthropometry were trying to measure "with scientific certitude" the inferiority of women. . . .

In the essay that follows this introduction, Steven Jay Gould focuses on anthropometry (the measuring of skulls) and then loops back to Eliot for his conclusion.

Conclusion

16   George Eliot well appreciated the special tragedy that biological labeling imposed upon members of disadvantaged groups. She expressed it for people like herself—women with extraordinary talent. I would apply it more widely—not only to those whose dreams are flouted but also to those who never realize that they may dream—but I cannot match her prose.

—**STEVEN JAY GOULD**, "Women's Brains"

Whatever technique you choose for your conclusion, provide readers with a sense of closure. Bear in mind that they may be wondering, "So what? Why have you told me all this?" Your conclusion gives you an opportunity to address that concern. If there is any chance that readers may not understand your purpose, use your conclusion to clarify why you have asked them to read what they have just read (see 7g(6)).

(3) A good title fits the topic and tone of an essay.

The title is the reader's first impression and, like the introduction, should fit the topic, tone, and orientation of the essay. Writers who are confident that they have chosen a topic likely to interest their audience might choose a title that simply announces the topic: "How to Pay for College" or "The Art of Getting a Good Night's Sleep." Other writers might draw attention with a title that involves a play on words, such as "Cents and Sensibility" or "Dressed to Thrill." A good title could also take the form of a question designed to arouse the reader's curiosity: "What Album Will Be Picked as Best of the Year?"

Some writers like to choose a title before they draft because they find that a good title provides a foothold for their writing and clarifies their direction. Other writers choose or revise their title later in the writing process. Whenever you decide to finalize the title of your essay, be sure to consider your thesis statement, your introductory and concluding paragraphs, your overall purpose, and any key words associated with your topic. And when revising your essay as a whole, consider whether you need to revise your title as well.

Exercise 3

Thumb through a magazine you enjoy, and skim the titles and introductions of all the articles. Select two titles and introductions that caught your attention. Copy them, word for word, and then consider the reasons *why* they interested you. What specific techniques for a title and an introduction did the authors use? Next, look through the same or another magazine for two effective conclusions. Copy these, and analyze their effectiveness as well. Be prepared to share your findings with the rest of the class.

3c | **When revising, make sure that your paragraphs are unified and coherent.**

Writers and readers alike recognize the importance of effective introductory and concluding paragraphs (see 3b(1)–(2)). But even when writers satisfy the audience's expectations at the beginning and end of an essay, they know they still have to clarify the relationships within the **body** of the essay, those paragraphs in between. When revising the body, writers are likely to find opportunities for further development (see **2d**) within each paragraph. In addition, each paragraph should be **unified;** that is, every sentence within the paragraph should relate to a single main idea, which most often appears in a topic sentence. After weeding out unrelated sentences, writers concentrate on **coherence,** ordering the sentences so that ideas progress logically and smoothly from one sentence to the next. A successful paragraph, then, is well developed, unified, and coherent.

(1) A topic sentence expresses the main idea of a paragraph.

Much like the thesis statement of an essay, a **topic sentence** states the main idea of a paragraph and comments on that main idea. Critical readers often notice that although the topic sentence is usually the first sentence in a paragraph, it can appear in any position within the paragraph—or not at all. Sometimes, the topic sentence is implied by something in all of the sentences. If you are new to writing or are making a special effort to improve your paragraphing, you might want to keep your topic sentences at the beginning of your paragraphs. Not only will they serve to remind you of your focus, but they're also obvious to your readers, who will grasp your main ideas immediately. More experienced writers try to avoid repeating the same paragraph patterns; they organize the sentences differently within different paragraphs.

When you announce your general topic and then provide specific support for it, you are writing **deductively.** Your topic sentence appears first, like the one in italics in paragraph 17, which announces that the author will discuss the purpose of topic sentences.

17 *Topic sentences establish a focus of attention at the beginning of a paragraph.* In a well-designed paragraph, the reader should be able to anticipate what is to come in the rest of the paragraph. Topic sentences orient readers by identifying what the paragraph is about and how it will be developed. When writers stay within the limits they establish, paragraphs are easier to follow. They feel unified, since they don't seem to digress or run off the point.

—**JOHN TRIMBUR,** *The Call to Write*

If you want to emphasize the main idea of a paragraph or give its organization some extra support, you can begin and conclude the paragraph with two versions of the same idea. This strategy is especially useful for long paragraphs—it gives readers whose attention may have wandered a second chance to grasp the main idea. In paragraph 18, both the first sentence and the last convey the idea that the perfect relationship is probably an illusion.

18   *We should not assume that there is a perfect relationship and that if only we could achieve it we would find, at least in this one place in the world, peace and contentment.* Rather, let us start by facing what seems to be a fact of modern life: Relationships are becoming more and more difficult. We might, as suggested, do well to ask why we attempt them at all. Phrased another way, what is loving another person all about? If we dwell on this question, we realize that expecting relationships to be completely free of fear may be the doorway through which fears enter our connections with others, because that expectation is an illusion. It is the illusion of imagining that people are not deeply hurt, that their past has been ideal, that no trauma has touched us, that all of our troubles will disappear once we have found the right relationship. Through this opening fear gets hold of us, compels us to try to make sure we get what we need from others, and allows us to lose sight of the basic spiritual dimension of relating—that we form bonds to be of help to others, not to ourselves. *We can begin to change this expectation by imagining being in a relationship exactly as we are, with all that we bring, by not expecting the relationship to heal the past, and by working to discover how we can love out of our woundedness.*   —**ROBERT SARDELLO,** *Freeing the Soul from Fear*

As you prepare to revise a draft, try underlining the topic sentences you can identify. If you cannot find a topic sentence, add a sentence stating the main idea of that paragraph. If you find that you open every paragraph with a topic sentence, you might try experimenting with another pattern, revising a paragraph so that the topic sentence appears at the end, as in paragraph 19.

19   I have been to big-money tribal casinos on both coasts and in Minnesota, and they tend to run together in the mind. They are of a sameness—the vast parking lots, the low, mall-like, usually windowless buildings, the arbitrary Indianish décor, the gleeful older gamblers rattling troves of quarters in their bulging pants pockets, the unromantic expressions in the employees' eyes. Also, going to a major Indian casino is so much like going to a non-Indian one, in Atlantic City or someplace, that you may have to remind yourself exactly why Indian casinos enjoy tax advantages non-Indian casinos don't. The idea of Indian tribal sovereignty, a bit elusive to begin with, can fade out entirely behind the deluge of generic gambling dollars. In the last few years, some state and federal legislators have begun to view tribal casinos in just this skeptical way. Their renewed attacks on tribal sovereignty usually include a

lot of rhetoric about the supposed great gambling wealth of Indian tribes nowadays. Regrettably, the resentment against Indian casinos, whose largest benefits go to only a few tribes, may end up threatening the sovereignty of all tribes. Many Indians have worried more about loss of sovereignty since the casino boom began. Some say that entering into compacts with the states is itself a wrong idea, because it accepts state jurisdiction where none existed before. Concern for sovereignty has been a main reason why the Navajo have rejected casino gambling. *A Navajo leader said that tribes who accept outside oversight of their gambling operations have allowed a violation of tribal sovereignty; he added, "The sovereignty of the Navajo nation and the Navajo people is not and should never be for sale."* —IAN FRAZIER, *On the Rez*

Placing the topic sentence toward or at the end of the paragraph works well when you are moving from specific supporting details to a generalization about those ideas, or writing **inductively.** Effective writers try to honor the expectations of their readers, which often include the anticipation that the first sentence will be the topic sentence; however, writers and readers alike enjoy an occasional departure from the expected.

(2) In a unified paragraph, every sentence relates to the main idea.

Paragraphs are **unified** when every sentence relates to the main idea; unity is violated when something unrelated to the rest of the material appears. Consider the obvious violation in paragraph 20.

20 New York has a museum to suit almost any taste. The Metropolitan Museum and the Museum of Modern Art are famous for their art collections. Other important collections of art can be found at the Frick, Guggenheim, and Whitney Museums. Visitors interested in the natural sciences will enjoy the Museum of Natural History. Those interested in American history should visit the Museum of the City of New York. *Getting around the city to visit the museums is easy once you have mastered the subway system.* Part of Ellis Island has become a museum devoted to the history of immigration. Exhibits devoted to social and cultural history can also be found at the Jewish Museum and the Asia Society.

Easy to delete, the italicized sentence about the subway system violates the unity of a paragraph devoted to New York's museums. If the overall purpose of the essay includes an explanation of how to use the city's public transportation for sightseeing, then the writer can simply develop "Getting around the city . . ." into a separate paragraph.

As you revise your paragraphs for unity, the following tips may help you.

TIPS FOR IMPROVING PARAGRAPH UNITY

Identify	Identify the topic sentence for each paragraph. Which topic sentences are stated? Which are implied?
Relate	Read each sentence in a paragraph, and decide if and how it relates to the topic sentence.
Eliminate	Any sentence that violates the unity of a paragraph should be cut (or saved for use elsewhere).
Clarify	Any sentence that "almost" relates to the topic sentence should be revised until it does relate. You may need to clarify details or add information or a transitional word or phrase to make the relationship clear.
Rewrite	If more than one idea is being conveyed in a single paragraph, either rewrite the topic sentence so that it includes both ideas and establishes a relationship between them or split the paragraph into two.

(3) Clearly arranged ideas make for coherent paragraphs.

Some paragraphs are unified (see 3c(2)) but not coherent. In a unified paragraph, every sentence relates to the main idea of the paragraph. In a **coherent** paragraph, the relationship among the ideas is clear and meaningful, and the progression from one sentence to the next is easy for readers to follow. The following paragraph has unity but lacks coherence.

21   The inside of the refrigerator was covered with black mold, and it smelled as if something had been rotting in there for years. I put new paper down on all the shelves, and my roommate took care of lining the drawers. The stove was as dirty as the refrigerator. *When we moved into our new apartment, we found that the kitchen was in horrible shape.* We had to scrub the walls with a brush and plenty of Lysol to get rid of the grease. The previous tenant had left behind lots of junk that we had to get rid of. All the drawers and cabinets had to be washed.

Although every sentence in paragraph 21 concerns cleaning the kitchen after moving into an apartment, the sentences are not arranged coherently. This paragraph can easily be revised so that the italicized topic sentence controls the meaningful flow of ideas—from what they saw to what they did:

22   *When we moved into our new apartment, we found that the kitchen was in horrible shape.* The previous tenant had left behind lots of junk that we had to get rid of. The inside of the refrigerator was covered with black mold, and it smelled as if something had been rotting in there for years. The stove was as dirty as the refrigerator. [New sentence:] So we set to work. All the drawers and cabinets had to be washed. I put new paper down on all the shelves, and my roommate took care of lining the drawers. We had to scrub the walls with a brush and plenty of Lysol to get rid of the grease.

Paragraph 22 is coherent as well as unified.

To achieve coherence and unity in your paragraphs, study the following patterns of organization (chronological, spatial, emphatic, and logical), and consider which ones you might easily adopt.

(a) Using chronological order, according to time

When you use **chronological order,** you arrange ideas according to the order in which things happened. This organizational pattern is particularly useful in narrations.

23   When everyone was finished, we were given the signal to put our silverware on our plates. Each piece of silverware had its place—the knife at the top of the plate, sharp edge toward us; then the fork, perfectly lined up next to the knife; then the spoon—and any student who didn't put the silverware in the right place couldn't leave the table. Lastly, our napkins were refolded and put in their original spot. When we stood, we pushed our chair under the table and waited for the signal to turn right. Then we marched outside, single file, while the kitchen staff started to clean the dining room.

—ANNE E. BOLANDER AND ADAIR N. RENNING, *I Was #87*

(b) Using spatial order, according to the movement of the eye

When you arrange ideas according to **spatial order,** you orient the reader's focus from right to left, near to far, top to bottom, and so on. This organizational pattern is particularly effective in descriptions. Often the organization is so obvious that the writer can forgo a topic sentence, as in the following paragraph.

24   The stores on Tremont Avenue seemed to be extensions of my domestic space. Each one had sensory memories that I associate with my mother. On the corner was the delicatessen. From its counter, which was like a bar complete with a brass footrest, came the deeply dark smell of cured meats, the tang of frankfurters, with the steaming background scent of hot knishes on the griddle.

—LENNARD J. DAVIS, *My Sense of Silence*

(c) Using emphatic order, according to importance

When you use **emphatic order,** you arrange information in order of importance, usually from least to most important. Emphatic order is especially useful in expository and persuasive writing (see **1e(1)** and chapter 7), both of which involve helping readers understand logical relationships (such as what caused something to happen or what kinds of priorities should be established).

In paragraph 25, the author emphasizes the future as the most important site for change.

25   Among the first things Goldsmith had taught the executive was to look only to the future, because, whatever he had done to make people angry, he couldn't fix it now. "Don't ask for feedback about the past," he says. Goldsmith has turned against the notion of feedback lately. He has written an article on a more positive methodology, which he calls "feedforward." "How many of us have wasted much of our lives impressing our spouse, partner, or significant other with our near-photographic memory of their previous sins, which we document and share to help them improve?" he says. "Dysfunctional! Say, 'I can't change the past—all I can say is I'm sorry for what I did wrong.' Ask for suggestions for the future. Don't promise to do everything they suggest—leadership is not a popularity context. But follow up on a regular basis, and you know what's going to happen? You will get better."

—**LARISSA MACFARQUHAR,** "The Better Boss"

(d) Using logical order, moving from specific to general or from general to specific

Sometimes the movement within a paragraph follows a **logical order,** from specific to general or from general to specific. A paragraph may begin with a series of details and conclude with a summarizing statement, as paragraphs 19 and 26 do, or it may begin with a general statement or idea, which is then supported by particular details, as occurs in paragraphs 22 and 27.

26   It was not the only disappointment my mother felt in me. In the years that followed, I failed her so many times, each time asserting my own will, my right to fall short of expectations. I didn't get straight As. I didn't become class president. I didn't get into Stanford. I dropped out of college.

—**AMY TAN,** "Two Kinds"

27   This winter, I took a vacation from our unfinished mess. Getting back to it was tough, and one morning, I found myself on my knees before the dish-

washer, as if in prayer, though actually busting a water-pipe weld. To my right were the unfinished cabinets, to my left the knobless backdoor, behind me a hole I'd torn in the wall. There in the kitchen, a realization hit me like a 2-by-4: for two years I'd been working on this house, and there was still no end in sight. It had become my Vietnam.

—**ROBERT SULLIVAN**, "Home Wrecked"

(4) Grammar contributes to coherence.

In addition to arranging your sentences in a clear pattern, you can also create a coherent paragraph by ensuring that each new sentence builds on either the subject or the predicate of the preceding one. (See chapter 16.) In one common pattern, links are established between the subject of the topic sentence and all subsequent sentences in the paragraph, as the diagram in figure 3.1 suggests.

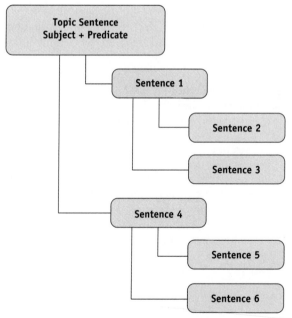

Figure 3.1. Linking a topic sentence to the rest of a paragraph.

Repeating or restating key words and phrases (or using synonyms and pronouns) is one grammatical way to build coherence in paragraphs. Note how many of the sentences in paragraph 28 refer back to *never,* the subject of the topic sentence.

28   ***Never*** is the most powerful word in the English language, or perhaps any language. It's magic. Every time I have made an emphatic pronouncement invoking the word ***never,*** whatever follows that I don't want to happen happens. **Never** has made a fool of me many times. The first time I remember noticing the powerful effect of this word I was a student at Indian school. My best friend, Belinda Gonzalez, and I were filling out our schedules for spring semester. She was Blackfeet, a voice major from Yakima, Washington. I was a painting major and checking out times for painting and drawing courses. She suggested I sign up for drama class with her. I said no, I will **never** get on a stage. Despite my initial protest I did sign up for drama class and soon was performing in one of the first all-native drama and dance troupes in the country, and now I make my living performing. **Never** is that powerful.   —**JOY HARJO**, "The Power of Never"

You can also link each new sentence to the preceding one by linking predicates or, as Annie Dillard does in paragraph 29, by creating links through both subjects and predicates.

29   Sir Robert Falcon Scott, who died on the Antarctic peninsula, was never able to bring himself to use dogs, let alone feed them to each other or eat them. Instead he struggled with English ponies, for whom he carried hay. Scott felt that eating dogs was inhumane; he also felt, as he himself wrote, that when men reach a Pole unaided, their journey has "a fine conception" and "the conquest is more nobly and splendidly won." It is this loftiness of sentiment, this purity, this dignity and self-control, which makes Scott's farewell letters—found under his body—such moving documents.   —**ANNIE DILLARD**, "An Expedition to the Pole"

The subject and predicate links in this paragraph can be mapped out as follows:

Subject Links

Sir Robert Falcon *Scott,* who
died on the Antarctic peninsula,

Instead *he*

Scott felt that eating dogs

he also felt, as he himself
wrote, that when men reach
a Pole unaided, their journey

It is this loftiness of sentiment,
this purity, this dignity and
self-control,

Predicate Links

was never able to bring himself to
use dogs, let alone feed them to
each other or eat them.

struggled with English ponies, for
whom he carried hay.

was inhumane;

has "a fine conception" and "the
conquest is more nobly and
splendidly won."

which makes Scott's farewell
letters—found under his body—
such moving documents.

3d | Transitions improve coherence within and between paragraphs.

Sentences can be arranged in a seemingly clear sequence (see 3c(3)), but
a single paragraph may lack internal coherence and a series of paragraphs
may lack overall coherence if transitions are abrupt or nonexistent.
When revising your writing, you can improve the coherence by using
transitional elements such as pronouns, repetition, conjunctions, other
transitional words or phrases, and parallel structure.

(1) Pronouns help establish links between sentences.

In paragraph 30, the writer explains the similarities of identical twins
raised separately. She mentions their names only once, but uses the pronouns *both, their,* and *they* to keep the reference to the twins always clear.

30   Jim Springer and Jim Lewis were adopted as infants into working-class Ohio families. **Both** liked math and did not like spelling in school. **Both** had law enforcement training and worked part-time as deputy sheriffs. **Both** vacationed in Florida, **both** drove Chevrolets. Much has been made of the fact that **their** lives are marked by a trail of similar names. **Both** married and divorced women named Linda and had second marriages with women named Betty. **They** named **their** sons James Allan and James Alan, respectively. **Both** like mechanical drawing and carpentry. **They** have almost identical drinking and smoking patterns. **Both** chew their fingernails down to the nubs.   —**CONSTANCE HOLDEN**, "Identical Twins Reared Apart"

(2) Repetition of words, phrases, or ideas can link a sentence to those that precede it.

In paragraph 31, the repetition of the key word *wave* links the sentences and also provides emphasis. (See 26e.)

31   The weekend is over, and we drive down the country road from the cottage to the pier, passing out our last supply of **waves.** We **wave** at people walking and **wave** at people riding. We **wave** at people we know and **wave** at people who are strangers.
                              —**ELLEN GOODMAN**, "Waving Goodbye to the Country"

Repeating a key word and using parallel structures (see chapter 25) are other common ways of establishing transitions between paragraphs, as in paragraphs 32 and 33.

32   I want a **wife** who will take care of *my* physical needs. I want a **wife** who will keep my house clean. A **wife** who will pick up after my children, a **wife** who will pick up after me. I want a **wife** who will keep my clothes clean, ironed, mended, replaced when need be, and who will see to it that my personal things are kept in their proper place so that I can find what I need the minute I need it. I want a **wife** who cooks the meals, a **wife** who is a *good* cook. I want a **wife** who will plan the menus, do the necessary grocery shopping, prepare the meals, serve them pleasantly, and then do the cleaning up while I do my studying. I want a **wife** who will care for me when I am sick and sympathize with my pain and loss of time from school. I want a **wife** to go along when our family takes a vacation so that someone can continue to care for me and my children when I need a rest and change of scene.

33   I want a **wife** who will not bother me with rambling complaints about a **wife's** duties. But I want a **wife** who will listen to me when I feel the need to

explain a rather difficult point I have come across in my course of studies. And I want a **wife** who will type my papers for me when I have written them.
—**JUDY BRADY**, "I Want a Wife"

In this case, the author wished to stress the expectations many people have about the role of a wife; by using *wife* fourteen times, she emphasizes how many details of a comfortable domestic life are often attended to by the wife.

(3) Conjunctions and other transitional words or phrases also contribute to coherence.

Conjunctions and transitional words or phrases demonstrate the logical relationship between ideas. In the following sentences, in which two clauses are linked by different conjunctions, notice the subtle changes in the relationship between the two ideas.

He laughed, **and** she frowned.

He laughed **while** she frowned.

He laughed **because** she frowned.

He laughed, **so** she frowned.

He laughed; **later** she frowned.

The following list of frequently used transitional connections, arranged according to the kinds of relationships they establish, can help you with your critical reading as well as your writing.

TYPES OF TRANSITIONAL CONNECTIONS

Alternative	or, nor, and, and then, moreover, besides
Addition	further, furthermore, likewise, also, too, again, in addition, even more important, next, first, second, third, in the first place, in the second place, finally, last
Comparison	similarly, likewise, in like manner
Contrast	but, yet, or, and yet, however, still, nevertheless, on the other hand, on the contrary, conversely, even so, notwithstanding, in contrast, at the same time, although this may be true, otherwise, nonetheless

(Continued on page 90)

(Continued from page 89)

Place	here, beyond, nearby, opposite to, adjacent to, on the opposite side
Purpose	to this end, for this purpose, with this object, in order to
Result or cause	so, for, therefore, accordingly, consequently, thus, thereupon, as a result, then, because, hence
Summary	to sum up, in brief, on the whole, in sum, in short, in any event
Repetition	as I have said, in other words, that is, to be sure, as has been noted
Exemplification	for example, for instance, to show, to see, to understand, in the case of
Intensification	in fact, indeed, to tell the truth
Time	meanwhile, at length, soon, after a few days, in the meantime, afterward, later, now, then, in the past, while

(4) Coherence can also be achieved through the use of parallel structures.

Parallelism is a key principle in writing coherent sentences and paragraphs. (See chapter **25**.)

> Human beings are more alike than unalike, and what is true anywhere is true everywhere, yet I encourage travel to as many destinations as possible for the sake of education as well as pleasure.
>
> —**MAYA ANGELOU**, *Wouldn't Take Nothing for My Journey Now*

The following checklist can guide you in revising your paragraphs.

CHECKLIST for **Revising Paragraphs**

- Does the paragraph have a clear topic sentence (**3c(1)**)? Does it need one?

- Do all the ideas in the paragraph belong together? Do sentences link to previous and later ones? Are the sentences arranged in chronological, spatial, emphatic, or logical order? Or are they arranged in some other pattern (**3c(2)**)?

- Are sentences connected to each other with effective transitions (3d)? What transitions are used?
- How does the paragraph link to the preceding and following ones (3d)?
- Is the paragraph adequately developed? How do you know? What idea or detail might be missing (3a(2))? What rhetorical methods have been used to develop each of the paragraphs (2d and 2e)?

When revising an essay, however, you must consider the effectiveness of the individual paragraphs at the same time as you consider how those paragraphs work (or don't work) together to achieve the overall purpose. Some writers like to revise at the paragraph level before addressing larger concerns; other writers cannot work on the individual paragraphs until they have grappled with larger issues related to the rhetorical situation (overall purpose, attention to audience, and context; see 1e) or have finalized their thesis (2b). All experienced writers use a process to write, but they do not all use exactly the same process. Since there's no universal, predetermined order to the writing process, you can follow whichever steps work best for you at the time you are revising. Be guided by the principles and strategies discussed in this chapter, but trust also in your own good sense.

3e | Writers benefit from having others read their drafts.

Because writing is a form of communication, writers benefit from checking whether they are communicating their ideas effectively to their readers. Instructors are, of course, one set of readers, but they are often the last people to see your writing. Before you submit your work to your instructor, take advantage of other opportunities for getting responses to it. Experienced writers *always* consult a trusted reader before they submit their work for evaluation. Why not follow their good example? You, too, can consult with readers—at the writing center, in your dorm, or in your classes—asking them for honest responses to your concerns. You have numerous options for getting feedback on your writing. Besides the opportunities on campus, there are a number of online writing groups and sites. Both writers and readers benefit from sharing and responding to writing; both gain a clearer sense of how they can improve their work.

(1) Clearly defined evaluation standards help both writers and reviewers.

Although you'll always write within a rhetorical situation (see 1b), you'll often address that situation in terms of an assigned task with specific evaluation standards. Instructors usually indicate their evaluation standards in class, on assignment sheets, or on separate handouts (see 1f(2)). Whether you're working with a small writing group from class or a single reader, such as a classmate or writing center tutor, you need to review evaluation criteria at the beginning of a working session and use them to indicate where you should focus your attention. For example, if your instructor has told you that your essay will be evaluated primarily in terms of whether you have a clear thesis (see 2b) and adequate support for it (7e), then those features should be your primary focus. Your secondary concerns will be sentence length and variety (see chapter 27) and the effectiveness of your introduction (3b(1)).

If you are developing your own criteria for evaluation, the following checklist can help you get started. Based on the elements of the rhetorical situation, this checklist can be easily adjusted so that it meets your specific needs for a particular assignment.

CHECKLIST for Evaluating a Draft of an Essay

- What is your purpose in the essay (1e(1))? Does the essay fulfill the assignment?

- Does the essay address a specific audience (1e(2))? Is that audience appropriate for the assignment?

- What is the tone of the essay (3a(3))? How does the tone align with the overall purpose, the intended audience, and the context for the writing (1e)?

- Is your topic sufficiently focused (2a(2))? What is the thesis statement (2b)?

- What assertions do you make to support the thesis statement? How do you support these assertions? What specific evidence do you provide?

- Are paragraphs arranged in an effective sequence (2c and 3d)? What order do you use? Is each paragraph thoroughly developed (2d)?
- Is the introduction effective (3b(1))? How do you engage the reader's attention?
- Is the conclusion appropriate for the essay's purpose (3b(2))? Does it draw the essay together, or does it seem disconnected and abrupt?

(2) You can help readers review your work by telling them about your purpose and your concerns.

When submitting a draft for review, you can increase your chances of getting the kind of help you want by introducing your work and indicating what your concerns are. You can provide such an orientation orally to a writing group, tutor, or peer reviewer in just a few minutes. Or, when doing so is not possible, you can attach a cover letter consisting of a paragraph or two—sometimes called a *writer's memo*—to your draft, especially if you are submitting it online. In either case, adopting the following model can help reviewers give you useful responses.

SUBMITTING A DRAFT FOR REVIEW

Topic and Purpose

State your topic and why you have chosen it. Explain what you hope to accomplish by writing about it. Describe your exigence for writing (see 1e). Indicate your thesis (2b), and explain in a sentence or two why you have taken this position. Providing this information gives reviewers useful direction.

Strengths

Mark the passages of the draft you are confident about. Doing so directs attention away from areas you do not want to discuss and saves time for all concerned.

Concerns

Being clear about your concerns is essential to the review process. Put question marks by the passages you find troublesome, and ask for specific advice wherever

(Continued on page 94)

(Continued from page 93)

possible. For example, if you are worried about your conclusion, say so. Or if you are afraid that one of your paragraphs may not fit the overall purpose, direct attention to that particular paragraph. You are most likely to get the kind of help you want and need when you ask for it specifically, and indicating your concerns tells readers that it is safe to discuss them with you.

(3) When you submit a draft for peer review, some responses may be more helpful than others.

When you write about your ideas, you are putting part of yourself on paper. So, hearing honest criticism of those ideas can be difficult. Sometimes writers feel anxious when they submit their work for evaluation.

Before asking for responses to a draft you are planning to revise, you may find it useful to remind both your readers and yourself that the work in question is *only a draft.* You and your readers may know this, but saying it explicitly is helpful. Then, your readers know that it is safe for them to criticize, and you feel reassured that they are responding to a piece that is not yet finished. You might do what many professional writers do: Type "DRAFT" into the header of your word-processing file.

Reviewers don't always know exactly how to help—or what to say that might be helpful—which is the best reason for you to provide some guidelines. But not even the most explicit guidelines will guarantee useful advice from reviewers every time. Whether the advice is helpful or not, try to listen to or read what your reviewers have to say about your work. Usually, you will go away with some measure of useful advice. After the reviewers have finished, however, you are responsible for evaluating their comments—rejecting those that would take you in a direction you do not want to pursue and applying those that will help you fulfill your purpose (see 1e(1)). Remind yourself that you are the author of the draft in question—you have the final say about what goes into an essay with your name on it. And remember that it's a rare writer who pleases everyone.

(4) You can help other writers by giving thoughtful responses to their work.

When you are asked to read a draft written by someone else, ask what concerns the writer has about it and how the writer would like you to respond to those concerns. Then, before you respond, read the draft carefully—at least twice, if possible. When you respond, be specific. Be sure to respond to the concerns the writer has expressed. If you see a major problem in the draft that the writer hasn't mentioned, ask the writer if she or he wants to discuss it at this time; if not, honor that decision. Be sure to praise whatever the writer has done well and to identify specific passages you think could be improved and *how.*

Whenever possible, frame your comments like those of a colleague rather than a judge. For example, if you tell a writer, "Your second page is confusing," you are making a judgment and putting yourself in the position of speaking for all readers. If, on the other hand, you say, "I have trouble following your organization on page two," you alert the writer to a potential problem while speaking only for yourself.

Remember, then, that it is possible to be honest without being unkind. You will not be helping a writer if you ignore problems in a draft you are reviewing. On the other hand, dwelling on every problem, big and small, or insisting that another writer follow all of your advice is unhelpful. Help writers write the essays they want to write, not the ones you want to write.

Computers can be used for peer review in a number of ways. If you can obtain a copy of an essay on a floppy disk or as an attachment to an email message, then you can read the draft on screen and make your comments directly in the file, which you can later return to your classmate. You should make your comments easy for the writer to distinguish from the original draft, by using boldface, caps, or a different font or color or by placing your comments in brackets. Most newer word-processing programs have a feature that enables you to insert comments in a draft without having them show on the original. The comments are indicated by colored highlighting on the screen but remain hidden in boxes that appear only when the writer clicks on the highlighted word or phrase. If both writer and reviewers are using one of these word-processing programs, the reviewers can all comment on a single draft without making the draft difficult for the writer to read. The writer can read the comments during revision, deleting each without affecting the original draft.

(5) Peer review usually improves as writers gain experience and build trust.

After freewriting, listing, and organizing her ideas into a working plan (see 2c), Melissa Schraeder submitted a draft for peer review in a first-year writing course. Melissa worked with a classmate, who was working on the same assignment, and a peer tutor from the university writing center as she drafted and revised her essay, using set criteria for peer evaluation. These students were just beginning to learn to respond helpfully in peer evaluations; therefore, their comments represent the range of responses you might receive in a similar situation. As members of writing groups gain experience and learn to employ the strategies outlined in 3e(1)–(4), their advice usually becomes more helpful.

As you read the assignment and then Melissa's draft, remember that it is only a first draft—not a model of perfect writing—and also that this is the first time the peer reviewers, Bob Geiger and Michelle Clewell, responded to it. Melissa sent her draft electronically to Bob and Michelle, who used Track Changes (a Microsoft Word editing function that can be found on the pulldown menu under Tools) to add suggested changes and comments throughout the essay.

Some instructors may require that students do peer review online using email or a computer network. You should always check with your instructor for specific peer-review guidelines and procedures, but here are some general suggestions for online reviewing.

- If you are responding to a classmate's draft via email, reread your comments before sending them to be sure that your tone is appropriate and that you have avoided the kinds of misunderstandings that occur with email (see 5b(3)).
- Always save a copy of your comments in case your email message is lost or inadvertently deleted.
- If you are responding to a classmate's draft using a special online program, such as WebCT or Blackboard, remember that your comments may be read by other classmates, too.
- Follow the advice in 3e(1) and 3e(4), just as you would if you were commenting on a paper copy of your classmate's draft.

The assignment Draft a three- to four-page, double-spaced essay in which you analyze the causes or consequences of a choice you have had to make in the last year or two. Whatever choice you analyze, make sure that it concerns a topic you can develop with confidence and without violating your own sense of privacy. Moreover, consider the expectations of your audience and whether the topic you have chosen will help you communicate something meaningful to readers. As you draft, then, establish an audience for your essay, a group that might benefit from or be interested in any recommendation that grows out of your analysis.

Melissa A. Schraeder   Bob

English 15   *Michelle*

Professor Glenn

Draft—Working toward a Degree

   When I first decided to pursue my college education at Penn State University, a key factor in my decision was that as a state university, Penn State offered a relatively low tuition. This first sentence doesn't seem to have much grounding. Maybe develop your own experience with choosing a school more, or use a different opening. Adding this factor to the giving financial support of my parents and my fortune at receiving several grants and scholarships, I initially believed that my college education would be easily affordable. When I started classes however, I soon found that with all the additional expenses of school such as the cost of books, technology fees, and spending money, going to school meant finding a job. Though hesitant at first about how holding a job might affect my studies, I soon took on a part-time job ~~where I worked~~, *working* about fifteen hours a week. Up until this point your sentences seem sort of long. Maybe you can condense these introductory sentences into a central idea that will get us more quickly to your thesis statement. See my suggestion. Based on my own experience, I feel confident in saying that balancing a part-time job with success in schoolwork is not only a manageable task, but also a valuable experience contributing to growth as a student and as an individual. ~~Since so many students of today need to work while going to school, I hope to show them that while holding a part-time job and doing well in school may seem difficult at first, in many ways these two undertakings are quite compatible~~. This sentence seems repetitive to me—I don't think it is needed.

   If you have the right attitude and some good advice about finding a part-time job, you will find that working while going to school *does not have to be a scary experience.* ~~is not as scary as it may sound at first.~~ As college students, the most important thing ~~that we~~

~~need~~ to remember is that ~~our~~ schoolwork must always be *your* ~~our~~ first priority. *I think you should keep your pronouns consistent. Since you started with the second-person voice, why not stick with it?* Keeping this in mind, as with most things in life, your own individual sacrifices in this balancing act will determine your success. One of the sacrifices that you might have to make is the need to limit or carefully schedule the time that you spend with your friends. *Since you are trying to show how work at school is both manageable and beneficial for a college student, maybe you shouldn't begin your evidence with such a negative example. Keep a consistent tone.* Not all sacrifices need to be so difficult though. A small sacrifice you can make is to bring your schoolbooks along with you to work and utilize your work breaks to get a ~~heads up~~ head start on your nightly schoolwork. In addition, ~~since part of your time is already committed to your employers, You~~ you will need to get a good handle on your school schedule and plan ahead ~~to determine the time you need to work on various assignments~~. *This section seems kind of vague. I think it would be better if you gave some of your own personal experiences with planning in order to show specific examples of this point.* This sacrifice however will have positive repercussions as it will encourage you to form early study and time management habits. *This is a good point, but I wonder if it might fit better on page three where you begin to discuss the positive repercussions of part-time work on the college experience.*

While it is important to make such sacrifices in balancing a part-time job with success in school, you need not put all of the pressure on yourself. In fact, a key factor in minimizing such pressure is to choose a job where you work for an understanding employer. *I don't like the way this is worded, it implies that you are putting pressure on the employer. Maybe rephrase "there are ways to limit the pressure that you might feel."* This is not always an easy task and is certainly easier said than done. You can, however, take advantage of the resources available to you such as older students, advisors, and internship coordinators in finding a student-friendly employer. You should look for an employer that understands the need to put schoolwork first and who values scholarship in employees. A good place to look for such an employer is in university-run businesses where supervisors are advised to view employees as students first and foremost. Planning ahead around exam or paper weeks, you should also look for a job that offers flexibility and variability in scheduling hours. Again, this is a feature that can be found in most university-related businesses or services since many of these follow the academic calendar in their hours of operation. For the understanding and flexibility that such jobs offer, you should take advantage of the many positions available within your own college or university. *This paragraph seems to repeat itself a little bit. I think you should condense this material and use a personal experience to drive home your point about university employment.* This paragraph is where you start to sound too "preachy." You say "you should" a few times. How about changing this to "I would recommend" or "based on my experiences, the following methods have been helpful" in order to make your tone less presumptuous?

Now that I have shown how college students can manage their schoolwork with a part-time job, I want to move on to demonstrating the ways in which the challenge of balancing work with school can be a valuable learning and growing experience for college students. First, this challenge provides students with a degree of self-discipline as working students need to prioritize their schoolwork carefully, thus learning the importance of realistic goal-setting and time management. *The tone of this is too definite. Remember that your previous paragraphs give good examples but are not the ultimate method for everyone.* Second, students who work to support their own education often develop a heightened sense of respect, value, and responsibility for that education. *Great point!* This means that working students often take their studies rather seriously and realize the importance of a timely completion of their degree. These two examples represent large-scale attitudes and outlooks on education, but part-time work can also have more immediate effects on the academic career of a college student.

Such immediate effects of part-time work can be categorized into two types of experiences ~~with part-time work~~, work which offers career experience and work which fuels academic and career motivation. The former category includes but need not be limited to arranged, paid internships or focused work programs implemented or overseen by your college or university. Career experience is also found in more unexpected ways, such as when a management student gets to observe her manager at work or when a communications student practices his skills in a sales job. While many students will be fortunate to have such experiences, others will find themselves working at jobs that have very little to do with their projected career goals. In such cases, there are still valuable lessons to be learned. Certain types of part-time work, such as factory, food service, or maintenance work, while less directly valuable to the education process, often have positive motivating effects on students' academic attitudes. A working student who faces boredom, monotony, or low wages in her or his part-time job, will often be motivated to achieve academic excellence as a means of moving beyond the scope of this part-time work. *I think you should add some personal experience here. Did you work at a job related to your major or that was monotonous yet motivating?*

With the right attitude and outlook, part-time work can have many positive effects on the experiences of a college student. Even the potential negativity of facing boredom or monotony at work can be used constructively to motivate students to do their best schoolwork. If your college years are the best and most important of your life, I assure you that combining work with academics will enrich that importance, as it will give you a greater appreciation for the education you worked doubly hard to receive. I like your conclusion. I think it is good that it ends on a very positive note and that it relates back to your title about "Working toward a Degree."

Melissa,

Generally, I think this is a very good essay. The overall progression of the paper going from "how to work and do well in school" to "why it is beneficial to work while in school" makes logical sense to me. I like that you emphasize the benefits of holding a job beyond just the obvious point of making money. I also think that you have strong credibility and show good will since you have personal experience with your topic. This credibility makes for a strong argument. Maybe it would behoove you to include specific examples of your working experiences in college. Although your credibility is strong, you might want to avoid being too "preachy" in your tone. I feel that this self-assured tone tends to weaken your argument. I do like, however, the way you note in your paper that not all work has to apply directly to your major in order for it to be valuable. And the way your working experiences reinforce this point. Finally, I like the point you make in the concluding paragraph about monotonous work motivating students to appreciate schooling and thus work harder at their education, as this is something that many college students don't think about. This is especially true for freshmen since many often take attending college for granted as they see it as the next logical step following high school.

—Bob Geiger

Melissa,

Your paper is well thought out and focused, yet combining several sentences and limiting the wordiness would intensify your point. The validity of the paper is strengthened because of your personal experience of holding a part-time job while attending college–tie some of these specific examples into your paper rather than using generic and general examples. This is a great draft–keep working, developing, and improving. Here are some specific suggestions for improvement.

—Michelle Clewell

- *First paragraph suggestion: "Because I decided to attend a state university, was fortunate to receive several grants and scholarships, and had the financial support of my parents, I initially believed my college education would be easily affordable. However, with all the additional expenses, such as the cost of books, technology fees, and spending money, going to school meant finding a part-time job."*
- *Paper has good structure and flow.*
- *Limit prepositional phrases and repeating yourself.*
- *Great points made about time management and valuing one's education.*
- *First half of the paper "you" is used talking directly to the student reading the paper, but the second half is written in a more generic third person. Try to be consistent with point of view.*
- *Add personal experiences and examples to strengthen points.*

Before revising, Melissa considered the comments she received from Bob and Michelle. Since she'd asked both of them to respond to her overall essay, addressing both big issues and small, she had to weigh all the comments and use the ones that seemed to be most useful for her next draft. For Melissa's own response to this draft, see pages 103–106. For Melissa's final draft, see pages 111–114.

Exercise 4

Reread "Working toward a Degree" and the comments it received. Identify the comments you think will be the most useful, and explain why. Are there any comments that seem to be less useful, even hurtful? Explain why. Are there any additional comments you would make if Melissa asked you to review her draft?

Exercise 5

Compose an evaluation sheet, with specific questions and guidelines, to use with a classmate as you review each other's draft for an assignment you're working on. You'll want to have questions about fulfilling the assignment, the overall purpose of the essay, the intended audience, and the thesis, among others.

After Melissa had time to reconsider her first draft and to think about the responses she received from readers (including the ones reprinted here), she made a number of large-scale changes concerning her attention to audience, improved her introduction and conclusion, and edited some of her paragraphs to make them more effective and clear. She also dealt with sentence-level issues of punctuation and word choice. The following pages show what her paper looked like midway through its revision. Melissa used the Track Changes function of her word-processing program as she revised so that she could see and track her changes.

Working toward a Degree

When I first decided to pursue my college education at Penn State University, a key factor in my decision was that as a state university, Penn State offered a relatively low tuition compared to other schools in the state, Temple, Pitt, Penn (of course), and many of the private schools. ~~That, together with my parent's support and the scholarships I'd won made me think that college would be easily affordable.~~ The relatively lower tuition, together with the generous financial support of my parents and my fortune to have received several grants and scholarships, led me to believe that my college education would be easily affordable. When I started classes, though ~~however~~, I soon discovered that unexpected expenses meant I'd have to find a job. What with the cost of books, technology fees, and simple spending money, I realized that, for me, going to school meant going to work. ~~I was shocked by how many unexpected expenses I continued to have at Penn State. I knew I was going to have to find a job.~~ Though initially nervous about how a job would affect my schoolwork, ~~Soon,~~ I took on a **part-time** job at the Penn State Creamery where I worked about 15 hours a week—and I **continue to do** ~~still did~~ well in my coursework. ~~So I can now say that balancing a part-time job with success in schoolwork is not only manageable but valuable for students. Since so many students of today need to work while going to school, I hope to show them that while holding a part-time job and doing well in school may seem difficult at first, in many ways these two undertakings are quite compatible.~~ Based on my own experience, I feel confident in assuring you hardworking students that not only can you, too, balance a part-time job with success in schoolwork, but that the experience can be a valuable, life-long lesson for you.

If you think it through and try to keep a positive attitude, you~~'ll~~ will find that working while going to school is not as scary as it may sound at first. As college students, the most important thing we all need to remember is that our schoolwork must always be our first priority. ~~Keeping this in mind, as with~~ After all, like most things in life, ~~y~~our own individual sacrifices in this balancing act will determine ~~y~~our success. One of the **first** sacrifices you ~~must~~ **might have** to make is to ~~cut out time~~ **limit**, schedule, or reimagine the free time you spend with your friends. ~~or schedule time with them (more about that below)~~. **After you start working, you won't be able to spend long hours in the coffee shop with your friends, but you can spend study time with them.** Not all sacrifices are difficult, **though.** Another small sacrifice might be to take ~~You can bring~~ your schoolbooks along with you to work and ~~utilize~~ **consistently think of** your work breaks ~~to get a heads up on~~ **as** pre-scheduled time to spend on your nightly schoolwork. **Using work breaks for study time will also help you plan ahead in terms of your various assignment deadlines.** ~~Besides, since you're already committed to work anyway, you'll need to get a handle on your school schedule and assignment deadlines. This sacrifice however will have positive repercussions early on because you'll immediately form better work and study habits.~~ **Such small sacrifices can lead to big gains: you can learn quickly how to manage your time so you work and study efficiently.**

While it is important to make such sacrifices in balancing a part-time job with success in school, you need not put all of the pressure on yourself. **One key factor in reducing pressure will be your ability (or luck) in finding a job that includes** ~~A key factor in reducing pressure is to find~~ an understanding employer. **Doing so is not easy,** but is surely ~~easier said than done,~~ so you might want to take advantage of some of the on-campus or campus-sponsored job opportunities. Older students, academic advisors, and internship coordinators can help you locate student-friendly employers, an employer who expects you to be a reliable employee at the same time that she accepts the fact that your major responsibility is schoolwork. In fact, it was my academic advisor who told me about openings at the Creamery, a ~~This is not always easy. So take advantage of the resources available to you on campus. You should look for an employer that~~

~~understands your need to put schoolwork first. A good place to look is in~~ university-run business where supervisors are advised to view employees as students first and foremost. The Creamery is one of a number of on-campus businesses that offer ~~You should also look for a job that offers~~ flexibility and variability in scheduling hours, ~~so take advantage of the many positions available within your own college or university,~~ especially during holiday breaks and finals' week. Again, this is a feature that can be found in most university-related businesses or services since they usually follow the academic calendar in their hours of operation. For these reasons, you should consider taking advantage of on-campus job opportunities.

Once you meet the challenge of balancing your schoolwork with the obligations of a part-time job, you'll find that the balancing act has its own rewards. First of all, this challenge provides you with self-discipline, the self-discipline that comes with prioritizing your schoolwork, setting realistic goals, managing your time, and becoming a reliable worker. ~~Now that I've shown how college students can manage their schoolwork with a part-time job, I want to move on to demonstatee the ways in which the challenge of balancing work with school can be a valuable learning experience for college students. First, this challenge provides students with self-discipline as they prioritize their schoolwork and learn to set realistic goals and time management.~~ Second, working students like us often value our education more because we've worked and paid (or helped pay) for it. Sometimes, we take more responsibility for our educations as well, which means that we study seriously enough to get out on time, even early. We understand the importance of a timely completion of our degree. ~~students who work value their education more. This means that working students take their studies seriously and realize the importance of a timely completion of their degree.~~ These two examples represent ~~large-scale~~ long-range attitudes and outlooks on education, but part-time work can also have more immediate effects on ~~the~~ your academic career as well. ~~of a college student.~~

Such immediate effects can be categorized into two types of experiences with part-time work~~,~~**:** work ~~which~~ **that** offers career experience, and work ~~which~~ **that** fuels academic and career motivation. The former category includes but need not be limited to arranged**,** paid internships or focused work programs implemented or overseen by your college or university. Career experience is also found in more unexpected ways, such as when a management student gets to observe her manager at work or when a communciations student practices his skills in a sales job. While many student~~s~~**-workers** will be fortunate to have such experiences, others, **like me,** will find themselves working at jobs that have very little to do with their projected career goals. In such cases, there are still valuable lessons to be learned. **While I'm grateful for my work environment, I don't plan to dip ice cream forever.** Thus, ~~c~~**C**ertain types of part-time work, such as factory, food service, or maintenance work, while less directly valuable to the education process, ~~often~~ **can** have positive motivating effects on **your** ~~students'~~ academic attitudes. **If you're a** ~~A~~ working student who faces boredom, monotony, or low wages in ~~her or his~~ **your** part-time job, **you might** ~~will~~ be motivated to achieve academic excellence as a means of moving beyond the scope of this part-time work.

With the right attitude and outlook~~,~~ **toward your** part-time work, **you might gain work experiences that are as positive as your academic ones. You can use the** ~~can have many positive effects on the experiences of a college student. Even the potential negativity of facing~~ boredom at work **as motivation** ~~can be used constructively to motivate students~~ to do **your** ~~their~~ best schoolwork **in order** to move steadily through **your requirements and graduate on time. You may also appreciate your career goals much more than someone who didn't work their way through school. Everyone tells us that our college years are the best years of our life—and I think they're right. By combining work with academics, we're earning a greater appreciation for our education, one we've worked doubly hard to receive.**

After several more revisions, more peer review, and some careful editing and proofreading, Melissa was ready to submit her essay to her instructor. Her final draft is on pages 111–114.

> ## 3f Editing makes ideas, sentences, and paragraphs clearer and more engaging.

If you are satisfied with the revised structure of your essay and the content of your paragraphs, you can move to the process of editing individual sentences for clarity, effectiveness, and variety (see chapters 27–30). Your writing group or tutor may have already alerted you to some of these editing issues, but if not, you can work alone. Consider combining choppy or unconnected sentences and reworking long, overly complicated ones. If you overuse some structures, say, introductory prepositional phrases, try experimenting with other patterns (see chapter 27). Eliminate any needless shifts in grammatical structures, tone, style, or point of view.

Examine your diction, and make sure that the words you have used are appropriate for this particular essay (see chapters 28 and 29). If any words leap out as much more formal or informal than your language as a whole, replace them with words that are more consistent with your style. Eliminate any redundant or repetitive words (see chapter 30). If you have experimented with words new to your vocabulary, make sure that you have used them accurately.

Check whether your punctuation is correct and whether you have followed standard conventions for mechanics. Even if you have already used a spell checker (see 36a), use it again because new errors may have been introduced in the revision process. Remember also that such software is never foolproof. Double-check that you are using such words as *there* or *their* and *who's* or *whose* correctly—and remember that even words that are spelled correctly might be the wrong words in a specific sentence.

The following checklist for editing contains cross-references to other chapters where you can find more specific information.

CHECKLIST for Editing

1 Sentences

- What is the unifying idea of each sentence (23)?
- Are ideas given appropriate emphasis within each sentence (26)?
- Are the sentences varied in length and in type (27)? How many words are in your longest sentence? Your shortest sentence?
- Are there any fragments (18)? Are there any comma splices or fused sentences (19)?
- How many of your sentences use subordination? Coordination? How are the ideas related in each of the sentences using these constructions (24)?
- Which sentences have parallel structure? Do any of your sentences have structures that should be parallel but are not (25)?
- Do any sentences contain misplaced or dangling modifiers (20)?
- Do any of your sentences shift in tone, style, or grammatical structure (23)? Is the shift intentional?
- Is every verb form appropriate (22)? Does each verb agree with its subject (22)? Does every pronoun agree with its antecedent (21d)?

2 Diction

- Have you repeated any words? Is your repetition intentional? Are each of your word choices exact, or are some words vague or imprecise (29a–c)? Have you used idioms correctly?
- Can you justify the necessity for every word or phrase (30)? Have any necessary words been left out by mistake?
- Is the vocabulary you've chosen appropriate for your audience, purpose, and context (1e and 28)?
- Have you defined any technical or unfamiliar words for your audience (29e)?

3 Punctuation and Mechanics

- Is all punctuation correct (31–35)? Are any marks missing?
- Are all words spelled correctly (36)?
- Is capitalization correct (37)?

- Are titles identified by either quotation marks (**34b**) or italics (**38a**)?
- Are abbreviations appropriate and correct (**39**)?

3g | Proofreading can make your final draft free from error.

Once you have revised and edited your essay, it's your responsibility to format it carefully and properly (see **6c–d**) and proofread it. Proofreading means making a special search to ensure that the final product you submit is free from error, or nearly so. An error-free essay allows your reader to read for meaning, without encountering spelling or punctuation errors that interfere with meaning. As you proofread, you may discover problems that call for further revision or editing, but proofreading is usually the last step in the writing process.

With a computer, you can easily produce professional-looking documents. Showing that you care about presentation indicates respect for your audience. (See chapter **6**.) However, presentation is only one feature of a successful paper. No matter how professional your paper looks when you print it, proofread it carefully. Mechanical mistakes can undermine your credibility.

Because the eye tends to see what it expects to see, many writers miss errors—especially minor ones, such as a missing comma or apostrophe—even when they think they have proofread carefully. To proofread well, then, you need to read your work more than once, read it aloud, pronouncing each syllable carefully, or read it backwards. Some people find they benefit from reading through the paper several times this way, checking for a different set of items on each pass.

An extra pair of eyes can also be helpful, so you might ask a friend for help. If someone else helps you proofread, this check should be in addition to your own. Moreover, if you ask someone to proofread your work, remember that you are asking for an error check only. If you want a more thoughtful response that could help you revise, you need to ask for it at an earlier point in the process (see **3e(2)**).

When using the proofreading checklist that follows, you may find it helpful to refer to the chapters and sections cited. Also, keep your dictionary at hand (see **28e**) to look up any words that puzzle you.

CHECKLIST for Proofreading

1 Spelling (36)

- Have you double-checked the words you frequently misspell and any the spell checker may have missed (for example, homophones or misspellings that still form words, such as *form* for *from*)?

- Have you double-checked the spelling of all foreign words and all proper names?

2 Punctuation (31–35) and Capitalization (37)

- Does each sentence have appropriate closing punctuation, and have you used only one space after each end punctuation mark (35)?

- Is all punctuation within sentences used appropriately and placed correctly (commas (31), semicolons (32), apostrophes (33), other internal marks of punctuation (35d–i), and hyphens (36f))?

- Are direct quotations carefully and correctly punctuated (34a)? Where have you placed end punctuation with a quotation (34d)? Are quotations capitalized properly (34a and 37d)?

- Are all proper names, people's titles, and titles of published works correctly capitalized (37a–c)?

Beyond the Rule

EDITING AND PROOFREADING

Editing and proofreading share many features: Both processes function to ensure a clear and error-free essay. For more information about the differences between the two processes, visit www.harbrace.com.

3h | The final draft reflects the care the writer took.

After producing the intermediate draft reprinted on pages 103–106, Melissa continued to revise and edit her essay. Each subsequent draft became stronger. The essay that Melissa ultimately submitted to her teacher follows.

Melissa A. Schraeder

English 15

Professor Glenn

Working toward a Degree

With many private universities approaching $40,000 per year for tuition, it is all too obvious that getting a higher education is expensive. Fortunately, financial aid programs and state-funded schools, where tuition costs are normally less than half of the average private school, have made higher education more affordable for Americans. When I decided to attend Penn State University, I was fortunate to receive several grants and scholarships as well as the promise of financial support from my parents. Little wonder that I initially believed that my college education would be easily affordable. When I started classes however, I soon found that with all the additional expenses of school such as the cost of books, technology fees, and spending money, going to school meant finding a job—even for someone with financial support. Though hesitant about how holding a job might affect my studies, I soon took on a part-time job at the Penn State Creamery where I work about fifteen hours a week—and continue to do well in my coursework. Based on my experience, I feel confident in assuring hardworking students that not only can they balance a part-time job with success in schoolwork, but that the experience can be a valuable, life-long lesson, contributing to their growth as students and individuals.

If you have the right attitude and some good advice about finding a part-time job, you will find that working while going to school does not have to be an overwhelming experience. As a college student, the most important thing to remember is that schoolwork must always be your first priority. After all, like most things in life, your individual sacrifices in this balancing act will determine your success. One of the first sacrifices you might have to make is to limit, schedule, or reimagine the free time you have with your friends. After you start working, you won't be able to spend long hours in the coffee shop with your friends, but you can study with them. Not all sacrifices are difficult, though. Another small sacrifice might be to take your schoolbooks along with you to work and consistently think of your work breaks as pre-scheduled time to spend on your nightly coursework. Using work breaks for study time will also help you plan ahead in terms of your various assignment deadlines. I usually set up a calendar where I indicate the dates of all my major exams and due dates for papers and then tailor my work schedule around these dates. Such small sacrifices can lead to big gains: you quickly learn how to manage your time so you work and study efficiently.

While it is important to make such sacrifices in balancing a part-time job with success in school, you need not put all of the pressure on yourself. One key factor in reducing pressure will be your ability (or luck) in finding a job that includes an understanding employer. Doing so is not easy, so you might want to take advantage of some of the on-campus or campus-sponsored job opportunities. Older students, academic advisors, and internship coordinators can help you locate a student-friendly employer, one that expects you to be a reliable employee at the same time that the employer accepts the fact that your major responsibility is your studies. In fact, it was my academic advisor who told me about openings at the Creamery, a university-run business where supervisors are advised to view employees as students first and foremost. Supervisors at the Creamery release a monthly newsletter in which they highlight the academic achievements of student employees as a means of encouragement. The Creamery is also one of a number of on-campus businesses that offer flexibility and variability in scheduling hours, especially during holiday breaks and finals' week. This scheduling feature can be found in most university-related businesses or services since they usually follow the academic calendar in their hours of operation. For the understanding and flexibility that such jobs offer, I recommend that you try to take advantage of the many positions available within your own college or university.

Once you meet the challenge of balancing your college studies with the obligations of part-time work, you'll find that the balancing act has its own rewards: it can be a valuable learning and growing experience for you. First, this challenge can provide you with self-discipline, the self-discipline that comes with prioritizing your schoolwork, setting realistic goals, managing your time, and becoming a reliable employee. Second, students who work to support their own education often develop a heightened sense of respect, value, and responsibility for that education because we've worked and paid (or helped pay) for it. Because we take more responsibility for our educations, we usually study seriously enough to graduate on time, even early. We realize the importance of the timely completion of a degree. These two examples represent forward-looking attitudes and outlooks, but part-time work can also have more immediate effects on your academic career as well.

Such immediate effects of part-time work can be categorized into two types of experiences with part-time work: work that offers career experience and work that fuels academic and career motivation. The former category includes but need not be limited to arranged, paid internships or focused work programs implemented or overseen by your college or university. But career experience can also be found in more unexpected ways, such as when a management student gets to observe her manager at work or when a communications student practices his skills in a sales job. While many student-workers will be fortunate to have such experiences, others, like me, will find themselves working at jobs that have very little to do with their projected career goals. My experiences with work at college have fallen into the latter category, but there are still valuable lessons to be learned. Although the food service work I perform at the Creamery has little relevance to my English and history majors, I enjoy my time there as a release from my studies. Working at the Creamery has also motivated me to do my best schoolwork, since I recognized that a food service job would not be fulfilling to me as a life-long career. If you find that the part-time work available to you is not

Schraeder 4

directly related to your education, such work can still have positive motivating effects on your academic attitudes. A working student who faces boredom, monotony, or low wages in her or his part-time job will often be motivated to achieve academic excellence as a means of moving beyond the scope of this part-time work.

With the right attitude, you might gain work experiences that are as positive as your academic ones. There are likely to be many jobs available within your university community that are student friendly and may even be directly related to your major area of studies. If that is not the case, you can use the less-than-fulfilling aspects of the work as motivation to do your best academic work in order to move steadily through your requirements and graduate on time. Any kind of employment may help you appreciate your career goals more than someone who isn't working their way through school. Everyone tells us that our college years are the best years of our life—and so far I think they're right. By combining part-time work with academics, we're not only earning a greater appreciation for our education, one we've worked doubly hard to receive, but we are also helping to pay for that education.

Exercise 6

Compare the three versions of "Working toward a Degree" reprinted in this chapter, and write a two-paragraph summary describing how Melissa revised her work. If she had shown her final draft to you, asking for your advice before submitting it for a grade, what would you have told her? Write a one-paragraph response to this draft.

Writing under Pressure

You won't always have the luxury of planning, drafting, revising, getting feedback from others, and editing a piece of writing over a stretch of days or weeks. Frequently, your college instructor or employer will ask you to produce an essay or report during a class period or within a day or two.

If the writing process is so valuable, why would anyone want to deny you its benefits? Traditionally, the in-class essay (or essay examination) has been standard practice in instructional settings, and the unscheduled writing assignment is often used for timely responses to a class experience, an ongoing discussion, or a monumental event. For instance, the September 11, 2001 destruction of the World Trade Center provided an occasion for many college students—in courses across the curriculum—to respond. It also served as the exigence for writing by architects, civil engineers, city planners, newspaper reporters, columnists, and government officials (see 1e(4)). Some writers submitted in-class essays; others quickly prepared reports, proposals, or analyses.

No matter how much time they have between an assignment and a due date, most writers feel some pressure. Some writers, however, experience added anxiety when they're asked to write quickly and on demand. If you belong to either or both of these groups of writers, you'll want to follow some general strategies for reducing stress: freewriting frequently (see 2a), making writing a part of your daily routine by keeping a journal (2a), and remembering that most rhetorical situations allow time for the writing process (chapters 2 and 3). The focus of this chapter, however, is how to write well when faced with time constraints, especially when you feel as though you have only one shot at success.

This chapter will help you

- work within deadlines (4a),
- abbreviate the writing process (4b),
- manage writer's block (4c),

- take essay examinations (**4d**), and
- write under pressure in the workplace (**4e**).

It is not always possible to engage in a writing process that stretches over a period of days or even weeks. Sometimes writers must respond almost immediately to email (see **15a**) or prepare a proposal for presentation at a hastily convened meeting. Few college students devote as much time as they ideally should to every writing assignment—especially if they're also working or parenting. And nearly everyone in a managerial or professional position faces writing deadlines that seem to come out of the blue. The key to succeeding in such situations is to use the available time as efficiently as possible.

4a | Deadlines can help you organize your work.

You will almost always be working with deadlines—whether for essays, business plans, or grant proposals with a specified due date or on in-class writing assignments, essay exams, or time-sensitive documents. Because missing deadlines often leads to penalties, you'll want to learn some techniques for managing your time wisely. These techniques will allow you to spend your intellectual energy on more important goals, such as demonstrating your knowledge of the subject and your writing ability.

Preparing ahead of time always helps. Even though an in-class essay exam may not be scheduled until midterm, start preparing on the first day of class. As you read your assignments and participate in class discussions, try to determine what is most important about the material you are learning. Pay attention to indications that your instructor considers certain material especially important. Whenever an instructor gives you instructions or questions, read them carefully, asking questions until you know exactly what is expected of you. If, however, an instructor intentionally makes an assignment open-ended or general in order to stimulate your creativity, start right away imagining how you might best respond to such an assignment. Devise your own reason (or exigence) for writing and your own guidelines for the assignment.

The best preparation for writing assignments is to write frequently for your own benefit—note taking (during class, meetings, or reading), regular journal writing, and freewriting. By writing regularly, you will be able to write more fluently when forced to write quickly. The second-best preparation for in-class or in-office writing assignments is reading the assignment carefully, looking for clues about how your instructor or supervisor wants you to respond to the subject or question (see 4d–e).

The best preparation for a writing assignment with a longer deadline, such as a research project or a progress report, is to start early. If you are choosing your own topic, begin early to narrow down your ideas (see 4b). The sooner you identify a subject (even if you continue to focus it more sharply), the sooner you can discuss it with your instructor or supervisor. You can make deadlines work for you by establishing your own time line, whether for all the assignments in a particular course or for the steps necessary to fulfill a business plan (see chapter 15). For an important project or report, you might even set yourself intermediate deadlines for writing an introduction with a thesis statement (see 3b(1)), composing a first draft, meeting with a classmate or colleague for review, revising your draft, and editing.

Whatever the deadline for a writing assignment, think about the form of the assignment and the best way to approach it. In fact, if you have the space to spread out your preliminary work (e.g., notes, research findings, relevant books and articles), you'll find that your mind will keep working on the assignment, whatever you're doing. If you carry a small notebook or hand-held computer with you, you'll always have a place to jot down notes and ideas.

4b | **It may sometimes be necessary to abbreviate the writing process.**

No matter how dependent you are on writing as a process, sometimes, you'll need to abbreviate that process. You'll have no other choice.

Students and employees are often expected to write well with little notice. If a controversial point is raised in an assigned reading, in a class, or during a meeting, chances are your instructor or supervisor will want you to respond to it in writing. You may be expected to write up a quick analysis of an argument or support a position for or against it.

When given little advance notice for writing, you can quickly focus on a topic. You might decide to write about something you already know about or an idea you already feel comfortable with—whatever doesn't require time-consuming library research. If you can adjust the assignment in such a way that it allows you to write from personal or professional knowledge, so much the better. Faced with a short deadline, try to narrow the topic to a manageable scope or to relate the assignment to past or present academic or work experiences, or personal knowledge or experience—but stay away, if at all possible, from a topic that requires time-consuming research. If you give your topic a sharp focus, you can write a thoughtful, in-depth analysis, rather than skimming the surface of a broader topic. Once you have a focused topic, finishing the writing assignment can be a simple matter of organizing and presenting your ideas about that topic.

The following tips will help you abbreviate the writing process.

TIPS FOR ABBREVIATING THE WRITING PROCESS

- If at all possible, brainstorm about the assignment or topic with a friend or colleague who is facing or has faced the same kind of deadline (see **2a**). That person can help you clarify your thinking, either by demonstrating where your line of reasoning is flawed or by helping you develop counterarguments (see **3e** and **7e**). As you brainstorm, take notes.

- Draft an introductory paragraph that frames your position or approach and includes a clear thesis statement. At this point, you might want to email your paragraph to your instructor or supervisor to make sure that it is acceptable: Is it addressing the right audience? Is it on track? If sending such an email is not an option, then ask a friend or colleague the same questions.

- If your thesis statement and basic approach have been approved, write down the main points you want to make, and try to flesh them out with examples and supporting text until you have a first draft.

- Read your draft aloud, slowly. Make sure that your topic sentences or bulleted points are clear. As you read aloud, you may discover that your writing needs transitional words or phrases to help your reader along. Now is the time to insert those.

- Write a strong conclusion, one that reiterates your main points but also suggests their implications, the directions in which they might point.

- Proofread one last time. Examine your writing closely to make sure that you've "pulled everything together"—that your writing fulfills the assignment you were given. Reread your introduction and conclusion to see whether they frame your piece. Reconsider your topic sentences and supporting paragraphs to make sure that they provide a shape for the piece, and to assess the overall effect on your audience.

- Submit your work on time.

You can use your computer to help you manage writing tasks efficiently.

- If you don't have much time for revising and editing, you can use the grammar checker and spell checker of your word-processing program to help you proofread, even while you are drafting (see 3g). You can usually adjust the settings on these functions so that errors or usage problems will be automatically highlighted (usually with colored squiggly underlining) and even corrected as you type.

- Keeping your notes for a writing assignment in a word-processing file will enable you to use the Search function to find key words or phrases quickly.

- A program such as Microsoft's Outlook can be used to schedule tasks and keep a calendar. You can set the Alarm function of this type of program to remind yourself to complete certain tasks for a writing assignment in time to meet the deadline.

- Many on-campus writing centers have the capability to receive drafts of student writing via email or through a Web site, and writing tutors can often respond to a draft within twenty-four hours. If the writing center on your campus offers such a service, you can use it to get helpful advice on short notice when you have a tight deadline.

4c | You can manage writer's block.

"You don't know what it is," wrote Gustave Flaubert, "to stay a whole day with your head in your hands trying to squeeze your unfortunate brain so as to find a word." Though exaggerated, Flaubert's complaint is one shared by all writers, whether they are teachers, students, or professionals. Writer's block can affect any writer at any time, no matter how experienced, no matter what the writing assignment. It helps to recognize writer's block for what it is and what it is not. First, it is not limited to inexperienced or unskilled writers. Many experienced and successful writers suffer from writer's block, which is nothing more than the inability to begin or continue writing for reasons other than lack of skill or commitment. Sometimes, it helps to stay put at the computer and keep typing away. Sometimes, it helps to write small sections of the writing assignment at a time. Other times, it helps to step away from the work. Although you may not be aware of it, whether you're at your computer or not, your mind will continue to develop ideas for a writing task.

Plan your time carefully. The stress that results from a looming deadline can be a major contributor to writer's block, and procrastination is one symptom of this problem. Of course, you have a good many demands your time—classes to attend, essays due in other courses, books that must be read, exams that must be studied for, not to mention the demands of your social life, family life, or job. Sometimes, setting priorities simply means finding a balance between what you'd like to do and what you need to do. But even if you budget your time carefully, you may not be able to give as much time to every assignment as you would like.

A number of factors can contribute to writer's block: You may not think you're a very good writer; you want the words to be "just right"; you cannot decide on a thesis statement, because there seem to be so many angles you could take; you find it difficult to obtain or organize information; you are worried about grammatical correctness; you want each sentence to be perfect before moving on to the next. Whenever you experience writer's block, try to identify its cause when it arises. The sooner you identify what you're worrying about, the sooner you can work to overcome it.

One of the most common causes for writer's block is striving for perfection. Of course, you want your writing to be as good as it can be, in terms of grammar, spelling, thesis statement, and development—but you must keep in mind that perfection is a goal rarely attained, even by experienced writers. Like them, you'll be better off turning in completed work that is less than perfect than submitting no work at all. This is not to say that you should use the excuse of your other responsibilities to submit half-finished or sloppy work. But when other responsibilities have claimed more of your time than you had planned or you haven't been able to muster much enthusiasm for the assigned topic, then it's time to admit that yours is a less-than-perfect piece of writing and vow to do better on the next assignment. In other words, do the very best you can, given your circumstances, and then move on. The deadline or due date is a reality that must be honored by all writers.

CHECKLIST for Managing Writer's Block

- Allot your time with thought and care.
- Prioritize your responsibilities, and allow time for each activity.

- Establish regular writing habits; write at the same time and in the same place whenever possible.

- For an out-of-class assignment, do not worry about getting the wording exactly right in the first draft. You can revise later.

- Do not stop the flow of your writing by worrying about mechanical problems (spelling or punctuation) in your first draft. You can check such errors later.

- For an essay exam, read each question slowly and jot ideas in the margin as you read down the page.

- When writing under pressure in the workplace, stay put at your keyboard. You need to get something on the screen that you can revise.

4d | You can prepare for essay examinations.

Essay exams have two basic parts: each individual question and your answer to each question. If your instructor has asked a question in such a way that you know what to write about, in what manner, and for how long, you're home free. All you have to do is write out your answer, framing it with a thesis statement, main points, and supporting arguments or examples. However, if a question does not make clear what is called for, ask your instructor for clarification (see 4d(5)). The steps described in this section will help you improve your ability to take essay examinations.

(1) Set up a time schedule.

If the exam has more than one question, the first thing to do is to figure out how much time to allot to each question. If you're faced with two questions that are worth the same number of points, the answer's easy: You give half the time to one and half to the other. When certain questions are weighted more heavily than others, however, you need to divide your time accordingly. If no relative weights are specified, the instructor may still indicate that he or she recommends spending more time on one question than on others.

For example, suppose you are expected to complete an essay examination in a fifty-minute class period. If there are three questions and one of them is worth half of the total points while the rest of the points are split between the other two, allow about twenty minutes for the more heavily weighted question and ten minutes for each of the others. That strategy leaves you about ten minutes to go back over your answers, revising and proofreading. When you have used up the time you have allotted for a question, leave room to complete it later and go on to the next, whether you are finished or not. Even if you cannot complete every question, partial answers to all questions will usually gain you more points than complete answers to only some of the questions. Furthermore, you can use the ten minutes you saved to put the finishing touches on any incomplete answers, even if you have to draw arrows to the margins or the back of the page, even if you have to supply rough notes (see 4d(3)). Your instructor will probably appreciate the extra effort. As you finalize your answers, use these strategies for completion; don't spend time recopying any of your answers.

(2) Read instructions and questions carefully.

Students who take time to read instructions carefully almost always do better than those who don't. Such students also carefully consider any choices they may have among questions, choosing to answer those that suit their knowledge best. Before you start writing, read the instructions carefully and note any specific directions. For example, realizing that you must "answer questions A *and* B" is very different from believing that you must "answer question A *or* B."

Invest a few minutes in studying each question so that you do not make a false start and waste time; you might even jot down a few notes in the margin next to the questions. If you have been asked to answer more than one question, decide whether your answers might overlap and how you might avoid doing that. Your goal is to answer only one question at a time.

Reread the question itself, one word at a time. You'll want to be able to put the question in your own words so that you know you really understand it and what it is asking you to do. If you feel confident that you understand the question, go ahead and get started. Otherwise, rethink your choice or your approach.

Most questions contain specific instructions about how, as well as what, to answer. Be alert for words such as *compare, define,* and *argue* which identify the writing task and provide specific cues for organizing your response (see chapter 2). Other words, such as *discuss* and *explain,* are less specific, so try to determine exactly what it is your instructor wants you to do.

When these more general directions appear, be tuned in to such accompanying words as *similar* or *different* (which signal, respectively, a comparison or a contrast), *identify* (which signals a definition or description), and *why* (which signals the need to identify causes). You'll also want to be clear as to whether you're being asked to call up course-related information from memory or to respond with your own ideas or in your own words. Words such as *think, defend,* and *opinion* signal that you are to frame a thesis (see 2b) and support it.

When you are asked to demonstrate your mastery of information or your critical thinking, you need to know exactly what approach your instructor expects you to take. Most essay exam questions begin with or contain one of the words in the following list and end with a reference to the information you are to consider or include.

TERMS USED IN ESSAY QUESTIONS

Compare (or **contrast**)	Examine the points of similarity (compare) or difference (contrast) between two ideas or things. See 2e(5).
Define	State the class to which the item to be defined belongs (see 2e(6)), and clarify what distinguishes it from the others of that class (2e(7)).
Describe	Use details in a clearly defined order to give the reader a clear mental picture of the item you are being asked to describe. See 2e(2).
Discuss	Examine, analyze, evaluate, or state pros and cons—in short, this word gives you wide latitude in addressing the topic and is thus more difficult to handle than some of the others, since you must choose your own focus. It is also the term that, unfortunately, appears most frequently. See 2d–e.
Evaluate	Appraise the advantages and disadvantages of the idea or thing specified. See 7d(2).
Explain	Clarify and interpret (see 2e(7)), reconcile differences, or state causes (2e(4)).
Illustrate	Offer concrete examples, or, if possible, create figures, charts, or tables that provide information about the item. See 2d(1)–(2).
Summarize	State the main points in a condensed form; omit details, and curtail examples. See 3b(2).
Trace	Narrate a sequence of events that show progress toward a goal or comprise a process. See 2e(1) and 2e(3).

(3) Decide how to organize your response.

Although time constraints will probably keep you from creating a formal outline when answering an essay exam question, you should be able to find time to draft a rough outline or jot down a few phrases for an informal working plan (see **2c**). Identify your thesis; then list the most important points you plan to cover. These might occur to you randomly, even while you're working on a different question, and you might later decide to rearrange them. But the first step is to get some ideas down on paper, a list that does justice to the topic. Before you begin to write the answer, quickly review the list, deleting any irrelevant or unimportant points and adding any better ones that come to you—keeping in mind how much time you've allotted to the specific question. Number the points in a logical sequence determined by chronology (reporting events in the order in which they occurred), by causation (showing how one thing led to another), or by order of importance (going from the most important point to the least important). Although arranging points in order of increasing importance is often effective, it can be risky in an exam situation because you might run out of time and not get to your most important point.

On the facing page is an example of a list of points that was quickly composed and edited during the first few minutes of an essay exam. It was jotted down in response to the following question: "Some readers believe that *The Scarlet Letter* is sexist. Discuss the treatment of Hester Prynne in this novel. Do you think her treatment was sexist, given the historical and social setting of the novel? Why or why not?"

Sometimes, the language of the question will tell you how you should organize your answer. Consider this example:

> Discuss how the two-party political system of the United States influenced the outcome of the Bush-Gore presidential election.

At first glance, this exam question might seem to state the topic without indicating how to organize a discussion of it. *To influence,* however, is to be responsible for certain consequences. In this case, the two-party political system is a cause, and you are being asked to identify its effects (see **2e(4)**). Once you have recognized this, you might decide to discuss different effects in different paragraphs.

Here is another example:

> Consider Picasso's treatment of the human body early and late in his career. How did his concept of the bodily form persist throughout his career? How did it change?

THESIS: The focus on Hester Prynne and her scarlet letter might seem like sexism, but instead it's a focus on the hypocrisy so prevalent in Puritan society.

1. Hester's situation. The reader always admires Hester's strength. —maybe end with this . . .

2. Hester is never evil, at least not by twenty-first century standards (though it might be unfair to judge past cultures by contemporary standards—???). PLUS she publicly confesses her sin (which shows that confession and forgiveness work together.

4. ~~The Church people~~ Some of the Church people are cruel to her; others, women and children especially, stay close to her because she takes care of them.

5. ~~3.~~ Hester has more dignity, loyalty, and religious conviction than the Puritan minister (Dimmesdale) who fathered her child, Pearl. (tie in with the other #5)

5. The men in her life (Dimmesdale and Chillingsworth, her husband) are far less respectable characters than she is. Dimmesdale is weak-willed and sneaky; Chillingsworth is also sneaky and vengeful.

3. Hester suffers, but she's always honest and loving.

5. Both men suffer (are punished?) for their behaviors, while Hester and her daughter (Pearl) happily go to Europe to continue helping the unfortunate. (tie in with the other two #5s)

The reference to two different points in the artist's career, along with the words *persist* and *change*, indicates that your task is to compare and contrast. You could organize your response to this question by discussing Picasso's concept of the bodily form when his paintings were realistic and when they were cubist—preferably covering the same points in the same order in each part of the response. Or you could begin by establishing similarities and then move on to discuss differences. There is almost always more than one way to organize a thoughtful response. Devoting at least a few minutes to organizing your answer can help you better demonstrate what you know.

(4) State main points clearly.

If you state your main points clearly, your instructor will see how well you have understood the assigned material and the important points in that material. Make your main points stand out from the rest of the answer to an exam question by identifying them. For instance, you can make a main point be the first sentence of each paragraph. Or you can use transitional words such as *first, second,* and *third.* You might even create headings to separate your points. By the time you have outlined your essay exam answer, you should know which points you'll want to highlight, even if the points change slightly as you begin drafting. Use your conclusion to summarize your main points. If you tend to make points that differ from those you had in mind when you started, try leaving space for an introduction at the beginning of the answer and then drafting it after you have drafted the rest. Or simply draw a line pointing into the margin (or to the other side of the paper), and write there.

(5) Stick to the question.

Always answer each essay exam question as precisely and directly as you can, perhaps using some of the instructor's language in your thesis statement. If your thesis statement implies an organizational plan, follow that plan as closely as possible. If you move away from your original thesis because better ideas have occurred to you as you write, simply go back and revise your thesis statement (see **2b**). If you find yourself drifting into irrelevant material, simply draw a line through it.

If you find yourself facing a vague or truly confusing question, construct a clear(er) question and then answer it. Rewriting the instructor's question can seem like a risky thing to do, especially if you've never done it before. But figuring out a reasonable question that is related to what the instructor has written is actually a responsible move if you can answer the question you've posed.

(6) Revise and proofread each answer.

Save a few minutes to reread each answer. Make whatever deletions and corrections you think are necessary. If time allows, think about what is not on the page: Ask yourself if there is anything you have left out that you can still manage to include (even if you have to write in the margins or on the back of the page). Unless you are certain that your instructor values neatness more than knowledge, do not hesitate to make additions and corrections. Simply draw a caret (∧), marking the exact place in the text where you want an addition or correction to be placed. Making corrections will allow you to focus on improving what you have already written, whereas recopying your answer just to make it look neat is an inefficient use of time (and you may have recopied only half your essay when the time is up). Finally, check spelling, punctuation, and sentence structure (see 3f).

Exercise 1

Write three questions that might be asked on an essay exam for a course you are currently taking. Practice answering one of the questions within the time you would have if you were taking the exam.

Exercise 2

Consider an exam you've taken in another course. Analyze the wording of each question in terms of what it asks—and how the answer is to be organized. Then describe how you went about answering each question that you chose and why you avoided the other questions. If this exam posed particular difficulties for you, be prepared to identify and discuss those difficulties.

4e You can use the writing process when you are writing under pressure in the workplace.

Much of the advice for writing under pressure at school applies to writing in the workplace as well. Whether you're writing emails, memos, letters, presentations, reports, or recommendations (see chapter 15), you need to meet planned as well as unexpected deadlines. Often, you'll find yourself juggling several writing deadlines at once. The steps described in this section will help you improve your ability to prepare for and execute your work-related writing tasks.

(1) Set up a time schedule.

Just as you do with academic obligations, you'll want to consider how much time to allot to each workplace writing assignment or task, especially when you're faced with more than one. Just as you weigh the importance of questions on an in-class essay examination, you'll want to weigh the significance of your on-the-job writing tasks, giving the most important one the most time and attention. Prioritize your tasks into a plan of work, giving yourself a schedule you can strive to keep. If writing a quick memo (see 15a) is one of your current tasks, do that before you begin any others that entail more thought. Checking just one item off your list can help reduce the pressure.

(2) Carefully consider the expectations for your writing.

What are you being asked to do: write yearly evaluations of employees, propose a marketing plan, pitch a new product, request a larger research budget? Once you determine what, exactly, your piece of writing should do, you can focus your attention on fulfilling *that* obligation. For example, if you are writing a letter of recommendation for an employee who wants to move up in the company, you'll want to describe the employee's accomplishments, strengths, and limitations. You won't want to use valuable time and space writing about the company's philosophy or your own role in either managing the company or mentoring the employee. If you have questions about a workplace writing project, make the inquiries necessary to form a clear picture of what you're being asked to write, for whom—and why.

Beyond the Rule

ESTABLISHING AUTHORITY

Workplace writers sometimes feel pressured to write what they think their supervisors want to hear. Although this isn't always a bad thing to do, workplace writers must understand their ethical obligations to balance the expectations of their supervisors with the needs of the organization, the other employees, the customers or clients, and the general public. To achieve this balance, writers will want to consider the context and audience of any specific business document in a wider sense, as more than just the supervisor and his or her expectations. For more information on establishing authority, visit www.harbrace.com.

(3) Determine the convention or format for your writing.

Workplace writing often follows established business conventions and formats. Memos, business letters, reports, résumés, and proposals all conform to certain formats (see chapter 15). You may be able to save time if you keep a sample of the kind of writing you're doing beside you as you plan and draft. Consulting a successful example can be quicker than looking up the format in an office manual or handbook. Once you've identified the format you want to use, you should draft a tentative thesis statement, a rough outline, and a few key phrases for your informal working plan (see 2c), just as you'd do for any kind of academic writing. Although you're condensing each step in the writing process, you're not skipping any. Spending a little time on each early step will make drafting go much faster. Once you've put your best ideas in a purposeful order, you can begin drafting (see 2d).

(4) State the main points clearly.

Business writing conforms to basic formats for one reason: so that it can be read efficiently. For that reason, you also want to state your main points clearly. You want your audience to realize immediately that your writing has done its job. Whether you make your main points in an introductory abstract, in topic sentences, or in bulleted lists, you want them to stand out from the rest of your text. In fact, you may be able to transfer your main points directly from your rough outline in order to save time.

(5) Compose a draft.

Find a place where you can concentrate without interruption (or put a sign on your door or cubicle), and draft your writing as quickly as possible. It's generally best if you can complete your first draft in one sitting. Stay put in front of your keyboard or paper. You need to get something down so that you will have time left for revision.

(6) Revise and proofread your writing.

If possible, lay aside your writing while you have lunch or even overnight so that you can return to it with greater objectivity. Reading it aloud to yourself will allow you to discover deletions and corrections you need to make. Reading aloud will also help you locate the best places to insert any information you've left out. Reread slowly to check for spelling, punctuation, and sentence structure (see 3g).

5 E-writing

Computers have become the standard tool for most writers because word-processing software can make it easy to develop ideas for writing (see **2a**), plan a writing task (**2b–c**), compose (**2d**), revise (**3a**), edit and proofread (**3f–g**), and produce professional-looking documents (chapter **6**). But a computer offers much more than word-processing capability. Using a computer can change your attitudes about writing tasks, enliven your prose, and widen your horizons as it allows you to participate in global as well as local communities.

In many ways, the computer is reinvigorating the rhetorical situation. For instance, a simple message such as the one in figure 5.1 can illustrate how the rhetorical situation shapes the emails you write. Meg Barry's audience (see **1e(2)**) is her editing group from a course on the history of the English language; the exigence (**1e(4)**) for her message is that the group is preparing for a midterm exam, and the context (**1e(3)**) includes Meg's careful attention to tone ("I hate to disagree . . ." and "Does anyone agree with me . . . ?"), her references to the textbook for the class, and her purpose for sending the message—to make sure that the group has the right information. The content of the message, therefore, responds to the rhetorical situation and not only demonstrates Meg's logical and careful work but also enhances her credibility (see **9a**) by showing her concern for her fellow students. Meg also paid attention to how she delivered her message. (**Delivery** refers to the way information is presented. In e-writing, this includes the interaction of visual elements with content. See also chapter **6**.) Two details indicate how conscientious Meg was about the delivery of her message—the word *but* is in full capitals (a signal of very strong emphasis in email), and she carefully spaces each part of her message so that it is easy to read—showing concern for her audience as well as attention to presentation. Notice how difficult it is to read the first email message in figure 5.1, even though it contains exactly the same words as the second one.

I hate to disagree with both Emily and Valerie, but I think the first real dictionary was published in 1604 (Kersey's didn't come out until 1702). If you look on page 10 of the notes, under the first heading called "Dictionaries" you will find "Earliest English-to-English dictionary 1604." Then the notes explain it. Also, the second-to-the-last paragraph on page 236 in the text talks about the 1604 dictionary. Kersey's dictionary is discussed later on page 10 of the notes under the heading "Dictionaries between 1604 and Johnson's Dictionary." Kersey's was the "first English-English dictionary to contain everyday words." And yes, I agree with Valerie that Bailey's was the "best dictionary before Johnson's" because it was the "first to show stress placement." BUT, the big clue for me that the 1604 dictionary is the first real dictionary of English is that both Kersey's and Bailey's are under the heading "Dictionaries between 1604 and Johnson's Dictionary." Therefore, 1604 was the first. Does anyone agree with me or am I the only one who feels this way?

Meg Barry

I hate to disagree with both Emily and Valerie, but I think the first real dictionary was published in 1604 (Kersey's didn't come out until 1702).

If you look on page 10 of the notes, under the first heading called "Dictionaries" you will find "Earliest English-to-English dictionary 1604." Then the notes explain it.

Also, the second-to-the-last paragraph on page 236 in the text talks about the 1604 dictionary.

Kersey's dictionary is discussed later on page 10 of the notes under the heading "Dictionaries between 1604 and Johnson's Dictionary." Kersey's was the "first English-English dictionary to contain everyday words." And yes, I agree with Valerie that Bailey's was the "best dictionary before Johnson's" because it was the "first to show stress placement."

BUT, the big clue for me that the 1604 dictionary is the first real dictionary of English is that both Kersey's and Bailey's are under the heading "Dictionaries between 1604 and Johnson's Dictionary." Therefore, 1604 was the first.

Does anyone agree with me or am I the only one who feels this way?

Meg Barry

Figure 5.1. Email and the rhetorical situation.

The computer is the gateway to the evolving world of electronic writing. Some e-writing tasks differ from those for writing essays or research papers in hard copy and call for different skills—many of which you already have. This chapter will help you

- compose effective Web documents (**5a**),
- use email effectively (**5b**),
- participate in online discussions (**5c**), and
- become familiar with online courseware and collaboration tools (**5d**).

| **5a** | **Composing for the Web puts all of your rhetorical skills to use.** |

The Web offers you the chance to communicate your ideas to many different audiences for a variety of purposes. As you respond to a particular writing situation and develop ideas to present in a Web document, you will use rhetorical strategies to enhance your message. Increasingly, the Web is becoming more than an electronic library for information and research; it is also a kind of global marketplace allowing people all over the world to exchange ideas.

Notice how Aaron Munk, the author of the Web page shown in figure 5.2, announces from the very first that he admires the courage and determination of African American soldiers who served in segregated units of the U.S. military before 1948. He continues that theme throughout this home page as well as on the other pages of the site (see **6c**). Munk's text appeals to a varied audience, composed partly of people of color and partly of military historians but also including any person who believes segregation was demeaning and inhumane. The attitudes so clearly displayed here contribute to Munk's credibility, help users of the site identify with his emotions, and support the logic that makes the site rewarding for those users. (See also **7h**.)

The home page of Munk's site introduces the main topics—the 54th Massachusetts Volunteer Infantry, the Buffalo Soldiers, and the Tuskegee Airmen—each of which is the subject of a separate page. (See page 161, for example.) Notice also that the arrangement (see **2c**) of the site is clear and easy to use: "Fighting for Integration" has links to all pages in the site at the bottom of each page, an example of how delivery can enhance content. Arrangement is involved in linking the word *desegregation* to a page of the Truman Library's Web site, which describes the events pre-

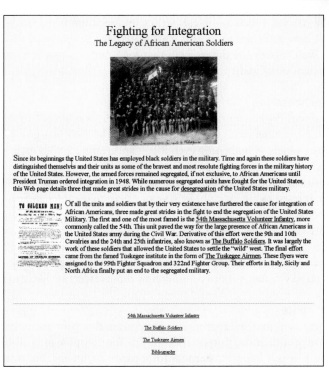

Fighting for Integration
The Legacy of African American Soldiers

Since its beginnings the United States has employed black soldiers in the military. Time and again these soldiers have distinguished themselves and their units as some of the bravest and most resolute fighting forces in the military history of the United States. However, the armed forces remained segregated, if not exclusive, to African Americans until President Truman ordered integration in 1948. While numerous segregated units have fought for the United States, this Web page details three that made great strides in the cause for <u>desegregation</u> of the United States military.

Of all the units and soldiers that by their very existence have furthered the cause for integration of African Americans, three made great strides in the fight to end the segregation of the United States Military. The first and one of the most famed is the <u>54th Massachusetts Volunteer Infantry</u>, more commonly called the 54th. This unit paved the way for the large presence of African Americans in the United States army during the Civil War. Derivative of this effort were the 9th and 10th Cavalries and the 24th and 25th infantries, also known as <u>The Buffalo Soldiers</u>. It was largely the work of these soldiers that allowed the United States to settle the "wild" west. The final effort came from the famed Tuskegee institute in the form of <u>The Tuskegee Airmen</u>. These flyers were assigned to the 99th Fighter Squadron and 322nd Fighter Group. Their efforts in Italy, Sicily and North Africa finally put an end to the segregated military.

<u>54th Massachusetts Volunteer Infantry</u>

<u>The Buffalo Soldiers</u>

<u>The Tuskegee Airmen</u>

<u>Bibliography</u>

Figure 5.2. Home page of "Fighting for Integration."

ceding and immediately following desegregation of the military. Finally, the centered picture at the top of the home page shows clearly that soldiers of color served in the U.S. military before 1948 in segregated units—a combining of arrangement and delivery. Another example of this blending is the image in the lower-left corner, which demonstrates that the U.S. military was actively recruiting for those segregated units.

(1) The rhetorical situation for a Web document expands the audience and the context.

When you plan a Web page or site, you make the same kinds of rhetorical choices you make when you plan an essay or a research paper: You identify your audience and your purpose, determine how they are affected by the context—time and place, writer, and medium (see **1e(3)**)—and decide how you want to present your material. The rhetorical situation for a Web page or site differs from that for an essay or paper mainly in the expansion of audience and context.

(a) Audience

As you would when writing any document, you should carefully analyze your audience (see **1e(2)**). But remember that the Web may give you access to a variety of audiences, even if you are creating a Web page or site for a class assignment. The potential audience for e-writing on the Web is vast—the number of possible readers far exceeds the number in any classroom, interest group, or club. So you may need to consider audience differently as you plan and put together a Web page or site. For example, if you are constructing a Web page for a course assignment, you obviously need to take into account as your main audience your instructor and probably your classmates. But the Web page may be seen by many other people, and so you may wish to consider how those readers are likely to react.

(b) Purpose

You also want to make appropriate decisions so that your document will achieve your intended purpose (see **1e(1)**). Your purpose for a Web document is much like your purpose for a paper document. For instance, you may want to express how you feel about something, create a mood, or amuse or entertain your readers. If you are more concerned with the information itself than with your feelings or your readers' responses, your purpose is to report information, as, for example, Nikki Krzmarzick does in her paper on sleep and memory (see **11d**), or to explain or evaluate the significance of information, as Nicole Hester does in her paper on race in the military (**11f**). Your purpose might be to analyze a situation, as Andy Pieper does in his paper on Starbucks (**11b**), to clarify a point, or to argue for a position or a course of action. For a Web site such as the one Aaron Munk developed, the purpose is much the same as for those papers—to inform the audience.

(c) Context

The advantages of hypertext (see **5a(2)**) and visual elements (**6a**) for presenting information constitute part of the context for a Web document, as do your background, your attitudes and beliefs, and your credibility. Another part of the context is the time—and timing—within which a

Web site or page is developed as well as any influence of place that may be relevant. For example, a Web site about terrorism produced before September 11, 2001 would be very different from one produced after that date, and a page that focused on the Pentagon would differ from one focused on the World Trade Center.

In addition to traditional considerations about audience, purpose, and context, then, you may wish to consider the following questions as you develop a Web document and seek guidance from your instructor if necessary.

CHECKLIST for Creating a Web Document

- Who is likely to visit my page or site?
- How might the fact that audiences other than my intended audience may view my page or site affect my purpose?
- Are there potential audiences I haven't considered?
- What influences do time and place have on the development of my page or site?
- What am I doing to take advantage of the fact that I am creating a Web document rather than a paper document?
- In what specific ways can a Web document help me achieve my purpose and reach my audience?
- Do I have particular strengths that I can use to advantage in developing this page or site?

---

(2) Planning Web documents involves working out an arrangement for presenting ideas.

More than a new vista, the opportunities available to you when you create a Web document open a new frontier. Because of the nature of the Web, you can have fun planning, drafting, and revising your Web documents.

It is important to distinguish between a Web page and a Web site. A Web page is a single document, or *node,* that can be displayed by a Web browser. While the user may need to scroll down the screen to read it all, a page can often be displayed in one screen. In some ways, constructing a Web site is a matter of constructing a set of related Web pages, and constructing a Web page requires you to think about arrangement (see **2c**) in ways that are significantly different from the ways in which you arrange your conventional print documents. Thus, with regard to matters of arrangement and delivery, planning and constructing a Web page or site may require you to think about the rhetorical situation in new and different ways.

There are two basic kinds of documents for the Web:

- True electronic documents are frequently constructed as Web pages or sites from the outset and are never intended to appear in print form.
- Print documents are sometimes converted to Web pages or sites; for example, an article in the *New York Times* is put on the newspaper's Web site, or a student essay is posted by an instructor on a course Web site.

The key element of presentation in Web documents is **hypertext**—a way of linking text, pictures, and sound into your document seamlessly. A true electronic document is planned and drafted with hypertext as well as images and even sound as integral parts of its arrangement and content, and it is delivered with all of those elements (see chapter **6**) integrated into the content. A document converted from print is first written on paper in the conventional way, then transformed into a Web page. Both kinds of Web documents allow you to use **hyperlinks** (elements that take you to another place in a Web site or to a different Web site); thus, a hypertextual document is significantly different from a print document because its arrangement allows for structuring and linking text and other kinds of elements in ways that are not available in conventional print documents.

Beyond the Rule

USING HTML

To create a Web page, you do not have to understand the computer codes that allow a browser to display your text. There are many programs that will do such coding for you automatically. But some writers find that knowing some of the basic HTML commands can be useful for troubleshooting a Web page. A number of tutorials are available on the Web. For additional information on HTML, visit www.harbrace.com.

Several important considerations will influence your use of hypertext as you work to create an effective Web document:

- Since the interests and personalities of those who read your Web document will prompt them to move through, or navigate, it in different ways, you will need to consider how user differences may affect the intended purpose of your document and arrange it accordingly.

- Because the inclusion of hyperlinks transfers control of the sequence of information from the writer to the reader, planning and composing a Web page or site requires a more fluid arrangement of the material than is typical in an essay. Since users may click links in any order they choose, Web documents offer them unlimited options for ordering the content.

- The visual elements included in a Web page or site may eliminate the need for some text or create a need for additional text. For instance, the second image on Aaron Munk's home page (see figure 5.2) relieves him of the necessity to comment specifically about the role of the U.S. government in recruiting men of color for segregated military units. You have to consider the rhetorical impact of visual elements on your Web document as you plan, compose, and revise it. (See chapter 6.)

As you develop your Web document, keep all the elements of the rhetorical situation (see 1b) in mind. Like a print document, a Web document can showcase the author's particular talents. It can also focus on the information itself or on the user's need to know the information. Planning and arranging a Web document involves some concerns about audience (What features can you expect users of a page or site to want?), some about information (How much and what kind of detail will you provide?), and some about purpose (What are you trying to achieve with your Web site?). The answers to those questions can involve content—both verbal and visual—as well as matters of how you will arrange it and what kinds of visual design and layout (see 6c) you will choose.

Another consideration involves aspects of both arrangement and audience. Users of your Web site may not all have sophisticated equipment or fast Internet connections. To accommodate less well-equipped users, you may wish to keep the design simple and use a limited number of graphical elements. These accommodations will make a Web site accessible to the greatest number of users.

Beyond the Rule

EVALUATING A WEB SITE FOR ACCESSIBILITY

Resources are available on the Web to help you evaluate whether your site is accessible to the users you want to reach. For additional information, visit www.harbrace.com.

You need to think about which ideas or information you wish to emphasize and how to arrange your Web document to convey those effectively. You might decide what supplementary links you want to use at the same time as you are generating material. But you don't have to do everything at once. You can fine-tune the visual design later. When you plan a Web site, you may find it helpful to create a visual representation (sometimes called a *storyboard*) of it. You can sketch plans on a sheet of paper or in a word-processing file if your site is fairly simple, or you can use index cards tacked to a bulletin board if it is more complex; you can also use the graphical capabilities of your word-processing program to help you map out your site. For instance, it is easy to draw a representation of how a linear site might be set up (see figure 5.3). Hierarchical and radial arrangements are more complex to develop. The hierarchical arrangement branches out at each level (figure 5.4), and the radial arrangement, in which individual pages can be linked in a variety of sequences, allows the user to determine the sequence in which pages are viewed (figure 5.5).

You can see that the possibilities for organizing a Web site are endless. The most important consideration is how the arrangement of your site will affect a user's experience in navigating it. However you decide to organize your site, try to represent each main element in your plan. You will find a good plan invaluable as you draft text, incorporate visual elements, and refine your arrangement.

Figure 5.3. Linear model of a Web site.

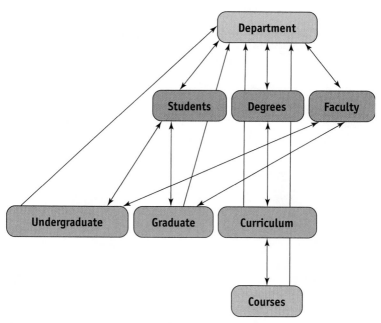

Figure 5.4. Hierarchical model of a Web site.

You may find it helpful to look at figure 5.2 and at the sample Web pages in chapter 6 (see pages 161–162) as you consider the following questions about planning a site and developing ideas for each page.

CHECKLIST for Planning a Web Site

- How will the arrangement of your site help you accomplish your purpose with your intended users?
- Should you devote each page to a single main idea or combine several ideas on one page?
- Can single pages be used to highlight the most important ideas or items of information?
- What will be the most effective way for users to navigate the site?
- What key connections between ideas or pieces of information might be emphasized through the use of hyperlinks?
- Where will key visual elements be placed to be most effective?

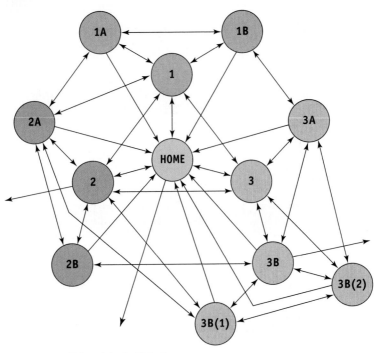

Figure 5.5. Radial model of a Web site.

(3) Hyperlinks help fulfill the rhetorical purpose of a Web document.

One of the distinguishing features of Web pages and sites, hyperlinks can be valuable tools for Web authors. Some basic principles can help you use hyperlinks effectively in your Web documents.

(a) Hyperlinks help make a Web document coherent.

A vital part of your organizational plan, hyperlinks are navigational tools that enable users to move from page to page in a site and from one Web site to others. Considering the ways in which users can exploit these links is an important part of your rhetorical strategy, and so you will want to use links skillfully. If your site is large, a site map is essential, and it can be helpful even for a compact site. Look back at figure 5.2. Notice that the main sections of the site are featured in a list of links arranged at the bottom of the home page. A link to a relevant external site—the Truman Library site—appears within the text. Hyperlinks between pages of a site can provide transitions based on key words, ideas, or divisions of the document. In other words, because these links provide coherence and help readers navigate your Web site, they are powerful rhetorical tools that aid you in creating an effective arrangement for your site (see 6d).

Consider carefully where you will place these navigational tools, especially those that appear on the home page of a site that contains several pages. Users should be able to locate hyperlinks quickly, and they should be able to get to any part of your site easily from every page within it. However, avoid peppering your pages with unnecessary links.

(b) Hyperlinks provide focus as well as coherence.

For example, on the home page in figure 5.2, the key phrases "The Buffalo Soldiers" and "The Tuskegee Airmen" are hyperlinks that reinforce the coherence of the site. Similarly, the key term "desegregation" links from this page chronicling the segregated military units to a page on another Web site that addresses the general topic of desegregation of the U.S. military. Such a link makes a rhetorical connection through the subject matter of both pages and allows users to navigate between those pages. But you may also want to have other links to pages that present information that is central to the purpose of your site. And at the top or bottom of every page in a site, you need to provide links to every other page in the site. Collectively, such links provide focus for your site and contribute to making it effective.

(c) Hyperlinks can be textual or graphical.

You can use individual words, phrases, or even entire sentences as textual hyperlinks. You can also use icons or other graphical elements instead of text. If you do use graphical links, be sure their appearance is appropriate for the kind of link you are making. On his home page, Aaron Munk could have made the recruiting poster a graphical link, but a photo of a buffalo would not have been an appropriate link for this page.

(d) External links can enhance Web documents.

Consider very carefully how many and what kind of external hyperlinks to include. Make sure that you have a clear reason for using each link. On his Web site, Aaron Munk provides a link to the Truman Library page on desegregating the military because he felt that the library had done a good job of presenting the steps the Truman administration followed between 1945 and 1950; Nicole Hester also used this source (see **11(f)**). For Hester's paper, the Truman Library site provides important information on desegregating the military. For Munk's Web site, the link explains what finally happened to the segregated military units—the end of the story.

When choosing external links, be sure to select those sites containing relevant, accurate, and well-presented information. You should also use any contact information on a site to ask permission to link to it and check your links periodically to be sure they are still active.

Above all, no matter how extensive a Web site is, it should be easy to use. As you develop your site, keep the following tips in mind.

TIPS FOR MAKING A WEB SITE EASY TO USE

- Make sure visitors to your site can easily find the information they are looking for without having to search through the entire site or click on many links to get to the page they want.

- If you know how to use frames, which allow you to divide the screen into several smaller screens and manipulate the content of each screen independently, they can help you organize your site and help users navigate it. But frames can diminish the size of the content window, can make it difficult for users to backtrack, and can make a site slow to download.

- Always provide navigational links that take users back to the home page of your site.

---

(4) Drafting Web documents can expand your options as a writer.

As you plan, draft, arrange, and revise a Web document, you will undoubtedly discover better material to include and better ways to include it. As you plan a Web site, you may draft text for it in a linear arrangement and then later break the text into separate sections for different pages and link them. However, you may find that arrangement and delivery issues force you to change your drafting process significantly. When you draft a Web site, it may be more efficient to write the text in chunks. You can write the text for a single page, then revise it, before moving on to the next page. As you revise each page, you can consider where you might place hyperlinks, or you can incorporate important links as you draft and then revise accordingly.

As you work on your site, remember that your plans may change. For instance, you may decide to replace some of your text with graphical elements. When that happens, the visual aspects of your site become part of your composing process rather than just decorative elements that are added later. (See 5a(2) and 6a.)

Once you have created and revised your site, it is a good idea to get feedback from your classmates or colleagues, just as you would for a draft of an essay or report (see 3e). Since Web sites are complex documents, however, you may want to seek responses not only about the content of your site but also about matters such as layout, graphics, and navigation (see chapter 6). Professional Web developers often put a site that is still in a draft stage on the Web and solicit reactions from users. The developers can then use those reactions to refine the site. Because Web sites are more interactive than printed texts, it's a good idea to seek such input from users as you develop a site. Getting this kind of feedback is a kind of peer review, and just as peer review helps writers iron out difficulties in their papers, feedback from users can help you iron out kinks in your Web site.

Find a place on your home page to include information about when you last updated the site and how users can contact you. Be careful, though, and consider your own security. If you are not comfortable giving out your primary email address, think about opening an account with a free provider such as Hotmail or Yahoo!. Finally, you must get permission for any text or graphics you draw from another source. Such material is often free on the Web, but it still requires acknowledgment. (See 10e.)

CHECKLIST for Developing a Web Site

- How would you like a user to navigate your Web site? For what purpose?
- What information or ideas should a user take away from your site?
- Will a user who follows external links be able to get back to your page?
- Will the experience of navigating the Web site be exciting and informative for the user?

(Continued on page 144)

(Continued from page 143)

- How might different users react to the arrangement of the site?
- Have you used Web-specific resources in creating your Web site so that it has more impact than a paper document?
- Do you need graphics—charts, graphs, pictures, cartoons, clip art, animations, and so on—to enhance the site so that it will accomplish your purpose?

Exercise 1

Plan and write out the information for a Web page that supports a paper you are writing for one of your classes. If you have access to a program that converts your document to a Web page, try that. Then, critique your page.

5b | Electronic mail (email) offers fast and easy communication.

Electronic mail has become common at school, in the workplace, and for personal communication. Because email messages are easy to create and are delivered very quickly, many people consider them superior to informal notes or letters. Using email is even more convenient than leaving a voicemail message because an email message is easy to file and creates a record. In business, email messages have almost entirely replaced paper memos.

Increasingly, email has become a medium for more than just simple communication. It is used for sharing ideas and information with coworkers and classmates, for exchanging documents of all kinds—including writing assignments—and for discussing and negotiating all types of course-related and business-related issues. Because the use of email for many different purposes is likely to continue to grow, you should understand both the advantages and the challenges of this medium.

(1) Email responds to the rhetorical situation.

The key thing about email is that it encourages rapid, concise communication. Because email's overriding purpose is communication with a specific audience, everything in it should serve that purpose. But the other elements of the rhetorical situation must also be considered. Audience (see 1e(2)) is at least as important as purpose, and exigence (1e(4)) influences both purpose and audience. Careful attention to those elements is critical. The ease and speed of email make it one of the most difficult media for establishing and maintaining tone—an essential consideration for addressing your audience effectively. When we write email, we often assume that our audience is only the person named in the "To" line, forgetting that email can easily be forwarded to many people. And we too often hit "Send" before we have thought about how the tone of our language will be perceived without facial expressions and tone of voice to modify it.

The basic rhetorical unit of an email message is the screen—not the paragraph or the page. Although computer screens come in a number of sizes, you should normally figure on having about twenty lines in which to present the address block that automatically comes with the message, any salutation ("Hi, Bill!"), your message, and your signature line(s). Since it is generally not a good idea to write messages that require the recipient to scroll down, it is important to get to the point as quickly as possible. You can follow your point with a few lines of explanation or argument. The most effective email messages generally contain a single point that is identified in the subject header. If you have two points to make, it may be better to send two messages. Longer messages are appropriate for the various kinds of online communication that are devoted to specialized topics, such as those that occur in academic and professional discussion groups.

Similarly, be aware that white space also contributes to your purpose and your concern for your readers. If you include adequate white space, you will make your email message easier to read than if you present large blocks of text. (See figure 5.1.) Large blocks are difficult to read. Ease of reading will help make your purpose clear, and if the purpose is clear, you are more likely to influence your audience.

In deciding on the appropriate language and style for an email message, consider the rhetorical situation as you would for any document (see 3a(3)): Who is your audience, and what do you hope to accomplish with your message? Conversational style may be acceptable for a message to a discussion group for your writing class, but a message to your instructor about the grade you received on an assignment or one to your supervisor about your annual performance review will probably have a more formal style. (See also **5c(3)**.)

Given the rapidly expanding use of email and the growing concerns about privacy, monitoring, and copyright, you should be aware that the emails you and your instructors or supervisors and other correspondents send through school or workplace accounts are neither private nor secure.

Beyond the Rule

WHO OWNS YOUR EMAIL?

Employers have been vindicated for reading employees' email, and there have been cases in which university legal counsels and administrators "confiscated" the emails of teachers or students when complaints were lodged about such things as grades. You should be sure to check your school's or employer's policy regarding the use of email. For additional information, visit www.harbrace.com.

(2) Attachments can be helpful if used with care.

Email attachments are an easy way to exchange word-processing and other kinds of files with classmates or coworkers. Because writers frequently share their drafts in this way, it's a good idea to become familiar with the procedures your email program uses for sending and receiving attachments.

People send files to each other as attachments because it is fast and convenient, and because email programs don't always preserve the formatting of text that is copied and pasted into a message. An attached document, in contrast, will arrive with paragraph breaks preserved and italics intact. Most email programs make it easy to attach a document (or an image) and send it anywhere in the world. The person receiving the attachment can then work on or respond to the document off line—giving an economical advantage if that recipient has to pay by the hour for Internet access.

When you are sending an attachment, consider the size of the file. A file created with one of the popular word-processing programs can be

large enough to clog the mailbox of the person you send it to. Ask a recipient if it's all right to send a file that's larger than 50K and specify the
size of the file you want to send.

You may sometimes encounter problems with attachments, however.
When the recipient uses a service that does not receive attachments, the
file will get lost—that is, it will not accompany the email message. You
also run the risk of sending an attachment to someone whose software is
not compatible with yours. This problem can be avoided, however, by
saving the document in *rich text format* (.rtf), which preserves most formatting and is recognized by most word-processing programs. (Check
the Help function of your word-processing program for specific instructions for saving a file in rich text format.)

Attachments are also notorious for transmitting computer viruses. You
should never open an attachment from someone you do not know. Mali-
cious viruses are often carried in messages that appear to offer sexy pictures,
love notes or poems, or "fantastic" business deals, but increasingly they accompany messages that appear normal and safe. Your best protection is to
get a reliable antivirus program and keep it up to date. You can also visit Web
sites such as www.symantec.com for information and updates on viruses.

Always log off after using your email account from a public location such
as a university computer lab or library. You can be held liable for repair-
ing any damage that may be caused by an unscrupulous person who gets
access to your account.

Exercise 2

Analyze the rhetorical situation—intended and likely audiences, purpose, and exigence—for an email you have received. Then, analyze the
rhetorical situation for an email you are sending.

5c   Online discussion groups or forums foster community.

People use email and the Web to help create and maintain many different kinds of online communities with their own conventions and

purposes. There are two main types of online discussion groups or forums. **Asynchronous groups** such as Listservs and newsgroups show a user a message at any time after it has been posted. A Listserv does not hold messages on its server (unless it also has a separate function to preserve the discussion in an archive). A forum—sometimes called a newsgroup—keeps messages on its server, organized by topic (or thread). **Synchronous groups** such as chat rooms and MUDs (Multi-User Dimensions) show a message only at the time the message is posted—that is, the user sees the message in real time.

Both asynchronous and synchronous forums are used by a variety of online communities—social groups, scholarly or special interest groups, and business groups. Both kinds of forums can also be used for course-related online discussions, as extensions of the classroom community. But when you work, volunteer, or take classes with the people in an online group, your rhetorical situation is somewhat different from that for online interactions with groups of strangers. It is often advisable to lurk (read the postings of others without participating) for a while to see what the conventions of an unfamiliar online community are; when you know the other participants in an online community, however, you can plunge right in—just remember to take your netiquette (see **5c(3)**) with you.

(1) Asynchronous (virtual-time) discussion groups offer a wealth of information.

There are two basic kinds of asynchronous groups for online discussions:

- Electronic mailing lists, or Listservs
- Newsgroups or Web-based bulletin boards

Electronic mailing lists, sometimes called Listservs, are online groups that enable you to receive any email messages sent to the list by any other member, or subscriber. The Internet supports thousands of Listservs, devoted to topics as diverse as political issues, sports, music, law, pets, and poetry. On some Listservs, a moderator reviews messages to eliminate inappropriate ones and reduce the possibility of **flaming**— an angry personal attack by one member of the group on another, often using profanity. Unmoderated Listservs automatically distribute any messages sent by subscribers.

Newsgroups and Web-based bulletin boards also exist for online discussion of any conceivable topic. Unlike mailing lists, newsgroups post messages to a specific site on the Internet, from which users then access the messages using a news-reader program (such as Outlook) or a Web browser (such as Netscape). In addition, because newsgroups and bulletin boards generally do not require you to subscribe to them, they are often more free-wheeling than online mailing lists. As you get to know the others in such a group through their messages, you also learn about the group's conventions regarding the length, tone, and content of messages.

Electronic mailing lists and newsgroups tend to involve specialized communities of people who share particular interests or perspectives but never meet face to face. Even though you don't meet the other members, you can develop important relationships in these communities, and you can even collaborate on projects, share ideas and information, and disseminate your work.

Both electronic mailing lists and newsgroups can be sources of a great deal of information about many different topics. Participating in such e-discussions is a good way to learn more about topics that interest you and to develop your skills and knowledge as a writer. But remember that one important skill as a writer is to be cautious and evaluate the information and advice you get on these forums as you would evaluate information from any other source (see chapter 9).

Exercise 3

Join a Listserv devoted to a subject you are interested in or one you will be researching for a class. Read the messages for a week. At the end of the week, introduce yourself to the members of the group, and ask a question related to one of the topics they have been discussing. Read the responses, and then write a paragraph describing the experience.

(2) Synchronous (real-time) discussion groups offer opportunities for immediate interaction.

Real-time (synchronous) discussions on the Internet are much more like live, face-to-face conversations than asynchronous discussions are. In a real-time discussion group, all users who are logged in see each other's messages as they are posted. If you have visited an Internet chat room or used a service like AOL's Instant Messenger, you have participated in a synchronous online discussion group and probably have a sense of its advantages and characteristics. These discussion groups offer a convenient way for people who are in different physical locations to come together. In business, for example, a project team in New York City can "meet" with members of another team in Los Angeles by using a program such as NetMeeting. Offering not only a text-based environment but also voice and video capability, business applications like this one have the advantages of immediacy and a sense of physical presence, even if the participants are in different locations across the country—or around the world.

All the varieties of real-time discussion groups allow users to engage in text-based discussions simultaneously. If you are using a Web browser such as Netscape, Web-based chat rooms make it easy to discuss specific topics or to engage in casual conversation, as is common on IRC (Internet Relay Chat) or with the various instant messaging programs. Special educational Web-based programs such as Blackboard and WebCT also have real-time chat functions, but these chat rooms are usually reserved for discussion of course topics or assignments and not used for casual conversation (see **5d**).

In addition, many sites on the Internet host **MUDs (Multi-User Dimensions)** or **MOOs (Multi-user dimensions, Object-Oriented)**—text-based environments that allow users to engage in real-time discussions but are also designed to simulate a physical environment. Thus, users can "move" from room to room and engage in "physical" activities through the use of specific text-based commands. The imaginative reconstruction of a physical environment provides context for the discussion. For example, "Joan moves to the corner of the room. Laughing gleefully, she says, 'Now I get it!' " MUDs or MOOs are primarily exploratory. They may be helpful in finding a topic and in planning your writing, but they are not useful for composing and revising drafts. Many instructors and students use MOOs for class discussions and collaboration, and occasionally MOOs are used for discussions with students at universities in different cities (see **5d**).

Engaging in real-time discussion can be disconcerting initially. Usually, several different discussions occur simultaneously in a real-time forum, and it can take time to get used to having all the comments from different participants appear on your screen as though they were part of a single conversation. Because of the speed of the discussions, conventions dictate that comments must be short and to the point—much more so than in newsgroups or Listservs. Users must join in judiciously so that other participants are not overwhelmed by

```
Christa Downer > that's like supporting your main points, right?
brittany randall > what about interesting beginnings--something to catch the
                   reader's attention?
Becky Adams > shouldn't the writing do something?
leeann church > i can talk about my points in like 2 pages. there's only five
                 paragraphs.
leeann church > good one brittany
brittany randall > yeah, like telling how something looks or feels or smells,
                   I think...
Becky Adams > serve a purpose, I mean.
brittany randall > thanks, lee
Christa Downer > what do you mean Becky?
Christa Downer > oh, okay
Becky Adams > our teacher is always saying our writing should have a
               purpose.
Becky Adams > so, it should do want we are wanting it to do.
brittany randall > what are those words called like first, next, third, etc...? Do
                   we need those?
Becky Adams > transitions?
```

Figure 5.6. Discussion group log.

too many messages. In the partial log of an online discussion session in figure 5.6, notice that some of the comments appear to be out of sequence.

(3) Netiquette is important.

Basically, netiquette is a set of successful practices that have been developed by people who use the Internet to regulate language and behavior online. The name is a combination of *Internet* and *etiquette,* the social behavior that is required by good manners. For the most part, if you try to convey respect, you will find electronic communication pleasurable.

Beyond the Rule

MORE ABOUT NETIQUETTE

Reasons for netiquette practices and additional information about how to employ them can be found at www.harbrace.com.

TIPS FOR NETIQUETTE IN EMAIL AND ONLINE DISCUSSION GROUPS

Audience

Be aware of the potential audience for your message—both those you intend it for and others who may read it.

Make the subject line of your message descriptive so that your reader(s) will know the topic.

Use a signature line for email to identify yourself and your institution or company.

Keep your message focused. Remember that your reader's time and bandwidth may be limited, and delete anything that isn't essential when you are replying—especially the previous message(s).

Give people adequate time to respond.

Respect privacy, and seek the sender's permission before forwarding email.

Respect copyright. Never send something written by someone else or pass it off as your own.

Don't send "junk mail" such as chain letters, petitions, and jokes unless you know the person likes that kind of material.

Style and Presentation

Make sure your tone is appropriate for your message and your audience.

Be sure of your facts.

Present ideas clearly and logically.

Pay attention to spelling and grammar in email messages.

Use emoticons (:>)) and abbreviations such as IMHO (in my humble opinion) only when you are sure your audience will understand them and find them appropriate.

Don't use all capital letters. OTHERWISE, YOU'll SEEM TO BE SHOUTING.

Abusive or profane language is never appropriate.

Context

Always use language and behavior acceptable for the community you are participating in.

Observe what others say and how they behave; see what kind of information participants find appropriate to exchange before you jump into an online discussion.

If someone is abusive, ignore that person or change the subject. Don't participate in flaming.

Understand that sarcasm and irony may appear to be personal attacks.

Credibility

Don't use your school's or employer's network for personal business.

Keep passwords secure.

If you have specialized knowledge, be willing to share it with your correspondents.

Be respectful of others even when you disagree, and be kind to new members of an online community.

Exercise 4

With a classmate or friend, join in a synchronous discussion. You can find such discussions on IRC (www.irc.com) or in a MUD or MOO. If you do not currently have access to a MUD or MOO, use your Web browser to go to Lingua MOO (lingua.utdallas.edu:7000). Write a paragraph about the experience.

5d | Online media provide new ways of writing and communicating in college courses and the workplace.

In addition to course-related email requirements (see **5b**), course-based Web sites are increasingly used to supplement or replace the traditional paper syllabus (see also **1f(1)**). Special Web-based educational programs, sometimes called *courseware,* include ways to present course assignments, policies, resources, and tests and also have email capability and chat room functions. These sometimes supplement conventional class meetings and assignments. Some courses, however, are offered exclusively online, through a combination of email, Web sites, courseware, and even video clips, completely replacing regular class meetings and face-to-face discussions. Even if you never take a course that is offered exclusively online, chances are that you will be required to go online to complete the requirements for some of your college courses.

Any online media skills you develop for courses will be useful in the workplace. Because businesses have almost entirely converted to e-writing for daily communication, it is almost certain that you will be required to use online media for writing you will do at work. Email has effectively replaced the interoffice memo; company reports are produced with word-processing and desktop-publishing software; NetMeeting and similar programs are widely used for conferring with coworkers; training programs are created using presentation software such as PowerPoint; and Web sites provide information about companies to the general public.

(1) Course-related email and online discussions sometimes substitute for class meetings.

Exchanging work via email eliminates the need to find time to meet, and submitting assignments via email instead of having to go to the instructor's office to do so can be convenient for both students and instructors. Most instructors have specific expectations about the use of online discussions in their courses, and you should be aware of these. How often will you be expected to participate in these discussions? Will the instructor provide specific questions to address or topics to discuss online? Should messages be short and informal, or will you be expected to post more formal kinds of comments? Will your online participation be graded? Because instructors will have different expectations for online course discussions, it's a good idea to ask these questions before participating.

Course-related online discussions can help create a greater sense of community and collaboration among students in a class, especially if the class is a large one. What you say in the online discussions can have an impact on class meetings. Although you may find that course-related online discussions may be somewhat more casual and less intimidating than face-to-face class discussions, you should nevertheless think of your online behavior as an extension of your classroom presence and participate accordingly. For instance, when responding to a classmate's draft, make sure your tone is as kind and respectful as possible while still conveying the necessary information. Whether commenting on a paper or continuing a class discussion, keep to the point.

The efficiency and convenience of online media have extended the conventional college course beyond the physical space of the classroom. When you participate in online class activities, you may find the following checklist helpful.

> **CHECKLIST for Participating in Online Class Activities**
>
> - Understand your instructor's expectations for course-related online discussions.
>
> - When communicating with an instructor or classmate via email, keep your message relevant, to the point, and respectful.
>
> - If you are submitting an assignment via email, check with your instructor about appropriate procedures for doing so. Some instructors prefer documents to be sent as attachments, and some have other requirements.
>
> - Engage in course-related online discussions appropriately.

(2) Courseware packages offer comprehensive course sites on the Web.

Many colleges and universities provide courseware packages such as Blackboard or WebCT instead of course-specific Web sites. In addition to the basic course information that normally appears on a syllabus, courseware packages allow instructors to include course assignments and supplementary material, such as handouts that can be downloaded, images to illustrate procedures or concepts, and video clips that supplement a reading assignment; these packages also enable students to upload and display word-processed documents and even files created by programs such as PowerPoint. With courseware packages, students can take tutorials and tests online, send emails, and use the chat function provided for online discussions.

One of the advantages of courseware packages is that they do not require you to learn new skills. The skills you have learned for e-writing—creating Web pages, writing email messages and attaching documents, and participating in asynchronous and synchronous discussion groups will serve you well when you use courseware packages. Another advantage of these packages is that students can gain access to all these resources by visiting a single site on the Internet. In fact, such packages are often used for courses that are offered exclusively online, and they can make those courses easier for students because they eliminate the need to learn to use several different media.

The first step is to be sure you can access the courseware site and verify that it will operate correctly on your computer. Generally, to access such a site, you must use a Web browser (such as Netscape or Internet Explorer) and type in the correct URL for the site. Once you access the site, you will probably be asked for a username and password. In most cases, instructors provide these to students in class or via email.

Since these courseware packages have many different features, some of which may be unfamiliar to you, it's a good idea to review the Help function for the package you are using. Find out which features (e.g., the chat function and the function for displaying student files) your instructor will require you to use, and be sure you know how to use them before you are required to do so for an assignment.

(3) Online media create new opportunities for collaborative writing.

If you have used any of the media described in this chapter, you probably realize that they offer many opportunities for writers to work together in ways that were once difficult or even impossible. For example, students can use a Web-based courseware package such as Blackboard or WebCT to share and comment on each other's drafts without having to meet physically. There are also special programs for networked classrooms, such as Daedalus, that enable students to work together simultaneously on the same document from different computers at different locations. These programs allow peer review to take place online by providing a way to share comments and suggestions for revision and by enabling users to exchange documents quickly and efficiently. (See also **3e**.) Programs such as NetMeeting (see page 150) have similar capabilities for use on the Web. Sometimes, an instructor will use a course-related newsgroup or Listserv to distribute drafts of essays to members of a class for comments.

In fact, online media facilitate collaboration among writers in ways that can help you improve your writing and give you the opportunity to help others do the same (see **3e**). And using email or online discussion groups can encourage you to see your own writing as something other than a solitary activity. The better you understand these media, the more possibilities you will see for engaging with other writers and enhancing your own ability as a writer.

E-designing 6

As the volume of information grows, so does the importance of its delivery—the visual design or format that gives readers the cues that lead them to the information they require and that makes your writing as readable as possible.

This chapter will help you

- use visual elements in Web design (**6a**),
- integrate graphics in Web design (**6b**),
- format documents to enhance content (**6c**), and
- format documents for readability (**6d**).

Far from being a surface detail that you take care of only after you have finished revising and proofing your document, delivery is important from the time you begin conceptualizing. Keeping in mind how you will present your ideas helps you develop them. Thus, delivery is closely related to arrangement (see **2c**), whether your document is intended for print or electronic distribution. The relationship between delivery and arrangement, however, is somewhat easier to understand in a Web document than in a print document.

Visual design sends messages to readers. It can invite them to explore at the same time as it reflects the rhetorical purpose. Consider the message that the uncluttered and inviting visual design of the award-winning Web page in figure 6.1 sends to those who view it.

Beyond the Rule

CRITERIA FOR WINNING AWARDS

For more information about the features that made the British Airways Web site the best of the Web in 2001, visit www.harbrace.com.

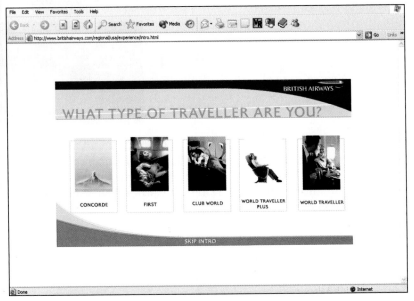

Figure 6.1. Award-winning British Airways Web site.

All of the elements of your document, whether it is a paper document or an electronic one, should contribute to making it easy to read. For a print document, one of the guiding principles of organization (see **2c** and **3c**) is grouping the parts of the document that go together. This is also true for Web documents. Notice how the designer of the British Airways Web site organized the information about types of travelers by embedding it in several clickable images. Make sure that there is a focal point for the reader's eye. In print, blocks of text—such as paragraphs (see **3c**) and block quotations (**34b**)—provide focal points. On the British Airways Web page, the focal point is the line of five images across the middle. The content flows from that focal point. Ample white space signals openness and availability by drawing the reader's eye to a focal point. White space on a page frames the material on the page and contributes to the balance. In print, a tightly packed page with narrow margins signals difficult material. Notice that the British Airways Web page has lots of white space, contributing to a user's impression that this page is easy to use and well organized.

6a | The visual elements of a Web document should serve a rhetorical purpose.

The Web provides opportunities for designing a wide range of documents. Web pages can be dynamically linked to other Web pages to form a new kind of document set that is very different from a book (see 5a). With today's technologies, the design and layout of a Web document can be extremely sophisticated. Relatively simple Web documents can also be effective, however, if you keep some basic principles in mind: Photographs and other kinds of visual elements can illustrate a key idea, present information, or help make a point, but these elements should not be merely decorative; they should be integral to achieving your purpose. Using a carefully chosen image can be a powerful way to evoke a feeling or make an argument. Similarly, a dramatic font style can be used to emphasize an idea. All the design elements of a Web document, like the tone and style of a printed one, are rhetorical tools that help you achieve your purpose and reach your intended audience. For example, a user's negative reaction to a photograph of dead sea lions on a Web site devoted to protecting wildlife can affect that user's view of the site in general. When you choose design elements such as photographs, try to anticipate how your audience may react.

The appearance of a well-designed site invites users to explore at the same time as it reflects the rhetorical purpose. To optimize the appearance of a Web document, keep in mind five basic design principles: balance, proportion, movement, contrast, and unity.

SOME BASIC DESIGN PRINCIPLES

- **Balance** involves the way in which elements in the design are spatially related to each other. Web pages with a symmetrical arrangement of elements convey a formal, static impression, whereas asymmetrical pages are informal and dynamic.

- **Proportion** has to do with the relative sizes of elements in a design. For example, large elements attract more attention than small ones and will be perceived as more important.

- **Movement** concerns the way in which our eyes scan a page for information. Most of us are accustomed to looking at the upper-left corner of a

(Continued on page 160)

(Continued from page 159)

page first and the lower-right corner last. Therefore, the most important information on a Web page should appear in those locations. Vertical or horizontal arrangement of elements on a page implies stability; a diagonal or zigzag arrangement suggests movement.

- **Contrast** between elements can be achieved by varying the focus or the size. For instance, a Web page on the dog breed the Siberian Husky might show the dog in sharp focus while blurring the background. The dog might also appear large relative to other elements on the page. You can also use contrasting fonts to emphasize an idea. For instance, a display font such as **kids** that looks like a child's writing or an elegant script font such as *Edwardian Script* might be used to highlight a contrast with something simpler and more direct. (Remember, though, that older Web browsers may not display all fonts properly.)

- **Unity** refers to the way all the elements (and pages) of a site combine to give the impression that they are parts of a complete whole. For instance, choose colors and fonts to reflect the tone you want to convey and use them consistently throughout your site. Creating a new design for each page of a Web site is almost certain to make the site seem chaotic and ineffective.

(1) Visual elements should be integrated with text in a Web document.

Rhetorically, Web pages are as much visual as they are verbal, and the most effective Web documents integrate both types of elements in such a way that they complement each other. Images and other visual elements extend and enhance the content of a Web document. Visual elements can be powerful tools, but selecting them and using them judiciously can be difficult. Too many visual elements may overwhelm viewers. Keep in mind that the basic design unit for a Web document is the computer screen, and put only as much on a page as a user can easily grasp within the space of a single screen. If you have too many images (or too much information) for one page, put some on another page or delete what is not essential.

Keep in mind that the visual impact of your Web site should be appropriate to its subject. Not only are the images on the pages from the "Fighting for Integration" site appropriate for an informative site, but they also help to tell the story and to involve readers in that story by

File Edit View Favorites Tools Help   Links »

The 54th Massachusetts Volunteer Infantry

While the 54th Massachusetts Infantry did posses a commendable battle history, most notably the assault on the Fort Wagner Battery and the rearguard action at the battle of Olustee, it is not the service record of the unit that made it famous. Rather the fame of the unit largely stemmed from the reason for its inception and the composition of its forces.

The 54th was composed mainly of free blacks from the northern states. The regiment came into existence through pressure that abolitionists placed on President Lincoln who as a result opened up the Military for black soldiers. Furthermore, several members of the 54th were the children of some of these same abolitionists. The organizing and commanding officer of the 54th, Robert Gould Shaw, was the son of prominent Boston abolitionists Francis Gould and Sarah Sturgis Shaw. Within the ranks of the recruits were two sons of Fredrick Douglass, a former slave and prominent abolitionist. The first was Sergeant-Major Lewis Douglass and the second, Charles Douglass. The assault on Fort Wagner was also where Sergeant William H. Carney earned his Congressional Medal of Honor saving the regiment's union flag from capture. He was the first African-American to receive such an honor.

The 54th had a clear purpose of helping to turn the war from one about state's rights to one about human rights. The regiment was as much a symbol as it was a fighting

Figure 6.2. The 54th Massachusetts Volunteer Infantry page.

arousing emotions. Notice especially the painting of the Black soldiers fighting under the Union flag in figure 6.2 and the photo of the lone Tuskegee airman in figure 6.3. Notice also how Aaron Munk, the creator of the site, placed the image in figure 6.2 at the top center of the page. Not only is this placement visually appealing and emotionally powerful, it is also informative. The prominent location in the center of the screen emphasizes that this regiment fought extremely hard in battle and was especially valorous, and it helps connect this page with the other pages on the site.

Because image files tend to be very large, they may download slowly on a user's Web browser, especially if the user has a slow connection to the Internet. For this reason, you should use them judiciously. Be sure that any image you include serves an important role in fulfilling your rhetorical purpose, especially if it is a large file. If a large file downloads too slowly, a user who is visiting your site may decide to abandon it before the download is even completed.

Web sites often incorporate audio or video elements. If you design a site devoted to rap music, for instance, you might want to include links

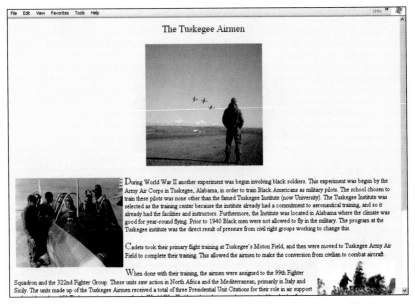

Figure 6.3. The Tuskegee Airmen page.

to audio clips of rap songs featured on the site. Or you might link to a video clip of a political speech on a site for a political science class. Such multimedia elements can help make your site more effective, but there are potential problems with their use. Audio and video clips are generally extremely large files that can take a long time to download. They also require special software in order to be heard or seen. As with the other elements of your Web document, consider the purpose of multimedia components carefully before incorporating them.

(2) Color and background play an important rhetorical role in a Web document.

Color and background can be used in a Web document to achieve various visual effects. Current Web standards allow the display of a wide array of colors for background, text, and frames. And it is easy to find thousands of background graphics on the Internet or to create them with special software. Like the other elements of a Web document, however, color and background should be considered rhetorical tools.

When deciding how to use color in your Web documents, keep the following considerations in mind:

- Designers recommend using no more than three main colors for a document (although you can use varying intensities, or shades, of a color, for example, light blue, dark blue, and medium blue). Using more than three colors can make your Web pages unappealing or confusing.
- Color can contribute to specific effects you wish to achieve. For example, bright colors such as red and yellow are more noticeable than light blue or brown, and you can use such colors on a Web page to emphasize a point or idea. In addition, some colors have associations you may wish to take advantage of. For instance, reds can suggest danger or an emergency, whereas brown shades such as beige and tan can create a formal atmosphere.
- Usually, textual hyperlinks appear in a color different from the surrounding text on a Web page. Also, a link that has not yet been clicked is one color, and a link that has already been clicked is a different color. For example, on a Web page with black text, a link not yet visited might be blue, and one that has been visited might be purple. Select the colors for textual hyperlinks to fit in with the overall color scheme of your document.

The background can also enhance your Web document, but there are some pitfalls to avoid when choosing one:

- A dark background can create a dramatic appearance, but it often makes text difficult to read and hyperlinks more difficult to see. A dark background can also cause a printout of a Web page to be blank. It is probably best not to use a dark background, but if you do, be sure that the color of the text is bright enough to be readable on screen and that you provide a version that will print clearly.
- A background with a pattern can also be dramatic but can make a Web page very difficult to read. If you want to use a pattern for your background, check the readability of the text. You may need to change the color of the text to make it easier to see. Notice how difficult it is to read the Web page in figure 6.4. Not only does the background produce a busy, crowded appearance without contributing to the purpose of the page, which is to teach close reading of a poem, it also is not related to the content. This page sends a false message that poetry is as difficult to read as the page itself is.
- You can use different background colors or patterns for different pages of your Web site, but be aware that doing so can create confusion. If you have a good rhetorical reason to alter the background from page

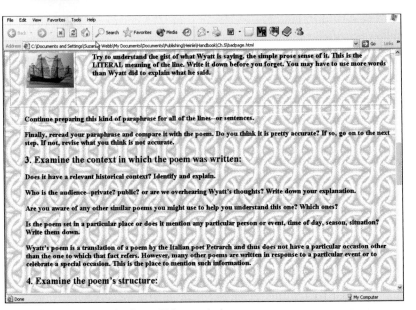

Figure 6.4. Example of poor Web page design.

to page of your site (as you might, for instance, if you were using a different color for each of several related categories of information), follow strictly the other design principles discussed on pages 159–160 so that your site still appears coherent to your audience.

For more detailed help with designing a Web site, you might look at some of the following.

Tim Berners-Lee, the creator of the World Wide Web, is the author of the following Web-based design manual: www.w3.org/Provider/Style/Introduction.html

Jeff Glover, the Web manager for XOOM.com, has good advice to offer at his Web site: jeffglover.com/ss.html

Check out library science professor Alastair Smith's list of nearly four dozen Web site evaluation guides: www.vuw.ac.nz/~agsmith/evaln/

If any of these Web addresses change, you may still be able to find the page by dropping the last element of the address and trying again. You may need to do that several times. If that doesn't work, you may be able to find the page by running a search (see **8c**) or looking at the links on other Web sites.

Beyond the Rule

HTML

Web pages are written in a fairly simple language called HyperText Markup Language (HTML). You insert HTML codes in a document to instruct a browser how to display the information in the document. For more information about HTML, visit www.harbrace.com.

CHECKLIST for Designing a Web Site

- Have you created a template to use for all of the pages in the Web site so that all of them are consistent?
- Have you chosen the background and text colors so that users can easily print copies of your pages?
- Have you used no more than three colors, but perhaps varied the intensity of one or more of them?
- Does a background pattern on your page make the text difficult to read?
- Have you chosen a single, easy-to-read font such as Times Roman for most of your text? If you use display fonts for titles or headings or for emphasis, are they suitable for the content and purpose? Are the type styles (bold, italic, and so on) used consistently throughout the document?
- Have you used visual elements sparingly? Are any image files larger than 30K, making it likely that they will take a long time to transfer? If so, can you shrink them by using a lower resolution or a smaller size?
- Are points indicated graphically by using bullets or numbers or by being divided into short blocks of text?
- Is any page crowded? Can users scan the information quickly on a single screen?
- Is there a site map or list of the site's sections on your home page? Are there links to get back to the home page from every other page in your site?

(Continued on page 166)

(Continued from page 165)

- Is the site too "text heavy"—that is, does each screen contain text of about the same density as in a book? If so, can you revise to provide more white space?
- Have you made sure that all links work?
- Have you identified yourself as the author and noted when the site was created or last revised?
- Have you run a spell checker?

Exercise 1

Using the Save as Web Page option of your word-processing program, create a simple Web page to accompany one of the papers you have written. Keep track of your reasons for making each design decision. State the rhetorical purpose for each visual element.

6b | Visual elements enhance understanding.

Visual elements help most readers understand complex information more readily. The ability of word-processing software to manage graphics easily has fostered an increase in the frequency with which writers use such elements. The danger, of course, is that visual elements can be overused. Most academic papers do not require these elements, and for many such papers, they may be inappropriate. But, for assignments in the natural and social sciences (see chapter 14), business (chapter 15), and education, tables, graphs, and charts are often essential. Becoming familiar with the creation and use of these elements will help you produce better documents for courses in these disciplines.

(1) Tables organize information to show relationships clearly.

Tables are particularly useful for presenting numerical information (see table 6.1). When you design a table, be sure to label all of the columns and rows accurately and to provide a title and a number. Table number and title appear above the table, but any notes or source information should be placed below it.

TABLE 6.1
Modified Monthly Tornado Statistics

Month	2002 Prelim.	2001 Final	2000 Final	1999 Final	3-Year Average
Jan	8	5	16	212	77
Feb	2	30	56	22	32
Mar	30	34	103	56	66
Apr	114	131	136	177	140
May	130	235	241	311	256
Jun	?	147	135	289	219
Jul	?	123	148	102	128
Aug	?	69	52	79	62
Sep	?	85	47	56	58
Oct	?	121	63	17	60
Nov	?	112	48	7	37
Dec	?	?	26	15	16
Total	290	1212	1071	1343	1151

Source: National Weather Service.

Word-processing programs have settings that let you insert a table wherever you need one. You can determine how many rows and columns the table will have, and you can also size each row and each column appropriately for the information it will hold. Tables can also be used to enhance page design.

(2) Charts and graphs demonstrate relationships among data.

Not only do charts and graphs demonstrate relationships among data, but they also show spatial concepts or call attention to particular information or comparisons. In paper documents, they should be used to support your text, not to replace any of it. In Web documents, they often substitute for text. (See page 158.) If you need many charts or graphs in a paper, consider placing all of them in an appendix.

Charts and graphs are often referred to as **figures.** Each figure in a document should be numbered and have a title. The figure number and title, as well as any source note, should be placed below the illustration. You can even create many figures with your word-processing program using a Chart function.

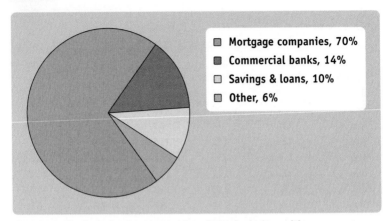

Figure 6.5. Pie chart showing issuers of mortgage-backed securities.
Source: GMAC Mortgage-Backed Securities.

Figure 6.6. Graph of nightly sleep stages.
Source: Jetlog 24x7.

Pie charts are especially useful for showing the relationship of parts to a whole (see figure 6.5).

Graphs show relationships over time. For instance, a graph can show the progression of sleep stages during a night (see figure 6.6), increases or decreases in student achievement or annual rainfall, or trends in financial markets.

Bar charts show other kinds of correlations. A bar chart might illustrate gross national product for several nations, the relative speeds of var-

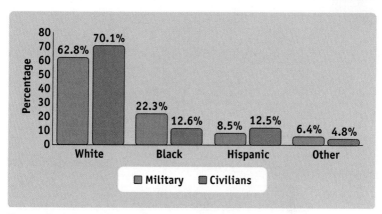

Figure 6.7. Bar chart illustrating the composition of the U.S. military.
Source: Seattle Times (seattletimes.nwsource.com/.../ military/new_military.html), 7/17/02.

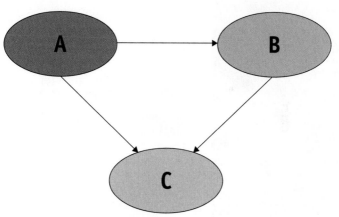

Figure 6.8. A diagram of the process from A to C.

ious computer processors, or statistics about the composition of the U.S. military (see figure 6.7).

(3) Diagrams, drawings, maps, and other illustrations help explain concepts.

Diagrams or drawings (see figure 6.8), maps (figure 6.9), and other kinds of illustrations help readers understand processes or concepts

Figure 6.9. A map showing Starbucks locations in China.
Source: Modified from CIA Fact Book.

Figure 6.10. A photograph that could add impact to a document.
Source: Photo courtesy of Roland Schlager.

"Indeed, your class attendance does give new meaning to the term 'distance learning.'"

Figure 6.11. A cartoon that brings humor to the discussion of a concept.
Source: Chronicle of Higher Education, 1999.

and visualize spatial dimensions and relationships, as well as other details pertinent to the topic of a document. Photographs can also have visual or emotional impact (see figure 6.10), and cartoons can add humor (figure 6.11).

| 6c | A well-designed document format contributes to the rhetorical purpose. |

Creating a balanced page and grouping related parts of a document are essential to good design. The advice here follows MLA guidelines. If your instructor has specified another style manual, check the most recent edition of that manual. (See the list of style manuals on pages 283–284.) In general, if your instructor asks you to use a particular style, follow the instructions for that style exactly.

(1) Indentation signals a change of ideas.

The first line of every paragraph should be uniformly indented. You can set your word-processing software to automatically indent the first line of a paragraph one-half inch. Indent block quotations one inch from the left margin (see figure 6.12).

If you use the tab key or space bar to create indentations, the format can change if you transfer your document to another computer or save it as a Web page. Thus, it is a good idea to learn to use the formatting controls in your word processor.

(2) All pages should be numbered.

Place arabic numerals—without parentheses or periods—on each page of a document. According to Modern Language Association (MLA) style, the number appears at the right margin, one-half inch from the top of the page. Put your last name immediately before the page number so that your instructor can identify any page that gets misplaced. (Notice the way the page number and last name appear in figure 6.12.) Similarly, American Psychological Association (APA) style calls for the page number to appear in the upper-right corner of the page after the running head (see 11c). *The Chicago Manual of Style* (CMS) does not specify the placement for page numbers, so ask your instructor for directions. Word-processing programs have a setting that will automatically insert the appropriate page number at the top or bottom of the page.

Pieper 3

the first outlet opened across from the city's famous opera house. Once some success is
accomplished, Starbucks buys enough of the foreign-owned branch to control the
company, and proceeds to enlarge rapidly throughout the country (Burke, Smith, and
Wosnitza 47).

Vienna, considered by many to be the birthplace of the coffeehouse tradition, is
legendary for its coffee culture. The first Viennese coffeehouses appeared after invading
Turks left sacks of coffee outside the city walls as they fled in 1683 (Pendergast 10).
Intellectual life abounded in elegant cafés by the nineteenth century, as they became
meeting places for early modernists such as Sigmund Freud and Gustav Klimt, as well as
for notable exiles such as Vladimir Lenin and Leon Trotsky. In Vienna, the people take
pride in the history and enjoy the culture that surrounds the coffeehouse tradition.
Austrians received the opening of Starbucks with mixed emotions:

> Many Viennese sniff that their culture has been infected, that Viennese use
> their 1,900 or so coffee shops to linger and meet, smoke and drink, savor the
> wonders of pastries with cream and marzipan, ponder the world, write books
> and read free newspapers. They drink from china cups and order from a
> waiter, usually in a stained black dinner jacket. (Erlanger B3)

Skeptics found it difficult to believe that an American brand such as Starbucks could
survive in an environment steeped in its own local history of coffee and pride in its
heritage, but these skeptics seem to have underestimated Starbucks.

There are several fundamental differences between the Starbucks experience and
the traditional experience found in Viennese coffeehouses. Instead of ordering through a
server, Starbucks patrons order at an American-style coffee bar. As opposed to more
traditional offerings such as Sachertorte and hot goulash, Starbucks sells American-style
sweets like blueberry muffins and chocolate-chip cookies. Furthermore, patrons are not
allowed to smoke in any Starbucks outlet in order to allow the aroma of coffee to fill each
store. Smoking, however, is a large part of the European coffeehouse experience.

These differences add up to two coffee cultures at a crossroads in Vienna. Traditional
American offerings are pitted against the offerings of Viennese coffeehouses that have

Figure 6.12. Example of indentation format.

(3) The first page of a document has a distinctive format.

Unless your instructor requires that you use a different style, follow
MLA guidelines and place your name, your instructor's name, the course
and section number, and the date in the top left-hand corner of the first
page of a paper (one inch from the top and one inch from the left edge
of the page), double-spacing after each line. You should also double-
space between the lines of a long title or between a main title and a subtitle. Center all lines of titles. Do not triple or quadruple space after the
title. (See figure 6.13.) Begin your first paragraph on the second line below the title (the first double-spaced line). (See also the models in chapters 3, 7, 11, 13, and 14.)

Figure 6.13. First page of a paper in MLA style.

Most papers do not require a title page, but if you use one, follow your instructor's directions about the format. The title page shown in CMS style in figure 6.14 may be suitable for use with an MLA-style paper if your instructor wants a title page. Figures 6.15 and 6.16 show first pages that follow APA and CSE/CBE styles, respectively.

(4) Headings help organize complex information.

Headings are necessary to help readers manage information in research papers, technical and business reports, and other kinds of complex documents. Headings highlight the organization of a long block of information and make it easy to combine several related statements. They are

Race in the U.S. Army: An Executive Order for Hope

Nicole Hester
American History 257
December 6, 2002

Figure 6.14. Title page in CMS style.

more commonly used for writing in the sciences and social sciences than in the humanities. Both APA and CSE/CBE styles have specific requirements for formatting headings. (See chapter 11.)

Short papers rarely require headings. If you use headings in a longer paper, make them consistent throughout your document. If you have two or more levels of headings, treat all occurrences of each level alike. For instance, headings in this book follow a pattern similar to that of an outline. The main sections are identified by a number and letter set at the left margin. Subsections are identified by numbers in parentheses, and subdivisions of these, where they appear, are indicated by letters in parentheses.

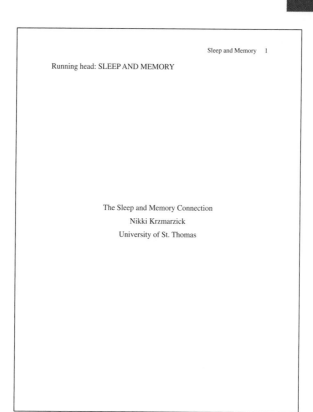

Figure 6.15. Title page in APA style.

Running head: SLEEP AND MEMORY

The Sleep and Memory Connection
Nikki Krzmarzick
University of St. Thomas

6d | A well-designed format enhances a document's readability.

Several formatting principles will help make your documents as attractive and easy to read as possible.

(1) Documents should follow a consistent format.

The conventions of academic writing require that all papers be double-spaced. Set margins of at least one inch (no more than one and one-half inches) on all sides of the text block to give your reader room for comments and to prevent a crowded appearance, and use eleven- or

---

Lab Report: Mitosis

Observations and Calculations of Onion Root Tip Cells

Heather Jensen

Texas Woman's University: Biology 101

June 7, 2002

ABSTRACT

This laboratory experiment examined *Allium* (onion) root tip cells in the five stages of mitosis. The five stages of mitotic division were identified and recorded, and a 50-cell sample was chosen for closer examination. Of those 50 cells, 64% were found to be in interphase, 20% in prophase, 6% in metaphase, 6% in anaphase, and only 4% in telophase. The results showed that onion root tip cells spend the majority of their life cycle in a rest period (interphase). Prophase was calculated to be the longest phase of active division, while telophase was the shortest. These results were consistent with the experiments completed by other students and scientists.

INTRODUCTION

This lab report outlines a laboratory experiment on mitosis, the division of the nucleus of a cell to form two new cells with the same number of chromosomes as the parent cell. Mitotic cell division consists of five visually identifiable stages: interphase, prophase, metaphase, anaphase, and telophase. The purpose of this laboratory experiment was to identify and observe cells in each phase of mitosis, as well as to calculate an estimation of the real time involved in each stage of mitosis in an onion root tip. The onion root tip was chosen for this experiment because of its easy availability and rapid growth. Rapid growth presented an easy opportunity to observe multiple

1

Figure 6.16. First page of a paper in CSE/CBE style.

twelve-point type. Also, resist the impulse to justify the right margin (i.e., to make it straight), unless a document will be printed without being reformatted, as is sometimes the case with business documents or documents intended for desktop publishing.

If you submit your work electronically (for instance, by email, in a Web document, or on a removable medium), follow your instructor's directions exactly. Check with your instructor about any special requirements, such as the need to provide your document in PC or Mac format. Always label disks clearly. Whatever requirements an instructor imposes, the computing facilities to meet them are probably available on campus at no cost. Employers will have their own formatting requirements and the equipment to produce your documents in the form they require.

(2) Type fonts are best kept simple.

Although word-processing software makes it easy to use a variety of different type sizes and fonts on a single page, using a variety detracts from your content. Most academic papers should be printed using a font that looks like typewriter type, such as Courier, or a simple proportional font, such as Times Roman. It is usually best to avoid sans serif fonts (those, such as Arial, in which letters lack cross-bars at the ends of strokes) and fancy display fonts, such as 𝔒𝔩𝔡 𝔈𝔫𝔤𝔩𝔦𝔰𝔥 and *Script*, because blocks of text printed in such fonts are hard to read.

Word-processing software makes it easy to use italics for titles and foreign words and phrases, but you should resist the temptation to use italics or boldfacing for emphasis. (See **38f**.) Follow the recommendations of the style manual for the specific discipline in which you are writing.

Although ink-jet printers offer the option of printing text in color, you should not do so unless there is some purpose to formatting in this way (as when creating a flyer or announcement). Most professors prefer that you use black ink (and a font such as Times Roman) for traditional academic assignments because it produces clear, dark text that is easy to read.

CHECKLIST for Formatting Paper Documents

- Have you used proper margins? Are the margins at least one inch wide or set according to your instructor's specifications?
- Is the first line of each paragraph indented one-half inch?
- Is each page numbered?
- Does the first page have the appropriate title and heading?
- Is the print dark, clean, clear, and legible?
- Are the lines double-spaced?
- Are all listed items numbered sequentially?

Exercise 2

Review the formatting decisions you have made for a paper you have submitted or that you are planning to submit. What, if anything, do you think needs to be changed? Why?

Writing Arguments

You write arguments on a regular basis. When you send your business partner a memo to tell her that a client needs to sign a contract, when you email your parents to ask them for a loan for a down payment, when you petition your academic advisor for a late drop, or when you demand that a mail-order company refund your money, you're writing an argument. You are expressing a point of view and then using logical reasoning to try to get a specific audience to accept that point of view or adopt a course of action. *Argument* and *persuasion* are often used interchangeably, but they differ in two basic ways. Traditionally, **persuasion** has referred to winning or conquering with the use of emotional reasoning, whereas **argument** has been linked with logical reasoning. But because much writing involves some measure of "winning"—even if it's only gaining the ear of a particular audience—and uses both emotion and reason, this book uses *argument* to cover the meanings of both terms.

When writing arguments, you follow the same process you use for all your writing: planning, drafting, revising, and designing (see chapters **2**, **3**, and **6**), as well as attending to audience and context (see **1e**). Argumentative writing is distinct from other kinds of writing in its focus on audience as inseparable from purpose. Recognizing and respecting the beliefs, values, and expertise held by a specific audience is the only way for you to achieve your purpose, which goes beyond victory over an opponent. Although the traditional purpose of argument has been winning, argument is now considered an important way to invite exchange, understanding, cooperation, consideration, joint decision making, agreement, or negotiation of differences. Thus, argument serves three basic and sometimes overlapping purposes: to analyze a complicated issue or question an established belief, to express or defend a point of view, and to invite or convince an audience to change a position or adopt a course of action.

This chapter will help you

- determine the purpose of an argument (7a),
- establish an arguable statement (7b),
- distinguish fact from opinion (7c),
- take a position or make a claim (7d),
- provide evidence to support your claims (7e),
- establish credibility (7f),
- appeal appropriately to the feelings of your audience (7f),
- arrange ideas (7g),
- use logical reasoning (7h),
- avoid rhetorical fallacies (7i), and
- learn from others' arguments (7j).

As you proceed, you'll understand the importance of determining your purpose, identifying your audience, marshaling your arguments, arguing ethically, and treating your audience with respect.

7a | Different arguments have different purposes.

What is your subject? Why are you arguing about it? What is at stake? What is likely to happen as a result of your making this argument? How important are those consequences? Who is in a position to act or react in response to your argument?

If you want to abolish spring break in order to get out of school earlier in the summer, the purpose of your argument is to analyze or question a complicated issue or established belief (in this case, an established institutional policy) with which you disagree. In this situation, you need to determine the appropriate audience for your argument, the person or group who can respond to your argument. Is it the college president, the members of the faculty senate, or student readers of the school newspaper? Who needs to reconsider the existence of spring break? Who is in the position to abolish or shorten it?

Perhaps your friends have asked how you still find time to attend church regularly now that you're in college. In this case, you may want to express or defend your point of view. You may need to explain to your friends that your attending church has more to do with your own religious beliefs and spiritual needs than how much coursework you have to do that day or where you are in terms of your education.

Or, let's say, you want to talk with your insurance agent about lowering your rates. She believes that you're a reckless driver because you've received two speeding tickets in the past two years; you know that you've stopped speeding, and you would like one last chance. Expecting your agent to change her business policy is not only unrealistic but undesirable; instead, your purpose is to invite or convince the agent (your audience, in this case) to consider another point of view, to modify her position, adjust her course of action, or allow some exceptions to the policy (in other words, give you one more chance). You'll need to provide the agent with the most compelling reasons you can think of, so that she begins to consider your point of view, the first step in changing her mind. Because you cannot always hope to defeat a position outright, your aim is sometimes to encourage slight movement, not radical change.

After you establish the relationship among your subject, purpose, and audience, you need to make that relationship clear in your introduction. Your readers (or audience) always expect to find the purpose of your argument in the introduction, and sometimes in the conclusion as well.

In argument, audience is integral to purpose. In fact, in certain circumstances, your audience might shape your purpose:

- If there is little likelihood that you can convince members of your audience to change a strongly held opinion, you might still achieve a great deal by simply inviting them to seriously consider and understand your position.
- If the members of your audience are not firmly and absolutely committed to a position, you might be able to convince them to agree with the opinion you are expressing or defending.
- If the members of your audience agree with you in principle, you might invite them to undertake a specific action—such as voting for the candidate you are supporting.

No matter how you imagine your audience responding to your argument, you must establish **common ground** with them, stating a goal toward which you both want to work or a belief, assumption, or value that you both share; in other words, common ground is a starting point of agreement. For instance, if you want to argue to a group of writing instructors that the first-year college writing course should no longer be a requirement, you might begin by stating that you agree that knowing how to write well is important to academic success. Once you have established agreement on this belief, you might be able to suggest and argue in favor of some alternatives to the required first-year writing course: writing-intensive courses across the curriculum, writing-across-the-curriculum practices, and/or an elective first-year writing course.

Exercise 1

Study the following paragraph by John Munzer, a columnist for *Esquire,* a men's magazine. As you read the paragraph, decide what Munzer's purpose seems to be and how it relates to the audience. (Be sure to note the title of the column.) Write a paragraph stating that purpose and including the specific information from the paragraph that helped you identify it.

[1]Remember that guy in college who told you, within ten minutes of meeting you, that he'd read *The Hobbit* 11 times before his 18th birthday and dressed up as Bilbo Baggins every year for Halloween? [2]I never trusted that guy. [3]I never trust any postpubescent man who spends his time reading about trolls, dastardly villains, and pint-sized sorcerers. [4]So you can imagine how my circle of friends has dwindled since J. K. Rowling and Lemony Snicket arrived on the scene. [5]It is now officially Worse Than Ever. [6]We're talking 50 million books sold between them, many of which were purchased by purported adults. [7]Rowling and Snicket are not to blame. [8]No, they probably just set out to tell the kiddies some stories, and what could be wrong with that? [9]Nothing is wrong with that. [10]But what *is* wrong is that grown men are buying these books, are *lining up around the block* to meet the authors, and are dropping words like *Muggles* and *Count Olaf* in casual conversation. . . . [11]Read a real book. . . . [12]Read Faulkner. [13]Read Márquez. [14]Read Ludlum. [15]Just don't read books that have accompanying merchandising lines. [16]The next time someone tells me that the Harry Potter books are "great beach reading," I will break down and cry. [17]Then I will tell them to grow . . . up.

—**JOHN MUNZER,** "The Complaint: Adults Reading Children's Books"

7b | Argument assumes the existence of differing views.

If everyone agreed on everything, there'd be no need for argument, for taking a position or questioning the position of someone else. But everyone doesn't agree. Thus, you'll find that a good deal of writing requires that you take a position on a topic, an arguable position. Almost everyone agrees that smoking is not a healthful practice—that's a widely shared belief that is nearly impossible to argue against. Such a widely held opinion could become a topic for an expressive or expository essay (see 1e(1)), such as "Why Smoking Is Harmful to Your Health" or "The Surgeon General's Latest Report on Smoking," but, in and of itself, this opinion lacks the element of controversy or disagreement that is essential to an argument. On the other hand, this topic could be reconceived into an arguable statement: "The pleasure of smoking outweighs the health hazards" or "Smoking is not healthful, but it's nearly impossible to quit." Thus, the first step toward finding a topic for argumentation is to consider issues that inspire different opinions.

Behind any effective argument is a question that can generate more than one reasonable answer. If you ask "Is there racism in the United States?" almost anyone will agree that there is. But if you ask "Why is there still racism in the United States?" or "What can Americans do to eliminate racism?" you will hear different answers. Answers differ because people approach questions with various backgrounds, experiences, and assumptions. Under these circumstances, they can be tempted to use reasoning that supports what they already believe. As a writer, you, too, will be tempted to employ such reasoning, and doing so is a good place to start. But as you expand and shape your argument, you'll want to demonstrate not only that you are knowledgeable about your topic but also that you are aware of and have given fair consideration to the diverse views about it (see 7e(2)). After all, the most honored speakers and writers have always been both eloquent and ethical as they have marshaled their knowledge of a given subject. To be both knowledgeable and yet respectful of others' views constitutes a worthy goal.

When you write an argument, then, you are trying to solve a problem or answer a question—with or for an audience. When you choose a topic for argumentation, you'll want to take a stance toward that topic that allows you to question, that provides you an exigence (or reason) for writing. Whatever general subject you're writing about, you'll focus on a topic (see **2a(2)**), on the part of the subject you'll address in your essay, and then pose a question. As you craft your critical question, you'll want to consider the following: (1) your own values and beliefs with respect to the question, (2) how your assumptions might differ from those of your intended audience, and (3) how you might establish common ground with members of your audience, while at the same time respecting any differences of opinion between you and them. The question you raise will evolve into your thesis, an arguable statement.

The most important criterion for choosing an arguable statement for an essay is knowledge of the topic: You must already have it or be willing to go out and get it. Either way, you'll be an informed writer, responsive to the expectations of your audience. When you're in a position to choose your own topic, you can draw on your knowledge of current events, politics, sports, fashion, or specific academic subjects. Even when you're watching a TV program or surfing the Web, topics may present themselves if you find yourself agreeing or disagreeing with what you hear and read. To find a topic, you can also try methods such as freewriting and listing (see **2a(1)**).

To determine if a topic might be suitable, make a statement about that topic and then check to see if that statement can be argued.

TIPS FOR ASSESSING A TOPIC AND AN ARGUABLE STATEMENT

- One thing I believe strongly about this topic is _____.
  List every reason you can think of to support your view.

- Who or what groups might disagree with my statement? Why?

- Do I know enough about this topic to discuss other points of view?
  Can I find out what I need to know?

- Mine is not the only belief on this topic. Other people believe
  _____. List all the reasons you can think of to support
  these other viewpoints.

- What is my purpose in writing about this topic?

- How does my purpose relate to my audience?

- What do I want my audience to do in response to my argument?
  In other words, what do I expect from my audience?

If you can answer all these questions to your satisfaction, then you should feel confident about your topic and move further into the writing process. If you cannot answer some of them, then reconsider your topic, your thesis statement, or the amount of research you may need to do to support your argument. As you research and explore your topic (see **2a**), by searching for information in the library or on the Web (see chapter **8**), you may be able to clarify your purpose and improve your thesis statement.

7c	**Preparing to write an argument requires the ability to distinguish between fact and opinion.**

When you explore your topic and consider how you want your audience to interpret it, you use both facts and opinions. It's important to distinguish between these two kinds of information so that you can use both to your advantage in argumentation. **Facts** are reliable pieces of information that can be verified through independent sources or procedures. **Opinions,** on the other hand, are assertions or inferences that may or may not be based on facts. Opinions that are widely accepted, however, may seem to be factual when actually they are not.

Just because facts are reliable does not mean that they speak for themselves. Facts are significant only when they are used responsibly to support a claim; otherwise, a thoughtful and well-informed opinion might have more impact. For instance, if you're driving down a hill at sixty-seven miles per hour in a sixty-five mile-per-hour zone, a police officer may think you're speeding, but you may not consider two miles per hour over the speed limit on a downhill run a traffic violation. Your opinion, rendered respectfully, that you picked up speed as you went down the hill, may convince the officer that you weren't really speeding. In this case, you're providing an interpretation of the facts. But if you argued simply from your opinion that you were not speeding, you could seriously damage your credibility—and get a ticket. The police officer might assume that you are not taking the speed limit seriously. By distinguishing facts from opinions, you not only use information effectively but establish your credibility (**7f(1)(a)**), an essential feature of successful argumentation.

To distinguish between fact and opinion, ask yourself questions about a statement you have read: Can it be proved? Can it be challenged? How often is the same result achieved? If a statement can consistently be proved true, then it is a fact. If it can be disputed, then it is an opinion.

Fact   Milk contains calcium.

Opinion   Americans should drink more milk.

To say that milk contains calcium is to state a well-established fact: It can be verified by consulting published studies or by conducting laboratory tests. Whether or not this fact is significant depends on how a writer chooses to use it. As an isolated fact, it is unlikely to seem significant. But to say that Americans need to drink more milk is to express an opinion that may or may not be supported by facts. When considering the statement "Americans should drink more milk," a thoughtful reader might ask: "How much calcium does a human need? Why do humans need calcium? Is milk the richest source of calcium? Might leafy green vegetables provide a richer source of calcium? Is cow's milk good for humans?" Anticipating questions such as these can help you develop an argument (see 7e).

Because facts can change over time, writers and readers need to remain flexible as they distinguish between fact and opinion. The erroneous belief that the sun revolves around the earth was once considered a fact, and Christopher Columbus's "discovery" of America was long undisputed. Describing what can easily happen in research, a distinguished physician writes that a good scientist must be prepared for the day when his or her life's work is suddenly called into question:

> All the old ideas—last week's ideas in some cases—are no longer good ideas. The hard facts have softened, melted away and vanished under the pressure of new hard facts.   —**LEWIS THOMAS**, "The Art of Teaching Science"

The most knowledgeable people are those who realize that the line between fact and opinion is not always clear. What appears to be factual (the earth is flat; earth, wind, fire, and water are the only elements; species are unchangeable) could be the result of inadequate research or assumptions that are so widely held that they have gone unchallenged. Knowledgeable people, then, are constantly assimilating new information and questioning old ideas.

Writers and readers of arguments are always prepared to interpret and assess the information before them; they evaluate the stance, the beliefs supporting such a stance, the kinds of sources used, and the objections that could be made to the argument. Careful writers and readers of arguments ask what kind of verification could establish the reliability of the information. For instance, if your dentist tells you that flossing is more important than brushing, you may not believe him. But if your dentist can verify this claim with reliable scientific evidence, by telling you that flossing helps remove the 35 percent of plaque that brushing cannot reach, you might be willing to change your morning teeth-cleaning habits.

Whether you are considering a fact or an opinion, prepare for writing a convincing argument by asking yourself, "What kind of evidence is necessary, how can that evidence be obtained, and what will happen if conflicting evidence is discovered?"

Exercise 2

Determine which of the following statements seem to be fact and which seem to be opinion. In each case, what kind of verification would you require in order to accept the statement as reliable? Explain your decisions in writing, and be prepared to discuss your choices in class.

1. Toni Morrison won the Nobel Prize in literature in 1993.
2. Women often earn less money than men holding the same positions.
3. *The Lion King* was the best movie ever made about animals.
4. Writing well is a gift, like musical genius.
5. A college degree guarantees a good job.
6. The oldest city in the United States is Santa Fe.
7. Running is good for your health.
8. The United States won the Second World War.
9. In combination, ammonia and chlorine bleach result in poisonous gas.
10. Researchers will find a cure for AIDS.

7d | An argument takes a position or makes a claim.

When making an argument, a writer takes a position on a particular topic. Whether analyzing, questioning, expressing, defending, inviting, or convincing, a writer of an argument makes that position clear. This position, called the **claim,** or **proposition,** clearly states what the writer wants the audience to do with the information being provided. This claim is the thesis (see **2b**) of the argument and usually appears in the introduction (see **7a** and **7g**) and sometimes again in the conclusion.

(1) Effective writers claim no more than they can responsibly support.

Claims vary in extent; they can be absolute or moderate, large or limited. A writer who makes an absolute claim needs to provide more, and more compelling, evidence than a writer who makes a moderate one. Absolute claims assert that something is always true or false, completely good or bad. Moderate claims make less sweeping assertions.

Absolute claim	College athletes are never good students.
Moderate claim	Most colleges have low graduation rates for their athletes.
Absolute claim	Harry S. Truman was the best president we've ever had.
Moderate claim	Truman's domestic policies helped advance civil rights.

Moderate claims are not necessarily superior to absolute claims. After all, writers frequently need to take a strong position in favor of or against something. But the stronger the claim, the stronger the evidence needed to support it. Be sure to consider the quality and the significance of the evidence you use (see **7c** and **7e**)—not just its quantity.

(2) Claims vary in kind as well as in how much they encompass.

(a) Substantiation claims assert that something exists.
Without making a value judgment, a **substantiation claim** makes a point that can be supported by evidence.

The job market for new Ph.D.'s in English is limited.

The post office is raising rates again.

(b) Evaluation claims assert that something has a specific quality.
According to an **evaluation claim,** something is good or bad, effective or ineffective, attractive or unattractive, successful or unsuccessful.

The graduation rate for athletes at Penn State is very high compared with that at the other Big Ten universities.

The public transportation system in Washington, D.C., is reliable and safe.

Jennifer Lopez is a great actress.

(c) Policy claims call for a specific action.

When making **policy claims,** writers call for something to be done.

We must find the funds to hire better qualified high school teachers.

We need to build a light-rail system linking downtown with the airport and the western suburbs.

Much writing involves substantiation, evaluation, and policy claims. When writing about the job market, you might tap your ability to substantiate a claim; when writing about literature (see chapter 13), you might need to evaluate a character. Policy claims are commonly found in arguments about social issues such as health care, social security, and affirmative action. They also occur in daily life, where they might take the form of asking your instructor to lift her attendance policy, asking your advisor to expand the list of electives, or asking your spouse to excuse you from attending a midsemester family gathering. Policy claims often grow out of substantiation or evaluation claims: First, you demonstrate that a problem exists (spending eight hours en route to and from a family gathering uses too much precious time); then, you establish the best solution for that problem (staying home that weekend to study for midterms and attending family gatherings during vacations).

TIPS FOR MAKING A CLAIM ARGUABLE

- Write down your opinion.
- Describe the situation that produced your opinion.
- Decide who constitutes the audience for your opinion and what you want that audience to do about your opinion.
- Write down the verifiable and reliable facts that support your opinion.
- Using those facts, transform your initial opinion into a thoughtful claim that considers at least two sides to the issue under discussion.
- Ask yourself, "So what?" If the answer to this question shows that your claim doesn't lead anywhere, start over with the first tip.

As an example of transforming an opinion into an arguable claim, consider the following scenario. Helen thinks that air pollution is a problem. She describes the situation that has inspired her opinion: She was jogging on a busy street and had difficulty breathing because of the excessive car exhaust. Describing this situation helps Helen focus her opinion; she decides to narrow her topic to reducing automobile emissions. Then, she imagines an audience for her topic, an audience who can *do* something about this issue. She decides to write to automobile manufacturers. Helen knows that she needs to do some research on this topic in order to write a convincing argument, so she researches the physics of automobile emissions and realizes that, with just a small amount of effort, car manufacturers could improve the efficiency of most automobile engines—and thereby reduce emissions. She also conducts a survey of fellow college students and learns that most of them would prefer to buy cars with more efficient engines. Helen now has a specific audience, a specific claim for them, and a specific reason for her audience to agree with her claim: Despite a slight increase in automobile price, automobile manufacturers should work to produce more efficient engines; if they do so, young adults will be more likely to purchase their automobiles.

Exercise 3

The following excerpt is from an argument analyzing racial strife in the United States, written by Cornel West, a scholar specializing in race relations. Evaluate the claims it presents. Are they absolute or moderate? Can you identify a substantiation or evaluation claim? What policy claim is implicit in this passage?

[1]To engage in a serious discussion of race in America, we must begin not with the problems of black people but with the flaws of American society—flaws rooted in historic inequalities and longstanding cultural stereotypes. [2]How we set up the terms for discussing racial issues shapes our perception and response to these issues. [3]As long as black people are viewed as a "them," the burden falls on blacks to do all the "cultural" and "moral" work necessary for healthy race relations. [4]The implication is that only certain Americans can define what it means to be American—and the rest must simply "fit in."

—**CORNEL WEST**, "Introduction," *Race Matters*

7e | An effective argument is well developed.

Effective arguments are well developed and supported. Although you may sometimes be able to write an effective argument directly from your own experience and observations, you are often likely to need to do some research to gain more information (see chapter **8**). In either case, you should explore your topic in enough depth to have the evidence to support your position intelligently and ethically (see **7b** and **7f(1)**). In addition, you'll want to take into consideration the reasons why other people might disagree with you and be prepared to respond to those reasons.

(1) An effective argument clearly establishes the thinking that leads to the claim.

If you want readers to take your ideas seriously, you must establish why you think as you do. That means communicating the reasons that have led to your position, as well as the values and assumptions that support your thinking. When you are exploring your subject, make a list of the reasons that have led to your belief without trying to edit them (see **2a(1)**). For example, when Laura Klocke was working on her argumentative essay (at the end of this chapter; see pages 216–222), she listed the following reasons for her belief that fair trade coffee should be used exclusively at her school:

> The average price of coffee is $12.00/lb., while the average coffee grower is paid only 20–40 cents/lb.
>
> The average latte costs $3.50, while the average coffee farmer makes $3.00/day.
>
> University of St. Thomas is committed to producing "morally responsible individuals who combine cultural awareness and intellectual curiosity."
>
> St. Thomas could easily support only fair trade coffee.

Although it is possible to base your argument on one good reason (such as "Buying fair trade coffee is the right thing to do"), doing so can be risky. If your audience does not find this reason convincing, you have no other support for your position. When you show that you have more than one reason for believing as you do, you increase the likelihood that your audience will find merit in your argument. For example, suppose you believe that all speakers and writers should use Standardized English and you write an argument stating that the United States is one nation that should have one language—Standardized English. Readers who are aware of the evidence showing that fluency in more than one language or dialect enriches cognitive abilities will dismiss your argument even if they find it well written. In this case, you'll need to introduce other reasons for supporting the use of Standardized English: perhaps because it is the language of wider communication or because it is the prestige dialect in the United States. When you introduce several reasons for your claim, you make a more complex argument, one that cannot be dismissed so readily.

Sometimes, however, one reason is stronger—and more appropriate for your audience—than several others you could advance. To develop an argument for which you have only one good reason (for instance, that Standardized English is the language of wider communication or the prestige dialect in the United States), explore the bases underlying your reason: the values and assumptions that led you to take your stand. By demonstrating the thinking behind the single reason on which you are building your case, you can create a well-developed argument.

Whether you have one reason or several, be sure to provide sufficient evidence from credible sources to support your claim:

- facts,
- statistics,
- examples, and
- testimony, often from personal experience or professional expertise.

This evidence must be accurate, representative, and sufficient. Accurate information should be verifiable by others (see 7c). Recognize, however, that a writer may provide you with information that is accurate but neither representative nor sufficient, because it was drawn from an exceptional case, a biased sample, or a one-time occurrence. If, for example, you are writing an argument about the advantages of using Standardized English but draw all of your supporting evidence from a proponent of the English-Only movement, your evidence represents only the views of that movement. If you draw all of your evidence from just one person (Bill Cosby, for instance, has strong views on the use of Standardized English, especially as a means to stamp out the Ebonics movement), your evidence is neither representative of all the support for the use of Standardized English, nor is it sufficient to support a thoughtful argument. In order to represent a wider viewpoint, you should gather supporting evidence from sociolinguists, speakers of other dialects and languages, education specialists, professors, and other experts. In other words, you need to consult a wider array of sources. (See chapter 8.)

When gathering evidence, you need to think critically about the information you find, especially the results of polls, interviews, authorities, and other statistics you plan to use. How recent and representative is the information, and how was it gathered? Is an authority you plan to quote qualified to address the topic under consideration? Is the authority likely to be respected by your readers? During the Great Depression, the editors of *Literary Digest* announced the results of a poll that predicted that Alf Landon would defeat Franklin D. Roosevelt in the U.S. presidential election. Because the poll was limited to people who were financially secure at that time (they owned cars and had telephone service), the poll was neither representative nor accurate. Roosevelt won by a landslide. Because Roosevelt advocated increased government spending on domestic programs, the participants in this poll were unlikely to vote for him, but the majority of American citizens did give him their votes.

As you consider survey statistics, you need to keep in mind that any set of statistics can be manipulated, whether the poll is representative or not. For instance, statistical surveys often report averages, such as the average income of sales managers. But there are three different types of averages, and they carry different meanings. As an example, consider the following (limited and hypothetical) list of salaries of sales managers: $50,000, $55,000, $60,000, $60,000, $95,000, $100,000, $120,000, $125,000, $150,000, $2,000,000. The most common type of average is the *mean,* for which all the figures in a set are added and the total is divided by the number of items. In this example, the mean is $270,000, and that figure could be "truthfully" reported as the average salary. But even a cursory glance at the list indicates that $270,000 seems too high as an accurate representation of these salaries. Another type of average is the *mode,* the figure that occurs most often in a set. In this example, the mode is $60,000, which seems too low to be representative. A third type of average is the *median,* the middle figure in a list of figures ordered from least to greatest. Here, the median figures are $95,000 and $100,000—numbers that seem to represent accurately the salaries listed. Knowing the differences among the uses of *average,* you can see which type of average—and which number, $270,000, $60,000, or $100,000—best represents the "average" salary of sales managers.

Whatever form of evidence you use—facts, statistics, examples, or testimony—you need to make clear to your audience exactly *why* and *how* it supports your claim. As soon as the relationship between your claim and your evidence is clear to you, make that connection explicit to your readers, helping them understand your thinking.

(2) Effective arguments respond to diverse views.

Issues are controversial—arguable—because good arguments can be made on all sides. Therefore, effective arguments consider and respond to other points of view, fairly and respectfully; they are never one-sided or distorted. As you list the reasons for believing as you do, you should also list any reasons others might have for believing otherwise. Some of these diverse views may come to you as you're establishing common ground with your audience.

In order for your argument to be convincing, your audience must realize that you are knowledgeable about points of view other than your own. The most common strategy for addressing opposing points of view is referred to as **refutation.** In the refutation, you introduce these diverse views and then respectfully demonstrate why you disagree with each of them. As you consider opposing points of view, you are likely to discover some you cannot refute, perhaps because they are based in a belief system markedly different from your own. You are also likely to discover that some of the other views have real merit, to the extent that they complicate and enrich your own point of view. Even if you sympathize with or understand the reasons behind opposing viewpoints, you will remain unconvinced by some of them and will need to demonstrate why.

When you find yourself agreeing with a point raised on another side of the issue, you can benefit from offering a **concession.** By openly admitting that you agree with opponents on one or more specific points, you demonstrate that you are fair-minded (see 7f(1)(a) and 9a) and at the same time increase your credibility. Concessions also increase the likelihood that opponents will be inclined to find merit in your argument.

Whether you agree or disagree with other positions, you need to recognize and assess them. It is hard to persuade people to agree with you if you insist that they are entirely wrong. If you admit that they are partially right, they are more likely to admit that you could be partially right as well. In this sense, then, argument involves working with an audience as much as getting them to work with you.

Arguments that are exchanged electronically—by email or in online discussion groups—can easily become one-sided when writers consider only the text before them and not the person sitting at another computer. The flame wars that often occur in online discussion groups or chat rooms develop when participants simply state their opinions or attack the opinions of others. These flame wars are rarely genuine arguments; rather, they are characterized by the rhetorical fallacies that weaken arguments (see 7i). Electronic communication has become so instantaneous that many writers click on Send before they've considered a crucial element of any rhetorical exchange: attention to audience. Even if you cannot see your readers or do not expect to meet them face-to-face, you will be more convincing if you imagine that they are in the same room with you and that you would like to continue your acquaintance.

When deciding what points to refute or to concede, consider how long your argumentative essay will be and what you know about the audience you are trying to persuade. In a short argument, you probably need to limit yourself to a brief discussion of opposing views. In a longer one, you can afford to explore such views more fully. In either case, however, think about what your audience is likely to believe, and write with those assumptions in mind. Address the most important concerns of your readers.

Although it may seem impolite to disagree openly with authority or to state personal views frankly, most readers in the United States are accustomed to such directness. They will expect you to state your opinion clearly and support it with various kinds of evidence.

Exercise 4

The following paragraph is taken from an argument by Martin Luther King, Jr., in which he defended the struggle for civil rights against public criticism from a group of prominent clergymen. Write a short analysis of this paragraph in which you note (a) an opposing viewpoint to which he is responding, (b) a refutation he offers to this viewpoint,

(c) a concession he makes, and (d) any questions this excerpt raises for you.

[1]You express a great deal of anxiety over our willingness to break laws. [2]This is certainly a legitimate concern. [3]Since we so diligently urge people to obey the Supreme Court's decision of 1954 outlawing segregation in the public schools, at first glance it may seem rather paradoxical for us consciously to break laws. [4]One may well ask: "How can you advocate breaking some laws and obeying others?" [5]The answer lies in the fact that there are two types of laws, just and unjust. [6]I would be the first to advocate obeying just laws. [7]One has not only a legal but a moral responsibility to obey just laws. [8]Conversely, one has a moral responsibility to disobey unjust laws. [9]I would agree with St. Augustine that "an unjust law is no law at all."

—MARTIN LUTHER KING, JR., "Letter from Birmingham Jail"

7f | Effective arguments use several rhetorical appeals.

Effective arguments always incorporate several appeals to the audience simply because logical reasoning—providing good reasons—is rarely enough (see 7c and 7e). Human beings do not believe or act on the basis of facts or logic alone; if we did, we would all agree, and we would act accordingly. We would not engage in unsafe practices (speeding, smoking, unprotected sex, and so on), and we would believe only that which can be proved. In reality, however, we believe and act on the basis of our own concerns, experiences, and needs. When we don't listen to another point of view, it's because we're not interested or not curious; we don't want to change our minds. An effective argument, then, is one that gets a fair hearing, an essential step in the argumentation process. If you want your views to be heard, understood, and maybe even acted on, you need to follow the necessary steps to gain a hearing.

(1) There are three classical rhetorical appeals.

Aristotle, a Greek philosopher who lived over two thousand years ago, was the first to help speakers shape effective arguments through a combination of three persuasive strategies: the rhetorical appeals of ethos, logos, and pathos. **Ethos** (an ethical appeal) establishes the speaker's or writer's credibility and trustworthiness. An ethical appeal demonstrates your goodwill toward your audience, your good sense or knowledge of the subject at hand, and your good character. Establishing common ground with your audience is another feature of ethos. When you take the time to establish common ground, your audience is more likely to continue considering your argument. But ethos alone rarely carries an argument; therefore, you also need to use **logos** (a logical appeal). Logos demonstrates your effective use of reason and judicious use of evidence, whether facts, statistics, comparisons, anecdotes, expert opinions, personal experiences, or observations. You employ logos in the process of supporting claims, drawing reasonable conclusions, and avoiding logical fallacies (see 7i). Aristotle also taught that persuasion comes about only when the audience feels emotionally stirred by the topic under discussion. Therefore, **pathos** (an emotional appeal) involves using language that will stir the feelings of the audience. If you misuse pathos in an attempt to manipulate your audience, it can backfire. But pathos can be used successfully when it establishes empathy and authentic understanding. Thus, the most effective arguments combine these three persuasive appeals responsibly and knowledgeably.

In the next three subsections, additional excerpts from Martin Luther King, Jr.'s "Letter from Birmingham Jail" illustrate how a writer can use all three of the classical rhetorical appeals.

(a) Ethical appeals establish a writer's credibility.

In his opening paragraph, King shows that his professional life is so demanding that he needs more than one secretary. He also indicates that he wishes to engage in "constructive work," thereby establishing common ground with his audience, toward whom he has goodwill. He also establishes that he will argue in good faith.

> My Dear Fellow Clergymen:
>   While confined here in the Birmingham city jail, I came across your recent statement calling my present activities "unwise and untimely." Seldom do I pause to answer criticism of my work and ideas. If I sought to answer all the criticisms that cross my desk, my secretaries would have little time for anything other than such correspondence in the course of the day, and I would have no time for constructive work. But since I feel that you are men of genuine good will and that your criticisms are sincerely set forth, I want to try to answer your statement in what I hope will be patient and reasonable terms.

(b) Logical appeals help an audience clearly understand the writer's ideas.

To help his audience understand why segregation is wrong, King defines key terms:

> Let us consider another example of just and unjust laws. An unjust law is a code that a numerical or power majority group compels a minority group to obey but does not make binding on itself. This is *difference* made legal. By the same token, a just law is a code that a majority compels a minority to follow and that it is willing to follow itself. This is *sameness* made legal.

(c) Emotional appeals can move the audience to a new way of thinking or acting.

As he moves toward his conclusion, King evokes feelings of idealism as well as guilt:

> I have travelled the length and breadth of Alabama, Mississippi and all the other southern states. On sweltering summer days and crisp autumn mornings I have looked at the South's beautiful churches with their lofty spires pointing heavenward. I have beheld the impressive outlines of her massive religious-education buildings. Over and over I have found myself asking: "What kind of people worship here? Who is their God? . . . Where were their voices of support when bruised and weary Negro men and women decided to rise from the dark dungeon of complacency to the bright hills of creative protest?" —MARTIN LUTHER KING, JR., "Letter from Birmingham Jail"

The full text of King's argument includes other examples of ethos, logos, and pathos.

Although ethos is often developed in the introduction, logos in the body, and pathos in the conclusion, these classical rhetorical appeals often overlap and appear throughout an argument. Once you start looking for them, you'll discover that these appeals appear in much of your reading and in your writing.

(2) Rogerian appeals show other people that you understand them.

Rogerian argument derives from the work of Carl R. Rogers, a psychologist who believed that many problems are the result of misunderstanding, which causes a breakdown in communication. In his book *On Becoming a Person* (1961), Rogers argues that people often fail to understand each other because of a natural tendency to judge and evaluate, agree or disagree. He emphasizes the importance of listening carefully to what others say and understanding their ideas. His model calls for suspending judgment until you are able to restate fairly and accurately what others believe. When each person in a conflict demonstrates this ability, the likelihood of misunderstanding is significantly reduced. One of the advantages of this model is that it can be initiated by a single person in a potentially explosive situation. Another advantage is that it can help foster personal growth.

Skills such as paraphrasing and summarizing (see **10d**) are essential to the Rogerian approach. Although this model can be used to achieve a number of goals, it is especially useful for building consensus. A writer making a Rogerian argument says, in effect, "I have heard your concerns, and I am responding to them to the best of my ability. I am also offering some ideas of my own from which we might both benefit. I want to work with you and will not try to push you around." This emphasis on being fair-minded and nonconfrontational gives ethos (see **7f(1)**) an essential place in the Rogerian approach. Because this approach emphasizes the importance of listening and speaking respectfully, it is also useful when writing groups discuss how to revise drafts. (See **3e**.)

To demonstrate that you have given fair consideration to the views of others, you begin a Rogerian argument by paraphrasing these views and demonstrating that you understand the thinking behind them. Then, you introduce your own position and explain why you believe it has merit. Because the Rogerian model is designed to build consensus, you conclude your argument by showing how everyone concerned about the issue could benefit from adopting your proposal.

The summary of benefits with which a Rogerian argument concludes gives you the opportunity to draw your threads together and appeal to your audience without simply restating what you have already said. In the following conclusion to an argument on public education, notice how the author cites benefits for students, teachers, and the public at large if her proposal is adopted.

> Reducing the maximum class size in our secondary schools from thirty students to twenty-five will not solve all the problems in our system, but it will yield important benefits. Students will get more individualized instruction. Better able to give their full attention to the students who remain with them, teachers will gain greater job satisfaction. And in an era when events like the recent killings in Littleton, Colorado, raise legitimate concerns about the safety of public schools, an improved student-teacher ratio reduces the risk of a troubled student being overlooked—a comfort to parents as well as

educators. Finally even those citizens who do not have children will benefit, because in the long run everyone benefits from living in a community where people are well educated. —**LAURA BECHDEL**, "Space to Learn"

For information on how to organize a Rogerian argument, see pages 200–201.

7g | Effective arguments are purposefully arranged.

No single arrangement is right for every written argument. Unless your instructor asks you to demonstrate a particular type of arrangement, the decisions you make about arrangement should be based on several factors: your topic, your audience, and your purpose. (See **1e**.) Writers often develop a good plan by simply listing the major points they want to make (see **2a(1)**), deciding what order to put them in, and then determining where to include refutation or concession (see **7e(2)**). They must also decide whether to place their thesis statement or claim at the beginning or the end of their argument.

In addition, there are a few basic principles that may be useful.

(1) Classical arrangement works well if your audience has not yet taken a position on your issue.

One way to organize your argument is to follow the plan recommended by classical rhetoric, which assumes that an audience is prepared to follow a well-reasoned argument. Use this plan if it seems appropriate for your rhetorical situation (see **1e**).

FEATURES OF THE CLASSICAL ARRANGEMENT

Introduction	Introduce your issue and capture the attention of your audience. Try using a short narrative or a strong example. (See **3b**.) Begin establishing your credibility (or ethos) and common ground.
Background Information	Provide your audience with a history of the situation, and state how things currently stand. Define any key terms. Even if you think the facts speak for themselves, draw the

(Continued on page 200)

(Continued from page 199)

	attention of your audience to those points that are especially important, and explain why they are meaningful.
Proposition	Introduce the position you are taking; in other words, present the argument itself, and provide the basic reasons for your belief. Frame your position as a thesis statement or claim. (See 2b and 7d.)
Proof or Confirmation	Discuss the reasons why you have taken your position. Each reason must be clear, relevant, and representative. Provide facts, expert testimony, and any other evidence that supports your claim.
Refutation	Recognize and disprove the arguments of people who hold a different position and with whom you continue to disagree.
Concession	Concede any point with which you agree or that has merit; in either case, show why this concession does not damage your own case.
Conclusion	Summarize your most important points, and appeal to your audience's feelings, making a personal connection. Describe the consequences of your argument in a final attempt to encourage your audience to consider (if not commit to) a particular course of action.

(2) Rogerian arrangement can help calm an audience strongly opposed to your position.

To write an argument informed by Rogerian appeals, you can be guided by the following plan.

FEATURES OF THE ROGERIAN ARRANGEMENT

Introduction	Establish that you have paid attention to views different from your own. Build trust by stating these views clearly and fairly.
Concessions	Reassure the people you hope to persuade by showing that you agree with them to some extent and do not think that they are completely wrong.
Thesis	Having earned the confidence of your audience, state your claim, or proposition.
Support	Explain why you have taken this position and provide support for it.

Conclusion	Conclude by showing how your audience and other people could benefit from accepting your position. Indicate the extent to which this position will resolve the problem you are addressing. If you are offering a partial solution to a complex problem, concede that further work may be necessary.

When following this plan, you will find that some parts require more development than others. For example, although you may be able to make concessions or to state your position within a single paragraph, you are likely to need several paragraphs to support your position.

(3) Refutation and concession are most effective when placed where readers will welcome them.

Classical arrangement places refutation after the proof or confirmation of the argument, an arrangement that works well for an audience familiar with this organizational model. But if you wait until the end of your confirmation to begin the refutation, to recognize views that differ from yours, it may be too late. Readers unfamiliar with classical arrangement may have decided that you are too one-sided—and may even have stopped reading. When writers are taking a highly controversial stand on a subject that has inspired strong feelings, they sometimes begin by establishing common ground and then acknowledge opposing viewpoints and respond to them. A variation on classical arrangement allows writers to begin by addressing opposing views on the grounds that readers will be unwilling to hear a new proposition unless they are first shown what is weak or incomplete about their current thinking.

In a Rogerian argument, a writer begins by reporting opposing views fairly and identifying what is valuable about them. The strategy here is not to refute the views in question but to concede that they have merit—thus putting the audience at ease before introducing a thesis or claim that might be rejected if stated prematurely.

However, sometimes readers may react negatively to a writer who responds to opposing views before offering any reasons to support his or her own view. These readers want to know from the start where an argument is headed. For this reason, writers often choose to state their position at the beginning of the argument and offer at least one strong reason to support it before turning to opposing views. They sometimes keep at least one other reason in reserve (often one responsibly laden with emotion, or pathos), so that they can present it after responding to opposing views, thereby ending with an emphasis on their confirmation.

Unless you are required to follow a specific arrangement, or organizational plan, you should respond to opposing views wherever your audience is most likely either to expect this discussion or to be willing to hear it. You must assess your readers carefully (see **1e(2)**), determining what opinions they are likely to have about your topic and how open they are to new ideas. If your audience is receptive, you can place refutation and concession after your confirmation. If your audience adheres to a different position, you should respond to their views toward the beginning of your argument.

(4) Separate reasons are best discussed in separate paragraphs.

As you sort out the reasons supporting your argument, consider how much development each of the reasons merits within your organizational plan. Whether you follow a classical or Rogerian arrangement, you are likely to need at least one full paragraph to develop any one reason for your claim (see **7d**). You might need two paragraphs to explain an important or substantial reason. If you try to develop two separate reasons in the same paragraph, it may lack unity and coherence. (See **3c**.) However, if the purpose of a paragraph is to summarize why you hold your position, you might list several reasons in that paragraph. In fact, writers sometimes include several reasons in a single paragraph near the conclusion if these reasons consist of additional advantages that do not call for detailed discussion.

When readers look at any paragraph, they should be able to see how it advances the argument that is being made. Whether you're discussing each of your reasons in separate paragraphs or using a summary paragraph, you'll want your readers to be able to follow your argument. No matter how many paragraphs you write, or how long any of them may be, make sure that every paragraph is unified and coherent (see **3c**).

(5) You can begin a paragraph with a view different from yours.

If you open a paragraph with an opposing view, you can use the rest of the paragraph for your response to that view. Readers will have to make only one shift between differing views. However, if you begin a paragraph with your view, then introduce an opposing view, and then move back to the development of your view, readers must shift direction twice and may miss the point you want them to get. If you use most of a paragraph to develop an opposing point of view, waiting until the very end of the paragraph to introduce your own, you may dilute the effect of your own view.

(6) Your conclusion can reinforce your purpose.

By the time you have reached your conclusion, you have clarified the connection between your purpose and your audience; you have also established common ground, an ethos, and a series of logical arguments. The most effective conclusions move beyond a mere summary of what has already been stated. When considering how to conclude an argument, then, you may want to imagine readers who are interested in what you've just said but remain unsure about what you expect from them. "So what?" they might ask. "How does all this affect me, and what am I supposed to do about it?" Whether your conclusion emphasizes a specific course of action you want your audience to take, an invitation to further understanding, or a purposeful restatement of your claim (see 3b(2)), it is the best place for you to introduce or reinforce an emotional, person-to-person, connection with your audience (see 7g). The conclusion is your last opportunity to explain to your audience the potentially useful, wonderful, harmful, or dangerous consequences of a particular belief or action. In other words, try to conclude by answering the question "So what?" The student paper by Laura Klocke at the end of this chapter (see pages 216–222) ends with a conclusion that not only reinforces her purpose but links her purpose with the stated mission of her university.

Exercise 5

Read the editorial pages of your community or college newspaper in several consecutive issues. Look for editorials that analyze or question an established belief, express or defend an opinion, invite consideration, or try to convince. Choose an editorial that strikes you as well argued, well developed, and well organized—even if it doesn't change your belief or action (it may only have changed your level of understanding). Bring several copies of the editorial to class, and be prepared to discuss its purpose, audience, use of appeals, and conclusion.

| 7h | Understanding logic can improve your ability to argue effectively and ethically. |

Because writers cannot argue on the basis of ethos alone, they need to understand the ways in which **logic**—the reasoning behind an argument—enhances or detracts from the argument. Logic is a means through which you can develop your ideas, realize new ones, and determine whether your thinking is clear enough to persuade readers to agree with you. By arguing logically, you increase the likelihood that your arguments will be taken seriously.

Studied as a separate discipline, logic entails highly specific exercises that are worked out with mathematical precision. When used in writing, however, logic is studied and used differently. When you evaluate the logic of an argument, you take into consideration the clarity of the thinking, the ethics of the reasoning, and the possible response to diverse views. Traditionally, logical arguments are classified as either inductive or deductive.

(1) Inductive reasoning is the process of using a number of specific facts or observations to make a generalization.

You use inductive reasoning on a daily basis. If you get a stomachache within fifteen minutes of eating ice cream, you might conclude that there's a connection. Perhaps you're lactose-intolerant. This use of evidence to form a generalization is called an **inductive leap,** and the leap should be in proportion to the amount of evidence gathered. It would be reasonable for you to stop eating ice cream if it consistently made you ill—especially if you sampled different brands and flavors of ice cream or if you didn't get a stomachache after eating tofu "ice cream." But if you conclude that ice cream is bad for everyone, then your claim is too large for the amount of evidence you have gathered.

Inductive reasoning involves moving (or leaping) from discovering evidence to interpreting it, and it can help you arrive at probable, believable conclusions (but not absolute, enduring truth). Making a small leap from evidence (a stomachache) to a probable conclusion (lactose-intolerance) is more effective and ethical than using the same evidence to make a sweeping claim that could easily be challenged (ice cream is bad for everyone) (see 7d(1)). Generally, the greater the weight of the evidence, the more reliable the conclusion.

When scientists use inductive reasoning, they refer to the process as the **scientific method.** For instance, early medical studies linked diets high in fat with coronary artery disease. The scientific community reserved judgment, since the early studies were based on only a small sample of men. However, later studies involving larger numbers of men and women confirmed the early reports. Although everyone with coronary artery disease cannot be studied, the sample became large enough and representative enough to allow researchers to draw the conclusion with more confidence. Nevertheless, a critical thinker should still examine the available evidence carefully and ask a number of questions about it: Is the conclusion equally applicable to premenopausal and post-menopausal women? Is the conclusion equally applicable to people of all races and all ages? To what extent have the researchers controlled all variables? Does the evidence support the conclusion that has been reached, or should the conclusion be modified? Because scientists understand the nature of inductive reasoning and have been trained to think critically, they are often motivated to ask followup questions and conduct further research.

When used in argument, inductive reasoning often employs facts (see 7c) and examples (see 2d(2)). When writers cannot cite all the information that supports their conclusions, they choose the evidence that is most reliable and closely related to the point they are making.

(2) Deductive reasoning is the process of applying a generalization (or generalized belief) to a series of specific cases.

At the heart of a deductive argument is a **major premise** (a generalized belief that is assumed to be true), which the writer applies to a specific case (the **minor premise**), thereby yielding a conclusion or claim. For example, if you know that all doctors must complete a residency and that Anna is in medical school, then you could conclude that Anna must complete a residency. This argument can be expressed in a three-part structure called a **syllogism.**

Major premise	All doctors must complete a residency. [generalized belief]
Minor premise	Anna is studying to become a doctor. [specific case]
Conclusion	Anna must complete a residency. [conclusion or claim]

Sometimes premises are not stated, for the simple reason that the writer assumes a shared belief with the audience.

Anna has graduated from medical school, so she must complete a residency.

In this sentence, the unstated premise is that all doctors must complete a residency. A syllogism with an unstated premise—or even an unstated conclusion—is called an **enthymeme.** Frequently found in written arguments, enthymemes can be very effective because they presume shared beliefs or knowledge. For example, the argument "We need to build a new dormitory because those we have are seriously overcrowded" contains the unstated premise that dormitories should house only the number of people for which they were designed.

Critical thinkers should examine enthymemes with care since the omitted statement may be inaccurate. "Racquel is from Texas, so she must speak Spanish" contains the unstated premise "Everyone from Texas speaks Spanish." This premise is unacceptable because there is no reason to assume that everyone from Texas knows how to speak Spanish—even though many people who live in Texas do speak Spanish. When you use deductive reasoning in your arguments, be sure to work from a reliable premise with which you and your audience can agree.

The conclusion of a deductive argument must be both true and valid. A **true conclusion** is based on well-backed premises generally accepted by your audience. A **valid conclusion** is based on logical thinking. The conclusion in the following syllogism is valid because it follows logically from the major and minor premises, but it is not true because the major premise is not generally accepted.

Major premise	All redheads are hotheaded.
Minor premise	Jamie is a redhead.
Conclusion	Jamie is hotheaded.

Because syllogisms can be logical without their conclusions being true and because they are too rigid and absolute to serve in arguments without absolute answers, they work more effectively as exercises in critical thinking than as outlines for written arguments. Nevertheless, familiarity with syllogistic reasoning can help you evaluate the arguments you read and write.

Exercise 6

Analyze the following enthymemes, supplying the missing premise for each of them. Then, determine if the conclusion is valid, true, both, or neither.

1. He must be healthy. He always has a good tan.
2. She is a good writer. She is easy to understand.
3. We need to restrict the use of water. We are suffering from a severe drought.
4. Omtronic Company must be well managed. Its earnings have grown steadily during the past few years.
5. Dr. Kordoff must be a good teacher. Her classes always fill up quickly.

Exercise 7

Study the following excerpt from the Declaration of Independence. Identify the assumptions on which this argument is based, and be prepared to explain how one assumption leads to another.

[1]We hold these truths to be self-evident, that all men are created equal, that they are endowed by their Creator with certain unalienable rights, that among these are life, liberty and the pursuit of happiness. [2]That to secure these rights, governments are instituted among men, deriving their just powers from the consent of the governed. [3]That whenever any form of government becomes destructive of these ends, it is the right of the people to alter or to abolish it, and to institute new government, laying its foundation on such principles and organizing its powers in such form, as to them shall seem most likely to effect their safety and happiness. —THOMAS JEFFERSON

(3) The Toulmin model of reasoning provides an alternative to inductive and deductive reasoning.

To create a working system of logic suitable for the needs of all writers, philosopher Stephen Toulmin moved away from the formal conventions of the syllogism. Instead, he defined *argument* as a logical progression, from the **data** (accepted evidence or reasons that support a claim), to the **claim** (a debatable or controversial statement), based on the **warrant** (the underlying assumption, like the major premise). If the warrant is controversial, it requires **backing** (support). Writers who assume that they are drawing their evidence from reliable authorities should be able to cite the credentials of those authorities. And writers who base an argument on the law or another written code that has been widely agreed upon (a university's mission statement, for instance) should be able to cite the exact statute, precedent, or regulation in question or even include the law or code in the essay itself.

Like deductive reasoning, Toulmin's method establishes a reasonable relationship between the data and the claim. The following argument may help explain the progression:

> Fair trade coffee should be served at the University of St. Thomas because doing so would foster social justice.

Data (or support)	Purchasing fair trade coffee promotes social justice.
Claim	The University of St. Thomas should purchase and serve only fair trade coffee.
Warrant	The University of St. Thomas seeks to promote social justice.

The warrant establishes a relationship with the data, providing a reasonable link with the claim that follows (see figure 7.1).

Of course, few arguments are as simple as this example. For instance, the University of St. Thomas may wish to promote social justice but cannot follow through on every opportunity to do so. In such cases, writers must make allowances for exceptions. Qualifiers such as *usually, probably, should,* and *possibly* show the degree of certainty of the conclusion, and rebuttal terms such as *unless* indicate exceptions.

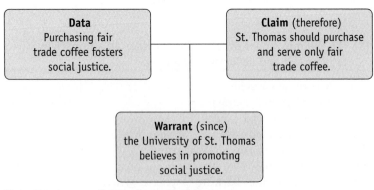

Figure 7.1. A warrant linking data and a claim.

Since the University of St. Thomas seeks to promote social justice, it **should** purchase and serve only fair trade coffee, **unless** it cannot pursue this course of action at this time.

When using the Toulmin model to shape your arguments, you may be able to identify the claim, the data, and the qualifiers more easily than the warrant. Like the unstated premise in an enthymeme (see 7h(2)), the warrant is often assumed and backed up by something left unsaid. In the example above, the backing is the university's mission statement, which calls for commitment to social justice. To determine your warrant, trace your thinking back to the assumptions with which you began. As you trace back, remember that warrants can take different forms. A warrant may be

- a requirement of a law or regulation (such as university regulations for student housing),
- an assumption that the data came from a reliable source (see chapters 9 and 10),
- an assumption that what is true of a sample is true of a larger group (see 7h(1)), or
- a moral, political, or economic value that is widely accepted in the writer's culture.

E x e r c i s e   8

A. Analyze the argument in the following excerpt by asking yourself the following questions:

1. What is the claim or conclusion? Is it implied or stated?
2. What data support the claim?
3. Does the author make more than one claim?
4. What is the warrant that underlies the argument?

[1]The movement to make English the official language of the United States is in no way a put-down of other languages or cultures. [2]But it is the language used predominantly by the print and electronic media; it is the tongue in which government at every level is conducted. [3]To be an effective citizen one ought to vote, and to do so intelligently one must be well informed. [4]Candidates, of course, present the issues and outline their platforms in English.   —**YOLANDA DE MOLA**, "The Language of Power"

B. Whatever your own position on language use may be, demonstrate that you understand the reasoning within the preceding excerpt by writing a two- to three-page essay in which you walk your reader through the steps in De Mola's argument.

Exercise 9

Review the excerpt from the Declaration of Independence in exercise 7. What kind of backing could be offered to support the warrants you find there?

7i | Rhetorical fallacies can weaken an argument.

Logical reasoning not only enhances the overall effectiveness of an argument, it also enhances the ethos of the speaker or writer. Almost as important as constructing an argument effectively is avoiding errors in argument, or **rhetorical fallacies.** Rhetorical fallacies signal to your audience that your thinking is not entirely trustworthy, that your argument is not well reasoned. Such fallacies may be lapses in logic that result from relying on faulty premises, appeals to the emotions of the reader in inappropriate situations, or misplaced emphases on the authority (or lack thereof) of the quoted sources.

Rhetoricians find it useful to distinguish among the different kinds of fallacies. As you read the arguments of others (see chapter 9) and revise the arguments you draft (chapter 3), try to keep the following common rhetorical fallacies in mind.

(1) *Non sequitur,* Latin for "it does not follow," is the basis for many fallacies.

Faulty
Eddie is smart; therefore, he'll do well in college. [This assertion is based on the faulty premise that *all* smart people do well in college. (See 7h(2).)]

(2) *Ad hominem* refers to a personal attack on an opponent that draws attention away from the issues under consideration.

Faulty

She is unfit to be a minister because she is divorced. [The fact that a woman is divorced may reveal the condition of a previous marriage, but a divorce has little if anything to do with her spiritual beliefs and principles that could benefit a congregation.]

(3) *Appeal to tradition* is an argument that says something should be done a certain way simply because it has been done that way in the past.

Faulty

We should not forbid fraternity hazings because they continue to be a memorable part of the pledge process. [Times change; what was considered good practice in the past is not necessarily considered acceptable now.]

(4) *Bandwagon* is an argument saying, in effect, "Everyone's doing or saying or thinking this, so you should too."

Faulty

Everyone drives over the speed limit, so why shouldn't we raise the limit? [The majority is not always right.]

(5) *Begging the question* is an argument that assumes what in fact needs to be proved.

Faulty

We need to fire corrupt officials in order to reduce the city's crime rate. [If there are corrupt officials in city government, this point needs to be established.]

(6) *Equivocation* is an assertion that falsely relies on the use of a term in two different senses.

Faulty

We know this is a natural law because it feels natural. [In the first use, *natural* means "derived from nature or reason"; when used again, it means "easy or simple because of being in accord with one's own nature."]

(7) *False analogy* **is the assumption that because two things are alike in some ways, they must be alike in others.**

Faulty

The United States lost credibility with other nations during the war in Viet Nam, so we should not get involved in the Middle East, or we will lose credibility again. [The differences between the war in Southeast Asia in the 1960s and 1970s and the current conflict in the Middle East may well be greater than their similarities.]

(8) *False authority* **is the assumption that an expert in one field can be credible in another.**

Faulty

We must stop sending military troops into Afghanistan, as Bruce Springsteen has argued. [Springsteen's expertise in music does not automatically qualify him as an expert in foreign policy.]

(9) *False cause* **is the assumption that because one event follows another, the first is the cause of the second—sometimes called** *post hoc, ergo propter hoc* **("after this, so because of this").**

Faulty

When Coach Joe Paterno turned 75, Penn State's football team had a losing season. [The assumption is that Paterno's age is solely responsible for the losing season, with no consideration given to the abilities and experience of the football players themselves.]

(10) *False dilemma* **(sometimes called the** *either/or fallacy***) is a statement that only two alternatives exist, when in fact there are more than two.**

Faulty

We must either build more nuclear power plants or be completely dependent on foreign oil. [Other possibilities exist.]

(11) *Guilt by association* **is an unfair attempt to make someone responsible for the beliefs or actions of others.**

Faulty

Jon Williams's family is a bunch of gamblers. [Several people can graduate from the same school, practice the same profession or religion, belong to the same family, or live in the same neighborhood without engaging in the same behavior.]

(12) *Hasty generalization* is a conclusion based on too little evidence or on exceptional or biased evidence.

Faulty
Ellen is a poor student because she failed her first history test. [Her performance may improve in the weeks ahead or be good in all her other subjects.]

(13) *Oversimplification* is a statement or argument that leaves out relevant considerations in order to imply that there is a single cause or solution for a complex problem.

Faulty
We can eliminate unwanted pregnancies by teaching birth control and abstinence. [Teaching people about birth control and abstinence does not guarantee the elimination of unwanted pregnancies.]

(14) *Red herring* (sometimes called *ignoring the question*) means dodging the real issue by drawing attention to an irrelevant one.

Faulty
Why worry about violence in schools when we ought to be worrying about international terrorism? [International terrorism has little if any direct relationship with school violence.]

(15) *Slippery slope* is the assumption that if one thing is allowed, it will be the first step in a downward spiral.

Faulty
Handgun control will lead to a police state. [Handgun control has not led to a police state in England.]

Beyond the Rule

RHETORICAL FALLACIES

What looks like a rhetorical fallacy may be acceptable under some circumstances. For examples of how and when to use rhetorical fallacies in an argument, visit www.harbrace.com.

Be alert for rhetorical fallacies in your own writing, perhaps by asking someone who is working on the same assignment to look for them in your draft. When you find such a fallacy, be sure to moderate your claim, clarify your thinking, or, if necessary, eliminate the fallacious point. Even if your argument as a whole is convincing, rhetorical fallacies can damage your credibility (see **7f** and **9a**).

Exercise 10

For each of the following statements, write one or two sentences in which you identify and explain the faulty reasoning. Then, identify circumstances under which you might find these statements convincing. Finally, rewrite each statement so that it avoids rhetorical fallacies, regardless of the circumstances (if possible).

1. You should go to Puerto Rico with us; the rest of us are going.
2. We must either build more dormitories or double up students in existing dormitories.
3. This car must be reliable; it's the kind my dentist drives.
4. If we censor neo-Nazi demonstrations, we will ultimately lose freedom of speech.
5. I know that store is badly managed. One of the salespeople there was rude to me.
6. If women dressed more conservatively, they would earn as much money as men.
7. You can't trust a guy like that; he comes from a poor family and bad neighborhood.
8. We should cut welfare because people on welfare are getting too many benefits.
9. The union is arguing for a cost-of-living raise, but its leaders are all a bunch of crooks.
10. Children would do a lot better at school if they didn't spend so much time watching television.

Read the following paragraph, a letter to *Esquire* magazine in response to Tom Carson's monthly movie-review column. Identify any rhetorical fallacies you find in it. Then, adopting the point of view of someone enthusiastic about the quality of Woody Allen's many films, write two or three paragraphs responding to the argument offered here.

[1]Once again, [Tom] Carson got it exactly right, this time on Woody Allen. [2]Taken in sum, Allen's work is like a carpet showroom: plenty of plush Berber right alongside plenty of indoor-outdoor crap. [3]You have to love that Woody wants it both ways—to make lots of movies and to make great movies. [4]But as Carson points out, the flaw is that he's so often making the same movie over and over again. [5]Personally, I gave up long ago. [6]I'm not going to line up anymore while Woody spins his tiny creative Rolodex, speed-dialing the same numbers in the same area code year after year. [7]Carson can wake me when the next *Zelig* arrives.

—TOM CHIARELLA

7j | You can improve your ability to write arguments by studying the written arguments of others.

The following paper was Laura Klocke's response to an assignment in argumentative writing. She was asked to write an essay that pointed to a specific problem at her living quarters, on her campus, in her town, or in the world at large, and then proposed a process, policy claim, or procedure for solving that problem.

As you read Laura's essay, consider whether—and how—she argued her case effectively. Note her use of classical rhetorical appeals (ethos, logos, and pathos) and arrangement and her inductive reasoning. Also, identify the kinds of evidence she uses (facts, examples, testimony, or authority).

Klocke 1

Just Coffee: A Proposal in the Classical Arrangement

Laura Klocke

Introduction

From the local café and the multinational chains to the gas station and the grocery story, you can buy lattes, cappucinos, fresh drip, and espresso. Everywhere and anywhere, it seems, coffee is "the best part of waking up."

Approximately 20 to 25 million people grow coffee for the world's drinkers and rely solely on coffee production for their income and survival. Coffee is a world beverage of choice, and this is perhaps most clearly evident in the United States, which consumes one-third of the world's coffee. Roughly $18 billion dollars is spent on coffee itself; almost just as much is invested in coffee equipment in the United States. It's not surprising, then, that coffee is the second-largest commodity traded on the market in the entire world, following oil (Dicum and Luttinger 3). With these large dollar figures and millions of cups of coffee in mind, you might wonder where all the money goes. Or, better yet, to whom?

The answer has mostly to do with coffee plantations known as *fincas,* a modern-day version of pre-Civil War Southern plantations. The coffee grown and processed is taken from the *fincas* and enters into what is called the "coffee chain." This chain continues from the *finca* and its workers to a local speculator, or "coyote." The coyote draws up a contract with an exporter, and the chain proceeds to the roaster, distributor, retail outlet, and, finally, your cup. The goal of this chain, like the goal of most business transactions, is to maximize the final profit. Unfortunately for those at the beginning--the peasant farmers of the *finca*--their livelihood

Background
Information

is not a consideration of their employer; the maximization of profit is the employer's sole concern. Grocery store gourmet coffee costs as much as $12.00 per pound, and yet some *finca* workers are paid only twenty to forty cents per pound. When considering that the average *finca* coffee farmer makes $3.00 a day, and the average latte is priced at $3.50 or more, it is clear that something doesn't add up in this coffee chain system (Rice and McLean 22). And, because the workers do not own the land, though they live and work on it in each stage of the coffee-growing production, they have relatively little say in their pay. Something akin to the sharecroppers of the past, the situation for those living on *fincas* is a present-day injustice. The emphasis for the world's production of coffee is on profit, and a speedy profit at that, which I will explain below.

When fair trade coffee organizations are part of the coffee-growing and coffee-selling equation, the emphasis is not only on speed and profit. Fair trade coffee organizations establish personal, gradually developing, and long-term buying relationships with coffee growers and encourage the farmers to organize into cooperatives, where they are free to live, work, and grow coffee in a community supported by a guaranteed fair and livable wage. Fair trade coffee eliminates the middle people in the chain and thereby allocates the money that had gone to the coyotes to the growers themselves. Instead of the twenty to forty cents per pound they earned on the *fincas,* the workers can earn a minimum of $1.20 per pound. This pay raise is accomplished by eliminating the middle people and ensuring that the workers are paid fairly for their labor--not by raising the price of coffee noticeably. With the guarantee of a livable wage, many farmers would be able to put money into their community, building schools, recreation centers, churches, and businesses, improving the lives of everyone in the region.

Proposition

Though I have never traveled to a *finca,* I am aware that my purchases are just one of the many ways that I can demonstrate my recognition of the inherent dignity of all people. Therefore, I do not want to support knowingly any flawed financial system with my purchases. My university is also working to make positive steps in its purchasing practices; however, with regard to fair trade food products, particularly coffee, the University of St. Thomas is not yet up to speed. In order to be fully engaged in ethical buying practices, St. Thomas must support a fully fair trade coffee supplier. Though the whole world may never be converted to the philosophy of fair trade, the sizable amount of money the university spends on coffee can still make a difference and set an example that other universities may want to follow.

Since the university can choose between selling fair trade or unfairly traded coffee at every food service location on campus, I advocate that our university sell only that coffee that has been provided from fair trade organizations. Such a university-wide decision will reflect the ethics and politics of the university's buying power as well as align with the commitment of our University Mission Statement.

Proof

The switch from coffee drinker to conscientious coffee drinker is not difficult. The mission of the University of St. Thomas includes a commitment to "develop morally responsible individuals who combine . . . cultural awareness and intellectual curiosity." In addition, the tradition of the school seeks to foster "a value-oriented education needed for complete human development and for responsible citizenship in contemporary

Klocke 4

society"; an "international perspective"; and an "appreciation for cultural diversity." Finally, "the university embraces its role and our responsibilities in the world community," a statement that clearly connects the University of St. Thomas and the fair trade issue. The commitment to ethical activities in the university supports not only a continuation of international learning and experience, but also reflects an understanding of the inherent dignity of work and the workers that grow and process the coffee the university serves. Not only are the workers valuable as members of the human race, but their work, also, has value to them, and to the world.

Many other groups already support the fair trade coffee movement, including the Audubon Society and the MacArthur Foundation, so the University of St. Thomas would join a wide movement of people and organizations who recognize that drinking fair trade coffee is in good taste--financially, politically, and ethically (Rice and McLean 38).

Unfortunately, this proposal for a change to a completely fair trade coffee offering at the University of St. Thomas has been met with several concerns from the administration. St. Thomas does not desire to terminate its contract with Dunn Brothers Coffee, a local Twin Cities company that currently provides several varieties of certified fair trade coffee, including Guatemalan and Mexican. Though Dunn Brothers offers these choices, they are not a solely fair trade coffee company. Through a gradual approach of switching to an entirely fair trade coffee company, Dunn Brothers would be given a chance to improve their offerings as well as help St. Thomas to address some of its major concerns, in particular, those from a cost standpoint. As a student of this university, and given

Refutation

my support of this mission statement, I prefer to approach this issue
from an ethical stand. However, it is easy to show that the serving of fair
trade coffee makes sense from a financial perspective as well.

First, however, to answer the concerns of the university is necessary.
University administrators argue that, by supporting a small local company
like Dunn Brothers, they are still using university money in an acceptable
way. I argue that the university could use its money in an even better way.
The fact that Dunn Brothers is not a solely fair trade company puts them at
odds with the university mission. Besides, there are several local fair trade
companies--Cloud Forest Initiatives and Peace Coffee, to name just two--
that are small enough for the university to support at the same time that it
does more with its buying power.

Next, the cost difference between fair trade and unfair trade coffee is
an understandable concern for St. Thomas. While the movement continues
to grow, fair trade coffee has the potential to cost slightly more (though
hardly noticeably more) per pound than unfairly traded coffee. However,
with an institution-sized order, many coffee cooperatives could be in a
position to provide a contract that could work in the best way, financially,
for both the growers and, in this case, the university. A worst-case scenario
would be an increase of almost five cents more per cup. In answering this
argument, however, the University of St. Thomas should recognize that the
price difference for fair trade coffee is negligible when compared to the cost
of unfairly traded coffee for communities, farmers, and families.

The last concern the administration of St. Thomas has expressed is
the fear of losing the recognizable Dunn Brothers' name. The
administration understandably wants to continue to sell coffee that is

Klocke 6

successfully marketed and doesn't yet know if students will support the move to fair trade coffee if there's no name recognition. To that objection, I would respond that relatively few students have taken an active interest in the coffee served at the University of St. Thomas (fair trade or otherwise). It is unlikely that once the switch to fair trade coffee is realized, my fellow students will notice--let alone protest against it. It seems that, at the heart, there is a discrepancy between the bottom lines in this issue. The University of St. Thomas would like to make the bottom line about cost, and yet the mission statement and foundation of the university clearly states otherwise. Also in response to this argument, it is worth mentioning that students are rarely consulted about the buying choices of the university. We live in a closed market system on campus, meaning, we have no choice about many of our food products (for example, the university is a "Pepsi" campus, and only Pepsi products are sold in beverage vending machines).

We at the University of St. Thomas have the chance not only to have our concerns answered but to affirm our mission statement and be a leader in the intra-campus community. We would convey a strong message with our purchase and sales of fair trade coffee, demonstrating that we are a community of concerned citizens. Our mission guides us in decisions that affect our local community as well as our global community. St. Thomas should be a leader in social justice as well as in academics.

Conclusion

We must support fair trade coffee growers and their communities, and, thereby, as a university, adhere to the mission that we profess. By helping to guarantee coffee growers a livable wage, the commitment to fair trade coffee at the University of St. Thomas is clearly the just choice.

Klocke 7

Works Cited

Dicum, Gregory, and Nina Luttinger. <u>The Coffee Book: Anatomy of an Industry from Crop to the Last Drop</u>. New York: New Press, 1999.

Rice, Paul D., and Jennifer McLean. "Sustainable Coffee at the Crossroads." <u>CCC Coffee Program</u>. 15 Oct. 1999. Consumer's Choice Council. 23 Oct. 2001. <http://www.consumerscouncil.org/coffee/coffeebook/coffee.pdf>.

University of St. Thomas. "Mission Statement." <http://www.stthomas.edu>.

Exercise 12

Reread Laura Klocke's essay to establish its grounding. What qualities or experiences has Klocke had that have shaped the values she reveals as she argues for fair trade coffee? In other words, what evidence in her essay might provide an explanation for her side of the argument? What are her unspoken but underlying values? What other sides of the argument might you be able to provide? What values do you bring to the argument?

Finding Sources Online, in Print, and in the Field

Good research skills are essential when you are required to incorporate outside sources into text that is clearly your own. (See chapters 10–11.) These skills may help with other writing assignments as well, since you will often need to obtain information even when you are not specifically required to do research. Moreover, good research skills are essential in most disciplines and professions (see chapters 14–15), and there will be many occasions when you simply want to find something out for yourself.

An inquiring mind is the best equipment you can bring to research. But to inquire efficiently, you need to develop specific skills in accessing information. Without these skills, you may find yourself without information you need or overwhelmed by more information than you can handle. Experienced researchers understand that it is easy to waste time looking for information in the wrong places or turning prematurely to sources they are not yet prepared to understand. Although different projects require different strategies—depending on the nature of the topic, your familiarity with it, and the time you have for research—you will benefit from developing effective research skills.

This chapter will help you

- assess your information needs and develop a research routine (8a),
- frame a research question (8b),
- use sources on the Web (8c),
- use library resources such as books and periodicals (8d), and
- conduct field research (8e).

While accessing information and developing your skills as a researcher, you also need to evaluate the material you discover. Strategies for evaluating sources are discussed in chapter 9.

8a | Writers need information.

Sometimes, you may have enough information from your own knowledge and experience to develop a good piece of writing. Frequently, however, you will need to search the Web or a library for material that can support and enrich your ideas.

Because downloading material from the Web can be easy and fast (see 8c), some people now go to it exclusively—overlooking other avenues that might give them better results. You can assume that there is information on the Web about most subjects, and knowing that all this information is at your fingertips can be reassuring. One of the advantages to searching the Web is that you can do so whenever you have access to a computer and can get online. You do not have to worry about whether the library is open or where you are going to park your car. But bear in mind that you will often benefit from stepping away from your computer and working elsewhere.

If you visit a college or university library, you will find thousands of documents that do not appear online. You will also find librarians who are knowledgeable in specific subject areas. They can help you focus your topic and can guide you to appropriate resources for your research. Meeting with a reference librarian can be useful if you are unsure about how to begin or feel overwhelmed by the number of resources available to you (see 8d).

As you proceed with research, be aware of whether sources are primary or secondary. **Primary sources** for topics in literature and the humanities are generally documents—such as old letters and records—and literary works. In the social sciences, primary sources can be field observations, case histories, and survey data. In the natural sciences, primary sources are generally empirical—measurements, experiments, and the like. **Secondary sources** are commentaries on primary sources. For example, a review of a new novel is a secondary source and so is a discussion of adolescence based on survey data. Experienced researchers usually consult both primary and secondary sources, read them critically, and draw on them carefully. (See 1a–d and chapter 9.)

In addition to examining information that has already been published (either on the Web or in print), you might benefit from discussing your research topic with other people. An authority on your topic could be teaching at your college, working in the next office, or accessible via email. Thoughtful conversation about your topic could even be generated in an online discussion group or forum (see 5c). And, of course, the instructor or supervisor who assigned your paper or project can help clarify what you need to do to complete it successfully.

(1) Different types of resources offer different advantages.

Much of the research people do in their daily lives involves looking in various places to find answers to questions. If you plan to buy a new car, for example, you may read reviews published in magazines or on the Web, talk to people familiar with the cars that interest you, and take a test drive or two. A similar strategy may be appropriate for research assignments in school or at work: read, interview, and observe.

The following box can help you see at a glance the advantages and disadvantages of different types of resources. (For additional information on developing a search strategy, see 8c–d.)

RESOURCE ASSESSMENT

Web Sites (see pages 228–231)

Advantages

The Web contains an amazing amount of recent material. Many sites have links to other relevant sites. The full text of a document can be downloaded and printed out on a personal computer.

Disadvantages

Researchers can be overwhelmed by the number of available sites and may waste time investigating sites that prove unhelpful. Many sites lack credibility. Sites can change or be removed without warning.

Library Catalog (see pages 232–235)

Advantages

A library catalog indexes books available on your campus. It may also link to catalogs at other schools. It identifies material that has been professionally edited, reviewed, and selected for purchase. Books can provide in-depth discussion.

(Continued on page 226)

(Continued from page 225)

Disadvantages

A library catalog does not include all books that exist. Books listed in the catalog may be checked out or lost. You may have to request an interlibrary loan, which is time-consuming.

Electronic Indexes to Periodicals (see pages 236–244)

Advantages

Electronic indexes enable you to find material focused specifically on your topic. They cover a high percentage of credible sources. The most recent citations are identified first, directing you to current work on your topic.

Disadvantages

Electronic indexes provide article citations, but an electronic version of the full text of an article is not always available. Articles must often be located in library holdings or through interlibrary loan. Scholarly articles can be difficult to read if you lack experience in a particular field of research.

Interviews and Dialogues (see pages 244–247)

Advantages

Interviews or dialogues can be conducted in person, by phone, or by email. An interview allows you to focus on a point you need to clarify. A dialogue can generate new ideas when you feel stuck.

Disadvantages

Ideas can be lost if not recorded. Misreporting is common. Sources may lack credibility.

(2) Establishing a research schedule helps you use time efficiently.

Planning ahead and scheduling your time are critical when writing research papers. Such papers are usually assigned several weeks before they are due, and the temptation to procrastinate or to fulfill other assignments with earlier due dates may be strong. Make sure to allow enough time for choosing a subject (see **2a**), reading extensively, taking notes (**10b**), preparing a working bibliography (**10c**), developing a thesis (**2b**), outlining (**2c(2)**), drafting (**2d**), revising (**3a–d**), and editing (**3f**). You must allow some time for each of these stages, no matter how much (or how little) time you have for the entire project. (For information about other stages in the process of writing a research paper, see chapters **9–11**.)

A **research log** can help you stay on schedule and keep you from having to repeat tasks. Such a log is a notebook or a computer file that includes everything related to your project: ideas for subjects, ways to refine topics, what you already know. Not only does a research log provide a central location for recording how your work is progressing, it can also help you keep track of the tasks you have yet to do or those you need to repeat. Knowing that you have useful records in your log can also help you work well under pressure and avoid writer's block (see chapter 4).

Beyond the Rule

THE RESEARCH LOG

A log is a record book devoted to information about performance history and other events—for example, a book in which sailors record navigational and weather information while on a voyage. For additional information on research logs and a sample log, visit www.harbrace.com.

8b | Researchers choose a topic and frame it as a question that needs to be answered.

You find a topic for a research paper in much the same way as you find a topic for any piece of writing: You are assigned a topic, or you choose a question you would like to answer. (See 2a and 7b.)

The exploration methods discussed in 2a(1)—freewriting, listing, clustering, and questioning—can help you find an interesting topic. Focusing on a specific topic is important since one of your main objectives is to show your ability to write in some depth within the time allowed and (usually) the length specified. But be flexible. Even if you begin research with a focused topic already in mind, be prepared to revise it if preliminary research leads you to a related issue that is more interesting or better documented.

As you do preliminary research, bear in mind that good research papers usually incorporate different kinds of materials. Reconsider any topic that would force you to rely exclusively on one type of source. Research drawn exclusively from books might overlook current information available online. Similarly, relying solely on electronic sources is unwise since there are excellent sources in print that do not appear online.

As you choose a topic, think in terms of a **research problem,** a question that can be resolved at least partly through research. Your investigation of this problem may lead you to a position you wish to argue (see chapter 7), but the question you initially pose should invite exploration rather than make a judgment. For example, the thesis statement "Animal experimentation is wrong" is not a research problem because it is a conclusion rather than a question. Someone interested in a research topic related to animal experimentation might begin with this question: "Are animals being treated responsibly in research labs?" or "Under what circumstances could animal experimentation be necessary?" Beginning with a question, rather than an answer, encourages you to look at diverse materials—not just material that reinforces what you already believe.

Exercise 1

Each of the following subjects would need to be narrowed down for a ten-page paper. To experiment with framing a research problem, compose two questions about each subject.

1. terrorism
2. the job market
3. gender differences
4. globalization
5. civil rights
6. health care

8c | Researchers understand how to navigate the Web.

The **Internet,** an international network of computers linked through telephone and fiber-optic lines and satellites, is the location of the **World Wide Web,** one of the most exciting tools available to researchers. The Web is a huge and rapidly expanding collection of information, much of which—once located—is useful for research papers. You may have been using this resource for years, but if you do not have experience with the Web, inexpensive, convenient help is readily available.

The computer center at your school may offer workshops that will teach you how to log on to the Internet, send an email message, sign up with an online discussion group, and access Web sites. The school library may also offer workshops on using the Web for research. If you have enough experience to log on to the Internet but don't know how to take advantage of the Web's potential for research, visit your library's Web site, which may contain advice and tutorials. Similarly, the company you work for may offer in-service training on using the Internet. Useful introductions to the Internet can also be found in bookstores and computer superstores.

The easiest way to find information on the Web is to use one of the many search tools, such as AltaVista, Google, Lycos, or Yahoo! After you type **keywords** (words that describe your research topic) into an on-screen text entry box, a search tool provides a list of electronic documents (Web sites) that meet the search criteria. Remember that no search tool searches all of the Web; each one searches a portion of it. Knowing how to use several search tools can make your Web searches more productive.

The opening page for Google, shown in figure 8.1, has a clear and inviting design (see **6d**) that includes relatively little text and emphasizes the space in which the user types the keywords for a search. The example shows the beginning of a search on Starbucks (the subject of the MLA-style paper in **11b**). Clicking on "Google Search" at this point would establish how many sites mention Starbucks and provide a list of the first ten. Clicking on "I'm Feeling Lucky" would take the user directly to the first site on the list. (In September 2002, when this search was made, Google listed 416,000 sites that mentioned Starbucks, demonstrating the need to narrow a keyword search.)

On the right side of Google's opening page, a link offers users an option called "Advanced Search." Undertaking an advanced search is often a good way to discover sites that are especially helpful. Doing so can also reveal the difference between surfing the Web and searching the Web. As the word suggests, surfing is informal and unpredictable. When **surfing the Web,** you simply enter a keyword, receive a list of sites, and scan them to determine which, if any, are worth consulting. This can be fun. It's a bit like going to the library (see **8d**), browsing the books on the shelves for a particular subject area, and taking a closer look at any book that seems appealing. **Searching the Web,** however, demands thinking carefully about keywords, identifying authorities you would like to locate, and deciding what dates are appropriate for the kind of data you need for a specific research project. When searching for information on

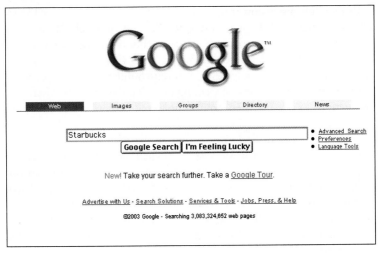

Figure 8.1. Google's opening page.

the Web, you can benefit from the strategies for broadening or narrowing a search that are often applied when looking for articles in scholarly journals (see pages 241–242).

There are important differences among the numerous tools available for searching the Web. Some, like Yahoo!, are **subject directories.** These match keywords against descriptions of Web sites submitted by sponsors or creators or entered by human indexers, who also classify sites into basic categories according to their content; these categories make it easy to browse for relevant sites. Other search tools are **search engines.** These use automatic programs called **spiders** that visit millions of Web sites to index the actual content of those sites by searching for keywords or phrases. Search engines, such as AltaVista, tend to be larger than subject directories. However, the distinction between subject directories and search engines is blurring, since many of the directories now link directly to one or more engines. For this reason, many people use the term *search engine* to refer to any Web-based search tool.

Search tools will return different results. One may search for only the titles of documents, another may look at document links, and a few search the full text of every document they index. Furthermore, some search tools cover only the Web, whereas others go into other areas of the

Internet (such as usenet newsgroups). For these reasons, one tool may be better for academic information, another for general information, and yet another for business information. Experiment with various search tools, and consult their Help functions when necessary.

The result of a successful search will be a list of Web addresses, or **Uniform Resource Locators (URLs),** which you can use to access the sites you need. As you proceed with your research, record in your research log (see 8a) the names and URLs of sites and the dates on which you visited them. Because sites change and even disappear, scholarly organizations such as the Modern Language Association (see 11a) and the American Psychological Association (see 11c) require that bibliographies include both the access date and the posting date for any site listed. When you print out material from the Web, the **access date** usually appears at the top or bottom of the printout. The **posting date** (the date when the site was last modified or updated) generally appears on the site itself. Some sites do not show a posting date, however, and some printouts will not have an access date. Keeping a separate record of this information in your research log can help you later, when you need to verify information on a site or list it in a bibliography (see 10c). If a site does not have a posting date, note in your log that it is undated; doing so will establish that you did not accidentally omit a piece of information. When you take notes directly from the screen, without making a printout, a separate record of sites and dates is essential.

Web pages usually combine text and images (see chapters 5 and 6) and include **hyperlinks** that take users to other pages. Identified by a different color from the text and/or by underlining, these links can appear anywhere in a Web site. To follow a link to another page or site, you simply click on it. For information on how to evaluate the credibility of Web sites, see 9c.

Exercise 2

Using at least three search tools and entering different keywords in each one, look on the Web for information about a topic you are interested in researching. Then, write a one- or two-page paper describing your search.

8d | Libraries house books, periodicals, and other important sources.

Libraries can provide a wide variety of materials that have been carefully selected and organized. These include books, periodicals (journals, magazines, and newspapers), videotapes, artwork, and unpublished documents and records (such as letters, minutes, and manuscripts). You can start working in a library before you even get there. Although information about resources in some small specialized libraries may be available only in those libraries, most large libraries provide information about their resources and services via the Web. But whether you uncover library resources from your desk at home, a table at an Internet café, or a terminal in a computer classroom, you will have to visit the library if you want to borrow or consult the print resources housed there. Once there, you will find terminals at which you can continue your search, as well as information specialists who can help you find what you need.

(1) Books often contain the results of extensive research.

A large bookstore stocks all sorts of books to sell to different kinds of customers, without claiming that the books available for purchase are of consistently high quality. Libraries do not make such a claim either. Municipal libraries select books likely to appeal to diverse citizens, and college and university libraries house some works that have become outdated. Nevertheless, a high percentage of the books available in a college or university library are reliable and informative because they have been chosen by trained librarians or ordered by professors with expertise in a specific field. In a sense, someone else has already done your shopping for you and left these purchases on a shelf waiting for you to use at your convenience. For information about how to determine the reliability of books, see chapter 9.

You locate a book by consulting the library's main catalog, which gives you the **call number** you need to find the location where the book is shelved. Most books are located in the **stacks** (one or more floors filled with bookshelves). Books put temporarily **on reserve** are located in a separate area and can be checked out for only a short period, if at all. Reference books, encyclopedias, and indexes—materials that cannot be checked out of the library—are located in the reference collection, but some of these materials may also be available online or on CD-ROMs.

Some libraries still maintain a **card catalog** consisting of cards arranged alphabetically in drawers. Each book has author, title, and subject cards, which are filed alphabetically. Most libraries, however, have **online catalogs,** which save space and make research more efficient. A library catalog, then, whether computerized or kept on cards, identifies books by author, title, and subject. Most online catalogs also allow researchers to locate sources by searching for other information, such as a keyword that may appear in the title or the text. Although the format of a computerized entry and a catalog card differ, both provide essentially the same information, including the call number.

If your library has both card and computerized catalogs, check with a librarian to see which is more current or complete. Libraries that have computerized their catalogs may have stopped including new acquisitions in their card catalogs, and libraries that have only recently computerized their catalogs may not yet have their entire collection online.

In addition to providing the author, title, publisher, and date of publication, an online record also reveals the book's status—information that can save a researcher time when a book has been moved to a special collection or checked out by someone else. If you need a book that has been checked out, you can request that the library put a hold on it when it is returned. A librarian will then notify you when the book is available.

The online catalog record shown in figure 8.2 was generated by the search that Nicole Hester, a student at Pennsylvania State University, did for her paper on desegregating the U.S. military (see **11f**). Expect to encounter variations from this example because the name of the library differs from one system to another and because libraries use different systems for computerizing their catalogs. Some computerized catalogs appear only on local networks, whereas others are Web-based to facilitate access from off-campus locations.

The information displayed on the screen can help you decide whether you want to examine the book itself or look for other books like it. Look at the terms, sometimes called *subjects,* listed for the book. Information specialists have chosen these standardized terms to characterize the contents of each book; you can thus click on the terms to find other books that may help you answer your research question.

(2) Reference books provide useful background.

When doing research, you may need to consult a variety of reference works. A general encyclopedia, such as *Encyclopaedia Britannica* (now available by subscription on the Web at www.eb.com), can provide useful background information for the early stage of your research. And you

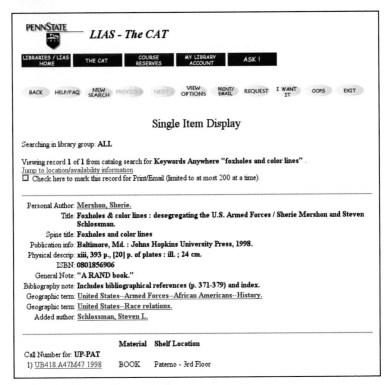

Figure 8.2. A record from an online catalog.

will almost certainly need to consult a dictionary. (See **28e** for a list of dictionaries.) You may be able to access an electronic encyclopedia or dictionary on your computer before turning to the Web, where many other reference works can be located.

Despite the ease with which many reference works can be accessed electronically, you may need to consult a specialized encyclopedia or dictionary in your college library to identify names and understand concepts in the books or articles you have discovered. Sources written for a specialized audience (see **1e**) assume that readers do not need help with basic terminology in the field. Reference books can help you fill in gaps that keep you from understanding the sources you have found.

For a detailed list of reference books and a short description of each, consult *Guide to Reference Books* by Robert Balay and *American Reference Books Annual* (*ARBA*). For titles of reference books for writing about literature, see page 415. A few of the most widely used reference books are listed here with abbreviated bibliographical information. Remember that these sources are useful for background information; refer to them for help, but do not use them as major sources for your research.

Special Dictionaries and Encyclopedias

Dictionary of American History. Rev. ed. 8 vols. 1976–1978. Supplements, 1996.

Dictionary of Art. Ed. Jane Turner. 34 vols. 1996.

Encyclopedia of Higher Education. Eds. Burton R. Clark and Guy R. Neave. 4 vols. 1992.

Encyclopedia of Psychology. Ed. Alan E. Kazdin. 2000.

Encyclopedia of Religion. Ed. Mircea Eliade. 16 vols. Also on CD-ROM.

Encyclopedia of U.S. Foreign Relations. Eds. Bruce W. Jentleson and Thomas G. Paterson. 4 vols. 1997.

International Encyclopedia of the Social and Behavioral Sciences. Eds. Neil J. Smelser and Paul B. Baltes. 26 vols. 2001.

McGraw-Hill Encyclopedia of Science and Technology. 8th ed. 20 vols. 1997. Yearbooks.

The New Grove Dictionary of Music and Musicians. Ed. Stanley Sadie. 2nd ed. 29 vols. 2001.

Routledge Encyclopedia of Philosophy. Eds. Edward Craig and Luciano Floridi. 10 vols. 1998.

Biographies

American National Biography. Eds. John A. Garraty and Mark C. Carnes. 24 vols. 1999.

Biography and Genealogy Master Index. 1980– . Also on CD-ROM.

Biography Index. 1946– .

Current Biography Cumulated Index. 1940– .

Dictionary of National Biography (British). 22 vols. 1882–1953. Rpt. 1981. Supplements.

Dictionary of Scientific Biography. 16 vols. 1970–1981. Supplements.

Notable American Women: 1607–1950. 3 vols. 1971. Supplements.

Notable Black American Women. 2nd ed. 1996.

Webster's New Biographical Dictionary. 1995.

Who's Who in America. 1899– . (See also Marquis's *Who's Who Publications: Index to All Books,* revised annually, 1976– .)

(3) Magazines, journals, and newspapers often contain recent information on a topic.

Periodicals (magazines, journals, and newspapers, in print or on microfilm) are typically held in a special section of the library. You can usually browse through issues from the past year. Older issues are generally stored elsewhere. To access information in periodicals, researchers use **electronic indexes.** Many periodicals are also available online, and some allow **full-text retrieval,** the option of downloading and printing out an entire article. Periodical literature is useful not only because it is timely, but also because it has been professionally reviewed and edited. For information on how to evaluate the credibility of periodicals, see **9b(2).**

Virtually every discipline and profession has its own **journals,** periodicals that generally provide much more detailed information than can be found in magazines or newspapers aimed at the general public. When conducting research on a topic, you should familiarize yourself with the indexes that direct you to work written by authorities on that topic and published in journals for the benefit of other authorities. You may not yet be an authority, but your knowledge and expertise will increase if you study serious scholarship.

With full-text retrieval becoming increasingly available, you will often be able to obtain the complete text of an article through your personal computer—whether directly from a periodical you subscribe to or through an electronic index available either via your library's Web site or, for InfoTrac College Edition, via your Web Browser and a password. On many occasions, however, you will need to visit a library to use an electronic or print index or to obtain a copy of an article in a periodical for which full-text retrieval is not available electronically.

(a) Choosing and using an electronic index

Electronic indexes, also frequently called *electronic databases,* can help you locate the titles and authors of articles. In addition, many of these indexes include *abstracts* (short summaries of articles; for an example of an abstract, see page 339). Some can even provide you with complete texts of articles. Selecting an appropriate index requires that you locate your topic within a field (such as psychology) or discipline (a group of related fields, such as the social sciences). For example, if you are researching the nature of memory, you could go directly to PsycINFO (see page 241), which is devoted exclusively to scholarship in psychology. If you are researching cases in which students have opened fire on their high school classmates, you could also go to PsycINFO. But if you recognize that sociologists and criminologists—as well as psychologists—are likely to have studied such cases, you might turn to SocialSciIndex for a broader range of materials (see page 240).

Many indexes are available on CD-ROM as well as on the Web. A CD-ROM offers you the convenience of searching for periodical literature from a personal computer when you do not have a link from your home or office to the electronic indexes available at a college library. But CD-ROM indexes have one disadvantage: Once published, the information cannot be updated unless a continuation is issued. If you need up-to-the-minute information, you might have to search through one of the online indexes to supplement what you find on the CD-ROM. With InfoTrac College Edition and a passcode, you can also conveniently search for periodical literature with the Web browser on your own computer. You do not have to be networked to your college library's Web site.

InfoTrac College Edition is often a good place to begin your search for periodical literature. It indexes more than 10 million articles in over 3,800 full-text journals, including the following:

Scholarly journals (such as the *Journal of Business Communication* and the *Journal of Social Psychology*)

Trade journals (such as *Adhesive Technology* and *Frozen Food Digest*)

General-circulation magazines (such as *Newsweek* and *Sports Illustrated*)

The InfoTrac screens in figures 8.3 and 8.4 illustrate part of the research conducted for the paper that appears in **11d**. Clicking in the box labeled "Mark" next to the article on the relationship between sleep and grade-point average, as shown in figure 8.3, and then clicking on "text and full content retrieval choices" brought up the complete article, whose first page appears in figure 8.4.

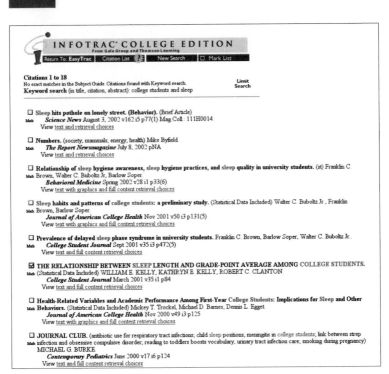

Figure 8.3. Example of an InfoTrac screen.

Beyond the Rule

USING INFOTRAC

Access to InfoTrac College Edition is available through your Web browser using a passcode packaged with new copies of this book. If your copy did not come with a passcode for InfoTrac and you would like to know more about this service, or if you have access to InfoTrac but have questions about it, visit www.harbrace.com.

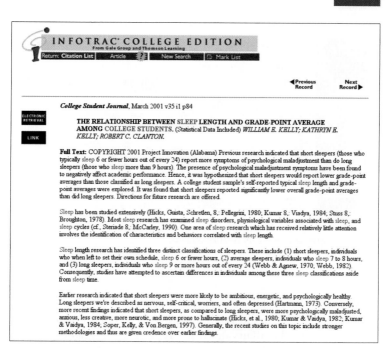

Figure 8.4. First page of an article found through InfoTrac.

As you continue your research, you may also benefit from consulting FirstSearch, a family of electronic indexes that is usually accessed through terminals in a school library or through personal computers linked to a school library via a local network or the Web. FirstSearch covers several broad topic areas (such as "Arts and Humanities" and "Business and Economics") and specialized databases (such as MEDLINE and GeoRefS). You will be asked to choose from among these topics and databases. FirstSearch also prompts you to enter keywords related to your topic.

To research the role of Starbucks in globalization, as Andy Pieper did for his paper (see **11b**), you could select one of the following topics: "General," "Business and Economics," or "Consumer Affairs and

Figure 8.5. Example of a screen from FirstSearch.

People." To research the status of African Americans in the U.S. military, as Nicole Hester did for her paper (see **11f**), you could select "General" or "Public Affairs and Law." To research the relationship between sleep and academic performance among college students, as Nikki Krzmarzick did for her paper (see **11d**), you could select "Life Sciences" or "Social Sciences."

Instead of selecting a topic, you can enter a database to search. Depending on the Web page you are viewing, you might have to choose a topic before choosing a database. The screen in figure 8.5 shows the choices available for "Social Sciences." By selecting "ECO," you could access a collection of scholarly journals; by clicking on "SocialSciIndex," you would also obtain journal articles, although this search might identify other kinds of articles as well. An effective search would probably include both. (Note that FirstSearch also provides access to books and Web resources through its WorldCat feature.)

The databases available through FirstSearch vary from one library to another. Librarians choose to subscribe to those databases that are best suited to their institution's needs and budget, taking into account the other electronic indexes that are available to their users. Similarly, the appearance of the opening screen for FirstSearch varies from one school to another. The example shown in figure 8.5 is from the library system through which Nikki Krzmarzick conducted her search.

Whether or not your school or library provides access to FirstSearch, check to see whether you can access other indexes or specialized databases. Some examples follow.

Literature	The MLA Bibliography indexes articles and books written in most modern languages and is essential for research in English and American literature.
Education	ERIC indexes articles and conference papers in all areas of education.
Psychology	PsycINFO provides short summaries, or abstracts, of articles in psychology in addition to the citations that will help you find the full article.
Life sciences	MEDLINE provides abstracts of articles in medicine and biology from more than seven thousand journals.

Another important electronic index is LexisNexis, a service that indexes legal documents and newspaper articles. Because this service is updated daily, and even includes information that will not be published in print until the following day, it is especially helpful for researchers working on current events.

Many electronic indexes permit keyword searches of their entire contents, not just limited searches by topic or by **controlled terms** (a vocabulary of official descriptors used to retrieve information). Even if a keyword is not one of the controlled terms, a search may turn up potential sources that use the keyword in a title or in some other part. If your search yields no records, try substituting or adding another closely related term. If your search turns up more records than you can handle, try locating those that are most relevant by adding other words to the keyword with which you began. A search result such as "Found 2,493,508 records containing the descriptor *film*" is as useless as one that reports "No records found." To narrow or broaden a search, you can use **logical operators** (also called **Boolean operators**):

or	broadens a search (For example, "Starbucks **or** Vienna" finds all records that contain information about either keyword.)
and	narrows a search ("Starbucks **and** Vienna" returns only those records that contain both keywords.)
not	excludes specific items ("Starbucks **and** Austria **not** Vienna" excludes any records that mention Austria's capital city.)

near   finds records in which the two keywords occur in close
proximity, within a preset number of words, and excludes
those in which the keywords are widely separated ("Starbucks
near globalization" lists only those records in which references
to both *Starbucks* and *globalization* occur in close proximity;
this option is often not available, however.)

Whether your library provides indexing and abstracting services online or on CD-ROMs, you can use the following search strategy to locate periodical literature.

TIPS FOR CONDUCTING A SEARCH FOR PERIODICAL LITERATURE

1. Identify keywords that clearly describe the topic.
2. Determine the databases to be searched.
3. Apply a basic search logic.
4. Log on and perform the search.
5. Identify the citations you want to keep.
6. Refine your search strategy if the first search returned too many or too
   few citations, or (worse) irrelevant ones.
7. Obtain the articles for which you have citations.

Exercise 3

Using InfoTrac or FirstSearch, identify at least two sources that seem useful for the research you began in exercise 2. Summarize what you learn
from these sources, and explain how you think you could use them for
the research question you have in mind. If you discover any sources that
seem unlikely to be useful, explain why you decided to exclude them.

(b) Searching indexes in bound volumes

Although searching electronic indexes is more efficient than searching
through bound and printed indexes, many college libraries continue to
purchase bound volumes along with the comparable electronic versions. They do so because computers malfunction, networks go down,

and Internet service is interrupted. Just as your computer may freeze, the entire computer system for a library can crash. Bound volumes provide essential backup when computers are out of service. Librarians also know that clients may need to access older information that is not available on electronic indexes. Searching through bound volumes takes more time than searching via computer, but it is preferable to having your research disrupted. Some of the most useful printed indexes, with their dates of beginning publication, are as follows.

> *Applied Science and Technology Index.* 1958– .
> *Art Index.* 1929– .
> *Biological and Agricultural Index.* 1946– .
> *Business Periodicals Index.* 1958– .
> *Cumulative Index to Nursing and Allied Health Literature* (*CINAHL*).
>   1982– .
> *General Science Index.* 1978– .
> *Humanities Index.* 1974– .
> *Index to Legal Periodicals.* 1908– .
> *Music Index.* 1949– .
> *Philosopher's Index.* 1967– .
> *Public Affairs Information Service (Bulletin).* 1915– .
> *Social Sciences Index.* 1974– .

When they publish electronic versions of their indexes, some publishers change the title: *Current Index to Journals in Education* (*CIJE*) and *Resources in Education* (*RIE*) are the bound volumes for research in education, and ERIC is the electronic version.

Consult the front of any bound volume for a key to the abbreviations used in individual entries.

(c) Using abstracting services

Although many abstracts are available through periodical indexes, others can be obtained through **abstracting services** that support specific academic disciplines (see chapter 12). Your library may provide access to *Academic Abstracts, Biological Abstracts, Chemical Abstracts,* and *Psychological Abstracts.* When using one of these services, you can quickly scan the short summaries they provide and decide which articles seem likely to be the most useful. As with many periodical indexes, you can usually find a list of citations, a list of citations with abstracts, and the full text of some articles. If your library does not provide electronic access to abstracting services, it may have bound volumes of abstracts; these can be useful even though they do not include abstracts of articles published since the last volume was printed.

Whether consulting abstracts electronically or in bound volumes, be aware that abstracting services sometimes cover material published in languages other than English. An abstract may be in English even if the article is not. When this is the case, the language in which the article was published is usually identified within the abstract.

Exercise 4

Continue the work you did for exercises 2 and 3 by consulting the main catalog in your library and at least one periodical index or abstracting service other than InfoTrac. Explore different ways of narrowing your topic. Then, write a short paper in which you (a) report two potential ways of narrowing your original topic, (b) explain which of the two paths you selected for further research, (c) report the number of sources that seem available, and (d) explain how these sources are different from those you were able to find on the Web.

8e | **Field research involves interviewing, corresponding, surveying, observing, and experimenting.**

For some topics, you may want to do field research—which once meant research done outside a library or office. An archeologist or geologist might work outside, literally in a field, and a social worker or political scientist might do field research by going door to door interviewing people in a specific neighborhood. Thanks to the opportunities for communication that the Internet provides, field research today can also take place indoors—even at your desk. Wherever it takes place, field research requires you to undertake an investigation to uncover data that are not already available in print or online.

The most common addition to Web-based or library research is an **interview.** Faculty members at your college or university, business and professional people, and even relatives and friends can provide important information and insights if they have relevant firsthand experience with the topic you are researching.

Since well-informed interviewers ask the best questions, you should consider an interview only after you have done some reading on your topic. Schedule the interview well in advance, and if you plan to use a tape recorder, ask permission. Take a professional approach to the interview: Have pens and paper ready for taking notes and fresh batteries and blank tapes for your tape recorder. Record the time and date of the interview on the tape or at the beginning of your notes.

To show that you have done some preparation, avoid asking for information that is already public knowledge. For example, if you are interviewing a novelist who is visiting your campus, you should not ask, "What have you published?" Anyone preparing to interview such a person should be able to find out this information in advance by checking the Web, a library catalog, or *Books in Print.* Try also to avoid asking questions that could be answered in a word or two, such as "Do you like to write?" Begin with questions that are broad enough to give someone room to reveal a special interest; then, follow up with more specific questions. You might ask a novelist, "When you sit down to write, what kind of process do you follow?" If the novelist says something about the importance of revision, you might then ask, "How do you respond to advice from editors?" But be prepared to depart from your list of questions whenever the person you are interviewing says something of particular interest that would be useful to pursue.

Less formal than an interview, a dialogue with one or more other people interested in your topic can also be useful. You may be able to have such a dialogue with people on your campus or in your community. Researchers often benefit, however, from using the Internet to exchange ideas with people in other parts of the world.

Online **discussion groups** or **forums** allow you to read messages posted to all the members of a group interested in a specific topic and to post messages yourself that those members can read. For instance, a writing teacher may belong to a specialized electronic mailing list, or **Listserv,** that is operated by the Alliance for Computers and Writing and called ACW-L. Participants discuss issues related to using computers to teach writing. Someone on this list can send email messages to the **Listserv address,** which redistributes them to hundreds of other writing teachers around the world, and then receive replies from any of those teachers.

Anyone who wants to discuss a topic can join a discussion list. (See chapter 5.) To find out if there are any lists that might discuss the topic you are researching, visit www.topica.com, a Web site that provides a directory for thousands of online discussion groups and instructions that can guide your search.

Electronic mailing lists can also give you a means of conducting an informal **survey,** in which you ask a number of people the same set of questions and then analyze the results. But a survey limited to people who are already familiar with a topic and have been discussing it will not yield results that are representative of other groups, such as the students at your school or the citizens of your state. For some research questions (see **8b**), you may get better results by designing a survey specifically for the kind of people whose views you wish to consider and directing it to that group.

You can administer a survey orally, like an interview, or you can distribute a written questionnaire by mail or in person. If you use a written questionnaire, be sure to distribute it well in advance of your deadline, as you cannot expect people to respond immediately. And since many people fail to respond to written surveys, send out at least twice as many questionnaires as you would like to receive back.

Once you have a clear idea of what you want to find out through a survey, you may find the following checklist helpful.

CHECKLIST for Creating Survey Questions

- Does each question relate directly to the purpose of the survey?
- Are the questions easy to understand?
- Are they designed to elicit short, specific responses?
- Are they designed to collect concrete data that can be analyzed easily?
- Have respondents been given enough space to write their answers?
- Can the questions be presented to the group you want to survey?

In addition to interviews, dialogues, and surveys, you may sometimes be able to draw directly on your own experience or observations. For example, if you have recovered from a learning disorder, your personal experience may be relevant to a research project on treating these disorders. Similarly, if you have lived or worked with someone who has a learning disorder, your observations of this person's behavior may be relevant. Or you could conduct observations in which you pay close attention to behavior other than your own during a specific time period. For example, if you are doing research on dyslexia, you might benefit from getting permission to observe a session in which a reading specialist works with a group of children who have been diagnosed as having this disorder. Or if you are doing research on a species of wildlife, you might benefit from observing the animals in their natural habitat. (For an example of a report based on observation, see 14c.) Although what you see is often shaped by subjective factors (see 1d), try to put your opinions and values aside when making observations so that you can focus on recording what happens as accurately as possible. You can interpret the events you witness later, if you wish. In any case, you should first check with your instructor or supervisor to see whether personal experiences or observations are appropriate for the assignment on which you are working.

You should also consult with your instructor or supervisor if you are planning to use laboratory experiments for researching a topic. When conducting laboratory experiments, chemists, physicists, and biologists use equipment that is expensive to purchase and maintain. You will almost certainly need permission to use such equipment, and you will need to schedule your use for a specific time. Waste material from many chemical and biological experiments needs to be disposed of with care. Other experiments, such as those conducted by biologists and psychologists, may involve the use of animals as subjects. Some researchers in the social sciences also conduct experiments using human participants. If you are planning to use equipment that does not belong to you, work with hazardous materials, or experiment on living subjects, you must conduct your research carefully, ethically, and legally.

Beyond the Rule

INSTITUTIONAL REVIEW BOARDS

Colleges and universities usually have committees or boards that review requests for experimentation involving animals or humans. Institutional review of this kind is intended to protect research subjects from abuse, and a researcher who proceeds to experiment with animals or humans without official permission could suffer serious penalties. For examples of review board guidelines, visit www.harbrace.com.

9 Evaluating Sources Online and in Print

As you search for sources that can help you resolve a research question (see **8b**), you need to be a critical reader (**1c–d**) and evaluate the credibility of the sources you discover. Credible writers are well informed and fair-minded about the topics they are discussing. Credible sources are posted or published by reputable institutions, organizations, and companies.

To evaluate sources, you need clear criteria for determining the credibility of authors and the works they publish. This chapter will help you

- assess authors' credibility (**9a**),
- evaluate publishers (**9b**),
- evaluate Web sites (**9c**),
- distinguish between bias and commitment (**9d**), and
- determine the relevance of a source (**9e**).

9a | Good writing conveys the author's credibility.

You can evaluate the credibility of authors by finding out how well they write, what their credentials are, and how other readers respond to their work.

(1) Authors achieve credibility through the way they write.

You can begin to determine an author's credibility by paying close attention to tone (see **3a**). If an author's tone seems thoughtful and considerate, chances are that the author is credible. If an author's tone sounds one-sided or disrespectful to readers, chances are that the author lacks credibility. However, a thoughtful tone does not necessarily indicate expertise, nor does an arrogant tone necessarily indicate unreliability. A writer who sounds honest and respectful could be working with erroneous data, and a writer who sounds abrupt and sarcastic could have expert knowledge. You must consider other factors in addition to tone.

To determine how credible a writer is, ask yourself the questions in the following checklist.

CHECKLIST for Evaluating an Author's Credibility

- Does the writer seem committed to communicating with readers? As a reader, do you feel that you are being addressed respectfully and that the writer is trying to establish common ground with you?
- Does the writer seem knowledgeable about the topic?
- Does the writer support claims with specific evidence?
- Does the writer reveal how and where supporting evidence was obtained?
- Does the work contain signs that the author is prejudiced in any way?
- Does the writer recognize that other points of view may be legitimate?
- Do lapses in reasoning undermine the writer's case (see 7i)?
- Has the writer reached a conclusion that is in proportion to the amount of evidence produced?

As you use sources (see chapter 10) to complete a research paper (chapter 11) or any other academic or professional assignment (chapters 7 and 12–15), establish your credibility by following the same guidelines you expect other good writers to follow. By focusing on your audience as well as on the information you discuss, you can see where you need to moderate a claim, develop a point more fully, or modify your statements.

(2) Credentials help establish an author's credibility.

When evaluating sources, consider whether the authors have credentials that are relevant to the topics they are addressing. Credentials take various forms, including academic or professional training, grants or honors, publication record, work experience, and personal experience. A college biology professor who specializes in genetics is likely to be credible when writing about genes, for example, and a civil engineer who specializes in bridges should have credibility when writing about how a particular bridge could be strengthened. However, given their areas of specialization, the biologist would not be considered a credible source of information on the foraging habits of black bears, and the engineer would not have credibility concerning the design of hydroelectric power plants.

When their experience is directly related to the topics they are addressing, credible authors may discuss that experience within the text itself. For the most part, however, they are likely to focus on their topics rather than themselves.

To find information about an author's credentials, look

- on the jacket of a book,
- on a separate page near the front or back of a book,
- in the preface of a book,
- in a note at the bottom of the first or last page of an article in print,
- on a separate page devoted to providing background on contributors to a periodical, or
- through a link on a Web site.

When assessing the level of an author's expertise, ask yourself the following questions.

CHECKLIST for Assessing an Author's Credentials

- What are the extent and nature of the author's education, and how does it relate to the subject of the work?
- What is the author's job? Is it related to the subject on which the author has written?
- What jobs has the author held in the past?
- With what institutions, organizations, or companies has the author been affiliated (see 9b)?
- What is the author's publishing record?
- Do other experts speak of the author as an authority (see 9a(3))?

Exercise 1

Find a one- to three-page article that seems credible because of the way in which it is written and because of the author's credentials. Distribute copies of the article to a group of fellow writers, and draw their attention to what impressed you favorably. Be prepared to explain why you found the article credible.

(3) Information about authors appears in the text of works by other writers.

If you invest time in researching a topic, you will often find that other writers mention authors who turned up in your preliminary search for sources. Consider how other writers refer to an author you wish to cite. If several writers offer negative evaluations of an author's work, there is a reasonable chance that that author is unreliable. If, on the other hand, several writers seem to benefit from the work of the author you are evaluating, then there is a good chance that you are considering a credible source.

(4) Information about authors appears in online sources.

You can learn more about authors by searching the Web (see **8c**) for information about them. Using a search engine such as Google, you can enter an author's name or the title of a book. Even if you do not find a site dedicated to the work you are thinking about using, you may find sites containing background information on the author or bibliographical information about his or her other works. You can also use InfoTrac College Edition or other electronic periodical indexes (see **8d(3)**) to locate book reviews or other articles about or by an author.

(5) Reviews contain information that can help you assess an author's credibility.

Book reviews often include useful information for readers who are looking for credible sources. When you are doing research, you may be able to determine the credibility of a work without consulting such reviews. But now that many reviews are available online, you can sometimes obtain a helpful review easily—especially if you are evaluating a recently published source.

When you read reviews, remember that being a credible source does not mean being a perfect source. A credible source may get some negative responses. Look for the main point (see **2b**) of a review, and decide whether that main point amounts to a positive or negative response to the book as a whole. For example, if an author is described as "entertaining but unreliable," the negative adjective is more important than the positive one when assessing that author's credibility. Or if an author is described as "dry but nevertheless informative," the praise outweighs the complaint.

Few writers please all reviewers all the time—hence your responsibility to read reviews carefully. Be willing to consider the work of a writer who is said to include more details than are necessary (because you do not always have to read an entire work to benefit from its contents) or to have taken a position that differs from that of recognized authority (because originality can be a merit). But dismiss from further consideration any writer whom more than one reviewer characterizes as ill-informed, careless with facts, biased (see **9d**), or dishonest in any way.

Beyond the Rule

BOOK REVIEWS

A book review might be shaped by the reviewer's religious or political affiliations, by professional rivalry, or by the requirements of a specific periodical. For additional information about the process of reviewing books, visit www.harbrace.com.

Exercise 2

Use Google to search for information about two or three authors whose credibility you are evaluating. Then, write a one-page assessment of one of these authors.

Exercise 3

Choose a book from the bestseller list published weekly in the *New York Times Book Review.* Locate at least two reviews of this book. Then, write a two-page paper in which you report what the reviews have in common and how they differ.

> **9b** | **Credible sources are published by reliable institutions, organizations, and companies.**

When you are doing research, consider not only the credibility of authors (see 9a) but also the credibility of the media through which their work is made available to you. Some publishers hold authors accountable to higher standards than others do.

(1) You can evaluate book publishers by considering whether they are commercial or academic.

When evaluating books, you can usually assume that university presses demand a high standard of scholarship. The more prestigious the university, the more reliable a source may be—but there are exceptions. Even such distinguished presses as the Harvard University Press and the University of California Press have published some works that were subsequently questioned by serious scholars. Editors at a university press, like those at a commercial press, may be influenced (if not to the same extent) by how many copies of the book are likely to sell. If an author with reasonably good credentials has written a book on a topic about which there is current interest that may soon pass, editors at a university press may be less careful than they should be when checking facts or editing sentences.

Problems such as these occur more frequently in works published by companies with stockholders, who are primarily concerned with profitability, so works published by commercial presses are sometimes taken less seriously by scholars than are works published by university presses. But there are many exceptions. Some commercial presses—such as Farrar, Straus & Giroux; Basic Books; and HarperCollins—have distinguished records. And books published by commercial presses frequently win awards such as the Pulitzer Prize and the National Book Award. When evaluating a work published by a commercial press, as when evaluating a work published by a university press, you must judge the case individually, considering not just the publisher's reputation but also the author's credibility (see 9a). Also be aware that fine works are sometimes published by small presses with which you may not be familiar (such as Milkweed in Minneapolis or Kitchen Table in Seattle).

Additional information about books and publishers can be found by searching the Web (see 8c). A directory of publishers that maintain sites on the Web can be obtained through Vanderbilt University (**www.library.vanderbilt.edu/law/acqs/pubr.html**).

(2) You can evaluate periodical literature by examining recent issues.

An article published in an **academic journal** is often more credible than one published in a popular magazine. Academic journals are usually published quarterly, which means that there are four issues a year; the time between issues allows for the careful selection and editing of articles. The most credible articles are usually those that appear in a **refereed journal,** which is an academic journal that publishes work recommended by external reviewers with expertise in the relevant field (as opposed to simply being chosen by the journal's editor). For every article appearing in a refereed journal, you can assume that at least three or four have been rejected. Information about the editorial policies of academic journals usually appears near the front of each issue.

Pieces that appear in **general-circulation magazines** (magazines that are published weekly or monthly and are sold in supermarkets and drugstores) may also be reliable, but they are usually written more quickly and chosen for publication by someone on the magazine's staff—not by an expert in the field. When evaluating an article in a general-circulation magazine, consider the quality of the article and the credibility of its author (see 9a). But also consider the substance and reputation of the magazine itself. Magazines such as the *Atlantic Monthly, Harper's,* and *Scientific American* publish more substantial articles than do magazines such as *GQ, People,* and *Seventeen.* If you are unfamiliar with general-circulation magazines, leafing through those you find in a bookstore or in the periodical room of a library should help you decide which of them can be taken more seriously than others.

For additional information about general-circulation magazines, you can also visit their Web sites or use a search engine such as Google to see if other readers have offered an assessment of them.

Similarly, some newspapers have more credibility than others. For example, critical readers consider the *New York Times,* the *Wall Street Journal,* the *Washington Post,* the *Miami Herald,* and the *Los Angeles Times* more credible than *USA Today* or the *New York Post.* If you examine issues of different newspapers in a library, you can gauge their credibility by considering the space devoted to various stories, the extent to which staff members (as opposed to wire services) are responsible for stories, and the tone of the commentary on the editorial pages. And, as with any informative or persuasive writing, examine the types of evidence used to support claims (see 7e).

When evaluating periodicals or books, you can benefit from considering the questions in the following checklist.

CHECKLIST for Evaluating Sources in Print

- Is the work recent enough to provide any up-to-date information you need?
- If you need information from another time period, is the work from the right period?
- Does the work provide documentation to support important points? Does this documentation indicate that the work is based on solid research?
- What can you discover about the company or organization that has published this work?

In books, the date of publication appears with other copyright information on a page near the front of the book, usually a left-hand page. Dates of periodicals appear on their covers and frequently on the top or bottom of pages throughout each issue. If you have failed to note the date of a periodical, you can usually find it by searching an electronic index (see 8d(3)).

| 9c | **Researchers need to evaluate Web sites and other online sources.** |

If you are evaluating periodical literature that you obtained online, you can follow the guidelines provided in (9b(2)). But if you are evaluating a Web site, you need to consider the nature of the site and its sponsor.

(1) You can evaluate a Web site by considering the content, timeliness, and author of the site.

When evaluating a Web site, you should consider how well the text is written (see 9a(1)), how often the site is updated, and who produces the content. Since Web sites can easily be kept up to date, look for evidence of frequent maintenance. Consider also whether you are viewing a site put together by a single individual or a team of people working for a reputable agency, institution, or organization. A site composed by a single author may be credible if that person has relevant credentials (see 9a(2)) and keeps the site current. A site maintained by a team of individuals may well be credible since different individuals can bring different credentials and different skills to composing and maintaining the site. However, its credibility will be weakened if it has not been updated in the past year or if it features links that lead nowhere.

The date on which a Web site was established or last updated frequently appears on the site, and the date on which you access it will usually appear on any hard copy that you print out. Do not confuse the access date with the posting date (see 8c).

(2) You can evaluate a Web site by considering the nature of its sponsor.

Consider the origin of a Web site as well as its content and timeliness. Although many sites are created by individuals working on their own, many others are sponsored by colleges or universities, professional organizations, and commercial enterprises. Such a sponsor is typically indicated in the site's address by a suffix that represents its domain. Colleges and universities are indicated by .edu, government departments and agencies by .gov, professional organizations by .org, and businesses by .com. An address that includes any one of these domains can take you to a credible and useful site, but you can benefit from considering whether a site with a specific type of domain is likely to have information relevant (see 9e) to your topic, purpose, and audience.

Suppose, for example, you were writing a paper about how corporate bankruptcies in 2002 revealed serious irregularities in the work of a major accounting firm. An education site could provide a scholarly analysis of the practices in question; a government site could contain data compiled by the Securities and Exchange Commission (SEC); an organization site could give you the viewpoint of an association of accountants; and a business site could convey information from the accounting firm in question. Each of these sites would offer different content, which would be shaped by the rhetorical situation (see 1b) as envisioned by each site's sponsor. For example, the SEC is an agency of the federal government that reports to the U.S. Congress, which, in turn, represents the citizens. Accordingly, the SEC's purpose is to show its audience that it is providing careful oversight of business practices. The commercial site of an accounting firm, on the other hand, has a vested interest in making the company look good to current customers and potential clients. Depending on the nature of your research paper, you can access any or all of the various types of sites. But, as you evaluate their content, remember that every site is shaped to achieve a specific purpose.

CHECKLIST for Evaluating a Web Site

- How often is the site updated?
- What do you know about the author? If no author is identified, what can you infer about the author from the site?
- What is the purpose of the site? How might this purpose affect the kind of information included on the site?
- Is the source located at an institution or sponsored by an organization about which information is available at other sites?
- Does the site include citations for other sources or links to other reliable documents?

Additional information on evaluating Web sites can be found at stcloudstate. edu/~killbornj/webvalidation.html (a site created at and sponsored by St. Cloud State University in Minnesota).

Exercise 4

Write a two- or three-page paper in which you define your evaluation criteria and then evaluate one print source and one Web site on a specific topic.

9d | Evaluating sources requires understanding how *bias* differs from *commitment*.

(1) Researchers recognize bias and commitment in print publications.

Some general-circulation magazines are straightforward about identifying their affiliations. For instance, *Mother Jones* reveals its political stance on its masthead, which identifies its namesake as "Mary Harris 'Mother' Jones (1830–1930), orator, union organizer, and hellraiser," and through its diction (see chapter 28) and tone (3a and 9a(1)).

> When the bombs explode at abortion clinics, when the tax protesters turn their guns on federal agents, the cynical politicos who mixed the cocktail of national convulsion won't be around to take the blame. In their plush backstage parlors, they will shake their heads in perfunctory pity before getting back to the business of slapping backs, trading business cards, and stirring the next round of drinks.
>
> —**WILLIAM SALETAN,** "What I Saw at the Decline of the Revolution"

Subscription forms for the *Conservative Chronicle,* the *Capitalist's Companion,* and the Conservative Book Club included in issues of the *American Spectator* reveal this magazine's political stance. Its conservativeness is also conveyed by the language used by the authors published in any issue.

> Just when you think you've got the rules of politics figured out—that liberal Democrats won't give up the theory, rhetoric and practice of class warfare, for example, until you pry their cold, dead fingers from the wallets of the rich—along comes a one-two-three punch to send you reeling.
>
> —**TOD LINDBERG,** "Growth Democrats"

These are fairly obvious examples. In other cases, however, an apparently well-reasoned article can reflect the values built into a periodical even if those values are not readily apparent in the article itself. For example, an article on malpractice suits in the *Journal of the American Medical Association* is likely to be sympathetic to physicians.

Recognizing that periodicals are likely to reflect the political values of their owners and editors does not mean, however, that you should necessarily distrust the information they contain. Journals and newspapers can be committed to certain values and still have high standards for what they publish.

It is important to distinguish between sources that are **committed** and those that are **biased.** A committed source represents a point of view fairly; a biased source represents it unfairly. The difference is a matter of ethos (see 7f). It is possible to argue ethically for ideas you believe in; it is also possible to twist facts and misrepresent events to make your point. If you read the *Wall Street Journal* over a period of several weeks, you will recognize that it has an editorial policy that is politically conservative and sympathetic to business interests. This paper is also committed to honest reporting and clear writing, however, so its articles are still generally reliable. Bias appears when politics interferes with honest reporting so that important elements of a story are ignored, distorted, or suppressed.

When distinguishing between bias and commitment, be careful not to dismiss a credible source simply because you disagree with what it says. If you immediately reject a committed source that challenges you to reconsider some of your own views, you may be displaying bias rather than thinking critically.

CHECKLIST for Discovering Bias

- Does the author make personal attacks on people?
- Does the author sound sarcastic or mean-spirited?
- Has the author used prejudiced language (see 28d)?
- Does the work include sweeping generalizations unsupported by verifiable data (see 7e)?
- Has the author oversimplified complex issues?
- Has the author ignored or belittled opposing views?

> ### CHECKLIST for Discovering Commitment
>
> - Does the author have clearly defined values?
> - Are the author's values worthy of respect?
> - Has the author addressed his or her audience (see 1e(2)) respectfully?
> - Has the author provided adequate support for all claims made (see 7e)?
> - Has the author recognized that the issue in question has more than one side?
> - Does the author treat opposing views fairly?

Exercise 5

Read the letters to the editor in at least three issues of your local news-paper. Choose a letter that seems biased and one that seems committed. Write a one-page paper explaining your evaluations and quoting words or passages that led you to make them.

(2) Researchers also recognize bias and commitment in online sources.

Understanding the distinction between *bias* and *commitment* is also use-ful when you search the Web. Many sites are created by organizations or individuals strongly committed to specific values and goals. If you visit the Web site for the American Cancer Society or the League of Women Voters, for example, you can expect to find information that advances the purpose of the organization. Similarly, if you visit the Web site of the Emily Dickinson International Society, you can expect to find informa-tion intended to advance interest in and scholarship about her poetry. A site designed by a teacher for a specific course is also likely to be com-mitted to certain values and goals that will be reflected not only in the grading and attendance policies but also in the texts chosen for study and the kind of writing assignments required. You can learn much from com-mitted sites such as these.

Keep in mind, however, that most Web sites are not subject to review; anyone can launch a site for any purpose. Even sites that seem professional and credible may be biased or contain erroneous information. You need to read critically (see 1c–d) and to remember that you are likely to encounter other points of view at other sites. You should not, however, assume that a site is biased just because it is committed. Look for the signs of bias described in the checklist on page 259. It is natural to expect the site of the Emily Dickinson International Society to be committed to that poet's work, but if your research takes you to a site that ridicules people who prefer other poets or that makes unsupported claims about Dickinson's personal life, then you are visiting a site where commitment has degenerated into bias. Much bias is the result of faulty logic, such as oversimplification or overgeneralization (see 7i).

Sometimes, however, bias and commitment can overlap. Consider the Web page shown in figure 9.1. Anyone visiting this site sponsored by the Organic Consumers Association should expect to find the site committed to promoting the consumption of healthy, naturally produced food. This commitment is conveyed by the association's logo, which features ripe vegetables and tools more likely to be used in a home garden than on a large commercial farm. Commitment to healthy food is also conveyed by one of the demands this site makes of Starbucks: "Remove genetically engineered ingredients from their food and dairy products on a worldwide basis."

Although a credible site could be devoted to both organic food and responsible business practices, the Web page excerpted here contains a disturbing sign of bias: By adapting the Starbucks logo into a "Frankenbucks" logo, the authors of this site evoke the idea of Frankenstein and imply that Starbucks is a kind of monster. The site might be useful for a research paper on social action, but anyone doing serious research on the kind of food products used by Starbucks would need to turn to other sites to verify the claim that Starbucks uses genetically engineered food and to discover whether this food is indeed unhealthy.

9e	Experienced researchers know how to identify relevant sources and key passages within them.

A source can be credible without being useful. It is useful when it is relevant to your research question (see 8b). Given the huge and ever-growing amount of information available on most topics, you should not be discouraged if you find that you have located a source that seems promis-

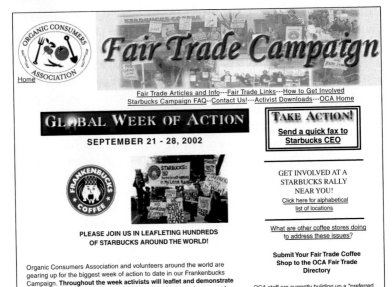

Figure 9.1 Web page for Fair Trade Campaign.

ing but fails to give you what you need. Plenty of other sources are available, and they can be located through the search strategies discussed in chapter 8. Be prepared to put aside a book or an article you have obtained. Some writers get off track because they cannot bring themselves to abandon a source they like, even if it is no longer relevant to their topic since—as often happens—their focus has changed during the process of conducting research, taking notes, drafting the paper, and revising it (see chapters 2, 3, 8, and 10). It's better to abandon an irrelevant source than to write a poorly focused paper.

While you may reject some sources altogether, you are likely to use only parts of others. Seldom will an entire Web site, book, or article be useful for a specific research paper. Do not assume that a source must be

100 percent relevant to be of use to you. A book may have a chapter or section focused on the topic you are researching, even if other chapters or sections are irrelevant. The table of contents can lead you to a relevant chapter or section, and the index can lead you to relevant pages. Once you find potentially useful material, read it with your research question (see 8b) in mind.

CHECKLIST for Establishing Relevancy

- Does the table of contents, index, or directory of the work include key words related to your research question?
- Does the abstract of a journal article contain information on your topic?
- If an abstract is not available, are any of the article's topic sentences relevant to your research question?
- Do the section heads of the source include information connected to your topic?

Using Sources Responsibly

To benefit from the sources you discover through research (see chapter 8), you must be able to preview efficiently (see **1c**) and to evaluate what you read (chapter **9**). Reading the directory of a Web site or the index of a book can help you decide which parts of the source to consult first. Whether a source appears in print or online, you can get a sense of its content by scanning section heads and topic sentences (see **3c(1)**). When you find ideas or information relevant to your research question (see **8b**), slow down and read critically (**1c–d**).

To write well using sources, you need to remember that you are a *writer*, not simply a compiler of data. *Yours* is the most important voice in a paper that has your name on it.

This chapter will help you

- determine the purpose of a research paper (**10a**),
- take notes accurately (**10b**),
- compose a working bibliography (**10c**),
- use direct quotations, paraphrase, or summarize (**10d**), and
- avoid plagiarism (**10e**).

To learn how to cite sources according to the rules established by different scholarly organizations and to read model research papers, see chapter **11**.

10a | A research paper makes or proves a point.

Like any other paper, a research paper must have a purpose—and that purpose must be appropriate for its audience and context. A research paper is more than a compilation of research findings or a list of works consulted (see **10c**). In a research paper, you build on what others have discovered. You do so by drawing these sources together in a conversation in which you play an essential role. That role is to bring a specific audience to a new understanding of the paper's topic. Accordingly, a research paper is either expository or argumentative. (See **1e**.)

When you discuss a research problem (see **8b**), your paper is **expository**; an expository paper explains

- the nature of the problem,
- its causes,
- its effects, or
- the way others are responding to it.

Your research paper is **argumentative** (see chapter 7) if it

- analyzes or questions a complicated issue,
- expresses or defends a point of view, or
- invites or convinces readers to consider another perspective or to make adjustments to their perspective.

Exposition and argumentation can overlap. You may need to explain the effects of a problem, for example, before you can convince readers to fix it. In other words, you may have more than one purpose, with the first serving to advance the second. As the writer of a research paper, you need to ask yourself, "What is the most important goal I want to achieve in this paper, and how can I best achieve that goal?" As you work toward fulfilling your purpose, be sure to present yourself as thoughtful and fair-minded. Whether your audience consists of a single instructor or some larger group, you must establish that you are a credible author (see **9a**). It is especially important to demonstrate that you have

- educated yourself about the topic,
- drawn accurately on the work of others (including diverse points of view),
- understood what you have discovered, and
- integrated research data into a paper that is clearly your own.

The rest of this chapter will help you fulfill these responsibilities.

10b Taking notes demands accuracy.

Taking good notes is an important skill both in the classroom and on the job. But this skill is especially critical when you are preparing to write a formal research paper in which you attribute specific words and ideas to others while taking credit for your own ideas. If you want to be a reliable note taker, choose a method of note taking that suits your individual learning style.

Some researchers are most comfortable taking notes in notebooks. Others like to write notes directly on pages they have photocopied or printed out from an online source (see 8c–d). Still others type notes directly in computer files or write them on index cards—two methods that allow notes to be rearranged easily. Each method has advantages and disadvantages, and your choice should be guided by the requirements of your project and your own work style.

(1) A ring binder can help you organize your notes.

A ring binder is an excellent organizational tool. When using one, you can combine pages of notes with photocopies or printouts of relevant source material. Moreover, you can add, remove, and rearrange material easily. Remember to identify the source on every page of notes and to use a fresh page for each new source. Be sure to distinguish direct quotations from paraphrases or summaries (see 10d), and keep your working bibliography (10c) separate from your notes.

(2) You can make notes on printouts and photocopies.

An easy way to take notes is to use printouts of sources from the Web (see 8c) or photocopies of articles and excerpts from books that you think you might quote directly. On a printout or photocopy, you can mark quotable material and jot down your own ideas. This method reduces the risk of including inaccurate quotations in your paper, because you have eliminated the step of copying quotes exactly as they appear in the original source. Printouts from the Web almost always indicate the source and the date of access, but you should also note the date on which the site was posted or last updated (see page 231). On photocopies, make sure to record the source if this information is not shown on what you have photocopied.

The example in figure 10.1 comes from the work Nicole Hester did for her research paper on the desegregation of the U.S. military (see 11f).

(3) You can keep notes organized in computer files.

You may find it efficient to use a computer for taking notes—recording them quickly and storing them safely. If you have a laptop, you can take it to the library or wherever you plan to work. Using a computer also makes it easy to copy and paste information into various files and ultimately into a draft of your paper.

It was the authors of the Declaration of Independence who stated the principles that all men are created equal in their rights, and that <u>it is to secure these rights that governments are instituted among men</u>.

= the purpose of gov't according to Truman

It was the authors of the Constitution who made it clear that, under our form of government, <u>all citizens are equal before the law</u>, and that the Federal Government has a duty to guarantee to every citizen equal protection of the laws.

= a radical idea for many Americans at the time

The Civil Rights Committee did more than repeat these great principles. It described a method to put these principles into action, and to make them a living reality for every American, regardless of his race, his religion, or his national origin.

background on the Civil Rights Committee link to Fahy

<u>When every American knows that his rights and his opportunities are fully protected and respected by the Federal, State, and local governments, then we will have the kind of unity</u> that really means something.

what Truman is after

Public Papers of the Presidents of the United States: Harry S. Truman, 1945–53, vol. 4 (Washington, D.C.: U.S. Government Printing Office, 1964), 923–5.

Figure 10.1. Photocopied source with notes.

Given the ease of computer use, it's important to remember to work slowly enough to digest the information in your sources so that you can use it effectively. It's also important to identify which records are direct quotations (see **10d(2)**), which are paraphrases (**10d(3)**), and which are your own thoughts. Following these two recommendations will help you derive as much benefit as possible from your sources while using them responsibly.

The tips in the following list can help you use your computer efficiently when taking and filing notes for a research paper.

- Create a separate master folder (or directory) for the paper.
- Create folders within the master folder for your bibliography, notes, and portions of drafts.
- Keep all the notes for each source in a separate file.
- Use a distinctive font or a different color to distinguish your own thoughts from the thoughts of others whom you are paraphrasing.
- Place direct quotations in quotation marks.
- When taking notes, record exactly where the information came from.
- When you discover new sources, add them to your working bibliography (see **10c**). Consider using the Annotation or Comment feature of your word-processing program to keep notes on sources you are using.

(4) Note cards are easy to arrange.

In the past, researchers usually took notes on index cards (also called three-by-five cards), which can still be useful if you are working in a library without your laptop or if you prefer handwritten notes that you can rearrange as your research proceeds.

If you are using this method, each card should show the author's name (and a short title for the work if the bibliography contains more than one work by that author) and the exact page number(s) from which the information is drawn. If you put no more than one note, however brief, on each card and a heading of two or three key words at the top, you can easily arrange your cards as you prepare to draft your paper.

Whatever method you use to create your notes, consider the questions in the following checklist.

CHECKLIST for Taking Notes

- Does every note clearly identify its source? Have you put the full bibliographic citation on the first page of every photocopy? Is the bibliographic information for every source accurate? Double-check to be sure.
- Have you taken down verbatim (that is, copied every word, every capital letter, and every punctuation mark exactly as it was in the origi-

nal) any useful passage you think you may quote? Have you been especially careful to put quotation marks around any words you copy directly? Failure to do so as you take notes may lead to unintended plagiarism (see 10d–e) when you draft your paper.

■ Have you used different fonts or different colors in computer files to make it easy to identify quoted text?

■ When a source has stimulated your thinking, have you identified both the source and the fact that the note is your own idea?

Exercise 1

Photocopy or print out an article you found using the research strategies discussed in 8c–d. Underline key passages, and make notes in the margins if possible. Then, while reading or rereading an assigned chapter in one of your textbooks, take notes in a notebook, in computer files, or on index cards. Review your notes with at least one classmate, and be prepared to discuss the advantages or disadvantages of the note-taking method you chose.

10c | A working bibliography lists sources.

A working, or preliminary, bibliography contains information (titles, authors, dates, and so on) about the materials you think you might use. Although you find sources (see chapter 8) and evaluate them (chapter 9) earlier in the research process—probably keeping informal lists and collecting printouts and photocopies as you do so—you will have a clearer sense of which sources you will actually draw on for your paper once you have taken notes (see 10b). If you have not already done so, this is a good time to draw these sources together into a single list.

Creating a working bibliography can help you evaluate the quality of your research. If you find that your most recent source is five years old, for example, or that you have relied exclusively on information from general-circulation magazines (see 8d(3)), you may need to find some other sources. If you find that you have gathered twenty sources for a ten-page paper, you probably need to weed some out by applying the evaluation criteria discussed in chapter **9**.

Some researchers find it convenient to put each bibliographic entry on a separate index card; this makes it easy to add or drop a card and to arrange the list alphabetically without recopying it. Others prefer to use a computer, which can sort and alphabetize automatically, making it easier to move material directly to the final draft.

It is also a good idea to follow the bibliographical format you have been instructed to use, consistently and right from the start. The bibliographic style of the Modern Language Association (MLA) is covered in **11a**, that of the American Psychological Association (APA) in **11c**, that from *The Chicago Manual of Style* (CMS) in **11e**, that of the Council of Science Editors (CBE/CSE) in **11g**, and that from *The Columbia Guide to Online Style* (COS) in **11i**. For each Web site you use, be sure to note the URL and the date on which you accessed the site—this information must be included in the finished bibliography that will accompany your paper or report.

E x e r c i s e 2

Prepare a working bibliography consisting of at least five sources you have already located. Use the bibliographic style from chapter **11** that is appropriate for the discipline in which you are conducting your research. Include all the necessary information about each source (this will vary, depending on the type of source being cited).

10d | Integrating sources fosters mastery of information.

Writers of research papers use sources in three ways: quoting the exact words of a source, paraphrasing those words, or summarizing them. With any of these methods, your writing will benefit if you are careful to integrate the material—properly cited, of course—into your own sentences and paragraphs. Whatever option you choose, be sure to use sources responsibly.

A research paper that consists primarily of material taken from other writers is unlikely to be effective even if the sources are carefully chosen (see chapter **8**) and meticulously cited (chapter **11**). Knowing how to evaluate sources (chapter 9) and take notes accurately (10b) is essential to research, but you must also understand how to integrate the information your research uncovers into a paper that is clearly your own. In a good paper, the sources support a thesis (see 2b) that has grown out of the writer's research. The sources do not obscure the writer's own ideas; they illuminate them.

(1) Writers introduce and discuss the sources they use.

When effective writers borrow material, they introduce it to readers by establishing the context from which the material came. For example, in a research paper about an advance in sports medicine, readers might find it useful to know that the author of a quotation praising a specific form of physical therapy is a Nobel laureate in physiology or medicine. A good way to introduce research is to use a phrase that indicates the importance of the information or your attitude toward it. The verbs in the following list are useful for integrating quoted, paraphrased, or summarized information with your own ideas.

Verbs for Integrating Research Information

acknowledge	complain	explain	reason
add	concede	express	refute
admit	conclude	find	reject
advise	concur	grant	remark
agree	confirm	illustrate	reply
allow	consider	imply	report
analyze	contend	insist	respond
answer	criticize	interpret	reveal
argue	declare	list	see
ask	deny	maintain	show
assert	describe	note	speculate
believe	disagree	object	state
charge	discuss	observe	suggest
claim	dispute	offer	suppose
comment	emphasize	oppose	think
compare	endorse	point out	write

Adding an adverb to one of the verbs in this list can emphasize your attitude toward the material you are introducing: *persuasively* argue, *briefly* discuss, *strongly* oppose. Although a paraphrase (see **10d(3)**) or a summary (**10d(4)**) should convey the content of what someone else has said in a neutral fashion, the language you use to introduce such material can reinforce your thesis and help readers understand your position.

As a general rule, anything worth quoting is worth discussing, and the longer the quotation, the greater your responsibility to discuss it. To use quoted material to your advantage, you need to indicate what is significant about the material (key terms, for instance), to interpret what the source is saying, or to indicate precisely how you agree or disagree with that position.

The examples of quotation, paraphrase, and summary presented in this section use the documentation style of the Modern Language Association (MLA), which is the style most frequently required for college English courses. For additional information on MLA style, see **11a–b**.

(2) Direct quotations draw attention to key passages.

Include a direct quotation in a paper only if

- you want to retain the beauty or clarity of someone's words,
- you need to reveal how the reasoning in a specific passage is flawed or insightful, or
- you plan to discuss the implications of what you quote.

Keep quotations as short as possible, and make them an integral part of your text. (For examples showing how this can be done, see **11b**, **11d**, and **11f**.)

Quote *accurately.* Any quotation of another person's words should be placed in quotation marks or, if longer than four lines, set off as an indented block. (See pages 315 and 363–366.) If you need to make any addition to or change in a quotation, place square brackets around the added or changed words.

> "In this role, he [Robin Williams] successfully conveys a diverse range of emotion."

If you want to omit part of a quotation, replace the deleted words with ellipsis points.

"Overseas markets . . . are critical to the financial success of Hollywood films."

When modifying a quotation, be sure not to alter its essential meaning. If the quoted material contains an error, insert *sic* (Latin for "thus" or "so") in square brackets after the word or phrase.

I giggled to myself at the only comment my teacher wrote on my paper: "Be sure to check your spelling and grammer [*sic*] before you turn in your final draft."

MLA style calls for parentheses instead of brackets when *sic* follows closing quotation marks.

Beyond the Rule

GETTING SICK OF *SIC*

Writers who use *sic* too frequently can seem more interested in identifying errors than in conveying meaningful thoughts. For more information on how to treat errors in quotations, visit www.harbrace.com.

Cite the exact source for any quotation. If you think your audience might be unfamiliar with a source, establish its authority the first time you refer to it. For example, the following sentence informs readers about Mike Rose's credentials, justifying him as a credible source.

Mike Rose, a nationally recognized authority on education, claims that learning is facilitated not by fear but by "hope, everyday heroics, the power and play of the human mind" (242).

The citation at the end of the quotation clearly establishes that the words came from page 242 of a work by Mike Rose; additional information about that work (such as the title, the publisher, and the city and date of publication) can be found in a list of works cited at the end of the paper. (See 11a.)

> **CHECKLIST for Using Direct Quotations**
>
> - Have you copied all the words accurately?
> - Have you copied all the punctuation accurately? (See **34d**.)
> - Have you followed a special format or used special spacing if required?
> - Have you used ellipsis points correctly to indicate anything you omitted? (See **35h**.)
> - Have you avoided using ellipsis points before quotations that are clearly only parts of sentences?
> - Have you used square brackets around anything you added to or changed in a direct quotation? (See **35g**.)
> - Have you used quotations sparingly? Using too many quotations suggests an inability to think independently or to synthesize material. Consider paraphrasing or summarizing the information instead.

(3) Paraphrasing enables you to convey another person's ideas in your own words.

A **paraphrase** is a restatement of someone else's ideas in approximately the same number of words. Paraphrasing allows you to demonstrate that you have understood what you have read; it also enables you to help your audience understand it. Paraphrase when you want to

- clarify difficult material by using simpler language,
- restate a crudely made point in more professional terms,
- use another writer's idea but not his or her exact words, or
- create a consistent tone (see **3a(3)**) for your paper as a whole.

Your restatement of someone else's words should honor two important principles. First, your version should be almost entirely in your own words, which should accurately convey the content of the original passage. Second, you must indicate where the paraphrase begins and ends. Adhering to these principles will improve your skills in critical reading (see **1c–d**) and demonstrate that you are in control of your material.

(a) Use your own words and sentence structure.

As you compare the source below with the paraphrases that follow, note the similarities and differences in both sentence structure and word choice.

Source   Cronon, William. "The Trouble with Wilderness." *Uncommon Ground: Toward Reinventing Nature*. New York: Norton, 1995. 80–81.

This, then, is the central paradox: wilderness embodies a dualistic vision in which the human is entirely outside the natural. If we allow ourselves to believe that nature, to be true, must also be wild, then our very presence in nature represents its fall. The place where we are is the place where nature is not.

Inadequate paraphrase

Here is the main problem: wilderness embodies a dualistic vision in which people have no place. When we convince ourselves that true nature must also be wild, then nature has no people in it. This means that we could never visit nature because as soon as we got to a natural place, it would no longer be natural (Cronon 80-81).

Adequate paraphrase

William Cronon has shown why it is problematic to associate "nature" with "wilderness." Wilderness refers to a place that is unspoiled by human presence. When we describe nature as wild, we are ultimately saying that people have no place in nature (80-81).

If you simply change a few words in a passage, you have not adequately restated it. You may be charged with plagiarism if the wording of your version follows the original too closely, even if you provide a page reference for the source. A page reference after an inadequate paraphrase acknowledges the source of the idea but not the extent of your debt to another writer's language.

(b) Maintain accuracy.

Any paraphrase must accurately maintain the sense of the original. If you unintentionally misrepresent the original because you did not understand it, you are being *inaccurate.* If you deliberately change the gist of what a source says, you are being *unethical.* Compare the original statements below with the paraphrases.

Source   Polsby, Daniel D. "Second Reading." *Reason* Mar. 1996: 33.

> Generally speaking, though, it must be said that even among enthusiasts who think about the Second Amendment quite a lot, there has been little appreciation for the intricate and nuanced way in which constitutional analysis is practiced, and has to be practiced, by judges and lawyers.

Inaccurate paraphrase

People who care about the Second Amendment don't really understand how hard judges and lawyers have to work (Polsby 33).

Unethical paraphrase

When writing about the Second Amendment, Daniel Polsby has claimed that nobody understands the issue as well as he does (33).

Accurate paraphrase

Daniel Polsby has claimed that public debate over the meaning of the Second Amendment seldom involves the kind of careful analysis that judges and lawyers have to practice when they try to interpret the Constitution (33).

Source   Doty, Mark. *Heaven's Coast.* New York: Harper, 1996. 159.

> We trivialize pain if we regard it as a preventable condition the spirit need not suffer. If we attempt to edit it out, will it away, regard it as our own creation, then don't we erase some essential part of the spirit's education? Pain is one of our teachers, albeit our darkest and most demanding one.

Inaccurate paraphrase

Pain can never be prevented. It is completely outside our control, but it makes us grow stronger (Doty 159).

Unethical paraphrase

Mark Doty argues that pain is the best teacher (159).

Accurate paraphrase

According to Mark Doty, pain cannot always be alleviated. In a spiritual sense, however, people can grow through suffering if they are willing to learn from what is happening to them (159).

(4) Summarizing enables you to convey ideas efficiently.

When you summarize, you condense the main point(s) of your source. Although a summary omits much of the detail the writer used in the original, it accurately reflects the essence of that writer's work. In most cases, then, a summary reports a writer's **main idea** (see **2b**) and the most important support given for it.

Whereas the length of a paraphrase (see **10d(3)**) is usually close to that of the original material, a summary is shorter than the material it reports. When you paraphrase, you restate another author's ideas in order to present or examine them in detail. When you summarize, you present just the gist of the author's ideas, without including background information and supporting details as well. Summaries can include short quotations of key phrases or ideas, but you must always enclose another writer's exact words in quotation marks when you blend them with your own.

Source   Kremmer, Christopher. *The Carpet Wars.* New York: Harper-Collins, 2002. 197.

> Iraq was once, like the United States today, a country of firsts. Sedentary society emerged in Mesopotamia around 5000 BC when people learned to plant, irrigate and harvest crops. Three thousand years before Christ, writing based on abstract symbols was invented to label the fruits of agricultural surplus. When a potter's wheel was turned on its side and hitched to a horse, modern transportation was born. It was where time was first carved into sixty minutes and circles into three hundred and sixty degrees. When in the ninth century the Arab caliph Haroun al-Rashid wanted to demonstrate his society's superiority over Europe, he sent Charlemagne a clock.

Summary

Iraq was once a center of innovation, where new methods of agriculture, transportation,

writing, and measurement were generated (Kremmer 197).

This example reduces six sentences to one, retaining the key idea but eliminating specific examples such as the clock. A writer who believes that the audience needs examples might decide to paraphrase the passage instead.

Whenever you are paraphrasing or summarizing, do not interject your own opinions into a restatement of ideas you are attributing to another writer. Be as objective as possible when restating material. You can convey your opinion of the material when introducing it (see pages 271–272) or when responding to it.

Exercise 3

Find a well-developed paragraph in one of your recent reading assignments. Rewrite it in your own words, varying the sentence structure of the original. Make your paraphrase approximately the same length as the original. Next, write a one-sentence summary of the same paragraph.

10e | Plagiarism is a serious offense.

Taking someone else's words or ideas and presenting them as your own leaves you open to criminal charges. In the film, video, music, and software businesses, this sort of theft is called **piracy**. In publishing and education, it is called **plagiarism** or **cheating**. Whatever it is called, it is illegal.

You may know of cases in which other students or colleagues have represented as their own words or ideas that they obtained elsewhere. People who plagiarize sometimes try to rationalize what they do by saying something like "It was accidental" or "Other people are doing it" or "My boss isn't really going to read this anyway." Such rationalizations are meaningless. They do not hold up under logical analysis (see 7h–i). If offered an opportunity to submit someone else's work as your own, do not compromise your integrity or risk your future.

Beyond the Rule

PLAGIARISM IN THE NEWS

If you follow the news, you may be aware of cases in which well-established writers have been accused of plagiarism. These stories demonstrate that plagiarism is not just an academic problem. For information about some of these cases, visit www.harbrace.com.

You would be putting yourself at a great disadvantage, though, if you avoided drawing on the work of others because you felt it was unsafe to do so. One purpose of this chapter is to help you use other writers' work responsibly so that you can enter into thoughtful conversation with them. The challenge is to ensure that your audience can distinguish among the different voices that have emerged through your research.

Honoring the principles discussed in this chapter will protect you from inadvertent plagiarism. There is, however, an act of plagiarism that is so blatant that no one could do it accidentally: submitting as your own an essay or paper written by someone else—obtained from a friend or a company that sells papers or simply downloaded from the Web. The way to avoid this kind of plagiarism is clear: *Never submit as your own a paper you did not write.*

Because the Web is such an extensive and easily accessible source of information, it has become a tool both for those who plagiarize and for those who try to prevent plagiarism. Although it is fairly easy to copy material from a Web site or even purchase a paper on the Web, it is just as easy for a teacher or employer to locate that same material on the Web and determine that it has been plagiarized. Many teachers routinely use Internet search tools such as Google (see 8c) or special services such as InSite (available from Heinle) if they suspect that a student has submitted a paper that was plagiarized.

Beyond the Rule

INTELLECTUAL PROPERTY

In some countries, anyone who has purchased a book can quote from it without citing the source or requesting permission. The rationale is that the person bought the words when he or she bought the book. People raised in one of those countries might get into trouble in the United States for following a practice that seemed normal to them. Similarly, some Americans believe that the words and ideas of others can be drawn on freely because they are part of a communal culture. However, even if there is a theoretical question as to whether words and ideas can be owned, anyone preparing to submit or publish a piece of writing in the United States should be mindful of this country's copyright laws. For more information about intellectual property, visit www.harbrace.com.

You must give credit for all information you use except common knowledge and your own ideas. **Common knowledge** includes well-known dates and other facts: "The stock market crashed in 1929." "Water freezes at 32 degrees Fahrenheit." It also includes information such as that reported in this sentence: "The *Titanic* sank on its maiden voyage." This event has been the subject of many books and movies, and some information about it has become common knowledge: The *Titanic* hit an iceberg, and many people died because the ship did not carry enough lifeboats. If, however, you are writing a research paper about the *Titanic* and wish to include the ship's specifications, such as its overall length and gross tonnage, you will be providing *un*common knowledge that must be documented. After you have read a good deal about a given subject, you will be able to distinguish between common knowledge and the distinctive ideas or interpretations of specific writers.

As for your own ideas, if you have been scrupulous about recording your own thoughts as you took notes, you should have little difficulty distinguishing between what you knew to begin with and what you learned through your research. When you use ideas or information provided by any other writer, be sure to provide appropriate documentation. To review how to draw responsibly on the words and ideas of others, consider the following examples.

Source   McConnell, Patricia B. *The Other End of the Leash.* New York: Ballantine, 2002. 142.

> Status in male chimpanzees is particularly interesting because it is based on the formation of coalitions, in which no single male can achieve and maintain power without a cadre of supporting males.

Undocumented copying

Male chimpanzees achieve status through the formation of coalitions, in which no single male can achieve and maintain power without a cadre of supporting males.

Undocumented paraphrase

By forming alliances with other male chimpanzees, a specific male can enjoy status and power.

Paraphrase with documentation

Patricia B. McConnell, an authority on animal training, notes that by forming alliances with other male chimpanzees, a specific male can enjoy status and power (142).

Whereas the first two examples lack documentation, the third includes not only the original author's name but also a parenthetical citation, which marks the end of the paraphrase and provides the page number on which the source can be found.

Quotation with documentation

Patricia B. McConnell, an authority on animal training, argues that male chimpanzees achieve status "based on the formation of coalitions, in which no single male can achieve and maintain power without a cadre of supporting males" (142).

Quotation marks show where the copied words begin and end, and the number in parentheses tells the reader the exact page on which those words appear. In this case, the sentence that includes the quotation identifies the author. An alternative is to provide the author's name within the parenthetical reference: (McConnell 142). If, after referring to the following checklist, you cannot decide whether you need to cite a source, the safest policy is to cite it.

CHECKLIST of Sources That Should Be Cited

- Writings, both published and unpublished
- Opinions and judgments not your own
- Statistics and other facts that are not widely known
- Images and graphics, such as works of art, drawings, charts and graphs, tables, photographs, maps, and advertisements
- Personal communications, such as interviews, letters, and email messages
- Public electronic communication, including television and radio broadcasts, motion pictures and videos, sound recordings, Web sites, and online discussion groups or forums

11

Citing Sources and Submitting Final Papers

When drafting and revising a research paper, acknowledge exactly where specific ideas and quotations in your paper have come from, and add a bibliography that provides detailed information about your sources. When editing a research paper (see **3f**), review your in-text citations and your bibliographic entries, making sure that you have followed the rules set forth by your instructor, your employer, or the appropriate professional organization.

This chapter will help you use

- MLA-style documentation (**11a–b**),
- APA-style documentation (**11c–d**),
- CMS-style documentation (**11e–f**),
- CSE/CBE-style documentation (**11g–h**), and
- COS-style documentation (**11i**).

In addition, three model research papers are included so that you can see different kinds of documentation within the context of writing.

 Many electronic sources, especially those on the Web, are relatively new and still evolving. Conventions for citing these sources are also evolving, so it can be difficult to know exactly how to cite information found in them. Because conventions change, the formats for electronic sources for all the documentation styles discussed in this chapter—MLA, APA, CMS, CSE/CBE, and COS—are periodically updated on the respective Web sites:

MLA   **www.mla.org**
APA   **www.apastyle.org**

CMS	www.press.uchicago.edu/Misc/Chicago/cmosfaq/cmosfaq.html
CSE/CBE	www.cbe.org
COS	www.columbia.edu/cu/cup/cgos/idx_basic.html

Different disciplines employ different documentation styles, so there is no single way to document sources or to prepare a bibliography that can be used in every academic or professional field. The manuals listed below discuss documentation formats in detail. If you are asked to use one of these manuals, look for it in your library's reference collection, and make sure that your notes and bibliography correspond exactly to the examples it provides.

Style Books and Manuals

American Chemical Society. *The ACS Style Guide: A Manual for Authors and Editors.* 2nd ed. Washington, D.C.: American Chemical Society, 1998.

American Institute of Physics. *AIP Style Manual.* 4th ed. New York: American Institute of Physics, 1990.

American Mathematical Society. *A Manual for Authors of Mathematical Papers.* Rev. ed. Providence, R.I.: American Mathematical Society, 1990.

American Medical Association. *American Medical Association Manual of Style.* 9th ed. Baltimore: Williams, 1997.

American Psychological Association. *Publication Manual of the American Psychological Association.* 5th ed. Washington, D.C.: American Psychological Association, 2001.

Council of Biology Editors. *Scientific Style and Format: The CBE Manual for Authors, Editors, and Publishers.* 6th ed. New York: Cambridge University Press, 1994.

Gibaldi, Joseph. *MLA Handbook for Writers of Research Papers.* 6th ed. New York: Modern Language Association of America, 2003.

Harvard Law Review. *A Uniform System of Citation.* 16th ed. Cambridge: Harvard Law Review, 1996.

Linguistic Society of America. *LSA Bulletin* (Dec. issue), annually.

Turabian, Kate L. *A Manual for Writers of Term Papers, Theses, and Dissertations.* 6th ed. Chicago: University of Chicago Press, 1996.

United States Geological Society. *Suggestions to Authors of the Reports of the United States Geological Survey.* 7th ed. Washington, D.C.: U.S. Government Printing Office, 1991.

United States Government Printing Office. *Style Manual.* Washington, D.C.: U.S. Government Printing Office, 2000.

University of Chicago Press. *The Chicago Manual of Style.* 14th ed. Chicago: University of Chicago Press, 1993.

Walker, Janice R., and Todd Taylor. *The Columbia Guide to Online Style.* New York: Columbia University Press, 1998.

11a | MLA-style documentation is required for papers submitted in English and other language or literature courses.

The Modern Language Association (MLA) supports teaching and scholarship in English and other languages spoken throughout the world. Its rules for documentation are used not only for literary analysis but also for research in composition studies.

Directory of MLA-Style Parenthetical Citations

(1) Parenthetical citations tell readers that a writer has drawn material from other sources.

Give proper credit by citing your sources. Traditionally, such citations took the form of notes numbered consecutively throughout the paper and placed either at the bottom of the appropriate page (**footnotes**) or all together at the end of the paper (**endnotes**). Although some disciplines still use a note system (see **11f** and **11i**), the MLA recommends placing citations in parentheses directly in the text. These parenthetical citations refer readers to a list of works cited at the end of the paper. The advantage of this system is that it is easy for both writers and readers to use. The MLA suggests reserving numbered notes for supplementary or explanatory comments. Superscript numbers are inserted in the appropriate places in the text, and the notes are gathered at the end of the paper. (For examples, see pages 313 and 321.)

The basic elements of the parenthetical citation are the author's last name and the page number of the material used in the source. However, it is not necessary to repeat any information that is already clearly provided. In other words, omit the author's name from the parenthetical citation if you have already mentioned it in the same sentence. For detailed information on parenthetical citation, study the following examples. See also the discussion of punctuation and mechanics that follows these examples (pages 290–292).

1. Work by one author

Set on the frontier and focused on characters who use language sparingly, Westerns often

reveal a "pattern of linguistic regression" (Rosowski 170).

In this citation, the author's name is included within the parentheses because it is not mentioned in the sentence. If there is only one work by Rosowski in the list of works cited, there is no need to place a title in the parentheses. Also included is a page number that directs readers to a specific page. Notice how the citation changes if the author's name does appear in the sentence.

Susan J. Rosowski argues that Westerns often reveal a "pattern of linguistic

regression" (170).

2. Work by two or three authors

Some environmentalists seek to protect wilderness areas from further development so that

they can both preserve the past and learn from it (Katcher and Wilkins 174).

Provide the last name of each author. Commas are necessary in a citation involving three authors, for example: (Bellamy, O'Brien, and Nichols 59).

3. Work by more than three authors

For a work by more than three authors, use either the first author's last name followed by the abbreviation *et al.* (from the Latin *et alii,* meaning "and others") or all the last names. (Do not italicize or underline the abbreviated Latin phrase.)

In one important study, women graduates complained more frequently about "excessive

control than about lack of structure" (Belenky et al. 205).

OR

In one important study, women graduates complained more frequently about "excessive

control than about lack of structure" (Belenky, Clinchy, Goldberger, and Tarule 205).

4. Multivolume work

When you cite material from more than one volume of a multivolume work, include the volume number (followed by a colon and a space) before the page number.

As Katherine Raine has argued, "true poetry begins where human personality ends"

(2: 247).

You do not need to include the volume number in the parenthetical citation if your list of works cited includes only one volume of a multivolume work.

5. More than one work by the same author

When your list of works cited includes more than one work by the same author, parenthetical citations of those works should include a shortened title that reveals which of them is being cited in a particular instance. Use a comma to separate the author's name from the shortened title when both are in parentheses. Underline the title.

According to Gilbert and Gubar, Elizabeth Barrett Browning considered poetry by women to be forbidden and problematic (Shakespeare's Sisters 107). That attitude was based on the conception that male sexuality is the "essence of literary power" (Gilbert and Gubar, Madwoman 4).

This passage cites two different books by the same authors. Sandra M. Gilbert and Susan Gubar wrote both *Shakespeare's Sisters: Feminist Essays on Women Poets* and *The Madwoman in the Attic: The Woman Writer and the Nineteenth-Century Literary Imagination.* Remember that the authors' names must appear in the citation if they are not mentioned earlier in the sentence.

You can often avoid cumbersome references by including information in the text that might otherwise have to appear parenthetically.

In both The Madwoman in the Attic and Shakespeare's Sisters, Sandra M. Gilbert and Susan Gubar argue that the infrequent appearance of women as literary figures is a result of the repression imposed by male sexuality.

In this case, no page numbers are necessary because reference is being made to an argument pervading both books. Titles and authors are clearly established in the sentence itself.

6. Works by different authors with the same last name

Occasionally, you will cite sources by two authors with the same last name—for example, rhetoricians Theresa Enos and Richard Enos. In such cases, use each author's first and last name.

Richard Enos includes a thirteen-page bibliography in Greek Rhetoric before Aristotle (141-54). In her collection of articles by prominent figures in modern rhetoric and philosophy, Professing the New Rhetorics, Theresa Enos mentions the considerable contemporary reliance on pre-Aristotelian rhetoric (25, 331-43).

In these references citing more than one page, "(141-54)" identifies continuous pages, and "(25, 331-43)" cites both a page and a set of pages.

7. Indirect source

If you need to include material that one of your sources quoted from another work and you cannot obtain the original source, use the following format (*qtd.* is the abbreviation for "quoted").

The critic Susan Hardy Aikens has argued on behalf of what she calls "canonical multiplicity" (qtd. in Mayers 677).

A reader turning to the list of works cited should find a bibliographic entry for Mayers (which was the source consulted) but not for Aikens (because the quotation was obtained indirectly).

8. Poetry, drama, and the Bible

When you refer to poetry, drama, or the Bible, you should give the numbers of lines, acts and scenes, or chapters and verses, rather than page numbers. This practice enables readers to consult an edition other than the one you have used.

Act, scene, and line numbers (all arabic) are separated by periods with no space before or after them. The MLA suggests that biblical chapters and verses be treated similarly, although some writers prefer to use colons instead of periods in such citations. In all cases, the progression is from larger to smaller units.

The following example illustrates a typical citation of lines of poetry.

Emily Dickinson concludes "I'm Nobody! Who Are You?" with a characteristically bittersweet stanza:

> How dreary to be somebody!
>
> How public, like a frog
>
> To tell your name the livelong June
>
> To an admiring bog! (lines 5-8)

Use *line* or *lines* in the parenthetical citation for the first quotation; subsequent quotations require only numbers.

Quotations of three or fewer lines of poetry can be placed in quotation marks and not set off as a block quotation. A slash with a space on each side indicates a line break.

The following citation shows that the famous "To be, or not to be" soliloquy appears in act 3, scene 1, lines 56–89 of *Hamlet.*

In <u>Hamlet</u>, Shakespeare presents the most famous soliloquy in the history of the English

theater: "To be, or not to be . . ." (3.1.56-89).

Biblical references identify the book of the Bible, the chapter, and the pertinent verses. In the following example, the writer refers to the creation story in Genesis, which begins in chapter 1 with verse 1 and ends in chapter 2 with verse 22.

The Old Testament creation story (Gen. 1.1-2.22), told with remarkable economy,

culminates in the arrival of Eve.

Names of books of the Bible are neither underlined (see chapter 38) nor enclosed in quotation marks (chapter 34). These books are frequently abbreviated (see chapter 39).

9. Sources produced for access by computer

Although electronic sources are treated differently from print sources in the list of works cited (see 11a(3)), many can be treated identically for parenthetical documentation in the text. For example, like a printed book, an online book could have both an author and page numbers.

If an electronic source does not have page numbers but uses another system of numbers, give those numbers. If paragraphs are numbered, cite the number(s) of the paragraph(s) after the abbreviation *par.* (for one paragraph) or *pars.* (for more than one). If a screen number is provided, cite that number after the word *screen* (or *screens* for more than one).

If an electronic source includes no numbers distinguishing one part from another, you should cite the entire source. In this case, to establish that you have not accidentally omitted a number, you can avoid using a parenthetical citation by providing what information you have within the sentence that introduces the material.

Raymond Lucero's Web site offers useful advice for consumers who are concerned about

transmitting credit card information over the Internet.

OR

Raymond Lucero's <u>Shopping Online</u> offers useful advice for consumers who are

concerned about transmitting credit card information over the Internet.

The Uniform Resource Locator (URL) for this site and additional information about it would be included in the list of works cited.

(2) MLA-style documentation calls for attention to punctuation, numbers, and placement.

(a) Punctuation

A comma separates the author's name from the title: (Brown, "Olivier's Richard III: A Reevaluation"). A comma also indicates an interruption in a sequence of pages or lines: (44, 47). A hyphen indicates continuous sequences of pages or lines: (44-47) or (1-4). A colon followed by one space separates volume and page numbers: (Raine 2: 247). Periods separate acts, scenes, and lines in drama: (3.1.56-89). A period distinguishes chapters from verses in biblical citations: (Gen. 1.1). No space follows the period.

Ellipsis points (see **35h**) indicate omissions within a quotation.

"They lived in an age of increasing complexity and great hope; we in an age of . . .

growing despair" (Krutch 2).

Brackets (see **35g**) enclose added words that are not part of the quoted material.

"The publication of this novel [Beloved] establishes Morrison as one of the most

important writers of our time" (Boyle 17).

When a question mark ends a quotation (see **34d**), place it before the closing quotation marks and add a period after the parenthetical citation.

Peter Elbow asks, "What could be more wonderful than the pleasure of creating or

appreciating forms that are different, amazing, outlandish, useless--the opposite of

ordinary, everyday, pragmatic?" (542).

(b) Numbers

The MLA favors arabic numbers in all citations, except for those referring to pages identified by roman numerals in the source itself (such as a page in the front matter of a book: Garner ix).

(c) Placement of citations

Wherever possible, place a citation right before a punctuation mark.

Richard Enos provides a bibliography of sources for the study of Greek rhetoric before

Aristotle (141-54), and Theresa Enos's edited collection, <u>Professing the New Rhetorics,</u>

includes Michael Halloran's essay "On the End of Rhetoric, Classical and Modern" (331-43).

The citation for Richard Enos's work falls just before a comma; that for Theresa Enos's work is just before a period. However, in a sentence such as the following, the citations follow the authors' names to keep the references separate.

Richard Enos (141-54) and Theresa Enos (25) address classical rhetoric from very

different perspectives.

(d) Lengthy quotations

When a quotation is more than four lines long, set it off from the text by indenting one inch (or ten spaces) from the left margin. Double-space the quotation. When you are quoting two or more paragraphs, indent each paragraph an extra quarter of an inch (or three spaces). Do not indent the first line of a single quoted paragraph. A colon may introduce a long quotation if the quotation is not an integral part of the structure of the preceding sentence.

In <u>Nickel and Dimed</u>, Barbara Ehrenreich describes the dire living conditions of the

working poor:

> The lunch that consists of Doritos or hot dog rolls, leading to faintness
>
> before the end of the shift. The "home" that is also a car or a van. The
>
> illness or injury that must be "worked through," with gritted teeth, because
>
> there's no sick pay or health insurance and the loss of one day's pay will
>
> mean no groceries for the next. These experiences are not part of a
>
> sustainable lifestyle, even a lifestyle of chronic deprivation and relentless
>
> low-level punishment. They are, by almost any standard of subsistence,
>
> emergency situations. And that is how we should see the poverty of millions
>
> of low-wage Americans--as a state of emergency. (214)

A problem of this magnitude cannot be fixed simply by raising the minimum wage.

Note that the period precedes the parenthetical citation at the end of an indented quotation.

(3) A complete list of the sources used in a paper helps readers locate and evaluate them.

For MLA-style papers, the list of sources from which you have cited information is called **Works Cited.** (Other documentation styles differ from the MLA style in the name and arrangement of the reference list—see **11c, 11e,** and **11g.**) The works cited list appears at the end of the paper.

When you are ready to produce your final draft, you need to prepare the list of works cited. Eliminate from your working bibliography (see **10c**) any sources that you did not use, and include only those sources for which there are citations in your paper. If you consulted a source but did not cite anything from it, it should not appear on the works cited list.

TIPS FOR PREPARING A LIST OF WORKS CITED

- Arrange the list of works alphabetically by author.
- If a source has more than one author, alphabetize by the last name of the first author.
- Type the first line of each entry flush with the left margin and indent subsequent lines one-half inch or five spaces (a hanging indent).
- Double-space throughout.

As you study the following MLA-style entries, which cover most of the types of sources you are likely to use, observe both the arrangement of information and the punctuation.

> **Directory of MLA-Style Entries for the Works Cited List**

BOOKS

ARTICLES

SOURCES VIEWED OR HEARD

SOURCES PRODUCED FOR ACCESS BY COMPUTER

BOOKS

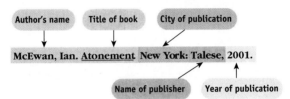

Author's name | Title of book | City of publication

McEwan, Ian. <u>Atonement</u> New York: Talese, 2001.

Name of publisher | Year of publication

Most book entries consist of three units separated by periods:

1. *Author.* Place the last name first, following it with a comma, the first name, and a period.

2. *Title.* Underline the title of the book, and capitalize all major words. (See **37c**.) Always include a book's subtitle if it has one. Use a colon to separate a main title and a subtitle. Make underlining continuous, not separate under each word. Do not underline the final punctuation mark.

3. *Publication data.* Provide the city of publication, a shortened form of the publisher's name, and the latest copyright date shown on the copyright page. If more than one city is listed on that page, mention only the first. Use a colon after the city and a comma after the publisher. (To shorten the name of the publisher, use the principal name: Alfred A. Knopf becomes Knopf; Random House becomes Random. For books published by university presses, abbreviate *University* and *Press* without periods: Harvard University Press becomes Harvard UP.)

1. Book by one author

Halberstam, David. <u>Firehouse</u>. New York: Hyperion, 2002.

2. More than one work by the same author

Angelou, Maya. <u>A Brave and Startling Truth</u>. New York: Random, 1995.

---. <u>Kofi and His Magic</u>. New York: Potter, 1996.

If you use more than one work by the same author, alphabetize the works by the first major word in each title. Give the author's name with the first title, but substitute three hyphens followed by a period for the name in subsequent entries.

3. Book by two authors

West, Nigel, and Oleg Tsarev. <u>The Crown Jewels: The British Secrets at the Heart of the</u>
<u>KGB Archives</u>. New Haven: Yale UP, 1999.

Invert the name of the first author, and place a comma after it. Do not invert the second name.

4. Book by three authors

Spinosa, Charles, Ferdinand Flores, and Hubert L. Dreyfus. <u>Disclosing New Worlds:</u>
<u>Entrepreneurship, Democratic Action, and the Cultivation of Solidarity</u>.
Cambridge: MIT P, 1997.

List all three authors in the same sequence used on the title page of the book.

5. Book by more than three authors

When a book has more than three authors, MLA style allows writers either to give all names in full as they appear on the title page or to use the abbreviation *et al.* (for *et alii,* meaning "and others") after the name of the first author.

Quirk, Randolph, Sidney Greenbaum, Geoffrey Leech, and Jan Svartvik. <u>A</u>
<u>Comprehensive Grammar of the English Language</u>. London: Longman, 1985.

OR

Quirk, Randolph, et al. <u>A Comprehensive Grammar of the English Language</u>. London:
Longman, 1985.

6. Book by a corporate author

Institute of Medicine. <u>Blood Banking and Regulation: Procedures, Problems, and</u>
<u>Alternatives</u>. Washington: Natl. Acad., 1996.

Alphabetize by the first major word in the corporate name. Omit any initial article (*a, an,* or *the*) from the name.

7. Book by an anonymous author

<u>Primary Colors: A Novel of Politics</u>. New York: Warner, 1996.

Begin the entry with the title. Do not use *Anonymous* or *Anon.*

8. Book with an editor instead of an author

Kachuba, John B., ed. <u>How to Write Funny</u>. Cincinnati: Writer's Digest, 2000.

9. Edition after the first

Murray, Donald. <u>The Craft of Revision</u>. 4th ed. Boston: Heinle, 2001.

10. Work from an anthology (a collection of articles or other writings by different authors)

Bishop, Wendy. "Students' Stories and the Variable Gaze of Composition Research."
<u>Writing Ourselves into the Story: Unheard Voices from Composition Studies</u>. Ed.
Sheryl I. Fontane and Susan Hunter. Carbondale: Southern Illinois UP, 1993.
197-214.

Use this form for an article or essay that was first published in an anthology, as well as for a story, poem, or play reprinted in an anthology.

For an article or essay that was published elsewhere before being included in an anthology, use the following form.

Chaika, Elaine. "Grammars and Teaching." <u>College English</u> 39 (1978): 770-83. Rpt. in
<u>Linguistics for Teachers</u>. Ed. Linda Miller Cleary and Michael D. Linn. New
York: McGraw, 1993. 490-504.

Note where the essay first appeared; then show where you read it. Use the abbreviation *Rpt.* for "reprinted."

Both of these forms require that you cite the complete range of pages on which the article or essay can be found, not just the pages from which you borrowed material. In the second form, you must cite both the pages of the original publication (770-83 in this case) and the pages of the anthologized version (490-504).

11. Translated book

Garrigues, Eduardo. <u>West of Babylon</u>. Trans. Nasario Garcia. Albuquerque: U of New
    Mexico P, 2002.

12. Republished book

Alcott, Louisa May. <u>Work: A Story of Experience</u>. 1873. Harmondsworth, Eng.: Penguin,
    1995.

The original work was published over a century before this paperback version. Use this form for books—even relatively recent ones—that have been reissued in a new format.

13. Multivolume work

Nowak, Ronald M. <u>Walker's Mammals of the World</u>. 2 vols. Baltimore: Johns Hopkins
    UP, 1991.

Cite the total number of volumes in a work when you have used material from more than one volume. If you use only one volume, include that volume's number (preceded by the abbreviation *Vol.*).

Browning, Robert. <u>The Complete Works of Robert Browning: With Variant Readings</u>
    <u>and Annotations</u>. Ed. John C. Berkey and Allan C. Dooley. Vol. 6. Athens: Ohio
    UP, 1996.

14. Reference book

Dreyer, Edward L. "Inner Mongolia." <u>Encyclopedia of Asian History</u>. Ed. Ainslee T.
    Embree. 4 vols. New York: Scribner's, 1988.

When the author of an article in an encyclopedia is indicated only by initials, check the table of contents for a list of contributors. When an article is anonymous, begin the entry with the article title; alphabetize the entry according to the first important word in the title.

Full publication information is not necessary for a well-known reference work organized alphabetically. Begin with the article title when the author is not identified.

Petersen, William J. "Riverboats and Rivermen." <u>The Encyclopedia Americana</u>. 1999 ed.

When citing a specific dictionary definition for a word, use the abbreviation *Def.* (for "Definition"), and indicate which one you used.

"Reactive." Def. 2a. <u>Merriam-Webster's Collegiate Dictionary</u>. 10th ed. 2001.

15. Book in a series

Kelly, Richard Michael, and Barbara Kelly. <u>The Carolina Watermen: Bug Hunters and Boat Builders</u>. Twayne English Author Ser. 577. Winston-Salem: Blair, 1993.

When citing a book that is part of a series, provide the name of the series and, if one is listed, the number designating the work's place in it.

16. Introduction, preface, foreword, or afterword to a book

Elbow, Peter. Foreword. <u>The Peaceable Classroom</u>. By Mary Rose O'Reilley. Portsmouth: Heinemann, 1993. ix-xiv.

Begin with the author of the introduction, preface, foreword, or afterword. Include the name of the book's author after the title. Note the pages at the end, using roman numerals if these are used in the work.

17. Pamphlet or bulletin

<u>Stucco in Residential Construction</u>. St. Paul: Lath & Plaster Bureau, 2000.

If the pamphlet has an author, begin with the author's name (last name first), as you would for a book.

18. Government publication

United States. Office of Management and Budget. <u>A Citizen's Guide to the Federal Budget</u>. Washington: GPO, 1999.

When citing a government publication, identify the government body (e.g., United States, Minnesota, Great Britain, or United Nations) and the agency that issued the work. Underline the title of a book or pamphlet. Indicate the city of publication. Federal publications are usually printed by the Government Printing Office (GPO) in Washington, D.C., but be alert for exceptions.

When the name of an author or an editor appears on a government publication, insert that name after the title and introduce it with the word *By* or the abbreviation *Ed.* to describe the person's contribution.

ARTICLES

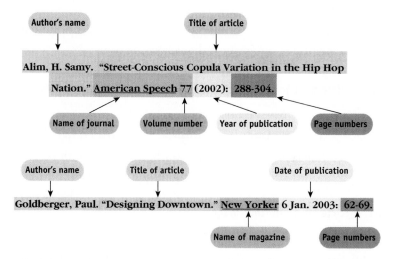

The documentation format for articles differs slightly from that for books. The three units are the same, and they are still separated by periods. Notice the differences in format for title and publication information.

1. *Author.* Place the last name first, following it with a comma, the first name, and a period.

2. *Article title.* Put the article title in quotation marks with the period inside the closing quotation marks. Capitalize all major words in the title, including the first and last word. (See 37c.)

3. *Publication data.* The publication information differs somewhat according to the type of periodical, but all entries provide the periodical title, the date of publication, and the page numbers on which the article appeared. Continuously underline the periodical title, and capitalize all major words. (See 37c.) Note that no punctuation follows the periodical title and that a colon introduces the inclusive page numbers. If a periodical entry requires both a volume number and a date, put the date in parentheses.

19. Article in a journal with continuous pagination

A **journal** is a scholarly publication written for a specific discipline or profession; a **magazine** is written for the general public.

Nair, Supriya. "The Caribbean Unbound: Cross-Atlantic Discourses on Slavery and

Race." <u>American Literary History</u> 14 (2002): 566-79.

Citing a specific issue (e.g., Fall 2002) is not necessary when a journal's pages are numbered continuously throughout the year.

20. Article in a journal with each issue paginated separately

Andrews, William L. "Postmodern Southern Literature: Confessions of a Norton

Anthologist." <u>Studies in the Literary Imagination</u> 35.1 (2002): 105-12.

When an issue is paginated separately (each issue begins with page 1), put a period after the volume number and add the issue number.

21. Article in a monthly magazine

Keizer, Garret. "How the Devil Falls in Love." <u>Harper's</u> Aug. 2002: 43-51.

In MLA style, the names of months (except for May, June, and July) are abbreviated. Volume numbers are unnecessary because specific dates are given. A period goes between the last word in the title and the closing quotation marks, unless the title ends with a question mark or an exclamation point, which makes an additional punctuation mark redundant. A space (without punctuation) separates the name of the magazine from the date of issue.

Magazine articles are often interrupted by advertisements or other articles. If the first part of an article appears on pages 45–47 and the rest on pages 92–94, give only the first page number followed by a plus sign: 45+.

22. Article in a weekly magazine or newspaper

Klotowitz, Alex. "The Trenchcoat Robbers." <u>New Yorker</u> 8 July 2002: 34-39.

Laing, Jonathan R. "The Bear That Roared." <u>Barrons</u> 28 Jan. 2002: 18-20.

23. Article in a daily newspaper

Moberg, David. "The Accidental Environmentalist." <u>Chicago Tribune</u> 24 Sept. 2002,

final ed., sec. 2: 1+.

When it is not part of the newspaper's name, the name of the city where the newspaper is published should be given in brackets after the title: *Star Tribune* [Minneapolis]. If a specific edition is not named on the masthead, put a colon after the date and then provide the page reference. Specify the section by inserting the section number or letter immediately before the page number, just as it appears in the newspaper (A7 or 7A, for example). When an article is continued elsewhere in the section (but not on the next page), add + to the page number to indicate this continuation.

24. Editorial in a newspaper or magazine

Beefs, Anne. "Ending Bias in the Human Rights System." Editorial. <u>New York Times</u>
    22 May 2002, natl. ed.: A27.

If the editorial is not signed, begin the entry with the title.

SOURCES VIEWED OR HEARD

25. Film

<u>My Big Fat Greek Wedding</u>. Dir. Joel Zwick. IFC, 2002.

The company that produced or distributed the film (IFC in this case) appears right before the date of release. It is not necessary to cite the city in which the production or distribution company is based.

When you want to highlight the contribution of a specific person rather than citing the film in general, put the person's name first. Other information can be included immediately after the title.

Gomez, Ian, perf. <u>My Big Fat Greek Wedding</u>. Screenplay by Nia Vardalos. Dir. Joel
    Zwick. IFC, 2002.

26. Radio or television program

"'Barbarian' Forces." <u>Ancient Warriors</u>. Narr. Colgate Salsbury. Dir. Phil Grabsky.
    Learning Channel. 1 Jan. 1996.

When referring to a specific episode, place quotation marks around its title. Underline the title of the program.

Finch, Nigel, dir. <u>The Lost Language of Cranes</u>. By David Leavitt. Prod. Ruth Caleb.

    Great Performances. PBS. WNET, New York. 24 June 1992.

To highlight a specific contributor, begin the entry with that person's name.

27. Play performance

<u>Proof</u>. By David Auburn. Dir. Daniel Sullivan. Walter Kerr Theater, New York. 8 Oct.

    2002.

Cite the date of the performance you attended.

28. Musical composition

Puccini, Giacomo. <u>Turandot</u>.

Rachmaninov, Sergei. Symphony no. 2 in E minor, op. 27.

Begin the entry with the name of the composer and the composition. When the composition is unnamed, use the number given to it by the composer (Symphony no. 2). Add the key when it has been specified by the composer (E minor), and conclude with the work number if available (op. 27 for "opus 27").

    However, if you are citing the published score of a musical composition, treat it like a book. Capitalize the abbreviations *no.* and *op.* when they are part of the title. Add the city of publication, publisher's name, and date of publication.

29. Sound recording on compact disc

Franklin, Aretha. <u>Amazing Grace: The Complete Recordings</u>. Atlantic, 1999.

Provide the full title of the compact disc, including the subtitle. For other kinds of sound recordings, identify the type (*Audiocassette* or *LP*).

Raitt, Bonnie. <u>Nick of Time</u>. Audiocassette. Capitol, 1989.

    When citing a recording of a specific song, begin with the name of the performer, and place the song title in quotation marks. Identify the author(s) after the song title. If the performance is a reissue from an earlier recording, provide the original date of recording (preceded by *Rec.* for "Recorded").

Horne, Lena. "The Man I Love." By George Gershwin and Ira Gershwin. Rec. 15 Dec.

    1941. <u>Stormy Weather</u>. BMG, 1990.

30. Lecture or presentation

Perl, Sondra. "Writing the Unwritten." Conf. on Coll. Composition and Communication
    Convention. Palmer House, Chicago. 21 Mar. 2002.

Scheiber, Andrew. Class lecture. English 215. Aquinas Hall, U of St. Thomas, St. Paul.
    30 Apr. 2003.

Identify the site and the date of the lecture or presentation. Use the title
if available; otherwise, provide a descriptive label.

31. Interview

Furstenheim, Ursula. Personal interview. 16 Jan. 2003.

Sugo, Misuzu. Telephone interview. 20 Feb. 2003.

Use these forms for interviews you have conducted, giving only the
name of the person you interviewed. If the interview was conducted by
someone else, add the name of the interviewer, as well as a title, if there
is one, and the name of the source.

Harryhausen, Ray. Interview with Terry Gross. <u>Fresh Air</u>. Natl. Public Radio. WHYY,
    Philadelphia. 6 Jan. 2003.

SOURCES PRODUCED FOR ACCESS BY COMPUTER

The information required to cite sources such as software programs or
databases that can be distributed on CD-ROM or other disks and the
information required to cite online sources differ in two important ways.
Citations for CD-ROM and other disks generally should identify the
publisher, the place, and the date of publication. Citations for information obtained online should state the Web address and the date of access.

    The main reason for citing any source is to give readers enough in-
formation so that they can consult the source on their own. Because electronic sources change more frequently than print sources do, the date
given for the creation or latest modification of a Web site and the date
on which you accessed it are both important. Further, because sites may
disappear overnight, it is wise to print out a hard copy of any site you use
as a source.

    The sixth edition of the *MLA Handbook for Writers of Research Papers*
(2003) recognizes that electronic sources continue to evolve—as does the
style for citing them. Check the MLA's Web site (<u>www.mla.org</u>) for up-

dates on formats for citations of online sources. This much, however, is certain: You must provide the correct URL for any Web site you use. By providing your readers with a complete address, including the protocol, or access identifier (**http, ftp, telnet, news**), all punctuation marks, and both path and file names, you are telling them how to locate the source.

<http://stanfordmag.org.marapril99/>
<ftp://beowulf.engl.uky.edu/pub/beowulf>

Although it is also important to include other information, such as the author's name, the name of the site, and the date you accessed it, the complete Web address is essential. It substitutes for the publication data that help readers find print sources. Place the address within angle brackets, < >, so that it is clearly separated from any other punctuation in your citation. Divide the address after a slash when it does not fit on a single line. Make sure that the address is accurate. Web browsers (such as Netscape) distinguish between uppercase and lowercase letters in a URL, and they recognize marks such as hyphens and underscores. If you inadvertently substitute a lowercase letter for an uppercase one, the Web browser will not be able to access the site you want to locate. Also keep in mind that the addresses of Web sites often change, which means that addresses can become out of date without warning. For that reason, double-check the URLs for any Web sites you cite before submitting your work.

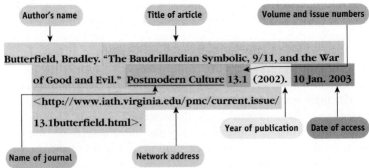

The information cited varies according to the type of online source. Arrange the information in the following sequence.

1. *Author.* Place the last name first, following it with a comma, the first name, and a period.

2. *Work title.* Capitalize all major words in the title, and either underline it or place it within quotation marks (see **34b**, **37c**, and **38a**). Begin with the title when there is no author.

3. *Publication data.* For online sources, include the date of publication, the name of the sponsoring organization, the date of access, and the URL. If the URL is extremely long, you may use the URL for the site's search page instead. If there is no search page, cite the document's home page, following it with the word *Path,* a colon, and the sequence of links you used. Separate the links with semi-colons. For a CD-ROM or diskette, include the city where the work was published, the name of the manufacturer, and the date of issue.

32. Online book

Ford, Jeffrey. <u>The Empire of Ice Cream</u>. 2003. <u>Scifi.com</u>. 2003. 28 Feb. 2003

ittp://www.scifi.com/originals/originals_archive/ford4/>.

In this case, the work was published in 2003 and accessed on February 28, 2003. Providing the date of publication tells readers how long the source has been available. Providing the date of access indicates how recently the site was still available, as well as the precise version used (since 'ine sources can be updated after publication).

33. Article in an online journal

Harnack, Andrew, and Gene Kleppinger. "Beyond the <u>MLA Handbook</u>: Documenting

Sources on the Internet." <u>Kairos</u> 1.2 (1996). 14 Aug. 1997 <http://www.english.ttu/

acw/kairos/index.html>.

The date of access follows the date of publication.

34. Article in an online magazine

Plotz, David. "The Cure for Sinophobia." <u>Slate</u> 4 June 1999. 4 June 1999

<http://www.slate.com/StrangeBedfellow/99-06-03/StrangeBedfellow.asp>.

Give the date of access after the date of publication, even if you consult the source the same day it is posted.

35. Article in an online newspaper

"Tornadoes Touch Down in S. Illinois." <u>New York Times on the Web</u> 16 Apr. 1998. 20

May 1998 <http://www.nytimes.com/aponline/a/AP-Illinois-Storms.html>.

When no author is identified, begin with the title of the article.

36. Review in an online newspaper

Koeppel, Fredric. "A Look at John Keats." Rev. of <u>Keats</u>, by Andrew Motion. <u>Nando</u>
<u>Times News</u> 16 Apr. 1998. 27 Aug. 1998 <http://www.nando.net/newsroom/
ntn/enter/ 041698/enter30_20804.html>.

37. Online government publication

United States. Dept. of State. Bur. of Democracy, Human Rights, and Labor. <u>Guatemala</u>
<u>Country Report on Human Rights Practices for 1998</u>. Feb. 1999. 1 May 1999
<http://www.state.gov/www/global/human_rights/1998_hrp_report/guatemal.html>.

Begin with the government responsible for the publication and the department or agency that issued it. If a subdivision of the larger organization is responsible, name that subdivision. If an author is identified,
provide the name between the title and the date of issue. Place the word
by before the name.

38. Online work of art

Vermeer, Johannes. <u>Young Woman with a Water Pitcher</u>. c. 1660. Metropolitan Museum
of Art, New York. 2 Oct. 2002 <http://www.metmuseum.org/collection/
view1.asp?dep=11&item=89%2E15%2E21>.

Place the date of the painting, sculpture, or photograph immediately after its title. If the precise date is not known, use the abbreviation *c.* (for
circa) to indicate an approximate date. Include the date of access after
the name and location of the institution or organization making the
work available for viewing.

39. Online map

"Virginia 1624." Map. <u>Map Collections 1544-1996</u>. Library of Congress. 26 Apr. 1999
<http://memory.loc.gov/cgibin/map_mp/~ammmem_8kk3::&title=Virginia++>.

Include the word *Map* followed by a period immediately after the map's
title.

40. Email

An email message is treated like a personal letter or memo. Provide the
name of the writer, a description of the message (usually the subject

line), and the name of the receiver (or use *the author* when the message is one you received directly). Conclude the message with the date. (Note that *e-mail* is hyphenated in MLA style.)

Peters, Barbara. "Scholarships for Women." E-mail to Rita Martinez. 10 Mar. 2003.

41. Discussion group or forum

Whenever possible, cite an archived version of a posting to an online discussion group or forum to make it easier for your readers to find the source.

Schipper, William. "Re: Quirk and Wrenn Grammar." Online posting. 5 Jan. 1995.

Ansaxnet. 12 Sep. 1996 <http://www.mun.ca/Ansaxdat/>.

Identify the name of the forum (in this case, Ansaxnet, a group of scholars interested in England before 1100 A.D.) between the date of posting and the date of access.

42. Newsgroup

May, Michaela. "Questions about RYAs." Online posting. 19 June 1996. 29 June 1996

<news:alt.soc.generation-x>.

Newsgroups are open forums, unconfined by a subscription list. Most have no moderator to ensure the quality of the postings, and messages are not usually retrievable after a few weeks. Ask whether your instructor wants you to make the source retrievable by including the email address of the person who posted the item or by printing out the posting.

43. Synchronous communication

To cite a synchronous communication, include the writer's name, event description, original date, forum (e.g., MediaMOO), access date, and URL.

Galin, Jeff. Netoric's Tuesday Café discussion "Teaching Writing in the Digital Age:

What Makes Teaching Good These Days?" 10 Sept. 1996. MediaMOO. 10 Sept.

1996 <telnet://purple-crayon.media.mit.edu/8888>.

If the discussion is archived, substitute the URL of the archive for that of the forum itself.

Galin, Jeff. Netoric's Tuesday Café discussion "Teaching Writing in the Digital Age:

What Makes Teaching Good These Days?" 10 Sept. 1996. MediaMOO. 12 Sept.

1996 <http://www.cs.bsu.edu/homepages/siering/netoric.html>.

44. CD-ROM

For a source on CD-ROM, provide the author (if available), title, publication medium, place of publication, publisher, and publication date.

"About Richard III." Cinemania 96. CD-ROM. Redmond: Microsoft, 1996.

45. Publication in more than one medium

English Poetry Plus. CD-ROM, diskette. New York: Films for the Humanities and

Sciences, 1995.

> **11b** | Studying a sample paper can help you learn the MLA style guidelines.

Although all good writing requires attention to detail, a research paper requires extra attention to ensure that sources are cited accurately and responsibly (see chapter 10). When preparing the final draft of an MLA-style paper, you must also check to make sure that you have adhered to MLA conventions for punctuation (see page 290) and documentation (see 11a).

(1) Submit a title page only if one is required.

The MLA recommends omitting a title page and instead providing the identification on the first page of the paper (see page 311). Some instructors require a final outline with a paper; this serves as a table of contents. If you are asked to include an outline, prepare a title page as well. A title page usually provides the title of the paper, the author, the instructor's name, the name of the course with its section number, and the date—all centered on the page.

A sample title page is shown in figure 11.1.

Starbucks in Vienna: Coffee Cultures at a Crossroad

Andy Pieper

English 299, Section 1
Professor Miller
27 November 2002

Figure 11.1. Sample title page for MLA-style paper.

(2) Studying a sample MLA-style paper prepares you for writing your own.

Interested in the effects of globalization, Andy Pieper decided to focus his paper on what happens when Starbucks opens coffee shops overseas. As you study his paper, notice how he develops his thesis, considers more than one point of view (see 7e(2)), and observes the conventions for an MLA-style paper.

COMMENTS

A. All pages (including the first one) are numbered with an arabic numeral in the upper right-hand corner, one-half inch from the top. The page number is preceded by the author's last name. Notice that no period follows the page number.

B. The name of the author, the name of the professor, the course number, and the date of submission—appearing in that order—begin one inch from the top of the page and flush with the left margin. A margin of one inch is provided at the left, right, and bottom.

C. Double-space between the heading and the centered title of the paper and also between the title and the first line of the text. (A title consisting of two or more lines is double-spaced, and each line is centered.)

D. Pieper provides background for his paper, establishing that Starbucks is part of a phenomenon that has economic and social consequences.

Andy Pieper   B

Professor Miller

English 299, Section 4

27 November 2002

Starbucks in Vienna: Coffee Cultures at a Crossroads   C

From St. Paul to Sao Paulo, from Rome to Riyadh, and from Johannesburg to Jakarta, world citizens are increasingly being pushed toward a global culture. We are being affected internationally through the media we experience, the food we eat, and the products we consume as multinational corporations act on a world stage (Rothkopf 38). People with disposable incomes can watch MTV in India, catch a Hollywood-produced movie in Australia, purchase a Mickey Mouse doll in Oman, use an Icelandic cell phone to call a friend in Malaysia, send an e-mail from an IBM computer in Russia, and purchase a bucket of Kentucky Fried Chicken in Japan.

All of these examples are signs of <u>globalization,</u> a term coined to describe the increasingly prominent role of large companies in the world marketplace. At the forefront of globalization is the multinational corporation, which David Korten, author of <u>When Corporations Rule the World</u>, defines as a business that takes "on many national identities, maintaining relatively autonomous production and sales facilities in individual countries, establishing local roots and presenting itself in each locality as a good local citizen" (125). Many of these multinationals originate and are headquartered in the United States or other Western nations, but they have means of production or outlets in countries all over the world.   D

Proponents of globalization claim that this process is advantageous because it makes business efficient and helps foster international ties. Opponents argue that local cultures are damaged and that globalization primarily benefits wealthy corporations in nations already rich. The Starbucks Coffee Corporation is one example of a multinational company involved in globalization. No matter what the long-term advantages or disadvantages of globalization prove to be, investigating how a Western company like

E. The thesis statement for this paper is placed where readers can easily locate it. The thesis statement for a paper can be placed anywhere, but readers usually expect to find it at the end of the first or second paragraph. The thesis for this paper emerged during the process of writing the paper. For earlier versions of this paper, visit www.harbrace.com.

F. A superscript numeral indicates that a note gives further information. The MLA recommends placing notes that provide explanation or additional information either at the bottom of the page or on a separate page at the end of the paper.

G. Pieper shows how Starbucks operates as a multinational corporation, building on the information he provided in the third paragraph. But he continues to emphasize the introduction of Starbucks into Viennese culture. He shows how his topic (Starbucks in Vienna) relates to a larger subject (globalization) so that readers can understand why the topic deserves attention.

Starbucks establishes itself overseas shows that a multinational corporation can succeed

in offering its own brand of culture, despite the strength or longevity of the local culture it

enters. The introduction of Starbucks to Vienna illustrates this point because Starbucks   E

offers an American-style coffee shop experience to a city that is already rich in its own

coffee traditions.

Throughout the 1990s, Starbucks sought to dominate the American coffee shop

market, and it succeeded. The company has skyrocketed since its stock debuted in 1992,

and within ten years went from revenues of $92 million to $2.6 billion at the end of fiscal

year 2001. Today, it has achieved status as an American brand that is nearly as familiar as

Coca-Cola and McDonald's. Starbucks has now expanded its goals to include leading the

world coffee shop market. With over 5,000 coffee shops already in operation--nearly

1,200 of which are located outside the United States--Starbucks hopes to reach revenues

of $6 billion by 2005 (Doherty 20). In order to accomplish this, the coffee corporation

intends to open an additional 5,000 stores worldwide (Scott 1). To reach its goals,

Starbucks will have to enter new markets in Africa, Asia, and the Middle East,[1] and   F

especially in Europe, where coffee is a staple of many countries. From the sidewalk cafés

of Paris to the espresso bars of Venice, Europeans have maintained a long love affair with

coffee--not only with the beverage itself, but also with their own coffeehouses. Therefore,

the continent represents both a challenge and an opportunity for Starbucks.

As part of its expansion plan, Starbucks had already opened European outlets in

Great Britain, Germany, and Switzerland by the time it opened a store in Vienna, the

capital of Austria, in the spring of 2002. Under this plan, Starbucks typically enters into a

joint-venture agreement with a local firm, initially holding a minority stake in the foreign

operation, usually twenty percent. This arrangement shields Starbucks from any large   G

losses incurred when stores are first opened. In this way, Starbucks presents itself as a

local company, when in fact it is a multinational with similar operations throughout the

globe. The local firm then sets up a few outlets, buying prime real estate and strategically

placing stores near symbols of historic and cultural significance[2]--as in Vienna, where

H. When referring to a work by three authors, Pieper correctly provides the last name for each.

I. Although the period follows the parenthetical citation in regular text, MLA style makes an exception for block quotations. For block quotations, indented one inch from the left margin, place the period before the parenthetical citation.

the first outlet opened across from the city's famous opera house. Once some success is accomplished, Starbucks buys enough of the foreign-owned branch to control the company, and proceeds to enlarge rapidly throughout the country (Burke, Smith, and   H
Wosnitza 47).

Vienna, considered by many to be the birthplace of the coffeehouse tradition, is legendary for its coffee culture. The first Viennese coffeehouses appeared after invading Turks left sacks of coffee outside the city walls as they fled in 1683 (Pendergast 10). Intellectual life abounded in elegant cafés by the nineteenth century, as they became meeting places for early modernists such as Sigmund Freud and Gustav Klimt, as well as for notable exiles such as Vladimir Lenin and Leon Trotsky. In Vienna, the people take pride in the history and enjoy the culture that surrounds the coffeehouse tradition. Austrians received the opening of Starbucks with mixed emotions:

> Many Viennese sniff that their culture has been infected, that Viennese use
> their 1,900 or so coffee shops to linger and meet, smoke and drink, savor the
> wonders of pastries with cream and marzipan, ponder the world, write books
> and read free newspapers. They drink from china cups and order from a
> waiter, usually in a stained black dinner jacket. (Erlanger B3)   I

Skeptics found it difficult to believe that an American brand such as Starbucks could survive in an environment steeped in its own local history of coffee and pride in its heritage, but these skeptics seem to have underestimated Starbucks.

There are several fundamental differences between the Starbucks experience and the traditional experience found in Viennese coffeehouses. Instead of ordering through a server, Starbucks patrons order at an American-style coffee bar. As opposed to more traditional offerings such as Sachertorte and hot goulash, Starbucks sells American-style sweets like blueberry muffins and chocolate-chip cookies. Furthermore, patrons are not allowed to smoke in any Starbucks outlet in order to allow the aroma of coffee to fill each store. Smoking, however, is a large part of the European coffeehouse experience.

These differences add up to two coffee cultures at a crossroads in Vienna. Traditional American offerings are pitted against the offerings of Viennese coffeehouses that have

J. Having decided to include a photo that illustrates the intersection of different coffee traditions in Vienna, Pieper analyzes the image so that it becomes an integral part of his paper—not just a decoration. The MLA does not require the use of images, but e-designing (see chapter 6) makes it easy for writers to include relevant graphics.

K. Ellipsis points indicate that Pieper has omitted words that can be found in the original source. (See page 319.)

L. Pieper reaches a well-balanced conclusion in keeping with what his research has shown. Without claiming that Starbucks is damaging the coffeehouse tradition in Vienna, he nevertheless notes that other American corporations are likely to succeed in overseas markets and that the long-term results of this trend cannot be predicted. (See page 319.)

Pieper 4

conducted business for centuries. Both Starbucks and independent Viennese coffeehouses sell good coffee, so the primary product being sold is fairly similar. But two essentially different aesthetic experiences and cultures are involved, and they now compete within the same locality. If Austrians had wanted the Starbucks experience previously, they would have had to seek it in other countries. Now, the Viennese cannot help but notice Starbucks. The two coffee cultures have thus become intertwined--competing against each other across not oceans, but streets.

Illustrating these differences is the picture at right of a ticket seller for the opera house across from the first Viennese Starbucks. On break from work, the man is dressed in aristocratic attire from the eighteenth century, but he is sipping his Starbucks coffee out of a paper cup rather than from the kind of china cup he would have received in a traditional Viennese coffeehouse. Moreover, he is smoking a cigarette outside instead of inside the store, as is customary in nearly all European coffeehouses. At first glance, this image appears harmless; it is a combination of new and old. Upon further

Photo courtesy of Roland Schlager.

examination, however, it is more than that. The Starbucks logo, the international symbol of the American company, hangs above the young man, with the angle of the photograph making him appear to be in a Starbucks advertisement. The similar color green in both the man's jacket and the Starbucks logo melts the two together even further. Also, the reflection of another man dressed in a business suit can be seen facing the subject of the photo, and looks to be walking straight toward him. The image can be interpreted as a sign of the times: Starbucks and its corporate chain of coffee shops, extending their reach and marching straight into the traditional independent cultures of other countries. The photograph also shows the apparent willingness of locals to embrace the products and service Starbucks provides even if it means abandoning a long-established cultural tradition of their own.

J

Starbucks has seen initial success in its Austrian operations with an estimated 100,000 patrons in its first two months of operation (Erlanger A1). This result is not uncommon since the market trend over the past decade has worked overwhelmingly in Starbucks' favor. The company has not failed in any of the markets into which it has introduced itself. A large part of the reason its expansion plans are on schedule in Europe is that Starbucks represents something different but nevertheless nonthreatening. In this case, a familiar product is being sold from one Western nation to another. The primary difference is in how that product is offered and what other products are offered along with it.

Starbucks also has played an inadvertent role in a movement that now exists throughout Europe, in which coffee shops are opening with an atmosphere noticeably reminiscent of Starbucks. Alwyn Scott, of the <u>Seattle Times</u> writes, "For proof of Starbucks' impact, look no further than its army of European imitators. New coffee chains are springing up with names--Chicago Coffee, San Francisco Coffee, Coffee Shop--that suggest American style, if not Seattle" (F1). Therefore, the traditional coffee cultures that reside in countries like Austria, France, and Italy compete with American culture from two fronts: Starbucks and Starbucks' imitators.

Competition alone is not necessarily bad. It is essential to capitalist economies. Without competition, there is no freedom of choice, and little innovation. People are left with the same options over and over again, while nothing new emerges. Free-market competition encourages companies to adapt to the changing needs and wants of populations. By opening stores in cities like Vienna, Starbucks could claim that it is simply offering the Viennese a choice that responds to their changing needs and that they are not compelled to accept this choice. It could even claim that it fosters diversity by increasing the options for consumers and creating an expanded coffee culture that includes not only the traditional coffeehouses but also the Americanized experience found in Starbucks and its imitators. However, Starbucks wields an immense amount of power in the regions where it establishes itself. This power is seen in its brand name--familiar from South Korea to Mexico--and in its wealth. Its coffee shops also present a powerful cultural experience, one that immerses the consumer in an American-style environment. By expanding its base to include countries all over the world, Starbucks is expanding the role of American culture abroad. This expansion diversifies the cultures of other countries, provides competition for existing coffee cultures, and offers new options to consumers. But, at some point, competition could become hegemony. In other words, the exportation of American culture occurs right along with the exportation of American products. Such expansion of American goods and services could overwhelm another culture, creating a more homogenous, Americanized culture that blurs the distinctiveness of the native one. Increasingly, foreign markets are becoming saturated with Western goods from multinational corporations, which have spread their products--whatever they may be--to places around the globe. Some suggest that this occurrence is working toward the establishment of a single global culture. According to Hugh Mackay, of the Open University, "that 'global culture' is not something which draws in any even or uniform way on the vast diversity of cultures in the world . . . but, rather, consists of the global dissemination of US or Western culture--the complete opposite of diversity" (60).

K

So far, Starbucks has been able to coexist with the traditional coffee culture in Vienna; the city's architecture, art, and beauty are likely to remain intact no matter how many stores Starbucks opens there. Because a relatively familiar product is passing from one Western nation to another in this case, and people have both the means to buy it and the freedom to reject it, cultural change may be limited to the Viennese getting used to drinking coffee out of paper cups and standing in the street to smoke. The social and economic effects of globalization may be more serious, as Mackay suggests, when multinational corporations operate in developing nations and limited means give people fewer choices. The lasting effects of globalization have yet to be seen. But it is clear that the already ubiquitous green mermaid, like the pervasive golden arches, is going to become even easier to find. And if Starbucks can flourish in an environment with a well-established local coffee culture of its own, then it is feasible that other multinational corporations will export not only their products but also the cultural experience that accompanies those products, no matter how strong the local culture may be.

L

M. Each note is coordinated with the related material in the text by a superscript number that matches the number used in the body of the paper. The number comes before the indented first line of the note. Although the MLA allows either footnotes (located on the bottom of the page) or endnotes (located on a separate page), Pieper has decided to use endnotes. He has centered the title "Notes" one inch from the top. Following MLA guidelines, he then double-spaces these notes, indenting them one-half inch (or five spaces) from the left margin.

Notes such as these provide writers with a way to present material they decide is too important to discard, even if they cannot incorporate it within the paper itself because they need to focus their ideas (see 2a(2)) and work within the length appropriate for a specific assignment. However, responsible writers do not use explanatory notes to preserve everything they decide to cut from their texts. Doing so could make excessive demands on the goodwill of their audience (see 1e(2)). When you add explanatory notes, remember that you are asking readers to turn away from your main text in order to make a side trip. Evaluate each of these detours by asking yourself whether they help you fulfill your rhetorical purpose (see 1e(1)).

Visit www.harbrace.com to see an earlier draft in which Pieper included a discussion of the Middle East and Asia in the body of the paper before deciding that he needed to narrow his focus.

N. When an online source does not include page numbers, writers cannot include a page reference within the parenthetical citation for it. (See page 289.)

Notes   M

[1]It should be noted that in Saudi Arabia, Starbucks, along with other multinational corporations, tries to conform to the existing cultural mores. Upon its introduction into Riyadh, Starbucks changed its logo (normally a crowned mermaid in a green circle) to one that did not include a depiction of a female since any representations of females are considered pornography (King, "Sellout"). In addition, stores make women enter through separate doors as well as drink their coffee in separate areas. The company has defended itself by stating, "While Starbucks adheres to the local customs by providing separate entrances, service and seating, all our stores provide equal amenities, service, menu and seating to both men and women" (King, "Arabia's" A27).

[2]In the fall of 2000, Starbucks opened an outlet in Beijing's Forbidden City, which was built early in the fifteenth century and listed as the world's largest imperial palace. Administrators of the site agreed to rent space to the Starbucks Chinese affiliate as a way of improving services. After news of the opening spread, a survey indicated that "over 70 percent of nearly 60,000 people surveyed were opposed to the café's entry . . . the main reason being the damaging effects to Chinese cultural heritage and its atmosphere" ("Starbucks").

     N

O. Center the title "Works Cited" one inch down from the top of the page, and double-space between this title and the first entry.

P. Include only those works you cited in the paper. If you consulted other sources but did not use them, do not include them in your list. Alphabetize entries according to the author's last name. Each entry should begin flush with the left margin. Lines after the first are indented one-half inch (or five spaces).

Q. When citing two or more sources by the same author, arrange them in alphabetical order determined by the first important and distinctive word in each title. Because *Saudi* appears in both article titles by King, the words used to alphabetize are *Arabia's* in the first entry and *Sellout* in the second. (These words are also used in parenthetical citations to distinguish the sources.) The author's name is given in the first entry; the second and subsequent entries begin with three hyphens, a period, and a space.

R. Pieper's works cited list includes entries from newspapers and magazines because he needed information about an event that was current when he wrote this paper: the opening of a Starbucks in Vienna. If you write about a current event, you may need to use sources like these. For other topics, however, other kinds of sources may have more credibility (see chapter 9).

S. Demonstrating that he did not rely exclusively on information from newspapers and magazines, Pieper cited *Foreign Policy,* one of the most respected journals in the country. He also cited three books and a Web site.

Works Cited   0

Burke, Greg, Stacey Vanek Smith, and Regine Wosnitza. "Whole Latte Shakin': Can   P
    U.S. Gourmet Coffee Chain Starbucks Convert Continental Europe's Café
    Society? It's Ready to Try." <u>Time International</u>. 9 Apr. 2001: 47.

Doherty, Jacqueline. "Make It Decaf: Despite Heavy Revenue Gains, Starbucks'
    Earnings Growth Is Slowing." <u>Barrons</u>. 20 May 2002: 20.

Erlanger, Steven. "An American Coffeehouse (or 4) in Vienna." <u>New York Times</u>.
    1 June 2002: A1+.

King, Colbert I. "Saudi Arabia's Apartheid (Cont'd)." Editorial. <u>Washington Post</u>.   Q
    19 Jan. 2002, final ed.: A27.

---. "The Saudi Sellout." Editorial. <u>Washington Post</u>. 26 Jan. 2002, final ed.: A23.   R

Korten, David C. <u>When Corporations Rule the World</u>. West Hartford, CT: Kumarian,
    1995.

Mackay, Hugh. "The Globalization of Culture?" <u>A Globalizing World? Culture,
    Economics, Politics</u>. Ed. David Held. New York: Routledge, 2000. 47-84.

Pendergast, Mark. <u>Uncommon Grounds: The History of Coffee and How It Transformed
    Our World</u>. New York: Basic, 1999.

Rothkopf, David. "In Praise of Cultural Imperialism?" <u>Foreign Policy</u> 107 (1997):   S
    38-52.

Scott, Alwyn. "A Shot of Americana; Starbucks Jolts Europe's Coffeehouses." <u>Seattle
    Times</u>. 19 May 2002: F1.

"Starbucks Café in Forbidden City Under Fire." <u>People's Daily Online</u>. 24 Nov. 2000.
    3 June 2002 <http://english.peopledaily.com.cn/200011/24/
    eng20001124_56044.html>.

11c	APA-style documentation is appropriate for research in education and the social sciences.

The American Psychological Association (APA) publishes a manual to guide writers of papers or articles in psychology. Its documentation system (sometimes called the *author-date style*) is also used for work in other disciplines such as education, economics, and sociology.

(1) APA-style parenthetical citations include dates of publication.

In APA style, the basic elements of a parenthetical citation in the text are the author's last name, the year of publication, and the page number(s) if the reference is to a passage quoted directly from the source. If the author's name is mentioned in the text of the paper, give the date alone or the date and the page number in parentheses. In the following examples, note the details of punctuation and the treatment of the page number.

1. Work by one author

A prominent neurologist has concluded, "Pushing back the age at which the widespread form of Alzheimer's strikes—from, say, age 70 to age 90—would be nearly tantamount to a cure" (Kosik, 1999, p. 17).

OR

Kosik (1999) has concluded, "Pushing back the age at which the widespread form of Alzheimer's strikes—from, say, age 70 to age 90—would be nearly tantamount to a cure" (p. 17).

Unlike MLA style, APA style requires the abbreviation *p.* (or *pp.* for "pages") before the page number(s). Use commas to separate the author's name from the date and the date from the page reference.

2. Work by two authors

Whether or not children spend time in day care, their development in early childhood is determined primarily by the nature of the care they receive from parents (Darvas & Walsh, 2002).

Use an ampersand (&) to separate the authors' names. A page number is not necessary unless the sentence includes a direct quotation from the source.

3. Work by more than two authors

One study has shown that people who fear failure are not susceptible to hypnosis (Manganello, Carlson, Zarillo, & Teeven, 1985).

For works with three to five authors, cite all the authors in the first reference, but in subsequent references give only the last name of the first author followed by *et al.* ("Manganello et al." for this example). For works with six or more authors, provide only the last name of the first author followed by *et al.,* even in the first citation.

4. Anonymous work

Use a shortened version of the title to identify an anonymous work.

Chronic insomnia usually requires medical intervention ("Sleep," 2003).

In this case, the author has cited a short article identified in the bibliography as "Sleep disorders: Standard methods of treatment."

5. Two or more works by different authors in the same parenthetical citation

Opponents of animal experimentation have traditionally argued that it is both unnecessary and cruel (Mayo, 1983; Singer, 1975).

Use a semicolon to separate citations, and arrange them in alphabetical order.

6. Two or more works by the same author in the same parenthetical citation

To determine the focus of a grammar lesson, teachers benefit from first examining the

three dimensions of a grammatical structure: form, meaning, and use (Larsen-Freeman,

1991, 1997).

Use a comma to separate the dates of publication, and order the dates from earliest to most recent.

7. Personal communication

State educational outcomes are often interpreted differently by teachers in the same

school (J. K. Jurgensen, personal communication, May 4, 2003).

Personal communications include letters, memos, email messages, personal interviews, and telephone conversations. These sources are cited in the text only; they do not appear in the reference list.

(2) An APA-style reference list follows specific conventions.

Whether you are submitting an APA-style paper in a college course or preparing a manuscript for publication, you can be guided by the format of the following entries. Each entry should be double-spaced with a hanging indent of five to seven spaces, or one-half inch. Arrange the entries alphabetically by the author's, or the first author's, last name. When two entries refer to the same author, arrange them according to the date of publication, placing the entry with the earliest date first. When an author's name appears both in a one-author entry and first in a multiple-author entry, place the one-author entry first.

Directory of APA-Style Entries for the Reference List

BOOKS

ARTICLES IN PRINT

SOURCES PRODUCED FOR ACCESS BY COMPUTER

OTHER SOURCES

BOOKS

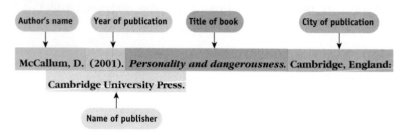

Author's name   Year of publication   Title of book   City of publication

McCallum, D. (2001). *Personality and dangerousness.* Cambridge, England:

Cambridge University Press.

Name of publisher

Most book entries consist of four units separated by periods.

1. *Author.* Place the author's last name first, followed by a comma and the first and middle (if used) initials. For entries that have more than one author, put commas after all last names and sets of initials, and put an ampersand (&) before the name of the last author.

2. *Date.* Place the date in parentheses after the author's name, and put a period after the closing parenthesis. By requiring the date to be near the beginning of the entry, APA style draws attention to its importance.

3. *Title.* Italicize the title of a book. Capitalize only the first word in titles and subtitles. Do not capitalize other words (except for proper names that would be capitalized in other contexts). Separate a title from a subtitle with a colon. For an article in an edited book, provide both the title of the article and the title of the book in which it appears.

4. *Publication data.* Identify the city of publication. Add the two-letter U.S. Postal Service abbreviation for the state unless the city is one of the following: Baltimore, Boston, Chicago, Los Angeles, New York, Philadelphia, or San Francisco. When a work has been published in a city outside the United States, add the country's name unless the city is Amsterdam, Jerusalem, London, Milan, Moscow, Paris, Rome, Stockholm, Tokyo, or Vienna—in these cases, the city alone is sufficient. Give only enough of the publisher's name so that it can be identified clearly.

1. Book by one author

Simmons, R. (2002). *Odd girl out: The hidden culture of aggression in girls.* New York: Harcourt.

Capitalize only the first word of the title and any subtitle (unless either includes a word that would be capitalized in other contexts).

2. Book by two or more authors

Beck, A. T., Emery, G., & Greenberg, R. L. (1990). *Anxiety disorders and phobias: A cognitive perspective.* New York: Basic Books.

Invert the names of all authors, and use an ampersand (&) before the name of the last author.

3. Book with editor(s)

Antony, M. M., Rachman, S., Richter, M. A., & Swinson, R. P. (Eds.). (1998). *Obsessive-compulsive disorder.* New York: Guilford Press.

Capitalize the abbreviation for editor or editors, and place it within parentheses.

4. Edition after the first

Hostetler, J. A. (1993). *Amish society* (4th ed.). Baltimore: Johns Hopkins University Press.

Identify the edition in parentheses immediately after the title.

5. Translation

Freud, S. (1999). *The interpretation of dreams* (J. Crick, Trans.). New York: Oxford University Press. (Original work published 1899)

A period follows the name of the publisher but not the parenthetical note.

6. Multivolume work, published over a period of more than one year

Copleston, F. (1993–1994). *A history of philosophy* (Vols. 1–9). New York: Doubleday.

7. Government report

National Institute of Mental Health. (1994). *Attention deficit hyperactivity disorder* (NIH Publication No. 96-3572). Washington, DC: U.S. Government Printing Office.

8. Selection from an edited book

Wolfe, A. (1996). Human nature and the quest for community. In A. Etzioni (Ed.), *New communitarian thinking* (pp. 126–140). Charlottesville: University Press of Virginia.

Italicize the book title but not the title of the selection.

9. Selection from a reference book

Wickens, D. (2001). Classical conditioning. In *The Corsini encyclopedia of psychology and behavioral science* (Vol. 1, pp. 293–298). New York: John Wiley.

ARTICLES IN PRINT

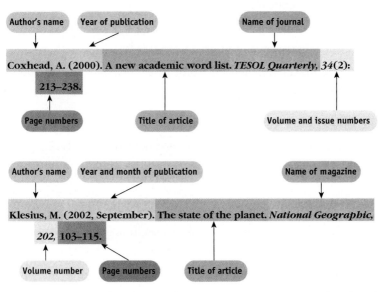

Capitalize only the first word and any proper nouns in an article title. (If the article has a subtitle, use a colon to separate the title and the subtitle, and capitalize the first word of each.) For an anonymous article, place the article title where the author's name would normally appear, and alphabetize the entry by the first important word in the title.

Each important word in a name of a journal is capitalized (in contrast to the title of an article or a book). Italicize the journal title and continue the italicizing so that it extends (without a break) to include the volume number. Include the issue number, when necessary, within parentheses, but do not italicize it. The point is to make volume and issue numbers visually distinct from page number(s).

10. Article from a journal with continuous pagination

Jazzmen, I. (2002). Previous behavioral control, self-efficacy, locus of control, and the
theory of planned behavior. *Journal of Applied Social Psychology, 32,* 635–685.

Italicize the volume number but not the page numbers.

11. Article with two authors in a journal with each issue paginated separately

Rudisill, J. R., & Edwards, J. M. (2002). Coping with job transitions. *Consulting
Psychology Journal, 54*(1), 55–62.

Add the issue number within parentheses immediately after the volume number.

12. Article with three to six authors

Frost, R. O., Steketee, G., & Williams, L. (2002). Compulsive buying, compulsive
hoarding, and obsessive-compulsive disorder. *Behavior Therapy, 33*(2), 201–213.

Include the names of all authors if the number of authors is no more than six.

13. Article with more than six authors

Reddy, S. K., Arora, M., Perry, C. L., Nair, B., Kohli, A., Lytle, L. A., et al. (2002).
Tobacco and alcohol use outcomes of a school-based intervention in New Delhi.
American Journal of Health Behavior, 26, 173–181.

After the name of the sixth author, use *et al.* to indicate that there are additional authors.

14. Article in a monthly or weekly magazine

Winson, J. (2002, June). The meaning of dreams. *Scientific American, 12,* 54–61.

For magazines published once a month, include the name of the month
after the year of publication. For magazines published weekly or bi-
weekly, add the day of the issue: (2003, May 8).

15. Article in a newspaper

Liptak, A. (2002, June 16). Polygamist's custody fight raises many issues. *New York
Times,* p. A20.

Include the letter indicating the section with the page number.

16. Letter to the editor

Mancall, M. (2002, June 17). Answer to cynicism [Letter to the editor]. *New York Times,* p. A20.

After the title, indicate within brackets that the work is a letter to the editor.

17. Book review

Kamil, M. L. (2002). The state of reading research [Review of the book *Progress in understanding reading: Scientific foundations and new frontiers*]. *American Journal of Psychology, 115,* 451–458.

SOURCES PRODUCED FOR ACCESS BY COMPUTER

The APA suggests the following formats for reference entries for electronic sources. Notice that the APA recommends following the same sequence of information as provided for print sources. Omit any information, such as volume or page numbers, that is not available. Information about when and how the source was retrieved appears at the end. Notice that the period that normally ends an entry is omitted after a URL because trailing periods can cause difficulty in retrieving files.

18. Online article based on a print source

Lindsay, D. S., & Poole, D. A. (2001). Children's eyewitness reports after exposure to misinformation from parents [Electronic version]. *Journal of Experimental Psychology: Applied, 7*(1), 27–50.

The words in square brackets indicate that the article came from the electronic version of a journal that is also published in print.

19. Article in a journal published only online

Yu, D. L., & Seligman, M. E. P. (2002, May 8). Preventing depressive symptoms in
    Chinese children. *Prevention & Treatment, 5,* Article 9. Retrieved June 15, 2002,
    from http://journals.apa.org/prevention/volume5/pre0050009a.html

If the article is numbered, indicate that number after the volume number.

20. Article in an online newspaper

McGrath, C. (2002, June 15). Father time. *New York Times.* Retrieved June 15, 2002,
    from http://nytimes.com/pages/science/index.html

21. Message posted to a newsgroup

Korniejczuk, V. (2002, June 11). Clinical psychology and psychiatry—What's the
    difference? [Msg 4]. Message posted to news://sci.psychology.theory

Provide the message number within square brackets after the message title.

22. Message posted to a forum or a discussion group

Ziegler, L. (2000, April 16). Dark vergence [Msg 15]. Message posted to
    http://groups.yahoo.com/groups/visualcognition/message/15

23. Article from a database

Kim, Y. (2002). Spirituality moderates the effect of stress on emotional and physical
    adjustment. *Personality and Individual Differences, 32*(8), 1377–1390. Retrieved
    June 21, 2002, from PsycINFO database.

Identify the database at the end of the entry.

OTHER SOURCES

24. Motion picture

Smith, M. (Producer/Writer), & Gaviria, M. (Producer/Director). (2001). *Medicating kids* [Motion picture]. (Available from the Public Broadcasting Service, 1320 Braddock Place, Alexandria, VA 22314)

Begin with the primary contributor(s), identifying the nature of the contribution. Follow with the release date, the title, and the descriptive label in square brackets. For a film with limited distribution, provide information within parentheses about how it can be obtained. For a widely distributed film, indicate the country where it was produced and the name of the studio (e.g., United States: Paramount Pictures).

25. Television program

Holt, S. (Producer). (2002, October 1). *The mysterious lives of caves* [Television broadcast]. Alexandria, VA: Public Broadcasting Service.

Give the title of the program in italics. If citing an entire series (e.g., *Nova* or *The West Wing*), cite the producer for the series as a whole and the network that originated it (e.g., WNET or NBC).

26. Music recording

McLachlan, S. (1989). Out of the shadows. On *Touch* [CD]. New York: Arista Records.

If the recording was made by an artist other than the song writer, begin the entry with the song writer's name, but place the artist's name in brackets (e.g., [Recorded by Diana Krall]) after the title of the song. Then, after the name of the record label, add the year the song was recorded in parentheses. No period follows the last parenthesis.

11d | Studying a sample paper can help you learn the APA style guidelines.

The APA makes a distinction between **final manuscript** (which a student submits to an instructor or a committee of professors) and **copy manuscript** (which an author submits to a journal for publication).

Both kinds of manuscript follow the rules for documentation explained in **11c.** The APA recognizes that a paper intended for publication may have to be modified so that the copy manuscript follows the requirements of the journal to which it is being submitted. Student papers may also require modification. According to the *Publication Manual,* "The purpose of theses, dissertations, and student papers and the nature of the reading audience (professor or committee members) may dictate variations from the requirements for manuscripts submitted for publication" (p. 322). The following section outlines the principal features and organization of a typical student paper. If you have any doubt as to what your instructor expects, find out what variations you should use.

In APA style, a **title page** includes a **manuscript page header** in the upper right-hand corner. It consists of the first two or three words of the title placed five spaces in front of the page number. The page number should be an inch from the right side of the paper and a half inch from the top. The manuscript page header appears on all subsequent pages. The title page is considered page 1.

Below the manuscript page header but on the left-hand side of the page is the **running head,** a shortened version of the title (no more than fifty characters). Letters in the running head are all uppercase. The title appears next in upper- and lowercase letters and is centered. The **author's name** appears below the title and is followed by the author's affiliation. If an instructor asks that the course name or number be included, it generally appears where the affiliation would be. Unless the instructor specifically requires it, the instructor's name and the date the paper is due are not included. All elements on the title page are double-spaced.

The title page is followed by a page containing an **abstract,** a summary of the paper in no more than 120 words. For advice on how to summarize, see **10d.** The body of the paper, as well as the abstract, is normally double-spaced. For information about how to organize a paper in the social sciences, see **14a–b.** A list of **references** follows the text, beginning on a separate page. This list includes only sources explicitly cited in the text. However, personal communications, such as email messages and interviews, are not listed in the reference list. Any other work that is especially pertinent or that informs the paper as a whole may be included in a separate bibliography. For additional examples of APA-style documentation, see the following student essay and the commentary printed on the left-hand pages.

COMMENTS

A. A **title page** includes five elements: the manuscript page header, the running head, the title, the author's name, and the author's affiliation. (The APA style does not include a date for the paper.) Double-space the title, the author's name, and the author's affiliation. Center the lines both horizontally and vertically on the page. For earlier versions of this paper, visit www.harbrace.com.

B. The **running head** is a shortened version of the title. It should not be more than fifty characters long.

C. If an instructor asks that a course name or number be included, it generally appears instead of the affiliation. Unless specifically required, the instructor's name is not included.

Running head: SLEEP AND MEMORY   B

The Sleep and Memory Connection

Nikki Krzmarzick

University of St. Thomas   C

D. An abstract is a short summary of a paper. Most papers submitted for publication in a journal include abstracts. Check with your instructor or supervisor to see whether an abstract is required for your paper.

E. An APA-style abstract should not exceed 120 words. Readers should be able to understand what a paper is about simply by reading the abstract. Devoted to summarizing the paper's content, the abstract does not include an evaluation of the paper's quality.

Abstract   D

Current research indicates that sleep plays a role in learning and memory. Results of

research cited within the paper suggest that sleep affects the acquisition of knowledge and

skills needed to perform perceptual, critical, and creative-thinking tasks. This topic's

relevance to college students is addressed, and practical application of findings to that end

are discussed. Further research is necessary to establish how the brain acquires,

consolidates, and organizes information for later retrieval.   E

F. The full title is centered at the top of the page below the running head. Double-space between the running head and the title.

G. Krzmarzick introduces her thesis, a claim that she supports in the rest of her paper.

The Sleep and Memory Connection   F

It's finals week. In 24 hours, Kyle Rosemount has a biology exam. He is not sure he is on track to pass the class, so a good grade is essential. He regrets not starting earlier in the week but has resolved to stay up all night reviewing course material. This method will afford him almost 16 hours of study time. Rosemount reasons that this amount of time will be sufficient and is almost positive he would not have spent more hours with the material had he started exam preparations the previous week.

This scenario is all too familiar to college students, and many have used the same logic as Rosemount in thinking that the total number of hours spent studying is more critical than when that studying takes place. It seems to make sense that the more time one spends studying the subject matter, the better one will retain the information. But current research on the possibility of a relationship between sleep and memory suggests that this assumption is not necessarily true. In fact, irregular sleep patterns and cram sessions may actually be sabotaging students' efforts.

If there is a connection between sleep and memory, then getting regular sleep may   G be essential for memory consolidation and for optimal performance on both critical- and creative-thinking tasks. An exploration of this possibility requires a basic understanding of the sleep cycle. To an observer, a sleeping person appears passive, unresponsive and essentially isolated from the rest of the world and its barrage of stimuli. While it is true that humans are unaware of most of what is happening around them during sleep, the brain is far from inactive. It can be as active during sleep as in a waking state. While asleep, the rate and type of neuronal firings (electrical activity) in the brain changes. The brain cycles through four sleep stages before moving into REM sleep. All of this occurs at relatively predictable intervals while the person is asleep. Generally, it takes about 90 minutes to cycle through the four stages of sleep and one REM episode, each with distinct neuronal characteristics (Hobson, 1989). Figure 1 graphs these stages for an 8-hour sleep period.

H. Following APA guidelines, Krzmarzick contacted the copyright holder for permission to reproduce this figure. In addition, she provided a source note below the figure. Reproduction of a table also requires a source note indicating that permission to reproduce the table was granted by the copyright holder (who may not always be the author).

I. When more than one source is included in a parenthetical citation, semicolons separate the sources.

J. The second source in this parenthetical citation includes five names. Because this is the first reference to this source, all of the authors' names are cited. Notice the comma before the ampersand.

Figure 1. Sleep stages. *Note.* From *Good sleep, good learning, good life,* by H
Piotr Wozniak, July 2000. Retrieved September 19, 2002, from
http://www.supermemo.com/articles/sleep.htm. Reprinted with permission.

  The first two stages of sleep are characterized by high-amplitude, low-frequency
neural waves, aptly named slow-wave sleep. During these phases the brain is relatively
inactive and fires at a baseline rate. Wave III and wave IV sleep are known as fast-wave
sleep, recognized on an electroencephalogram readout by low-amplitude, high-frequency
neuronal activity. REM sleep is characterized by rapid motion of the eyes beneath closed
lids. This is the stage of sleep associated with vivid dreams, and thus it is sometimes
called dream sleep. Some dreams may occur within other stages as well, but they lack the
rich visual and emotional content of REM dreams. The function of this fascinating
phenomenon remains at least a partial mystery.

  Current research examines links between sleep, or stages of sleep, and memory or
learning. Some studies suggest that all-night cram sessions, such as the one Rosemount is
planning, do not improve performance and may even have the opposite effect (Kelly, Kelly,
& Clanton, 2001; Pilcher & Walters, 1997). The idea that sleep is linked to learning is I
supported by studies showing that certain types of learning are hampered by sleep
disruption or deprivation (Horne, 1988; Karni, Tanne, Rubenstein, Askenasy, & Sagi, 1994). J

K. A quotation of forty or more words is set off as an indented block, one-half inch from the left margin (the equivalent of an indent for a new paragraph). This example includes a citation within a citation. Krzmarzick has followed the APA rule given in the *Publication Manual:* "Do not omit citations embedded within the original material you are quoting. The works cited need not be included in the list of references (unless you happen to cite them elsewhere in your paper)" (p. 121). This example also includes numbers. The *Publication Manual* states that writers should use figures for all numbers 10 and above. Words can be used for numbers below 10, unless they indicate precise measurements or appear in a set with other numbers.

L. Because Krzmarzick has already cited the full list of authors for this source (on page 4 of her paper), she follows APA style by including in this citation only the first author's name followed by *et al.* (abbreviation for the Latin phrase meaning "and others").

Some studies implicate REM sleep as having a particularly important role in memory consolidation (Karni et al., 1994). Early research showed the importance of REM sleep for rats. Hunt (1989) summarizes a few of these early studies that indicate the importance of the timing of REM sleep:

> Over the past few years Carlyle Smith (1981) has studied the REM augmentation following learning in rats over several days and has found that these increases occur as regular "windows" that climb steadily over a six-day period (Smith & Lapp, 1984). Deprivation of REM during these specific windows of augmentation was at its most effective in disrupting prior learning between 48 and 60 hours after training (Smith & Kelly, 1986). (p. 28)

Research involving human participants has yielded similar results. Karni et al. (1994) showed that performance on a procedural task improves "neither during nor immediately after practice but rather 8 to 10 hours after a training session has ended" (p. 679). Hunt (1989) reports confirmation of the "window" phenomenon by noting that in 1985 Epstein found participants in his study reporting life events as dream content 2 or 3 days after the experiences. Epstein's findings differ in nature from those of Karni et al. (1994) in that they are more difficult to quantify because his data depend on dream recall, which is subjective. While Epstein's observations are not the most scientifically sound support for optimal timing of REM sleep, they are worth noting and could be significant when pooled with other findings supporting the idea that the brain processes new information and experiences over the course of a few days. In addition to the timing of sleep following training, the amount of REM sleep may play a role. Toward the end of the entire sleep cycle, time spent in REM sleep increases. When people are deprived of REM sleep, their brains react by going into REM sleep more frequently or by staying at the REM stage longer during a sleep-recovery phase (Hobson, 1989).

Although there is no definitive answer as to which type of sleep is needed for memory consolidation, studies show that lack of sleep hinders learning in various ways. Pilcher and Walters (1997) noted its negative impact on participant performance on a test of cognitive ability. Horne (1988) found that participants performed creative-thinking tasks at a decreased capacity when compared with a control group. Karni et al. (1994) observed the damaging effect of sleep deprivation on perceptual learning.

Some studies include a self-report measure for perceived effort, concentration, and the like (e.g., Buboltz, Brown, & Soper, 2001; Pilcher & Walters, 1997). Participants are asked to report how confident they are in their performance and to rate that performance. Findings from these self-report measures are somewhat disturbing. It appears that the tendency exists, when a person is sleep-deprived, to overestimate performance. Surprisingly, although Pilcher and Walters (1997) noted that sleep deprivation negatively affected the ability of participants to perform on a test, the participants overestimated their performance. They also rated themselves as having expended more effort than participants in the control group did. Perhaps such skewed perception partially explains why college students often deprive themselves of sleep. If their perception is that performance is not hindered, there is no incentive to make sleep a priority.

The studies outlined above illustrate multiple types of learning and memory that may be affected by sleep. It is noteworthy that many of these studies used variables and methodologies that are realistic: They involve tasks similar to those that college students are asked to perform. For example, it is common for students to be asked to employ creative problem-solving skills in a classroom setting. Visual discrimination tasks, too, are common in college courses. Students may be required to recognize a painting by sight and then name the artist in an art history course. This line of research offers an obvious link between science and real-life situations.

Clearly there is a need for more research on this topic. The fact that an adequate amount of sleep is necessary for a person's health and well-being is well-established. We now have sufficient evidence to warrant a closer look at just how important the role of sleep is. Further research may establish that all stages of sleep play an important role in optimal functioning, or that one or two stages are particularly important. The exact relationship between sleep and memory is not yet known.

College students have notoriously bad sleeping habits, often because they are attempting to balance schoolwork, part-time jobs, extracurricular activities, and a social life. Known for their irregular sleep patterns, they are often sleep-deprived and/or suffer from some type of disturbed sleep (e.g., difficulty falling, or staying, asleep) (Hicks, Fernandez, & Pellegrini, 2001).

Based on the current body of research literature, it appears that there is a link between sleep and optimal functioning. For this reason, it is important for college students to manage their time in a way that allows them to study material over a period of a couple of days or longer and to have adequate sleep time in order to maximize retention. The consequences of inadequate sleep go beyond simply feeling sleepy. It is alarming that the self-reported sleep habits and quality of sleep of over 1,500 college students has worsened over the last decade (Hicks et al., 2001), indicating that necessary precautions are not being taken to ensure that at the very least students are educated regarding the importance of sleep.

It is evident that Kyle Rosemount is not doing himself any favors by delaying his studying until the last minute. Ideally, Rosemount should have studied in shorter blocks of time over a week, or at least a couple of days, allowing more time to process the information and commit it to memory. It may be that the sleep deprivation college students inflict upon themselves, particularly around finals time, may lead them to overestimate performance while actually hindering it.

M. The reference list is organized alphabetically and begins on a new page. The word *References* is centered at the top of the page. Double-space the reference list.

N. After the first line of each entry, use a hanging indent of five spaces.

O. The last name is always given first, followed by initials for the first and middle names (if available). The date of publication is always given parenthetically, immediately after the author's name. (See 11c(2).)

P. Observe the use of periods and commas, the capitalization for book and article titles, and the use of italics for book and journal titles. The volume number for a journal is also italicized.

Sleep and Memory 8

References

Buboltz, W. C., Brown, F. C., Jr., & Soper, B. (2001). Sleep habits and patterns of
college students: A preliminary study. *Journal of American College Health, 50*(3),
131–135.

Hicks, R. A., Fernandez, C., & Pellegrini, R. J. (2001). The changing sleep habits of
university students: An update. *Perceptual and Motor Skills, 93*(3), 648.

Hobson, J. A. (1989). *Sleep.* New York: Scientific American Library.

Horne, J. A. (1988). Sleep loss and divergent thinking ability. *Sleep, 11*(6), 528–536.

Hunt, H. T. (1989). *The multiplicity of dreams: Memory, imagination, and
consciousness.* New Haven, CT: Yale University Press.

Karni, A., Tanne, D., Rubenstein, B. S., Askenasy, J. M., & Sagi, D. (1994, July 29).
Dependence on REM sleep of overnight improvement of a perceptual skill.
Science, 265, 679–682.

Kelly, W. E., Kelly, K. E., & Clanton, R. C. (2001). The relationship between sleep
length and grade-point average among college students. *College Student Journal,
35,* 84–86.

Pilcher, J. J., & Walters, A. S. (1997). How sleep deprivation affects psychological
variables related to college students' cognitive performance. *Journal of American
College Health, 46*(3), 121–126.

Wozniak, P. (2000, July). *Good sleep, good learning, good life.* Retrieved September 19,
2002, from http://www.supermemo.com/articles/sleep.htm

11e | **CMS provides a widely used system for using footnotes and endnotes.**

The Chicago Manual of Style (CMS) has been an indispensable resource for writers since 1906. The manual provides detailed information about preparing a manuscript for publication. For documentation, it recommends using either endnotes or footnotes and a bibliography. The information in notes is condensed if a bibliography mentions all the sources used in the paper. When no bibliography is provided, a full citation is necessary.

Both footnotes and endnotes require that a superscript number be placed wherever documentation of a source is needed. The number should be as close as possible to whatever it refers to, following the punctuation that appears at the end of the direct quotation or paraphrase.

Footnotes should be single-spaced four lines below the last line of text on the same page where the documentation is necessary (in other words, at the foot of the page). Double-space between footnotes if more than one appears on any page. Endnotes should be double-spaced on a separate page headed "Notes," and this heading should be at the top center of the page. Endnotes appear after the last page of text and before the bibliography, if there is one. See the model CMS paper on pages 361–371 for an example.

Directory of CMS Note and Bibliographic Forms

BOOKS

BOOKS

Full note form

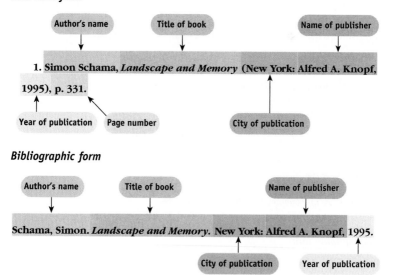

Bibliographic form

Author's name Title of book Name of publisher

Schama, Simon. *Landscape and Memory.* New York: Alfred A. Knopf, 1995.

City of publication Year of publication

Most book entries consist of the author's name, the title of the book, and publication data (city of publication, publisher's name, and date of publication). This information appears in both full footnotes and full endnotes and in the bibliography at the end of the paper.

The principal differences are these:

- In a note, the author's name appears with the first name first; in a bibliographic entry, the author's name (or the name of the first author when there is more than one author) is inverted so that the last name is first.
- In a note, commas separate the author's name from the book title, and the book title from additional information (such as a translator's name) that appears before the publication data. In a bibliographic entry, periods follow the author's name and the book title.
- The publication data in a note appear within parentheses. Parentheses are not used in bibliographic references.
- When information cited is found on a specific page in the text, the page number is placed at the end of the footnote or endnote. A bibliographical reference ends with the date of publication.

Remember that when you provide a full bibliography, the full note form is not required. Instead, use condensed citations, which include only the author's last name, the title (if long, shortened to four words), and the relevant page number(s). See the model on pages 369 and 370 for examples of shortened note forms. Both CMS note form and CMS bibliographic form are provided for the examples that follow.

1. Book with one author

Full note form

1. Carlo D'Este, *Eisenhower: A Soldier's Life* (New York: Holt, 2002), 417–18.

Shortened note form

1. D'Este, *Eisenhower: A Soldier's Life* , 417–18.

Bibliographic form

D'Este, Carlo. *Eisenhower: A Soldier's Life.* New York: Holt, 2002.

The author's last name appears first. Put a period (rather than a comma) after the author's first name and a period after the title. Do not place parentheses around publication information.

2. Book with two authors

Full note form

2. Cathy Scott-Clark and Adrian Levy, *The Stone of Heaven* (Boston: Little, Brown, 2001), 28.

Any specific page references should be placed after the publication data.

Bibliographic form

Scott-Clark, Cathy, and Adrian Levy. *The Stone of Heaven.* Boston: Little, Brown, 2001.

Invert the order of the first author's name only. Place a comma after this name, and use the conjunction *and* (not an ampersand, &).

In the publisher's name, do not include words such as *Company* or *Corporation* or abbreviations such as *Co.* or *Inc.* For example, *Little, Brown & Co.* becomes *Little, Brown* (a comma separates the two words in this publisher's name only because it is part of the publisher's name).

3. Book with three authors

Full note form

3. Xue Litai, John W. Lewis, and Sergei N. Goncharov, *Uncertain Partners: Stalin, Mao, and the Korean War* (Palo Alto, CA: Stanford University Press, 1993).

Use commas after the names of the first and second authors. CMS recommends writing out *University Press,* although the abbreviation *Univ.* is acceptable if it is used consistently.

Bibliographic form

Litai, Xue, John W. Lewis, and Sergei N. Goncharov. *Uncertain Partners: Stalin, Mao, and the Korean War.* Palo Alto, CA: Stanford University Press, 1993.

4. Book with an editor

Full note form

4. Hanna Schissler, ed., *The Miracle Years* (Princeton, NJ: Princeton University Press, 2001).

Bibliographic form

Schissler, Hanna, ed. *The Miracle Years.* Princeton, NJ: Princeton University Press, 2001.

In both forms, the abbreviation *ed.* appears after the editor's name.

5. Book with an author and an editor

Full note form

5. Ayn Rand, *The Art of Fiction,* ed. Tore Boeckmann (New York: Plume, 2000).

Use the abbreviation *ed.* for "edited by."

Bibliographic form

Rand, Ayn. *The Art of Fiction.* Edited by Tore Boeckmann. New York: Plume, 2000.

Write out the words *Edited by.*

6. Translated book

Full note form

6. Murasaki Shikibu, *The Tale of Genji,* trans. Royall Tyler (New York: Viking, 2001).

Use the abbreviation *trans.* for "translated by."

Bibliographic form

Shikibu, Murasaki. *The Tale of Genji.* Translated by Royall Tyler. New York: Viking, 2001.

Write out the words *Translated by.*

7. Edition after the first

Full note form

7. Edward O. Wilson, *On Human Nature,* 14th ed. (Cambridge: Harvard University Press, 2001).

Bibliographic form

Wilson, Edward O. *On Human Nature.* 14th ed. Cambridge: Harvard University Press, 2001.

8. One volume in a multivolume work

Full note form

8. Thomas Cleary, *Classics of Buddhism and Zen,* vol. 3 (Boston: Shambhala Publications, 2001), 116.

Bibliographic form

Cleary, Thomas. *Classics of Buddhism and Zen.* Vol. 3. Boston: Shambhala Publications, 2001.

9. Government document

Full note form

9. Department of Commerce, Census Bureau, *Statistical Abstract of the United States,* 120th ed. Bureau of the Census (Washington, DC, 2000), 16.

Bibliographic form

U.S. Bureau of the Census. *Statistical Abstract of the United States.* 120th ed. Bureau of the Census. Washington, DC, 2000.

10. Selection from an anthology

Full note form

10. Elizabeth Spencer, "The Everlasting Light," in *The Cry of an Occasion,* ed. Richard Bausch, 171–182 (Baton Rouge: Louisiana State University Press, 2001).

Bibliographic form

Spencer, Elizabeth. "The Everlasting Light." In *The Cry of an Occasion,* edited by
Richard Bausch, 171–182. Baton Rouge: Louisiana State University Press, 2001.

When only one selection from an anthology is used, inclusive page numbers precede the place of publication.

11. Published letter

Full note form

11. Lincoln to George McClellan, Washington, DC, 13 October 1862, in *This Fiery Trial: The Speeches and Writings of Abraham Lincoln,* ed. William E. Gienapp (New York: Oxford University Press, 2002), 178.

Bibliographic form

Lincoln, Abraham. Abraham Lincoln to George McClellan. Washington DC, 13 October
1862. In *This Fiery Trial: The Speeches and Writings of Abraham Lincoln,* edited by
William E. Gienapp, 178. New York: Oxford University Press, 2002.

ARTICLES

Like CMS forms for books, the two forms for articles include essentially the same information, with minor differences in punctuation. The principal difference is that both the full note form and the bibliographic form for articles end with page number(s). A note ends with the specific page or pages being cited; a bibliographic entry ends with the full range of pages on which the article can be found.

12. Article in a journal with continuous pagination

Full note form

12. Y. C. Wong and Joe Leung, "Community-based Service for the Frail and Elderly in China," *International Social Work* 45 (2002): 212.

Use initials for first or second names only when the author's name appears that way in the original publication.

Bibliographic form

Wong, Y. C., and Joe Leung. "Community-based Service for the Frail and Elderly in China." *International Social Work* 45 (2002): 205–16.

Pages establishing the full length of the article appear at the end of the citation.

13. Article in a journal with issues paged separately

Full note form

13. Andreas Schedler, "The Menu of Manipulation," *Journal of Democracy* 13, no. 2 (2002): 48.

Bibliographic form

Schedler, Andreas. "The Menu of Manipulation." *Journal of Democracy* 13, no. 2 (2002): 36–50.

14. Article in a popular (general-circulation) magazine

Full note form

14. John O'Sullivan, "The Overskeptics," *National Review,* June 17, 2002, 23.

This example shows a magazine published weekly. For a magazine published monthly, include only the month and the year.

Bibliographic form

O'Sullivan, John. "The Overskeptics." *National Review,* June 17, 2002, 22–26.

15. Newspaper article

Full note form

15. Rick Bragg, "An Oyster and a Way of Life, Both at Risk," *New York Times,* 15 June 2002, national edition, sec. A.

If the city of publication is not part of the newspaper's name, it should be added at the beginning of the name and italicized as if part of the title: *St. Paul Pioneer Press.* If the city is not well known or could be confused with another city with the same name, add the state name or abbreviation within parentheses after the city's name. If the paper is a well-known national one, such as the *Wall Street Journal,* it is not necessary to add the city of publication.

Bibliographic form

Bragg, Rick. "An Oyster and a Way of Life, Both at Risk." *New York Times,* June 15,

2000, national edition, sec. A.

When reference is made in the text to the name of the newspaper and to the date of publication, no bibliographic entry is needed.

OTHER SOURCES

16. Interview

Full note form

16. Yoko Ono, "Multimedia Player: An Interview with Yoko Ono," interview by
Carolyn Burriss-Krimsky, *Ruminator Review,* no. 10 (Summer 2002): 28.

Bibliographic form

Ono, Yoko. "Multimedia Player: An Interview with Yoko Ono." By Carolyn Burriss-

Krimsky. *Ruminator Review,* no. 10 (Summer 2002): 26–29.

Although an interview is not always listed in the bibliography, if you are required to include one, begin with the name of the person being interviewed; next, include the title of the interview and the name of the person who conducted it, followed by information about where the interview can be found.

17. Videocassette

Full note form

17. *Araby,* VHS, produced and directed by Dennis J. Courtney (Los Angeles, CA:
American Street Productions, 1999).

Bibliographic form

Araby. VHS. Produced and directed by Dennis J. Courtney. Los Angeles, CA: American
Street Productions, 1999.

18. Indirect (secondary) source

Full note form

18. Toni Morrison, *Playing in the Dark* (New York: Vintage, 1992), 26, quoted in
Jonathan Goldberg, *Willa Cather and Others* (Durham, NC: Duke University Press,
2001), 37.

Bibliographic form

Morrison, Toni. *Playing in the Dark,* 26. New York: Vintage, 1992. Quoted in Jonathan
Goldberg, *Willa Cather and Others* (Durham, NC: Duke University Press, 2001), 37.

If you cite a work indirectly, you must cite both the original work and
the secondary source in which you found it quoted. Begin with the author you have quoted, and provide information about this work (which
should be available in the notes or bibliography of the indirect source
you used); follow with information about the source from which you obtained the quotation.

19. Journal database

Full note form

19. Samuel Guy Inman, "The Monroe Doctrine and Hispanic America," *Hispanic
America Historical* Review 4, no. 4 (1921): 635. http://links.jstor.org/sici?sici=0018-
2168%28192111%294%3A4%3C635%3ATMDAHA%3E2.0.CO%3B2-8.

Bibliographic form

Inman, Samuel Guy. "The Monroe Doctrine and Hispanic America." *Hispanic America
Historical* Review 4, no. 4 (1921): 635-81. http://links.jstor.org/sici?sici=0018-
2168%28192111%294%3A4%3C635%3ATMDAHA%3E2.0.CO%3B2-8.

If the URL is one that may change or one that is cumbersome to reproduce, use just the URL for the database's main Web page (for the previous example, http://www.jstor.org/).

20. Online document

Full note form

20. Wisconsin Constitution, art. 2, sec. 2, http://www.legis.state.wi.us/
rsb.2wisconsin.html (accessed March 15, 2003).

Bibliographic form

Wisconsin Constitution, art. 2, sec. 2. http://www.legis.state.wi.us/rsb.2wisconsin.html
(accessed March 15, 2003).

When a URL is unlikely to change, it may not be necessary to include an access date.

11f | Studying a sample paper can help you learn CMS style for courses in history and political science.

The following student paper addresses an important development in the Civil Rights movement. To read earlier versions of this paper, visit www.harbrace.com. Although CMS does not provide guidelines for a title page, one is shown in figure 11.2 as a sample.

Race in the U.S. Army: An Executive Order for Hope

Nicole Hester

American History 257

December 6, 2002

Figure 11.2. Sample title page for CMS-style paper.

While students of the Civil Rights movement are often familiar with the Supreme Court decision *Brown* v. *The Board of Education,* which acknowledged the inherent inequality in separate but equal practices, that decision would not happen until 1955, nearly eight years after President Harry S. Truman issued an executive order to integrate the federal government and, in particular, the United States military. Although the earlier Thirteenth (1865), Fourteenth (1868), and Fifteenth (1870) Amendments redefined freedom, citizenship, and voting, these amendments were diluted by Supreme Court

1

decisions in the nineteenth and early twentieth centuries. In cases like *Plessy* v. *Ferguson,* the court established the precedent of "separate but equal," which legally allowed the separation of races in public facilities.[1] Thus, Truman's executive order in 1948 became an important step in the long-term struggle for civil rights.

Like American schools, the United States Army was segregated, and this segregation remained in place until after the Second World War (1941–1945). In July of 1948, by executive order, President Truman demanded equal treatment and equal opportunity in the armed forces, setting into motion a series of events that would force change, however slow it might be:

> It is hereby declared to be the policy of the President that there shall be equality of treatment and opportunity for all persons in the armed services without regard to race, color, religion or national origin. This policy shall be put into effect as rapidly as possible, having due regard to the time required to effectuate any necessary changes without impairing efficiency or morale.[2]

With such language as "all persons" and "as rapidly as possible," Truman showed that his statement was more than a publicity stunt. While understanding the scale of the change he was demanding, Truman was also aware of the sentiment of the American people and numerous government officials. Examining the desegregation of the Army from the viewpoints of those who sought to keep the races segregated and those who wanted integration leads to understanding how the law can begin to secure the pathways to justice and freedom.[3] Truman's executive order in 1948 illustrates how the government can be a vehicle for social change.

Historically, approximately 200,000 Blacks enlisted to fight in the Civil War, but their involvement was strongly influenced by the need for manpower.[4] After the Civil War, the Army maintained only four Black regiments. Although there were 380,000 Blacks in the Army during the First World War, no more than 42,000 actually served in combat units; most Blacks served as laborers.[5] The end of the First World War ushered in a time of analysis and redefinition of the roles of Blacks in the armed forces. The Selective Service Act of 1940 would forbid discrimination because of race with regard to enlisting and being inducted into the armed forces.[6] However in October 1940, Robert P. Patterson, the Secretary of War, stated that the Selective Service Act would not eliminate segregation within the armed forces; instead, it would allow Blacks to serve in segregated units:[7]

> The policy of the War Department is not to intermingle colored and white enlisted personnel in the same regimental organizations. This policy has been proven satisfactory over a long period of years and to make changes would produce situations destructive to morale and detrimental to the preparations for national defense.[8]

Patterson's statement followed the idea of "separate but equal," and ultimately undercut any effect the Selective Service Act could have had on integration. The enlistment of Blacks was increasing, but their advancement was not, no doubt because they were restricted to separate units. The existence of segregation, stemming from earlier war practices and later defined by War Department policy, would become the norm in the Second World War. From the perspective of those in the War Department, the policy was working effectively, and to "experiment" with its segregated structure would be detrimental to all within military ranks.[9]

These beliefs were reinforced by unreliable data. Supporting the policy outlined by the War Department, results from the U.S. Army General Classification Tests (AGCT), which tested general learning ability, showed 45 percent of Blacks and only 5 percent of Whites in the lowest class of exam scores. However, the War Department did not assess any reasons *why* the test results showed the deficit. Because of the "differences in opportunity and background," Blacks generally did not receive the same level of educational opportunity as Whites, so a difference in overall level of performance in standardized testing was bound to exist.[10] Although the Army was correct in its statement about the difference in test results, it ignored the direct effect that segregation and social constraints were having on the academic performance of Black Americans.

The testing issue, however, was only an excuse for preventing integration. For those who believed that segregation was *right,* allowing Blacks equal opportunities in the armed services would enable them to "achieve equality in America by force."[11] Simply

3

put, separatists were afraid that the growing political power of Blacks would lead to a revolt, bringing about the end of segregation, which threatened what separatists thought was right. More importantly, the Army did not believe the government should intervene, forcing desegregation within an otherwise segregated nation. In January 1948, nearly seven months before Truman's executive order, a Gallup poll showed that 81 percent of Southerners had heard of Truman's civil rights plan, and 58 percent felt that it should *not* be passed in Congress, compared to the 14 percent in the New England and Middle Atlantic region who felt that Truman's civil rights initiative should not be passed. In the same survey, Southern Whites responded 5-to-1 in an overwhelming show of support for segregation.[12] In a memorandum from December 1941, when the United States entered the Second World War, Chief of Staff General George C. Marshall reflected the sentiment that existed in the country and explained the Army's resistance to promote social change. In his words, integrating the U.S. Army

> would be tantamount to solving a social problem which has perplexed the American people throughout the history of this nation. The army cannot accomplish such a solution, and should not be charged with the undertaking. The settlement of vexing racial problems cannot be permitted to complicate the tremendous task of the War Department and thereby jeopardize discipline and morale.[13]

When Truman asked for the equal treatment of soldiers regardless of "race, color, religion, or national origin,"[14] he was essentially asking the government to ignore the widespread sentiment of White Americans. Undoubtedly, there were significant numbers of Blacks, Whites, and others craving freedom, but the nation as a whole was not ready for what Truman demanded. After so many years of segregation and prejudice, Truman was fighting a widely supported status quo.

Knowing the greatness of the change he had demanded, Truman established a committee that would be known as the Fahy Committee. Named after its chairman, Charles H. Fahy, the multiracial committee consisted of seven men, including Black leader Lester Granger and the executive secretary of the Urban League, John H.

Sengstacke, who were responsible for examining the existing procedures and practices of the armed forces to devise a way to carry out the president's new policy.[15] The Fahy Committee set out to show the ways in which segregation was hurting the "effectiveness" of the armed forces and to establish the positive results that would follow from integrating the armed forces, particularly the Army.[16]

The Fahy Committee wrestled tirelessly with the Army to put an end to the quota system, which limited the number of Black enlistees to 10 percent, as well as the segregation that prevented the advancement of Blacks within the Army.[17] Essentially the Army needed to use every individual within its ranks as effectively as possible, regardless of race, but the quota system and segregation made this impossible.[18] Because the skills of Black soldiers could be used only in Black units, White units sometimes had to leave essential positions unfilled.

When the Army could no longer deny the statistical and practical truth that segregation was inefficient and ineffective, Adjutant General of the Army Edward F. Witsell finally announced on March 27, 1950 that *all* appointments would be open to *all* applicants without regard to race or color.[19] As Mershon and Schlossman discuss in *Foxholes and Color Lines,* by assessing the integration of the armed forces, the Fahy Committee helped Truman to fight segregation and essentially prepare Americans for change.[20] Having the law on their side, Blacks were encouraged in their pursuit of equal opportunity, and they could hope that the equality being fostered in the federal government would eventually affect state practices. After changing the laws, Blacks hoped that prejudice and bigotry would begin to fade.

However, changing the minds of individuals is an entirely different task from changing the laws. Lee reports the statement of an unnamed White officer requesting relief in 1945 from the Ninety-Second Division, an engineer battalion where Black troops worked with Whites:

> Although I can still find such interest in a few specific individuals, for the rank and file I can feel only disgust for their inherent slovenliness, and their extreme indolence, indifference and frequent insolence. . . . I am likewise convinced that

> with few exceptions colored officers with whom I have come into contact are
> thoroughly incompetent, and for the most part are to be viewed in a light little
> different from enlisted men.[21]

This statement shows that while the law can create an environment in which freedom can exist, the law cannot change racist hearts and minds.

Knowing that legal equality was far off and that a deeply changed society was a hope for the distant future, Blacks in the military were then faced with daunting questions about their dual role as Blacks and as Americans. From their perspective, they enlisted to defend a country that would not defend them. For what reason should Blacks then enlist? What were they fighting for? Who were they really fighting against? The simplified answer to these questions came for Blacks in what would become known as the Double V Campaign: victory abroad and victory at home. In early 1942, this campaign was explained in the Black newspaper the *Courier* as a "struggle to remove the contradiction between the claims of American democratic ideology and the racial inequalities evident in American life."[22] Blacks were fighting for what they knew America was capable of, and ultimately created for, even while being bound by the racial policies of the Army; they still had a larger vision of what America could truly be. Fighting on the battlefields of foreign countries for a nation that rejected them in so many ways, the pursuit of freedom and equality came at a high emotional cost for Blacks in the Army. Hubert Humphrey used a quotation by James Baldwin, who served in the Second World War, to exemplify the Black experience and struggle:

> You must put yourself in the skin of a man who is wearing a uniform of his
> country, is a candidate for death in its defense, and who is called a "nigger"
> by his comrades-in-arms and his officers . . . and who watches German pris-
> oners of war being treated by Americans with more human dignity than he
> has ever received at their hands. And who, at the same time, as a human be-
> ing, is far freer in a strange land than he has even been at home. HOME! The
> very word begins to have a despairing and diabolical ring. You must consider
> what happens to this citizen, after all he has endured, when he returns—home;
> search, in his shoes, for a job, for a place to live; ride, in his skin, on segre-

gated buses; see, with his eyes, the signs saying "White" and "Colored," and especially the signs that say "White Ladies" and "Colored Women" . . . imagine yourself being told to "Wait." And all of this happening in the richest and freest country in the world, and in the middle of the twentieth century.[23]

Between fighting for the freedom of others in the war and hoping justice would permeate the policies and social hierarchies in America, Black soldiers had an immense struggle that would not end after the war.

However, Blacks were not alone, there were others fighting along with them, and President Truman was certainly one of them. By issuing executive order 9981 in 1948, Truman clearly established his position concerning racial bias within the government by "tak[ing] significant unilateral action to alter the stance of the federal government toward minority groups . . . demonstrat[ing] dedication to the legal equality for racial minorities without waiting for congressional approval."[24] In short, Truman's order required action within the armed forces to end racial bias and to do so within a reasonable amount of time.[25] Sidestepping a conservative Congress and the prejudice of many Americans, Truman supported Blacks in their struggle for advancement and equality in the armed forces, even though he moved the law to a place where the American people were not necessarily ready to follow.

Understanding Truman's order concerning segregation, we are left to wonder why he would take such a political risk. Why should Truman be any different from other government officials or separatists that surrounded him? What could Truman gain from alienating himself from the legislative branch? Of course, Truman undoubtedly gained the support of Black voters because of his bold stance concerning race, but could that be the entirety of his motivations? What Truman *really* thought or felt is something we can never know, but in October 1948 in an address in Harlem, New York, where he would receive the Franklin Roosevelt Award, Truman had this to say:

> It was the authors of the Declaration of Independence who stated the principle that all men are created equal in their rights, and that it is to secure these rights that governments are instituted among men.

7

>It was the authors of the Constitution who made it clear that, under
>our form of government, all citizens are equal before the law, and that the
>Federal Government has a duty to guarantee to every citizen equal protection
>of the laws.[26]

In his own words, Truman stated what the founding documents of this nation intended, and he was determined to see those principles put into action. Truman's biographer, David McCullough, describes Truman as "the kind of president the founding fathers had in mind for this country."[27] Yet Truman himself reveals that growing international concerns such as the Cold War were also influencing him:

>Today the democratic way of life is being challenged all over the world.
>Democracy's answer to the challenge of totalitarianism is its promise of
>equal rights and equal opportunities for all mankind.
>
>The fulfillment of this promise is among the highest purposes of
>government.
>
>Our determination to attain the goal of equal rights and equal opportu-
>nity must be resolute and unwavering.
>
>For my part, I intend to keep moving toward this goal with every
>ounce of strength and determination that I have."[28]

Simply, Truman effected the change in government because he was compelled by the same truth that compelled individuals in the Civil Rights movement and that compels individuals today to stand against injustice and discrimination.

Despite politics and despite the prevailing attitudes of many Americans, Truman initiated change. Beginning a process that would affect the Civil Rights movement, Truman established the grounds by which the government could step beyond the stance of most White Americans. Truman's executive order in 1948 showed how the action of one president can work against injustice and encourage those in the midst of a growing struggle for freedom. Legally free to advance in all branches of the armed forces, Blacks were able to prove the truth that they had been proclaiming for so long—that equality in humanity transcends racial differences.

Notes

1. *Plessy* v. *Ferguson,* 163 U.S. 537 (1896).

2. Merrill, *Documentary History*, 11:741.

3. It is beyond the scope of my paper to discuss all the non-Whites who were affected by Truman's order. In this essay, I focus on the effect of Truman's order on people whom I refer to as Black.

4. Lee, *Employment of Negro Troops*, 4.

5. Ibid., 73–74.

6. Mershon and Schlossman, *Foxholes and Color Lines*, 44–45.

7. Ibid., 73–77.

8. Nalty and MacGregor, *Blacks in the Military*, 108.

9. Ibid.

10. Lee, *Employment of Negro Troops,* 141.

11. Reddick, "Negro Policy," 12.

12. Gallup, *Public Opinion 1935–1971,* 2:782–83.

13. Nalty and MacGregor, *Blacks in the Military,* 114–15.

14. Merrill, *Documentary History,* 11:741.

15. Gardner, *Truman and Civil Rights*, 114.

16. Billington, "Freedom to Serve," 273.

17. Mershon and Schlossman, *Foxholes and Color Lines,* 209.

18. Nalty and MacGregor, *Blacks in the Military,* 289.

19. Ibid., 269.

20. Mershon and Schlossman, *Foxholes and Color Lines,* 217.

21. Lee, *Employment,* 187.

22. Osur, *Blacks in the Army Air Forces*, 11–12.

23. Quoted in Hubert H. Humphrey. *Beyond Civil Rights*, 19. Humphrey provides no indication of the source of Baldwin's statement, and I have been unable to track it down.

24. Mershon and Schlossman, *Foxholes and Color Lines,* 167–68.

25. Mayer. *Stroke of a Pen*, 4.

26. Harry Truman, *Public Papers*, 923–25.

27. McCullough, *Truman*, 991.

28. Truman, *Public Papers,* 923–25.

Bibliography

Billington, Monroe. Freedom to Serve: "The President's Committee on Equality of Treatment and Opportunity in the Armed Forces, 1949–1950." *Journal of Negro History* 51, no. 4 (1966): 262–74. http://links.jstor.org/sici?sici= 0022-2992%28196610%2951%3A4%3C262%3AFTSTPC%.

Gallup, George H. *The Gallup Poll Public Opinion 1935–1971.* Vol. 2. New York: Random House, 1972.

Gardner, Michael R. *Harry Truman and Civil Rights: Moral Courage and Political Risks.* Carbondale and Edwardsville: Southern Illinois University Press, 2002.

Humphrey, Hubert H. *Beyond Civil Rights: A New Day of Equality.* New York: Random House, 1968.

Lee, Ulysses. *The Employment of Negro Troops.* Washington, DC: Center of Military History, 1963.

Mayer, Kenneth. *With the Stroke of a Pen: Executive Orders and Presidential Power.* Princeton and Oxford: Princeton University Press, 2001.

McCullough, David. *Truman.* New York: Simon & Schuster, 1992.

Merrill, Dennis, ed. *Documentary History of the Truman Presidency.* Vol. 11. Bethesda, MD: University Publishers of America, 1996.

Mershon, Sherie, and Steven Schlossman. *Foxholes and Color Lines.* Baltimore: Johns Hopkins University Press, 1998.

Nalty, Bernard C., and Morris J. MacGregor. *Blacks in the Military.* Wilmington, DE: Scholarly Resources, 1981.

Osur, Alan M. *Blacks in the Army Air Forces During World War II.* Washington, DC: Office of Air Force History, 1941.

Plessy v. *Ferguson,* 163 U.S. 537 (1896).

Reddick, L. D. "The Negro Policy of the United States Army, 1775–1945." *Journal of Negro History* 34, no. 1(1949): 9–29. http://www.jstor.org/search/ 8dd55340.10427454971/1-10?configsortorder=SCORE&frame=noframe&dpi= 3&config=jstor.

Truman, Harry. *Public Papers of the Presidents of the United States: Harry S. Truman, 1945–53.* Vol. 4. Washington, DC: GPO, 1964.

| **11g** | **The CSE/CBE style is used by writers of scientific and mathematical publications.** |

The Council of Science Editors (CSE), formerly the Council of Biology Editors (CBE), has established guidelines for writers in the life sciences, the physical sciences, and mathematics. The CSE/CBE manual—*Scientific Style and Format: The CBE Manual for Authors, Editors, and Publishers*—covers both general conventions for spelling and punctuation and specific conventions for such items as chemical names and formulas. In addition, the manual presents two formats for citing and documenting sources: the citation-sequence system and the name-year system. To determine which format to use, consult your instructor, your supervisor, or the current submission guidelines for a journal in your field.

The citation-sequence system for in-text citation requires that each mention of a source be followed by a number, usually a superscript to distinguish it from other numbers used in the text. The number is placed immediately following the word or phrase indicating the source: Herbert's original method[1] was used. The order of numbers corresponds to the order in which the sources are introduced: Both Li[1] and Holst[2] have shown. . . . A source mentioned more than once is represented by the same number. When more than one source is mentioned, the numbers are separated by commas, or, when more than two numbers occur in sequence, the first and the last are separated by an en-dash: The early studies[1,2,4–7] . . . .

The name-year system for in-text citation requires both the author's last name and the year of publication to be placed in parentheses following the mention of a source: In a more recent study (Karr 2002), these findings were not replicated. The author's name may be omitted from the parenthetical citation if it appears in the text preceding it: In Karr's study (2002), these findings were not replicated. Multiple citations are separated by semicolons and ordered chronologically when the publication years are different but alphabetically when they are the same: (Li 1998; Holst 2001) but (Lamont 1998; Li 1998).

Regardless of the format you use, your reference list should have the heading *References* or *Cited References*. If you choose the citation-sequence system, you should list the sources in the order in which they were introduced in the text. See page 380 for an example. If you decide to follow the name-year system, your reference list is ordered alphabetically according to the author's last name. See page 378 for an example.

Entries for the reference lists differ only in the placement of the year of publication: The name-year system calls for the date to be placed after the author's name; the citation-sequence system calls for the date to be placed after the publisher's name in entries for books and after the periodical's name in entries for articles. Use the directory to help you find sample entries for the citation-sequence system. The reference list on page 378 shows sample entries for the name-year system.

Directory of CSE/CBE Reference Systems

BOOKS

ARTICLES

ELECTRONIC SOURCES

BOOKS

Citation-sequence system

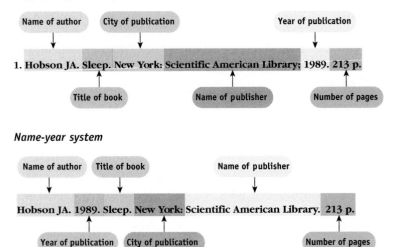

Name-year system

Citation-sequence system

References to books include four pieces of information.

1. *Name(s) of author(s) or editor(s).* Begin the entry with the author's or editor's last name; follow it with just the initials (no periods) for the first and middle names. Alternatively, you may use full first names with middle initials. When listing more than one name, follow the same format and use commas to separate the names. Add *editor* or *editors* after the last name.

2. *Title of book.* Use the title found on the book's title page. Capitalize only the first word of the title and any proper names or adjectives. If the book is a second or later edition, follow the title with a numeric indication: 3rd ed.

3. *Publication information.* Include the place of publication, the publisher's name, and the year of publication. The place of publication can usually be found on the title page. If more than one city is mentioned, use the first one listed. If the city is not well known, clarify the location by indicating the state, province, or country as well. The publisher's name should be listed next, separated from the place of publication by a colon and one space. (Standard abbreviations for publishing companies may be used. These are listed in

Appendix 2 of *Scientific Style and Format.*) After the publisher's name, list the year of publication, separating it from the publisher's name with a semicolon and one space.

4. *Number of pages.* Provide the total number of pages, excluding preliminary pages with roman numerals. Use the abbreviation *p* for *pages.* When *p* precedes a number, it indicates a specific page or sequence of pages.

1. Book with one author

1. Thompson JN. The coevolutionary process. Chicago: Univ Chicago Pr; 1994. 376 p.

2. Book with two or more authors

2. Shrader-Frechette KS, McCoy ED. Method in ecology: strategies for conservation. Cambridge: Cambridge Univ Pr; 1993. 328 p.

3. Book with an organization listed as author

3. World Commission on Environment and Development. Our common future. New York: Oxford Univ Pr; 1987. 383 p.

4. Book with editor(s)

4. Pimentel D, Westra L, Noss RF, editors. Ecological integrity. Washington: Island Pr; 2000. 428 p.

5. Chapter or part of an edited book

5. Hall SJ, Raffaelli DG. Food web patterns: what do we really know? In: Gange AC, Brown VK, editors. Multitrophic interactions in terrestrial systems. Oxford: Blackwell Science; 1997. p 395–418.

ARTICLES

References to articles include three pieces of information.

1. *Name(s) of author(s).* Begin the entry with the last name; follow it with just the initials for the first and middle names. Alternatively, you may use full first names with middle initials. When listing more than one name, use commas to separate the names.

2. *Title of article.* Capitalize only the first word of the title and any proper nouns or adjectives.

3. *Publication information.* For journal titles of more than one word, use standard abbreviations; for example, abbreviate *Scientific American* as *Sci Am.* For a list of abbreviations, see www.library.uq.edu.au/endnote/biosis/html. Use one space after the journal title; then indicate the date of publication, the volume and issue numbers, and the page numbers of the article. Place a semicolon between the date of publication and the volume number, and place a colon between the issue number and the page number(s). Put the issue number in parentheses. An issue number is not required for articles in journals with continuous pagination. Page numbers should be expressed as a range, with the second number shortened as much as possible: 237–45 or 430–4.

6. Article in a journal with continuous pagination

6. Goldwasser L, Roughgarden J. Construction and analysis of a large Caribbean food web. Ecology 1993;74:1216–33.

7. Article in a journal with issues paginated separately

7. Milad MR, Quirk GJ. Neurons in medial prefrontal cortex signal memory for fear extinction. Nature 2002;420(6911):70–3.

8. Article in a popular (general-circulation) magazine

8. Morell V. Kings of the hill? National Geographic 2002 Nov:100–20.

9. Article in a newspaper

9. Goleman D. The experience of touch: research points to a critical role. New York Times 1988 Feb 2;Sect C:1(col 2).

ELECTRONIC SOURCES

Because the CSE/CBE manual was last published in 1994, it refers users to another scientific manual for guidance in documenting electronic sources: *National Library of Medicine Recommended Formats for Bibliographic Citation.* According to this guide, entries for electronic sources are similar to those for books and articles; however, they also include three additional pieces of information:

1. The word *Internet* is placed in square brackets after the title of the book or the name of the journal to indicate that the work is an online source.

2. The date the source was cited is also given in square brackets after the date of publication.

3. The Internet address (URL) is included at the end of the entry.

10. Online book

10. Nielsen C. Interrelationships of the living phyla [Internet]. New York: Oxford Univ Pr; 1995 [cited 2002 Oct 30]. 467 p. Available from: http://emedia.netlibrary.com/reader/reader.asp?product_id=22950

11. Article in an online journal

11. Van Lunteren E, Torres A, Moyer M. Effects of hypoxia on diaphragm relaxation rate during fatigue. J Appl Physiol [Internet]; 1997 [cited 2002 Dec 2];82(5):1472–8. Available from: http://jap.physiology.org/cgi/content/full/82/5/1472

12. Article in an online newspaper

12. Forero J. As Andean glaciers shrink, water worries grow. New York Times on the Web [Internet]. 2002 Nov 23 [cited 2002 Dec 7]:[about 31 paragraphs]. Available from: http://www.nytimes.com/2002/11/24/international/americas/24BOLI.html?pagewanted=1

13. Web site

13. Corvus corax [Internet]. Bay Shore (NY): Long Island Ravens MC; c2000–2002 [updated 2001 Dec 3; cited 2003 Jan 3]. Available from: http://www.liravensmc.org/About/about_ravens.htm

14. Listserv posting

14. Reed T. Patient Safety News. In: MEDLIB-L [Internet]. [Chicago: Medical Library Assoc]; 2002 Nov 18, 9:46am [cited 2002 Nov 30]:[1 paragraph]. Available from: MEDLIB-L@LISTSERV.ACSU.BUFFALO.EDU

Name-year system

The following sample entries for a reference list in the name-year format correspond to those listed in the section on the citation-sequence format. However, the list is ordered alphabetically. The individual entries for books and articles differ from those in citation-sequence format only in the placement of the date. According to the name-year system, the date follows the author's name. Because the National Library of Medicine provides only one format for online sources, the entries for these sources are not shown in the name-year format.

References

Goldwasser L, Roughgarden J. 1993. Construction and analysis of a large Caribbean food web. Ecology 74:1216–33.

Goleman D. 1988 Feb 2. The experience of touch: research points to a critical role. New York Times;Sect C:1(col 2).

Hall SJ, Rafaelli DG. 1997. Food web patterns: what do we really know? In: Gange AC, Brown VK, editors. Multitrophic interactions in terrestrial systems. Oxford: Blackwell Science. p 395–418.

Milad MR, Quirk GJ. 2002. Neurons in medical prefrontal cortex signal memory for fear extinction. Nature 420(6911):70–3.

Morell V. 2002 Nov. Kings of the hill? National Geographic:100–20.

Pimental D, Westra L, Noss RF, editors. 2000. Ecological integrity. Washington: Island Press. 428 p.

Shrader-Frechette KS, McCoy ED. 1993. Method in ecology: strategies for conservation. Cambridge: Cambridge Univ Pr. 328 p.

Thompson JN. 1994. The coevolutionary process. Chicago: Univ Chicago Pr. 376 p.

World Commission on Environment and Development. 1987. Our common future. New York: Oxford Univ Pr. 383 p.

11h | Studying a sample paper can help you learn the CSE/CBE style guidelines.

Writers preparing reports in the sciences follow the CSE/CBE style guidelines. Such reports are generally divided into six main sections: **abstract, introduction, methods and materials, results, discussion,** and **references** (see **14c–d**). The following sample report written by Geoff Rutledge for a course in comparative anatomy and physiology includes excerpts from his abstract and introduction along with the references page. Because the CSE/CBE guidelines were not written for classroom use, your instructor or supervisor will likely provide directions for writing title pages. To read the complete report, "The Effect of Nicotine Chewing Gum on Cardiovascular Function in Nonsmokers," visit www.harbrace.com.

The Effect of Nicotine Chewing Gum on Cardiovascular Function in Nonsmokers

Geoff Rutledge

Comparative Anatomy and Physiology 350

April 26, 2002

1

Abstract

Nicotine, the primary addictive substance in tobacco, affects cardiovascular function primarily through its binding to sympathetic postganglionic nicotinic acetylcholine receptors. This binding stimulates the release of norepinephrine, which in turn stimulates heart rate, ventricle contraction strength, and vasoconstriction of blood vessels. This study examined the cardiovascular effects in nonsmokers who chewed 4mg of nicotine gum for 20 min.

[The abstract continues.]

2

Introduction

Nicotine, the primary addictive substance found in tobacco,[1] is a drug known to have both stimulant and depressant impacts, thus producing complex changes in the body.[2] However, in most clinical settings, nicotine's sympathetic impact has been found to strongly dominate any parasympathetic activity.[3] Nicotine's stimulatory mode of action involves activating a release of catecholamines directly through the adrenal medulla and also stimulating postganglionic sympathetic nerve endings.[3] These postganglionic sympathetic nerve endings are normally stimulated by a release of acetylcholine (Ach) from the preganglionic neuron. However, nicotine mimics Ach and binds to the nicotinic acetylcholine receptors, thus stimulating the release of the sympathetic neurotransmitter norepinephrine (Nor) into the body.[3] In addition to producing this release of Nor from the sympathetic nervous system, nicotine also produces a release of Nor and the sympathetic neurotransmitter epinephrine (Epi) from the adrenal medulla, thus strengthening the stimulatory mode of action.[2]

[Text omitted.]

This experiment tested the effects of nicotine chewing gum on cardiovascular function in nonsmoking individuals. Previous studies have shown significant increases in heart rate, systolic blood pressure, and diastolic blood pressure of smokers within 30 min of being exposed to nicotine from cigarettes, oral snuff, chewing tobacco, and nicotine gum.[5] This study investigated the effect of nicotine chewing gum on nonsmokers, in order to determine the effects of isolated nicotine (free from other toxins present in cigarette smoke) on human cardiovascular systems not acclimated to its presence. Because of the stimulatory effects of nicotine on the sympathetic release of Nor and Epi, the hypothesis tested was that individuals exposed to nicotine would experience increases from normal testing values in both heart rate and blood pressure.

[The introduction continues and is followed by the remainder of the paper.]

11

References

1. Tanus-Santos JE, Toledo JCY, Cittadino M, Sabha M, Rocha, JC, Moreno H. Cardio-vascular effects of transdermal nicotine in mildly hypertensive smokers. Am J Hypertens 2001;14:610–4.

2. Goodman LS, Gilman A. The pharmacological basis of therapeutics. 5th ed. New York: Macmillan; 1975. 1704 p.

3. Haass M, Kuhler W. Nicotine and sympathetic neurotransmission. Cardiovasc Drug Ther 1997;10:657–65.

4. Silverthorn DU. Human physiology: an integrated approach. 2nd ed. Upper Saddle River (NJ): Prentice Hall; 2001. 816 p.

5. Benowitz NL, Porchet H, Sheiner L, Jacob P. Nicotine absorption and cardiovascular effects with smokeless tobacco use: comparison with cigarettes and nicotine gum. Clin Pharmacol Ther 1988;44:23–8.

6. Nyberg G, Panfilov V, Sivertsson R, Wilhelmsen L. Cardiovascular effects of nicotine chewing gum in healthy nonsmokers. Eur J Clin Pharmacol 1982;23:303–7.

7. Benowitz NL, Gourlay SG. Cardiovascular toxicity of nicotine: implications for nicotine replacement therapy. J Am Coll Cardiol 1997;29:1422–31.

11i | COS provides a style for documenting sources accessed by computer.

Recognizing that increasing numbers of writers conduct much of their research online, Columbia University Press published *The Columbia Guide to Online Style* (COS) in 1998. As the manual's title suggests, this system of documentation focuses exclusively on sources produced for access by computer. COS provides both a humanities style intended to complement MLA or CMS style and a scientific style to complement APA or CSE/CBE style.

Because it is relatively new, COS is less well known than MLA (see 11a–b), APA (11c–d), CMS (11e–f), or CSE/CBE style (11g–h). But that doesn't mean that it lacks authority. It is published by a distinguished university press (see 9b) and supported by a Web site:

www.columbia.edu/cu/cup/cgos/idx_basic.html

(1) COS-style parenthetical citations offer a useful alternative format.

COS emphasizes that parenthetical citations can rarely include navigational aids such as page or section numbers because of the nature of online sources: "On the WWW, . . . a given site is always one page, regardless of its length. Pagination is thus an element of print publication that has little or no meaning in electronic documents and files" (p. 36). Specific passages in a document can be located, when necessary, by doing an online search for a keyword or phrase in the document. Accordingly, COS parenthetical citations in the humanities typically consist of an author's name (or the document title when an author is not listed). COS parenthetical citations in the sciences usually include the author's name and a date—the date of publication or modification, when available, or the date of access, when no other date is available. Here again, the document title can be substituted for the author's name when an author is not identified in the document. The title, or a shortened version of it, should be either italicized or enclosed between quotation marks, depending on the nature of the document.

In COS humanities style, parenthetical citations look like these:

Individual author (Erdrich)
Document title ("Shamengwa")

However, when an online source does include the kind of information usually associated with print publication, you can incorporate that information into the parenthetical citation.

Author and page number (Ferguson, p. 5)
Author with section number (Weiland, sec. 2)
Author with paragraph number (Chew, par. 14)

In COS scientific style, the parenthetical reference includes the date of publication (or the date of access if no publication date is available).

Author and year (Kavanaugh, 2003)
Author and specific date (Whitmore, 27 Aug. 2003)
Document title and date (Office systems, 14 May 2003)

Place the day of the month before the month. Abbreviate the names of months that have more than four letters. As in COS humanities style, add navigational aids—such as page and section numbers—only when they appear in the source itself.

(2) The specifications for a COS-style bibliography depend on whether you are writing in the humanities or in the sciences.

When composing a COS-style bibliography for a work in the humanities, include

- the author's full name (last name first), followed by a period;
- the title of the document, followed by a period and placed within quotation marks;
- the title of the larger work (in italics) of which the document is a part;
- the version or file number (if available);
- the document date or date of last modification (if different from the access date);
- the protocol and address through which the document can be accessed; and
- the date you accessed the source (within parentheses and followed by a period).

When composing a COS-style bibliography for a work in the sciences, include

- the author's last name and initials for first and middle names;
- the date the document was published or last modified, if different from the date accessed;
- the title of the document followed by a period (but without quotation marks);
- the italicized title of the complete work of which the document is a part;
- the version or file number (if available);
- the edition or revision (if any);
- the protocol and address through which the document can be accessed; and
- the date you accessed the source (within parentheses and followed by a period).

In short, COS calls for essentially the same information in humanities and scientific style. The principal differences involve

- the treatment of the first and middle names of authors,
- the placement of publication or modification date (when that information is available and differs from the access date), and
- the capitalization and punctuation of titles.

The COS scientific style calls for capitalizing only the first letter of the first word in any title or subtitle and any word that would be capitalized outside of the title. Document titles do not appear in quotation marks. Italics are used for the titles of complete works (such as book and journal titles). For both styles, double-space the entire reference list.

The COS recognizes that online sources frequently omit one or more of the elements necessary for a full citation. It recommends that writers composing a bibliography should work with what information they have and arrange it so that it follows the sequence required for a full entry.

Directory of COS-Style Entries for a Bibliography

1. Web site with a group or organization as author

Humanities style

Scientific style

Humanities style

American Lung Association. "Tobacco Product Advertising and Promotion." 2000.

> http://www.lungusa.org/tobacco/advertising_factsheet99.html (27 Oct. 2002).

List the sponsoring organization as the author when a specific author is not identified. When citations run to more than one line, indent all lines after the first line a half inch or five spaces.

Scientific style

American Lung Association. (2000). Tobacco product advertising and promotion.

> http://www.lungusa.org/tobacco/advertising_factsheet99.html (27 Oct. 2002).

This example includes a date of publication as well as a date of access. When a date of publication (or modification) is not available, do not substitute the date of access. Although that date can be used in a parenthetical citation when a date of publication or modification is not available (see page 383), it should always appear at the end of a bibliographic entry.

2. Web site with an individual author

Humanities style

Luce, Dianne C. *Cormac McCarthy: A Bibliography.* Mod. 13 Feb. 2001.

> http://www.mid.tec.sc.us/edu/ed/eng/biblio.htm (7 Jul. 2002).

Begin any entry with the author's name when an author's name is available. Use the abbreviation *Mod.* or *Rev.* to indicate a modified or revised site.

Scientific style

Kyle, S. P. (2001). Digital elevation model of the Hartnett study site. *The Hartnett site: A case study in soils and land use.* http://www.uwec.edu/Academic/ Curric/runningl/350_2001/DIGITALELEVATION.htm (14 Jan. 2003).

3. Database

Humanities style

Rickford, John R. "The Ebonics Controversy in My Backyard." *Journal of Sociolinguistics.* May 1999: 267–276. Synergy +Ebonics (15 Jan. 2003).

Check whether your instructor or supervisor wants you to include the keyword(s) you used as well as the name of the database. *Ebonics* is the keyword in this example.

Scientific style

Inger, R. F., & Voris, H. K. (2001, July). The biological relations of the frogs and snakes of Sundaland. *Journal of Biogeography,* 863–891. Synergy +frogs (15 Jan. 2003).

4. Telnet site

Humanities style

Taylor, Richard. "Guidelines for the Debate." *National Capital Freenet.* May 1997. telnet://telnet.ncf.carleton.ca (5 Jul. 2002).

Indicate that the protocol is "telnet" even if that word is part of the address for the site.

Scientific style

Taylor, R. (May 1997). Guidelines for the debate. *National capital freenet.* telnet://telnet.ncf.carleton.ca (5 Jul. 2002).

5. Gopher site

Humanities style

United Nations Office of Public Information. "Universal Declaration of Human Rights."
United Nations, What It Is and What It Does. 1994. gopher://gopher.undp.org/
(23 Jul. 2002).

Indicate that "gopher" is the protocol even if that word is part of the address.

Scientific style

United Nations Office of Public Information. (1994). Universal declaration of human
rights. *United Nations, what it is and what it does.* gopher://gopher.undp.org/
(23 Jul. 2002).

In this case, the first letter of *Nations* is capitalized in the title of the work because it is part of the name of the international organization.

6. Posting to a discussion list

Humanities style

Mitchell, Nicole Dayo. "Spanish Colonization in Trinidad." 29 June 2002. *H-Caribbean
Discussion List.* h-caribbean@msu.edu (2 Jul. 2002).

Italicize the name of the discussion list in which the document was posted.

Scientific style

Mitchell. N. D. (29 June 2002). Spanish colonization in Trinidad. *H-Caribbean
discussion list.* h-caribbean@msu.edu (2 Jul. 2002).

7. Email message

Humanities style

Kresbach, John. "A Change in the First Year Advising Program." Personal email
(15 May 2002).

Identify the document as email immediately after the subject heading, which serves as the title. Include the date of publication after the author's name only if it differs from the access date. In this case, the document was accessed the same day it was sent.

Scientific style

Kresbach, J. A change in the first year advising program. [personal email].

(15 May 2002).

Email messages are usually not included in scientific bibliographies. Before you include messages you have received, consult your instructor, your supervisor, or the guidelines for the journal to which you plan to submit your paper.

8. Article in an online journal

Humanities style

Anderson, Craig A., and Karen E. Dill, "Video Games and Aggressive Thoughts,
Feelings, and Behavior in the Laboratory and in Life." *Journal of Personality and
Social Psychology* 78.4 (2000). http://www.apa.org/journals/psp/psp784772.html
(2 Jul. 2002).

Scientific style

Anderson, C. A., & Dill, K. E. (2000). Video games and aggressive thoughts, feelings,
and behavior in the laboratory and in life. *Journal of Personality and Social
Psychology, 78*(4). http://www.apa.org/journals/psp/psp784772.html (2 Jul. 2002).

9. Article in an online encyclopedia

Humanities style

Linsky, Bernard. "Logical Constructions." *Stanford Encyclopedia of Philosophy.* Ed.
Edward N. Zalta. Stanford, CA: Metaphysics Research Lab, 2002.
http://plato.stanford.edu/entries/logical-construction/ (2 Jul. 2002).

Include both the article title and the title of the reference work, as well as any information about print publication that is provided. Begin with the article title when an author is not given.

Scientific style

Linsky, B. (2002). Logical constructions. In E. N. Zalta (Ed.), *Stanford encyclopedia of philosophy*. Stanford, CA: Metaphysics Research Lab.
http://plato.stanford.edu/entries/logical-construction/ (2 Jul. 2002).

10. Book originally published online

Humanities style

Cliff, Steven, ed. *E-Democracy E-Book: Democracy Is Online*. 2000.
http://www.publicus.net/ebook/ (2 Jul. 2002).

When a book has an editor rather than an author, place a comma after the editor's name and insert the abbreviation *ed.*

Scientific style

Cliff, S. (Ed.). (2000). *E-democracy e-book: Democracy is online.*
http://www.publicus.net/ebook/ (2 Jul. 2002).

11. Book previously published in print, now online

Humanities style

Cather, Willa. *My Antonia*. Boston: Houghton Mifflin, 1918. 2000. *American Literary Classics*. http://www.americanliterature.com/MA/MAINDEX.HTML (6 Jul. 2002).

Immediately after the title, include publication information (city of publication, publisher, and date) for the original print version. Follow with the date of the online version. Italicize both the book title and the online document of which it is a part.

Scientific style

Darwin, C. (1910/2000). *Coral reefs.* London: Ward Lock. *Project Gutenberg.*
    http://www.ibiblio.org/gutenberg/etext01/coral10.txt (21 Feb. 2003).

Place the dates of the original publication and the online version after
the author's name.

12. Government publication

Humanities style

U.S. Department of State. Bureau of Public Affairs. "Political and Security Situation of
    Women in Afghanistan." May 2002. http://www.state.gov/g/wi/rls/10023.htm
    (2 Jul. 2002).

Begin with the name of the government agency. If possible, indicate
what part of it is responsible for the publication.

Scientific style

U.S. Department of State. Bureau of Public Affairs. (2002, May). Political and security
    situation of women in Afghanistan. http://www.state.gov/g/w/rls/10023.htm
    (2 Jul. 2002).

Writing Academic Discourse

Effective communication is necessary in every academic discipline and in most professions. Professionals in every discipline—whether they work in colleges, companies, or organizations—value the basic elements of good writing: coherent organization and structure (see chapter 2), sound reasoning (chapter 7), appropriate use of evidence and detail (chapter 10), clear expression (chapters 23–27), a strong sense of audience (chapter 1), grammatical correctness (chapters 16–22), and an understanding of the conventions of the discipline or the profession.

This chapter will help you

- understand what various disciplines recognize as evidence (12a),
- understand how disciplines use evidence (12b),
- be aware that the language and writing style of disciplines differ (12c), and
- recognize the documents and formats used in several disciplines (12d).

12a	Disciplines are distinguished according to what they consider evidence to be.

Like members of a culture, people working in a discipline share certain attitudes, values, patterns of speech, and, occasionally, patterns of thought. The way each disciplinary culture generates and delivers knowledge depends to a large extent on its values and the various sources of evidence it considers worthwhile.

Traditionally, there have been three disciplinary cultures: humanities, social sciences, and natural sciences. It's fair to say that people who work in the **humanities** study expressions of human experience. Broadly speaking, the humanities include the fields of literature and language, history, philosophy and religion, art, music, drama, and film.

The humanities focus on understanding and interpreting imagination, ideas, emotions, values, and ideals.

People who work in the **social sciences** are interested in observing, recording, and interpreting human behavior in a systematic way. They study human interactions and make inferences about the causes and effects of those interactions on the basis of data they collect. The social sciences include such fields as psychology, sociology, political science, education, economics, and business.

People working in the **natural sciences** attempt to quantify and understand phenomena in the world around them, especially deviations from the norm. The natural sciences include mathematics, the biological sciences of botany and zoology, the physical sciences of chemistry and physics, and the earth sciences of geology, geography, and astronomy. The natural sciences also include the applied sciences: medicine and allied health studies, engineering, and computer science. The natural sciences are problem-solving disciplines, which explain the natural world using provable information derived from meticulous observation and experimentation.

12b	Disciplines are distinguished according to how they use evidence.

Evidence, or **data,** includes anything that might be used to prove a point in a discipline, including language and numbers. The kind of evidence that each discipline accepts as proof depends on its specific cultural values. For instance, natural scientists consider **empirical evidence**—that is, facts that can be measured or tested—to be the only kind of evidence that leads to truth. Those working in the social sciences accept **inferences** and **opinions** as well as facts (see 7c). Writers in the humanities accept both of these kinds of evidence as well as **logic** and **argumentation** (see chapter 7)—the data we employ when we use language.

Natural scientists and social scientists both claim allegiance to **inductive reasoning** (see 7h), but they carry out this process differently. Natural scientists generally begin an investigation with a **hypothesis,** an idea that serves as a basis for experimentation. The experiment either validates the hypothesis or shows it to be in error. Social scientists, on the other hand, collect evidence from which they develop a hypothesis. Thus, you could say that natural scientists reason from a hypothesis, and social scientists reason to a hypothesis. Both use a version of the scientific method (see **14c**). Humanists, however, use both inductive reasoning and **deductive reasoning** (see **7h**). They begin with an idea, collect evidence, and then use both types of reasoning to arrive at a conclusion—an interpretation of what the evidence means.

Whereas all disciplines demand that you establish your credibility (see **9a**) and use logic and sound reasoning as you develop your findings and report your conclusions, they differ in their acceptance of what constitutes support. In the natural sciences, you rely on **quantitative data**—numerically based evidence—as is evident in the excerpt from Jennifer York's lab report.

From Jennifer York's lab report,
"Sex-Linked Inheritance, Sex Determination"

Virgin female flies were mated to male flies by placing several pairs together in a vial. One week later, the parent flies were removed to prevent them from mating with their own progeny and the vial was checked for larvae to indicate that successful mating had occurred.

York describes her method.

Week 1:

Cross 1:

P: 3 ♂ (++/YB)　　　×　　3 ♀ (yw/yw)

　　　Tan body, red　　　　　Yellow body, white

　　　bar eye　　　　　　　　round eye

She reports quantitative data numerically.

Cross 2:

P: 4 ♂ (yw/YB)　　　×　　3 ♀ (++/++)

　　　Yellow body, white　　　Tan body, red round

　　　bar eye　　　　　　　　eye

Cross 3:

P: 3 ♂ (yw+/YB)　　　×　　3 ♀ (y+f/y+f)

　　　Yellow body, white　　　Yellow body, red round

　　　bar eye, long bristles　　eye, short bristles

You will generally report quantitative evidence in a tightly formatted piece of writing that permits your readers to replicate (that is, repeat) the results of your study. The format for such reporting includes an introduction, a description of methods, a summary of findings, and a discussion of results. An example of a scientific report—Heather Jensen's lab report for a first-year biology course—appears in 14d. (Another example of scientific discourse, Jennifer York's report on fruit flies for a third-year biology course, is available online. See www.harbrace.com.)

In the social sciences, you rely on quantitative data such as statistics you develop from laboratory research or the results of surveys you conduct, but you are also likely to use **qualitative data**—evidence based on your observations of behavior, interviews you conduct, and the like. You can report qualitative evidence in a format that includes an introduction, a subject identification, a description of methods, an analysis of behaviors, and conclusion. In this kind of report, as in reports written by natural scientists, you minimize personal involvement. (Notice the language in the excerpt from Mike Demmon's field report.) You can also report qualitative data in thick analysis, where you are an active agent, observing phenomena and then describing in detail what you have observed in an ethnographic report or case study.

**From Mike Demmon's field report,
"Quantitative Analysis of Diving Ducks"**

Demmon makes an inference to produce qualitative data.

With the exception of human-induced movements, it appeared that there were no significant interactions between any of the species. As may have been expected, the Buffleheads also appeared to be courting at times. The data above also show that the majority of the birds that were paired or followed by the other sex were Buffleheads.

Beyond the Rule

MORE ABOUT THICK ANALYSIS

Thick analysis comes from the idea of "thick description," first introduced by philosopher Gilbert Ryle and adapted for ethnographic research by Clifford Geertz. For more information, visit www.harbrace.com.

Thick analysis is often arranged to permit persuasion. Background material is presented before the narrative, which is then followed by data and explanation, in an arrangement similar to classical arrangement (see 2c). Thus, while you cannot generalize successfully from qualitative research studies, such studies often produce "findings" that you can then test with more control and objectivity in quantitative research studies. Nikki Kzmarzik's discussion of the relationship between sleep and memory (see 11d) and Mike Demmon's environmental science field report on the behavior of diving ducks are both examples of writing in the social sciences (although environmental science is often classified as a natural science discipline).

In the humanities, you rely almost entirely on qualitative evidence that you derive from careful observation and analysis of texts—including musical scores and paintings or sculptures, as well as literary texts and historical documents. This handbook includes two examples of writing in the humanities: Nicole Hester's paper about President Truman's desegregation of the U.S. military (see 11f) and Josh Otis's essay on *The Things They Carried* (13g).

From Nicole Hester's essay, "Race in the U.S. Army"

> In July of 1948, by executive order, President Truman demanded equal treatment and equal opportunity in the armed forces, setting into motion a series of events that would force change, however slow it might be:

Hester summarizes Truman's statement.

It is hereby declared to be the policy of the President that there shall be equality of treatment and opportunity for all persons in the armed services without regard to race, color, religion or national origin. This policy shall be put into effect as rapidly as possible, having due regard to the time required to effectuate any necessary changes without impairing efficiency or morale.[2]

Hester relies on the evidence of language. She infers what Truman understood about the situation and the attitudes of others.

With such language as "all" and "as rapidly as possible," Truman showed that his statement was more than a publicity stunt. While understanding the scale of the change he was demanding, Truman was also aware of the sentiment of the American people and numerous government officials.

From Josh Otis's essay, "Friendship in *The Things They Carried*"

Otis provides context for his evidence.

He presents the evidence from his source.

Otis explains the evidence.

Just after Tim arrives in Vietnam, there is an incident in which the men find a dead farmer in an abandoned village. One by one, the soldiers go up and shake the old man's hand, but Tim refuses. His refusal makes him the object of harassment, but he persists. That night Kiowa approaches him and says, "You did a good thing today. That shaking hands crap, it isn't decent. The guys'll hassle you for a while, especially Jensen--but just keep saying no. Should've done it myself. Takes guts, I know that" (257). Kiowa's sense of what is morally sound and his support of actions in accordance with his beliefs help explain why he and Tim become so close.

12c | Each discipline has a particular language and writing style.

Each discipline has a vocabulary that you will learn when you take courses in its specific subject areas. For example, if you take a course in the social sciences, you will learn the difference between quantitative and qualitative research studies and between a field study and a laboratory study. You will also understand what is meant by the term *theory* and be able to distinguish between thin and thick description. (Unlike writers of thick description who use a kind of personal narrative of the sequence of events and observations that occur in an experiment, writers of thin description present an impersonal distillation of those events.) If you take a course in the natural sciences, you will learn how to collect and process quantitative data. In both the social and the natural sciences, you will learn the term *replicability* and understand its importance. In courses in the humanities, you will learn to recognize the difference between primary and secondary sources (see chapter 8). In addition to the language of a discipline, you will master a wide range of technical terms specific to its subject areas: sociology and psychology, chemistry and zoology, or literature and music, to name a few (see 28c(4)).

Learning the language of a discipline has an important benefit. The purpose of a specialized vocabulary is to make communication between those who work in a discipline precise and efficient, and it is thus the language that experts in that discipline use regularly. When you use the specialized vocabulary of a discipline, you establish yourself as knowledgeable in that discipline and as credible in writing about it; that is, you establish your professional ethos.

Each discipline has developed a distinctive writing style and tone. Writers in the natural sciences use language sparingly to convince an audience of the viability of research findings. Social scientists report ethnographic inquiry and case studies using thick descriptions, which are fundamentally rhetorical (see 12b), but they use language more sparingly when writing thin descriptions to report the results of surveys and experiments. In thin descriptions, writers in both the social and the natural sciences present themselves as impartial and objective; in doing so, they strive to avoid the first-person pronoun *I* (see 29d), a practice that often results in the use of the passive rather than the active voice (22c). Writers in both the social and the natural sciences also use visual elements such as charts, graphs, and tables (see **6b**) more often than writers in the humanities do. Writers in the humanities may allow their personalities to show in their texts more than do writers in the social and natural sciences (unless the latter are using thick description). And writers in the humanities tend to see rhetorical analysis as a viable means of conducting research and rhetorical and theoretical argumentation as an acceptable way of reporting evidence. Further, although disciplines differ concerning the best length for sentences and paragraphs, they all expect sentences to be complete (see chapters **16** and **18**) and paragraphs to be coherent (chapter **3**).

Each discipline also has conventions for formatting documents. Writers in the humanities make minimal use of headings (see **6c(4)**), and they format documents in traditional ways. Writing in the humanities is also less dependent on a prescribed approach than is writing in the social or natural sciences, where research generally must follow specific procedures and be reported in a predetermined sequence. And writers in any discipline are expected to adhere to that discipline's approved documentation and bibliographical style (see chapter **11**). Literary studies, modern languages, and rhetoric follow the style guidelines of the Modern Language Association (MLA) (see **11a–b**). History, art, and music follow *The Chicago Manual of Style* (see **11e–f**). Linguistics and most of the social sciences use some form of the style recommended by the American Psychological Association (APA) (see **11c–d**). The Council of Science Editors (formerly the Council of Biology Editors) encourages natural scientists to use either a name-date system that is similar to the APA and MLA systems or a citation-sequence system that calls for listing sources in the order in which they occur in the document (see **11g–h**).

12d Each discipline favors specific kinds of documents and formats.

In the natural sciences, you will write two important kinds of documents: the lab report (see **14d**) and the literature review. In the social sciences, you will also write literature reviews, in addition to several kinds of reports, among them field reports, observational reports, and case studies. The excerpt from a literature review by Rebecca Abraham follows APA documentation style.

**From Rebecca Abraham's literature review,
"Thinking Styles as Moderators of Role Stressor–
Job Satisfaction Relationships"**

Sternberg and Grigorenko's (1993) 16-item, forced choice thinking styles inventory was employed. Their Cronbach alpha reliabilities for the judicial, hierarchical, global and liberal thinking styles were 0.73, 0.81, 0.83 and 0.88 and were all above the 0.70 threshold of acceptability. Sternberg and Grigorenko (1993) established construct validity through a five-factor structure accounting for 77% of the variance in the data. Factors (loadings in parentheses) elicited included legislative-executive (-0.78 and 0.58), judicial-oligarchic (0.7 each), external-internal (0.72 and 0.80), global-local (-0.82 and 0.92) and hierarchic (0.86). Convergent validity was established through correlations with the Myers-Briggs type indicator as well as the Gregorec measure of mind styles. For the former, 30 of 128 correlations were significant, whereas for the latter, 22 of 52 were significant. The judicial, global and liberal styles correlated positively with SAT math, but not with SAT verbal. Consequently, styles are largely distinct from intelligence or aptitude.

Abraham summarizes the work of a research team.

For humanities classes, you can expect to write papers that describe your experiences or argue for the correctness of your observations. These papers may be creative texts such as poems, interpretive texts that offer interpretations of literary, musical, or artistic works, or theoretical essays that attempt to understand something in a larger context (how a poem reflects the age in which it was written, for example). Remember, however, that interpretations must be logical arguments based on support and proof (chapter 7).

It is worth noting that all disciplines are dynamic entities, constantly developing new approaches and new attitudes. For instance, the acceptance of thick description in the social sciences is a relatively recent phenomenon, and such description is beginning to achieve acceptance in the natural sciences (particularly in medical writing). Similarly, writers in the humanities have borrowed techniques from the social and natural sciences. Rhetoricians report ethnographic research, musicians analyze the physiological effects of sound, and painters and sculptors discuss experiments that test the physical properties of the media they use. Generalizations made about the characteristics of specific disciplines are, like all generalizations, incomplete at best.

Exercise 1

Read an article in a professional journal on a topic you are studying in another course or one you are simply interested in. Then, answer the following questions about it.

a. What kind of evidence is the research reported in the article based on? How do you know?
b. How is the evidence presented in the article?
c. Comment on the kind of language used in the article.
d. What kind of article is it (e.g., literature review, interpretation, case study)? Identify its main characteristics.

Writing to Interpret Literature

Ever since you wrote your first book report, you've been interpreting and writing about literature, talking about plot, characters, and setting. When you write about literature in college, regardless of the literary genre involved—fiction, drama, poetry, essays, personal narratives, manifestos, or memoirs—you'll still discuss plot, characters, and setting. But you'll also apply many of the same interpretive strategies you use to write about other topics: You'll explore and focus your subject (see 2a), formulate a thesis statement (see 2b) that can be supported from the literary work itself, and arrange your thoughts in the most effective way.

This chapter will help you

- recognize the various genres of literature (13a),
- use the specialized vocabulary for discussing literature (13b),
- employ various critical approaches for interpreting literature (13c),
- understand specific terms that define the purpose of an interpretation (13d),
- realize the value of a careful reading (13e), and
- apply the special conventions for writing about literature (13f).

13a | Literature can be divided into various genres.

Like all specialized fields, literature can be divided into categories, which are referred to as **genres** (from the French word for "kind" or "type"). A genre can be identified by its particular features or conventions, which develop within a specific cultural context. Some genres, such as drama and poetry, appear to be timeless and universal; others, detective fiction, for example, seem to be more recent Western cultural phenomena. In fact, your cultural background can affect how easily you recognize and understand any specific genre. If you grew up in a family in which poems were read aloud, chances are that you'll understand poetry more easily than someone who hasn't heard much poetry. If you and your family are opera buffs, you'll recognize the conventions of drama more readily than someone whose family reads mostly detective fiction.

Just as you can recognize film genres—action, suspense, horror, romantic comedy, comedy, animated, Western, and science fiction—you can recognize literary genres, from poetry and drama to essays and narratives. And just as film genres sometimes overlap (for example, when an action film is partially animated), so do literary genres: Some poems are referred to as prose poems, whereas some plays are written in poetic verse. But even when genres overlap, the identifiable features of each genre are still evident.

Some of the most widely studied literary genres are fiction, drama, and poetry, though many forms of nonfiction (including personal essays and memoirs, literacy narratives, and documents such as manifestos) are gaining attention in college courses. Although all imaginative literature is fiction, the term **fiction** is applied specifically to novels and short stories. These works express truth about the human condition through such components as setting, character, and plot (see **13b**).

Drama differs from other imaginative literature in one specific way: It is meant to be performed—whether on stage, on film, or on television—with the director and actors imprinting the play with their own interpretations. Like fiction, nonfiction, and poetry, however, drama can be read; in which case, you bring your interpretative abilities to the printed page. Drama has many of the same elements as fiction (setting, character, and plot) but is distinguished by its method of presentation. In a novel, you often find extensive descriptions of characters and setting, as well as passages revealing what characters are thinking. In a play, you learn what a character is thinking when he or she shares thoughts with another character in dialogue or presents a **dramatic soliloquy** (a speech delivered to the audience by an actor alone on the stage).

Poetry shares many of the components of fiction and drama. It too may have a narrator with a point of view. Dramatic monologues and narrative poems sometimes have a plot, a setting, and characters. But poetry is primarily characterized by its concentrated use of connotative language, imagery, allusions, figures of speech, symbols, sound, and rhythm.

13b | The specialized vocabulary for discussing literature helps writers understand its elements.

Like all specialized fields, literature has a unique vocabulary, which describes the various features of literary texts and concepts of literary analysis. As you learn this vocabulary, you'll learn more than just a list of terms: You'll learn how to understand, interpret, and write about literature.

(1) Characters carry the plot forward.

The **characters** are the humans or humanlike personalities (aliens, creatures, robots, animals, and so on) who carry the plot forward; they usually include a main character, called a **protagonist,** who is in external conflict with another character or an institution or in internal conflict with himself or herself. This conflict usually reveals the **theme,** or the central idea of the work (see **13b(7)**).

Because writing about literature often requires character analysis, you need to understand the characters in any work you read. You can do so by paying close attention to their appearance, their language, and their actions. You also need to pay attention to what the narrator or other characters say about them. Whether you are writing about characters in novels (Tony Hillerman's Joe Leaphorn or David Morrell's Rambo), in plays (William Shakespeare's Hamlet or Lorraine Hansberry's Mrs. Young), or in poems (Gwendolyn Brooks's cool school skippers or William Blake's young chimney sweep), you'll want to concentrate on what those characters do and say—and why.

(2) Imagery is conveyed by descriptive language.

The **imagery** in a piece of literature is conveyed by **descriptive language,** or words that describe a sensory experience. Notice the images in "Portrait," a prose poem by Pinkie Gordon Lane that focuses on the life—and death—of a mother.

> My mother died walking along a dusty road on a Sunday morning in New Jersey. The road came up to meet her sinking body in one quick embrace. She spread out like an umbrella and dropped into oblivion before she hit the ground. In that one swift moment all light went out at the age of forty-nine. Her legacy: the blackened knees of the scrub-woman who ransomed her soul so that I might live, who bled like a tomato whenever she fought to survive,

who laughed fully when amused—her laughter rising in one huge crescendo—and whose wings soared in dark despair. . . .
—**PINKIE GORDON LANE,** *Girl at the Window*

The dusty road, the sinking body, the quick embrace—these images convey the loneliness and swiftness of death. The blackened knees, bleeding tomato, and rising laughter, in contrast, are images of a life of work, struggle, and joy.

(3) The narrator tells the story.

The **narrator** of a literary work tells the story, and this speaking voice can be that of a specific character (or of characters taking turns telling, as in William Faulkner's *The Sound and the Fury*), can seem to be that of the work's author (but should not be confused with the author), or can be that of an all-knowing presence that transcends both characters and author. Whatever the case may be, the diction and sentence structure reveal the narrator's **tone,** or attitude toward events and characters and even, in some circumstances, toward readers. By determining the tone and the impact it has on you as a reader, you can gain insight into the author's purpose. (See 3a(3).)

(4) Plot is the sequence of events and more.

The **plot** is what happens in the story, the sequence of events or the narrative. Plot is those things—and more. The plot establishes how events are patterned or related in terms of conflict and resolution. Narrative answers "What comes next?" and plot answers "Why?" Consider this example:

> **Narrative** The king died, and then the queen died.
> **Plot** The queen was beheaded after she killed the king.

Plot usually begins with a conflict, an unstable situation that sets events in motion (for instance, a state of tension or animosity between the king and the queen). In what is called the **exposition,** the author introduces the characters, setting, and background—the elements that not only constitute the unstable situation but also relate to the events that follow. The subsequent series of events leads to the **climax,** the most intense event in the narrative. The climax is also referred to as the **turning point** because what follows is **falling action** (or **dénouement**) that leads to a resolution of the conflict and a stable situation.

(5) Setting involves place and time.

Setting involves place—not just the physical setting, but also the social setting (the morals, manners, and customs of the characters). Setting also involves time—not only historical time, but also the length of time covered by the narrative. Setting includes atmosphere, or the emotional response to the situation, often shared by the reader with the characters. For example, Boston in the nineteenth century is a markedly different setting from Boston in the twenty-first century. Not only has the physical appearance of the city itself changed, but so has the social setting and the atmosphere. Being aware of these features of the setting will help you better understand the story, whether it's written as prose fiction, drama, or poetry.

(6) Symbols resonate with broader meaning.

Frequently used by writers of fiction, drama, and poetry, a **symbol** is an object, usually concrete, that stands for something else, usually abstract. For example, at the beginning of *A Streetcar Named Desire,* a play by Tennessee Williams, one of the main characters buys a paper lantern to cover a naked light bulb. During the scenes that follow, she frequently talks about light, emphasizing her preference for soft, attractive lighting. At the end of the play, another character tears off the lantern, and a third character tries to return the ruined lantern to the main character as she is being taken away to a mental hospital. Anyone seeing this play performed or reading it carefully would note that the lantern is a symbol. It is what it is (a paper lantern), but it also stands for something more than it is (a character's determination to avoid harsh truths).

When you write about a particular symbol, first note the lines, paragraphs, or passages in which it appears in the literary work. Then consider why it appears in those places and to what effect: What might this particular symbol mean? When you have an idea, trace the incidents in the literary work that reinforce that idea.

(7) The theme is the main idea of a literary work.

The main idea of a literary work is its **theme.** Depending on how they interpret a work, different readers may identify different themes. To test whether the idea you have identified is central to the work in question, check to see if it is supported by the setting, plot, characters, and symbols. If you can relate these components to the idea you are considering, then that idea can be considered the work's theme. The most prominent literary themes arise out of conflict: person versus person, person versus self, person versus nature, or person versus society.

When you believe you have identified the theme, state it as a sentence—and be precise. A theme conveys a specific idea; it should not be confused with a topic.

Topic	family conflict
Vague theme	*King Lear* is about family conflict.
Specific theme	*King Lear* reveals a conflict between a father who yearns for respect and daughters who have lost confidence in his judgment.

For additional definitions of literary terms and conventions, see **13d** and **13f**.

Beyond the Rule

OTHER USEFUL LITERARY TERMS

As you draft and revise your essays about literature, you may want to use some of the literary terms available at www.harbrace.com.

CHECKLIST for Interpreting a Literary Work

- From whose point of view is the story or poem told?
- Who is the protagonist? How is his or her character developed?
- With whom or what is the protagonist in conflict?
- How are the characters depicted and distinguished through dialogue?
- What is the theme?
- How does the author use setting, plot, characters, and symbols to establish the theme?
- What symbols, images, or figures of speech does the author use? To what effect?
- How do the various elements combine to convey meaning?

13c | Critical approaches to literature can serve as the basis for interpretation.

Writing a paper about a literary work usually requires you to focus on the work itself and to demonstrate that you have read it carefully—a process known as **close reading.** (Compare close reading with critical reading, see chapter 1.) Through close reading, you can offer an **interpretation** of what the work means to you. An interpretation can be shaped by your personal response to what you have read, a specific type of critical theory, or the views of other readers, which you wish to support or challenge.

In recent years, there has been growing interest in **literary theory**— scholarly discussion that tries to explain how the meaning of literature can be determined. Literary theory ranges from approaches that focus almost exclusively on the text itself (its language and structure) to approaches that show how the meaning of the text relates to historical, economic, social, and other cultural factors. Familiarity with literary theory can enrich your reading of literature as well as your understanding of the books and essays about literature that you discover when you do research (see 8d). Literary theory can also help you decide how you want to focus your writing about literature.

This section discusses some of the most popular critical approaches to literature. Although these approaches overlap somewhat, each has a different primary focus: the reader, some aspect of the cultural context, the text itself, or the author or characters. It's important to keep in mind that interpreting literature involves a responsible reliance on one or more of these critical approaches. Literary interpretation doesn't mean that anything goes, nor does it mean that there's only one correct interpretation. But whatever your interpretation, the text should support it.

(1) Reader-response theory focuses on the reader.

Reader-response theory argues that a literary work is incomplete in and of itself; a reader is necessary to complete its meaning. Readers construct meaning as they read and interact with the elements within the text, with each reader bringing something different to the text. Readers bring different intellectual values and life experiences to a work each time they read it. Thus, meaning is not fixed on the page; meaning depends more on what each reader brings *to* the page every time he or she encounters it. For example, a feminist (whether male or female) might doubt the universality of Henry David Thoreau's *Walden,* and any sensitive reader might wonder about the relationship between Celie and Shug in Alice Walker's *The Color Purple* (see more about feminist and gender-based criticism in **13c(2)**). Furthermore, the same reader can have different responses to the same literary work when rereading it after a number of years: A father of teenagers might find Gwendolyn Brooks's "we real cool" more disturbing than it had seemed when he first read it in high school. Although a reader-response approach to literature encourages diverse interpretations, you must be able to support your interpretation by showing how it interacts responsibly with the text to shape the meaning you describe. You cannot simply say, "Well, that's what this work means to me" or "That's my interpretation." You must demonstrate to your audience how each element of the work supports your interpretation.

(2) Both feminist and gender-based literary criticism focus on issues related to sex, gender, or sexual orientation.

Both feminist and gender-based literary criticism focus on the significance of sex, gender, or sexual orientation within a particular social context. To determine the purpose of a literary work or to analyze its characters, these theories enable a reader to analyze the ways the work promotes or challenges the prevailing intellectual or cultural assumptions of its day regarding issues related to gender and sexuality, including patriarchy and compulsory heterosexuality. For instance, Edith Wharton's *The Age of Innocence* compares two upper-class nineteenth-century women in terms of the specific social pressures that shaped and constricted their lives and loves. A feminist critic might emphasize the oppression of these women and the repression of their sexuality. Another critic, using a gender-based approach, might focus on the positive features of the domestic relationship between Olive and Verena, two financially independent women in Henry James's *The Bostonians*; that same critic might also try to explain why Jake Barnes in Hemingway's *The Sun Also Rises* bonds with some men and is contemptuous of others.

(3) Race-based literary criticism focuses on issues related to race relations.

A useful form of race-based literary criticism, **critical race theory** focuses on the significance of race relations (race, racism, and power) within a specific historical and social setting in order to explain the experience and literary production of peoples whose history is characterized by political, social, and psychological oppression. Not only does this theoretical approach seek out previously neglected literary works, but it also illuminates the ways in which race, ethnicity, and power inform many works. Previously neglected works such as Zora Neale Hurston's *Their Eyes Were Watching God,* Rudolpho Anaya's *Bless Me, Ultima,* and Frederick Douglass's *Narrative,* each of which demonstrates how racism affects the characters' lives, have taken on considerable cultural value in the last twenty years. **African American literary criticism,** for example, has been particularly successful in invigorating the study of great African American writers, whose works can be more fully appreciated when readers consider how some of their literary elements (see 13a) have been informed by the social forces that helped produce them. Closely associated with critical race theory is **postcolonial theory,** which takes into account the relationship of the colonized with the colonizer and the ways a text challenges the dominant powers at a particular time and place, asserting a drive toward the liberation of oppressed social groups. Joseph Conrad's *Heart of Darkness,* Jean Rhys's *Wide Sargasso Sea,* Daniel Defoe's *Robinson Crusoe,* and E. M. Forster's *A Passage to India* can all be read productively using postcolonial theory.

(4) Class-based literary criticism focuses on socioeconomic issues.

To explain the conflict between characters in a work of literature or between a character and a community or institution, **class-based literary criticism** draws on the work of Karl Marx, Terry Eagleton, and other theorists who have addressed the implications of social hierarchies and the accompanying economic tensions. These theorists argue that differences in socioeconomic class—in the material conditions of daily life— divide people in profoundly significant ways, much more so than differences in race, ethnicity, culture, and gender. Thus, a class-based approach can be used to explain why Emma Bovary is unhappy, despite her "good" (i.e., financially advantageous) marriage, in Gustave Flaubert's *Madame Bovary,* why Bigger Thomas gets thrown into such a confused mental state in Richard Wright's *Native Son,* or why a family loses its land in John Steinbeck's *The Grapes of Wrath.*

(5) Text-based literary criticism focuses on the work itself.

Text-based literary criticism demands concentration on the piece of literature itself; with this approach, only the use of concrete, specific examples from the text validates an interpretation. The reader must pay careful attention to the elements within the literary work—plot, characters, setting, tone, dialogue, imagery, and so on (see **13b**)—to evaluate their interaction, overall effect, and meaning. The reader requires nothing more than what is contained within the text itself—not information about the author's life or other cultural productions of the time—in order to understand and appreciate the text's unchanging meaning. Readers may change, but the meaning of the text does not. A close reading of the work is essential, then, in order to account for all of its particularities, including the ways in which the language and the structure fit within a specific literary genre. According to text-based literary criticism, F. Scott Fitzgerald's *The Great Gatsby* is the story of unfulfilled longing, richly told with haunting imagery.

(6) Context-based literary criticism focuses on the time and place in which a work was created.

Context-based literary criticism considers the historical period in which a work was written and the cultural and economic patterns that prevailed during that period. For example, recognizing that Willa Cather published *My Antonia* during World War I can help account for the darker side of that novel; similarly, understanding that Arthur Miller wrote *The Crucible* in response to the accusations of the House Un-American Activities Committee in the 1950s helps explain why that play generated so much excitement when it was first produced. Critics who use a context-based and class-based approach known as **cultural studies** consider how a literary work interacts with economic production, socioeconomic class, and other cultural artifacts (such as songs or fashion) from the period in which it was written.

(7) Psychoanalytic theories focus on psychological factors affecting the writing and the reading of literature.

Psychoanalytic theories, which focus on the psychological states of the author and characters as well as the reader, seek to explain human experience and behavior in terms of sexual impulses and unconscious motivations (drives, desires, fears, needs, and conflicts). When applied to literary criticism, these theories (based on the work of Nancy Chodorow, Hélène Cixous, Sigmund Freud, Melanie Klein, Jacques Lacan, Herbert Marcuse, and Juliet Mitchell, among others) help readers discern the motivations of characters, envision the psychological state of the author as implied by the text, and evaluate the psychological reasons for their own interpretations. Critics may apply the psychoanalytic approach to explain why Hamlet is deeply disturbed by his mother's remarriage, why Holden Caulfield rebels at school (in *Catcher in the Rye* by J. D. Salinger), or why Rochester is blinded (in Charlotte Brontë's *Jane Eyre*).

Critics who use the work of psychiatrist Carl Jung to explore **archetypes** (recurring figures or patterns in literature) are also using a psychoanalytic approach to interpret literature, whether the literary form is a fairy tale, fable, epic poem, Greek drama, postmodern novel, or movie script. Archetypal figures include the hero, the earth mother, the scapegoat, the outcast, and the cruel stepmother; archetypal patterns include the quest, the initiation, the test, and the return.

13d | Specific types of literary interpretation differ in purpose.

An interpretation that attempts to explain the meaning of one feature of a literary work is called an **analysis.** To analyze a work of literature, a writer divides it into elements, examines such elements as setting and characters, and determines how one element contributes to the overall meaning. A common form of analysis is **character analysis,** in which a writer interprets one or more aspects of a single character. An analysis can also focus on a single scene, symbol, or theme.

An interpretation that attempts to explain every element in a literary work is called an **explication** and is usually used only with poetry. When explicating William Wordsworth's "A Slumber Did My Spirit Seal," a writer might note that the *s* sound reinforces the hushed feeling of sleep and death in the poem. But it would also be necessary to consider the meanings of *slumber, spirit,* and *seal,* as well as why these words are arranged as they are (as opposed to "A Slumber Sealed My Spirit" or "My Spirit Was Sealed by Slumber").

An **evaluation** of a work gauges how successful the author is in communicating meaning to readers. The most common types of evaluation are book, theater, and film reviews. A writer can also evaluate a work by focusing on how successfully one of its parts contributes to the meaning conveyed by the others. Like any other interpretation, an evaluation is a type of argument in which a writer cites evidence to persuade readers to accept a clearly formulated thesis. (See chapters 2 and 7.) An evaluation of a literary work should consider both strengths and weaknesses, if there is evidence of both.

Although summarizing a literary work can be a useful way to make sure you understand it, do not confuse a summary with an analysis, interpretation, or evaluation. Those who have read the work are unlikely to benefit from reading a summary of it. Do not submit one unless your instructor has asked for it.

Exercise 1

Attend a film, a play, or a poetry reading at your school or in your community. Write a two- to three-page essay evaluating the work, using one of the theoretical approaches discussed in this chapter.

13e | Careful reading is essential to the process of writing about literature.

You can interpret and write effectively about a work of literature if you read it carefully (see chapter 1). As you read, take notes on your personal response, either in a notebook or in the margins of your book. As you plan your essay, think critically about your impressions—and how you might interpret them.

(1) Writing about literature begins with active, personal engagement with what you read.

As you read, trust your own reactions. Which characters do you admire? Did you follow the plot? Did the work remind you of any experience of your own? Did it introduce you to a different world in terms of historical or geographical setting, or did you encounter a familiar cast of characters? Were you amused, moved, or confused? These first impressions can provide the seeds from which strong essays will grow, even if they are modified by your thinking later on.

You can also engage a text you own by **annotating** it—marking key passages and raising questions that occur as you read (see **10b**). In addition, you can benefit from **freewriting** about your first impressions (see **2a(1)**), from keeping a journal in which you record your reactions to and questions about reading assignments (see **2a(1)**), or from practicing various planning and focusing techniques (chapter **2**). These methods of exploring a subject can help you discover what you think, what you want to understand, and what you need to research. Therefore, when using any of these methods, simply let yourself explore.

(2) You can understand your response by considering how it is shaped by your identity.

When reflecting on your response to a work of literature, you can clarify your thinking by considering how your reading might be shaped by the factors that make you who you are and the critical approaches to literature you are consciously or unconsciously using (see **13c**). For example, if you find yourself responding positively or negatively to a character in a novel or play, you could ask yourself whether this response has anything to do with your

- psychological makeup,
- political beliefs,
- gender or sexual orientation,
- race,
- social class,
- religion, or
- geographic region.

Thinking along these lines can help you decide how to focus your paper and prepare you for using one or more critical approaches (see **13c**) as the basis for your interpretation.

(3) After choosing a topic, you need to develop it.

If you are choosing your own topic, your first step should be to reflect on your personal response (see **13c–d**) and the way you've decided to focus the subject. Reviewing these responses may enable you to narrow your focus as well as formulate a tentative thesis statement. Not only must you begin to shape a thesis, you also need to consider how to convince your readers of the validity of your interpretation and how to use specific evidence from the text to explain and support that interpretation.

For these reasons, you want to choose a topic that interests you and your readers. Because most readers will be interested in what *you* think, you need to discover a way to demonstrate your originality in terms of a subject that you can develop adequately and responsibly. Apply strategies of development, singly or in combination (see 2e). You might define why you consider a character heroic, classify a play as a comedy of manners, or describe a setting that contributes to a work's meaning. Perhaps you can compare and contrast two poems on a similar subject or explore cause-and-consequence relationships in a novel. Why, for example, does an apparently intelligent character make a bad decision? You can even combine two or more development strategies when you have a clear focus. For instance, you might show how the description of a family's house in a novel defines that family's values or reveals the effects of an underlying conflict.

(4) Rereading a literary work enhances your understanding of it.

A literary work can provoke different responses (see chapter 1) from different readers for different theoretical reasons (13c). Moreover, you can have a significantly different response when rereading a work—even a work you think you understand already. For instance, if you're rereading John Milton's *Paradise Lost* in order to write an essay about it, your response may differ from what you felt and thought while racing through it, cramming for an exam. Reread any work you are planning to write about—or, at least, reread the chapters, passages, or scenes that impressed you as especially important or problematic.

With your tentative thesis in mind, annotate the text a second time for evidence that supports *or* detracts from that thesis. You are likely to find evidence that you did not notice on your first reading or that will help you modify and sharpen your thesis. To establish yourself as a credible author (see 9a), use evidence appropriate for your purpose (see 7d–e), and present it fairly. Remember that a good way to note evidence, ideas, and concerns is to engage actively in the reading process (see 1c–d).

(5) Research can reveal the ways other readers have responded to a literary work.

You will undoubtedly anchor your essay on your personal response or interpretation. But if you read literary criticism by others, visit online discussion groups or forums (see 5c), participate in class discussions, or become active in a book club, you can engage in a dialogue that can enrich your own ideas. Many instructors will want you to advance your own ideas at the same time as you use and give credit to outside sources (see **8c–d**). Although it's tempting to lean heavily on the interpretations of experts, remember that your readers are mainly interested in your interpretation and the ways you use the sometimes conflicting interpretations of others (including the other members of your class) to support your own points. To that end, you need to read critically (see chapter **1**) as you formulate your thesis (**2b**).

Chapters **8**, **9**, and **10** explain how to conduct research. To locate material on a specific writer or work, consult your library's catalog (see **8d**) and *The MLA International Bibliography,* an index of books and articles about literature that is an essential resource for literary studies and that can be consulted in printed volumes or online. (See page 241.)

In addition to having books and articles about specific writers, your school or public library is also likely to have a number of reference books that provide basic information on writers, books, and literary theory. Works such as *Contemporary Authors, The Oxford Companion to English Literature,* and *The Princeton Handbook of Poetic Terms* can be useful when you are beginning your research or when you have encountered terms you need to clarify.

You can also access information for an essay about a literary topic by searching the Web. Scholars and societies interested in specific writers have created Web sites to encourage reading and discussion. Many journals devoted to the study of literature also maintain sites that contain articles and other resources. Instructors teaching a specific work sometimes create chat rooms to foster online discussions. And some contemporary writers have their own Web sites or pages. Links from these sites can lead you to additional information. As a general rule, however, a Web-based search can supplement but not entirely replace a search in the *MLA Bibliography.* (See chapters **8** and **9**.)

Exercise 2

Study the following poem, and try to capture its literal meaning in a sentence or two. Then, paying close attention to the words used and their arrangement, write a two- to three-page explanation of what the poem means to you.

The Sick Rose
O Rose, thou are sick!
The invisible worm
That flies in the night,
In the howling storm,
Has found out thy bed
Of Crimson joy,
And his dark secret love
Does thy life destroy.   —WILLIAM BLAKE

Exercise 3

Conduct research on William Blake by using the *MLA Bibliography* (see page 241) or by visiting the William Blake Archive at the University of Virginia (jefferson.village.virginia.edu/blake/). Prepare a working bibliography (see **10c**) consisting of five sources that discuss the poem in exercise 2.

13f	**Writing about literature follows certain special conventions.**

Writing about literature involves adhering to several conventions.

(1) The first person is typically used.

When you're writing your analysis of a piece of literature, you can use the first-person singular pronoun, *I:*

> Although many critics believe Sethe had no choice other than to kill her daughter, I think she could have . . . .

In this case, you are showing how your opinion differs from a popular one; you are owning your opinion. But in order to own an opinion, belief, or interpretation responsibly, you must support it with specific evidence from the text itself.

Some writers use the first-person plural pronoun, *we,* thereby creating a relationship with the reader, as though reader and writer were moving together through the steps in the argument. (See also **29d**.)

(2) The present tense is used in discussions of literary works.

Use the present tense when discussing a literary work, since the author of the work is communicating to the reader at the present time. (See 22b(1).)

> In "A Good Man Is Hard to Find," the grandmother reaches out to touch her killer just before he pulls the trigger.

Similarly, use the present tense when reporting how other writers have interpreted the work you are discussing.

> As Henry Louis Gates demonstrates in his analysis of . . . .

(3) Documentation of sources follows certain formats.

When writing about a work assigned by your instructor, you may not need to give the source and publication information. However, if you are using an edition or translation that may be different from the one your audience is using, you should indicate this. One way of doing so is to use the MLA (Modern Language Association) format for listing works cited, as explained in section 11a, although in this case your bibliography will consist of only a single work—the one you are discussing. (See the example on page 422.)

An alternative way of providing the source and publication information is by acknowledging the first quotation in an explanatory note and then giving all subsequent references to the work in the body of the paper.

> [1]Dorothy Allison. "Believing in Literature." *Skin: Talking about Sex, Class, and Literature.* (Ithaca: Firebrand, 1994) 165-82. All subsequent references to this work will be by page number within the text.

If you use this note form, you may not need a list of works cited to repeat the bibliographical information. Check with your instructor about the format he or she prefers.

Whichever format you use for providing source and publication data, you must indicate specific references whenever you quote a line or passage. According to MLA style, quotations from short stories and novels are identified by page number, for example:

> "A man planning to spend money on me was an experience rare enough to feel odd" (Gordon 19).

Quotations from poems are referenced by line number, as in

> "O Rose, thou are sick!" (Blake 1).

And references to plays usually give the act, scene, and line numbers:

> "How much better it is to weep at joy than to joy at weeping" (*Much Ado About Nothing* I.i.28).

This bibliographic information should be placed in the text in parentheses directly after the quotation, and the period or comma should follow the parentheses. (See **34d** and **10d(2)**.)

(4) Quoting poetry involves several conventions

For poems and verse plays, type quotations involving three or fewer lines in the text and insert a slash (see **35i**) with a space on each side to separate the lines.

> "Does the road wind uphill all the way? / Yes, to the very end"—Christina Rossetti opens her poem "Uphill" with this two-line question and answer.

Quotations of more than three lines should be indented and double-spaced. Do not use slashes at the ends of lines, and make sure you follow the original for line breaks, special indenting, or spacing.

(5) Authors' names are referred to in standard ways.

Use the full name of the author of a work in your first reference and only the last name in all subsequent references. For instance, refer to "Charles Dickens" or "Willa Cather" the first time, and after that, use "Dickens" or "Cather." Never refer to a female author differently than you do a male author: Use "Robert Browning and Elizabeth Barrett Browning" or "Browning and Barrett Browning" (not "Browning and Mrs. Browning").

13g	**Study a student essay as an example of a literary interpretation.**

The following student essay, which illustrates a reader-response interpretation (see **13c**) of a novel by Tim O'Brien, was submitted in the first semester of a first-year English course on writing about literature. When given the opportunity to choose his own topic for a paper on O'Brien's novel, Josh Otis decided to focus (see **2a(2)**) on a specific friendship, showing how this friendship illustrates moral concerns.

Josh Otis

Professor Miller

English 199, Section 1

10 May 2002

Friendship in <u>The Things They Carried</u>

In Tim O'Brien's novel <u>The Things They Carried</u>, love blossoms in the death-filled rain forests of Vietnam. Throughout the war, soldiers are expected to remain indifferent, for unless they are indifferent they risk their own lives. Yet the friendship between Kiowa and Tim runs so deep that it can only be described as love. Their relationship shows how a soldier who preserves his morals and ability to feel compassion can help another man survive immersion in death and decadence.

Kiowa is an experienced soldier with a strong sense of self, while Tim (not to be confused with the author) is an inexperienced young man thrust into the war and unsure about whether he will succeed as a soldier. Just after Tim arrives in Vietnam, there is an incident in which the men find a dead farmer in an abandoned village. One by one, the soldiers go up and shake the old man's hand, but Tim refuses. His refusal makes him the object of harassment, but he persists. That night Kiowa approaches him and says, "You did a good thing today. That shaking hands crap, it isn't decent. The guys'll hassle you for a while, especially Jensen--but just keep saying no. Should've done it myself. Takes guts, I know that" (257). Kiowa's sense of what is morally sound and his support of actions in accordance with his beliefs help explain why he and Tim become so close.

Kiowa carries a Bible with him, and perhaps his faith is part of the reason that he is able to behave honorably during a war. Kiowa shares a religious conversation with Henry Dobbins in the chapter titled "Church." As the men are preparing to bivouac in an abandoned pagoda (a Buddhist shrine), Kiowa says, "it's bad news

. . . you don't mess with churches" (133). Kiowa is a man at war, killing people, yet he still considers a foreign religious shrine sacred. During the conversation with Henry, Kiowa describes the feeling of escape he gets when he is in a church. "It feels good when you just sit there," he explains, "like you're in a forest and everything is really quiet, except there's this sound you can't hear" (136). These are the types of conversation Kiowa has in <u>The Things They Carried</u>, meaningful ones that deal with moral and religious issues.

When Tim kills a young boy near My Khe and freezes, staring at what he has just done, Kiowa is supportive. This is a traumatic moment for Tim. As he stares at the dead boy, he is confronted with what he has become: a killer. Although it is war, and he is there to kill the enemy, killing wasn't quite real until that moment. As a soldier, Tim has heard all the terms designed to distance men from the reality of what they are doing--"zapped," "wasted." But he fully understands that he has killed someone. It is Kiowa who tries to help him deal with the moral crisis he now faces. Kiowa knew the import of what he was looking at, that the dead boy could easily destroy his friend's moral base. Kiowa tries to comfort Tim as he stares at the boy he has just killed. "Tim, it's a war. The guy wasn't Heidi--he had a weapon, right? It's a tough thing for sure, but you got to cut out that staring" (141). That is the voice of a friend, trying to help Tim deal with what is probably the most traumatic experience of his life. He offers other words, but all had the same end: trying to help a friend he loves make sense of the horror he has just created.

If Kiowa represents the moral center of this novel, then his death represents what can happen to morals in war. Like the morals of some of the men beside whom he fought, Kiowa is also fragile. Kiowa's death is as much an accident as an act of war. A young kid makes a mistake; he turns on a flashlight and marks their position for the enemy. In an instant, Kiowa is dead; the flick of a switch triggers the mortar rounds that kill him. The morals of the soldiers could also be destroyed by small, unintentional acts. Kiowa's body sinking in the mud represents what Vietnam did to the morals of many of these men; they were sucked under all the muck and decay that surrounded them. Once their morals were sucked away, it was a tough fight to pull them back, and sometimes, no matter how hard the men pulled, their morals could not be recovered.

Tim speaks of his loss in the chapter titled "Field Trip." In this chapter, Tim goes back to the field twenty years later to take his friend's moccasins and bury them under the muck in the spot where Kiowa had died so long ago. Tim says, "In a way, maybe, I had gone under with Kiowa, and now after two decades I'd worked my way out" (212). Tim works himself out by facing the battlefield, by being able to face his painful memories instead of burying them with his friend.

Throughout the book, O'Brien creates a combination of anger, grief, and fear so that readers can begin to imagine what American soldiers experienced. They killed and often died alongside their best friends and yet knew little about them. Most were very young and had not had their morals, faith, or emotions tested to any serious extent, let alone through killing other people and watching their friends die. These experiences created a strong bond between men of very different backgrounds. The bond between Tim and Kiowa was so strong that Tim goes back to the field twenty years later, willingly reliving the horror and death of his past, to take Kiowa his moccasins. As Tim wedges them into the muck, he thinks, "I wanted to tell Kiowa that he'd been a great friend, the very best, but all I could do was slap hands with the water" (212). Yet even that gesture was unable to capture for Tim the combined sense of love and loss he felt for his friend.

It took Vietnam veterans a long time to recover from the war, and it left some with scars that will never heal. In The Things They Carried, O'Brien shows how

Otis 4

these veterans were forced to dig long and hard through horror and squalor to make

sense of what they had done. But throughout the ordeal they faced in recovering,

nothing would help them more than the friendships they had forged in the fields and

jungles of Vietnam.

Otis 5

Work Cited

O'Brien, Tim. <u>The Things They Carried</u>. New York: Penguin, 1991.

Exercise 4

Based on your reading of Josh Otis's paper on *The Things They Carried,*
what personal or political values do you think this writer brought to interpreting that text? Which of the critical approaches to literature did he
use as the basis for his interpretation (see **13c**)? Write a one- to two-page
paper analyzing Otis's interpretation of the novel.

Writing in the Social and Natural Sciences

In both the social and natural sciences, writers report the results of investigations carried out in a systematic way. Both of these disciplines have traditionally relied heavily—though not exclusively—on the **scientific method** for collecting and evaluating data. Most scientific research is a product of careful adherence to this method, which has long been accepted among scientists.

Beyond the Rule

THE SCIENTIFIC METHOD

The scientific method consists of six steps: (1) statement of the problem, (2) collection of evidence, (3) formation of a hypothesis, (4) experimentation to prove or disprove the hypothesis, (5) analysis of results, and (6) statement of conclusions. To see how researchers make use of the scientific method and learn what each step includes, visit <u>www.harbrace.com</u>.

This chapter will help you

- write reports for social science courses (14a–b) and
- write reports for natural science courses (14c–d).

Researchers today hesitate to claim that any reporting can be completely objective. Everything we do is affected by our perception of ourselves, others, and the world around us. Although scientists want to control their experimental methods to filter out as much bias as possible, even that desire is subjective in some important ways. The tight control scientists exert over their experiments is an effort to remain objective by monitoring human judgment and subjectivity. It is also the only way scientists can design research studies that can be replicated (repeated by others).

When you write for courses in either the social or the natural sciences, you make use of evidence (data) from two kinds of sources. Data you have developed by observing or by conducting surveys, interviews, or laboratory experiments are from **primary sources.** Data you have collected from the reports of other researchers' work are from **secondary sources** (see **8a**).

| **14a** | **Writers in the social sciences report systematic investigations of behavior.** |

The **social sciences** include psychology, sociology, political science, economics, business, education, and some aspects of environmental science. Social scientists study behavior, human interactions, and the environment, especially the relationship between human beings and the environment. In this discipline, evidence that helps researchers understand observable behavior or something about human consciousness is considered usable evidence. You can use data in the social sciences (see **8d**) to prove or disprove a particular belief (participation/observation), to develop a theory about behavior (survey/interview), to quantify a large body of information (statistics), or to test a hypothesis (laboratory experiments). These research activities produce related qualitative and quantitative information. Statistics and laboratory experiments generally yield numerical data that researchers can manipulate to show various kinds of relationships. Statistical and experimental information is quantitative. Qualitative information is derived from observation and may include inferences drawn from such observation. The relationship between these two kinds of information lies in the fact that qualitative evidence can be tested in laboratory experiments or through surveys and interviews to provide statistical and other kinds of quantitative data.

When the research you undertake seeks quantitative evidence, you begin with a **hypothesis,** a prediction of what the results of the experiment will be. You set up the experiment to remove or mitigate all sources of bias, and you must make the report of your work as objective as you can. Obviously, you cannot entirely eliminate the influence of your own thoughts or ideas; if you could, you would have nothing to say. But you can strive to be impartial, and you can avoid language that makes value judgments. Your report should follow a particular format—introduction to the problem, description of methods and materials, statement of findings, and discussion of implications.

When the research you undertake seeks qualitative evidence, you do not begin with a hypothesis. Instead, you observe some phenomenon and note what you see. Although you still strive to maintain an impartial stance, you need not exclude your own attitudes. As in a report of quantitative information, you begin your report with an introduction to the problem, but then you move on to identify the subject of your observation. A discussion of your methods precedes the analysis of the behavior you observed, and the report ends with your conclusions.

14b	Reports in the social sciences follow prescribed formats to present evidence.

In courses in the social sciences, you will most often be asked to write applications of theory, library research reports, case studies, and observation reports. An **observation report** such as Mike Demmon's field report on diving ducks (see pages 428–430) contains the standard elements of scientific reports (see 14c). However, Demmon's instructor asked that the order of presentation be modified slightly and that the elements be labeled differently.

- Introduction (placed after "Experiment" in Demmon's field report and called "Objectives")
- Definitions (not required for Demmon's report)
- Methods and materials (placed first in Demmon's report and called "Experiment")
- Results (called "Procedures" and "Data" in Demmon's report)
- Discussion and critique (Demmon's "Conclusions" and "Adjustments for Future Research")

When you write an **application of theory,** you use the perspective of a particular theory to analyze information you have gathered using appropriate methods, or you use a theory you have studied to interpret the behavior of some person or group. This kind of report includes an introduction, which states the research question, followed by a discussion of previous research and a description of the theory to be applied. The report then generally identifies the subject of the study and discusses how the theory applies to the behavior of that subject, before coming to a conclusion about the subject and/or the theory.

Writing a **library research report** requires that you read a wide variety of sources on a specific topic and then summarize, critique, and integrate those sources. Library reports generally include the following elements:

- Statement of the research question or thesis
- Presentation of background information using sources
- Discussion of major findings available in the sources
- Application of findings to the specific research question
- Conclusions
- References

An example of such a report is briefly excerpted in figure 14.1. Notice that the author, P. A. Blissitt, includes an abstract and uses headings to identify the sections of her report.

Abstract: The relationship of sleep to memory and learning is complex. Sleep affects memory, and memory must be present for learning to occur. A number of studies have been conducted to increase our understanding of their relationship. In addition to the numerous scientific investigations of each concept separately, sleep, memory, and learning have been studied together to determine (a) the effect of sleep on memory and learning, (b) the effect of sleep deprivation in general on memory and learning, (c) the effect of rapid eye movement (REM) sleep deprivation on memory and learning, (d) the effect of memory and learning on REM sleep, and (e) the effect of non-REM sleep loss on memory and learning. Neuro-anatomic correlates have been pursued as well with most attention to the hippocampus. Despite considerable efforts to date, many of the studies reveal contradictory or inconclusive findings. Much remains unknown, and additional work is needed. Implications for nursing include those that have a direct effect on the patient, the nurse, and nursing science.

Sleep, memory, and learning are most often studied as individual concepts. As separate unrelated concepts, much remains unknown about each of them. Yet, despite our lack of knowledge about each individually, the relationship of sleep to memory and learning has been and continues to be investigated in animals and humans. As result of these studies, our knowledge of the relationship of sleep to memory and learning is increasing. This article reviews knowledge about the relationship of sleep to memory, including (a) the effect of sleep on learning and memory, (b) the relationship of sleep deprivation in general to memory, (c) the effect of rapid eye movement (REM) sleep deprivation on memory, (d) the effect of memory and learning on REM sleep, (e) the effect of non-REM sleep deprivation on memory and learning, (f) neuro-anatomic correlates, and (g) implications for nursing practice and research. Only human studies are included. Studies conducted on patients with insomnia are not included because their pattern of cognitive deficits may be different [27]

Sleep, Memory, and Learning

Sleep, memory, and learning are each complex multidimensional biobehavioral systems. Sleep, for example consists of several distinct phases: Stage 1--transitional sleep, Stage 2--light sleep, Stages 3 and 4--slow wave sleep, and Stage 5--REM sleep. Together, Stages 1-4 are called non-REM sleep. Non-REM sleep often is compared with REM sleep. Each of these stages occurs five to six times nightly with a complete cycle of stages lasting 60-90 minutes. One sleep cycle consists of a progression from Stage 1 through Stage 4 of non-REM sleep followed by a return to Stages 3 or 2 of non-REM sleep, then REM sleep. [38, 42] The amount, type, timing, and quality of sleep are all important considerations.

Figure 14.1. Excerpt from a library research report.

You may need to identify the elements in a research report with headings such as "Introduction" and "Background." However, Nikki Krzmarzick's paper on sleep and memory (see pages 336–349) is relatively short, and her organization is clear; therefore, headings were not necessary. Notice how Krzmarzick presents her thesis (paragraph 3) and follows with a description of the importance of sleep stages—the background information (paragraphs 3–4). In paragraph 5, she refocuses the paper on the specific problem—the effects of sleep deprivation on college students. In paragraphs 6–9, she discusses the findings of several researchers; in paragraphs 10–12, she applies those findings to her specific research question. Her conclusions follow in paragraph 13. Notice also that Krzmarzick uses her first paragraph to gain her reader's interest with a scenario about a particular college student's sleep deprivation and frames her paper by concluding with a paragraph about the same student.

Throughout her paper, Krzmarzick maintains a neutral stance that lends an impression of impartiality, although the argument clearly shows that she is committed to her point of view. Notice that she achieves this neutral tone just as the APA recommends, by using active verbs and the past tense (see 22b) rather than the passive voice (22c) to report findings. (Blissitt's language in the report in figure 14.1 conveys the same kind of impartiality.) Krzmarzick's references page documents her sources according to APA guidelines.

Mike Demmon's field report for an advanced environmental science course demonstrates how advanced students are expected to present data for original research. (Environmental science is often considered a natural science, but Demmon's report is included here because it is a report on behavior.) His report includes a description of the experiment, a table listing the data, and a discussion of his findings. Because Demmon's work was original field research, he was not required to use secondary sources; thus, his report does not include a references page. Although Demmon calls his report a quantitative analysis, it includes some qualitative elements: For example, he allows subjectivity to intrude when he uses the adverb *surprisingly* to qualify his observation about how late it was when the ducks began to be active. Another intrusion of subjective comment is one required by the assignment—the adjustments section. Throughout this report, Demmon's own voice is evident—a personalization that writers generally strive to avoid in scientific reports but a feature that makes this report lively and interesting.

Mike Demmon

Avian Ecology and Management

December 11, 2000

Quantitative Analysis of Diving Ducks

Experiment

This section states the method.

Follow a specific duck for a 10-minute time period and record diving

patterns, times, and frequency of dives. Stagger the species being watched to

create an equal representation of each species within the

data. Try not to follow the same duck in any two 10-minute intervals.

Objectives

The goals are stated separately.

To determine whether any of the species have evolved to share limited

resources of the environment. To look for evidence of these species having

evolved within the same environment.

Procedures

This section corresponds to "Results."

During the class field trip to Eagle Lake, I participated in a quantitative

evaluation of several diving duck species. During this time we monitored

several different variables to see whether feeding practices were staggered

between species, whether frequencies of dives were different between species,

and whether any of the species interacted with each other. The three species

we studied were the Ruddy Duck (*Oxyura jamaicensis*), the Redhead Duck

(*Aytheya americana*), and the Bufflehead Duck (*Bucephala albeola*).

Avian Ecology 2

Data

Time	Species	Sex	Number of Dives	Dive Time (seconds, respectively)	Other Activities
8:30–8:40	Bufflehead	Male	0	N/A	Preening & sleeping
8:45–8:55	Bufflehead	Female	1	Lost after 4 minutes	Preening & followed by 2 males
9:00–9:10	Ruddy	Female	4	21, 27, 33, 19 lost after 5 minutes	Paired with 2 females, ran males off, preening
9:15–9:25	Redhead	Male	13	45, 46, 13, 49, 17, 13, 24, 14, 33, 47, 49	N/A
9:30–9:40	Ruddy	Male	3	6, 33, 17	Following a female
9:45–9:55	Bufflehead	Female	7	9, 13, 11, 22, 20, 29, 19	Followed by 2 males
10:00–10:10	Redhead	Female	8	12, 14, 14, 13, 18, 21, 18, 26	N/A
10:15–10:25	Redhead	Female	11	17, 13, 14, 22, 19, 20, 17, 21, 24, 23, 19	Following 2 males
10:30–10:40	Bufflehead	Female	3	21, 11, 17	Sleeping & follow 1 male
10:45–10:55	Ruddy	Male	7	9, 12, 22, 27, 16, 11, 15	N/A
11:00–11:10	Redhead	Male	10	10, 18, 22, 11, 19, 27, 20, 31, 17, 14	N/A
11:15–11:25	Ruddy	Female	6	15, 13, 21, 29, 18	Preening
11:30–11:40	Bufflehead	Male	4	12, 18, 15, 19	Followed a female

Demmon summarizes the quantitative data in this table.

Avian Ecology   3

This section corresponds to "Discussion." Demmon comments on the data—a feature of qualitative research.

Conclusions

As the data above show, there is no evidence that these species practice any variation in diving time or frequency of dives, or that any of the species directly and intentionally interact. Surprisingly, the data do seem to show that activities do not begin until mid-morning. When we arrived, about 8 a.m., a large percentage of the birds were still sleeping. Once the birds awaken, it appears as though they ritually preen themselves before feeding. With the exception of human-induced movements, it appeared that there were no significant interactions between any of the species. As may have been expected, the Buffleheads also appeared to be courting at times. The data above also show that the majority of the birds that were paired or followed by the other sex were Buffleheads.

Adjustments for Future Research

This section corresponds to "Critique." Comments in this section verge on qualitative information.

In order to refine this study, it would be advantageous to develop a better, easier method to follow each individual bird. I found that it was very difficult to follow a diving duck for prolonged periods of time. Also, looking through a monocular spotting scope for 10-minute segments can be very aggravating. It would also be advantageous to get closer to the birds being observed. Finally, the study time is possibly too long. It should be possible to observe more specimens and get a better sampling in half the time.

14c | **Writers in the natural sciences report empirical evidence about the natural world.**

The natural sciences include mathematics, the biological sciences botany and zoology, the physical sciences chemistry and physics, and the earth sciences geography (including the more physical branches of environmental science), geology, and astronomy. The applied sciences include medicine and allied health studies, engineering, and computer science. The natural and applied sciences are problem-solving disciplines that approach the natural world using the scientific method. The information you report when writing in these disciplines must be empirical—that is, provable evidence derived from meticulous observation and experimentation. Interpretation is controlled and, as far as possible, neutral.

Among the kinds of writing you will do in natural and applied science courses is the **literature review,** in which you report on the most current knowledge about a topic, critiquing what has been done, pointing out what needs to be done, and classifying related themes. Another kind of scientific writing is the **journal critique,** in which you examine and evaluate the parts of a specific journal article. A relatively new form of scientific writing is the **microtheme**—a few paragraphs in response to an open-ended question—which allows you to use your creativity and writing ability to display your understanding of the scientific principles involved.

The most frequent kind of writing you will do in the natural sciences, however, is the **scientific report**—usually in the form of a **laboratory report** (or perhaps a **lab summary,** an informal version of a lab report). Depending on whether an abstract is required, most scientific reports include five or six main sections.

- The **abstract** states the problem and summarizes the results. (You may not have to include an abstract if your report is short or if your instructor does not require it.)
- The **introduction** states the problem clearly and concisely, explains the scientific basis for the study, and provides brief background on the subject of the study and the techniques to be used. The introduction usually makes use of sources.
- The **methods and materials** section is a narrative that describes how the experiment was conducted. It lists the materials that were used, identifies where the experiment was conducted, and describes the procedures that were followed. (Your lab notes should help you remember what you did. Anyone who wants to repeat your work should be able to do so by following the steps described in this section.)
- **Results** are reported by describing (but not interpreting) major findings and supporting them with properly labeled tables and graphs showing the empirical data.
- The **discussion** section analyzes the results, showing how they are related to the goals of the study and commenting on their significance.

This is where you would formulate a hypothesis, report any problems you encountered, and suggest ways to test the results further.

■ The final section lists sources, the **literature cited.** It includes only works that were used in the study or referred to in the report. The comprehensiveness and the accuracy of this list allow readers to evaluate the quality of your work and put it into a relevant context.

Scientific writing depends on the clear and accurate presentation of facts, and every fact must have a source—your own experimentation, studies published by other researchers, surveys, and so on. These facts are the data. Scientific writing focuses on such objective data and keeps the writer's actions and responses in the background. Thus, instead of saying "I found . . . ," a scientific report might say something like "The data reveal . . . ."

An example of scientific writing (Heather Jensen's lab report for a first-year biology course) appears in the next section, and another example of scientific discourse (Jennifer York's report on fruit flies for a third-year biology course) is available online at www.harbrace.com.

Jensen's lab report is typical of a report based on an experiment outlined in a lab manual. It includes a brief example of each element of a typical scientific paper. The report includes graphics—drawings of the various stages of mitosis and a graph showing the results. The Council of Science Editors (CSE/CBE) approves two documentation formats: the citation-sequence format and the name-year format. Jensen used the citation-sequence format. The sixth edition of the CSE/CBE manual, *Scientific Style and Format: The CBE Manual for Authors, Editors, and Publishers,* does not give examples for citations of most electronic sources. It is likely that the next edition will do so. For more information about CSE/CBE style, see **11g**.

14d | **Writing in the natural sciences is impartial and follows a prescribed format.**

Most of the time when you write for natural science courses, you will be required to follow the standard format for scientific writing (see **14c**). That format is required because experiments must be conducted and reported in such a way that they can be repeated over and over for verification—a principle called *replicability.* You will almost certainly be evaluated in terms of both your ability to execute experiments and your ability to follow the prescribed format and maintain impartiality. Heather Jensen's lab report contains all of the required elements in the proper format and is written so as not to reveal her own attitudes.

Observations and Calculations of Onion Root Tip Cells

Heather Jensen

Biology 101

June 7, 2002

ABSTRACT

This laboratory experiment examined *Allium* (onion) root tip cells in the five stages of mitosis. The five stages of mitotic division were identified and recorded, and a 50-cell sample was chosen for closer examination. Of those 50 cells, 64% were found to be in interphase, 20% in prophase, 6% in metaphase, 6% in anaphase, and only 4% in telophase. The results showed that onion root tip cells spend the majority of their life cycle in a rest period (interphase). Prophase was calculated to be the longest phase of active division, while telophase was the shortest. These results were consistent with the experiments completed by other students and scientists.

INTRODUCTION

This lab report outlines a laboratory experiment on mitosis, the division of the nucleus of a cell to form two new cells with the same number of chromosomes as the parent cell. Mitotic cell division consists of five visually identifiable stages: interphase, prophase, metaphase, anaphase, and telophase. The purpose of this laboratory experiment was to identify and observe cells in each phase of mitosis, as well as to calculate an estimation of the real time involved in each stage of

1

Jensen summarizes the experiment in an abstract.

The introduction states the problem, explains the basis for the experiment, describes the method, and provides background on the subject of the experiment.

mitosis in an onion root tip cell. The onion root tip was chosen for this experiment because of easy availability and rapid growth. Rapid root growth resulted in an easy opportunity to observe multiple cells in the phases of mitosis in a small sample, on one or two slides. Onion root cells complete the entire cycle of division in 80 minutes,[1] and it was expected that larger numbers of cells would be found in interphase because the majority of a life cycle is spent performing normal cell functions.

MATERIALS AND METHODS

The materials required for this experiment include a compound microscope and prepared slides of a longitudinal section of *Allium* (onion) root tip.

First, the slides were placed on a compound microscope under low power, a 40x magnification level. The end of the root tip was located; then the cells immediately behind the root cap were examined. These cells appeared as a darker area under low power. This area of cells was identified as the apical meristem,[1] an area of rapid growth and division in the onion root tip. This area of cells was examined while keeping the microscope on low power, to find and identify cells in interphase, prophase, metaphase, anaphase, and telophase.[2] Then high power, a 400x magnification, was used to further examine and record the appearance of these cells.

After the multiple phases of mitosis were observed, a large area of 50 cells in mitosis was selected for further examination. This area was located under low power in order to assess rows of cells in an easily countable space. Then the number of cells in each stage of mitosis was counted. These numbers were then divided by the total number of cells examined, or 50 cells, and multiplied by 100 in order to calculate the percentage of cells in each phase of mitosis. For example, if 10 cells were observed in interphase, then $10/50 = 0.20$

This footnote refers to the first source.

Jensen lists the materials used in the experiment and describes the procedures followed.

The footnote after "meristem" refers to the first source again, and the one after "telophase" to the second source.

and $0.20 \cdot 100 = 20\%$ of cells were in interphase. The actual time of each phase of mitosis in this sample of cells was calculated by multiplying the percentage by the total time of the division cycle, 80 minutes for the onion root tip cell.[1] For example, if 20% of cells were observed in interphase, then 20% (20/100) $\cdot$ 80 minutes = 16 minutes total time spent in interphase.

RESULTS

Drawings and Observations

INTERPHASE

This phase lasts from the completion of a division cycle to the beginning of the next cycle. All regular cell functions occur in this phase (except reproduction).[3]

Figure 1   Two cells observed in interphase

PROPHASE

Technically the first phase of mitosis, this stage is marked by the thickening and shortening of chromosomes, which makes them appear visible under a compound microscope. The nucleus appears grainy at first and then the chromosomes appear more clearly defined as prophase progresses.

Figure 2   Two cells observed in prophase

Jensen describes what she observed and supports her descriptions with appropriately labeled drawings.

This footnote refers to the third source.

METAPHASE

This phase is identified by the lining up of double chromosomes along the center line, the equator, of the cell.

Figure 3   Two cells observed in metaphase

ANAPHASE

This phase is classified by the separation of the double chromosomes. They will begin to pull apart to opposite poles of the cell.

Figure 4   Two cells observed in anaphase

TELOPHASE

In telophase, the chromosomes have reached the opposite poles of the cell, and the connection between the chromosomes begins to break down as the nuclear membrane begins to form around each chromosomal clump. At the end of telophase, cytokinesis, or the division of the cytoplasm, takes place. In plant cells, a cell plate begins to form in the center of the cell and then grows outward to form a new cell wall, completely dividing the old cell into two new cells, both with a complete set of chromosomes.

4

Figure 5   Two cells observed in telophase

Table 1 shows the number of cells found in each phase of mitosis.

Table 1   Number of cells in each phase

Interphase	Prophase	Metaphase	Anaphase	Telophase
32 cells	10 cells	3 cells	3 cells	2 cells

Jensen uses tables to summarize her findings.

Table 2 shows the calculated percentage of cells in each phase of mitosis.

Table 2 Percentage of cells in each phase

Interphase	Prophase	Metaphase	Anaphase	Telophase
64% of cells	20% of cells	6% of cells	6% of cells	4% of cells

Figure 6 shows the actual time cells spent in each phase of mitosis.

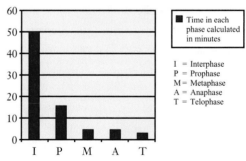

She also graphs part of her data.

Figure 6   Time spent in each phase of mitosis

5

DISCUSSION

This laboratory experiment provided firsthand experience with the phases of cell division. The five phases became more easily recognizable as each cell was examined and classified. Cells often looked like they could be classified in interphase or prophase or like they were between phases. Observation led to the confirmation that mitosis is a fluid process and not just a series of distinct phases. During the experiment, difficulties with overdyed and gray areas caused uncertainty because visual indications of phase were impossible to detect. This problem was lessened through the careful selection of clear patches of cells for observation. The expectation that a large number of cells would be found in interphase was confirmed by the numbers of cells counted in the cell sample of the onion root tip. Online comparison of the results of this experiment to those of other similar experiments confirmed the results found here as typical of an onion (*Allium*) root tip.[4] This indicated that the careful selection of clear patches of cells for sampling proved an effective method for eliminating error that might have been caused by the incorrect labeling of cells or the poor visibility of cells in overdyed or gray areas. Further studies might include larger samples of cells. Experiments with larger numbers of cells would offer additional evidence to confirm the results found in this experiment.

REFERENCES

[1] Schraer WD, Stoltze H. Biology: the study of life. 4th ed. Needham (MA): Prentice Hall; 1991. Mitosis and asexual reproduction. p 397–415.

[2] Smith DW, Maier CGA. Plant biology lab manual. Dubuque (IA): Kendall/Hunt; 1995. Topic 5, The plant cell. p 52–66.

[3] Alexander GM, Goodson P, Hanneman PJ, Melear, CT. Scott, Foresman biology. Glenview (IL): Scott, Foresman; 1985. Information storage and transfer in cells. p 117–43.

[4] Yesnik A, Jaster K. The bio 1 super virtual lab book [Internet]. Washington DC: Sidwell Friends School; 1998 [modified 2002; accessed 2002 Jun 7]. Mitosis lab. Available from: http://www.sidwell.edu/us/science/vlb/mitosis/.

Using the citation-sequence format, Jensen lists the references in the order in which they are referred to in the paper. Notice that the only words capitalized in titles are the first word and any proper names.

CBE/CSE currently recommends using *Library of Medicine Recommended Formats for Bibliographic Citation, Supplement: Internet Formats* for electronic sources.

7

Exercise 1

Revise a document you have written for a course in the social or natural sciences. Make sure that your language is as impartial as you can make it and that you have used one of the formats outlined in this chapter.

15 Writing in Business

Writing in business requires the same attention to audience, purpose, and context as does writing in any other situation; however, the reasons for that attention are somewhat different. The most important reason is that the writing you do in a business situation projects an image of your employer and therefore must be absolutely clear and correct. Furthermore, you will typically have less time to produce each document in the workplace than in an academic setting, so you must learn to make the best use of your time.

This chapter will help you

- realize the need for efficiency when writing for business (**15a**),
- write a business plan (**15b**),
- produce a professional-looking résumé (**15c**),
- compose a letter of application (**15d**), and
- write a grant proposal (**15e**).

15a | Writing in business requires efficiency.

When you write in a business situation, time is often limited. The more efficient you are in planning, drafting, and revising, the better use you will make of the time you have. And your time is not the only consideration in the business environment; to accommodate the busy schedules of your colleagues and supervisor, you will need to state the purpose of your document at the beginning, come right to the point, and be as concise as possible without obscuring that point.

Writers in businesses produce a wide variety of documents, not just letters, résumés, and memos. Business writing also includes reports similar to those produced for social science courses (see **14a–b**), business plans, grant proposals, and feasibility studies, among other formats.

BUSINESS WRITING FORMATS

A number of widely accepted business writing formats prescribe how letters, memos, and email messages should look. For examples of these formats, visit www.harbrace.com.

Although the company you work for is likely to have its own formats and style, the kind of document you are producing dictates how you handle the content. For example, the business plan Roxanne Kirkwood prepared for her advanced management class has the typical elements of any business plan, and the grant proposal Alicia Obaldo prepared for her family science class also contains the elements required in any grant proposal.

15b | **Writing a business plan is crucial when starting a company.**

Business plans have three main purposes: (1) to ensure that the writer of the plan has considered all the potential risks as well as benefits, (2) to persuade lenders and potential investors that their money will be safely invested because the writer has planned realistically and has sufficient expertise, and (3) to help the new business stay on track during its early development. To fulfill those purposes adequately, a business plan should be well researched, clearly written, and complete—that is, it should provide all the information a loan officer or investor might need.

When Roxanne Kirkwood received an assignment in a management course that required her to research and write a proposal for an actual business, she chose to write about a coffee shop where people could socialize and engage in conversation. Because the plan was a course assignment, she was not required to include her personal worth in the financial data or to supply the supporting documents that would be important elements of an actual plan. Though brief, her business plan contains all of the other elements that would be needed for a much larger company. With minor modifications, it could be used as part of a loan application.

ELEMENTS OF A BUSINESS PLAN

- Cover page, including the name and address of the business
- Title page
- Table of contents
- Executive summary. Usually written last, this is a brief statement of the objectives of the business plan and a description of the business. The executive summary also indicates who will own the business and under what form of ownership (partnership, corporation, or sole proprietorship). Finally, it explains why the business will be successful.
- Description of business. This section identifies the kind of business (service or retail), explains why the business is distinctive, and briefly describes its market.
- Business location. This section discusses lease or sale terms, the need for and costs of renovation, and features of the neighborhood.
- Licenses and permits. This section explains what kinds of licenses and permits must be obtained and whether the business name is registered.
- Management. This section includes information about managers' experience and education, the organizational structure, proposed salaries and wages, and any other pertinent management resources (accountant, attorney, and so on).
- Personnel. This section lists the personnel needed—full- or part-time, skilled or unskilled—and explains whether training will be required and how it will be provided.
- Insurance. This section describes insurance needs and potential risks.
- Market. This section characterizes the market—size and potential growth, typical customers—and describes how the business will attract customers—advertising, pricing, product quality, and/or services.
- Competition. This section analyzes any competitors and describes how the business is unique.
- Financial data. This section includes a current balance sheet and income statement and projected (or actual) income statements by month and quarter for two years, as well as cash flow and balance sheet projections.
- Supporting documents, including résumés, financial statements, and letters of reference for the owner(s) as well as letters of intent from suppliers, leases, contracts, deeds, and other legal documents.

Roxy's   1

ROXY'S COFFEE SHOP

The cover page
contains the
business name
and address
and the date.

1819 S. University Avenue

Little Rock, AR 72204

May 25, 2002

Roxy's   2

Table of Contents

The table
of contents
helps readers
find
information
easily.

The executive
summary gives
an overview
of the
business plan.

Executive Summary

Roxy's Coffee Shop will provide a desirable service for University of Arkansas at Little Rock (UALR) students, staff, and faculty, as well as for area residents. The purpose of this business plan is to secure financial backing for Roxy's for the first year. Roxanne Kirkwood will be the sole proprietor of the business and will be the general manager. She will hire an experienced coffee shop manager to oversee the actual operation of the business.

Students, staff, and faculty at UALR have requested an establishment like Roxy's for many years. The UALR campus is near a main shopping area for the city and several working-class neighborhoods which are being revitalized. There is also a major hospital a block away on University Avenue. Roxanne Kirkwood is asking for a loan of $60,000 to open the shop and help with operating expenses until it makes a profit. The loan will be repaid in monthly installments beginning in the first month of the second year of business and will be secured using the borrower's home as collateral. Roxy's Coffee Shop will offer a useful, desirable service to a university community that continues to grow as well as to a revitalized neighborhood that has the potential for providing more consumers.

Roxy's will offer a somewhat limited menu. Focusing on coffee as the main sale item will allow for the greatest amount of profit. Serving a few other high-demand hot and cold drinks as well as some desserts will support the main focus on coffee. The shop will be intentionally kept small to provide the best service with the lowest prices while offering excellent quality. The research carried out for this proposal shows that Roxy's has an ideal location, is practically planned, and offers a product that is in demand.

Roxy's   4

Description of Business

Roxy's will be a small, independently owned coffee shop serving regular and specialty coffee. Although juice, smoothies, hot chocolate, tea, bottled water, carbonated beverages, fruit, and desserts such as pie, cake, cookies and brownies will also be served, premium quality, free trade coffee will be marketed at a reasonable price as the primary menu item. Although Little Rock has a number of coffee shops, none are easily accessible from the UALR campus.

Roxy's primary market will be UALR students, faculty, and staff, since the restaurants on campus all close by 7:00 in the evening and the campus coffee kiosk closes at 2:00 in the afternoon. People who live close to the campus in the surrounding neighborhoods will form a secondary market. These people will benefit from having a place nearby to enjoy coffee. In addition, Roxy's will appeal to shoppers and businesspeople frequenting the nearby malls and businesses. Situated on University Avenue, Roxy's will have an ideal location on a main thoroughfare going through the center of UALR campus, so it is convenient for morning commuter traffic.

Once financial backing for the company has been secured, all suppliers are willing to begin delivery. Restaurant supplies will be obtained through AbestKitchen.com, and a merchant account will be provided by Redwood Internet.

Business Location

Roxy's will be located at 1819 S. University Avenue, a main thoroughfare in Little Rock. This location is one block from the main campus on University, near Highway 630, which runs through the heart of Little Rock. This location is ideal because UALR students, staff, and faculty can walk to the

This section describes the business in detail.

This section gives details about the location of the business.

coffee shop from campus. In addition, tourists and businesspeople can find the location easily and park without trouble. Roxy's will be open most of the hours that the UALR library is open.

The 250-square-foot space will be leased for one year at $2,500 a month, with the option to renew and renegotiate terms at the end of that time. No walls will be moved, and electrical service and plumbing lines are to be used as is. Renovations will involve only surface changes such as wall treatments, decorations, and furniture. The estimated cost for these changes, as noted in the financial data section of this business plan, is projected to be $5,000. Although the rent may seem high, the location of the building— only a couple of blocks from a major intersection in Little Rock offering access to traffic and potential customers—makes the cost worthwhile. It is a freestanding building located directly on the street and has a private parking lot. The building is convenient not only for UALR students, staff, and faculty, but also for shoppers from the two major malls in Little Rock as well as for staff and visitors from a major hospital located on University Avenue. On either side of University Avenue are neighborhoods consisting of mostly working-class homes. Owners are struggling to rejuvenate these neighborhoods and keep them from being overtaken by commercial and business properties. Homeowners, attempting to keep a neighborhood feel, should welcome a local spot such as Roxy's as a place to meet socially.

Licenses and Permits

All necessary licenses and permits will be obtained. The State of Arkansas leaves most decisions up to the county in which the business is located. The Little Rock Small Business Administration is gathering information on licenses and permits.

Roxy's   6

Management

Roxy's general manager will be Roxanne Kirkwood, and a business

manager will be hired to assist with business operation and marketing. The

general manager will work 40 hours a week for an annual salary of $30,000.

The general manager will alternate day and night shifts with the business

manager Monday through Friday. The business manager will work 40 hours

a week for an annual salary of $25,000. Salaries will increase only when

the business becomes clearly profitable.

This section covers the responsibilities and compensation for the managers.

Personnel

Other than the managers, Roxy's will hire two part-time employees who

will work 15 hours per week at $8.00 an hour. These employees will be

responsible for the shop 16 hours on Saturdays and 14 hours on Sundays,

including getting ready to open and cleaning up before closing. Managers

will be on call.

This section summarizes personnel requirements.

Insurance

Roxy's will have the standard liability and property insurance. Although

exact numbers are still being negotiated, costs are estimated at $100 per

month. Roxy's main insurance needs include liability coverage for any

accident on the property affecting customers or employees and coverage for

property losses resulting from fire, theft, or vandalism. The business will

not provide health insurance for employees.

This section notes the extent of insurance coverage for the business.

The Market

Roxy's target market is UALR students, staff, and faculty. Although the

campus has on-site food vendors, including a coffee vendor, these vendors

close early. A large portion of UALR's student body attends night classes,

which begin long after the coffee vendor's closing time of 2:00 in the

This section identifies the market for the proposed business.

afternoon. Many of these students visit the library, which is open until 11:00 on weeknights. In addition, a large neighborhood surrounds the campus, and a main street borders the campus, moving a large amount of traffic right past Roxy's. Because of Roxy's location near the intersection of 630 and University, the ability to attract shoppers, tourists, and hospital staff and visitors is guaranteed.

This section identifies the competition for the proposed business.

Competition

Little Rock has not yet been inundated with coffee shops as many American cities have. There is one chain, Coffey Beanery, which has a stand in one mall and one shop halfway across town in West Little Rock, off Chenal. There are no Starbucks and only a few independently owned establishments. The other independently owned shops are located in neighborhoods nowhere near UALR or University Avenue.

Roxy's   8

Financial Data

Table 1

Estimated Expenses for First Year of Operation

Expense	Startup only	Monthly	Yearly
Equipment including crockery	X		$15,000
Furniture, fixtures and remodeling	X		10,000
Inventory including coffee beans and food		$2,000	24,000
Rent		2,500	30,000
Insurance		100	1,200
Advertising	$800	100	2,000
Utilities		1,000	12,000
Licenses and permits			500
Miscellaneous		200	2,400
General manager			30,000
Business manager		2,083.33	25,000
Part-time employees		960	11,520
Total needed for first year		$11,443.33	$163,620
Total needed for startup costs		$80,000	(approximately 3 months operating costs, plus a small emergency reserve)
Total supplied by borrower		$20,000	
Total supplied by lender		$60,000	

A table summarizes the projected financial data for the first year of operation.

15c | Persuasive, professional-looking résumés command attention.

A résumé lists your qualifications for a job and is enclosed with a letter of application. The résumé highlights your experience and abilities and should include

- personal data (name, mailing address, telephone number, email address, and fax number, if available),
- educational background, and
- work experience.

Like a letter of application (see **15d**), a résumé is an argument (chapter 7) designed to emphasize your qualifications for a job and get you an interview. Since almost every job has more than one applicant, your résumé should make the most of your qualifications. If you create and save your résumé as a word-processing file, you can easily tailor it for each job, presenting your qualifications in the best light.

Writing a résumé requires planning and paying attention to detail. First, make a list of the jobs you have had, the activities and clubs you have participated in, and the offices you have held. Amplify these items by adding dates, job titles, and responsibilities. Omit tangential information such as a list of hobbies.

A résumé can be organized in a number of ways. One approach is to list experience and activities in reverse chronological order, so that your most recent experience comes first. This format works well if you have a steady job history and if you want to emphasize your most recent experience because it is closely related to the position for which you are applying. If less recent experience is more directly relevant to the job for which you are applying, you can emphasize it by giving your work history chronologically. An alternative way to organize a résumé is to list experience in terms of job skills rather than jobs held. This format, called an **emphatic résumé,** is especially useful when your work history is modest or you are applying for a position in a field in which you have skills but limited experience.

Software programs that allow you to select the kind of résumé you need and then prompt you to complete the different sections of it can be helpful. When using a computer to write your résumé, you can also view the document in its entirety on screen and redesign it if necessary.

However you choose to organize your résumé, remember that document design is important (see chapter 6). An unprofessional-looking résumé is likely to be overlooked now that computers make effective presentation so easy. Your résumé is, in effect, going to someone's office for a job interview, so make sure that it is dressed for success. It is usually best to design the résumé to fit on a single page. Use good-quality paper (preferably white or off-white) and a laser printer. Use boldface type or even a different font for headings. Resist the impulse to make the design unnecessarily complicated, however. When in doubt, opt for simplicity.

TIPS FOR RÉSUMÉ WRITING

- Make sure to include your name, address, telephone number, and an email address or fax number, if available.

- Identify your career objective simply, without elaborating on future goals. Reserve details about your plans until asked about them during an interview (and even then make sure they enhance your appeal as a candidate). Try to match your qualifications to the employer's needs.

- Mention your college or university degree and any pertinent areas in which you have had special training.

- Do not include personal data such as age and marital status.

- Even if an advertisement asks you to state a salary requirement, any mention of salary should usually be deferred until an interview.

- Whenever possible, establish a clear relationship between jobs you have had and the job you are seeking.

- The names and addresses of references are not usually listed on a résumé. Job candidates are advised to take a list of references to interviews. If there is some reason for including the names and addresses of references, include their phone numbers and/or email addresses as well. List people who have agreed to speak or write on your behalf. Make sure that these individuals understand the nature of the position you are seeking.

- To show that you are well organized and thoughtful, use a clean, clear format.

- Make sure to proofread the résumé carefully.

Exercise 1

Prepare a résumé for a job that interests you.

Emphatic résumé

Karen Tran
10363 East 10th Avenue
Little Rock, AR 72204
(501) 328-6974
ktran@hotmail.com

CAREER OBJECTIVE:

A full-time management position specializing in food and beverage services.

Pertinent skills **MANAGEMENT SKILLS:**

Familiarity with all contemporary models of effective management; good writing and communication skills; experience with planning and evaluating food service operations; experience with operating a coffee shop.

Relevant work
experience **EXPERIENCE IN FOOD SERVICE:**

Assisted in the transfer of data on development of new restaurant locations for a major restaurant development firm; developed and provided customer service information to employees; worked for three years in food service.

Brief summary **ADDITIONAL EXPERIENCE:**

Worked with students, parents, and faculty at Western Ozark University as an information specialist; helped edit the yearbook; gave campus tours.

Degree and major **EDUCATION:**

Western Ozark University, B.S. with honors, 2002; majored in Business Administration with an emphasis in Management; minor in Nutrition; Phi Beta Kappa.

EXTRACURRICULAR:

Active in Management Club and yearbook.

List if relevant References available on request.

Beyond the Rule

THE APPLICATION PACKAGE

An application package consists of a résumé and a letter of application. Both of these documents are important tools for any job search. To see a sample chronological résumé and get further information on application letters, résumés, and interviews, visit www.harbrace.com.

15d | Letters of application make first impressions.

Writing a letter of application is an essential step in applying for a job. Your letter of application gives a prospective employer a first impression of you. This letter usually accompanies a résumé (see 15c), and it should do more than simply repeat information that can be found there. Your letter of application provides you with the chance to sound articulate, interesting, and professional. Make the most of it.

Address your letter to a specific person. If you are responding to an advertisement that mentions a department without giving a name, call the company and find out who will be doing the screening and how that person spells his or her name. Assume that your audience will be screening many applications, and try to keep your letter to one page or two at most (see chapter 30).

In your opening paragraph, you should identify the position you are applying for, explain how you learned about it, and—in a single sentence—state why you believe you are qualified to fill it. In the paragraphs that follow, describe the experience and abilities that qualify you for the job. If your experience is extensive, establish that fact and then focus on how you excelled in one or two specific situations. Mention that you are enclosing a résumé, but do not summarize it. Your goal is to get a busy person, who will not want to read the same information twice, to look at your résumé.

In addition to stating your qualifications, your letter of application might also indicate why you are interested in the company or organization

Model letter of application

Return address
and date

10363 East 10th Avenue
Little Rock, AR 72204
April 19, 2003

Inside
recipient's
address

Ms. Roxanne Kirkwood
Roxy's Coffee Shop
1819 S. University Avenue
Little Rock, AR 72204

Salutation

Dear Ms. Kirkwood:

I am writing to apply for the position of Business Manager of Roxy's Coffee Shop advertised in this morning's *Arkansas Democrat-Gazette*. My education and experience are well suited to this position, and I'd welcome the chance to work full-time at making a new business successful.

Body of
the letter

As you can see from my résumé, I majored in Business Administration with an emphasis in management; I am continuing my education by pursuing an MBA at UALR. Whenever possible, I have found campus activities and jobs that would give me experience in working with people. As an assistant in the Admissions Office at Western Ozark University, I worked successfully with students, parents, alumni, and faculty. The position required both a knowledge of university regulations and an understanding of people with different needs.

I also benefited from working as an intern last summer for Brinker Enterprises, a firm that has established many different chains of restaurants around the country. When I was working there, a new template for customer service was developed. Because I have experience with a variety of people, I was able to help develop the new manual. More important, I improved my knowledge of what it takes to make a food service business successful.

I am very much interested in putting my training to use at Roxy's because it is close to school and I can draw upon skills I already have. The location makes it possible for me to fulfill two objectives at the same time. I hope that we can schedule an interview sometime during the next few weeks. I will be here in Little Rock except for the week of May 7, but I will be checking my phone and email messages daily when I am out of town, and you should have no difficulty reaching me.

Complimentary
close

Sincerely,

Signature

Karen Tran

Typed name

Karen Tran

Enclosure

enc.

Beyond the Rule

WRITING ON THE JOB

It is likely that you will do most of your own writing on the job, and you will always be responsible for anything that is sent from your office with your signature on it. You will need to pay particular attention to audience (see 1e(2)) and purpose (1e(1)) as well as to conciseness (chapter 30), correctness, and format. For further information, visit www.harbrace.com.

in question. Demonstrating that you already know something about it will help you appear to be a serious candidate. Extensive information on most companies is available in their annual reports. You can also find information by searching LexisNexis (see page 241) or the Web.

In your closing paragraph, offer any additional useful information, and make a specific request for an interview. Be sure to tell your reader how and where you can be reached. Indicate that you would enjoy the opportunity to exchange information.

Exercise 2

Write a letter of application to accompany the résumé you wrote in exercise 1.

15e | A grant proposal is an application for funding for a project.

As a college student, businessperson, or community activist, you may at some time need to write a grant proposal. Grants are available to support academic research, creative writing, performance art, new businesses, and community service projects. Your school may have a grants specialist who can advise you about funding opportunities. You can also find information about specific funding agencies on the Web. In addition, your school or public library is likely to have directories of available grants, as well as books devoted to grant writing.

Funding agencies usually supply applicants with literature that explains how to apply for grants and frequently lists what the reviewers expect to find in the proposal. Because these agencies often have their own forms, which they require applicants for funds to use, the content and format of grant proposals vary. Read the Request for Proposals (RFP) closely, and contact the organization that issued it if you have any questions.

Most grant proposals, however, contain

- an abstract, or summary of the project,
- a narrative describing the project's purpose and nature,
- a description of the methodology that will be used,
- a schedule for completing the work or for evaluating the project, and
- a budget.

Writing a grant proposal usually involves writing for a diverse audience (see **1e(2)**). Although the review committee may include a member with expertise in the field in which the project is based, it is likely to include people with different kinds of expertise. For example, the review committee of a foundation supporting work in the sciences may include physicists, chemists, biologists, and software engineers, as well as an administrator whose background may be in business or the humanities. When you prepare a grant proposal, it is important to write clearly and simply, avoiding jargon and defining any technical terms you use.

The following grant proposal was written by Alicia Obaldo for a family science course. This proposal does not include graphics (see chapter 6), which are seldom required for simpler projects, although they are likely to be used for more complicated ones. Many software programs are available to help you create graphics and import them into text documents.

The style used for this proposal follows guidelines established by the American Psychological Association (APA) except that the title page was adjusted to comply with requirements of the foundation to which the proposal is addressed. Variations of the APA style are used widely for writing in the social sciences. (Other examples of the use of APA style can be found on pages 336–349 and 428–430.)

Model grant proposal

Texas Woman's University Childcare Center

Capital Fund Grant Request for Renovation

Texas Woman's University Education

for Success Program

304 Administration Drive

Denton, TX 76201

(940) 898-2000

Alicia Obaldo

The first page lists expanded author information, name of the funding agency, and amount of request.

Submitted to: Kresge Foundation

Project Dates

August 2003–August 2004

Requesting $15,000 for project

May 30, 2003

Capital Fund Grant   2

The abstract summarizes the project.

Abstract

The Texas Woman's University Childcare Center will provide childcare services to students of the University while they attend classes. This service will help to assure students that their children are well cared for. Students will then be better able to focus on furthering their educations to expand and improve professional opportunities. The facility will be located in an existing home, which needs renovation for safety, convenience and code requirements. A playground must also be built on the property. Although the program will begin with a small staff and serve a limited number of families, the university has planned for growth in all areas. Texas Woman's University is a university primarily for women, and it enrolls a large number of nontraditional students, many of whom are limited in their class options or are in danger of dropping out because of family responsibilities. Providing on-campus childcare would assist current students and appeal to prospective students, encouraging them to pursue educational goals where they can be assured their children are safe and happy.

Capital Fund Grant 3

Narrative

The Texas Woman's University (TWU) Education for Success Program is
asking the Kresge Foundation for a capital fund grant of $15,000 for
renovation and building costs associated with opening the TWU Childcare
Center. The TWU Education for Success Program is a nonprofit joint
venture between the Student Government Association (SGA) and the
university administration that works to recruit and retain students who
might not be able to finish their college degrees without help. The goal of
the Education for Success Program is to enable students to finish college so
that they may attain their professional goals. The Kresge Foundation has
established a reputation for providing capital funds for universities striving
to provide enrichment in the lives of students; the TWU Childcare Center is
the kind of program the foundation has supported in the past.

In an effort to help TWU students who have children and to appeal to
potential students who have children, TWU Childcare Center plans to
provide childcare services for a number of at-risk students taking classes at
the university. Since TWU is a university primarily for women (over 91%),
with nearly 90% of the student population age 20 or older, it is reasonable
to assume that many of the students have children. Some of these children
may be school age, but many are not. Even parents of school-age children
need childcare if they take late afternoon or night classes. Open from 7:40
a.m. until 9:10 p.m., the TWU Childcare Center will provide short-term
care for TWU students' children so that the parents may obtain a college
education, thereby increasing their professional opportunities.

This section describes the nature and purpose of the project.

Obaldo identifies the project's goals.

This paragraph stresses the project's importance to an underserved group.

Obaldo establishes the limits of the project.

The project as proposed here would be limited in size and scope for a trial period of 2 years. Provided that evaluation of the program is successful, TWU Childcare Center will expand its scope as detailed in Methodology. This project will appeal to the TWU student community by offering convenient, easy childcare.

Staff

Personnel qualifications and available resources are noted.

The TWU Childcare Center will use two full-time experienced childcare administrators supervising TWU graduate students to staff the facility. The graduate students will work as paid part-time employees or as interns earning credit from their departments. Because of TWU's wide variety of degree offerings, children will be offered instruction at the center in dance, music, art, reading, and exercise, in addition to traditional childcare (see Table 1 for activities schedule). The Family Sciences Department and the Education Department will provide teachers for the children. In addition to staff employed by the facility and interns, the TWU Childcare Center will maintain a board made up of representatives from the vested departments, student representatives, administrative representatives, and the facility directors. This board will hire the two facility directors and will determine the success of the program, based on established criteria determined before the facility opens.

Capital Fund Grant   5

Table 1

TWU Childcare Center Activities Schedule

A table presents a tentative schedule for children.

8:00–9:20	Free play/exercise/music
9:30–10:50	Dance/art
11:00–12:20	Lunch
12:30–1:00	Nap or story time/free play
1:00–2:30	Dance/music
2:30–3:50	Snack time/free play/exercise
4:00–5:20	Story time/dance
5:30–6:00	Supper
6:00–8:50	Free play/story time/music/art

The TWU Childcare Center will follow the guidelines below for student/ teacher ratio. These guidelines exceed Texas Day-care Center Minimum Standards & Guidelines.

This paragraph shows compliance with state guidelines.

- At any time, at least 1 full-time and 2 part-time staff members will be on duty at the facility.
- The facility will maintain a 5:1 child/teacher ratio.
- No more than 10 children will be scheduled at any time.
- No more than 35 children will be enrolled at the facility per semester.

Evaluation

The TWU Childcare Center will provide limited service for 2 years while the success of the program is evaluated. Upon successful completion of the evaluation period, the program will look at beginning planned expansion projects (discussed below). The TWU Childcare Center will open with the following guidelines:

- Children must be registered for TWU Childcare Center services 1 week before a semester begins.

- Parents must schedule times when children will be at the center. The program will not be a drop-off facility.
- Children may be scheduled for no more than 4.5 hours on one day and attend no more than 13 hours in a week.
- Parents will provide meals and snacks for children.
- Children may be dropped off 20 minutes before their scheduled starts and picked up 20 minutes after their scheduled departures.

Obaldo provides for the evaluation of the project.

Evaluation of the TWU Childcare Center will be based on compliance with Texas Day-care Center Minimum Standards & Guidelines, satisfaction of and demand from TWU students using the facility, and an acceptable profit margin determined by the facility's board.

The methodology section shows how the center will operate.

Methodology

Children from 24 months to 10 years of age will be accepted at the TWU Childcare Center. The children will be separated into two groups, 24 months to 5 years in one group and 6 years to 10 years in another group. The charge for the services of the TWU Childcare Center will be $4 per hour, payable weekly or biweekly, depending on the agreement signed by the parent at the time of enrollment. This amount is in line with area daycare programs charging an average of $135 a week.

She details possible uses for grant money.

The TWU Childcare Center will be located behind the Multi-Purpose Classroom building in a renovated 2800-square-foot home acquired by the university from a former faculty member at a discounted price. The home will be renovated to meet all building and safety code requirements.

Capital Fund Grant   7

Currently, the two-story home has one bathroom, two large rooms and a small room downstairs, which will be kept intact for the children's activities. There is also a small kitchen that will be left intact for staff use. Upstairs are four bedrooms, two baths, and an office, which will be used for storage and office space for staff and as a sick room for children until parents can be notified. The fenced backyard will be planted with soft turf, and outdoor play equipment will be installed. In addition to these minor renovations, the facility will need a sign out front and additional miscellaneous changes for parent and staff convenience. The home is easily accessible from campus so that parents may visit their children between classes.

The TWU Childcare Center's plans for future expansion include providing meals and snacks that will be planned and prepared by the Nutrition and Food Science Department, providing part-time care for the children of staff and faculty, and hiring more full-time staff for the growing needs of the facility. After these changes have occurred, the TWU Childcare Center will begin adding more teachers and children, including older and younger children, as the demand grows.

This paragraph addresses plans for the future.

Schedule

A time line has been established so that the TWU Childcare Center can open in time for the fall semester in 2004 (see Table 2).

This time line gives the plan for completion.

Table 2

TWU Childcare Project Time Line

August 2003	Submit required state forms for operating childcare facility
September 2003	Organize and meet with facility board
October 2003	Obtain written commitments and plans from all departments for support of facility
November 2003	Begin renovation of facility
February 2004	Begin inspection of facility
April 2004	Confirm all license and permits completed
May 2004	Begin job search for facility director
June 2004	Begin interviewing part-time teachers
August 2004	Open TWU Childcare Center

Budget

A budget has been established to show estimates of funds needed and already supplied (see Table 3). The university has agreed to provide $5,000 in seed money, and the alumnae association has pledged another $5,000. Plans are in place for a fundraiser to raise another $5,000. The TWU Childcare Center is requesting $15,000 from the foundation.

This table presents the budget.

Table 3

Estimated Opening Budget

Building renovations	−$22,000
Toys and child development materials	− 1,500
Playground equipment	− 5,000
Sign for front porch	− 500
Licenses and permits	− 1,000
Total cost	− 30,000
Seed money from university	5,000
Alumnae contributions	5,000
Campus fundraiser	5,000
Total grant request	$15,000

Exercise 3

What new facility might be offered at your school or workplace for students or employees? For instance, is there a music listening room where students can relax or study? Does your workplace have a fitness room? Write a proposal for funding the new facility; address the proposal to your school or employer or to an agency or foundation that supports such improvements.

Grammar

Using a Grammar Checker

Most word-processing programs have features that help writers identify many grammar errors as well as various problems with usage and style.

But these grammar checkers have significant limitations. Because they are programmed according to certain basic rules, they search for violations of those rules. They usually will identify

- fused sentences, sometimes called run-on sentences (chapter 19),
- some misused prepositions (chapter 29c),
- wordy or overly long sentences (chapter 30), and
- missing apostrophes in contractions (chapter 33).

Most grammar checkers will suggest one or more ways to correct the errors they find, and you can incorporate or modify those suggestions as you revise a draft. However, grammar checkers frequently miss

- sentence fragments (chapter 18),
- problems with adverbs or adjectives (chapter 20),
- dangling or misplaced modifiers (chapter 20),
- problems with pronoun-antecedent agreement (chapter 21),
- errors in subject-verb agreement (chapter 22), and
- misused or missing commas (chapter 31).

Since these problems weaken your credibility as a writer, you should never rely solely on a grammar checker to find them. Grammar checkers cannot distinguish between true errors and choices you make deliberately to suit your rhetorical situation (see chapter 1). As a result, they often miss subtle problems with usage and style or flag words or phrases that you have chosen intentionally.

Used carefully, a grammar checker can be a helpful tool, but keep the following advice in mind.

- Adjust the settings on your grammar checker to look only for errors you make frequently. (However, even if used in this way, a grammar checker may miss some errors.)

- Always evaluate any sentences flagged by a grammar checker to determine whether there is in fact a problem.

- Carefully review the revisions proposed by a grammar checker before accepting them. Sometimes, the proposed revisions create entirely new errors.

- Use a grammar checker only in addition to your own reading. When in doubt, consult the appropriate chapters in this handbook.

Sentence Essentials

Sentences serve a number of purposes. Writers state facts or report information with **declarative sentences.** They give instructions with **imperative sentences.** Questions, or **interrogative sentences,** introduce topics and elicit information. **Exclamatory sentences** express emotion.

Declarative	The runners from Kenya won the race.
Imperative	Compare their times with the record.
Interrogative	Who were those runners whose victory surprised the world?
Exclamatory	What a tough race that was!

For guidelines on how to punctuate sentences, see chapter 35. To write effective sentences, though, you will also benefit from knowing their essential elements.

Beyond the Rule

SENTENCE TYPES

Each type of sentence can be used for a variety of purposes. For example, imperative sentences are used not only to give directions, but also to make suggestions *(Try using a different screwdriver),* to issue invitations *(Come in),* to extend wishes *(Have a good time),* and to warn others *(Stop).* Furthermore, a single purpose, such as making a request, can be achieved with more than one type of sentence.

Imperative	Close the window, please.
Declarative	We should close the window.
Interrogative	Would you please close the window?

For further discussion of sentence types, visit www.harbrace.com.

This chapter will help you

- recognize the essential parts of a sentence (**16a**),
- identify verbs (**16b**),
- identify subjects and complements (**16c**), and
- recognize basic sentence patterns (**16d**).

For explanations of any unfamiliar terms, consult the **Glossary of Terms.**

16a | **A sentence contains a subject and a predicate.**

A sentence consists of two parts: a **subject** and a **predicate.**

SUBJECT + PREDICATE

The subject is generally someone or something that either performs an action or is described.

> The **quarterback** + passed the ball to his wide receiver. [subject performs an action]
>
> **He** + is talented. [subject is described]

The predicate expresses the action initiated by the subject or makes a comment about the subject.

> The goalie + **has blocked** the shot. [predicate expresses the action]
>
> She + **is quick.** [predicate makes a comment about the subject]

The central components of the subject and the predicate are often called the **simple subject** (the main noun or pronoun) and the **simple predicate** (the main verb and any accompanying verbs). They are underlined in the examples above.

Compound subjects and compound predicates include a connecting word such as *and, or,* or *but.*

> **The Republicans <u>and</u> the Democrats** are debating the issues. [compound subject]
>
> The candidate **stated his views on abortion <u>but</u> did not discuss stem-cell research.** [compound predicate]

Generally, sentences have the pattern subject + predicate. However, writers often vary this structure to provide emphasis or cohesion.

He + elbowed his way into the lobby and paused.
[subject + predicate]

From a far corner of the lobby came + shrieks of laughter.
[predicate + subject]

In the second sentence, the predicate contains information related to the first sentence and is thus placed at the beginning of the sentence. The placement of the subject at the end of the sentence allows the information it contains to be emphasized. To learn how writers commonly vary sentence structure, see chapters 26 and 27.

E x e r c i s e   1

Identify the subject and the predicate in each sentence, noting any compound subjects or compound predicates.

1. A naturalist gave us a short lecture on the Cascade Mountains.
2. He showed slides of mountain lakes and heather meadows.
3. David Douglas explored much of the Northwest.
4. Douglas fir predominates in the Cascade forests.
5. Mountaineers and artists have long considered the North Cascades the most dramatic mountains of the range.
6. Timberlines are low because of the short growing season.
7. Mt. Rainier is the highest volcano in the range.
8. Huckleberries taste sweet.
9. The waxing and waning of the glaciers have eroded the mountain walls.
10. People wishing to camp by the Enchantment Lakes must apply for a special pass.
11. Hikers to this area should pack warm clothing.
12. The National Wilderness Act banned motorized travel in many areas.

13. My friend lent me his map of the Pacific Crest Trail.
14. The trail begins in southern California and ends in British Columbia.
15. We found the naturalist's advice useful.

All of the sentences in exercise 1 are declarative. Write five more sentences that are imperative, interrogative, or exclamatory.

Bring to class a paragraph of at least five sentences that you find interesting. In each sentence, label the subject and the predicate. Place an asterisk by any sentence that does not follow the subject + predicate pattern. State possible reasons for the variation.

16b The central part of the predicate is the verb.

A **verb** indicates action or signals a state of being (see chapter 22). A verb may be a single word, or it may be accompanied by one or more **auxiliary verbs,** also called *helping verbs.* The most common auxiliaries are *be (am, is, are, was, were, been), have (has, had),* and *do (does, did).* Others, including *can, may,* and *might,* are called **modal auxiliaries.** These auxiliary verbs convey various meanings, such as ability or possibility.

They **work** as volunteers. [single-word verb]

They **have been working** as volunteers. [verb with two auxiliaries]

They **might work** as volunteers. [verb with modal auxiliary expressing possibility]

Other words, usually adverbs, may intervene between the auxiliary and the main verb.

They have **always** worked as volunteers.

Have you **ever** volunteered?

Because verbs are essential parts of a sentence, choose them with care. The more precise, the better. Exactness is a characteristic of good writing. (See chapter 29.)

Exercise 4

Review the sentences in exercise 1, identifying all main verbs and auxiliary verbs.

Exercise 5

Review the sentences in the paragraph you chose for exercise 3. Identify all main verbs and auxiliary verbs.

16c | Subjects and complements take different positions in a sentence.

In most sentences, the subject refers to someone or something performing an action and usually appears before the verb.

$$\overset{s}{\text{The \underline{chair} of the committee}} \overset{v}{\text{presented}} \text{ his plans for the new year.}$$

Complements are parts of a sentence required by the verb to make the sentence complete. For example, the sentence *The chair of the committee presented* is incomplete without the complement *his plans.* There are four different types of complements: direct object, indirect object, subject complement, and object complement. A **direct object** usually receives the action expressed by the verb. It appears after the verb.

The committee members questioned **the <u>chair</u>.**

An **indirect object** also comes after the verb. It generally indicates to whom or for whom something is done.

The chair sent **the committee <u>members</u>** an agenda for the meeting.

A **subject complement** describes, identifies, or classifies the subject. Like a direct or indirect object, it follows the verb.

He is **the <u>chair</u> of the committee.**

The chair of the committee is **<u>reasonable</u>.**

An **object complement** follows a direct object, describing, identifying, or classifying it.

They elected him **<u>chair</u>.**

They consider him **quite <u>reasonable</u>.**

You will find it useful to be able to identify the main word in subjects and complements, especially when you are checking for agreement (see **21d** and **22e**). The main word in each of the examples above is underlined. Sometimes, a main word is a noun that consists of more than one word. Examples of such **compound nouns** are *Labor Day, swimming pool,* and *ice cream.*

Subjects and complements are generally pronouns, nouns, or noun phrases. The term **noun phrase** refers to the main noun and any modifiers that provide additional information about the noun (see **17a**). A pronoun can stand in for an entire noun phrase. In fact, you can use a pronoun test to help you recognize subjects and objects: Simply substitute a pronoun for the noun phrase. Common pronouns used for this test are *he, she, it, they, him, her, them, this,* and *that.*

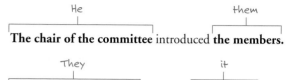

The chair of the committee introduced **the members.**

The committee members discussed **the proposal.**

(1) Subjects are usually pronouns, nouns, or noun phrases.

Grammatically complete sentences contain a subject. Except for imperatives, in which the subject, *you,* is understood, most subjects take the form of a pronoun, noun, or noun phrase.

My best friend is a nutritionist. [noun phrase]

She works at a clinic. [pronoun]

Eat plenty of fruits and vegetables. [understood *you*]

To identify the subject of a sentence, find the verb and then use it in a question beginning with *who* or *what,* as shown in the following examples.

Jennifer works at a clinic.	Meat contains cholesterol.
Verb: **works**	Verb: **contains**
WHO works? **Jennifer**	WHAT contains? **Meat**
(not the clinic) **works.**	(not cholesterol) **contains.**
Subject: **Jennifer**	Subject: **Meat**

Some sentences begin with the **expletive** *there* or *it.* Such a word occurs in the subject position, forcing the true subject to follow the verb.

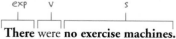

There were **no exercise machines.**

A subject following the expletive *it* is often a noun clause rather than a noun phrase. You will learn more about this type of clause in chapter 17.

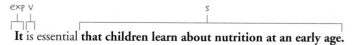

It is essential **that children learn about nutrition at an early age.**

In sentences beginning with the expletive *there*, the verb comes before the subject. The verb *are* is often hard to hear, so be careful that you do not omit it (see **23f**).

                    are
There ∧ many good books on nutrition.

---

(2) Objects are usually pronouns, nouns, or noun phrases.

Objects complete the meaning begun by the subject and verb.

> My roommate writes **movie scripts.** [The object *movie scripts* completes the meaning of the sentence.]

Whether an object is required in a sentence depends on the meaning of the verb. Some sentences have no objects at all; others have one or even two objects.

> The robins are migrating. [A sentence with no object.]
>
> She lent **me** her **laptop.** [*Me* is one object; *laptop* is another.]

(a) Direct objects

The direct object of a verb showing action either receives the action or shows the result of the action.

> I. M. Pei designed **the East Building of the National Gallery.**
>
> Steve McQueen invented **the bucket seat** in 1960.

Compound direct objects include a connecting word, usually *and.*

> Thomas Edison patented **the phonograph and the microphone.**

To identify a direct object, find the subject and the verb and then use them in a question ending with *what* or *whom.*

Marie Curie discovered radium.	They hired a new engineer.
Subject and verb: **Marie Curie discovered**	Subject and verb: **They hired**
Marie Curie discovered WHAT? **radium**	They hired WHOM? **a new engineer**
Direct object: **radium**	Direct object: **a new engineer**

Some direct objects are clauses (see 17b).

> Researchers found **that patients responded favorably to the new medication.**

(b) Indirect objects

Some verbs can have both a direct object and an **indirect object.** Indirect objects are typically pronouns, nouns, or noun phrases that name the recipient of the direct object. Verbs that commonly take indirect objects include *bring, buy, give, lend, offer, sell,* and *send.*

> The supervisor gave **the new employees** computers.
>
> She sent **them** contracts in the mail.

Like subjects and direct objects, indirect objects can be compound.

> She offered **Elena and Octavio** a generous benefits package.

(3) Subject and object complements are usually pronouns, nouns, noun phrases, adjectives, or adjectival phrases.

Like objects, complements can be pronouns, nouns, or noun phrases. However, they can also be **adjectives** or **adjectival phrases,** phrases in which the main word is an **adjective** (a word that classifies or describes a noun or pronoun). The adjective may be accompanied by a word that softens or intensifies its meaning (such as *somewhat, very,* or *quite*).

(a) Subject complements

A **subject complement,** which identifies, classifies, or describes the subject, follows a **linking verb** (see 22c). The most common linking verb is *be* (*am, is, are, was, were, been*). Other linking verbs are *become, seem, appear,* and the sensory verbs *feel, look, smell, sound,* and *taste.*

> The game is **a test of endurance.** [noun phrase]
>
> The winner is **you.** [pronoun]
>
> The game rules sound **quite complicated.** [adjectival phrase]

(b) Object complements

An **object complement** identifies or describes the direct object. Object complements help complete the meaning of verbs such as *call, elect, make, name,* and *paint.*

Sports reporters called the rookie **the best player of the year.**
[noun phrase]

News of the strike left the fans **somewhat disappointed.**
[adjective phrase]

Beyond the Rule

VERBS AND NOUNS

The verb you choose affects how many and what kinds of nouns are in a sentence. Some verbs, such as *sleep,* are never followed by an object. Other verbs take an object in some contexts (*I passed the exam*) but not in others (*Time passed slowly*). For more information, visit www.harbrace.com.

(4) Vocatives or appositives usually consist of pronouns, nouns, or noun phrases.

Sometimes, the pronouns, nouns, or noun phrases in a sentence are not subjects or complements. If they are used to address someone directly, they are **vocatives.** If they are placed near other nouns to identify them or otherwise supplement their meaning, they are **appositives.**

Arlese, would you repeat your question? [vocative]

Arlese, **my elder sister,** attends Jacksonville University. [appositive]

Exercise 6

Review the sentences in exercises 1 and 3, identifying all direct objects, indirect objects, subject complements, and object complements. Then, write five sentences that contain either expletives, vocatives, or appositives.

16d | There are five basic sentence patterns.

Understanding basic sentence patterns and variations will help you recognize subjects and complements. The following box summarizes the five basic sentence patterns. Each pattern is based on the type of verb the sentence includes. You have already been introduced to linking verbs (such as *be, seem, sound,* and *taste*). Linking verbs are followed by subject complements. Verbs that are not linking are either transitive or intransitive (see **22c**). Notice that *trans* in the words *transitive* and *intransitive* means "over or across." Thus, the action of a **transitive verb** carries across to an object, but the action of an **intransitive verb** does not. Intransitive verbs have no complements, although they are often followed by adverbs or phrases functioning as adverbs.

BASIC SENTENCE PATTERNS

Pattern 1   SUBJECT + INTRANSITIVE VERB

Pattern 2   SUBJECT + TRANSITIVE VERB + DIRECT OBJECT

Pattern 3   SUBJECT + TRANSITIVE VERB + INDIRECT OBJECT + DIRECT OBJECT

The student teacher read them a story.

Pattern 4   SUBJECT + TRANSITIVE VERB + DIRECT OBJECT + OBJECT COMPLEMENT

The new leaders declared the country a separate nation.

(Continued on page 480)

(Continued from page 479)

Pattern 5   SUBJECT + LINKING VERB + SUBJECT COMPLEMENT

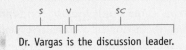

Dr. Vargas is the discussion leader.

Some languages, such as French and Cantonese, have sentence patterns similar to those you have learned for English. These languages are called SVO (subject-verb-object) languages, even though not all sentences have objects. The patterns for other languages vary. SOV (subject-object-verb) languages and VSO (verb-subject-object) languages are also common. Keep the SVO pattern in mind to help guide you through English sentences.

SOV (Japanese): *Watakushi wa soko de Okutsu san o mimashita.*
["I saw Mr. Okutsu there."]

VSO (Tongan): *Na'e tāmate'i 'e Tēvita 'a Kōlaiate.*
["David killed Goliath."]

When declarative sentences, or statements, are turned into questions, the subject and the auxiliary verb are inverted; that is, the auxiliary verb is moved to the front of the sentence, before the subject.

Statement: A Chinese skater (has) won a gold medal.

Question: Has a Chinese skater won a gold medal?

Often, a question word such as *what* or *why* opens an interrogative sentence. Nonetheless, the auxiliary verb still comes before the subject.

Question: What has a Chinese skater won?

If a statement does not include an auxiliary verb or a form of the linking verb *be,* then a form of *do* is added to the corresponding question. Once again, the auxiliary verb is placed in front of the subject.

Statement: A Chinese skater won a gold medal.

Question: Did a Chinese skater win a gold medal?

English is one of a few languages in which subject and verb are inverted in questions. Most languages rely on intonation to indicate that a question is being asked, without a change in word order. (English speakers occasionally use uninverted questions to ask for clarification or to indicate surprise.) Another frequently occurring option for making a statement into a question is to add a particle, such as the Japanese *ka.*

You have learned five basic sentence patterns in this section. However, as you study sentences more closely, you will find other patterns as well. For example, some patterns require mention of a destination or location. The sentence *The town lies* is incomplete without a phrase such as *between a mountain and a river*; similarly, the sentence *I put the documents* needs a phrase such as *on your desk.* Other sentences have phrases that are not essential but do add pertinent information. These phrases can sometimes be moved. For example, the phrase *on Friday* can be placed either at the beginning or at the end of a sentence.

I finished my assignment **on Friday.**

On Friday, I finished my assignment.

To learn how to write effective sentences by varying their structure, see chapters 26 and 27.

Exercise 7

Identify the basic pattern of each sentence in exercises 1 and 3. Note any nonessential phrases. Then, write a question corresponding to each of the sentences. Put a check mark next to those questions in which a subject and a verb are inverted.

Phrases and Clauses in Sentences

Within a sentence, groups of words form phrases and clauses. Like single words, these larger units function as specific parts of speech: nouns, verbs, adjectives, or adverbs. By understanding how word groups function, you will be able to make your sentences clear, concise, and complete. You will also be able to vary sentence structure so that your paragraphs are rhythmic and cohesive. (For explanations of any unfamiliar terms, see the **Glossary of Terms**.)

This chapter will help you

- recognize phrases (**17a**),
- recognize clauses (**17b**), and
- use different sentence forms (**17c**).

Beyond the Rule

DEFINITION OF *PHRASE*

There are two definitions of the word *phrase*. The traditional definition is that a *phrase* is a sequence of grammatically related words without a subject, a predicate, or both. However, there is another definition used by linguists. According to them, a *phrase* is a unit that has one word as its main part. This word is called the *head* of the phrase. A noun phrase, then, is a phrase with a noun (or a pronoun) as its head. Technically, *people, a shy person, everyone in the room,* and *me* are all noun phrases. The traditional definition allows only multiword groupings to be phrases; the linguists' definition also allows phrases to consist of single words. In most composition handbooks, including this one, the traditional definition is used. For more information on phrases, visit <u>www.harbrace.com</u>.

> **17a** | A phrase is a group of words that can function as a single unit in a sentence.

(1) A noun phrase consists of a main noun and any accompanying determiners (*a, an, the, that*), adjectives, or other modifiers.

Noun phrases serve as subjects and complements. They can also be objects of prepositions such as *in, of, on, at,* and *to.* (See **17a(4)** for a longer list of prepositions.)

The heavy frost killed **many fruit trees.** [subject and direct object]

My cousin is **an organic farmer.** [subject and subject complement]

His farm is in **eastern Oregon.** [subject and object of the preposition *in*]

In these sentences, the determiners *the* and *an* as well as the adjectives *heavy, fruit, organic,* and *eastern* add specificity. For example, the noun phrase *an organic farmer* tells the reader more than *farmer* alone would. Most writers move between general nouns (*businesses*) and more specific noun phrases (*small businesses, local small businesses*). Choose the noun or noun phrase that best serves your purpose. By choosing noun phrases carefully, you will make your sentences more precise and cohesive.

Much of Greenland lies within the Arctic Circle. ~~The area~~ is owned ^This large island^

by Denmark. Its ^native^ name is Kaballit Nunaat.

[*The area* could refer to either Greenland or the area within the Arctic Circle. *This large island* clearly refers to Greenland. *Its native name* is more precise than just *Its name.*]

 In noun phrases with nouns referring to individual items that can be counted (**count nouns**), such as *student* and *document,* some determiners are chosen according to whether the nouns are singular or plural:

a student, **an** opportunity, **that** opportunity [determiners used with singular count nouns]

some students, **few** students, **fewer** students, **those** opportunities, **many** opportunities [determiners used with plural count nouns]

Determiners such as *less* and *much* are used with nouns representing abstract concepts or masses that cannot be counted (**noncount nouns**):

> **less** time, **less** water, **much** energy, **much** coffee [determiners used with noncount nouns]

Some nouns, especially abstract or plural generic nouns, do not have any determiners.

> **Patience** is a virtue. [abstract noun]
>
> **Customers** can be demanding. [plural generic noun]

Other languages that have determiners may not use them as they are used in English. For example, in Italian, the definite article, equivalent to the English *the,* is used with abstract nouns.

> *La pazienza è una virtù.* [The definite article *La* precedes the noun *pazienza.*]

For more information on the use of determiners, see **23e**.

(2) A verb phrase is an essential part of the predicate.

The predicate says something about the subject and contains a word that expresses action or state of being—a verb (see **16a–b**). Besides a main verb, a verb phrase may also include **auxiliaries,** sometimes called *helping verbs,* such as *be, have, do, will,* and *should.*

> The trees **blossomed.** [main verb]
>
> The fruit **has ripened.** [auxiliary verb + main verb]

For a complete discussion of verb structure, see chapter **22**. For more information on using verbs to convey meaning effectively, see **23d**, **23f**, **26d**, and **27d**.

(3) Verbal phrases may be used as nouns or as modifiers.

Verb forms used as nouns or as adjectives or adverbs (see chapter **20**) are called **verbals.** Because of their origin as verbs, verbals in phrases often have their own objects and modifiers.

> He wanted **to finish the task quickly.** [The object of the verbal *to finish* is *the task. Quickly* is a modifier.]

Verbal phrases are divided into three types: gerund phrases, participial phrases, and infinitive phrases.

Central to **gerund phrases** are *-ing* verb forms (see **22a**). Gerund phrases function as nouns, usually serving as subjects or objects.

> **Writing a bestseller** was her only goal. [subject]
>
> My neighbor enjoys **writing about distant places.** [object]

Because gerund phrases act as nouns, pronouns can replace them.

> **That** was her only goal.
>
> She enjoys **it.**

Participial phrases can be divided into two subtypes. The first includes a present participle (*-ing* form). The second subtype includes a past participle (*-ed* form for regular verbs or another form for irregular verbs). (See **22a** for more information on verb forms.)

> <u>**Planning**</u> **her questions carefully,** she was able to hold fast-paced and engaging interviews. [present participle]
>
> <u>**Known**</u> **for her interviewing skills,** she was asked to host her own radio program. [past participle]

Participial phrases function as modifiers. They may appear at various points in a sentence: beginning, middle, or end.

> **Fearing a drought,** all the farmers in the area used less irrigation water.
>
> All the farmers in the area, **recognizing the signs of drought,** used less irrigation water.
>
> Farmers used less irrigation water, **hoping to save water for later in the season.**

The commas setting off each participial phrase in the preceding examples signal that the phrase is not necessary for identifying the noun it modifies. Instead, the phrase adds extra information to the sentence. Sometimes, however, the participial phrase is essential for meaning. The details it provides help the reader identify the noun being referred to.

> The reporter **providing the most accurate account of the war** was once a soldier. [The participial phrase helps distinguish this reporter from others.]

A present participle (*-ing* form) cannot function alone as the main verb in a sentence. When an *-ing* form is the main verb, it is generally preceded by a form of *be* (*am, is, are, was,* or *were*).

are
They thinking about the future.
   ∧

Infinitive phrases serve as nouns or modifiers. The form of the infinitive is distinct: the infinitive marker *to* followed by the base form of the verb.

The company intends **to hire twenty new employees.** [direct object]

To attract customers, the company changed its advertising strategy. [modifier of the verb *changed*]

We discussed his plan **to use a new packing process.** [modifier of the noun *plan*]

When an infinitive follows a form of *make* or sometimes a form of *have*, the marker *to* is omitted.

The coach **made** the new recruit **repeat** the drill.

The coach **had** the new recruit **run** an extra lap.

For advice on the punctuation of verbal phrases, see **31b** and **31d–e.**

The infinitive marker *to* does not follow modal auxiliaries.

You **should to** revise your paper.

They **must to** address the need for more energy sources.

Some verbs in English are followed by a gerund, some are followed by an infinitive, and some are followed by either.

(Continued on page 488)

(Continued from page 487)

Verbs followed by a gerund

admit	deny	finish
avoid	dislike	miss
consider	enjoy	suggest

Example: She enjoys playing the piano.

Verbs followed by an infinitive

agree	hope	prepare
decide	need	promise
deserve	plan	seem

Example: She promised to play the piano for us.

Verbs followed by a pronoun, noun, or noun phrase

advise	encourage	persuade
allow	invite	require
cause	order	teach

Examples: Her father taught her to play the piano. A good friend persuaded the young pianist to audition for the city orchestra.

Verbs followed by either a gerund or an infinitive

begin	like	remember
continue	love	stop
hate	prefer	try

Examples: She likes to play the piano. She likes playing the piano.

Although both gerund phrases and infinitive phrases can serve as direct objects, their meanings may be different.

We stopped **discussing the plan.** [The discussion has ended.]

We stopped **to discuss the plan.** [The discussion has not yet started.]

Good dictionaries such as those mentioned on pages 660 and 662 provide both definitions and examples.

Beyond the Rule

SPLIT INFINITIVES

Some grammarians advise against putting words between the infinitive marker *to* and the base form of the verb.

Be sure **to ~~carefully~~ proofread** your paper ~carefully~ .

This advice is based on Latin grammar, which says that infinitives are never split. And it is good advice to remember if the intervening words create a cumbersome sentence.

~Under the circumstances, the~
~The~ jury was unable **to, ~~under the circumstances,~~ convict** the defendant.

However, most writers today recognize that an adverb splitting an infinitive can provide emphasis.

It was a relief **to finally finish** my history project.

For more information on split infinitives, visit www.harbrace.com.

(4) Prepositional phrases are generally used as modifiers.

Prepositional phrases provide information about time, place, accompaniment, cause, manner, and so on.

With great feeling, Martin Luther King expressed his dream **of freedom.** [*With great feeling* describes the manner in which the speech was delivered, and *of freedom* specifies the kind of dream.]

King delivered his most famous speech **at a demonstration in Washington, D.C.** [Both *at a demonstration* and *in Washington, D.C.* provide details about place.]

A **prepositional phrase** consists of a **preposition** (a word such as *around, at, in,* or *near*) and a noun, noun phrase, or pronoun (**object of**

the preposition). A prepositional phrase modifies another element in the sentence.

> The professor's lecture **on censorship** stirred controversy. [*On censorship* modifies the noun phrase *the professor's lecture.*]
>
> Everyone **in the class** was upset. [*In the class* modifies the pronoun *everyone.*]
>
> Some students met the professor **after class.** [*After class* tells when the action of the verb occurred.]

A prepositional phrase can also occasionally serve as a subject.

> **After supper** is too late!

When the object of the preposition is a pronoun such as *whom* or *what,* the preposition may follow rather than precede its object, especially in questions.

> **What** was the book **about?** [The object of the preposition is *what.* COMPARE The book was about what?]

SOME COMMON PREPOSITIONS

about	behind	during	off	to
above	below	except	on	toward
across	beneath	for	out	under
after	beside	from	outside	unlike
against	between	in	over	until
among	beyond	inside	past	up
around	by	into	regarding	upon
as	concerning	like	round	with
at	despite	near	since	
before	down	of	through	

Some prepositions, called **phrasal prepositions,** consist of more than one word.

Except for the last day, it was a wonderful trip.

PHRASAL PREPOSITIONS

according to	due to	in spite of
along with	except for	instead of
apart from	in addition to	on account of
as for	in case of	out of
as to	in front of	with reference to
because of	in lieu of	with regard to
by means of	in place of	with respect to
by way of	in regard to	with the exception of

Some pairs of prepositions, such as *by/until* and *except/besides,* pose special problems. *Until* indicates a continuing situation that will come to an end at a definite time in the future. *By* indicates an action that will happen before a particular time in the future.

I will be away **until** next Tuesday.

I will finish my work **by** six o'clock.

Besides means "in addition to" or "plus," and *except* means "but" or "minus."

Besides a salad, we had soup and crackers. [We ate soup and crackers in addition to salad.]

Everyone **except** Alice attended the luncheon. [Everyone but Alice was there.]

For other information about prepositions, consult the Glossary of Usage or one of the ESL resources listed on page 662.

In English, some verbs, adjectives, and nouns combine with prepositions to form idiomatic expressions (see **29c**).

Verb + Preposition	Adjective + Preposition	Noun + Preposition
apply to	fond of	interest in
rely on	similar to	dependence on
trust in	different from	fondness for

For more information on such combinations, consult a specialized dictionary such as those listed on page 662. Specialized dictionaries include commonly occurring combinations with the entries for verbs, adjectives, and nouns.

(5) An appositive can expand the meaning of a noun or noun phrase.

Appositives (usually nouns or noun phrases) identify, explain, or supplement the meaning of other nouns or noun phrases. When appositives provide essential information, no commas are used.

> Jonathan Weiner's book ***The Beak of the Finch*** won a Pulitzer Prize. [The appositive identifies the book being referred to.]

When an appositive phrase provides extra details, commas set it off.

> *The Beak of the Finch*, **a book by Jonathan Weiner,** won a Pulitzer Prize. [The appositive provides extra details about the book.]

By using appositives carefully, you will add variety to your writing (see **27a–b**). For more information on how to punctuate nonessential appositives, see **31d**.

(6) Absolute phrases provide descriptive details or express causes or conditions.

An **absolute phrase** is usually a noun phrase modified by a participial phrase or a prepositional phrase.

> She left town at dawn, **all her belongings packed into a Volkswagen Beetle**. [*Belongings* is the main noun; *packed into a Volkswagen Beetle* is the modifying verbal phrase.]

Her guitar in the front seat, she pulled away from the curb. [*Guitar* is the main noun; *in the front seat* is the modifying prepositional phrase.]

These absolute phrases provide details. An absolute phrase can also express cause or condition.

More vaccine having arrived, the staff scheduled its distribution.

To learn how to use absolute phrases to make your writing concise, see **30b**. For information on how to punctuate absolute phrases, see **31d**.

Exercise 1

Identify the underlined phrases in the following sentences as noun phrases, verb phrases, prepositional phrases, or verbal phrases. For verbal phrases, specify the type: gerund, participial, or infinitive. Next, identify any appositive phrases or absolute phrases in the sentences.

1. <u>Most museums</u> acquire, preserve, and exhibit objects <u>with artistic, historical, or scientific value.</u>
2. Nontraditional museums abound <u>in the United States and Canada.</u>
3. You <u>can learn</u> the history of <u>the potato</u> at the Food Museum.
4. <u>Established in 1849,</u> the Mutter Museum, in Philadelphia, displays <u>pathological specimens.</u>
5. Some of the paintings in <u>the Museum of Bad Art</u> <u>were donated.</u>
6. For those interested in various methods for <u>making toast,</u> the Cyber Toaster Museum can be visited <u>via the Internet.</u>
7. <u>Located within the Science Museum of Minnesota,</u> the Museum of Questionable Medical Devices displays objects <u>ranging from weight-reduction glasses to the age-reversing McGregor Rejuvenator.</u>
8. <u>To learn more about funeral vehicles,</u> consider <u>visiting the National Museum of Funeral History,</u> a museum dedicated to providing the public with information on a common cultural ritual.
9. A large collection <u>of footwear,</u> including a pair of Queen Victoria's ballroom slippers, is on display at <u>the Bata Shoe Museum.</u>
10. Their curiosity piqued, some tourists travel <u>great distances</u> <u>to see collections of unusual objects.</u>

Exercise 2

Add details to the following sentences, using prepositional phrases, verbal phrases, appositive phrases, and absolute phrases. Then, label the phrases you added.

1. The team ran onto the field.
2. The president delivered his speech.
3. The detective slowly opened the door.
4. I slept late.
5. Roy pushed the button.

> **17b** | A clause is a group of related words that contains a subject and a predicate.

(1) Independent clauses can stand alone.

An **independent clause,** sometimes called a *main clause,* has the same grammatical structure as a simple sentence: Both contain a subject and a predicate.

> The students earned high grades. [The complete subject is *the students.* The complete predicate is *earned high grades.*]

> They were able to apply for scholarships. [The complete subject is *they.* The complete predicate is *were able to apply for scholarships.*]

Independent clauses combine with other clauses to form longer, more detailed sentences.

(2) Dependent clauses are attached to an independent clause.

A **dependent clause** resembles an independent clause. It, too, has a subject and a predicate. However, it cannot stand alone; it must be attached to an independent clause. A dependent clause functions as a noun, an adjective, or an adverb.

We know **who won the gold medal**.

The athlete **who won the gold medal** was from Argentina.

Maria received the gold medal **because her performance was flawless.**

(a) Dependent clauses used as subjects or objects

Clauses that serve as subjects or objects are called **noun clauses** (or *nominal clauses*). They are introduced by *if, that,* or a *wh-* word such as *why, what,* or *when.* Notice the similarity in usage between noun phrases and noun clauses.

Noun Phrases	Noun Clauses
The testimony may not be true. [subject]	**What the witness said** may not be true. [subject]
We do not understand **their motives.** [direct object]	We do not understand **why they did it.** [direct object]
Send the money to **a charity.** [object of the preposition]	Send the money to **whoever needs it most.** [object of the preposition]

When no misunderstanding would result, *that* can be omitted before a noun clause.

The scientist said **she was moving to Australia.** [*that* omitted]

However, *that* should always be retained when there are two noun clauses.

The scientist said **that she was moving to Australia** and **that her research team was disbanding.** [*that* retained in both noun clauses]

(b) Dependent clauses used as modifiers

Two types of dependent clauses—adjectival (relative) clauses and adverbial clauses—serve as modifiers. Any clause that answers the question

Which one? or *What kind of. . . ?* about a noun or a pronoun is an **adjectival clause.** Such clauses, which nearly always follow the words they modify, usually begin with a relative pronoun (*who, whom, that, which,* or *whose*) but sometimes begin with a relative adverb (*when, where,* or *why*). Notice the similarity in usage between adjectives and adjectival clauses.

Adjectives	Adjectival Clauses
Nobody likes **malicious** gossip. [answers the question *What kind of gossip?*]	Nobody likes news reports **that pry into people's private lives.** [answers the question *What kind of news reports?*]
Some **diligent** students begin their research early. [answers the question *Which students?*]	Students **who have good study habits** begin their research early. [answers the question *Which students?*]
The **public** remarks were troubling. [answers the question *Which remarks?*]	The remarks **that were made public** were troubling. [answers the question *Which remarks?*]

As objects in adjectival clauses, relative pronouns can be omitted as long as the meaning of the sentence is still clear.

Mother Teresa was a woman **the whole world admired.** [*Whom,* the object in the adjectival clause, is omitted.]

She was someone **who cared more about serving than being served.** [*Who,* the subject in the adjectival clause, is not omitted.]

The relative pronoun cannot be omitted when the clause is set off by commas.

Mother Teresa, **whom the whole world admired,** cared more about serving than being served.

An **adverbial clause** usually answers a question about a verb: *Where? When? How? Why? In what manner?* Adverbial clauses are introduced by subordinating conjunctions such as *because, although,* and *when.* (For a list of subordinating conjunctions, see page 499.) Notice the similarity in usage between adverbs and adverbial clauses.

Adverbs	Adverbial Clauses
Occasionally, the company hires new writers. [answers the question *When?*]	**When the need arises,** the company hires new writers. [answers the question *When?*]
She acted **selfishly.** [answers the question *How?*]	She acted **as though she cared only about herself.** [answers the question *How?*]

In an adverbial clause that refers to time or establishes a fact, both the subject and any auxiliary verb or linking verb are frequently omitted.

While fishing, he saw a rare owl. [The subject *he* and the auxiliary verb *was* have been omitted.]

Though tired, they continued to study for the exam. [The subject *they* and the linking verb *were* have been omitted.]

When using such **elliptical clauses,** be sure that the omitted subject is the same as the subject of the independent clause.

While reviewing your report, $_\wedge$ a few questions ~~occurred to me~~. [*I thought of* inserted above]

For more information on the use of elliptical clauses, see **30d.**

(3) Conjunctions and conjunctive adverbs link and relate clauses.

Conjunctions are connecting words used to signal transitions such as addition, comparison, and contrast. For a list of transitional connections, see **3d.**

Coordinating conjunctions join single words and phrases, but they also link clauses.

tired **yet** excited [The coordinating conjunction *yet* joins two adjectives and signals contrast.]

in the boat **or** on the pier [The coordinating conjunction *or* joins two phrases and marks them as alternatives.]

We did not share a language, **but** somehow we communicated. [The coordinating conjunction *but* joins two independent clauses and signals contrast.]

Coordinating conjunctions can also join sentences.

In the more open places are little lavender asters, and the even smaller-flowered white ones that some people call beeweed or farewell-summer.

And in low wet places are the richly flowered spikes of great lobelia, the blooms an intense startling blue, exquisitely shaped.

—**WENDELL BERRY,** *Home Economics*

Correlative conjunctions, consisting of two or more words, also join single words, phrases, and clauses. However, they do not join sentences.

either you **or** I [The correlative *either . . . or* joins two words and marks them as alternatives.]

neither on Friday **nor** on Saturday [The correlative *neither . . . nor* joins two phrases and marks them as negative alternatives.]

Not only did they run ten miles, **but** they **also** swam twenty laps. [The correlative *not only . . . but also* joins two independent clauses and signals addition.]

Generally, a correlative conjunction links similar structures. The following sentence has been revised because the correlative conjunction was linking a phrase to a clause.

did he save
Not only ~~saving~~ the lives of the accident victims, **but** he **also** prevented any spinal injuries.

For more information on ensuring clarity when using correlative conjunctions, see **23e**.

COORDINATING AND CORRELATIVE CONJUNCTIONS

Coordinating and, but, for, nor, or, so, yet

Correlative both . . . and, either . . . or, neither . . . nor, not only . . . but also

---

A **subordinating conjunction** marks a clause as dependent. It also signals a connection—for example, temporal or causal—that exists between the dependent clause and the main clause.

She studied Spanish **so that** she would be able to work in Costa Rica. [*So that* signals a purpose.]

Unless the project receives more funding, the research will stop. [*Unless* signals a condition.]

For a list of the types of transitions signaled by subordinating conjunctions, see **3d**.

SUBORDINATING CONJUNCTIONS

after	in case	supposing that
although	in that	than
as (far/soon) as	inasmuch as	though
as if	insofar as	till
as though	lest	unless
because	no matter how	until
before	now that	when, whenever
even if	once	where, wherever
even though	provided (that)	whether
how	since	while
if	so that	why

Conjunctive adverbs—such as *consequently, however, nevertheless, then,* and *therefore*—link independent clauses. Like coordinating and subordinating conjunctions, these adverbs signal relationships such as cause, condition, and contrast. Unlike coordinating and subordinating conjunctions, however, some conjunctive adverbs may appear in the middle or at the end of a clause.

Heat the oil; **then** add the onions. [*Then* begins the clause and signals another step in a sequence.]

He made copies of the report for members of the committee. He **also** sent copies to the city council. [*Also* appears in the middle of the clause and signals an additional action.]

My mother and father have differing political views. They rarely argue, **however.** [*However* ends the clause and signals contrast.]

For more information on conjunctive adverbs, see **3d** and **20b**. For specific information on punctuation, see **32a**.

Exercise 3

A. Identify the dependent clauses in the following paragraph. Specify whether each is a noun, adjectival, or adverbial clause.
B. Identify all coordinating conjunctions, correlative conjunctions, subordinating conjunctions, and conjunctive adverbs.

[1]With the goal of crossing both the North Pole and the South Pole alone, Børge Ousland started his 1,240-mile trek on March 3, 2001. [2]He had already crossed the South Pole in 1997, so this time he planned to walk, ski, and swim across the North Pole. [3]When he left Cape Arkticheskiy in Russia, he weighed 214 pounds. [4]When he reached Ward Hunt Island in Canada on March 23, he weighed only 177 pounds. [5]Although Ousland had prepared for the most grueling triathlon imaginable, he had no way of predicting what he would have to endure. [6]One night huge chunks of ice forced upward from the packed surface almost destroyed his camp, and the next morning he had to search hard for snow that he could melt into fresh water. [7]About a week into his trip, Ousland's sledge started to break down. [8]Ousland considered canceling his trip at that point, but instead he steeled himself and ordered a new sledge, which did not arrive until several days later. [9]Ousland also had to swim across leads, shoot at approaching polar bears, and endure the pain of frostbite and strained tendons. [10]Despite all the misery, Ousland continually took cues from his surroundings. [11]Whenever he came to a lead, he asked himself what a polar bear would do. [12]When crossing treacherous pack ice, he thought as a fox would, making each step count. [13]Ousland said the key to surviving such a rigorous journey was perseverance. [14]He never gave up.

17c	Identifying clauses helps you understand the types of sentences they form.

You can identify the form of a sentence by noting the number and kinds of clauses it contains.

(1) A simple sentence consists of a single independent clause.

A **simple sentence** is equivalent to one independent clause. Essentially, then, it must have a subject and a predicate.

> The lawyer presented her final argument. [The complete subject is *the lawyer*. The complete predicate is *presented her final argument*.]

However, you can expand a simple sentence by adding prepositional phrases or verbal phrases.

The lawyer presented her final argument **in less than an hour.**
[A prepositional phrase adds information about time.]

Encouraged by the apparent sympathy of the jury, the lawyer
presented her final argument. [A verbal phrase adds detail.]

(2) A compound sentence consists of at least two independent clauses but no dependent clauses.

Two or more independent clauses form a **compound sentence.** The independent clauses are most commonly linked by a coordinating conjunction. However, punctuation may sometimes serve the same purpose. (See 32a and 35d.)

The Democrats proposed a new budget, **but** the Republicans opposed it. [The coordinating conjunction *but* links two independent clauses and signals contrast.]

The Democrats proposed a new budget; the Republicans opposed it. [The semicolon serves the same purpose as the coordinating conjunction.]

(3) A complex sentence has one independent clause and at least one dependent clause.

Sentences consisting of an independent clause and at least one dependent clause are called **complex sentences.** The dependent clause may be a noun clause, an adjectival clause, or an adverbial clause.

Because he was known for architectural ornamentation, no one predicted **that the house <u>he designed for himself</u> would be so plain.** [This sentence has three dependent clauses. *Because he was known for architectural ornamentation* is an adverbial clause. *That the house he designed for himself would be so plain* is a noun clause. *He designed for himself* is an adjectival clause within the noun clause. The relative pronoun *that* has been omitted.]

(4) A compound-complex sentence consists of at least two independent clauses and at least one dependent clause.

The combination of a compound sentence and a complex sentence is called a **compound-complex sentence.** This type of sentence contains two or more independent clauses and one or more dependent clauses.

Because it had snowed hard in October that year, the ski resorts opened early, **and** the skiers and snowboarders flocked to them. [*Because* signals the dependent clause; *and* connects the two independent clauses.]

Exercise 4

Return to exercise 3, and identify each sentence in the paragraph as simple, compound, complex, or compound-complex.

Exercise 5

A. Write a sentence exemplifying each type listed below. (If you do not understand the terms *declarative, interrogative, imperative,* and *exclamatory,* see page 469.

   1. a declarative simple sentence
   2. a declarative compound sentence
   3. a declarative complex sentence
   4. an imperative simple sentence
   5. an imperative compound sentence
   6. an imperative complex sentence
   7. an interrogative simple sentence
   8. an interrogative complex sentence
   9. a declarative compound-complex sentence
   10. an exclamatory simple sentence

B. In each of your sentences from part A, bracket the dependent clause. Label it as a noun clause, an adjectival clause, or an adverbial clause. Circle and label the coordinating and subordinating conjunctions. Your instructor may ask you to identify phrases as well.

Exercise 6

Take a paragraph from your own writing or from a book you are currently reading. Label each of the sentences as simple, compound, complex, or compound-complex.

Sentence Fragments

This chapter can help you

- revise fragments resulting from incorrectly punctuated phrases (**18a**) and clauses (**18b**) and
- recognize effective fragments (**18c**).

As its name suggests, a **sentence fragment** is only a piece of a sentence; it is not complete. Whereas a complete sentence consists of a complete subject and a complete predicate (see **16a**), a fragment may be missing either or both of these parts. Notice how the following boldfaced fragments have been revised.

Magazines often include articles about alternative medicine. **Usually** *, usually* **covering both the benefits and the drawbacks of particular methods.**

Occasionally, alternative medical treatment includes hypnosis. **The** *, the* **placement of a patient into a sleeplike state.**

Most patients, however, respond better when in a normal state of consciousness. **According to most psychiatrists practicing today.** *, according*

Alternatively, a fragment may have the essential sentence components but begin with a subordinating conjunction or a relative pronoun (see **17b**).

Subordinating Conjunction

Most people can be hypnotized easily. **Although the depth of the** *, although* **trance for each person varies greatly.**

Relative Pronoun

Hypnosis is usually induced by a hypnotist. *, who* ∧**Who gives repetitive,**

monotonous commands.

Because a fragment generally depends on the sentence preceding it to be meaningful, it can often be connected to that sentence. It can also be rewritten as a complete sentence.

> Fragment: Most people can be hypnotized easily. Although the depth of the trance for each person varies greatly.

> Revision: Most people can be hypnotized easily. However, the depth of the trance for each person varies greatly.

Note that imperative sentences (see chapter **16**) are not considered fragments. Although not written, the subject *you* is implied. In fact, the subject of an imperative sentence is often called the *understood you*.

> Imperative: Find out as much as you can about alternative treatments. (*You* find out as much as you can about alternative treatments.)

 In some languages, subject pronouns are dropped when there is no risk of misunderstanding. In Japanese, a sentence such as *Sushi o tabemasu* ("eat sushi") is permissible when the subject pronoun can be determined from the context. In Spanish, the verb form reveals information about the subject; unless needed for clarity or emphasis, a subject pronoun can be dropped, as in *Trabajo en un banco* ("I work in a bank"). However, subject pronouns must be included in all English sentences, except imperative sentences (see chapter **16**).

Be verbs (*am, is, are, was, were, been*) can be omitted in some languages. In English, however, they are necessary.

Sentence without an auxiliary verb: The population ∧*is* growing.

Sentence without a linking verb: It ∧*is* quite large.

For more information on auxiliary verbs and linking verbs, see **22a** and **22c**.

If you have trouble with fragments, you should not rely on a grammar checker to flag all of the fragments in your writing (see page 468). The grammar checker used in producing this chapter recognized only half of the fragments serving as examples. Instead of relying on a grammar checker, use the following methods.

FOUR METHODS FOR IDENTIFYING FRAGMENTS

Fragments may be difficult to find within the context of neighboring sentences. If you have trouble recognizing fragments, try one or more of these methods:

1. Read each paragraph backwards, sentence by sentence. When you read your sentences out of order, you may more readily note the incompleteness of a fragment.

2. Locate the essential parts of each sentence. First, find the main verb and any accompanying auxiliary verbs. Remember that verbals cannot function as main verbs (see $17a(3)$). After you find the main verb, find the subject by asking *Who?* or *What?* (see $16c(1)$). Finally, check to see that the sentence does not begin with a relative pronoun or a subordinating conjunction (see $17b$).

Test sentence: Striving to provide educational opportunities for African Americans.

Test: Main verb? *None. "Striving" and "to provide" are both verbals.* Subject? *None.*

[Because there is no subject or main verb, this test sentence is a fragment.]

Test sentence: Striving to provide educational opportunities for African Americans, Mary McLeod Bethune opened a small school in 1904.

Test: Main verb? *Opened.* Subject? *Mary McLeod Bethune.* Relative pronoun or subordinating conjunction? *None.*

[This test sentence contains a subject and a verb, and it does not begin with a relative pronoun or subordinating conjunction. It is therefore complete.]

3. Put any sentence you think might be a fragment into this frame: They do not understand the idea that _____ . Only a full sentence will make sense in this frame. If a test sentence, other than an imperative, does not fit into the frame, it is a fragment.

(Continued on page 506)

(Continued from page 505)

Test sentence: Depending on availability of food.

Test: They do not understand the idea that *depending on availability of food.*

[The sentence does not make sense; therefore, the test sentence is a fragment.]

Test sentence: The number of tiger sharks grows or shrinks depending on availability of food.

Test: They do not understand the idea that *the number of tiger sharks grows or shrinks depending on availability of food.*

[The sentence does make sense; therefore, the test sentence is a complete sentence.]

4. Rewrite any sentence you think might be a fragment as a yes/no question. Only full sentences can be rewritten this way.

Test sentence: Which is made from the leaves of the foxglove plant.

Test: *Is which made from the leaves of the foxglove plant?*

[The question does not make sense; therefore, the test sentence is a fragment.]

Test sentence: Some heart patients take digitalis, which is made from the leaves of the foxglove plant.

Test: *Do some heart patients take digitalis, which is made from the leaves of the foxglove plant?*

[The question does make sense; therefore, the test sentence is a complete sentence.]

Exercise 1

Identify the sentence fragments in the following paragraph. Be prepared to explain how you identified each fragment. Revise the fragments by attaching them to related sentences or by recasting them as full sentences.

[1]One of the most versatile American sculptors of the twentieth century, Alexander Calder (1898–1976) is best known for his mobiles. [2]Playfully balanced arrangements of abstract or organic forms. [3]As a young man, Calder first studied mechanical engineering. [4]Even

though he came from a family of sculptors. **⁵**It was not until four years after he earned his degree that he enrolled in an art school. **⁶**Shortly thereafter, Calder moved to Paris. **⁷**Where his wire sculptures won him worldwide recognition. **⁸**During the 1930s, he began to experiment with motion. **⁹**Eventually developing the mode of sculpture that most people think of when they hear the name Calder.

18a | Fragments are often phrases incorrectly punctuated as sentences.

Certain types of phrases (see **17a**) may be mistakenly written as sentence fragments. You can revise such a fragment by attaching it to a related sentence, usually the one preceding it. This method creates a strong link between the fragment and the independent clause it follows. If you are unsure of the correct punctuation to use with phrases, see **31b** and **31d**.

Verbal Phrase

Early humans valued color. *, creating* **C̶r̶e̶a̶t̶i̶n̶g̶ permanent colors with natural pigments.**

Prepositional Phrase

For years, the Scottish have dyed sweaters with soot. *, originally* **O̶r̶i̶g̶i̶n̶a̶l̶l̶y̶ from the chimneys of peat-burning stoves.**

Compound Predicate

Arctic foxes turn white when it snows. *and* **A̶n̶d̶ thus conceal themselves from prey.**

Appositive

During the Renaissance, one of the most highly valued pigments was ultramarine. *—an* **A̶n̶ extract from lapis lazuli.**

Appositive List

In order to derive dyes, we have always experimented with what we
find in nature. ~~:~~ **Shells,** roots, insects, flowers.

: shells,

Absolute Phrase

The deciduous trees of New England are known for their brilliant
autumn color. ~~.~~ **Sugar** maples dazzling tourists with their deep

, sugar

orange and red leaves.

Instead of attaching a fragment to the preceding sentence, you can re-cast the fragment as a full sentence. This method of revision elevates the importance of the information conveyed in the fragment.

Fragment: Early humans valued color. **Creating permanent colors with natural pigments.**

Revision: Early humans valued color. They created permanent colors with natural pigments.

Fragment: Humans painted themselves for a variety of purposes. **To attract a mate, to hide themselves from game or predators, or to signal aggression.**

Revision: Humans used color for a variety of purposes. For example, they painted themselves to attract a mate, to hide themselves from game or predators, or to signal aggression.

E x e r c i s e   2

Revise each fragment by attaching it to a related sentence or by recasting it as a full sentence.

1. The first person to produce an artificial dye commercially was William Perkin. A nineteen-year-old Englishman.
2. At one time in Europe, mummy was a popular pigment. Made by crushing the remains of Egyptian mummies.
3. Many food producers package their products in red. Believing that it attracts consumers.

4. Red causes the release of adrenaline in humans. As well as in other animal species.

5. Crayola assigns the colors of crayons unusual names. Including Outer Space and Pig Pink.

6. There are three colors on the Italian flag. Green on the left side, red on the right side, and white in the center.

7. One of Marie Antoinette's favorite shades was puce. The French word for "flea."

8. At times, the pigment saffron was quite popular. And worth its weight in gold.

9. The pigment carmine was in high demand. Spanish conquistadors making vast fortunes on its production.

10. Sir Isaac Newton showed that white light comprised all the visible colors of the spectrum. By passing a beam of sunlight through a prism.

18b | **Fragments are often dependent clauses incorrectly punctuated as sentences.**

Dependent clauses that are punctuated as if they were independent clauses are sentence fragments. An adverbial clause or an adjectival clause (see 17b) is a common culprit. Such a fragment can be revised by attaching it to a related sentence, usually the sentence preceding it. By linking the fragment to the independent clause, you explicitly indicate their relationship—cause and effect, for example.

Adverbial Clause

The iceberg was no surprise. ~~Because~~ the *Titanic*'s wireless operators had received reports of ice in the area.

[Edit marks: period struck, replaced with "because" inserted below]

Adjectival Clause

More than two thousand people were aboard the *Titanic*. ~~Which~~ was the largest ocean liner in 1912.

[Edit marks: period replaced with ", which"]

The shipbuilders first constructed the keel. ~~Which~~ was considered the backbone of the ship.

[Edit marks: period replaced with ", which"]

Two other methods can be used to revise these types of fragments. You can recast the fragment as a full sentence by removing the subordinating conjunction or relative pronoun and supplying any missing elements. This method of revision draws more attention to the information conveyed in the fragment.

> Revision: The iceberg was no surprise. The *Titanic's* wireless operators had received reports of ice in the area.

> Revision: More than two thousand people were aboard the *Titanic*. In 1912, this ocean liner was the largest ever to have been built.

You can also reduce the fragment to a participial phrase (see **17a(3)**) or to an appositive phrase (see **17a(5)**) and then attach the phrase to a related sentence. When you link a phrase to a sentence, you establish a certain relationship between the two. Unlike adverbial clauses, however, participial and appositive phrases suggest relationships less directly because they do not include subordinating conjunctions or relative pronouns.

> Revision: More than two thousand people were aboard the *Titanic,* the largest ocean liner in 1912. [reduced to an appositive phrase]

> Revision: The shipbuilders first constructed the keel—considered the backbone of the ship. [reduced to a participial phrase]

If you are unsure of the correct punctuation to use with phrases or dependent clauses, see chapter **31**.

Exercise 3

Revise each fragment by attaching it to a related sentence or by recasting it as a full sentence.

1. The iceberg was hard to see. Because there was no wind causing waves to splash against it.
2. The lookouts on the *Titanic* did not spot the iceberg. Until it was too late.
3. The name given to the large ocean liner was *Titanic*. Which means "of great size."
4. One of the most reliable eyewitnesses was Jack Thayer. Who gave his report shortly after he was rescued.
5. Moviegoers raved about the film *Titanic*. Which was based on the ship's story.

18c | Fragments can be effective when used judiciously.

When used judiciously, fragments—like short sentences—emphasize ideas, add surprise, or enhance the rhythm of a paragraph. Fragments are not appropriate for all types of writing, however. They are generally permitted only when the rhetorical situation allows the use of an intimate or playful tone.

The room is full of sunlight. **Yellow. Cream. Gold. White.** These colors cover two-thirds of its surface, which is also awash with lavenders and reds falling in sun-filled stripes from the curtains, the walls, the man, the table, the chair, the dresser.   —**ELAINE SCARRY,** *On Beauty and Being Just*

Narrow, shoulderless highway 61 looked as if a tar pot had overturned at the summit and trickled a crooked course down. **A genuine white-knuckled road.**   —**WILLIAM LEAST HEAT-MOON,** *Blue Highways*

Beyond the Rule

SENTENCE FRAGMENTS

You encounter sentence fragments every day—in conversations, in email messages, and even in some instructional materials. In conversation, someone might ask you, "Going anywhere tonight?" And you might respond, "Maybe." To end an email message, you might write, "See you later." When preparing a meal, you have probably read instructions similar to these: "Just heat and serve." "Cook to golden brown." The writers of such instructions expect you to know what is to be heated or browned. These kinds of fragments, in which words that can be understood from the context are omitted, are called *abbreviated sentences*. For other examples of abbreviated sentences, visit www.harbrace.com.

Exercise 4

Locate the fragments in the following excerpts. Explain why the authors may have decided to use them.

1. Any theory that can tame the quintessentially unruly English irregular past-tense system with only three rules, each delicately adjusting a single feature, is undeniably brilliant. But is it true? Not necessarily. —STEVEN PINKER, *Words and Rules*

2. I am standing in water for some moments before I am aware of its caress, before I can separate the pain in my feet from its soothing. A little farther on I hear the gurgle of springs. More water, running from beneath the Sierra de San Martín. I squat down to feel the expanse of the shallow flow. Headwaters of the Oso.

   —BARRY LOPEZ, *Field Notes*

Exercise 5

Advertisements often contain sentence fragments. Find a newspaper or magazine advertisement that contains several fragments. Rewrite the advertisement so that it consists of complete sentences; then, write a short paragraph explaining why you think the advertiser may have used the fragments.

Exercise 6

Follow the guidelines in this chapter to locate and revise the fragments in the following passage. If you find it necessary, make other changes to enhance the paragraph as well. Be prepared to explain your revisions.

[1]A giant hairy animal has caught the fascination of many people. [2]Including normally skeptical citizens and scientists. [3] They are all interested in the phenomenon of Sasquatch. [4]Also commonly called Big Foot. [5]*Sasquatch* comes from the Salish word *saskehavas*. [6]The North American Sasquatch has a counterpart. [7]The Himalayan Yeti. [8]Both have been studied by cryptozoologists. [9]Who research undiscovered animals. [10]In our country, most sightings of Sasquatch occur in the Pacific Northwest. [11]From northern California to central Alaska. [12]Although reports have come from almost every state. [13]During the settlement of the United States, stories of hairy ape-men were told by Native Americans. [14]And later on by trappers. [15]Teddy Roosevelt recorded one such story.

Comma Splices and Fused Sentences

Comma splices and fused sentences are similar sentence-level mistakes; both result from weak or missing punctuation between two sentences. Such errors are sometimes hard to find because the sentences involved sound natural together: Their content and purpose are closely related. Nonetheless, because comma splices and fused sentences do not follow punctuation conventions, they may distract your readers from understanding what you have written.

This chapter will help you

- recognize comma splices and fused sentences (19a) and
- learn ways to revise them (19b, 19c, 19d).

Although grammar checkers identify many comma splices and some fused sentences, they routinely miss many others. In fact, a grammar checker could not reliably identify the comma splices and fused sentences in this chapter. For example, the grammar checker failed to identify any of the comma splices in exercise 5 on page 526. See Using a Grammar Checker on page 468.

A **comma splice,** or *comma fault,* refers to the incorrect use of a comma to separate two independent clauses (see 17b).

Most stockholders favored the merger, the management did not.

This kind of error can be easily fixed. Because a comma is a weak mark of punctuation, usually joining words and phrases (see chapter 31), it is not conventionally used to join independent clauses. For this purpose, you should use connecting words, stronger marks of punctuation, or both.

Most stockholders favored the merger, but the management did not.

OR

Most stockholders favored the merger; the management did not.

A **fused sentence** consists of two independent clauses run together without any punctuation at all. This type of sentence is sometimes called a *run-on sentence.*

The first section of the proposal was approved however the budget will have to be resubmitted.

Revising a fused sentence is also easy. All you have to do is include appropriate punctuation and any necessary connecting words.

The first section of the proposal was approved; however, the budget will have to be resubmitted.

In case you are unfamiliar with or unsure about the conventions of punctuating independent clauses, here is a short review.

- A comma and a coordinating conjunction can join two independent clauses (see 17b–c). The coordinating conjunction indicates the relationship between the two clauses. For example, *and* signals addition, whereas *but* and *yet* signal contrast. The comma precedes the conjunction.

  [Independent clause], and [independent clause].

  The new store opened this morning, and the owners greeted everyone at the door.

- A semicolon can join two independent clauses that are closely related. A semicolon generally signals addition or contrast.

  [Independent clause]; [independent clause].

  One of the owners comes from this area; the other grew up in Costa Rica.

- A semicolon may also precede an independent clause that begins with a conjunctive adverb such as *however* or *nevertheless.* A comma follows this type of connecting word.

  The store will be open late on Fridays and Saturdays; however, it will be closed all day on Sundays.

- A colon can join two independent clauses. The second clause usually explains or elaborates the first.

  [Independent clause]: [Independent clause].

  The owners extended a special offer: Anyone who makes a purchase during the opening will receive a 10 percent discount.

- A period separates clauses of unequal length, different structure, or unrelated content.

  [Independent clause]. [Independent clause].

  The store is located on the corner of Pine Street and First Avenue. It was formerly an insurance office.

- Occasionally, commas are used (instead of semicolons or periods) between independent clauses, but only when the clauses are short, parallel in form, and unified in meaning.

  They came, they shopped, they left.

- Commas are also used to separate a statement from an attached question (also called a *tag question*).

  You went to the grand opening, didn't you?

For more information on punctuating sentences, see chapters 31, 32, and 35.

| 19a | Two different methods can be used to identify comma splices and fused sentences. |

If you have trouble recognizing comma splices or fused sentences, try one of these methods:

1. Locate a sentence you are unsure about. It may have a comma or no punctuation at all. Put the sentence in this frame: They do not understand the idea that _____. Only complete sentences will make sense in this frame. If only part of a test sentence fits into the frame, you have probably located a comma splice or a fused sentence.

   Test sentence: The wild Bactrian camel, a two-humped camel living in the Gobi Desert, can drink salt water.

Test: They do not understand the idea that *the wild Bactrian camel, a two-humped camel living in the Gobi Desert, can drink salt water.* [The sentence makes sense. No revision is necessary.]

Test sentence: Male proboscis monkeys have oddly shaped large noses, they also have unusual webbed paws.

Test: They do not understand the idea that *male proboscis monkeys have oddly shaped large noses, they also have unusual webbed paws.* [The sentence does not make sense because there are two sentences completing the frame, rather than one. Therefore, the test sentence needs to be revised: *Male proboscis monkeys have oddly shaped large noses. They also have unusual webbed paws.*]

2. Locate a sentence you are unsure about. It may have a comma or no punctuation at all. Try to rewrite it as a question with a yes or no answer. If only part of the sentence makes sense, you have likely found a comma splice or a fused sentence.

Test sentence: The Arctic tern migrates from the Arctic to Antarctica.

Test: *Does the Arctic tern migrate from the Arctic to Antarctica?* [The question makes sense. No revision is necessary.]

Test sentence: Meerkats use their claws to forage for food they frequently prey on scorpions.

Test: *Do meerkats use their claws to forage for food they frequently prey on scorpions?*

[The question does not make sense because only one of the two sentences has been made into a question. The test sentence should be revised: *Meerkats use their claws to forage for food. They frequently prey on scorpions.*]

Once you have identified a problematic sentence, you can determine whether the problem is a comma splice or a fused sentence by following these steps.

1. Notice how many pairs of grammatical subjects and verbs are in the sentence (see **16a–c**).

   a. Find the verbs.

   b. Match verbs to subjects.

   $$\overset{\text{S}}{}\quad\overset{\text{V}}{}\qquad\qquad\overset{\text{S}}{}$$

   (1) Male proboscis <u>monkeys</u> <u>have</u> oddly shaped large noses, <u>they</u> also

   $\overset{\text{V}}{}$
   <u>have</u> unusual webbed paws. [two pairs]

       S   V   S   V

(2) <u>Meerkats</u> <u>use</u> their claws to forage for food <u>they</u> frequently <u>prey</u>

on scorpions. [two pairs]

2. Look for the punctuation that separates the pairs of subjects and verbs (if there are at least two). Sentence (1) has a comma. Sentence (2) has no punctuation.

3. If no punctuation separates the pairs, you have found a fused sentence, unless there is a dependent clause present (see **17b**). Sentence (2) is a fused sentence.

                                    . They

Meerkats use their claws to forage for food ⌄t̶h̶e̶y̶ frequently prey on scorpions.

Notice, however, that the following sentence includes a dependent clause and is not fused.

Meerkats use their claws to forage for food, which frequently consists of scorpions and beetles.

4. If a comma separates the pairs of subjects and verbs, you may have found a comma splice.

   a. If the comma is followed by a coordinating conjunction or a nonessential (nonrestrictive) dependent clause (see **31d**), the sentence does not contain a comma splice.

      Male proboscis monkeys have oddly shaped large noses, and they also have unusual webbed paws.

      A male proboscis monkey has an oddly shaped large nose, whose size may attract mates.

   b. If there is not a coordinating conjunction or a nonrestrictive dependent clause, the sentence does contain a comma splice. Sentence (1) contains a comma splice.

                                             . They

      Male proboscis monkeys have oddly shaped large noses⌄,̶ t̶h̶e̶y̶ also have unusual webbed paws.

You can also find comma splices and fused sentences by remembering that they commonly occur in certain circumstances:

- With transitional words and phrases such as *however, therefore,* and *for example* (see also **19c**)

  Comma splice: The director is not able to meet with you this week**;**
  however**,** next week she will have time on Monday and Tuesday.

  [Notice that a semicolon replaces the comma.]

- When an explanation or an example is given in the second sentence

  Fused sentence: The cultural center has a new collection of spear
  points**. Many** of them were donated by a retired anthropologist.

- When a positive clause follows a negative clause

  Comma splice: A World Cup victory is not just an everyday
  sporting event**. It** is a national celebration.

- When the subject of the second clause is a pronoun whose antecedent is in the preceding clause

  Fused sentence: Lake Baikal is located in southern Russia**. It** is 394
  miles long.

19b | **A comma splice or a fused sentence can be revised in a number of ways.**

If you find comma splices or fused sentences in your writing, try one of the following methods to revise them.

1. Link clauses by using a comma and a coordinating conjunction such as *and* or *but.* By linking clauses in this way, you signal the relationship between them (addition or contrast, for example).

   Fused sentence: Joseph completed the first experiment**, and** he will
   complete the other by Friday.

Comma splice: Some diplomats applauded the treaty,‸*but* others

opposed it vehemently.

2. Link clauses by using a semicolon (see **32a**) or colon (**35d**), or separate them with a period (**35a**). When you link clauses with a semicolon, you signal their connection indirectly. There are no explicit conjunctions to use as cues. The semicolon usually indicates addition or contrast. When you link clauses with a colon, the second clause serves as an explanation or an elaboration of the first. A period indicates that each clause is a complete sentence, distinct from surrounding sentences.

Comma splice: Our division's reports are posted on our Web page, hard copies are available by request.

Revision 1: Our division's reports are posted on our Web page; hard copies are available by request.

Revision 2: Our division's reports are posted on our Web page. Hard copies are available by request.

Fused sentence: His choice was difficult‸*: He* he would either lose his job

or betray his ethical principles.

3. Rewrite one clause as a phrase (see **17a**) or as a dependent clause (**17b**). A dependent clause includes a subordinating conjunction such as *although* or *because,* which indicates how the dependent and independent clauses are related (in a cause-and-effect relationship, for example). Phrases suggest relationships less directly because they do not include conjunctions.

Comma splice: The wind had blown down trees and power lines, the whole city was without electricity for several hours.

Revision 1: **Because of the downed power lines,** the whole city was without electricity for several hours. [using a phrase]

Revision 2: **Because the wind had blown down power lines,** the whole city was without electricity for several hours. [using a dependent clause]

4. Integrate one clause into the other. When you integrate clauses, you generally retain the important details and omit or change some words in one of the clauses.

Fused sentence: The proposal covers all but one point it does not describe how the project will be assessed.

Revision: The proposal covers all the points except assessment procedures.

As you edit fused sentences and comma splices, you will find that you are refining the connections between your sentences, making them clearer and more cohesive. By taking the time to revise, you will be helping your readers follow your train of thought. For more information on joining clauses, see chapter 24.

The following checklist will help you find and fix comma splices and fused sentences.

CHECKLIST for Comma Splices and Fused Sentences

1 Common Sites for Comma Splices or Fused Sentences

- With transitional phrases such as *however, therefore,* and *for example*
- When an explanation or an example occurs in the second clause
- When a positive clause follows a negative clause
- When the subject of the second clause is a pronoun whose antecedent is in the preceding clause

2 How to Identify a Comma Splice or a Fused Sentence

1. Notice how many pairs of subjects and verbs (see 16a–c) are in the sentence.
   a. Find the verbs.
   b. Match verbs to subjects.
2. Look for the punctuation that separates the pairs of subjects and verbs (if there are at least two).
3. If no punctuation separates the pairs and no dependent clause is present, you have found a fused sentence.
4. If a comma separates the pairs, you may have found a comma splice.
   a. If there is a coordinating conjunction or a nonessential dependent clause, there is no comma splice.

b. If there is no coordinating conjunction or nonessential dependent clause, there is a comma splice.

3 How to Fix Comma Splices and Fused Sentences

- Link the clauses with a comma and a coordinating conjunction.
- Link the clauses by using a semicolon or a colon.
- Separate the clauses by punctuating each as a sentence.
- Make one clause dependent.
- Reduce one clause to a phrase.
- Rewrite the sentence, integrating one clause into the other.

Exercise 1

Connect each pair of sentences in two of the following ways: (a) join them with a semicolon or colon, (b) join them with a coordinating conjunction, (c) reduce one to a phrase or dependent clause (see 17b(3) for a list of subordinating conjunctions), or (d) integrate one clause into the other.

1. Our national parks offer a variety of settings. They attract millions of visitors every year.

2. The Grand Teton National Park includes a sixteen-peak mountain range. It offers extensive hiking trails and wildlife-viewing opportunities.

3. Yellowstone National Park is generally full of tourists. The geysers and cliffs are worth the visit.

4. Hikers especially enjoy their vacations at Yellowstone National Park. The park consists of two million acres of backcountry perfect for hiking.

5. Vacationers enchanted by cascading water should visit Yosemite National Park. The waterfalls at Yosemite reach heights of more than two thousand feet.

E x e r c i s e   2

Revise each comma splice or fused sentence. Do not edit a sentence that is correctly punctuated.

1. Bats are the only mammals that fly, their modified arms and hands serve as wings.
2. Bats have a highly evolved system of echolocation, which makes them excellent hunters.
3. Many bats shriek and listen for returning echoes to determine the location of prey, this is the most common type of echolocation.
4. To avoid deafening themselves, these bats shriek in pulses.
5. Leaf-nosed bats have a more sophisticated location system they emit a continuous sound that does not require listening for echoes.
6. Some bats eat the nectar from plants others feed on amphibians or insects.
7. The majority of bats eat insects, they live in tropical regions, where insects are abundantly available.
8. Bats that roost in colonies produce huge amounts of guano, in the past phosphorus and nitrogen extracted from bat droppings were used to make explosives.

19c	**Transitional words and phrases can be used to join independent clauses.**

Another way to revise comma splices and fused sentences is to use transitional words (**conjunctive adverbs**) or transitional phrases (see list below). These words and phrases may begin new sentences.

Fused sentence: Sexual harassment is not just an issue for women ‸ men

. After all,

can be sexually harassed too.

Transitional words or phrases may also join two clauses into one sentence. In these sentences, a semicolon appears after the first clause (before the transition); a comma appears after the transition. If a sentence contains a transitional word or phrase without the appropriate punctuation, it may be a fused sentence or contain a comma splice.

Comma splice: The word *status* refers to relative position within a group, however it is often used to indicate only positions of prestige.

Conjunctive Adverbs

also	however	next
anyhow	incidentally	otherwise
anyway	indeed	similarly
besides	instead	still
consequently	likewise	then
finally	meanwhile	therefore
furthermore	moreover	thus
hence	nevertheless	

Transitional Phrases

after all	even so	in fact
as a result	for example	in other words
at any rate	in addition	on the contrary
at the same time	in comparison	on the other hand
by the way	in contrast	that is

A transitional word or phrase may either begin a clause or take another position within it. When it appears within the clause, the transitional word or phrase is set off by commas.

She believed that daily exercise has many benefits; **however,** she couldn't fit it into her schedule. [The conjunctive adverb begins the second independent clause and is positioned after a semicolon and before a comma (see also **32a**).]

She believed that daily exercise has many benefits; she couldn't, **however,** fit it into her schedule. [The conjunctive adverb appears later in the second clause. In this position, it is set off by commas.]

Beyond the Rule

PUNCTUATING SENTENCES WITH CONJUNCTIVE ADVERBS

A comma used to set off a conjunctive adverb is sometimes omitted when there is no risk of misreading.

The sea was unusually hot; **thus** the coral turned white. [No misreading is possible, so the comma can be omitted.]

He was so nervous that his stomach was churning. **However,** he answered the question calmly and accurately. [The comma is needed. Without it, *however* might be interpreted as meaning "in whatever way" rather than "in contrast." COMPARE However he answered the question, he would offend someone.]

For more examples, visit www.harbrace.com.

Exercise 3

Connect each pair of sentences by including a transitional word or phrase and any necessary punctuation.

1. Discoveries in neuroscience have yielded many benefits. Researchers have developed medication for schizophrenia and Tourette's syndrome.
2. The average human brain weighs about three pounds. The average brain of a sperm whale weighs seventeen pounds.
3. Researchers studying brain hemispheres have found that many professional musicians process music in their left hemisphere. The notion that musicians and artists depend on the right side of their brain is considered outmoded.
4. The brain needs water to function properly. Dehydration commonly leads to lethargy and hinders learning.
5. The body of a brain cell can move. Most brain cells stay put, extending axons outward.

Exercise 4

Revise each comma splice or fused sentence. Do not edit a sentence that is correctly punctuated.

1. According to Rick Gore in "Ancient Ashkelon," artifacts found by archaeologists reveal much about the Canaanites who lived in Ashkelon around 1850 B.C. For example, people at that time buried their relatives in chambers.

2. Some people do not want skeletons to be disinterred thus they have staged protests against archaeological excavations in the area around Ashkelon.

3. Ashkelon is a relatively unknown beachside city in Israel, however it was a major seaport over five thousand years ago.

4. Families left a corpse in the chamber for several months, then they placed the bones in corners.

5. In 1850 B.C., Ashkelon had a population of fifteen thousand, the population of Babylon at the same time was around thirty thousand.

6. The word *Philistine* is often used to label an enemy of the arts, the decorated pottery found in recent excavations suggests that the Philistines living in Ashkelon between 1175 B.C. and 604 B.C. valued beauty.

7. Many artifacts are similar to Greek artifacts consequently some researchers believe that the Philistines were immigrants from Mycenaean Greece.

8. Biblical descriptions of Samson are similar to those of the Greek mythical hero Heracles. Likewise, the story of Samson's loss of strength echoes a Greek myth.

9. The Philistines ruled Ashkelon for almost six hundred years, nevertheless, their empire was destroyed by Nebuchadnezzar in 604 B.C.

10. The archaeological excavation of Ashkelon has yielded many artifacts, even so much of Ashkelon's history remains unknown.

19d | Divided quotations require special attention.

When you divide quotations (see chapter 34) with attributive tags such as *he said* or *she asked,* be sure to use a period between independent clauses.

> Comma splice: "Beauty brings copies of itself into being," states Elaine Scarry, "it makes us draw it, take photographs of it, or describe it to other people."

> [Both parts of the quotation are complete sentences; thus, the attributive tag is attached to the first, and the sentence is punctuated with a period. The second sentence stands by itself.]

A comma separates two parts of a single quoted sentence.

> "Musing takes place in a kind of meadowlands of the imagination," writes Rebecca Solnit, "a part of the imagination that has not yet been plowed, developed, or put to any immediately practical use."

> [Because the quotation is a single sentence, a comma is used.]

Exercise 5

Revise the following paragraph so that no comma splices remain. Some sentences may not need revision.

[1]In the introduction to his book of true stories, *I Thought My Father Was God,* Paul Auster describes how he was able to collect these accounts of real and sometimes raw experience. [2]In October 1999, Auster, in collaboration with National Public Radio, began the *National Story Project,* during an interview on the radio program *Weekend All Things Considered,* he invited listeners to send in their stories about unusual events—"true stories that sounded like fiction." [3]In just one year, over four thousand stories were submitted, Auster read every one of them. [4]"Of the four thousand stories I have read, most have been compelling enough to hold me until the last word," Auster affirms, "Most have been written with simple, straightforward

conviction, and most have done honor to the people who sent them in." [5]Some of the stories Auster collected can now be read in his anthology, choosing stories for the collection was difficult, though. [6]"For every story about a dream or an animal or a missing object," explains Auster, "there were dozens of others that were submitted, dozens of others that could have been chosen."

Exercise 6

After reviewing this chapter and chapter 18, rewrite the following paragraph so that no fragments, comma splices, or fused sentences remain. Change the wording if necessary.

[1]In 1959, a jazz sextet formed by trumpeter Miles Davis recorded an album it would later be titled *Kind of Blue*. [2]Jazz critics worldwide consider this album one of the most important of its time. [3]Selling millions both here and abroad. [4]The words most frequently used to describe the album's music include *sublime, transcendent, poetic,* and *heavenly,* even the liner notes by the sextet's pianist Bill Evans have been praised for their insightful tranquility. [5]Instead of giving biographies of the musicians and a description of the music's superiority, Evans wrote a short essay comparing the creation of music through group improvisation to *suibokuga*. [6]A style of Japanese ink painting. [7]"As the painter needs his framework of parchment," writes Evans, "the improvising musical group needs its framework in time." [8]Using their frameworks, *suibokuga* artists and improvisational jazz musicians are expected to be spontaneous yet deliberate, simple yet complex. [9]Through these paradoxes in *Kind of Blue,* as Evans observes in his original draft for the liner notes. [10]"Perhaps those who hear well will find something captured which escapes contemplation."

20 Modifiers

Adjectives and adverbs are modifiers; that is, they qualify, restrict, or intensify the meaning of other words. They also describe degrees of comparison.

This chapter will help you

- recognize adjectives and understand how to use them (**20a**),
- recognize adverbs and understand how to use them (**20b**),
- use the comparative and superlative forms correctly (**20c**),
- know when to use a group modifier (**20d**),
- place modifiers near the words they modify (**20e**),
- avoid dangling modifiers (**20f**), and
- revise double negatives (**20g**).

Adjectives modify nouns and pronouns; **adverbs** modify verbs, adjectives, and other adverbs.

Adjectives	**Adverbs**
a **quick** lunch	eat **quickly**
armed squads	**heavily** armed squads
She looked **angry.**	She looked **angrily** at me.

In traditional grammar, the determiners *a, an,* and *the* are often classified as adjectives since they identify or describe a noun. See **23e(1)** for the use of articles.

Because adjectives and adverbs work as modifiers, can be similar in form, and generally occur near one another, they can be difficult to tell apart. If you need to distinguish an adjective from an adverb, you consider the form of the word and its function in the particular sentence.

20a | Adjectives either modify nouns or pronouns or function as complements.

Adjectives answer any of several questions: *What kind? How many? Which one(s)?*

What kind?   **simple** one
How many?   **several** men
Which one?   **writing** class

Beyond the Rule

A TEST FOR ADJECTIVES

If you need to determine whether a word is an adjective, you can use a simple test. To learn more about this test, which can identify many but not all adjectives, visit www.harbrace.com.

 In some languages, adjectives and nouns agree in number. In Spanish, for example, when a noun is plural, the adjective is plural as well: *vistas claras.* In English, however, adjectives do not have a plural form: *clear views.*

Sometimes a verbal (see 17a(2)), for instance, an infinitive or a participle, serves as an adjective.

a determin**ing** factor   a determin**ed** effort   a chicken **to eat**

Do not omit the *-d* or *-ed* ending of a past participle used as an adjective. (See 22a(1)–(2).)

The dog was too frighten_{ed} to go to him.

Both present participles and past participles are used as adjectives; however, they cannot be used interchangeably. To express emotion, you use a present participle with a noun referring to someone or something that is the cause of the emotion. In the phrase *the exciting tennis match,* the tennis match is the cause of the excitement. You use the past participle with a noun referring to someone who experiences the emotion. In the phrase *the excited crowd,* the crowd is experiencing the excitement.

Here is a list of commonly confused participles:

annoying, annoyed
boring, bored
confusing, confused
embarrassing, embarrassed
frustrating, frustrated
interesting, interested
surprising, surprised
tiring, tired

Adjectives generally, but not always, come before the words they modify.

When I write, I appreciate a **quiet** house.
Tom found the house **quiet.**

 In English, two or more adjectives modifying the same noun are used in a particular order based on their meanings. (The use of more than three consecutive adjectives is rare.) The following list shows the usual order of adjectives and gives examples. Notice that determiners precede all of the adjectives.

Determiner	a, an, the, this, these, those, my, our, much, many, five
Evaluator	fascinating, painful, sad
Size	large, small, tiny, miniscule
Shape	square, round, triangular
Age	young, old, aged, newborn, antique

Color	black, white, green, brown
Nationality or geography	Arabian, Cuban, Peruvian, Slavic
Religion	Jewish, Catholic, Protestant, Buddhist
Material	silk, paper, pine, rubber

We stayed in **a simple old country** inn.

Have you seen **those large pine** trees?

Marquita wrapped **three blue silk** scarves around the post.

(1) Adjectives can often be recognized by their endings.

Because many adjectives are formed from other parts of speech, you can often determine that a word is an adjective by looking at its ending: *-able, -al, -ful, -ic, ish, -less,* and *-y* are commonly used to make an adjective from a noun or a verb.

accept**able**   rent**al**   event**ful**   angel**ic**   sheep**ish**   effort**less**   sleep**y**

Certain adjectives formed from nouns have the ending *-ly* (*cost, costly*).

(2) Adjectives used as subject or object complements are easily confused with adverbs.

An adjective used as a **subject complement** completes the meaning of the verb by describing the subject of the sentence. A common error is to use an adverb as a subject complement.

The actor looked ∧ **angrily.** [*Angry* is an adjective that tells something

about *actor.*]

The actor looked up ∧ **angry.** [*Angrily* is an adverb that tells something

about *looked up.*]

He felt **bad** about the mistake. [Using *badly* in this sentence would be a *hypercorrection*—introducing an error in an attempt to be correct.]

His leg hurt **badly** after he broke it. [an acceptable use of *badly*]

Adjectives that modify the direct object in sentences with such verbs as *call, consider, find, make,* and *name* are **object complements.** (See **16c(3)**.)

They *named* the baby **Fred.**

They *considered* the restaurant **expensive.** [The adjective *expensive* refers to the direct object *restaurant* and completes the meaning of the verb *considered.*]

E x e r c i s e 1

Using adjectives as complements, write two sentences that illustrate each of the following patterns.

Oranges	*taste*	*good.*	
Subject	+ linking verb	+ subject complement	

They	*called*	*us*	*friendly.*
Subject	+ verb	+ direct object	+ object complement

20b | Adverbs modify verbs, adjectives, and other adverbs.

Adverbs answer any of several questions: *How? When? Where?*

How did Vassily answer her?	Vassily answered her **playfully.**
When did she plan to leave?	She planned to leave **early.**
Where did I put the cat?	I put the cat **outside.**

An adverb that modifies a verb commonly describes the circumstances—how (manner), when (time), or where (place)—under which an action or event occurred.

Manner	We walked **quietly.**
Time	We arrived **later.**
Place	We walked **home.**

Adverbs of frequency (such as *always, never, sometimes,* and *often*) appear before one-word verbs.

He **rarely** <u>goes</u> to horror movies.

However, these frequency adverbs appear after a form of *be* when it is the main verb.

Movies based on Stephen King novels <u>are</u> **always** popular.

When a sentence contains more than one verb in a verb phrase, the adverb of frequency is placed after the first auxiliary verb.

My friends <u>have</u> **never** <u>seen</u> *The Shining*.
I <u>have</u> **seldom** <u>been</u> frightened by a movie.

Adverbs can also modify verbals (gerunds, infinitives, or participles) or whole clauses. (See **17b**.)

Walking rapidly is good for you. [The adverb *rapidly* modifies the gerund *walking,* which is the subject.]

Whole clauses can even function as adverbs. (See **17b**.)

When I was seven years old, my family began our tradition of spending every summer in Colorado. [The adverbial clause of time modifies the verb *began*.]

Infinitives can also serve as adverbs.

studied **to pass**   happy **to leave**   afraid **to speak**

Beyond the Rule

KINDS OF ADVERBS

Adverbs can be said to have four basic relationships to other words in a sentence. *Subjuncts* (such as *very* and *only*) are those adverbs that expand, intensify, or diminish the subject, verb, or complement. *Adjuncts*

(Continued on page 534)

(Continued from page 533)

(such as *quietly, outside,* and *under the table*) give additional information about other sentence elements. *Disjuncts* are adverbs (such as the sentence modifier *Yes* in *Yes, they were late*) that are not clearly attached to other elements of a sentence. *Conjuncts* (such as *however* and *therefore*) show relationships between parts of a sentence. For additional information, visit www.harbrace.com.

Because many adverbs are formed by adding *-ly* to an adjective, you can often spot an adverb by looking for that ending.

> Monique wrote her name **carefully.** [The adverb *carefully* modifies the verb *wrote.*]

> The plane departs at an **unpleasantly** early hour. [The adverb *unpleasantly* modifies the adjective *early.*]

> The computer was priced very **reasonably.** [The adverb *very* modifies the adverb *reasonably.*]

If an adverb is formed from an adjective ending in *-y,* the *-y* is changed to *-i* before *-ly* is added.

> eas**y** [adjective]   eas**ily** [adverb]

If an adjective ends in *-le,* the *-le* is dropped before *-ly* is added.

> simp**le** [adjective]   simp**ly** [adverb]

The *-ly* ending is usually associated with adverbs formed from adjectives. A few adverbs have two acceptable forms (*quick, quickly; slow, slowly*). When in doubt, look in a dictionary for the label *adv* and any usage notes.

A number of words—for example, *fast* and *well*—can function as either adjectives or adverbs. When in doubt, consult a dictionary for the labels *adj* and *adv* and any usage notes.

> She likes **fast** cars. [adjective]

> We ran **fast** to catch the bus. [adverb]

Most dictionaries still label *sure* for *surely, real* for *really,* and *good* for *well* as *colloquial* (see **28e**), meaning that you may hear them in conversation but should avoid using them in writing.

Conversational	Marcy is a **real good** swimmer. [The usual meaning of *real* is "not artificial" rather than "very."]
Written	Marcy swims **really well.** [appropriate in both written and conversational usage; see **28c(2)**]

Exercise 2

Revise the following sentences to use adverbs considered conventional in college writing. Replace any that are colloquial or unconventional. Do not change any sentence that does not need editing.

1. The boat's engine roared loud throughout Puerto Vallarta Bay.
2. We were looking for the local known island protected as a wildlife refuge.
3. The man next to me explained that he didn't scuba dive as regular as he would like.
4. With everyone participating in scuba diving and snorkeling, the boat seemed abnormal quiet.
5. My sister and I certainly enjoyed watching everyone.

20c	Many adjectives and adverbs change form to show relative quality, quantity, or manner (the degree of comparison).

Degree refers to the quantity, quality, or manner of items being compared. Both adjectives and adverbs show the quality, quantity, or manner of a single element (positive) or the relationship between two elements (comparative) or among three or more elements (superlative).

Positive	Comparative	Superlative
large	larger	largest
quickly	more quickly	most quickly

It can be difficult to know when to add the suffix -*er* or -*est* to show degree and when to use *more/less* or *most/least,* but the following guidelines can help you.

Generally, the endings -*er* for the comparative and -*est* for the superlative are added to one-syllable adjectives and adverbs. Two-syllable adjectives with the stress on the first syllable sometimes take -*er* and -*est*. (If the base word ends in -*y*, don't forget to change the -*y* to -*i* when adding the comparative or superlative ending: *lucky, luckier, luckiest*. See **36d(4)**.) Other two-syllable adjectives, longer adjectives, and most adverbs use *more* (or *less*) for the comparative and *most* (or *least*) for the superlative.

> tall, taller, tallest [one-syllable adjective]
>
> fast, faster, fastest [one-syllable adverb]
>
> pretty, prettier, prettiest [two-syllable adjective with stress on the first syllable]
>
> quickly, more/less quickly, most/least quickly [two-syllable adverb]
>
> fortunate, more/less fortunate, most/least fortunate [three-syllable adjective]
>
> rapidly, more/less rapidly, most/least rapidly [three-syllable adverb]

For some two-syllable adjectives, the comparative and the superlative can be formed in both ways. Examples are *able, angry, clever, common, cruel, friendly, gentle, handsome, narrow, polite, quiet,* and *simple*. Use *the* rather than *a* or *an* with the superlative.

A few common modifiers have irregular forms.

> little, less, least
>
> good/well, better, best
>
> bad/badly, worse, worst
>
> far, further/farther, furthest/farthest (See the Glossary of Usage.)

When in doubt, consult a dictionary.

(1) The comparative denotes two elements in a comparison.

The **comparative** is used with two elements in a comparison. Make sure to complete every comparison (see **23g**), and always make clear what the first element is being compared with. The conjunction *than* often signals the second element being compared.

> The metropolitan area is much **bigger** now **than** it was five years ago.
>
> Dried apples are **more** nutritious per pound **than** fresh apples.
> [a comparison of two groups]

The comparison may be implied by the context.

> She wrote **two** papers, and the instructor gave her a **better** grade on the second.

The comparative form used with *other* sometimes refers to more than two.

> Bert can run **faster** than the *other* players can.

(2) The superlative denotes three or more elements in a comparison.

The **superlative** shows the relationship among three or more elements in a comparison.

> Bert is the **fastest** of the three runners.

> OR

> Bert is the **fastest** runner of all.

The superlative occasionally refers to fewer than three, as in "Put your *best* foot forward!"

Beyond the Rule

ABSOLUTE MODIFIERS

General usage and dictionaries accept comparative forms of many adjectives or adverbs with absolute meanings, as in *a more perfect society, the deadest campus,* and *less completely exhausted.* But careful writers rarely use such comparisons. Also, most still consider *unique* an absolute adjective—one without degrees of comparison—and thus do not write *more unique* or *most unique.* For more information, visit www.harbrace.com.

(3) A double comparative or superlative is redundant.

> This bus stop is **more** cold**er** than the one around the corner.
> That was the **most** smart**est** thing anybody ever said.

Exercise 3

Provide the correct comparative or superlative form of each modifier within parentheses.

1. Amphibians can be divided into three groups. Frogs and toads are in (common) group.
2. Wormlike caecilians are (common) of the amphibians.
3. Because they do not have to maintain a specific body temperature, amphibians eat (frequently) than mammals do.
4. Reptiles may look like amphibians, but their skin is (dry).
5. During the Devonian period, (close) ancestors of amphibians were fish with fins that looked like legs.
6. In general, amphibians have (few) bones in their skeletons than other animals with backbones.
7. Color markings on amphibians vary, though the back of an amphibian is usually (dark) than its belly.
8. Frogs are known for their leaping ability. (Long) jump recorded is seventeen and a half feet.
9. The skin on a frog is usually (smooth) than the dry, warty skin of a toad.
10. Once fairly common, frogs of many species are becoming (rare) due to the effects of pollution.

20d | A noun or a word group can be used as a modifier.

Many nouns or word groups effectively modify other nouns (as in *reference manual, windfall profits tax, House Ways and Means Committee*), especially when appropriate adjectives are not available. Avoid such forms, however, when they are awkward or confusing.

Many candidates entered the president͵ial race.

~~The~~ Representative Landor͵'s ~~recess~~ maneuvers͵during the recess led to victory.

Occasionally, a group of words linked with hyphens (a compound adjective) modifies a noun. (See 36f(1).)

I threw away the **half-eaten** apple.

The students did very well on a **harder-than-average** examination.

Nouns used as modifiers are almost always singular: *sophomore students, executive decision.*

20e | **Placing modifiers near the words they modify clarifies meaning.**

The meaning of the following sentences changes according to the position of the modifier.

Butch **just** sat down at the table with his hat on.

Just Butch sat down at the table with his hat on.

Butch sat down at the table with **just** his hat on.

The student **who fell** had tried to help his friend.

The student had tried to help his friend **who fell.**

To keep the meaning clear, place modifiers such as *almost, even, hardly, just, merely, nearly,* and *only* immediately before the words they modify.

The flight ~~only~~ costs $\overset{only}{\wedge}$ $380.

Drew ~~even~~ spent $\overset{even}{\wedge}$ his tuition money.

Similarly, prepositional phrases and adjectival clauses should be placed so that what they modify is clear.

Bobby Joe sings $\overset{in\ the\ first\ stanza}{\wedge}$ that his heart is broken ~~in the first stanza~~.

We noticed the movie $\overset{that\ we\ had\ seen\ on\ Friday}{\wedge}$ was not playing at the same theater ~~that we had seen on Friday.~~

Constructions that could modify either of two elements in a sentence should be revised so that they refer clearly to either a preceding or a following element.

The next day he
He agreed ~~the next day~~ to pay what he owed.

the next day
He agreed ~~the next day~~ to pay what he owed .

Exercise 4

Improve the clarity of the following sentences by moving the modifiers. Some sentences may not require editing.

1. In 1665, Sir Isaac Newton devised three laws about moving objects that are still discussed today.
2. According to one of the laws, an object only moves when force is applied.
3. Once in motion, something must force an object to slow down or to speed up; otherwise, it will continue at a constant speed.
4. Another law explains the variables affecting an object's movement.
5. Another of Newton's contributions is the law about action and reaction that engineers use to plan rocket launchings.
6. Scientists still use the laws of motion formulated by Newton over three hundred years ago to understand moving objects.

20f | **Modifiers that refer to no particular element in a sentence need to be revised.**

Although any misplaced word, phrase, or clause can be said to dangle, a dangling modifier is generally a verbal phrase that does not refer clearly and logically to another word or phrase in a sentence. The words in the sentence can be rearranged, or words can be added, to make the meaning clear.

Dangling participial phrases have no clear word to which to refer.

millions of voters listened to
Tuning the television to CNN, the State of the Union speech ~~reached~~ ~~millions of voters~~.

Because they tuned
Tuning the television to CNN, the State of the Union speech reached millions of voters.

Placed after the main independent clause, the participial phrase in the first revision below refers to the subject, but the revision changes the emphasis of the sentence. The second revision clarifies the relationship between the main clause and the modifier.

We passed the
~~The~~ afternoon ~~passed~~ very pleasantly, **lounging in the shade and reminiscing about our childhood.** [shifts the focus to *we*]

while we were
The afternoon passed very pleasantly, lounging in the shade and reminiscing about our childhood. [maintains the focus on *afternoon,* as in the original sentence]

A dangling modifier containing a gerund or an infinitive needs a logical word to refer to. (See **17a(3).**)

Theo was surprised at
On **entering** the stadium, the size of the crowd ~~surprised Theo~~.

a person must read
To write well, good books ~~must be read~~.

Elliptical clauses often dangle because they imply words that are not stated. (See **17b(2).**)

I was
When only a small boy, my father took me with him to Chicago. [The elliptical clause in the original sentence refers to *father,* not to the speaker.]

Sentence modifiers and absolute phrases are not considered to be dangling. (See **17a(6)** and the **Glossary of Terms.**)

Marcus played well in the final game, **on the whole.**

Considering all she's been through this year, Marge is remarkably cheerful.

Grammar checkers rarely catch problems with dangling or misplaced modifiers. A grammar checker identified no problems with the sentences in exercises 4 and 5 in this chapter. Careful proofreading, not the use of a grammar checker, is the best way to avoid problems with modifiers. For more information about grammar checkers, see **Using a Grammar Checker** on page 468.

Exercise 5

Revise the following sentences to eliminate misplaced and dangling modifiers. Some sentences may not require editing.

1. Climbing a mountain, fitness becomes all-important.
2. Getting to the top must be in doubt to make the climb a true adventure.
3. Having set their goals, the mountain must challenge the climbers.
4. In determining an appropriate challenge, considering safety precautions is necessary.
5. Taking care to stay roped together, accidents are less likely to occur.
6. Even when expecting sunny weather, rain gear should be packed.
7. Knowing how to rappel is necessary before descending a cliff.
8. Although adding extra weight, climbers should not leave home without a first-aid kit.
9. Climbers should not let themselves become frustrated if they are not immediately successful.
10. By taking pains at the beginning of a trip, agony can be averted at the end of a trip.

20g | A double negative is redundant.

Most words that express negation are modifiers. The term **double negative** refers to the use of two negative words within a sentence or clause to express a single negation.

He didn't keep ~~no~~ records.
                 ^any

OR

He didn't ~~keep~~ no records.
          ^kept

Beyond the Rule

THE ORIGINAL DOUBLE NEGATIVES

In spoken and written English several centuries ago, two—or even three, four, or five—negative words were used to make a negative statement more emphatic. In the eighteenth century, grammarians decided that this practice was incorrect because the second negative was redundant at best and likely to be confusing (based on the mathematical idea that two negatives make a positive). Double negatives are common in many other languages and in some nonprestige English dialects and song lyrics ("I can't get no satisfaction"). For more information, visit www. harbrace.com.

Because *hardly, barely,* and *scarcely* denote severely limited or negative conditions, using *not, nothing,* or *without* with any of these modifiers creates a double negative.

I could**n't hardly** quit in the middle of the job.

OR

I could**n't** ~~hardly~~ quit in the middle of the job.

The motion passed with **not scarcely** a protest.

OR

The motion passed with ~~not scarcely~~ ^little^ a protest.

Rarely, emphasis in a sentence requires the use of two negatives, and such a construction is not considered a double negative.

It would**n't** be safe **not** to install smoke detectors. [This construction is permissible when *not* is being emphasized. Otherwise, the sentence should be revised. COMPARE It would be dangerous not to install smoke detectors.]

Exercise 6

Using what you have learned in this chapter, revise the following sentences to remove modifier errors.

1. As a woman in the twentieth century, the life of Gertrude Bell was unusual.
2. Young, wealthy, and intelligent, many people were impressed by the red-headed Bell.
3. She was among the first women to graduate from Oxford and couldn't hardly be satisfied with domestic life.
4. Instead, Bell traveled to what were considered the most remotest countries in the world, saw the wonders of the Ottoman Empire, and explored the desert of Iraq.
5. Several of the Arab sheiks who knew Bell thought that she acted bold.
6. The war in Iraq didn't give Bell no time to pursue her research.
7. She became an Arab rebellion supporter.
8. While traveling in Iraq, meetings with important politicians took place.
9. In 1921, Winston Churchill invited Bell to a conference in the Middle East because the other Great Britain conference participants knew little about Iraq.
10. When the photo of the conference participants was taken, Bell looked elegantly in her feathered hat and silk dress among the thirty-six black-suited males.

Pronouns

This chapter will help you

- identify the various kinds of pronouns (**21a**),
- determine the forms of pronouns (**21b**),
- know how to use *who* and *whom* (**21c**),
- make sure pronouns agree with the nouns they refer to (**21d**), and
- ensure clear pronoun references (**21e**).

A **pronoun** is commonly defined as a word that can replace either a noun or a phrase acting as a noun. Unlike nouns, which change form only to become plural or possessive, pronouns change form to show their relationship to other words in a sentence. Each of a pronoun's forms is a **case.** You can see how a pronoun changes form (case) in the examples that follow. When a pronoun changes case, that change signals a different relationship.

He wants his cousin to help him.	**Hugh** wants his cousin to help him.
He wants **his** cousin to help him.	He wants **Hugh's** cousin to help him.
He wants his cousin to help **him.**	He wants his cousin to help **Hugh.**

Grammar checkers often provide minimal help in identifying case errors. A grammar checker found nothing wrong with this sentence: *Carol and me agree that Mark is a good athlete.* And it identified a word order problem, not a case error, in this sentence: *Me and Carol agreed that Mark is a good athlete.* In addition, grammar checkers miss as many errors involving *who/whom* as they find (see **21c(2)**), and they almost never find problems with pronoun-antecedent agreement (**21d**). See **Using a Grammar Checker** on page 468.

> **21a** | **Being familiar with the various kinds of pronouns helps writers use them correctly.**

English has several different kinds of pronouns: personal, relative, interrogative, and reflexive pronouns.

(1) Personal pronouns identify the speaker, the person spoken to, and the person or thing spoken about.

The first-person pronoun (*I* or *we*) identifies the speaker, the second-person pronoun (*you*) identifies the person spoken to, and the third-person pronoun (*he, she, it,* or *they*) identifies the person or thing spoken about. Personal pronouns change form to reflect their relationship to other words in a sentence. The subject of a sentence appears in the subjective case, the object appears in the objective case, and a word showing possession appears in the possessive case. (See **33a**.)

	Subjective		**Objective**		**Possessive**	
Person	**Singular**	**Plural**	**Singular**	**Plural**	**Singular**	**Plural**
First person	I	we	me	us	my mine	our ours
Second person	you	you	you	you	your yours	your yours
Third person	he she it	they	him her it	them	his hers its	their theirs

Notice that the second-person pronoun *you* has the same form for both singular and plural and for the subjective and objective cases. The third-person pronoun *it* has the same form for the subjective and objective cases. The possessive form of *it* is *its,* without an apostrophe (*it's* means "it is"). All the other personal pronouns reflect person, number, and case. (And the third-person singular forms also reflect the last vestige of gender in English usage. See **21d(1)** and **28d(1)**.)

Beyond the Rule

THE TERRITORIES OF CASES

It can be useful to think in terms of territories to distinguish the
subjective and objective cases. That is, the part of a sentence before the
verb is "subject territory," and pronouns in that position appear in
subjective case. The rest of the sentence is "object territory," and the
pronouns in that part of the sentence almost always appear in objective
form. The only exception occurs when the verb is a form of *be.* For
additional information on case, visit www.harbrace.com.

(2) A relative pronoun relates a dependent clause to a noun in the main clause.

Relative pronouns (*who, whom, whoever, whomever, which, whose,* and
that) introduce clauses that refer to a noun in a main clause.

Mike Schildt, who carved my stone bear, lives in Taos.

Mike Schildt, about **whom** I know only that he lives in Taos, carved my
stone bear.

Graham explained his invention to whoever would listen. [*Whoever* is the
subject of its own clause.]

Graham explained his invention to whomever he could get to listen.
[*Whomever* is the object of the preposition *to.*]

Who, whose, and *whom* ordinarily refer to people; *which* refers to things;
that refers to either people or things. The possessive pronoun *whose* (used
in place of the awkward *of which*) sometimes refers to things.

The poem, **whose** author is unknown, has recently been set to music.
[COMPARE The poem, of which the author is unknown, has . . .]

	Refers to people	Refers to things	Refers to either
Subjective	who	which	that
Objective	whom	which	that
Possessive			whose

Do not confuse *who's* and *whose. Who's* is a contraction for *who is,* and *whose* indicates possession.

(3) Interrogative pronouns introduce questions.

Like their relative counterparts, the interrogative pronouns *who* and *whom* change form to reflect their grammatical use in a sentence.

> **Who** asked the question? [subjective case for the subject of the sentence]
>
> **Whom** did she give the book to? [See **21c(2)** for the approved use of the subjective case in such sentences.]

Which and *that* do not change form.

(4) Reflexive pronouns direct the action back on the subject or the agent; intensive pronouns are used for emphasis.

Reflexive and intensive pronouns are formed by combining personal pronouns with *-self.* The reflexive pronouns *myself, ourselves, yourself, himself, herself, itself,* and *themselves* refer to the subject of the clause in which they appear. Intensive pronouns are used primarily for emphasis and are indistinguishable from the reflexive forms.

> Jake saw a picture of **himself.** [reflexive]
>
> Jake, **himself,** brought the plant here. [intensive]

When these pronouns refer to a noun or pronoun already mentioned in the sentence, they always immediately follow the person or thing to which they refer.

Do not use *myself* or *me* in place of *I* in a compound subject.

Jake and **myself** brought the plant here.
(I inserted above "myself")

Jake and I
Me and Jake brought the plant here.

Hisself and *theirselves,* although logical forms for reflexive pronouns (possessive plus *-self* as in *myself, yourself,* and *herself*), are inappropriate in college or professional writing. Instead, use *himself* and *themselves.*

themselves
Tommy and Mike painted the house by **theirselves.**

Attempts to create a gender-neutral singular reflexive pronoun have resulted in such forms as *themself;* these forms are also inappropriate in college or professional writing.

21b | Pronouns change form to indicate the subjective, objective, or possessive case.

In English, most of what there is to say about case applies to the pronouns that change form to show their relationship to other words in a sentence. For example, the different cases of the boldfaced pronouns below, all referring to the same person, show their different uses.

He [the subject] wants **his** [modifier showing possession] cousin to help **him** [direct object].

He, the subject, is in the *subjective* case; *his,* showing possession, is in the *possessive* case; and *him,* the object, is in the *objective* case.

Pronouns also have singular and plural forms.

They [plural subject] want **their** [plural modifier showing possession] cousins to help **them** [plural direct object].

(1) Subjects and subject complements with linking verbs are in the subjective case.

A **subject complement** is a word that renames the subject. A **linking verb** is a form of *be* (*am, is, are, was, were*), a verb expressing sensation (*look, sound, feel, taste, smell*), or a verb conveying a state or condition (*become, grow, prove, remain, seem, turn*). A linking verb relates the subject to the subject complement. (See **22c(1)**.) Pronouns that are subject complements or subjects are in the subjective case.

The ones in charge were ~~him and me~~ *he and I*. [compound subjective complement, *he and I,* in the subjective case]

Russell and ~~me~~ *I* were in charge. [compound subject of the sentence, *Russell and I,* in the subjective case]

In conversational English, "It's *me*" (or *him, her, us,* or *them*) is acceptable.

In some languages, a noun and a pronoun can both be the subject of a clause. In English, though, only one of these can be in the subject position.

My roommate ~~he~~ works in the library for three hours a week.

(2) All objects are in the objective case.

Whenever a pronoun is an object—a direct object, an indirect object, or the object of a preposition—it takes the **objective case.**

Direct object	Miguel loves **her.** [The direct object, *her,* is in the objective case. COMPARE Miguel loves Martha.]
Indirect object	Miguel gave **her** his love. [The indirect object, *her,* is in the objective case. COMPARE Miguel gave Martha his love.]
Object of a preposition	Miguel cares deeply for **her.** [The object of the preposition, *her,* is in the objective case. COMPARE Miguel cares deeply for Martha.]

(3) The possessive case indicates ownership.

Modifiers that indicate ownership or a comparable relationship are in the **possessive case.** A few possessive pronouns (such as *mine* and *theirs*) sometimes function as nouns.

That book is **mine.** [COMPARE That book is my book.]

Their and *they* can be confused in spoken English. *Their* is the possessive pronoun; *they* is in the subjective case. These must be distinguished in written English.

   their   their
  ~~they~~ book   ~~they~~ house
  ^   ^

See the Glossary of Usage to clear up confusion among *their, there,* and *they're.*

Beyond the Rule

CASE MATTERS

When an offending pronoun is in the possessive or objective case, people notice the lack of agreement (see 21b) more often and find it more objectionable than when the incorrect pronoun is in the subjective case. For examples, visit www.harbrace.com.

21c | The use of a pronoun in its own clause determines its case.

(1) Pronouns in compound constructions have the same case as they would if the construction were not compound.

Pronouns in compound subjects or subject complements are in the subjective case.

I thought **he or Dad** would come to my rescue. [*He* is part of the compound subject of the clause that acts as the direct object. COMPARE I thought **he** would come to my rescue.]

It was **Maria and I** who solved the problem. [compound subject complement; see **21b(1)**]

She and her father buy groceries on Saturday morning. [compound subject containing two pronouns, one subjective and one possessive]

You can test the case of any pronoun in a compound construction by eliminating the accompanying noun or pronoun and the conjunction.

(Lou and) I like to watch *Star Wars* movies. [subject]

They elected (George and) me to the board. [direct object]

Gabriel gave it to (Edwyn and) me. [object of the preposition]

The first-person pronoun *I* occurs last in a compound construction. (See **29d** for ways to use the first-person pronoun effectively.)

~~Me and~~ Ricardo _{and I} are good friends.

As compound objects of prepositions, pronouns are in the objective case.

between him and ~~I~~ ^{me}   with Amanda and ~~he~~ ^{him}

Beyond the Rule

YOU AND ME, OR YOU AND I?

The subjective case has come to be viewed as more formal and thus more prestigious than the objective case. Perhaps in an effort to lend more prestige to their speech, some people incorrectly use *I* as the second element in compound objects.

The supervisor asked John and ~~I~~ ^{me} to lead the discussion.

Between you and ~~I~~ ^{me}, he talks too much.

For additional information, visit www.harbrace.com.

Compound objects of verbs or verbals and subjects of infinitives are also in the objective case.

Clara may appoint **you or me.** [direct object]

They lent **Tom and her** ten dollars. [indirect object]

He gets nowhere by scolding **Bea or him.** [object of the gerund]

Dad wanted **Sheila and me** to keep the old car. [subject of the infinitive in a verbal phrase, which is the direct object of the sentence]

If an appositive (a word that renames a noun or pronoun) follows a pronoun, normal case rules apply.

We
~~Us~~ students need this.
∧

us
The director told we extras to go home.
∧

To test the case of a pronoun that is followed by an appositive, remove the appositive.

We
~~Us students~~ need this.
∧

us
The director told ~~we extras~~ to go home.
∧

Exercise 1

Revise the following paragraph, using appropriate cases for pronouns. Some sentences may not require editing.

¹When I was twelve, my family lived in Guatemala for a year. ²My parents taught English at a university; me and my younger brother went to a local school. ³Although the Spanish language was new to both Sam and I, we learned to speak it quickly. ⁴At first, we couldn't understand much at all, but with the help of a tutor, who we met every day after school, we started learning "survival" Spanish. ⁵Sam had better pronunciation than me, but I learned vocabulary and grammar faster than him. ⁶After we learned to ask and answer some basic

questions, we started making friends, whom eventually introduced us to they're own version of Spanish. **7**They taught us slang words that our tutor didn't even know. **8**However, though Sam and me benefited from all our Spanish lessons, we learned the language so quickly because, unless we were with our parents or by ourself, we listened to it, read it, wrote it, and spoke it all day long.

(2) *Who/whoever* and *whom/whomever* are often misused.

You may be able to avoid confusion about the correct usage of *who/whoever* and *whom/whomever* if you remember that the case of any pronoun is determined by its grammatical function in the clause in which it appears. The subject of a verb in a dependent clause takes the subjective case, even if the whole clause is used as an object.

> I remembered **who** won the Academy Award that year. [*Who* is the subject of the clause *who won the Academy Award that year.* The clause is the object of the verb *remembered.*]

> She offered help to **whoever** needed it. [*Whoever* is the subject of the clause *whoever needed it.* The clause is the object of the preposition *to.*]

When the pronoun is the direct object or the object of a preposition, *whom* is *always* the correct form. See **16c(2)**.

> They helped the people ~~who~~ whom they liked. [direct object]

> Gabriel happily greeted ~~whoever~~ whomever he met that day. [direct object]

> This is a friend ~~who~~ whom I write to once a year. [*Whom* is the object of the preposition *to.* COMPARE I write to him once a year.]

> I don't know ~~who~~ whom he voted for. [*Whom* is the object of the preposition *for.* COMPARE He voted for *him.*]

> Hemingway's seventh novel is titled For **Whom** the Bell Tolls. [objective case for the object of a preposition]

Whom may be omitted (or replaced by *that*) in sentences where no misunderstanding would result.

The friend he relied on moved away. [*Whom* has been omitted after *friend*.]

The friend *that* he relied on moved away. [*That* has been substituted for *whom*.]

Beyond the Rule

WHO AND WHOM

Although many writers still prefer the objective case, *whom* or *whomever*, dictionaries have approved the use of *who* or *whoever* when the pronoun begins a clause.

I wondered **who** she gave the book to.

Give the book to **whoever** he wants to have it.

Who do you plan to vote for?

Who were you speaking of?

In college writing, it is better to use *whom* as the object even when it is the first word in a sentence or a clause.

Whom will they elect president?

For additional information, visit www.harbrace.com.

Exercise 2

Following the guidelines for college and professional writing, choose the appropriate form of each pronoun in parentheses. Remember to choose *whom* when the pronoun functions as an object and *who* when it functions as a subject or a subject complement.

1. The United States Equestrian Team's training program allows visits by interested individuals (who/whom) arrive when the stables are open.
2. The organization considers supporting (whoever/whomever) can provide their own horses and exhibit the skills to win.

3. Amateurs and professionals (who/whom) apply to the United States Equestrian Team are evaluated by (whoever, whomever) the organization accepts as skilled judges.

4. The American Horse Shows Association can nominate a professional rider (who/whom) it thinks would be an asset to the United States Equestrian Team.

5. (Whoever/Whomever) the organization finances for competition must surely be thankful that supporters, (whoever/whomever) they may be, were able to make contributions to the United States Equestrian Team.

(3) The use of *who* or *whom* with an interpolated expression depends on the pronoun's grammatical function.

Such interpolated expressions as *I think, he says, she believes,* and *we know* can follow either *who* or *whom.* The case of the pronoun still depends on its grammatical function in the clause. To make sure that you have used the correct form, delete the intervening phrase.

Walter picked Jan, **who** ~~he knows~~ speaks well. [*Who* is the subject of the verb *speaks.*]

Walter picked Jan, **whom** ~~he knows~~ we all respect. [*Whom* is the object of the verb *respect.*]

(4) The choice of pronoun form can determine the meaning of the sentence.

In sentences with implied (rather than stated) elements, the pronoun form can determine the meaning of the sentence.

She likes Clarice more than **I.** [subjective case, meaning "more than I like Clarice"]

She likes Dana more than **me.** [objective case, meaning "more than she likes me"]

He talks to Jerry as much as **her.** [objective case, meaning "as much as he talks to her"]

(5) Pronouns used with infinitives are in the objective case.

A pronoun grouped with an infinitive takes the objective case.

> They wanted Dave and me to help **him.** [object of the infinitive, in the objective case]
>
> Alex wanted Elizabeth and **me** to rent a bigger apartment. [subject of the infinitive, in the objective case]
>
> Bill wanted **us** to play more music that features the bassoon. [subject of the infinitive, in the objective case]
>
> Their guide tried to steer **them** around the dangerous rapids. [object of the infinitive in the objective case]

(6) A pronoun that precedes a gerund takes the possessive case.

Just like a noun, a pronoun follows the convention of taking a possessive form when it occurs before a **gerund** (a verb form ending in -*ing* and used as a noun).

> I appreciated Tom's helping Denise.
>
> I appreciated him helping Denise.

[*his* written above, with caret replacing *him*]

The -*ing* ending marks both gerunds and participles. A **participle** is a verbal used as an adjective.

> The man **sitting** [participle modifying *man*] at the next table annoyed us. [The participle *sitting* tells more about which man annoyed us.]

A gerund is a verbal used as a noun.

> The man's **sitting** [gerund acting as subject] at the desk annoyed us. [The gerund *sitting* indicates that it was the act of sitting that annoyed us.]

Notice that the possessive case is used before gerunds, but not before participles.

Exercise 3

Revise the following sentences, using correct pronoun cases. Some sentences may not require editing.

1. The board of directors has asked you and I to conduct a customer survey.
2. They also recommended us hiring someone with extensive experience in statistical analysis.
3. You understand statistics better than me.
4. Although the board asked me to be in charge, I would like you to recruit and interview candidates.
5. The directors recognize your expertise and will surely approve of you taking the lead.

21d | **A pronoun and its antecedent agree when they have the same number and gender.**

A pronoun and the noun or other pronoun to which it refers, the **antecedent,** must agree in number (singular or plural).

Singular A **wolf** has **its** own language. [*Wolf* and *its* agree.]

Plural **Wolves** have **their** own language. [*Wolves* and *their* agree.]

A pronoun also agrees with its antecedent in gender (masculine, feminine, or neuter).

the **boy** and **his** sister [masculine antecedent]

the **girl** and **her** brother [feminine antecedent]

the **garden** and **its** weeds [neuter antecedent]

 The possessive pronouns (*his, her, its, their, my, our,* and *your*), sometimes called *possessive determiners,* agree with their antecedents, not with any noun they modify.

Ken Carlson brought ^his her young daughter to the office today.

[The possessive pronoun *his* agrees with the antecedent, *Ken Carlson,* not with the following noun, *daughter.*]

(1) Agreement is still necessary when the antecedent is an indefinite pronoun or a generic noun.

Indefinite pronouns are generally singular.

Everybody has to live with ~~themselves~~. [OR Rephrase using the plural: *himself or herself* *People have* to live with themselves.]

Each student has the combination to ~~their~~ own locker. *his or her*

Because many readers consider the use of *his or her* awkward, it is usually best to rewrite your sentence so that a generic noun is plural.

Singular   A lawyer represents **his or her** clients.
Plural   Lawyers represent **their** clients.

A pronoun that refers to one of the following words should be singular: *man, individual, woman, person, everybody, one, anyone, each, either, neither, sort,* and *kind.*

Each of these companies had ~~their~~ books audited. *its*

When the gender of the antecedent is clear, use the appropriate personal pronoun.

Masculine   John represents **his** clients.
Feminine   Mary represents **her** clients.

When the gender of the antecedent is not clear or when the noun could refer to either gender, rewrite the sentence to make the noun plural or use a form of *his or her* or *himself or herself.*

College students who support themselves have little free time.
[COMPARE A college student who supports *himself or herself* has . . . .]

When using a word such as *student,* which can refer to either a man or a woman, you can avoid agreement problems by dropping the pronoun, making the antecedent plural, or, as a last resort, rewriting the sentence using the passive voice. (See **22c**.)

Each student has the combination to a private locker. [no pronoun]
Students have the combinations to their private lockers. [plural]
The combination to a private locker is issued to each student. [passive voice]

In spoken English, a sentence such as the following is considered easy and natural; in college and professional writing, however, it is not accepted.

Everyone was invited to dinner, ~~but they~~ had already eaten.
[above "was" is inserted: who]

[The revision avoids the agreement problem.]

Beyond the Rule

INCLUSIVE USE OF PRONOUNS

Be careful not to introduce errors into your writing because you are trying to avoid sexist usage. (See 28d(1).)

Whenever ~~a~~ driver lets their license expire, they have to take the driving test.
[marks "s" above "driver" and "license"]

For more information on pronouns and nonsexist usage, visit www.harbrace.com.

(2) The pronoun agrees with the nearer of two antecedents joined by *or* or *nor*.

Did **Mark or Gordon** lose **his** enthusiasm?

If one of two antecedents joined by *or* or *nor* is singular and the other is plural, the pronoun usually agrees with the nearer antecedent.

Neither the **president nor** the **senators** had announced **their** decision. [*Their* is closer to the plural antecedent *senators*.]

When gender makes it awkward to follow the rule, as in *Roger or Betty will bring his or her book,* recast the sentence to avoid the problem: *Roger will bring his book, or Betty will bring hers.*

(3) Agreement with collective nouns as antecedents can be tricky.

When the antecedent is a collective noun, special care should be taken to avoid treating it as both singular and plural in the same sentence.

The choir is writing ~~their~~ [its] own music. [Because the choir is working as a unit, *choir* is regarded as singular.]

The group of students disagree on methods, but **they** unite on basic aims. [Because the students in the group are behaving as individuals, *group* is regarded as plural.]

PRONOUN-ANTECEDENT AGREEMENT

Antecedent	Singular Pronoun	Plural Pronoun	Option
Indefinite pronoun such as *anybody, each, everyone, either,* or *someone*	✔		
Collective noun such as *committee* or *audience*	✔	(✔ only if referring to individuals within a group)	
Word that refers to a member of a class, such as *student* or *employee*	✔		
Compound construction such as *brother and sister* or *family and friends*			✔ (refers to nearest element)

Exercise 4

Revise the following sentences so that they have correct agreement between pronouns and antecedents.

1. A researcher relies on a number of principles to help him make ethical decisions.
2. Everyone should have the right to participate in a study only if she wants to.
3. A team of researchers should provide its volunteers with informed-consent forms, in which they describe to the volunteers the procedures and risks involved in participation.

4. Every participant should be guaranteed that the information they provide will remain confidential.

5. Institutions of higher education require that a researcher address ethical issues in their proposal.

21e | A pronoun must refer clearly to a specific antecedent.

The main rhetorical principle to keep in mind regarding pronoun reference is clarity. Clarity requires making sure that pronoun references are not ambiguous or unclear, remote or awkward, broad or implied, or impersonal.

Each boldfaced pronoun below clearly refers to an italicized noun or pronoun—its **antecedent**—which can be a word group or a single word.

Nevertheless, it is the same dedication to family that has always tied *women* to the home that today urges **them** into the workplace.

Our ranching operation keeps *cattle* year-round in the same pastures where **they** are bred, born, and raised.

Losing weight has become more than a national occupation; **it** is a national obsession.

Without any loss of clarity, a pronoun can often refer to a noun that follows it.

Unlike **their** ancestors, the *soldiers* of today do not travel on their feet.

The meaning of each pronoun in a sentence should be immediately obvious. To avoid confusion, repeat the antecedent, use a synonym for it, or rewrite the sentence so that the pronoun and the antecedent are clearly related.

(1) Ambiguous or unclear pronoun references can confuse readers.

When a pronoun could refer to either of two possible antecedents, the ambiguity confuses, or at least inconveniences, your readers. To make the antecedent clear, replace the pronoun with a noun or rewrite the sentence.

Sue pointed out ~~to Lou that since her~~ cat was shedding, ~~she~~ had cat
that because Lou's (above "out to Lou that since her") — *Lou* (above "she")

hair all over her suit. [In the unrevised sentence, it is not clear who

owns the cat and who has cat hair on her suit.]

A pronoun may clearly refer to two or more antecedents.

Jack and Jill lost **their** tickets.

(2) Remote or awkward references can cause readers to misunderstand.

If a pronoun is too far away from its antecedent, the reader may have to back-track to get the meaning. A pronoun that refers to a **modifier** (a word that explains or gives more details about another word) or to another pronoun in the possessive case (see **21b(3)**) can also obscure the meaning. Rewriting the sentence to bring a pronoun and its antecedent closer together or substituting a noun for the obscure pronoun will clarify the meaning.

who was not a joiner of organizations
The **sophomore** found herself the unanimously elected president of a

group of animal lovers~~, who was not a joiner of organizations~~. [*Who* is

too far removed from its antecedent *sophomore*. See **20e.**]

all the Indian jewelry
Before Ellen could get to the jewelry store, it was ~~all~~ sold. [*It* could refer

to *store* but probably refers to *jewelry.*]

The Kiwanis Club sells tickets for the **fireworks** ~~on the Fourth of July~~
on the Fourth of July
that it sponsors . [The pronoun refers to a distant antecedent.]

(3) Broad or implied references can make writing vague.

Pronouns such as *it, such, this, that,* and *which* may refer to a specific word or phrase or to the sense of a whole clause, sentence, or paragraph.

The weight of the pack was manageable, once I became used to **it.** [*It* refers specifically to *weight.*]

Large corporations may seem to be more trustworthy than individuals, but **that** is not true. [*That* refers to the sense of the whole first clause.]

When used carelessly, broad references can interfere with clear communication. To ensure clarity, make each pronoun refer to a specific word. Unless the meaning is clear, avoid reference to the general idea of a preceding clause or sentence.

> When class attendance is compulsory, some students feel that education
> ~~perception~~
> is being forced on them. This is not true. [*This* has no clear antecedent.]

Express the idea referred to rather than merely implying it.

> He wanted his teachers to think he was above average, as he could have
> his intelligence   his
> been if he had used it to advantage. [*It* has no expressed antecedent.]
> Teaching music
> My father is a music teacher. It is a profession that requires much
>
> patience. [*It* has no expressed antecedent.]

(4) The use of the impersonal pronoun *it* can result in wordiness or ambiguity.

The use of *it* without a specific antecedent postpones the actual subject of the sentence and can be wordy or awkward.

> Trying   useless
> ~~It was~~ ~~no use trying~~.

Avoid the placement of *it* near another *it* with a different meaning.

> Staying in the old apartment
> It would be simpler ~~to stay in the old apartment~~, but it is too far from
>
> my job. [The first *it* is an expletive (see the **Glossary of Terms**); the
>
> second *it* refers to *apartment*.]

E x e r c i s e   5

Edit the following sentences to make all references clear. Some sentences may not require editing.

1. It is remarkable to read about Lance Armstrong's victories.

2. A champion cyclist, a cancer survivor, and a humanitarian, it is no wonder that Lance Armstrong is one of the most highly celebrated athletes in the world.

3. Armstrong's mother encouraged his athleticism, which led to his becoming a professional triathlete by age sixteen.

4. Though you might not believe it, Armstrong was only a senior in high school when he started training for the Olympic developmental team.

5. By the time he was twenty-five, Armstrong was ranked as the top cyclist in the world.

6. Not long afterward, because of intense pain, he sought medical attention, and they told him he had testicular cancer.

7. The cancer had spread to his lungs and brain; thus, they said his chances for recovery were slim.

8. Armstrong underwent dramatic surgery and aggressive chemotherapy; this eventually helped him recover.

9. Armstrong started training five months after their diagnosis and went on to win major championships, including the Tour de France.

10. For Lance Armstrong, it hasn't only been about racing bikes; he has become a humanitarian as well, creating the Lance Armstrong Foundation to help cancer patients and to fund cancer research around the world.

Verbs

Choosing precise verbs to convey what you observe or think is the first step toward writing clear and effective sentences. The next step is to ensure that the verbs you choose conform to the conventions your audience expects you to follow.

This chapter will help you

- identify conventional verb forms (**22a**),
- use verb tenses to provide information about time (**22b**),
- distinguish between the active voice and the passive voice (**22c**),
- use verbs to signal the factuality or likelihood of an action or event (**22d**), and
- ensure that subjects and verbs agree in number and person (**22e**).

22a | A verb has three or more forms.

Most English verbs have four forms, following the model for *walk.*

walk, walks, walking, walked

However, English also includes irregular verbs, which may have as few as three forms or as many as eight forms:

let, lets, letting   **be, am, is, are, was, were, being, been**

(1) Regular verbs have four forms.

A regular verb has a **base form.** This is the form you find in a dictionary. *Talk, act, change,* and *serve* are all base forms.

The second form of a regular verb is the **-s form.** To derive this form, add to the base form either *-s* (*talks, acts, changes, serves*) or, in some cases, *-es* (*marries, carries, tries*). See **36d** for information on spelling changes that accompany the addition of *-es.*

The third form of a regular verb is the **-*ing* form,** also called the **present participle.** It consists of the base form and the ending -*ing* (*talking, acting*). Depending on the verb, spelling changes may occur (*changing, chatting*). (See 36d.)

The fourth form of a regular verb consists of the base form and the ending -*ed* (*talked, acted*). Again, spelling may vary when the suffix is added (*changed, served, chatted*). (See 36d.) The -*ed* form has two names: When it is used without the auxiliary verb *have* or *be,* it is called the **past form** (*We **talked** about the new plan*). When the -*ed* form is used with one of these auxiliary verbs, it is called the **past participle** (*We **have talked** about it several times. A committee **was formed** to investigate the matter*).

Verb Forms of Regular Verbs

Base Form	-s Form	-*ing* Form (Present Participle)	-*ed* Form (Past Form or Past Participle)
work	works	working	worked
play	plays	playing	played
watch	watches	watching	watched
apply	applies	applying	applied
stop	stops	stopping	stopped

When verbs are followed by words that begin with similar sounds, you may find their endings (-*s* and -*ed*) difficult to hear. In addition, these verb endings may seem unfamiliar because your dialect does not have them. Nonetheless, you should use -*s* and -*ed* when you write for an audience that expects these endings:

She **seem** satisfied with the report.

He **live** seven blocks from the university.

I **use** to play the saxophone.

We were **suppose** to receive the results yesterday.

(2) Irregular verbs have from three to eight forms.

Some irregular verbs, such as *write*, have forms similar to some of those for regular verbs: base form (*write*), *-s* form (*writes*), and *-ing* form (*writing*). However, the past form (*wrote*) and the past participle (*written*) vary from the regular forms. In fact, some irregular verbs have two acceptable past forms and/or past participles (see *awake* and *beat* in the following chart). Other irregular verbs have only three forms because the same form serves as the base form, the past form, and the past participle (see *let* and *put* in the chart). If you are unsure about verb forms, consult a dictionary or this chart.

Verb Forms of Irregular Verbs

Base Form	-s Form	-ing Form (Present Participle)	Past Form	Past Participle
awake	awakes	awaking	awaked, awoke	awaked, awoken
bear	bears	bearing	bore	borne, born
beat	beats	beating	beat	beaten, beat
begin	begins	beginning	began	begun
break	breaks	breaking	broke	broken
bring	brings	bringing	brought	brought
choose	chooses	choosing	chose	chosen
come	comes	coming	came	come
dive	dives	diving	dived, dove	dived
do	does	doing	did	done
dream	dreams	dreaming	dreamed, dreamt	dreamed, dreamt
drink	drinks	drinking	drank	drunk
drive	drives	driving	drove	driven
eat	eats	eating	ate	eaten

Base Form	-s Form	*-ing* Form (Present Participle)	Past Form	Past Participle
fall	falls	falling	fell	fallen
forget	forgets	forgetting	forgot	forgotten
freeze	freezes	freezing	froze	frozen
get	gets	getting	got	gotten, got
give	gives	giving	gave	given
go	goes	going	went	gone
hang (suspend)	hangs	hanging	hung	hung
hang (execute)	hangs	hanging	hanged	hanged
hold	holds	holding	held	held
know	knows	knowing	knew	known
lay (see the Glossary of Usage)	lays	laying	laid	laid
lead	leads	leading	led	led
let	lets	letting	let	let
leave	leaves	leaving	left	left
lend	lends	lending	lent	lent
lie (see the Glossary of Usage)	lies	lying	lay	lain
lose	loses	losing	lost	lost
pay	pays	paying	paid	paid
put	puts	putting	put	put

(Continued on page 570)

(Continued from page 569)

Base Form	-s Form	-ing Form (Present Participle)	Past Form	Past Participle
rise (see the Glossary of Usage)	rises	rising	rose	risen
see	sees	seeing	saw	seen
set (see the Glossary of Usage)	sets	setting	set	set
sit (see the Glossary of Usage)	sits	sitting	sat	sat
speak	speaks	speaking	spoke	spoken
stand	stands	standing	stood	stood
steal	steals	stealing	stole	stolen
strike	strikes	striking	struck	struck
swim	swims	swimming	swam	swum
take	takes	taking	took	taken
teach	teaches	teaching	taught	taught
tell	tells	telling	told	told
wear	wears	wearing	wore	worn
write	writes	writing	wrote	written

Beyond the Rule

IRREGULAR VERBS

Irregular verbs follow seven basic patterns. Once you know these patterns, you can predict the forms for most irregular verbs. For more information on irregular verb patterns, visit www.harbrace.com.

The verb *be* has eight forms.

be	**Be** on time!
am	I **am** going to arrive early tomorrow.
is	Time **is** of the essence.
are	They **are** always punctual.
was	The meeting **was** scheduled for 10 A.M.
were	We **were** only five minutes late.
being	He is **being** delayed by traffic.
been	How long have we **been** here?

(3) A phrasal verb consists of a main verb and an adverbial particle.

A **phrasal verb** is a combination of a verb and an **adverbial particle** such as *up, out,* or *on.* Such a verb + particle unit is often idiomatic, conveying a meaning that differs from the common meanings of the individual words. For example, the definitions that first come to mind for the words *blow* and *up* are not likely to help you understand the phrasal verb *blow up* when it means "to enlarge": *She **blew up** the photograph so that she could see the faces better.* However, the meanings of other phrasal verbs are similar to common definitions; the adverbial particles just add a sense of completion: *They **finished up** the report by six o'clock.* The particle *up* in *finish up* does not refer to a direction; instead, it emphasizes the completion of the report. Other phrasal verbs retain the common meanings of the verb and the particle: *The protesters **hung up** a banner.*

Most phrasal verbs may be separated by short noun phrases or pronouns.

She **called** the meeting **off.**

The student **turned** it **in** yesterday.

Some phrasal verbs are not separable, however.

The group **went over** the proposal.

I **came across** an interesting fact.

Adverbial particles that add little meaning are often deleted, especially if they seem redundant.

I **sent out** the invitations.

You may have trouble finding the definitions for phrasal verbs in conventional dictionaries. Instead, use a specialized dictionary that provides both definitions and information about the separability of these verbs. See page 662 for a list of dictionaries.

(4) Auxiliary verbs combine with main verbs.

The auxiliary verbs *be, do,* and *have* combine with main verbs, both regular and irregular:

be	am, is, are, was, were writing
	am, is, are, was, were surprised
do	does, do, did call
	doesn't, don't, didn't spend
have	has, have, had prepared

When you combine auxiliary verbs with main verbs, you alter the meanings of the main verbs in some subtle ways. The resulting verb combinations may provide information about time, emphasis, or action in progress. (See **22b.**)

Be, do, and *have* are not just auxiliary verbs, though. They may be used as main verbs as well.

be	I **am** from Texas.
do	He **does** his homework early in the morning.
have	They **have** an apartment near a park.

A sentence may even include one of these verbs as both an auxiliary and a main verb.

They **are being** careful.

Did you **do** your taxes by yourself?

She **has** not **had** any free time this week.

Another type of auxiliary verb is called a **modal auxiliary.** By combining a modal auxiliary such as *will, should,* or *could* with the base form of a main verb, you can make a request, give an instruction, or express certainty, doubt, necessity, obligation, possibility, or probability: *we shall overcome, you can dream, she must sleep, they should laugh.*

Although English verbs are often followed by the infinitive marker *to* (as in *want to go* and *plan to leave*), modal auxiliaries do not follow this pattern.

We **should ~~to~~** finish our report by Friday.

Each modal auxiliary has more than one meaning. For example, *may* can indicate permission or probability.

The instructor said we **may** have an extension. [permission]

The weather **may** improve by tomorrow. [probability]

The box provides examples of the use of modal auxiliaries to convey common meanings.

COMMON MEANINGS OF MODAL AUXILIARIES

Meaning	Modal Auxiliary +	Main Verb	Example
Ability	can, could	afford	They can afford to buy a small house.
Certainty	will	succeed	We will succeed by dint of our hard work.
Obligation	must	return	You must return your books by the due date.
Advice	should	talk	He should talk with his counselor.
Permission	may	use	You may use the computers in the main office.

When a modal auxiliary occurs with the auxiliary *have* (*must have forgotten, should have known*), *have* frequently sounds like the word *of*. When you proofread, be sure that modal auxiliaries are not followed by *of*.

        have
They **could of taken** another route.
      ∧

(Continued on page 574)

(Continued from page 573)

Writers generally do not combine modal auxiliaries unless they want to portray a regional dialect.

> be able to
> We **might** c̶o̶u̶l̶d̶ plan the meeting for after the holidays.
>   ∧

 English also has **phrasal modals,** or auxiliary verbs consisting of more than one word. They have meanings similar to those of one-word modals.

be able to (ability): We **were able to** find the original document.

have to (obligation): To complete the application, you **have to** include your test results.

Other common phrasal modals are *be going to, be supposed to, had better, used to,* and *ought to.* Most phrasal verbs have more than one form (*am able to, is able to, were able to*). Only *had better, ought to,* and *used to* have a single form.

(5) Participles are accompanied by auxiliary verbs.

Present participles (*-ing* verb forms) are used with the auxiliary verb *be* (*We **were waiting** for the next flight*). Depending on the intended meaning, past participles can be used with either *be* or *have* (*We **have waited** for an hour. The first flight **was canceled***). If a sentence contains only a participle, it is probably a fragment (see **18a**).

> We were dreaming
> ∧ D̶r̶e̶a̶m̶i̶n̶g̶ of far-off places.

When a participle is part of a verbal phrase, it often appears without an auxiliary verb (see **17a(3)**).

Swatting at mosquitoes and **cursing** softly, the campers quickly packed up their gear.

Exercise 1

Supply the correct form of each verb in parentheses.

1. I (awake) early that morning.
2. Jason said we were (suppose) to leave at 5:00 A.M.
3. I wasn't (use) to getting up before dark, but I (manage) to be at the bus stop on time.
4. The sun was just (begin) to rise.
5. My backpack (be) heavy, so I (lay) it next to the other gear that was (lie) in a heap.
6. Without my pack on, though, I (be) cold.
7. I had (forget) how chilly mornings (be) in the desert.
8. Jason (see) me shivering and (lend) me his jacket.
9. "(Be) you okay?" he (ask).
10. "Yes," I (lie). It (be) early, it (be) cold, and I (be) nervous.

Exercise 2

Revise the following sentences. Explain any changes you make.

1. Any expedition into the wilderness suffer its share of mishaps.
2. The Lewis and Clark Expedition began in May 1804 and end in September 1806.
3. The Fates must of smiled on Meriwether Lewis and William Clark, for there were no fatalities under their leadership.
4. Lewis and Clark lead the expedition from St. Louis to the Pacific Ocean and back.
5. President Thomas Jefferson commission the expedition in 1803 in part because he was interest in finding the Northwest Passage—a hypothetical waterway connecting the Atlantic and Pacific Oceans.
6. By 1805, the Corps of Discovery, as the expedition was call, included thirty-three members.

7. The Corps might of lost all maps and specimens had Sacajawea, a Native American woman, not fish them from the Missouri River.
8. Sacajawea could of went off with her own people in Idaho, but she accompany Lewis and Clark to the Pacific.
9. When the Mandans had finish inspecting York, William Clark's African American servant, they assume he was the expedition's leader.
10. The success of the expedition depend on its members' willingness to help one another.

22b | Verb tenses make time relationships clear.

Verb tenses provide information about time. For example, the tense of a verb may indicate that an action took place in the past or that an action is ongoing. Verb tenses are labeled as present, past, or future; they are also labeled as simple, progressive, perfect, or perfect progressive. The chart shows how these labels apply to the tenses of *walk*.

Verb Tenses

	Present	Past	Future
Simple	walk, walks	walked	will walk
Progressive	am, is, are walking	was, were walking	will be walking
Perfect	has, have walked	had walked	will have walked
Perfect progressive	has, have been walking	had been walking	will have been walking

Some of the tenses have more than one form because they depend on the person and number of the subject. **Person** refers to the role of the subject. First person (*I, we*) indicates that the subject of the verb is the writer or writers. Second person (*you*) indicates that the subject is the audience. Third person (*he, she, it, they*) indicates that the subject is someone or something other than the writer or audience. **Number** indicates whether the subject is one or more than one (*I/we, building/ buildings*). In the following subsections, conjugation tables are used to show how person and number influence the forms of the regular verb *work*.

(1) Simple tenses have many uses, not all related to specific points in time.

The conjugation for the simple present tense includes two forms of the verb: the base form and the *-s* form. Notice that the third-person singular form is the only form with the *-s* ending.

Simple Present Tense

	Singular	Plural
First person	I **work**	We **work**
Second person	You **work**	You **work**
Third person	He, she, it **works**	They **work**

Tense is not the same as time. Although the words *present, past,* and *future* may lead you to think that these tenses refer to actions happening now, in the past, and in the future, this strict separation does not always hold. For example, the simple present tense is used to indicate a current state, a habitual action, or a general truth.

We **are** ready. [current state]

Dana **uses** common sense. [habitual action]

The sun **rises** in the east. [general truth]

The simple present tense is also commonly used to add a sense of immediacy to historical actions and to discuss literary and artistic works (see **13f**).

In 1939, Hitler's armies **attack** Poland. [historical present]

Joseph Conrad **writes** about what he sees in the human heart. [literary present]

On occasion, the simple present tense is used to refer to future time.

My bus **leaves** in twenty minutes.

The simple past tense of regular verbs has only one form: the base form with the *-ed* ending. The past tense for irregular verbs varies (see 22a(2)).

Simple Past Tense

	Singular	Plural
First person	I **worked**	We **worked**
Second person	You **worked**	You **worked**
Third person	He, she, it **worked**	They **worked**

The simple past tense is used to refer to completed past actions or events.

He **traveled** to the Philippines. [past action]

The accident **occurred** several weeks ago. [past event]

Like the simple past tense, the simple future tense has only one form: the base form accompanied by the auxiliary *will.*

Simple Future Tense

	Singular	Plural
First person	I **will work**	We **will work**
Second person	You **will work**	You **will work**
Third person	He, she, it **will work**	They **will work**

The simple future tense refers to future actions or states.

I **will call** you after work today. [future action]

The video **will be** ready by Friday. [future state]

(2) Progressive tenses indicate that events have begun but have not been completed.

The present progressive tense of a verb consists of a form of the auxiliary verb *be* and the present participle (*-ing* form) of the main verb.

Present Progressive Tense

	Singular	Plural
First person	I **am working**	We **are working**
Second person	You **are working**	You **are working**
Third person	He, she, it **is working**	They **are working**

Notice that the present participle remains the same regardless of person and number, but the auxiliary *be* appears in three forms: *am* for first-person singular, *is* for third-person singular, and *are* for the other person-number combinations.

The present progressive tense signals an activity in progress or a temporary situation.

> The doctor **is attending** a conference in Nebraska. [activity in progress]
>
> We **are living** in a yurt right now. [temporary situation]

The present progressive tense can refer to a future event when it occurs with a word indicating time.

> Tomorrow we **are leaving** for Alaska. [*Tomorrow* indicates a time in the future.]

Like the present progressive, the past progressive tense is a combination of the auxiliary verb *be* and the present participle (*-ing* form) of the main verb. However, the auxiliary verb is in the past tense, rather than in the present tense.

Past Progressive Tense

	Singular	Plural
First person	I **was working**	We **were working**
Second person	You **were working**	You **were working**
Third person	He, she, it **was working**	They **were working**

The past progressive tense signals an action or event that occurred in the past and was repeated or ongoing.

The new member **was** constantly **interrupting** the discussion. [repeated past action]

We **were eating** dinner when we heard the news. [ongoing past action]

The future progressive tense has only one form. Two auxiliaries, *will* and *be*, are used along with the *-ing* form of the main verb.

Future Progressive Tense

	Singular	Plural
First person	I **will be working**	We **will be working**
Second person	You **will be working**	You **will be working**
Third person	He, she, it **will be working**	They **will be working**

The future progressive tense refers to actions that will occur in the future.

She **will be giving** her report at the end of the meeting. [future action]

Some verbs that do not express actions but rather mental states, emotions, conditions, or relationships are not used in the progressive form. These verbs include *believe, belong, contain, cost, know, own, prefer,* and *want*.

The book is ~~containing~~ contains many Central American folktales.

He is ~~knowing~~ knows many old myths.

(3) Perfect tenses indicate action performed prior to a particular time.

The present perfect tense is formed by combining the auxiliary *have* with the past participle of the main verb.

Present Perfect Tense

	Singular	Plural
First person	I **have worked**	We **have worked**
Second person	You **have worked**	You **have worked**
Third person	He, she, it **has worked**	They **have worked**

The participle remains the same regardless of person and number; however, the auxiliary has two forms: *has* (for third-person singular) and *have* (for the other person-number combinations). The present perfect tense signals a time prior to the present. It can refer to a situation originating in the past but continuing into the present. It can also refer to a past action that has current relevance.

They **have lived** in New Zealand for twenty years. [situation originating in the past and still continuing]

I **have read** that book already. Do you have another? [past action that is currently relevant]

The past perfect tense is also formed by combining the auxiliary *have* with the past participle. However, the auxiliary is in the past tense. There is only one form of the past perfect for regular verbs.

Past Perfect Tense

	Singular	Plural
First person	I **had worked**	We **had worked**
Second person	You **had worked**	You **had worked**
Third person	He, she, it **had worked**	They **had worked**

The past perfect tense refers to an action completed at a time in the past prior to another past time or past action.

Before 1990, he **had worked** in a shoe factory. [past action prior to a given time in the past]

I **had studied** geology before I transferred to this school. [past action prior to another past action]

The future perfect tense consists of two auxiliaries, *will* and *have,* along with the past participle of the main verb. There is only one form of the future perfect tense.

Future Perfect Tense

	Singular	Plural
First person	I **will have worked**	We **will have worked**
Second person	You **will have worked**	You **will have worked**
Third person	He, she, it **will have worked**	They **will have worked**

The future perfect tense refers to an action that is to be completed prior to a future time.

By this time next year, I **will have finished** medical school.

(4) Perfect progressive tenses combine the forms and meanings of the progressive and the perfect tenses.

The present perfect progressive tense consists of two auxiliaries, *have* and *be,* plus the present participle (*-ing* form) of the main verb.

Present Perfect Progressive Tense

	Singular	Plural
First person	I **have been working**	We **have been working**
Second person	You **have been working**	You **have been working**
Third person	He, she, it **has been working**	They **have been working**

The form of the auxiliary *have* varies with person and number. The auxiliary *be* appears as the past participle. The present perfect progressive signals that an action, state, or event originating in the past is ongoing or incomplete.

I **have been feeling** tired for a week. [ongoing state]

We **have been organizing** the conference since April. [incomplete action]

The past perfect progressive tense follows the pattern *had* + *been* + present participle (*-ing* form) of the main verb. The auxiliary *have* is in the past tense.

Past Perfect Progressive Tense

	Singular	Plural
First person	I **had been working**	We **had been working**
Second person	You **had been working**	You **had been working**
Third person	He, she, it **had been working**	They **had been working**

The past perfect progressive tense refers to a situation or action occurring over a period of time in the past prior to another past action or time.

She **had been living** so frugally all year that she saved enough money for a new car. [past situation prior to another action in the past]

The future perfect progressive tense follows the pattern *will* + *have* + *been* + present participle (*-ing* form) of the main verb.

Future Perfect Progressive Tense

	Singular	Plural
First person	I **will have been working**	We **will have been working**
Second person	You **will have been working**	You **will have been working**
Third person	He, she, it **will have been working**	They **will have been working**

The future perfect progressive tense refers to action that is occurring in the present and will continue to occur for a specific amount of time.

In one more month, I **will have been working** on this project for five years.

(5) The auxiliary verb *do* is used to question, negate, or emphasize.

Unlike *be* and *have,* the auxiliary verb *do* does not occur with other verbs to indicate tense. Instead, it is used to question, negate, or emphasize.

> **Do** you have any questions? [question]
>
> I **do** not have any questions. [negation]
>
> I **do** have a few questions. [emphatic sentence]

The auxiliary *do* is used only in the simple present (*do, does*) and the simple past (*did*).

Exercise 3

Explain what the verb tenses used in the following paragraph reveal about the time or duration of the actions expressed by the main verbs.

[1]Professor Alex Cohen and his literature students are leaving on Friday for Oxford University. [2]While there, they will study Keats and Wordsworth. [3]Although they have been studying these poets since September, Professor Cohen believes that the students will gain greater insight into English poetry because they will have access to important archives. [4]Professor Cohen studied in Oxford when he was an undergraduate, earning a degree in English and classics. [5]This is the first trip he has planned for students. [6]However, with the help of a university grant, he will be planning many more. [7]He is already exploring the possibility of taking students from his mythology class to Greece next year.

Exercise 4

For each sentence, explain how the meaning of the sentence changes when the verb tense changes.

1. The Asian elephant (roams/does roam/had been roaming) freely in the jungles of Thailand.
2. The elephant's harsh habitat and treatment in domesticity (have endangered/will have endangered) the species very soon.
3. The Thai Elephant Conservation Center (has treated/had treated) hundreds of cases in its hospital since 1994.

4. Some of the afflicted elephants (ate/did eat/were eating) bananas containing amphetamines.

5. In *Gone Astray: The Care and Management of the Asian Elephant in Domesticity*, Richard Lair (wrote/writes) about the disappearing Thai jungle and the rapidly declining numbers of Asian elephants.

Exercise 5

In a paragraph from one of your recent writing assignments, underline all the verbs and identify the tenses you used. Explain why they are appropriate.

(6) Tense forms should appear in logical sequence.

When you combine tense forms in a single sentence, you give readers information about how actions and events are related in time and duration.

> Whenever he **calls** on me, I **stutter** nervously. [Both forms indicate habitual actions.]

> When the speaker **had finished,** everyone **applauded.** [The past perfect tense *had finished* indicates a time before the action expressed by *applauded.*]

Infinitives and participles (see 17a(3)) can be used to express time relations within a sentence. The present infinitive (*to* + base form) of a verb expresses action occurring at the same time as or later than the action expressed by the main verb.

> We **like to write** about sports. [Both actions occur at the same time.]

> They **want to design** a new museum. [The action of designing will take place in the future.]

The perfect infinitive (*to* + *have* + past participle) signals that an action did not occur.

> The governor **would like to have postponed** the vote. [The postponement did not occur.]

The present participle (*-ing* form) indicates simultaneous or previous action.

Laughing loudly, the old friends **left** the restaurant arm in arm. [The friends were laughing as they were leaving.]

Hearing that she was distressed, I **rushed** right over. [The action of hearing occurred first.]

The perfect participle (*having* + past participle) expresses action completed before that conveyed by the main verb.

Having learned Spanish at an early age, she **spoke** to the Mexican diplomats in their native language.

The past participle can be used to express either simultaneous action or previous action.

Led by a former Peace Corps worker, the volunteers **provided** medical assistance. [Both actions occur simultaneously.]

Encouraged by job prospects, he **moved** to Atlanta. [The encouragement preceded the move.]

Exercise 6

Revise the following sentences so that all verbs occur in logical sequences.

1. We expected the storm to have bypassed our town, but it didn't.
2. We would like to have prior notice; however, even the police officers were taken by surprise.
3. Not having known much about flooding, the emergency crew was at a disadvantage.
4. Having thrown sandbags all day, the volunteers had been exhausted by 5 P.M.
5. They went home, succeeding in preventing a major disaster.

22c | **Voice indicates the relationship between a verb and its subject.**

When a verb is in the **active voice,** the subject is generally a person or thing performing an action. When a verb is in the **passive voice,** the subject is the *receiver* of the action.

Susan Sontag **wrote** the essay. [active voice]

The essay **was written** by Susan Sontag. [passive voice]

(1) Verbs may be linking, intransitive, or transitive.

A **linking verb** relates the subject and a word referring to the subject (the complement). (See **16c**.) A linking verb may be a verb referring to the senses (such as *feel, look, smell, sound,* or *taste*) or a verb that indicates being (*be*), seeming (*seem, appear*), remaining (*remain, keep, stay*), or becoming (*become, grow, turn*).

Claudia **is** studious.

She **sounds** authoritative.

She **seems** responsible.

Linking verbs are used only in the active voice.

An **intransitive verb** does not take an object. In other words, there is no noun following the verb and receiving its action.

Claudia **studies** hard.

Like linking verbs, intransitive verbs are used only in the active voice.

In contrast to an intransitive verb, a **transitive verb** takes a direct object; that is, a noun follows the verb and receives its action.

Claudia **wrote** the prize-winning essay.

Transitive verbs can be used in the passive voice. When they are, the recipient of the action is the subject, not the object, of the sentence.

The prize-winning essay **was written** by Claudia.

(2) The active voice emphasizes the actor and the action.

Sentences that have the active voice are generally clearer and more vigorous than their passive counterparts. To use the active voice to emphasize actor and action, first make the actor the subject of the sentence, and then choose verbs that will help your readers see what the actor is doing.

Passive voice: The graduation ceremony was planned by a group of students. A well-known columnist was invited to give the graduation address.

Revised: A group of students planned the graduation ceremony. They invited a well-known columnist to give the graduation address.

For more information on using the active voice to write forceful sentences, see **26d**.

(3) The passive voice highlights the recipient of the action.

The passive voice differs from the active voice in three ways. First, the subject is the recipient of the action, not the actor.

The **construction** of the Guggenheim Museum was finished in 1959.

Second, if an actor is mentioned, that noun or pronoun is placed in a prepositional phrase beginning with the preposition *by*.

The Guggenheim Museum was designed by **Frank Lloyd Wright.**

Finally, the verb form is different. A verb in the passive voice consists of a form of the auxiliary verb *be* and the past participle. Depending on the verb tense, the auxiliaries *have* and *will* may appear as well. The following are the most common tense forms for the passive voice for *call*.

Simple present: *am called, is called, are called*
Simple past: *was called, were called*
Simple future: *will be called*
Present progressive: *am being called, is being called, are being called*
Past progressive: *was being called, were being called*
Present perfect: *has been called, have been called*
Past perfect: *had been called*
Future perfect: *will have been called*

Use the passive voice when you want to stress the recipient of the action, rather than the actor, or when the actor's identification is unimportant or unknown. For example, you may want to emphasize the topic of a discussion.

Tuition increases will be discussed at the next board meeting.

Or you may be unable to identify the actor who performed some action.

The lights were left on in the building last night.

Exercise 7

Identify the voice in each sentence as active or passive.

1. In a recent *National Geographic* report, Tom O'Neill describes the discovery of ancient art in Guatemala.
2. Archaeologist William Saturno recently discovered the oldest known Maya mural.
3. The mural was found in a tunnel used by looters.
4. The tunnel was actually a small room attached to a pyramid.
5. The small room was covered with debris; its exact dimensions were hard to gauge.
6. The archaeologist found the mural by accident.
7. The mural was dated to about 150 years before the beginning of the Maya Classic period.
8. For protection from further looting, the research crew posted guards outside the small room.
9. Pigments and wall plaster were gathered for analysis.
10. The details of the mural have not yet been interpreted.

Exercise 8

Rewrite the sentences in exercise 7, making active verbs passive and passive verbs active. Add or delete actors when necessary. If one version of a sentence is better than the other, explain why.

22d | **The mood of a verb expresses the writer's attitude toward an action, a state, or an event.**

The mood of a verb expresses the writer's attitude toward the factuality of what is being expressed. The **indicative mood** is used for statements and questions regarding fact or opinion. The **imperative mood** is used to give commands or directions. The **subjunctive mood** is used to state requirements, make requests, express wishes, and signal hypothetical situations. By using moods correctly, you can show your readers how you feel about the content of your sentences—certain, confident, doubtful, hesitant, ambivalent, and so on.

Indicative	We will be on time.
Imperative	Be on time!
Subjunctive	The director insists that we be on time.

(1) Verb forms signal moods.

Verb forms for the indicative mood are described in **22b**. The verb form for the imperative is simply the base form. Verb forms used for the subjunctive mood are the present subjunctive, the past subjunctive, and the perfect subjunctive. The **present subjunctive** is the base form of the verb.

> The doctor recommended that he **go** on a diet.

> The curator requested that I **be** at the museum by five o'clock.

In the passive voice, the present subjunctive form consists of *be* and the past participle of the main verb.

> We demanded that you **be reimbursed.**

The **past subjunctive** has the same form as the simple past (for example, *had, offered, found,* or *wrote*). However, the past subjunctive form of *be* is *were,* regardless of person or number.

> If they **offered** me the job, I would take it.

> She acts as if she **were** the employer rather than the employee.

To form the passive voice of the past subjunctive, use *were* and the past participle.

> Even if he **were given** a large amount of money, he would not change his mind.

Although it is labeled "past," the past subjunctive refers to the present or the future.

The **perfect subjunctive** verb has the same form as the past perfect tense: *had* + past participle. The perfect subjunctive signals that a statement is not factual.

> I wish I **had known** about the scholarship competition.

To form the passive of the perfect subjunctive, add the past participle to *had been.*

If she **had been awarded** the scholarship, she would have quit her part-time job.

(2) The subjunctive is mainly used in dependent clauses.

Although you may not use the subjunctive when you are speaking with your friends, using it in your writing shows your readers how you feel about your claims. In addition, your audience may expect you to follow the conventions for formal writing. The following guidelines should help you avoid pitfalls in the use of the subjunctive.

TIPS FOR USING THE SUBJUNCTIVE

- In clauses beginning with *as if* and *as though,* use the past subjunctive or the perfect subjunctive.

  He acts as if he **was** the owner. [*were*]

  She looked at me as though she **heard** this story before. [*had*]

- In nonfactual dependent clauses beginning with *if,* use the past subjunctive or the perfect subjunctive. Avoid using *would have* in the *if* clause.

  If I **was** rich, I would buy a yacht. [*were*]

  If the driver ~~would have~~ **checked** his rearview mirror, the accident would not have happened. [*had*]

- Notice that *if* does not always mark a clause as nonfactual.

  If it is sunny tomorrow, I'm going fishing. [indicative mood]

- In dependent clauses following a verb that expresses a wish, requirement, or request, use the past subjunctive or the perfect subjunctive.

  I wish I **was** taller. [*were*]

  My brother wishes he **studied** harder years ago. [*had*]

Beyond the Rule

STATUS OF THE SUBJUNCTIVE MOOD

Some linguists believe that certain subjunctive forms are disappearing from the English language. For more information, visit www.harbrace.com.

Grammar checkers catch some missing verbs, some mismatches between auxiliary verbs and main verbs, and some missing *-ed* endings on verbs, but they skip over at least as many as they find. Furthermore, they can identify some misused infinitives but seldom find misused present participles or gerunds (see 17a(3)). They cannot distinguish between a true passive construction, such as *have been seen,* and a form of *be* followed by an adjective, such as *have been healthy;* thus, they incorrectly flag the latter as a passive construction. In addition, they cannot tell when passive constructions are appropriate and so generally advise writers to "correct" them. They cannot identify improper tense forms or problems with conditional clauses, and they occasionally flag properly used subjunctives as agreement errors (see 22e). For more information about grammar checkers, see **Using a Grammar Checker** on page 468.

Exercise 9

Use subjunctive verb forms to revise the following sentences.

1. The planners of Apollo 13 acted as if the number 13 was a lucky number.
2. Superstitious people think that if NASA changed the number of the mission, the astronauts would have had a safer journey.
3. They also believe that if the lunar landing would have been scheduled for a day other than Friday the Thirteenth, the crew would not have encountered any problems.
4. The crew used the lunar module as though it was a lifeboat.
5. If NASA ever plans a space mission on Friday the Thirteenth again, the public would object.

22e | Verbs must agree with their subjects.

A verb must agree with its subject in **number.** That is, when a subject is plural, the verb must have a plural form; when the subject is singular, the verb must have a singular form. The subject and verb must also agree in **person.** First-person subjects require first-person verb forms, second-person subjects require second-person verb forms, and third-person subjects require third-person verb forms. Notice in the following examples that the singular third-person subject takes a singular verb and that the plural third-person subject takes a plural verb. (If you cannot easily recognize verbs and their subjects, see chapter **16.**)

Singular	The **car** in the lot **looks** new. [*Car* and *looks* are both singular.]
Plural	The **cars** in the lot **look** shabby. [*Cars* and *look* are both plural.]

You can refer to the following subsections for guidance on ensuring subject-verb agreement in particular situations:

- when words come between the subject and the verb (**22e(1)**),
- when two or more subjects are joined by conjunctions (**22e(2)–(3)**),
- when word order is inverted (**22e(4)**),
- when the subject is a relative pronoun (**22e(5)**), an indefinite pronoun (**22e(6)**) or a collective noun (**22e(7)**), and
- when the subject is a noun that is plural in form but singular in meaning (**22e(8)**).

Standardized English requires the addition of *-s* to mark most nouns as plural but most verbs as third-person singular. (Modal auxiliaries are the exception.) Be careful not to confuse the verb ending and the noun ending.

The **students** need attention. [noun + *-s*]
The student **needs** attention. [verb + *-s*]

Except for *be,* verbs change form to indicate the number and person of their subjects only in the simple present tense.

Simple present tense of *be*: *am, is, are*

Simple past tense of *be*: *was, were*

Simple present tense of other verbs: base form or base form + *-s* or *-es* (*read/reads, push/pushes*)

Because of the possibility of confusing the two forms, most problems with subject-verb agreement occur when the present tense is used. When you edit your writing, watch for the following potential pitfalls.

(1) Agreement errors are likely when other words come between the subject and the verb.

The **rhythm** of the pounding waves **is** calming. [*Waves* is the object of the preposition *of*.]

Certain phrases commonly occur between the subject and the verb; however, they do not affect the form of the verb:

accompanied by　along with　as well as　in addition to

not to mention　no less than　including　together with

Her **salary,** together with tips, **is** just enough to live on.

Tips, together with her salary, **are** just enough to live on.

(2) Subjects joined by *and* usually take a plural verb.

Writing on a legal pad and **writing with a computer are** not the same at all.

A compound subject that refers to a single person or thing takes a singular verb.

The **founder and president** of the art association **was** elected to the board of the museum.

Red beans and rice is the specialty of the house.

(3) Agreement errors are common when subjects are joined by *or* or *nor*.

When singular subjects are linked by *or, either/or,* or *neither/nor,* the verb is singular as well.

The provost or the dean usually **presides** at the meeting.

Neither the car nor the motorcycle **is** for sale.

Either her accountant or her lawyer **has** the will.

If one subject is singular and one is plural, the verb agrees with the subject closer to the verb.

Neither the basket nor the **apples were** expensive.

Neither the apples nor the **basket was** expensive.

The verb also agrees in person with the nearer subject.

Either Frank or **you were** going to make the announcement.

Either you or **Frank was** going to make the announcement.

(4) Inverted word order may lead to agreement errors.

In most sentences, the subject precedes the verb.

The large **cities** of the Northeast **were** the hardest hit by the subzero temperatures.

The subject and verb can sometimes be inverted for emphasis (see 26f); however, they must still agree.

Hardest hit by the subzero temperatures and snow **were** the large **cities** of the Northeast.

When the expletive *there* begins a sentence, the subject and verb are also inverted; the verb still agrees with the subject, which follows it (see 16c(1)).

There **are** several **cities** in need of federal aid.

(5) Adjectival clauses are common sites for agreement errors.

In an adjectival clause (see 17b(2)), the subject may be a relative pronoun (*that, who,* or *which*). To determine whether a relative pronoun is singular or plural, you must find its antecedent (the noun it refers to). When the antecedent is singular, the relative pronoun is singular; when the antecedent is plural, the relative pronoun is plural.

singular   singular
antecedent   verb

This is the only **store that gives** triple coupons.

plural   plural
antecedent   verb

Those are the **books that are** out of print.

singular   singular
antecedent   verb

It is not bigger discounts but better **service that makes** a store successful.

plural   plural
antecedent   verb

The Starion is one of the new **models that include** air conditioning as standard equipment.

Beyond the Rule

ONE AS A POSSIBLE ANTECEDENT

According to traditional grammar, in sentences containing the pattern *one* + *of* + plural noun + adjective clause (such as the sentence just before this box), the antecedent for the relative pronoun (*that,* in this case) is the plural noun (*models*). The verb is thus plural as well. However, professional writers often consider *one,* instead of the plural noun, to be the antecedent of the relative pronoun and thus make the verb singular:

The Starion is **one** of the new models that **includes** air conditioning as standard equipment.

For more information on this variation, visit www.harbrace.com.

(6) Agreement errors frequently occur with indefinite pronouns.

The indefinite pronouns *each, either, everybody, one,* and *anyone* are considered singular and so require singular verb forms.

Either of them **is willing** to lead the discussion.

Each has bought a first-class ticket.

Everybody in our apartment building **has** a parking place.

Other indefinite pronouns, such as *all, any, some, none, half,* and *most,* can be either singular or plural, depending on whether they refer to a unit or quantity (singular) or to individuals (plural).

plural plural
antecedent verb

My sister collects comic **books; some are** very valuable.

singular singular
antecedent verb

The bank would not take all the **money** because **some was** foreign.

Singular subjects that are preceded by *every* or *each* and joined by *and* require a singular verb.

Every cat and dog in the county **has** to be vaccinated.

Each fork and spoon **has** to be polished.

However, placing *each* after a plural subject does not affect the verb form. The verb should agree with the plural subject.

Colleges and vocational schools each **have** their advantages.

When an indefinite pronoun is followed by a prepositional phrase beginning with the preposition *of* (see 17a(4)), the verb agrees in number with the object of the preposition.

plural plural
object verb

None of **those are** spoiled.

singular singular
object verb

None of the **food is** spoiled.

singular singular
object verb

More than half of the **population** in West Texas **is** Hispanic.

plural plural
object verb

More than half of the **people** in West Texas **are** Hispanic.

Beyond the Rule

AGREEMENT WITH *NONE*

Some grammarians reason that, like *no one, none* is singular and thus should be followed by a singular verb:

None of the grant requests **has** been rejected.

Nonetheless, many reputable writers have used *none* with plural verbs, leading to the widespread acceptance of this usage:

None of the grant requests **have** been rejected.

For more information, visit www.harbrace.com.

(7) Collective nouns and measurement words often cause agreement difficulties.

Collective nouns and measurement words require singular verbs when they refer to groups or units. They require plural verbs when they refer to individuals or parts.

Singular (regarded as a group or unit)	**Plural (regarded as individuals or parts)**
The **majority rules.**	The **majority** of us **are** in favor.
Ten million gallons of oil **is** more than enough.	**Ten million gallons** of oil **were spilled.**
The **number is** insignificant.	A **number** of workers **were** absent.

Although the use of *data* and *media* as collective nouns has gained currency, treat *data* and *media* as plural in most academic writing. (See the Glossary of Usage.)

The data **are** in the appendix.

The media **have** shaped public opinion.

(8) Words ending in -s are sometimes singular.

Individual titles that are plural in form (for example, *Star Wars* and *Dombey and Son*) are treated as singular because they refer to a single book, movie, recording, or other work.

> *Lilo and Stitch* **is** now out on video and DVD.

A reference to a word is also considered singular.

> *Beans* **is** a slang word for "a small amount": I don't know beans about football.

A few nouns ending in -s are actually singular. Examples are *linguistics, news,* and *Niagara Falls.*

> The **news is** encouraging.

Some nouns (such as *athletics, politics, electronics, measles,* and *deer*) can be either singular or plural, depending on their meanings.

Singular	Plural
Statistics is an interesting subject.	**Statistics are** often misleading.
A **series** of natural disasters **has** occurred recently.	Two **series** of natural disasters **have** occurred recently.

 Although grammar checkers do flag agreement errors, they are only occasionally correct, and they frequently flag acceptable sentences and recommend bizarre alternatives. For instance, one grammar checker flagged *What I think is my own business,* suggesting that *is* should be changed to *am* to agree with *I*. Because a grammar checker cannot distinguish separate clauses, it first compares *think* to *I* and finds agreement, but then compares *is* with *I* as well and finds a problem. For more information about grammar checkers, see <span class="navigation">Using a Grammar Checker on page 468.</span>

Exercise 10

In each sentence, choose the correct form of the verb in parentheses. Make sure that the verb agrees with its subject according to the rules of academic and professional writing.

1. Attitudes about money (vary/varies).
2. Neither time nor affluence (remove/removes) memories of childhood poverty.
3. Experiences of poor children (illustrate/illustrates) how significant money and status (is/are) in our society.
4. Children with unhealthy attitudes toward money often (remember/remembers) their parents' arguments about paying bills.
5. Some adults (think/thinks) their mother or father (was/were) responsible for their attitudes about money.
6. Their current understanding of their parents' past problems with money often (provide/provides) little solace.
7. A number of adults (overcome, overcomes) the stigma of having been poor as children.
8. However, some (do/does) not succeed.
9. There (is/are) affluent children who also (develop/develops) unhealthy attitudes about money.
10. Problems such as these (is/are) less likely to occur if at least one of the parents (talk/talks) to the children about money issues.

Exercise 11

Complete the following sentences, making sure that subjects and verbs agree.

1. Applying for college and enrolling in courses . . .
2. Erik is one of the students who . . .
3. Either of them . . .
4. Neither the president nor the senators . . .
5. The list of volunteers . . .
6. There . . .
7. Hidden beneath the stairs . . .
8. The teacher, along with her students, . . .
9. Ten months . . .
10. Politics . . .

Effective Sentences

23 Sentence Unity

Good writing is unified (see **2a** and **3c**). It is composed of unified sentences that are consistent, clear, and complete. They have no unnecessary shifts in structure, tone, style, or person, and they omit no necessary words. If you want to write unified sentences, this chapter can help you

- recognize unrelated ideas (**23a**),
- avoid excessive detail (**23b**),
- revise mixed metaphors and constructions (**23c**),
- correct faulty predication (**23d**),
- use articles, pronouns, conjunctions, and prepositions effectively (**23e**),
- include all necessary verbs and auxiliaries in a sentence (**23f**), and
- complete comparisons (**23g**) and intensifiers (**23h**).

> **23a** | **Relating ideas clearly in a sentence helps readers understand your meaning.**

Occasionally, a sentence needs an additional phrase or two to establish such relationships as time sequence, location, and cause.

Unrelated	Jason gave his girlfriend a bracelet for her birthday, and she went out to dinner with her parents.
Related	Jason gave his girlfriend a bracelet for her birthday, and she **wore it when they** went out to dinner with her parents. [The additional information establishes why the bracelet and the dinner belong in the same sentence.]
Unrelated	An endangered species, tigers live in India, where there are many people.

Related   An endangered species, tigers live in India, **where their natural habitat is shrinking because of population pressure.** [The revised clause clarifies the cause-and-effect relationship between the tigers' habitat and their endangerment.]

Exercise 1

Adding words where necessary, rewrite the sentences to indicate a logical relationship between their apparently unrelated ideas. If you cannot establish a close relationship, put the ideas in separate sentences.

1. Firefighting is a dangerous job, but there are many high-tech devices and fire-resistant materials.
2. Wildfires can trap firefighters. Fire shelters are being developed to withstand temperatures as high as 2,000 degrees.
3. NASA developed Uninhabited Aerial Vehicles. Firefighters need accurate information fast.
4. Firefighters have difficulty seeing through smoke. A thermal imaging camera detects differences in heat and distinguishes between humans and surrounding objects.
5. Opticom is a traffic-control system, so firefighters can get to a fire quickly. They can change a red light to green from 2,000 feet away.

23b | **Choosing and arranging details can make sentences clear and complete.**

Details help you create effective sentences (see **2d**). If you try to include too many details within a single sentence, however, your readers may lose sight of your main point. Include only those details that develop your point.

Excessive   When I was only sixteen, I left home to attend a college in California that my uncle had graduated from twenty years earlier.

Clear   I left home when I was only sixteen to attend college in California. [If the detail about the uncle is important, include it in another sentence. If not, delete it.]

When considering how much detail to include, remember that lengthiness alone does not make a sentence ineffective. Sometimes you may need a long sentence in which every detail contributes to the central thought. Parallel structure (see chapter 25), balance, rhythm, effective repetition of connecting words, and careful punctuation can make a paragraph-length sentence interesting and coherent. The challenge is to make no sentence longer or more complex than it has to be to fulfill your rhetorical purpose (see 1b and 1e(1)), while keeping in mind that readers enjoy variety in sentence length and type (see chapter 27).

Exercise 2

Revise each sentence in the following paragraph to eliminate excessive detail.

¹Shortly before the end of the year 1997, I returned to the place where I had lived for years as a child with my father, mother, and our two cats, an old farm that had been built decades before my birth, which actually took place there. ²The farm had been passed along by various family members such as my uncle Rick and aunt Louise and later by my cousins Sam and Bernie, who, though they all cherished living there, had done little in the way of upkeep and improvement. ³The farmhouse had been considered a model of technological advances in 1950, and it was probably coveted by neighboring farmers, but when I lived there with my family, it was in need of paint and repair. ⁴Because it was so dilapidated, though not because of our lack of care, my parents decided to renovate it completely, which meant that we had to move to an apartment in a dreary suburb of a nearby city. ⁵The renovation of the house lasted only a year, though it seemed much longer than that, and I remember constantly asking my mother when it would be finished. ⁶Still, watching the slow transformation of the house made me appreciate the care that had gone into its original construction, which many people fail to recognize when they look at old houses.

23c | When revising, writers correct mixed metaphors and mixed constructions.

(1) A mixed metaphor combines different images and creates an illogical comparison.

Mixed	If you are on the fast track up the corporate ladder, it is best to keep your nose to the grindstone.
Revised	If you are on the fast track to a brilliant corporate career, it is best to keep working as hard as you can.
	OR
	If you are trying to become a successful business executive quickly, you will need to work as hard as you can.

As this example shows, mixed metaphors often include clichés (see **29c**). When writers use clichés without picturing what they convey, readers can be confused. One cliché may be at odds with another. For example, it's hard to picture someone quickly climbing a ladder while his or her nose is held against a grindstone. Mixed metaphors are not limited to clichés, however; they can arise when you create your own metaphors if you don't think about what you are asking readers to picture. Every metaphor should be fresh. When revising a mixed metaphor, don't simply remove one cliché and leave another in place.

(2) Mixed constructions are illogical.

A sentence that begins with one kind of construction and shifts to another is a **mixed construction** (see also **23d**). Mixed constructions often omit the subject or the predicate.

Mixed	By practicing a new language every day will help you become proficient.
Revised	Practicing a new language every day will help you become proficient.
	OR
	Daily practice with a new language will help you become proficient.

Mixed	It was a young, frisky puppy but which was generally well behaved.
Revised	It was a young, frisky puppy, but it was generally well behaved.

23d In a good sentence, the predicate follows logically from the subject.

When drafting, writers sometimes compose sentences in which the subject cannot logically perform the action of the predicate, a problem called **faulty predication.** You can fix faulty predication by changing either the subject or the predicate.

Faulty	One book I read believes in eliminating subsidies. [A book does not believe.]
Revised	The author of one book I read believes in eliminating subsidies.
Faulty	One kind of discrimination is a salesclerk who refuses to help an elderly customer. [The refusal of help, not the salesclerk, is an example of discrimination.]
Revised	One kind of discrimination is a salesclerk's refusal to help an elderly customer.

23e Articles, conjunctions, or prepositions are sometimes necessary for clarity.

(1) Omitting an article (*a, an,* or *the*) can confuse your audience.

The following sentence is ambiguous. Without the indicated revision, it could mean that either one person or two people are standing nearby.

A friend and ᵃ helper stood nearby.
    ∧

The indefinite articles *a* and *an* classify the singular nouns they precede. Use *a* before a consonant sound (*a* yard, *a* university). Use *an* before a vowel sound (*an* apple, *an* hour).

The teacher asked me to buy **a** writing journal.

In this sentence, *a journal* is a general term meaning a certain type or class of notebook; it does not refer to a specific journal. Indefinite articles are used for classification in the following common contexts.

- With the first mention of a noun: Use an indefinite article when you introduce a singular noun for the first time.

  I bought **a** writing journal for my English class. It was not very expensive.

- With the expletive *there:* Use an indefinite article when you introduce a topic that includes a singular noun.

  There is **a** good reason for using journals to improve your English.

- For a generalization: When you are referring to a singular noun in a general way, use an indefinite article.

  A journal is a notebook for you to write in without worrying about grammar.

If a noun is plural or if it cannot be counted, no article is needed.

Journals are useful.   **Writing** is an important skill.

The definite article *the* can precede singular or plural nouns. It is used for identification.

The students in the class write in their journals every day.

The students referred to in this sentence are identified as specific students. The definite article is used for identification in the following common contexts.

- For a subsequent mention: Once a noun has been introduced, use the definite article to refer back to it.

  I wrote an entry about whales. **The** entry included facts about the size, shape, and color of whales.

Subsequent mention does not always involve exact repetition of a noun. However, the noun used in the subsequent mention must be clearly related to the content of the previous clause or sentence.

  The teacher grades us on our work, but **the grade** isn't based on grammatical correctness. [*The grade* is close in meaning to the verb *grades*.]

(Continued on page 608)

(Continued from page 607)

- For shared knowledge: When a reference is to something that is part of common knowledge, use the definite article.

  One teacher asked her students to write about **the** moon in their journals.

  The moon is considered part of common knowledge because there is only one and everyone knows what is meant by a reference to it. Other nouns like *moon* include *universe, solar system, sun, earth,* and *sky.* In certain contexts, there may be other nouns that everyone recognizes because they cannot be confused.

  My friend wrote about her experience at **the** airport.

- For abstract classes: *The* is used with a noun that refers to an abstract class.

  The writer's journal has become a mainstay in the composition classroom.

---

(2) When conjunctions or prepositions are omitted, clarity suffers.

In sentences like the following example, *of* is often omitted in speech but never in writing.

We had never tried that brand ^of film before.

We discussed a couple ^of issues at the meeting.

When a sentence has a compound verb (two verbs linked by a conjunction), you may need to supply a different preposition for each verb to make your meaning clear.

I neither believe ^in nor approve of those attitudes.

In the following sentence, use a comma when the conjunction *and* is omitted.

Habitat for Humanity built the house, (**and**) then later painted it. [COMPARE Habitat for Humanity built the house and later painted it. (See **31g(2)**.)]

23f | Verbs sometimes omitted in speech are necessary in writing to clarify meaning.

When speaking, we sometimes drop—or "swallow"—unemphatic words. If you try to write like you talk, you may mistakenly omit words from your writing because you simply do not hear them. These words are necessary in writing, however, to make your meaning clear. Although effective writing often seems natural, as if you are hearing a voice speaking to you, that voice is usually more formal than speech and includes more detail.

She ^has^ seen the movie three times.

A grammar checker will sometimes alert you to a missing word, but it will just as often fail to do so. It may also tell you that an article is missing when it is not. You are better off proofreading your work yourself. (See 3g.)

Providing all necessary verbs eliminates the awkwardness in the following sentence.

Voter turnout has never ^been^ and will never be 100 percent.

Although forms of the verb *be* may not be used in speech, they should be included in writing.

Lamont ^is^ strong and very tall.

In sentences with two short clauses that include the same verb, the second instance of the verb can be omitted (see 30d).

The storm was fierce and the thunder (**was**) deafening.

Beyond the Rule

SPEECH AND WRITING

Although a good piece of writing sounds fine when it is read aloud, a good speech does not necessarily read well if written down exactly as it was spoken. For more information about how speech and writing differ, visit www.harbrace.com.

23g | **Complete comparisons are needed to convey meaning if it is not provided by the context.**

Comparisons can be completed by words or phrases later in the sentence, by other sentences in the paragraph, or by the context.

He is taller **than his brother.**

Most people think television is more violent **than it used to be.**

Occasionally, an incomplete comparison can be understood by readers.

Craig is exercising more.

Most readers will interpret this to mean that Craig is exercising more than he used to exercise, not that he is exercising more than someone else whose name has been omitted from the sentence. However, if there is any chance that someone in your audience could misunderstand a comparison, be sure to make it complete.

Craig is exercising more than he did last season.

OR

Craig is exercising more than the rest of the team.

23h | **The intensifiers *so*, *such*, and *too* require a completing phrase or clause.**

My hair is **so** long **that I must get it cut today.**

Julian has **such** a hearty laugh **that it makes everyone feel good.**

It is just **too** much **for me to try to do.**

When writers approximate speech, they sometimes omit a completing phrase after the intensifier *so*, *such*, or *too* when it is used for emphasis.

> My hair is **so** long.
>
> Julian has **such** a hearty laugh.
>
> It is just **too** much.

In academic and professional writing, *so* and *such* are usually considered too informal. In these contexts, use another intensifier, such as *very, unusually,* or *extremely.* (See chapter **20**.)

Exercise 3

Revise the following sentences to make them clear and complete. Some sentences may not require editing.

1. By studying the villains' faces in the *Star Wars* movies can reveal popular notions about the look of evil.
2. To design the character of Darth Maul for *The Phantom Menace,* Iain McCaig started by illustrating a picture of his worst nightmare.
3. He drew generic male face with metal teeth and long red ribbons of hair falling in front of it.
4. This drawing did not satisfy the movie's producer, George Lucas, who asked McCaig to think of another nightmare.
5. Although McCaig always found the painted faces of clowns frightening, he decided to draw masks instead.
6. The preproduction period was such a long time. It lasted three years, so in the end McCaig had time to experiment with designs for both masks and painted faces.
7. Ralph McQuarrie sketched designs for R2D2 and Darth Vader, including his mask. McCaig wanted to create something scarier.
8. When after arriving at many dead ends, McCaig finally had an idea of what he wanted to do.
9. He designed a face that looked as though it been flayed.
10. The evil visage of Darth Maul was so horrible. To balance the effect, McCaig added elegant black feathers.
11. However, the need to add beauty was not shared by others on the production team, and the feathers eventually became small horns.

Subordination and Coordination

Subordination and coordination help readers understand the relative importance of different ideas by making the structure of sentences clearer. This chapter will help you

- combine short, choppy sentences (**24a**),
- revise long, stringy sentences (**24b**), and
- avoid faulty or excessive subordination (**24c**).

Coordinate means "being of equal rank." When two ideas are expressed in coordinate structures—in two independent clauses, for example—they are grammatically equal and thus seem of equal importance.

Independent Clause		Independent Clause
SUBJECT + **PREDICATE,**	Coordinating Conjunction	**SUBJECT +** **PREDICATE.**
The company was losing money,	but	the employees knew nothing about it.

Coordinate structures can also give equal importance to words and phrases.

a **stunning** and **unexpected** conclusion [coordinate adjectives]

in the attic or **in the basement** [compound prepositional phrases]

Subordinate means "being of lower rank." Subordinate structures make the ideas they express seem less important than the ideas expressed in the structures to which they are subordinate, regardless of which structure comes first in a sentence. In the following sentences, two facts of potentially equal importance are alternately made subordinate by being placed in dependent clauses.

Dependent Clause	**Independent Clause**
Although the company was losing money,	**the employees knew nothing about it.**
Although the employees knew nothing about it,	**the company was losing money.**

Notice that when the clauses are reversed, the emphasis changes. The first sentence subordinates the financial problem; the second subordinates the employees' knowledge. In addition to dependent clauses, phrases and appositives are often used as subordinate structures. (See 17a–b for an explanation of the differences between phrases and clauses and between independent and dependent clauses.)

24a | Subordination can help you combine two or more short, related sentences into one effective sentence.

Short sentences can be effective (see 26h), but too many of them in a row can make your writing seem choppy.

Choppy   I was taking eighteen hours of course work. I wanted to graduate in three years. Such a schedule turned out to be impossible for me. I also had a full-time job at a newspaper office. I just did not have enough time to finish my homework. I had to make a decision. I had to decide what was important. Was money more important? Or was graduating early more important? I really had hoped to have a degree in three years. Then, I decided to drop a course. That way, I could keep my job. I could also pay for tuition.

Revised   I was taking eighteen hours of course work because I wanted to graduate in three years. However, such a schedule turned out to be impossible for me. Since I already had a full-time job at a newspaper office, I did not have enough time to finish my homework. So I had to decide whether money or early graduation was more important. Even though I had hoped to have a degree in three years, I decided to drop one course so that I could both keep my job and pay for tuition.

When combining related sentences, select the main idea, express it in the structure of a simple sentence (subject + predicate), and use any of the following subordinate structures to relate the other ideas to the main one.

(1) Related sentences can be reduced to single words or phrases.

Choppy	The lake was surrounded by forest. It was large and clean. It looked refreshing.
Better	**Surrounded by forest,** the **large, clean** lake looked refreshing. [participial phrase and coordinate adjectives]
Choppy	Season the ground beef with garlic and Italian herbs. Use a lot of garlic. Go lighter on the herbs. Brown it over low heat.
Better	**After seasoning** the ground beef **heavily** with garlic and **lightly** with Italian herbs, brown it **slowly.** [prepositional phrase and adverbs]
	OR
	Season the ground beef **heavily** with garlic and **lightly** with Italian herbs, and brown it **slowly.** [adverbs]
Choppy	His face was covered with white dust. So were his clothes. The man looked like a ghost.
Better	**His face and clothes white with dust,** the man looked like a ghost. [The first two sentences are combined in an absolute phrase (see 17a(6).)]
Choppy	Philip's behavior consisted of a series of foolish acts. They were noticed. But they were not criticized.
Better	Philip's behavior—**a series of foolish acts—was noticed** but **not criticized.** [An appositive phrase and a compound predicate reduce the choppiness.]

(2) A related sentence can become a dependent clause.

Dependent clauses are linked to main clauses by subordinating conjunctions or relative pronouns. These subordinators signal how a dependent clause is related to the main idea: in terms of **time** (*after, before, since, until, when, while*), **place** (*where, wherever*), **reason** (*as, because, how, since, so that*), **condition** (*although, if, unless, whether*), or **additional information** (*that, which, who, whose*). (See pages 499 and 547 for lists of subordinating conjunctions and relative pronouns.)

Choppy	The thunderstorm ended. Then we saw a rainbow. It seemed to promise a happy future.
Better	**When the thunderstorm ended,** we saw a rainbow, **which seemed to promise a happy future.** [adverbial clause and adjectival clause]

If English is not your native language, be sure to check your adverbial clauses to make sure that you have used a subordinating conjunction rather than a preposition.

My friend lived in Mexico for a year **because of** he wanted to improve his Spanish.

Because is a subordinating conjunction; *because of* is a two-word preposition that should be followed by a noun or noun phrase.

24b | Using subordination or coordination is preferable to stringing independent clauses together.

If you overuse coordinating conjunctions (*and, but, or,* and *so*), your writing may lack emphasis (see chapter 26) and variety (chapter 27). Methods of subordination that apply to combining two or more sentences also apply to revising faulty or excessive coordination in a single sentence.

(1) Subordination makes one idea less prominent than another.

When information is strung out over a series of independent clauses, readers may not be able to tell what really matters to the writer. Effective writers usually put what they consider the most important information in an independent clause and place minor points or supporting details in a dependent clause.

In the following examples, the independent clauses are boldfaced; the dependent clauses are italicized. Notice how the ideas expressed in the dependent clauses in the revisions are subordinate to the ideas in the independent clauses.

Stringy	**Jim had a good job** and **he lost the election,** but **he really didn't mind.** [three independent clauses strung together]
Better	*Since he already had a job,* **Jim didn't really mind losing the election.** [one dependent clause and one independent clause]
Stringy	**It was Friday,** and **the crew leader picked us up early,** and **we ate breakfast together at a local diner.**
Better	*On Friday, after the crew leader picked us up early,* **we ate breakfast together at a local diner.** [one dependent clause and one independent clause]

Sometimes, however, the most important information appears in an embedded dependent clause that is an essential part of the independent clause.

The weather service announced *that a tornado was headed straight for town.* [The dependent clause is the direct object of the sentence.]

We didn't know *how far the farm was from the train station.* [The dependent clause is the direct object of the sentence.]

Beyond the Rule

SUBORDINATING IMPORTANT IDEAS

Writers sometimes use subordination to draw attention away from information whose importance they want to play down. For more information about this strategy, visit www.harbrace.com.

(2) Coordinate elements give ideas equal importance.

The band came back onstage, and the audience was pleased. [Independent clauses place equal emphasis on the band and the audience.]

COMPARE The audience was pleased when the band came back onstage. [Subordinating the action of the band emphasizes the reaction of the audience.]

OR The band came back onstage, pleasing the audience. [Subordinating the reaction of the audience emphasizes the action of the band.]

(3) Choosing precise conjunctions enhances readability.

The meanings of some conjunctions are more specific than those of others. For example, the coordinating conjunction *so* indicates a cause-and-effect relationship better than *and* does.

The rain continued to fall, ~~and~~ the tournament was canceled.
[inserted above: so]

Accurate coordination calls for precise coordinating conjunctions. Simmilarly, effective subordination requires carefully chosen subordinating conjunctions. In the following sentence, the use of *as* is distracting because it can mean either "because" or "while."

[inserted above: Because]
~~As~~ time was running out, I randomly filled in the remaining circles on

the exam sheet.

When introducing an adjectival clause, do not use *but* or *and* before *which, who,* or *whom.*

It was a large can of olive oil, ~~and~~ which was very expensive.

 In English, connections between clauses are signaled with coordinating conjunctions or subordinating conjunctions but not with both.

Even though I took aspirin, ~~but~~ I still have a sore shoulder.

Because he had a severe headache, ~~so~~ he went to the health center.

Alternatively, coordinating conjunctions, rather than subordinating conjunctions, can be used to connect clauses.

I took some aspirin, but I still have a sore shoulder.

He had a severe headache, so he went to the health center.

24c | Faulty or excessive subordination can confuse readers.

Faulty subordination	Chen was a new player, winning more than half of his games.
Better	Although Chen was a new player, he won more than half of his games. [*Although* establishes the relationship between the ideas in the sentence's two clauses.]
Excessive subordination	Some people who are insecure and who act superficially miss opportunities for making interesting friends.
Better	Some insecure, superficial people miss opportunities for making interesting friends. [The ideas in two subordinate clauses are reduced to adjectives.]

Exercise 1

Using coordination and subordination, revise the sentences in the following paragraph so that they emphasize the ideas you think are important.

[1]The Lummi tribe lives in the Northwest. [2]The Lummis have a belief about sorrow and loss. [3]They believe that grief is a burden. [4]According to their culture, this burden shouldn't be carried alone. [5]After the terrorist attack on the World Trade Center, the Lummis wanted to help shoulder the burden of grief felt by others. [6]Some of the Lummis carve totem poles. [7]These carvers crafted a healing totem pole. [8]They gave this pole to the citizens of New York. [9]Many of the citizens of New York had family members who were killed in the terrorist attacks. [10]The Lummis escorted the totem pole across the nation. [11]They made stops for small ceremonies. [12]At these ceremonies, they offered blessings. [13]They also offered songs. [14]The Lummis don't believe that the pole itself heals. [15]Rather, they believe that healing comes from the prayers and songs said over it. [16]For them, healing isn't the responsibility of a single person. [17]They believe that it is the responsibility of the community.

Exercise 2

Revise the following sentences to eliminate faulty or excessive subordination. Be prepared to explain why your sentences are more effective than the originals.

1. The Duct Tape Guys usually describe humorous uses for duct tape, providing serious information about the history of duct tape on their Web site.
2. Duct tape was invented for the U.S. armed forces during World War II to keep the moisture out of ammunition cases because it was strong and waterproof.

3. Duct tape was originally called "duck tape" as it was waterproof and ducks are like that too and because it was made of cotton duck, which is a durable, tightly woven material.

4. Duck tape was also used to repair jeeps and aircraft, its primary use being to protect ammunition cases.

5. When the war was over, house builders used duck tape to connect duct work together, so the builders started to refer to duck tape as "duct tape" and eventually the color of the tape changed from the green that was used during the war to silver, which matched the ducts.

Parallelism

Parallelism contributes to clarity by making ideas that are parallel in meaning parallel in structure. It also gives your writing rhythm. This chapter will help you

- balance similar grammatical elements (**25a**),
- use parallel structures within sentences (**25b**),
- use parallel structures to link sentences (**25c**),
- establish parallelism with correlative conjunctions (**25d**), and
- use parallelism for emphasis (**25e**).

Parallel elements frequently appear in lists or series.

I like **running, hiking,** and **swimming.**

Their goals are **to raise awareness of the natural area, to build a walking path near the creek running through it,** and **to construct a nature center at the east end of the parking lot.**

Parallel elements are often linked by a coordinating conjunction (such as *and, but,* or *or*) or by a pair of correlative conjunctions (such as *neither/nor* or *whether/or*), sometimes referred to as *correlatives.* In the following examples, the conjunctions are in italics, and the parallel elements are in boldface.

She is both **smart** *and* **efficient.** [A coordinating conjunction links two adjectives.]

Whether **mortgage rates rise** *or* **building codes change,** the real estate market should remain strong this spring. [Correlative conjunctions join two clauses.]

To learn *a new language* is **to understand** *another culture.* [Verbals in parallel form are used as subject and subject complement.]

Ideas that are equal in importance should be presented in parallel structures.

>   *what*
> We are not so much what we eat as ~~the thoughts~~ we think.

> OR

>   *the food*
> We are not so much ~~what~~ we eat as the thoughts we think.

If elements are not parallel in meaning, you may have to add words or otherwise revise rather than just changing the form of existing words.

>   *coaching*
> His favorite activities are playing golf, baseball, and watching TV.

25a | Similar grammatical elements should receive similar treatment.

To achieve parallelism, balance grammatical elements—nouns with nouns, prepositional phrases with prepositional phrases, adjectival clauses with adjectival clauses, and so on. In the examples that follow, repetition emphasizes the balanced structures.

(1) Balance parallel words and phrases.

> I traded **wealth for simplicity,**
>   and **smugness for satisfaction.**

> The dean emphasized his commitment to **academic freedom,**
>   **professional development,**
>   **cultural diversity,** and
>   **social justice.**

(2) Balance parallel clauses.

> Eventually, she came to understand Ted,
> **who longed for love,**
> **who worried about rejection.**

(3) Balance parallel sentences.

> **When I interviewed for the job, I tried not to sweat.**
> **When I got the job, I managed not to shout.**

Making sentences parallel can help make paragraphs coherent. (See 3c.)

Exercise 1

Write two sentences that illustrate each of the following structures: parallel words, parallel phrases, and parallel clauses. Use the examples in this section as models.

25b | Parallel structures help readers grasp ideas within a sentence.

Repeating a preposition, an article, the infinitive marker *to,* or the introductory word of a phrase or clause can improve the parallel structure in a sentence and clarify meaning.

> For about fifteen minutes, I have been stalking about my house,
>   hands **on** my hips,
> a scowl **on** my face,
>   **trying to** remember where I put my car keys,
>   **trying to** retrace my movements last night.

> The satisfaction came not **from the money**
>   but **from the recognition.**

> The team vowed **that they would stick together,**
>   **that they would play their best,**
>   and **that they would win the tournament.**

25c | Parallel structures can establish a relationship between two or more sentences.

Repeating a pattern emphasizes the relationship of ideas (see 23a). The following example comes from the conclusion of "Letter from Birmingham Jail" (see 7f).

> **If I have said anything** in this letter **that overstates the truth and indicates an** unreasonable **impatience, I beg you to forgive me. If I have said anything that understates the truth and indicates** my having **a patience** that allows me to settle for anything less than brotherhood, **I beg God to forgive me.** —MARTIN LUTHER KING

Almost every structure in the second sentence is parallel with a structure in the first. To create this parallelism, King repeats some words and phrases. But the second sentence would still be parallel with the first if some of its words were changed. For example, substituting *written* for the second *said* and *reveals* for the second *indicates* would result in a sentence that was still parallel with the first sentence—although these changes would lessen the impact of the passage.

In addition to using parallelism to establish the relationship between sentences in a paragraph, you can also use it to create a transition between paragraphs by making the first sentence of a paragraph parallel with the last sentence of the preceding paragraph (see **3d**).

25d | Correlative conjunctions require parallel structures.

Correlative conjunctions (or *correlatives*) are pairs of words that link ideas of equivalent importance:

- both . . . and
- either . . . or
- neither . . . nor
- not only . . . but also
- whether . . . or

Readers expect these pairs to be associated with parallel structures.

Either **you pass the final** *or* **you repeat the course.**

Whether **at home** *or* **at work,** she was always busy.

The team not only practices
~~Not only practicing~~ at 6 A.M. during the week~~,~~ but ~~the team~~ also scrimmages on Sunday afternoons.

OR

does the team practice   it
Not only ~~practicing~~ at 6 A.M. during the week, but ~~the team~~ also scrimmages on Sunday afternoons.

25e | Parallel structures can help you emphasize key ideas.

Although parallel structures could be used to link all the sentences in a paragraph, readers are likely to grow bored with a pattern that is repeated too many times. The use of parallel structures can contribute to emphasis (see **26g**). But if you try to emphasize every point you make, none of your points will stand out from the rest. Using parallelism is especially effective when you are writing the conclusion of a paragraph or of an essay.

The first of the following examples comes from the conclusion of an article criticizing the amount of attention many Americans give to trying to look young; the second is from the conclusion of an essay on cowboys.

> Advances in **science** and **medicine** have come to this: **the tattooing of permanent eyeliner, the bleaching of teeth, the lasering of sun spots.**
> —ANNA QUINDLEN, "Leg Waxing and Life Everlasting"

> **Because these men work** with **animals,** not **machines, because they live** outside in landscapes of torrential beauty, **because they are confined** to **a place** and **a routine** embellished with awesome variables, **because calves die** in the arms that pulled others into life, **because they go** to the mountains as if on a pilgrimage to find out what makes a herd of elk tick, **their strength** is also a **softness, their toughness,** a rare **delicacy.**
> —GRETEL EHRLICH

Similarly, parallel structures can be effective in the introduction to an essay or as the topic sentence of a paragraph (see **3b–c**).

The following example is the first paragraph in a chapter of a book about how advertising affects women.

> **While men are encouraged to fall in love with their cars, women are more often invited to have a romance,** indeed an erotic experience, with **something** closer to home, **something** that truly does pump the valves of our hearts—**the food we eat.** And the consequences become even more severe as we enter into the territory of **compulsivity** and **addiction.**
> —JEAN KILBOURNE

Contrasting men with women, the author establishes that the chapter will discuss the relationship between women and food.

Departing from the use of parallel structures after "romance," the author builds some suspense before introducing her topic. During this break, however, a degree of parallelism is maintained by the repeated use of "something."

> COMPARE While men are encouraged to fall in love with cars, women are encouraged to fall in love with food.

Although this sentence is more completely parallel than the original, it lacks some of the playfulness of that version. The key point is that you can use parallelism effectively without necessarily making every word or phrase parallel with another one. But a break in parallelism should contribute to the effect you are trying to achieve—rather than undermining that effect by appearing to be a careless slip.

Beyond the Rule

PARALLELISM AND POLITICS

Because parallelism helps make ideas easy to grasp and remember, it is frequently used by politicians when giving speeches. Some parallel structures have been used so often that they have become clichés. But others have helped win elections or define important moments in world history. For examples, visit www.harbrace.com.

Exercise 2

Make the structures in each sentence parallel.

1. Helen was praised by the vice-president, and her assistant admired her.
2. Colleagues found her genial and easy to schedule meetings with.
3. When she hired new employees for her department, she looked for applicants who were intelligent, able to stay focused, and able to speak clearly.

4. At meetings, she was always prepared, participating actively yet politely, and generated innovative responses to department concerns.

5. In her annual report, she wrote that her most important achievements were attracting new clients and revenues were higher.

6. When asked about her leadership style, she said that she preferred collaborating with others to work alone in her office.

7. Although dedicated to her work, Helen also recognized that parenting was important and the necessity of cultivating a life outside of work.

8. She worked hard to save money for the education of her children, for her own music lessons, and investing for her retirement.

9. However, in the coming year, she hoped to reduce the number of weekends she worked in the office and spending more time at home.

10. She would like to plan a piano recital and also have the opportunity to plan a family vacation.

26 Emphasis

You can emphasize ideas by using subordination and coordination (see chapter 24), parallelism (chapter 25), exact word choice (chapter 29), and concise sentence structure (chapter 30).

There are several other ways to add emphasis to your writing. This chapter will help you

- place words where they receive emphasis (26a),
- use periodic sentences (26b),
- arrange ideas in climactic order (26c),
- use active, forceful verbs (26d),
- repeat words effectively (26e),
- invert word order in sentences (26f),
- balance similar grammatical elements (26g), and
- vary sentence length (26h).

26a | Placing words at the beginning or the end of a sentence emphasizes them.

Words at the beginning or the end of a sentence—especially the end—receive emphasis.

~~In today's society, most~~ good *Good* jobs *today* require a college education ~~as part of the background you are supposed to have.~~

Traffic roared
~~I could hear the roar of traffic~~ outside my hotel room in Chicago ~~when I was there.~~

As these examples show, you can often make sentences more concise (see chapter 30) by revising them so that important words fall at the beginning or the end. Sometimes, however, you may need to add a few words to make a sentence emphatic.

Because the semicolon (see chapter 32) is a strong mark of punctuation, most often used to separate independent clauses, the words placed immediately before and after it tend to be emphasized. Either a colon or a dash also often precedes an emphatic ending. (See also 35d–e.)

> By "power" I mean precisely the capacity to do what force always does: coerce assent. —CYNTHIA OZICK

> By 1857, miners had extracted 760 tons of gold from these hills—and left behind more than ten times as much mercury, as well as devastated forests, slopes and streams. —REBECCA SOLNIT

Exercise 1

Find the most important idea in each set of sentences. Then, combine each set into one sentence so that the most important idea is emphasized. Be prepared to explain your changes.

1. Snowboarding is a new sport. It debuted at the Olympics in 1998. The Olympics were held in Nagano, Japan, that year.
2. Snowboarders came from around the world. Some competed in the giant slalom. Others participated in the halfpipe.
3. Snowboarding has increased in popularity. Each year more and more people go snowboarding. It attracted 50 percent more participants in 2000 than it did in 1999.
4. Snowboarding is a fast-growing sport. The number of snowboards sold each year has increased dramatically.
5. However, the inventor of the snowboard is hard to identify. People have been sliding down hills on sleds for a long time.
6. Some sources credit M. M. "Jack" Burchet. Burchet tied his feet to a piece of plywood in 1929.
7. Sherman Poppen is most frequently cited as the inventor of the snowboard. His Snurfer went into production in 1966. (The name is a combination of the words *snow* and *surf*.)
8. Poppen created the Snurfer for his daughter. He bound two skis together. He also fixed a rope at the nose.
9. Snowboarding originated as a sport for kids. It eventually became a competitive sport.

10. The United States snowboarding team won two medals in the 1998 Olympic Games. The team won five medals in the 2002 Olympic Games.

26b | A periodic sentence can contribute to emphasis.

In a **cumulative sentence,** the main idea (the independent clause, or sentence base) comes first; less important ideas or details follow. In a **periodic sentence,** however, the main idea comes last, just before the period.

Cumulative   History has amply proved that large forces can be defeated by smaller forces superior in arms, organization, morale, and spirit.

Periodic   That large forces can be defeated by smaller forces superior in arms, organization, morale, and spirit is one important lesson of history.

Cumulative   Memory operates by way of the senses, by way of detail, which is the stuff of fiction, the fabric of good stories.
—DAVID HUDDLE

Periodic   In a day when movies seem more and more predictable, when novels tend to be plotless, baggy monsters or minimalist exercises in interior emotion, it's no surprise that sports has come to occupy an increasingly prominent place in the communal imagination.
—MICHIKO KAKUTANI

Both types of sentence can be effective. Because cumulative sentences are more common, however, the infrequently encountered periodic sentence is often more emphatic.

26c | When ideas are arranged from least to most important, the last idea receives the most emphasis.

Arranging your ideas in **climactic order**—from least important to most important—encourages your audience to read the entire sentence. If you place your most important idea first, the sentence may seem to trail off. If you place it in the middle, readers may not recognize its full significance.

> They could hear the roar of the artillery, the crash of falling timbers, the shrieks of the wounded.

> Benefiting from much needed rest, moderate medication, and intensive therapy, he eventually recovered.

> The applicants relaxed when they saw that she was charming, friendly, and kind.

Beyond the Rule

PLACING THE LEAST IMPORTANT IDEA LAST

Placing the least important idea last can be effective when you are trying to be humorous, as in the following example:

> Contemporary man, of course, has no such peace of mind. He finds himself in the midst of a crisis of faith. He is what we fashionably call "alienated." He has seen the ravages of war, he has known natural catastrophes, he has been to singles bars. —WOODY ALLEN

For additional examples, visit www.harbrace.com.

Exercise 2

Arrange the ideas in the following sentences in the order you consider to be least to most important.

1. Juan is known for his wisdom, humor, and efficiency.
2. He became a social worker because he wanted to understand people, inspire them, and influence them.
3. In his work, he has found that alcoholism destroys families, ruins health, and leads to erratic behavior.
4. His clients include abused children, single mothers, crack addicts, ex-convicts, and laid-off workers.
5. Unless the city invests more money in social services, several neighborhoods will become dangerous, unattractive, and unlivable.

26d | Active, forceful verbs can add emphasis to sentences.

(1) Active voice is more emphatic than passive voice.

Active voice emphasizes the *doer* of the action by making that actor the subject of the sentence. **Passive voice** emphasizes the *receiver* of the action, minimizes the role of the doer, and results in wordier sentences. (See **22c**.) One sign of a passive construction is the addition of a form of the verb *to be* to the main verb. The preposition *by* before a noun also often indicates the passive voice.

Active	Sylvia won the race.
Passive	The race **was** won **by** Sylvia.
Active	All citizens should insist on adequate medical care.
Passive	Adequate medical care should **be** insisted on **by** all citizens.

Because whoever or whatever is responsible for the action is not the subject, a sentence in the passive voice is often less precise. It is grammatically correct but stylistically undesirable to write *The requirement was waived.* Such a sentence does not tell the reader *who* waived the requirement. Politicians sometimes favor the passive voice because it allows them to avoid responsibility—by using constructions like *a meeting has been called* and *your taxes have been raised.*

The passive voice is appropriate, however, when the person or thing performing the action is unknown or unimportant to the main idea of the sentence.

Passive	My television set was stolen. [The thief is unknown, or there is a reason to withhold the person's identity.]
Passive	We couldn't watch the Super Bowl because our television set had been stolen. [Given the emphasis of the sentence, the identity of the thief is unimportant.]

Unless they have a rhetorical reason for using the passive voice, effective writers prefer the active voice because it is clearer and more emphatic.

Beyond the Rule

THE PASSIVE VOICE AND OBJECTIVITY

When reporting the results of research or scientific experiments, writers often choose to use the passive voice to project an objective tone and to emphasize the work being done rather than whoever is doing it. (See chapter 14.)

> **Passive** The experiment was conducted under carefully controlled conditions over several months.

Keep this in mind when using a grammar checker. Most grammar checkers are programmed to flag sentences in the passive voice, and they usually suggest changing those sentences to the active voice. For examples of the passive voice in scientific writing, visit www.harbrace.com.

(2) Action verbs and forceful linking verbs are more emphatic than forms of *have* or *be*.

When used without an action verb, forms of *have* or *be* rob your writing of energy and forcefulness. In sentences lacking an action verb, the action is often suggested by a noun or a verbal phrase.

Our college ~~is always~~ wins ~~the winner of~~ the conference. [The action suggested by the noun *winner* is conveyed more forcefully by the action verb *win.*]

The meat ~~has a~~ smells rotten ~~smell~~. [The action is more directly expressed by the linking verb *smells* than by the noun *smell.*]

You can ~~be more effective at~~ solve a problem more effectively if you understand ~~by understanding~~ it first. [The verbals (*solving* and *understanding*) contain the action, which main verbs can convey more forcefully.]

E x e r c i s e   3

Make each sentence more emphatic by changing passive voice to active (you may have to invent an actor) or by substituting a more forceful verb for a form of *have* or *be*.

1. Both teachers and parents acknowledged that every student has the right to high-quality education.
2. All the teachers in our district will have the responsibility for more students next year.
3. A petition is being circulated to reduce class size in elementary schools.
4. To cover the costs of more students and smaller classes, a tax increase was recommended by the school board.
5. The outcome of a referendum on school funding will be decided by voters in the fall.

26e | Repeating important words gives them emphasis.

Although effective writers avoid *unnecessary* repetition (see chapter 30), they also understand that *deliberate* repetition emphasizes key words or ideas.

> We **forget** all too soon the things we thought we could never **forget.** We **forget** the loves and betrayals alike, **forget** what we whispered and what we screamed, **forget** who we are.   —JOAN DIDION

In this case, the repetition of *forget* emphasizes how easy it is to forget things, reinforcing the author's point.

When you decide to repeat a word for emphasis, make sure that that word conveys an idea central to your rhetorical purpose. (See 3d(2).)

26f | Inverting word order in a sentence provides emphasis.

At the back of the crowded room sat a newspaper reporter. [COMPARE A newspaper reporter sat at the back of the crowded room.]

Fundamental to life in New York is the subway.
[COMPARE The subway is fundamental to life in New York.]

When you invert standard word order (subject before predicate) for emphasis, you should make sure that the sentence has not become so awkward or artificial that it is difficult to read.

 English sentences are inverted in various ways. Sometimes, the main verb in the form of a participle is placed at the beginning of a sentence. The subject and the auxiliary verb(s) are then inverted.

part *aux* *s*
Lying under the doormat was a house key. [COMPARE A house key was lying under the doormat.]

part *aux* *s*
Carved into the bench were someone's initials. [COMPARE Someone's initials were carved into the bench.]

An adjective may also begin a sentence. In this type of sentence, the subject and the linking verb are inverted.

adj *linking verb* *s*
Crucial to our success was the dedication of our employees.
[COMPARE The dedication of our employees was crucial to our success.]

In other inverted sentences, the auxiliary verb comes before the subject. Sentences beginning with a negative adverb (such as *never, seldom, rarely,* or *barely*) require this type of inversion.

aux *s*
Rarely have we experienced such bad weather!

Both the auxiliary and the main verb, in normal order, are placed before the subject in sentences beginning with prepositional phrases and containing verbs of location.

aux *v* *s*
On top of the chimney was perched a huge owl.

26g | Balanced construction gives a sentence emphasis.

A sentence is balanced when similar grammatical elements—often parallel independent clauses—express contrasting or similar ideas. (See 25a.) The length and rhythm of different parts of a balanced sentence mirror each other, thus emphasizing the contrast or similarity of ideas.

> Gospel is for the mornings; jazz is for the evenings. Gospel inspires you; jazz relaxes you.

26h | A short sentence following one or more long ones gains emphasis.

Readers often grasp the meaning of a sentence more easily if it is short than if it is long. If all your sentences are short, however, no single sentence will stand out, and your writing may seem choppy (see 27a). To give a short sentence emphasis, lead up to it with a long sentence.

> After organizing the kitchen, buying the groceries, slicing the vegetables, mowing the lawn, weeding the garden, hanging the decorations, and setting up the grill, I was ready to have a good time when my guests arrived. Then the phone rang.

Exercise 4

Add emphasis to the following sentences by repeating words, inverting words, using balanced constructions, or using short sentences after long ones. You may have to add some words and delete others.

1. Wilma Rudolph was in leg braces in 1946. In 1960, she was on the Olympic podium.
2. Rudolph tied the world records in the 100-meter race and the 400-meter relay. She broke the record in the 200-meter race. She also won the hearts of fans from around the world.
3. Some sports reporters described Rudolph as a gazelle because of her beautiful stride.

4. Rudolph's Olympic achievement is impressive, but her victory over a crippling disease is even more spectacular.

5. Rudolph was born prematurely, weighing only four and one-half pounds. As a child, she suffered from double pneumonia, scarlet fever, and then polio.

6. Every day, her brothers and sister massaged her legs. In addition, her mother drove her to a hospital for frequent therapy sessions.

7. Her siblings' willingness to help was essential to her recovery, as were her mother's vigilant care and her own determination.

8. After she recovered, her passions became basketball and track.

9. Rudolph set a scoring record in basketball and an Olympic record in track. She also established the standard for future track and field stars.

10. Since Rudolph's time, other female athletes, such as Florence Griffith Joyner and Jackie Joyner-Kersee, have won Olympic medals and broken Olympic records. Many of them have said that Wilma Rudolph was an inspiration.

Variety

Relying too heavily on a few familiar sentence structures can make your writing seem predictable and repetitious. Varying the kinds of sentences you use can make your writing seem lively and distinctive. For example, if most of your sentences follow the familiar pattern subject + predicate, varying your sentence structure may help you keep your readers' attention.

This chapter will help you

- combine choppy sentences (27a),
- vary the beginnings of sentences (27b),
- revise ineffective compound sentences (27c),
- insert words or phrases between a subject and a verb (27d), and
- use questions, commands, or exclamations instead of statements (27e).

Both of the following paragraphs express the same ideas in virtually the same words, both use acceptable sentence patterns, and both are grammatically correct. Variety in the structure and length of the sentences, however, gives one paragraph more rhythm and impact than the other.

Sentences Not Varied

I am going to start with taste. I want you to imagine your first taste of honey or sugar on your tongue. I want you to imagine it as an astonishment. I want you to imagine it as intoxication. I'm thinking of my son's first experience with sugar. It was in the icing on the cake on his first birthday. I have the testimony of Isaac's face to go by. I also know that he was determined to repeat the experience. It was plain that his first encounter with sugar had intoxicated him. He was in ecstasy, in the literal sense of the word. He was beside himself with pleasure. He was no longer here with me. He was in a different time and space. He gazed at me between bites. He was on my lap. His mouth was gaping. I was feeding him ambrosial forkfuls. His expression showed that he was surprised to taste something sweet. He also seemed to want to dedicate his life to eating sweet food. (He has done that basically.) I remember thinking that desire like this is not minor. I wondered if sweetness could be the prototype of *all* desire.

The paragraph becomes much more interesting if sentence variety is employed.

Variety in Sentence Structure and Length

Start with the taste. Imagine a moment when the sensation of honey or sugar on the tongue was an astonishment, a kind of intoxication. The closest I've ever come to recovering such a sense of sweetness was secondhand, though it left a powerful impression on me even so. I'm thinking of my son's first experience with sugar: the icing on the cake at his first birthday. I have only the testimony of Isaac's face to go by (that, and his fierceness to repeat the experience), but it was plain that his first encounter with sugar had intoxicated him—was in fact an ecstasy, in the literal sense of the word. That is, he was beside himself with the pleasure of it, no longer here with me in space and time in quite the same way he had been just a moment before. Between bites Isaac gazed up at me in amazement (he was on my lap, and I was delivering the ambrosial forkfuls to his gaping mouth) as if to exclaim, "Your world contains *this?* From this day forward I shall dedicate my life to it." (Which he basically has done.) And I remember thinking, this is no minor desire, and then wondered: Could it be that sweetness is the prototype of *all* desire?

—**MICHAEL POLLAN,** *The Botany of Desire*

In addition to commands and questions, the second paragraph has simple sentences, complex sentences, and a compound-complex sentence—as well as a sentence fragment (see **18c**). Moreover, the sentences begin in different ways and have different lengths. The content remains the same, but now a paragraph about pleasure *sounds* pleasurable. Repetitious sentence structure made the first version predictable; the revision is surprising.

If you have difficulty distinguishing between various types of sentence structures, review the fundamentals in chapter **16** and in **17b**.

Although a grammar checker will flag long sentences, it cannot determine whether they contribute to variety. But identifying long sentences can allow you to decide if you have used them effectively. See **Using a Grammar Checker** on page 468.

27a │ A series of short, simple sentences sounds choppy.

To avoid the choppiness produced by a series of short sentences, you can lengthen some of them by using subordination or coordination to show how the ideas are related. (See chapter 24.)

Choppy   Minneapolis and St. Paul are called the Twin Cities. The Mississippi River is a boundary between them. They differ in many ways.

Effective   Separated only by the Mississippi River, Minneapolis and St. Paul are called the Twin Cities even though they differ in many ways. [use of subordination to combine sentences]

Choppy   Some people study everything on the menu. Next, they ask about how various dishes are made. Then, they contemplate the possibilities for a few minutes. Finally, they order exactly what they had the last time. The idea is to seem interested in food without taking any risks.

Effective   To seem interested in food without taking any risks, some people study everything on the menu, ask how various dishes are made, contemplate the possibilities, and end up ordering exactly what they had the last time. [use of subordination and coordination to combine sentences]

Beyond the Rule

THE VIRTUE OF BREVITY

Occasionally, a series of brief sentences can be used for special effect. For example, a writer may have a rhetorical reason for conveying a sense of abruptness; thus, what might seem choppy in one situation seems dramatic in another. For examples, visit www.harbrace.com.

Exercise 1

Convert each set of short, simple sentences into a single longer sentence. Use no more than one coordinating conjunction in the revised sentence.

1. It was the bottom of the ninth inning. The score was tied. The bases were loaded. There were two outs.
2. A young player stepped up to the plate. This was his first season. He had hit a home run yesterday. He had struck out his last time at bat.
3. He knew the next pitch could decide the game. He took a practice swing. The pitcher looked him over.
4. The pitch came in high. The batter swung low. He missed this first pitch. He also missed the second pitch.
5. He had two strikes against him. The young player hit the next ball. It soared over the right-field fence.

| 27b | Writing sounds monotonous when too many sentences begin the same way. |

Most writers begin more than half of their sentences with the subject. Although this pattern is common for English sentences, relying on it too heavily can make your writing dull. Experiment with the following alternatives for beginning your sentences.

(1) Begin with an adverb or an adverbial clause.

Immediately, the dentist stopped drilling and asked me how I was doing. [beginning with an adverb]

Although the company offers only two weeks of paid vacation time, it offers other benefits that appeal to employees. [beginning with an adverbial clause]

When you use email to correspond with someone you are dating, you can get the impression that you are more involved than you really are. [beginning with an adverbial clause]

(2) Begin with a prepositional or verbal phrase.

In the auditorium, electricians installed a new lighting system. [beginning with a prepositional phrase]

To win, candidates need to convey a clear message to voters. [beginning with an infinitive phrase]

Looking south from the top of the Empire State Building, we can still imagine where the twin towers of the World Trade Center once stood. [beginning with a participial phrase]

(3) Begin with a connecting word—a coordinating conjunction, a conjunctive adverb, or a transitional phrase.

In each of the following examples, the connecting word shows the relationship between the ideas in the pair of sentences. (See also 3d.)

Many restaurants close within a few years of opening. **But** others, which offer good food at reasonable prices, become well established. [*But* is a coordinating conjunction.]

Difficulty in finding a place to park is one of the factors that prevent people from shopping downtown. **Moreover,** public transportation has become too expensive. [*Moreover* is a conjunctive adverb.]

This legislation will hurt the economy. **In the first place,** it will cost thousands of jobs. [*In the first place* is a transitional phrase.]

(4) Begin with an appositive, an absolute phrase, or an introductory series.

A town of historic interest, Santa Fe also has many art galleries. [beginning with an appositive; see 17a(5)]

His fur bristling, the cat attacked. [beginning with an absolute phrase; see 17a(6)]

Light, water, temperature, minerals—these affect the health of plants. [beginning with an introductory series; see 35e]

E x e r c i s e 2

Rewrite each sentence so that it begins with anything except the subject.

1. John Spilsbury was an engraver and mapmaker from London who made the first jigsaw puzzle in about 1760.

2. He pasted a map onto a piece of wood and used a fine-bladed saw to cut around the borders of the countries.
3. The jigsaw puzzle was first an educational toy and has been a mainstay in households all over the world ever since its invention.
4. The original puzzles were quite expensive because the wooden pieces were cut by hand.
5. Most puzzles are made of cardboard today.

27c Varying the structure of compound sentences is often effective.

Writers who draft a series of short, simple sentences sometimes revise them by using a conjunction such as *and* or *but* to turn two simple sentences into a compound sentence. This technique works well if the two ideas are of equal importance (see 24b(2)). Frequently, however, one idea is less important than another; when this is the case, subordination (see 24a) is a creative way to add variety in sentence structure and retain readers' interest. To revise an ineffective compound sentence, you can use one of the following methods.

(1) Make a compound sentence complex.

| Compound | Seafood is nutritious, and it is low in fat, and it has become available in greater variety. |
| Complex | Seafood, which is nutritious and low in fat, has become available in greater variety. |

(2) Use two or more verbs with the same subject.

| Compound | Marie quickly grabbed a shovel, and then she ran to the edge of the field, and then she put out the fire before it could spread to the trees. |
| Simple | Marie quickly grabbed a shovel, ran to the edge of the field, and put out the fire before it could spread to the trees. |

(3) Use an appositive.

Compound	Matthew Shepard was a college student in Wyoming, and his brutal murder captured national attention.
Simple	The brutal murder of Matthew Shepard, a college student in Wyoming, captured national attention.

(4) Add a prepositional or verbal phrase.

Compound	The snow was thick, and we could not see where we were going.
Simple	In the thick snow, we could not see where we were going.
Compound	The plane pulled away from the gate on time, and then it sat on the runway for two hours.
Simple	After pulling away from the gate on time, the plane sat on the runway for two hours.
Compound	The town is near the interstate, and it attracted commuters, and it grew rapidly.
Simple	The town, located near the interstate, attracted commuters and thus grew rapidly.

Beyond the Rule

REPETITION OF CONJUNCTIONS

Effective writers sometimes add stylistic interest by exaggerating what could be considered a flaw. By using a number of conjunctions in close succession, you can slow the pace and dignify material that might otherwise seem unremarkable. Rhetoricians call this technique *polysyndeton*. For examples, visit www.harbrace.com.

Exercise 3

Revise the following paragraph, using any of the methods for varying compound sentences.

[1]Onions are pungent, they are indispensable, and they are found in kitchens everywhere. [2]China is the leading producer of this vegetable. [3]Libya is the leading consumer, and on average a Libyan eats over sixty-five pounds a year. [4]One hundred billion pounds of onions are produced each year, and they make their way into a variety of foods. [5]Raw onions add zest to salads, but they also add zest to burgers and salsas. [6]Cooked onions give a sweetness to pasta sauces, and they can also be added to soups and curries. [7]The onion is a ubiquitous ingredient, yet its origin remains unknown.

27d | **Separating the subject and the verb in a sentence can introduce variety.**

Although it is usually best to keep the subject next to the verb so that the relationship between them is clear, breaking this pattern on occasion can lead to variety. In the following examples, subjects and verbs are in boldface.

Subject-verb	**Great Falls was** once a summer resort, but **it has become** a crowded suburb.
Varied	**Great Falls,** once a summer resort, **has become** a crowded suburb.
Subject-verb	The **fans applauded** every basket and **cheered** the team to victory.
Varied	The **fans,** applauding every basket, **cheered** the team to victory.

An occasional declarative sentence with inverted word order can also contribute to sentence variety. (See **26f**.)

There but for the grace of God go I.

27e | **When surrounded by declarative statements, a question, an exclamation, or a command adds variety.**

When you have written a long series of declarative statements, you can vary the paragraph by introducing another type of sentence: *interrogative, exclamatory,* or *imperative.* (See page 469.)

(1) Raise a question or two for variety.

> If people could realize that immigrant children are better off, and less scarred, by holding on to their first languages as they learn a second one, then perhaps Americans could accept a more drastic change. What if every English-speaking toddler were to start learning a foreign language at an early age, maybe in kindergarten? What if these children were to learn Spanish, for instance, the language already spoken by millions of American citizens, but also by so many neighbors to the South? —**ARIEL DORFMAN**

You can either answer the question or let readers answer it for themselves, according to your rhetorical situation (see **1b**).

(2) Make an exclamation for variety.

> But at other moments, the classroom is so lifeless or painful or confused—and I so powerless to do anything about it—that my claim to be a teacher seems a transparent sham. Then the enemy is everywhere: in those students from some alien planet, in the subject I thought I knew, and in the personal pathology that keeps me earning my living this way. What a fool I was to imagine that I had mastered this occult art—harder to divine than tea leaves and impossible for mortals to do even passably well! —**PARKER PALMER**

Effective writers make their sentences exciting without always resorting to exclamation points (see **35c**). As a result, the introduction of an exclamatory sentence can contribute to variety.

(3) Include a command for variety.

> Now I stare and stare at people shamelessly. Stare. It's the way to educate your eye. —**WALKER EVANS**

In this case, a one-word imperative sentence provides variety. Because few people enjoy being ordered around, use commands with care.

E x e r c i s e 4

Consider how you could improve sentence variety in one of your recent papers. Identify the kind of sentence you use most frequently. Then, revise three of those sentences by using one of the strategies discussed in this chapter.

Exercise 5

Prepare for a class discussion on the sentence variety in the following paragraph.

[1]It is too much that with all those pedestrian centuries behind us we should, in a few decades, have learned to fly; it is too heady a thought, too proud a boast. [2]Only the dirt on a mechanic's hands, the straining vise, the splintered bolt of steel underfoot on the hangar floor—only these and such anxiety as the face of a Jock Cameron can hold for a pilot and his plane before a flight, serve to remind us that, not unlike the heather, we too are earth-bound. [3]We fly, but we have not "conquered" the air. [4]Nature presides in all her dignity, permitting us the study and the use of such of her forces as we may understand. [5]It is when we presume to intimacy, having been granted only tolerance, that the harsh stick falls across our impudent knuckles and we rub the pain, staring upward, startled by our ignorance.

—BERYL MARKHAM, *West with the Night*

Diction

Good Usage

Using the right words at the right time can make the difference between having your ideas taken seriously and seeing them brushed aside. In academic or professional writing, it is important for you to sound well informed and respectful. In conversation with friends, it is just as important to sound casual; otherwise, your friends may think that you are cold or snobbish. Whatever the occasion, choosing the right words will help you connect with your audience. Effective writers avoid sounding too casual or too stuffy, and they usually avoid slang and jargon (see **28c**) when writing for a diverse audience (**1e(2)**). But for an academic or professional audience, they use a specialized vocabulary, thus enhancing their credibility (see **9a**). When you edit your writing, be sure that your words can be understood by everyone in your audience.

This chapter will help you

- understand how word choice is related to the rhetorical situation (**28a**),
- write in a clear, straightforward style (**28b**),
- choose words that are appropriate for the audience, the purpose, and the context (**28c**),
- use inclusive language (**28d**), and
- realize the benefits of dictionaries (**28e**) and thesauri (**28f**).

28a | **Language varies according to audience, purpose, and context.**

The words you use vary from situation to situation. How you talk to a loan officer differs from how you talk to your best friend. A discussion with a loan officer would probably be relatively formal, while a conversation with a friend would be less so. Understanding such differences in tone and making word choices that reflect them are especially important in writing because readers cannot see your body language, hear the inflections of your voice, or interrupt to say that they are having trouble following you. Instead, readers respond to the words on the page or the screen. You can help them understand your ideas by choosing words that they know (or that you can explain to them) and that also help you fulfill your purpose in a particular context.

When drafting (see chapter 2), use words that come immediately to mind. Sometimes, these words will be good choices. When revising (see chapter 3), you can identify any that need to be replaced. Remembering your rhetorical situation (see 1b and 1e) will help you use the right word at the right time.

28b | A clear, straightforward style is easy to read.

Although different styles are appropriate for different situations—depending, for example, on purpose, audience, and context (see 1b and 1e)—you should usually keep your writing simple and straightforward. An ornate and wordy style takes more time to read and could make you seem stuffy or pretentious.

Ornate   The majority believes that the approbation of society derives primarily from the diligent pursuit of allocated tasks.

Simple   Most people believe that success results from hard work.

A simple writing style does not indicate that you are a simplistic thinker. Instead, it shows that you can write clearly and do not want to waste your readers' time. Active, forceful verbs can help you to create this style (see 26d). Using words that are precise (see 29a) and sentences that are concise (chapter 30) will also help you write simply and directly.

Beyond the Rule

THE PLAIN STYLE

Western rhetoricians have discussed the advantages of a plain, straightforward style for thousands of years, while also recognizing the

(Continued on page 652)

(Continued from page 651)

advantages of an ornate style. The plain style became dominant in the twentieth century, influenced by the value people in the modern era placed on efficiency. In the future, new standards for usage will emerge as style preferences evolve. For more information about the history of style, visit www.harbrace.com.

Exercise 1

Revise the following sentences for an audience that prefers a simple, straightforward style.

1. Expert delineation of character in a job interview is a task that is not always possible to achieve.

2. In an employment situation, social pleasantries may contribute to the successful functioning of job tasks, but such interactions should not distract attention from the need to complete all assignments in a timely manner.

3. Commitment to an ongoing and carefully programmed schedule of physical self-management can be a significant resource for stress reduction in the workplace.

4. Employees troubled by dysfunctions in interpersonal relationships can benefit from monthly workshops conducted by an independent expert therapeutic counselor contracted as a consultant by the human resources department.

5. Individuals released from their obligation to fulfill their professional responsibilities within this corporate sector can navigate their search for another employment opportunity by surveying on a regular basis the listings for unfilled staffing needs published in various media.

28c | Making appropriate word choices establishes common ground with your readers.

Unless you are writing for a specialized audience and have good reason to believe that this audience would welcome slang (and other kinds of informal language) or jargon, the following advice can help you achieve good usage.

(1) Slang is effective in only a few rhetorical situations.

Slang is usually defined as words used primarily by people in a particular age group, locality, or profession. Slang, in fact, covers a wide range of words that are variously considered casual, facetious, or fashionable—any of which can either appeal to readers or alienate them. For example, using *shrink* for "psychiatrist" may convey disrespect for a field of medicine. Although such words are often used in private conversation, they are not appropriate for academic or professional writing (see chapters 12–15). A clear sense of your audience is essential if you want to use slang effectively. If a slang word or expression is newly coined, your audience may not understand what you mean. If it has been around for a long time, your use of it can make you seem out of touch with popular culture. Frequent use of *whatever, awesome,* or *dude,* for example, can make you sound as if you are still living in the twentieth century.

(2) Conversational (or colloquial) words are usually too informal for academic and professional writing.

Words labeled *colloquial* in a dictionary (see 28e) are fine for casual conversation and can be used by writers when composing dialogue or a personal essay on a light topic. Such words may sometimes be used for special effect in academic writing, but you should usually replace them with more appropriate words. For example, conversational terms such as *dumb, belly button,* and *kid* can be replaced by *ignorant, navel,* and *tease.*

Contractions (such as *you'll* for "you will" and *she's* for "she is") reflect the sound of conversation and can be useful for engaging a specific audience in a particular context (see 33b). Some readers find them too informal for academic or professional writing.

(3) Regionalisms can be fun to read.

Regionalisms—such as *tank* for "pond" and *sweeper* for "vacuum cleaner"—can make writing lively and distinctive, but they are effective only when the audience can understand them in a specific context. Moreover, many readers consider regionalisms too informal for use in academic and professional writing (see chapters **12–15**). Consider your rhetorical situation (see **1b** and **1e**) before using regionalisms.

(4) Technical words are essential when writing for specialists who understand them.

When writing for a diverse audience (see **1e(2)**), an effective writer will not refer to the need for bifocals as *presbyopia*. However, technical language is appropriate when the audience can understand it (as when one physician writes to another) or when the audience needs to learn the terms in question.

Jargon is technical language tailored specifically for a particular occupation. Jargon can be an efficient shortcut for conveying specialized concepts, but you should use it only when you can be sure that you and your readers share an understanding of the terms. *Splash,* for example, does not always refer to water or an effect (as in *making a splash*); the word also signifies a computer screen that can appear after you click on a Web site but before you view its opening page. Keep in mind that spell checkers cannot recognize jargon.

Beyond the Rule

FROM JARGON TO ACCEPTABILITY

Terms that originate as jargon sometimes enter mainstream usage because nonspecialists begin to use them. As computer use has grown, for example, technical terms such as *download* and *mouse* have become commonly understood. For additional examples of widely adopted jargon, visit www.harbrace.com.

for Assessing Usage within a Rhetorical Situation

- Do your words convey the meaning you intend?
- Can your audience understand the words you have used?
- Do you explain any words your audience might not understand?
- Have you used any words that could irritate or offend members of your audience?
- Do any of your words make you sound too casual or too formal?
- Do your words help you to fulfill your rhetorical purpose?
- Are your words appropriate for the context in which you are writing?
- Are your words appropriate for the context in which they will be read?

28d | Using inclusive (nonprejudiced) language increases your credibility.

By making word choices that are inclusive rather than exclusive, you invite readers into your writing. Not only does prejudiced or derogatory language have no place in academic or professional writing, using it undermines your authority as a writer. Even if you are writing for one person you think you know well, do not assume that you know everything about that person. A close colleague at work might have a gay uncle, for example, or his sister might be married to someone of a different race or religion. Do not try to justify demeaning language on the grounds that you meant it as a joke. Take responsibility for the words you use.

(1) Nonsexist language respects both men and women.

Effective writers show equal respect for men and women. For example, they avoid using *man* to refer to people in general because they feel that the word excludes women.

Man's achievements in science are impressive.

Sexist language has a variety of sources, such as contempt for the opposite sex and the unthinking repetition of words used by others. Words that characterize someone in terms of sexual attraction (such as *babe, hunk,* and *hottie*) can be demeaning, even if they could be taken as compliments in some contexts.

Stereotyping can also lead to sexist language. Women, like men, can be *firefighters* or *police officers*—terms that are increasingly used as gender-neutral replacements for *firemen* and *policemen.* Even though some sexist usage remains embedded in the English language, it is gradually being reduced, as illustrated by the widespread avoidance of the once common practice of using *he* or *mankind* to refer to both men and women.

A grammar checker can find sexist words ending in *-ess (authoress)* or *-man (policeman)* and almost always flags *mankind.* Unfortunately, it also erroneously identifies as sexist many appropriate uses of the words *female, woman,* and *girl,* but not similar uses of *male, man,* and *boy.*

Being alert for sexist language and knowing how to revise it will help you gain acceptance from your audience, whatever its demographics. As the following box shows, revising to remove sexist language is relatively straightforward.

TIPS FOR AVOIDING SEXIST LANGUAGE

When you review your drafts, revise the following:

■ **Generic *he:*** A doctor should listen to *his* patients.

A doctor should listen to **his or her** patients. [use of the appropriate form of *he or she*]

Doctors should listen to **their** patients. [use of plural forms]

By listening to patients, **doctors gain information they can use in their diagnoses.** [elimination of the pronoun by revising the sentence]

■ **Occupational stereotype:** Glenda, a female engineer at Howard Aviation, won the best-employee award.

Glenda, an engineer at Howard Aviation, won the best-employee award. [removal of the unnecessary gender reference]

- **Terms such as man and mankind or those with -ess or -man endings:** Labor laws benefit the common *man*. *Mankind* benefits from philanthropy. The *stewardess* brought me some orange juice.

  Labor laws benefit **working people.** [replacement of the stereotypical term with a neutral term]

  Everyone benefits from philanthropy. [use of an indefinite pronoun]

  The **flight attendant** brought me some orange juice. [use of gender-neutral language]

- **Stereotypical gender roles:** I was told that the university offers free tuition to faculty *wives*.

  I was told that the university offers free tuition to faculty **spouses.** [replacement of the stereotypical term with a neutral term]

- **Inconsistent use of titles:** *Mr. Holmes* and his *wife*, Mary, took a long trip to China.

  Mr. and Mrs. [or Ms.] Holmes took a long trip to China. [consistent use of titles]

  OR **Peter and Mary Holmes** took a long trip to China. [removal of titles]

  OR **Peter Holmes** and **Mary Wolfe** took a long trip to China. [use of full names]

- **Unstated gender assumption:** Have your *mother* make your costume for the school pageant.

  Have your **parents** provide you with a costume for the school pageant. [replacement of the stereotypical term with a neutral term]

 Languages vary in the ways they indicate gender, so translations may result in unintentionally sexist usage. For example, the German word *Mann* means both "man" and "husband." However, in English, *man and wife* is considered sexist because the word *wife* indicates a woman's relationship to a man as well as her gender, whereas the word *man*

(Continued on page 658)

(Continued from page 657)

indicates a person's gender only. The unbiased version of this expression is *husband and wife*. If you are unsure of the possible bias in a gender-marked word, ask a teacher, classmate, or colleague for advice.

E x e r c i s e 2

Make the following sentences inclusive by eliminating sexist language.

1. The ladies took a tour of the city while the executive managers met for a business conference.
2. The old boys run the city's government.
3. Mothers should read to their small children.
4. Some fans admired the star because he was a hunk; others praised him for his environmental activism.
5. For six years, he worked as a mailman in a small town.

(2) Nonracist language promotes social equity.

Rarely is it necessary to identify anyone's race or ethnicity in academic or professional writing. However, you may need to use appropriate racial or ethnic terms if you are writing a demographic report, an argument concerning existing racial inequities, or an expository essay on the history of a particular ethnic group. Because language changes, the terms used to refer to various racial and ethnic groups also change. Although Americans of African descent are no longer referred to as *colored* or *Negro*, those terms persist in the names of important organizations such as the National Association for the Advancement of Colored People and the United Negro College Fund. And whether to refer to *African Americans* or *Blacks* is now sometimes determined by the generation to which your audience belongs. People of Spanish-speaking descent in different parts of the United States have preferences concerning the usage of *Latino/Latina, Chicano/Chicana, Hispanic, Latin American, Mexican American,* or *Puerto Rican*. Many descendants of indigenous peoples prefer *Native American* to *American Indian,* and *Asian American* has supplanted *Oriental.* Use the term the group or individual prefers on those infrequent occasions when you need to identify race or ethnicity.

Because of the sensitivity of this usage issue, many writers now use *person(s) of color* to describe individuals who are other than white. Writers of any race or color should also be mindful that *white* is widely considered a race even if different cultures have had different criteria for deciding who is "white." Racist terms for white people are no more acceptable than racist terms for people of any other color. Remember that race is a complex concept, that increasing numbers of people cannot be identified by a single race, and that mentioning race in a piece of writing is often unnecessary.

(3) Respectful writers do not use homophobic language.

Terms such as *faggot* or *dyke* should never be used to describe men or women who are gay, lesbian, bisexual, or transgendered—or to demean heterosexuals who appear or act as though they may be other than heterosexual. Like sexist and racist language, homophobic language is inappropriate for academic or professional writing.

Words associated with sexual orientation often function better as adjectives than as nouns. Describing a man as *a gay,* for example, implies that he is defined by his sexuality. When used as one among other identifying adjectives, however, *gay* (or *lesbian, bisexual,* or *transgendered*) functions simply as one of the words describing someone: *a conservative, gay, white attorney.*

Beyond the Rule

INCLUSIVE LANGUAGE

Members of a social minority may choose to reclaim as their own words that have been used against them. For more information about prejudicial language and the power people have to change usage that hurts them, visit www.harbrace.com.

(4) Respectful writers are sensitive to matters of ability, age, class, religion, and occupation.

Although referring to persons with physical disabilities as *handicapped* may be insensitive, being overly cautious about references to disabilities can be demeaning. Someone who is blind might object to being called *visually impaired* because the phrase is imprecise. Many older people dislike being called *senior citizens* (imagine how most young people would resent being called *junior citizens*). Labels such as *preppie* and *redneck* are clearly class-based references that reduce individuals to stereotypes.

A secular calendar that marks Christmas and Easter with no mention of Yom Kippur or Ramadan is exclusionary. Although some attempts to enhance the prestige of manual labor (such as making up a term like *deforestation technician* to describe a member of a logging team) could be considered patronizing, using the terms that are preferred by the people who perform the labor shows sensitivity. In all instances, avoid the stereotyping that careless use of language can create.

Exercise 3

Find a short piece of writing that includes words or phrases that bother you because they are unclear, unnecessarily ornate, or potentially hurtful. Share your choice with a group of peers or colleagues, explaining what you dislike and why.

28e | Dictionaries can help you make good writing decisions.

A good dictionary is an indispensable tool for writers. Desk dictionaries such as *The American Heritage Dictionary* and *Merriam-Webster's Collegiate Dictionary* do much more than provide the correct spellings of words; they also give meanings, parts of speech, plural forms, and verb tenses, as well as information about pronunciation and derivation (how a word originated and how its meaning evolved). In addition, a reliable dictionary also includes labels that can help you decide whether words are appropriate for the purpose, audience, and context of your writing. Words labeled **dialect, slang, colloquial, nonstandard,** or **unconventional**, as well as those labeled **archaic** or **obsolete** (meaning that they are no longer in common use), are usually inappropriate for college and professional writing. If a word has no label, you can safely assume that it can be used in writing for school or work. But whether the word is appropriate depends on the precise meaning a writer wants to convey (see **29a**).

Because language is constantly changing, it is important to choose a dictionary with a recent copyright date. Many dictionaries are available—in print, online, or on CD-ROM. Pocket dictionaries, which are useful for checking spellings and definitions, omit important information on usage and derivation. The dictionaries incorporated into most word-processing programs are equivalent to pocket dictionaries and may be out of date.

(1) Words and expressions labeled *nonstandard* or *colloquial* should not be used in college and professional writing, except possibly in direct quotations.

For example, *ain't* should not be used for *am not,* nor should *irregardless* be used for *regardless.* Usage such as this might be appropriate, however, if you are quoting someone you interviewed (see **8e**) or a character from a piece of literature (**13f**).

(2) Using words labeled *archaic* can make you sound silly or pretentious.

All dictionaries list (and give meanings for) words that have long since passed out of general use. Such words as *rathe* ("early") and *yestreen* ("last evening") are still found in dictionaries because they occur in literature from the past and so must be defined for the modern reader; these words are no longer used, however. A number of obsolete or archaic words—such as *worser* (for *worse*) or *holp* (for *helped*)—are still in use but are considered nonstandard.

(3) When you want a thorough understanding of a word, you can benefit from consulting an unabridged or special dictionary.

Unabridged Dictionaries

The Oxford English Dictionary. 2nd ed. 20 vols. 1989– . CD-ROM. 1994.

Webster's Third New International Dictionary of the English Language. 1995.

Special Dictionaries

Cowie, Anthony Paul, and Ronald Mackin. *Oxford Dictionary of Current Idiomatic English.* Vols. 1–2. 1975, 1984.

Follett, Wilson. *Modern American Usage: A Guide.* 1998.

Morris, William, and Mary Morris. *Harper Dictionary of Contemporary Usage.* 2nd ed. 1985, 1992.

Partridge, Eric, and Paul Beale. *Dictionary of Catch Phrases.* 1992.

Dictionary of American Slang, 3rd ed. 1994.

Merriam-Webster's Dictionary of English Usage. 1994.

 The following dictionaries are recommended for nonnative speakers of English.

Collins Cobuild Dictionary. 1995

Longman Dictionary of Contemporary English. 1996. (*Longman Dictionary of American English,* 1997, is the American abridgment.)

Longman Dictionary of English Language and Culture. 2000.

The Newbury House Dictionary of American English. 4th ed. 2004.

Oxford Advanced Learner's Dictionary of Current English. 1998. (*Oxford ESL Dictionary,* 1994, is the American edition.)

Two excellent resources for ESL students are the following:

Longman Language Activator. 1993. (This book supplies definitions, usage, and sample sentences: It is a cross between a dictionary and a thesaurus.)

Swan, Michael. *Practical English Usage.* 1995. (This is a practical reference guide to problems encountered by those who speak English as a second language.)

(4) Reading the introductory material and noting any special abbreviations will help you understand the information a dictionary provides.

Figure 28.1 shows sample entries from the tenth edition of *Merriam-Webster's Collegiate Dictionary*. The type of information these entries provide can be found in almost all desk dictionaries, although sometimes in a different order. Notice that *answer* is listed twice—first as a noun, then as a verb.

(a) Spelling, syllabication, and pronunciation
Dictionaries describe both written and spoken language. You can check spelling and word division (syllabication), as well as pronunciation of an unfamiliar word. A key to sound symbols appears at the bottom of each page and also in the introduction. Alternative pronunciations usually represent regional differences.

(b) Parts of speech and inflected forms
Dictionaries identify the possible functions of words in sentences—for instance, *n* for "noun" or *vi* for "intransitive verb." Meanings will vary depending on the part of speech identified. Dictionaries may also identify inflected forms, especially irregular ones: *fly, flew, flown, flying, flies* or *good, better, best.*

(c) Word origin, or etymology
The origin of a word—also called its *derivation* or *etymology*—can be useful in understanding its meaning. It can also lead to an appreciation of the many cultures that have influenced, and continue to influence, the English language.

(d) Date of first occurrence
A date in parentheses (such as *bef. 12c* for "before the twelfth century" in the examples in figure 28.1) is the first known occurrence of the word in written English.

(e) Definition(s)
The order of definitions varies from dictionary to dictionary. In figure 28.1, the oldest meaning is listed first. Often, however, meanings are ordered according to how common they are.

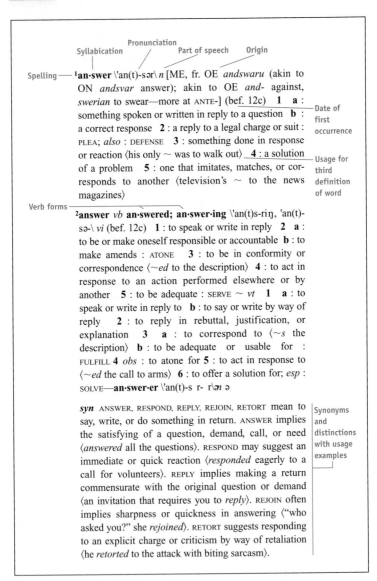

Figure 28.1. Example of dictionary entries.

(f) Usage

Most dictionaries give guidance on usage and include quotations showing how the word has been used in several contexts.

(g) Synonyms

Dictionaries always list synonyms and sometimes provide detailed explanations of subtle differences in meaning. When such lists of synonyms are used in conjunction with a thesaurus, they are extremely helpful. Notice in figure 28.1 that the second entry for *answer* lists four one-word synonyms (following *syn*) and provides information about their meanings and usage.

Exercise 4

Study the definitions for the pairs of words in parentheses. Then, choose the word you think best completes each sentence. Be prepared to explain your answers.

1. Sixteen prisoners on death row were granted (mercy/clemency).
2. The outcome of the election (excited/provoked) a riot.
3. The young couple was (covetous/greedy) of their neighbors' estate.
4. While she was traveling in Muslim countries, she wore (modest/chaste) clothing.
5. The president of the university (authorized/confirmed) the rumor that tuition would be increasing next year.

28f | A thesaurus provides alternatives for frequently used words.

Unlike a dictionary, which explains what a word means and how it evolved, a thesaurus provides only a list of words that serve as possible **synonyms** for each term it includes. A thesaurus can be useful, especially when you want to jog your memory about a word you know but cannot recall. A thesaurus usually includes every possible synonym, so you need to choose the one that is most appropriate for your audience, purpose, and context. You may use a word incorrectly if you simply pick it from a list in a thesaurus. If you find an unfamiliar word that intrigues you, look it up in a dictionary before you use it.

Several thesauri are available in print. Among them are *Roget's International Thesaurus* (1999) and *Merriam-Webster's Collegiate Thesaurus* (1995). Most word-processing programs include a thesaurus, and other thesauri are available online. Whether you consult a print or electronic thesaurus, remember that you must take responsibility for the language you use. Learning new words is beneficial. Using them accurately (see chapter 29) is essential.

E x e r c i s e 5

Review two or three of your recent papers, and look for a word you used frequently. Look up that word in a thesaurus, and then check each possible synonym in a dictionary. Use one of these synonyms appropriately in a sentence, and explain your usage. If you are unable to find an adequate synonym, explain why the words listed in the thesaurus are inappropriate.

Exactness

Make words work for you. By choosing the right word and putting it in the right place, you can communicate exactly what you mean and make your writing memorable. When drafting (see chapter 2), choose words that express your ideas and feelings. Then, when revising (see chapter 3), make those words exact, fresh, and natural. Use the words you already know effectively, but add to your vocabulary regularly so that you will be able to pick the exact word that suits your purpose, audience, and context.

This chapter will help you

- master the denotations and connotations of words (**29a**),
- use fresh, clear expressions (**29b**),
- understand how to use idioms (**29c**),
- use the first- and second-person pronouns appropriately (**29d**), and
- compose clear definitions (**29e**).

29a | Accurate and precise word choice conveys meaning clearly.

(1) Denotations establish precision.

The **denotation** of a word refers to what it names, not what it suggests. In other words, denotations are definitions of words, such as those that appear in dictionaries (see **28e**). For example, the noun *beach* denotes a sandy or pebbly shore. Select words that convey your point exactly.

The Alaskan wilderness is ~~really great~~. astonishingly beautiful

[Because *great* can mean "extremely large" as well as "outstanding" or "powerful," its use in this sentence is imprecise.]

The speaker _^*inferred* that the team attracted many new fans this year.
> *implied*

[*Infer* means "to draw a conclusion from evidence," as in *From the figures before me, I* **inferred** *that the team attracted many new fans this year. Imply* means "to suggest," so *implied* is the exact word for the sentence as drafted.]

(2) Connotations enrich meaning.

The **connotation** of a word is what the word suggests or implies. *Beach,* for instance, may connote natural beauty, surf, shells, swimming, tanning, sunburn, or crowds. The context affects the connotations a word evokes. In a treatise on shoreline management, *beach* has scientific and geographic connotations; in a fashion magazine, it evokes images of bathing suits. Most readers carry with them a wealth of personal associations that can influence how they respond to the words on a page. The challenge for writers is to choose the words that are most likely to evoke the appropriate connotations from their readers in the given context.

One of the reasons I am recommending Mr. Krueger for this job is that

he is so _^~~relentless.~~ [*Relentless* has negative connotations that are inappro-
> *persistent*

priate for a recommendation.]

I love the _^~~odor~~ of freshly baked bread. [Many odors are unpleasant;
> *aroma*

aroma sounds more positive, especially in association with food.]

He gets into trouble sometimes because he is so _^~~innocent.~~ [*Innocent* sug-
> *naive*

gests virtue; *naive* suggests a lack of judgment.]

Your ability to recognize connotations will improve as your vocabulary increases. When you learn a new word that seems to mean exactly what another word means, study the context in which each word is used. Then, to help you remember the new word, create a phrase or a sentence in which the word is used in an appropriate context. If you are confused about the connotations of specific words, consult an ESL dictionary or ask a native speaker for help.

(3) Specific, concrete words provide readers with helpful detail.

A **general word** is all-inclusive, indefinite, and sweeping in scope. A **specific word** is precise, definite, and limited in scope.

General	Specific	More Specific/Concrete
food	fast food	cheeseburger
entertainment	film	*Gladiator*
place	city	Atlanta

An **abstract word** refers to a concept or idea, a quality or trait, or anything else that cannot be touched, heard, or seen. A **concrete word** signifies a particular object, a specific action, or anything that can be touched, heard, or seen.

Abstract democracy, evil, strength, charity

Concrete mosquito, hammer, plastic, fog

Some writers use too many abstract or general words, making their writing vague and lifeless. As you select words to fit your context, you should be as specific and concrete as you can. For example, instead of the word *bad,* consider using a more precise adjective.

bad neighbors: rowdy, snobby, nosy, fussy, sloppy, dangerous

bad meat: tough, tainted, overcooked, undercooked, contaminated

bad wood: rotten, warped, scorched, knotty, termite-ridden

To test whether or not a word is specific, you can ask one or more of these questions about what you want to say: *Exactly who? Exactly what? Exactly when? Exactly where? Exactly how?* In the following examples, notice what a difference specific, concrete words can make in expressing an idea and how adding details can expand or develop it.

Vague She has kept no reminders of performing in her youth.

Specific She has kept no sequined costume, no photographs, no fliers or posters from that part of her youth.   —LOUISE ERDRICH

Vague He realized that he was running through the cold night.

Specific He found himself hurrying over creaking snow through the blackness of a winter night.   —LOREN EISELEY

Vague	When I was younger, I could eat a lot of food without getting fat.
Specific	When I worked on farms as a boy, loading hay bales onto wagons and forking silage to cows, shoveling manure out of horse barns, digging postholes and pulling barbed wire, I could eat the pork chops and half-dozen eggs my neighbors fed me for breakfast, eat corn bread and sugar in a quart of milk for dessert at lunch, eat ham steaks and mashed potatoes and three kinds of pie for supper, eat a bowl of hand-cranked ice cream topped with maple syrup at bedtime, and stay skinny as a junkyard dog.

—SCOTT RUSSELL SANDERS

As these examples show, sentences with specific details are often longer than sentences without them. But the need to be specific does not necessarily conflict with the need to be concise. (See chapter **30**.) Simply substituting one word for another can often make it far easier for your readers to see, hear, taste, or smell what you are hoping to convey.

> fell out of the canoe   land a muskie
> I ~~had an accident~~ while trying to ~~catch a fish~~.

Writers use general and abstract words successfully when such words are vital to communicating ideas, as in the following sentence about what happens when a plague comes to an end.

> We expect a catharsis, but we merely find a transition; we long for euphoria, but we discover only relief, tinged with, in some cases, regret and depression. —ANDREW SULLIVAN

Abstract words are exact when they are used to express abstractions—such as *spirit, compassion, sacrifice, endurance, freedom,* and *terrorism.* When you use abstract words, make sure you do so deliberately and with good reason.

(4) Figurative language can contribute to exactness.

Commonly found in nonfiction prose as well as in fiction, poetry, and drama, figurative language involves using words in an imaginative rather than a literal sense. Similes and metaphors are the chief **figures of speech.** A **simile** is the comparison of dissimilar things using *like* or *as.* A **metaphor** is an implied comparison of dissimilar things without *like* or *as.*

Similes

He was **like a piece of rare and delicate china which was always being saved from breaking and finally fell.** —ALICE WALKER

She sat **like a great icon** in the back of the classroom, tranquil, guarded, sealed up, watchful. —REGINALD MCKNIGHT

Metaphors

His **money was a sharp pair of scissors** that snipped rapidly through tangles of red tape. —HISAYE YAMAMOTO

The injured **bird was a broken handled flag** waving in the grass.
—TRACY YOUNGBLOM

Single words can be used metaphorically.

These roses must be **planted** in good soil. [literal]

Keep your life **planted** wherever you can put down the most roots. [metaphorical]

Similes and metaphors are especially valuable when they are concrete and describe or evoke essential relationships that cannot otherwise be communicated. Similes and metaphors can also be extended throughout a paragraph of comparison, but be careful not to mix them. (See 23c.)

E x e r c i s e   1

Study the paragraph below and prepare to discuss in class your response to the author's choice of words—his use of both exact and figurative language to communicate his ideas.

[1]A single knoll rises out of the plain of Oklahoma, north and west of the Wichita range. [2]For my people, the Kiowas, it is an old landmark, and they gave it the name Rainy Mountain. [3]The hardest weather is there. [4]Winter brings blizzards, hot tornadic winds arise in the spring, and in summer the prairie is an anvil's edge. [5]The grass turns brittle and brown, and it cracks beneath your feet. [6]There are green belts along the rivers and creeks, linear groves of hickory and pecan, willow and witch hazel. [7]At a distance in July or August the steaming foliage seems almost to writhe in fire. [8]Great green and yellow grasshoppers are everywhere in the tall grass, popping up like corn to sting the flesh, and tortoises crawl about on the red earth, going nowhere in plenty of time.
—N. SCOTT MOMADAY, "The Way to Rainy Mountain"

Exercise 2

Choose five of the items below, and use them as the bases for five original sentences containing figurative language, exact denotations, and appropriate connotations.

1. the look of someone's hair
2. a hot summer day
3. studying for an exam
4. your favorite food
5. buying a car
6. an empty street
7. college athletes
8. a heavy rain
9. a traffic jam
10. the way someone talks

29b | **Fresh expressions can capture the attention of readers.**

Such expressions as *bite the dust, breath of fresh air,* and *smooth as silk* were
once striking and effective. Excessive use, however, has drained them of
their original force and made them **clichés.** Faddish or trendy expressions such as *to put a spin on something* and *to think outside the box* have
also lost their vitality because they are overused. Many political slogans
and the catchy phrases used in advertisements have also become hackneyed. Some **euphemisms** (pleasant-sounding substitutions for more
explicit but possibly offensive words—for example, *correctional facility*
for *jail* or *pre-owned* for *used*) are not only trite but wordy or awkward.

Clichés are so much a part of the language, especially the spoken language, that nearly every writer uses them from time to time. But effective writers often give a fresh twist to an old saying.

> I seek a narrative, a fiction, to order days like the one I spent several
> years ago, on a gray June day in Chicago, when I took a roller-coaster
> ride on the bell curve of my experience.   —GAYLE PEMBERTON

> [Notice how much more effective this expression is than frequent
> references elsewhere to "being on an emotional roller coaster."]

Variations on familiar expressions from literature, many of which have become part of everyday language, can often be used effectively in your writing.

Now is the summer of my great content. —KATHERINE LANPHER

[This statement is a variation on Shakespeare's "Now is the winter of our discontent. . . ."]

Good writers, however, do not rely too heavily on the words of others; they choose their own words to communicate their ideas.

Beyond the Rule

CLICHÉS

Some scholars have defended clichés on the grounds that they convey widely accepted ideas in a direct way and can thus help writers to communicate effectively with certain readers in specific rhetorical situations. For information about this position, visit www.harbrace.com.

Exercise 3

From the following list of trite expressions, select five that you often use or hear and replace them with carefully chosen words or phrases. Then, use the replacements in sentences.

EXAMPLES

beyond the shadow of a doubt   *undoubtedly*
slept like a log   *slept deeply*

1. a crying shame
2. after all is said and done
3. at the crack of dawn
4. bored to tears/death
5. in the last analysis
6. avoid like the plague
7. beat around the bush
8. the powers that be
9. in this day and age
10. the bottom line

29c | Exact word choice requires an understanding of idioms.

An **idiom** is an expression whose meaning is peculiar to a community or class or differs from the individual meanings of its word parts. Most academic and professional writing assignments call for the use of idiomatic Standardized English, not unidiomatic approximations. *She talked down to him* is idiomatic. *She talked up to him* is not. Occasionally, the idiomatic use of prepositions can be difficult. If you do not know which preposition to use with a given word, check the dictionary. For instance, *agree* may be followed by *about, on, to,* or *with.* The choice depends on the context. Writers sometimes have trouble with the idioms in the following list.

MASTERING IDIOMS

Instead of	Use
abide **with**	abide **by** the decision
according **with**	according **to** the source
bored **of**	bored **by** it
comply **to**	comply **with** rules
conform **of/on**	conform **to/with** standards
differ **to**	differ **with** them
in accordance **to**	in accordance **with** policy
independent **to**	independent **of** his family
happened **on**	happened **by** accident
plan **on**	plan **to** go
superior **than**	superior **to** others
type **of a**	type **of** business

Many idioms—such as *all the same, to mean well,* and *to pay attention to*—cannot be understood from the individual meanings of their words. Others—such as *turning something over in one's mind*—are metaphorical. Such expressions cannot be meaningfully translated word for word into another language. Used every day, they are an important part of the English language. As you encounter idioms that are new to you, master their meanings just as you do for words you are adding to your vocabulary.

Grammar checkers can find some unidiomatic expressions but will not find all of them. Further, although a grammar checker will not flag a nonsense sentence such as *These books must be broiled in the hope,* it will flag *Is a squirrel in the tree* and point out "*Is* usually begins a question." The problem with this sentence, however, may not be an omitted question mark but rather an omitted expletive such as *there.* You must decide for yourself when and how to correct an unidiomatic expression.

When learning how to use idioms, study how writers use them. The context in which idioms appear can often help you understand their meaning. For example, if you read *I never eat broccoli because I can't stand it,* you would probably understand that *not to be able to stand something* means "to dislike something intensely." As you learn new idioms from your reading, make a list of them, and then use them in your writing. If you are confused about the meaning of a particular idiom, check a dictionary of idioms (see page 662.)

Exercise 4

Write sentences using each of the following idioms correctly. Use your dictionary when necessary.

1. hang up, hang out
2. differ from, differ with
3. wait on, wait for
4. get even with, get out of hand
5. on the go, on the spot

29d | **The use of first- and second-person pronouns can help writers be exact.**

Using *I* is appropriate when you are writing about personal experience. In academic and professional writing (see chapters 12 and 15), the use of the first-person singular pronoun is also a clear way to distinguish your own views from those of others or to make a direct appeal to readers. However, if you frequently repeat *I feel* or *I think,* your readers may start to feel that you do not understand much beyond your own experience or that you are more interested in talking about yourself than about your topic.

We, the first-person plural pronoun, is trickier to use correctly. When you use it, make sure that your audience can tell which individuals are included in this plural. For example, if you are writing a paper for a college professor, does *we* mean you and the professor, you and your fellow students, or some other group (such as all Americans)? If you are using *we* in a document you are drafting in the workplace, are you intending to include the entire company, your group within it, or you and a specific individual? When drafting (see chapter 2), you may inadvertently use *we* when you are thinking of more than one group of people. You will confuse readers if you move carelessly from one kind of *we* to another. When editing (see 3f), check to see whether you have used the first-person plural pronoun consistently and, if not, revise or clarify any change of meaning.

Beyond the Rule

WHO IS PART OF *WE*?

Writing specialists have been discussing how the use of *we* can blind writers to differences of gender, race, religion, region, class, and sexual orientation. Readers sometimes feel excluded from works in which the first-person plural pronoun has been used carelessly. For more information about this debate, visit www.harbrace.com.

Using the second-person pronoun (*you*) is a way to address readers. When using the second-person pronoun, be sure that you have specific readers in mind, that you are not using it to refer to anyone outside your audience, and that you are not accidentally shifting from a reference to a single member of your audience to the audience as a whole without clearly establishing that you are making a deliberate shift. Consider your rhetorical situation (see 1b and 1e) to determine if the second-person pronoun is appropriate for the work you are drafting.

If you are not allowed to use first- or second-person pronouns in a particular rhetorical situation and feel frustrated by this restriction, you might be able to relax and draft successfully by giving yourself temporary permission to use *I, we,* or *you.* Later, when revising and editing (see chapter 3), you can find replacements for these words or eliminate the need for using them. Some writers find that this approach helps them in drafting and leads to better final drafts.

For additional advice on using pronouns, see chapter 21.

E x e r c i s e   5

Revise the following paragraph to eliminate the use of the first- and second-person pronouns.

¹In my opinion, some animals should be as free as we are. ²For example, I think orangutans, African elephants, and Atlantic bottlenose dolphins should roam freely rather than be held in captivity. ³We should neither exhibit them in zoos nor use them for medical research. ⁴If you study animals such as these you will see that, like us, they show emotions, self-awareness, and intention. ⁵You might even find that some use language to communicate. ⁶It is clear to me that they deserve the right to freedom.

29e | Definitions help establish exact meanings.

Because words often have more than one meaning, you must clearly establish which meaning you have in mind in a particular piece of writing. By defining terms, you can help make your writing exact.

In this paper, I use the word *communism* in the Marxist sense of social organization based on the holding of all property in common.

By stipulating your meaning in this way, you set the terms of the discussion.

A formal definition first states the term to be defined, then puts it into a class, and finally differentiates it from other members of that class.

A *phosphene* [term] is a luminous visual image [class] that results from applying pressure to the eyeball [differentiation].

A short dictionary definition may be adequate when you need to define a term or convey a special meaning that may be unfamiliar to readers. (See **28e**.)

Here *galvanic* means "produced as if by electric shock."

Giving a synonym may also clarify the meaning of a term. Such synonyms are often used as appositives.

Machismo, confidence with an attitude, can be a pose rather than a reality.

Writers frequently show—rather than tell—what a word means by giving examples.

Many homophones (such as *be* and *bee, in* and *inn,* or *see* and *sea*) are not spelling problems.

You can also formulate your own definition of a concept you wish to clarify.

Knowledge is seasoning for the mind's palate.
Clichés could be defined as thoughts that have hardened.

When writing definitions, do not confuse readers with **faulty predication** (placing a predicate with a subject that is not logically connected to it). (See **23d**.) Constructions that combine *is* or *are* with *when, where,* or *because* are often illogical because forms of *to be* signify identity or equality between the subject and what follows.

Faulty   The Internet is when you look at text and images from across the world.

Revised   The Internet allows you to look at text and images from across the world.

Faulty   A grocery store is where people go to buy food.

Revised   A grocery store is a place where people go to buy food.

E x e r c i s e   6

Using your own words, define any two of the following terms in full sentences.

1. collaboration   3. party   5. globalization
2. honesty   4. style   6. terrorism

Conciseness 30

Using words economically is fundamental to writing clearly because unnecessary words or phrases distract readers and blur meaning. Good writers know how to make their points concisely. This chapter will help you

- make each word count (**30a**),
- combine and simplify phrases and clauses (**30b**), and
- avoid unnecessary repetition (**30c** and **30d**).

In some situations, repeating a word or a phrase can be useful. (See **3d(2)** and **26e**.) In most cases, however, repetition is inefficient.

Wordy	In the early part of August, a hurricane was moving threateningly toward Houston.
Concise	In early August, a hurricane threatened Houston.
Repetitious	This excellent baker makes excellent bread.
Concise	This baker makes excellent bread.

30a | Every word should count; omit words or phrases that add nothing to the meaning of a sentence.

Many people feel overwhelmed by the huge amount of information that technology has made easily available (see chapters **5**, **6**, and **8**). You show respect for others by not asking them to read ten pages when five would make your point.

(1) Redundancy contributes to wordiness.

Restating a key point in different words can help readers understand it. (See **10d**.) But there is no need to rephrase readily understood terms. If you do, your work will suffer from redundancy—repetition for no good reason.

Ballerinas auditioned ~~in the tryouts~~ for *The Nutcracker.*

Each actor has a unique talent for ~~and ability that he or she uses in his or her~~ acting.

Although they are often small ~~in size~~, women gymnasts are extremely strong.

USELESS WORDS IN COMMON PHRASES

yellow [in color]	circular [in shape]
at 9:45 A.M. [in the morning]	return/refer [back]
[basic] essentials	rich [and wealthy] nations
bitter[-tasting] salad	small[-size] potatoes
connect [up together]	[true] facts
because [of the fact that]	was [more or less] hinting
[really and truly] fearless	by [virtue of] his authority
fans [who were] watching TV	the oil [that exists] in shale

You should also avoid grammatical redundancy, as in double subjects (*my sister [she] is*), double comparisons ([*more*] *easier than*), and double negatives (*could[n't] hardly*).

 Review your adjectival clauses to make sure that they do not include a personal pronoun as well as a relative pronoun referring to the same antecedent.

The drug that we were testing ~~it~~ has not been approved by the Food and Drug Administration.

The principal investigator, whom we depended on ~~her~~ for guidance, had to take a medical leave before the project was completed.

(2) Delete unnecessary words.

Watch for empty or vague words such as *area, aspect, element, factor, feature, field, kind, situation, thing,* and *type.* They may signal wordiness.

> Effective
> ~~In an employment situation, effective~~ communication is essential at work.

> If
> ~~In the event that~~ taxes are raised, voters will complain ~~expect complaints on the part of the voters.~~

SOME ONE- OR TWO-WORD REPLACEMENTS FOR COMMON EXPRESSIONS

at all times	**always**
at this point in time	**now**
by means of	**by**
for the purpose of	**for**
in an employment situation	**at work**
in spite of the fact that	**although**
on account of the fact that	**because**
somewhere in the neighborhood of $2,500	**about $2,500**

One exact word can say as much as several inexact ones. (See **29a**.)

spoke in a low and hard-to-hear voice	**mumbled**
persons who really know their particular field	**experts**

(3) The constructions *there are* and *it is* can often be deleted.

There followed by a form of *be* is an **expletive**—a word that signals that the subject of the sentence will follow the verb. (See **26f**.) Because expletives shift emphasis away from the subject, they can result in unnecessary words. They can also be imprecise because they substitute a form of *be* for a forceful verb.

> Three   were
> ~~There were three~~ children playing in the yard.

When the pronoun *it* has no word to refer to and is followed by a form of *be, it* also is an expletive.

Learning to ski
∧It is easy ~~to learn to ski~~.

Exercise 1

Substitute one or two words for each of the following phrases, and use your choice in a sentence.

1. in this day and age
2. has the ability to sing
3. was of the opinion that
4. in a serious manner
5. prior to the time that
6. did put in an appearance
7. located in the vicinity of
8. has a tendency to break
9. during the same time that
10. involving too much expense

30b | **Combining sentences or simplifying phrases and clauses can eliminate needless words.**

Notice how the following sentences have been edited to make every word count.

A carpet of blue-green grass
~~The grass was like a carpet. It~~ covered the whole playing field. ~~The color~~

~~of the grass was blue green.~~

cheating
Some ~~phony~~ unscrupulous brokers are ~~taking money and savings from~~
out of their pensions. ∧
elderly ~~old~~ people ∧~~who need that money because they planned to use~~

~~it as a retirement pension.~~

30c Repetition is useful only when it contributes to emphasis, clarity, or coherence.

~~One week was like the next week~~. Each week was as boring as the last.

She hoped Alex understood that her comment did not reflect her feelings. ~~the complaint she made did not mean she was complaining because she disliked him.~~

In the preceding examples, repetition serves no useful purpose; in the following example, it provides emphasis.

We will not rest until we have pursued **every** lead, inspected **every** piece of evidence, and interviewed **every** suspect. [The repetition of *every* is effective because it emphasizes the writer's determination.]

(See also **3d(2)**, **25b**, and **26e**.)

30d Using pronouns and elliptical constructions can eliminate unnecessary repetition.

Instead of repeating a noun or substituting an inexact synonym, you can use a pronoun as long as the reference is clear (see **21e**).

The hall outside the office was empty. It ~~The hall~~ had dirty floors, and its the walls ~~of this corridor~~ were covered with graffiti.

An **elliptical construction** (the omission of words that are readily understood) helps make the following sentence concise.

Speed is the goal for some swimmers, endurance [is the goal] for others, and relaxation [is the goal] for still others.

Sometimes, as an aid to clarity, commas mark omissions in elliptical constructions.

My family functioned like a baseball team: My mom was the coach; my brother, the pitcher; and my sister, the shortstop.

As these examples show, parallelism reinforces elliptical constructions. (See chapter **25**.)

Revise the following paragraph to eliminate wordiness and needless repetition.

[1]When I look back on my high school career, I realize that I wasn't taught much about international affairs in the world in spite of the fact that improved communications, the media, the Internet, travel, trading with different foreign countries, and immigration have made the world smaller. [2]Nonetheless, because both international affairs and business interest me, I decided to major in political science now that I am in college and to study marketing as my minor. [3]There are advantages to this combination of a major and a minor in my job situation at work as well, for I am now currently working part-time twenty hours a week for a company that imports merchandise into the United States and exports products to other countries. [4]Eventually, at some future time, when I have graduated and received my bachelor's degree, I may go on to law school and pursue my interest in politics, unless, on the other hand, my supervisor makes the recommendation that I develop my skills in marketing by spending time overseas in one of the company's foreign offices. [5]The opportunity to work overseas would provide me with a knowledge, an understanding, and an appreciation of the world economy. [6]Such an understanding is essential for anyone hoping to succeed in business.

Punctuation

P

The Comma

Punctuation signals meaning. It lends to written language the flexibility that facial expressions, pauses, and variations in voice pitch give to spoken language. For instance, a pause after *called* in the first of the following examples would make it clear that the spoken sentence refers to only two people: the recruiter and Kenneth Martin. In the second example, a pause after *Kenneth* would let the listener know that the sentence refers to three people: the recruiter, Kenneth, and Martin. In written text, the same meanings can be established by commas.

When the recruiter called, Kenneth Martin answered.

When the recruiter called Kenneth, Martin answered.

But pauses are not a reliable guide for comma use because commas are often called for where speakers do not pause and pauses occur where no comma is called for. Knowing some basic principles of comma usage works better.

Beyond the Rule

HISTORY OF THE COMMA

Ancient Greeks referred to a short section of a speech as a *comma*. During the Middle Ages, scribes used a special mark to signal a pause in speech. By 1566, a mark recognizable as a comma was being used in Italy to clarify relationships between phrases and clauses. For more information about the history of the comma, visit www.harbrace.com.

This chapter will help you understand that commas

- come before coordinating conjunctions when they link independent clauses (**31a**),
- follow introductory clauses and, usually, introductory phrases (**31b**),
- separate items in a series (**31c**),
- set off nonessential (nonrestrictive) elements (**31d**),
- set off parenthetical elements (**31e**),
- contribute to ease in reading (**31f**), and
- can be overused or misplaced (**31g**).

31a | A comma comes before a coordinating conjunction that links independent clauses.

A comma must come before a coordinating conjunction (*and, but, for, nor, or, so,* or *yet*) that links two independent clauses. An **independent clause** is a group of words that can stand as a sentence (see **17b(1)**).

INDEPENDENT CLAUSE,	CONJUNCTION	INDEPENDENT CLAUSE.
	and	
	but	
	for	
Subject + predicate,	nor	subject + predicate.
	or	
	so	
	yet	

American pottery of the Southwest reveals an artistic heritage**, and** it unlocks the history of the indigenous people of the region.

Most Southwestern pottery comes from Arizona and New Mexico**, but** some also comes from Nevada, Utah, Colorado, and Texas.

Pottery provides important archaeological artifacts**, for** it is abundant, identifiable, and well preserved.

No one knows exactly how many types of Southwestern pottery there are**, nor** is there a list of even the most common.

A classification system based on culture and historical period has been developed**, so** archaeologists can at least establish a time line.

Studying pottery seems simple at first, **yet** it has challenged archaeologists and art historians for decades.

No matter how many clauses are in a sentence, a comma comes before each coordinating conjunction.

No one knows exactly how many types of Southwestern pottery there are, **nor** is there a list of even the most common, **but** scientists are working to change that.

When the independent clauses are short, the comma can be omitted before *and, but,* or *or,* but not usually before *for, nor, so,* or *yet.*

I liked my lessons **but** Annie hated hers.

Howie worked hard on calculus, **for** he wanted to be an engineer.

Sometimes a semicolon instead of a comma separates two independent clauses, especially when the second one already contains commas or when it reveals a contrast. (See also 32a.)

Most archaeologists study the pottery in connection with a particular culture; **but** it should be possible, I think, to study one type of pottery across several cultures.

Not all coordinating conjunctions, however, are preceded by commas. A common error is to place one before *and* when that conjunction links parts of a compound predicate rather than two clauses. (See chapter 17.)

She **slapped** the hamburger patty onto the grill **and seasoned** it liberally before taking my order. [no comma before *and* in a compound predicate]

Exercise 1

A. Combine the following sentences by using coordinating conjunctions and inserting commas where appropriate. (Remember that not all coordinating conjunctions link independent clauses and that *but, for, so,* and *yet* do not always function as coordinating conjunctions.)

B. Explain why you used each of the conjunctions you chose.

1. Dinosaurs lived for 165 million years. Then they became extinct.
2. No one knows why dinosaurs became extinct. Several theories have been proposed.

3. Some theorists believe that a huge meteor hit the earth. The climate may have changed dramatically.
4. Another theory suggests that dinosaurs did not actually become extinct. They simply evolved into lizards and birds.
5. Yet another theory suggests that they just grew too big. Not all of the dinosaurs were huge.

31b | A comma usually follows an introductory word, phrase, or clause.

(1) A comma follows an introductory clause that precedes an independent clause.

INTRODUCTORY CLAUSE,   INDEPENDENT CLAUSE.

When you write, you make a sound in the reader's head.
—RUSSELL BAKER

Although the safest automobile on the road is expensive, the protection it offers makes the cost worthwhile. [dependent clause preceding independent clause]

Although you can always include a comma after any introductory clause, you can omit one if the clause is short.

If I shout someone will hear me.

(2) A comma follows an introductory phrase that appears before an independent clause.

INTRODUCTORY PHRASE,   subject + predicate.
          OR
INTRODUCTORY WORD,   subject + predicate.

(a) Introductory prepositional phrases

From our porch, I could not hear what my father was saying, but I could hear the sound of my mother's laughter, throaty and rich with joy.

If the comma after an introductory prepositional phrase is not necessary to prevent misreading, it can be omitted.

> For safety the university installed call boxes linked directly to campus security.

(b) Other types of introductory phrases

> **Having traveled nowhere,** she believed the rest of the world was like her own small town; **having read little,** she had no sense of how other people think. [participial phrases before both independent clauses; see 17a–b]
>
> **The language difference aside,** life in Germany doesn't seem much different from life in the United States. [absolute phrase; see 31e(4)]

Commas are not used after phrases that begin inverted sentences. (See 26f.)

> With marriage came responsibilities. [COMPARE Responsibilities came with marriage.]
>
> Of far greater concern than censorship of bad words is censorship of ideas. —**DONNA WOOLFOLK CROSS**

(c) Introductory words

> **Furthermore,** the person who designs the best logo will win an award. [transitional word]
>
> **Well,** come on in and join the party. [interjection]
>
> **Yes,** I have a valid inspection sticker. **No,** I did not forget to renew it. [introductory *yes* or *no*]

E x e r c i s e   2

Insert commas wherever necessary in the following paragraph. Explain why each comma is needed. Some sentences may not require editing.

[1]If you had to describe sound would you call it a wave? [2]Although sound cannot be seen people have described it this way for a long time. [3]In fact the Greek philosopher Aristotle believed that sound traveling through air was like waves in the sea. [4]Envisioning waves in the air he hypothesized that sound would not be able to pass through a vacuum because there would be no air to transmit it. [5]Aristotle's hypothesis was

not tested until nearly two thousand years later. ⁶In 1654 Otto von Guericke found that he could not hear a bell ringing inside the vacuum he had created. ⁷Thus Guericke established the necessity of air for sound transmission. ⁸However although most sound reaches us through the air it travels faster through liquids and solids.

A grammar checker can be helpful for discovering places where you may have skipped a necessary comma. For instance, a grammar checker found two of the missing commas in exercise 2. Be sure to use your own comma sense when you proofread. For Web sites that can give you help with commas, visit www.harbrace.com.

31c | Commas separate parallel elements, such as items in a series.

A **series** contains three or more parallel elements. (To be parallel, elements must be grammatically equal. See chapter 25.) The punctuation of a series depends on its form.

> The sky was cloudless, bright, and blue. [A comma is preferred before *and*.]
>
> The sky was cloudless, bright, blue. [A comma is essential when *and* is omitted.]
>
> The sky was cloudless, bright and blue as a sapphire. [This sentence does not contain a series.]

(1) Commas separate words, phrases, or clauses in a series.

A comma appears after each item in a series except the last one.

> Many dogs are affectionate, trusting, obedient, and intelligent. [words in a series]
>
> My job allows me to start work at 7 A.M., to drive to three charming villages every day, and to be home by 4 P.M. [phrases in a series]
>
> My idea of a great vacation spot is one where no telephone rings, someone else fixes me great food, and I sit on the porch in the cool shade all day and read mystery novels. [clauses in a series]

If items in a series contain internal commas, you can make the meaning clear by separating the items with semicolons. (See 32b.)

> The main reasons our ancestors smiled were to reinforce social bonds; to reduce tensions in stressful situations; and, most of all, to express pleasure.

For emphasis, writers sometimes use commas when coordinating conjunctions link all the items in a series.

> We cannot put it off for a month, or a week, or even a day.

(2) Commas separate coordinate adjectives.

Two or more adjectives that modify the same noun or pronoun are called **coordinate adjectives.** One way to test for coordinate adjectives is to switch them; another is to put *and* between them. If the meaning does not change, the adjectives are coordinate.

> Crossing the **rushing, shallow** creek, I stepped on a rock and sank above my boot tops into a **small, still** pool. [*Rushing* and *shallow* modify *creek,* and *small* and *still* modify *pool.*]

Commas separate coordinate adjectives only when the adjectives are not linked by a coordinating conjunction.

> The pool of water that I stepped in was small and still.

Exercise 3

Using commas where necessary, write sentences in which coordinate adjectives modify any five of the following ten words.

EXAMPLE

metric system   Most countries use the familiar, sensible metric system to measure distances.

1. bagel	6. college
2. music	7. tree
3. steak	8. skyscraper
4. painting	9. truck
5. software	10. highway

31d | Commas set off nonessential (nonrestrictive) elements.

Nonessential (nonrestrictive) clauses or phrases give supplemental information about a noun or pronoun. To set off a nonessential word or word group, use two commas, unless the element is at the beginning (see 31b) or the end of the sentence. Of course, not all words preceded and followed by commas are nonessential.

> Some people lie**,** **as my grandmother observed,** because they don't know how to tell the truth. [COMPARE As my grandmother observed, some people lie because they don't know how to tell the truth. OR Some people lie because they don't know how to tell the truth, as my grandmother observed.]

Restrictive clauses or phrases follow and limit the words they modify. They are essential to the clear identification of the word or words they refer to. Restrictive clauses make the meaning more specific. When a restrictive clause follows an independent clause, a comma is unnecessary.

> Dinosaurs may have become extinct because their habitat was destroyed. [*Because,* a subordinating conjunction, introduces a dependent clause.]

If a dependent clause is not essential to understanding the sentence, a comma can precede it.

> My neighbor is now retired**,** **although she works every day at the food bank.**

Beyond the Rule

NONESSENTIAL ELEMENTS

If you are having difficulty deciding whether a particular clause or phrase is nonessential, visit www.harbrace.com.

(1) Commas set off nonessential elements used as modifiers.

Clauses and phrases that *describe* the meaning of a noun or pronoun but are not essential to that meaning are supplemental (nonrestrictive). Set off by commas, they are nonessential elements that could be omitted without changing the meaning of the sentence.

> My sister, who lives in Denver, is visiting me. [I have only one sister, and she happens to live in Denver.]
>
> We climbed Mt. McKinley, which is over 15,000 feet high. [There is only one Mt. McKinley, so it doesn't need further identification.]

Clauses and phrases that *limit* a noun or pronoun by providing essential identifying information are restrictive. Not set off by commas, they identify the noun or pronoun they modify by telling which specific one (or ones). Restrictive clauses and phrases are essential elements that may not be omitted from a sentence.

> My sister who lives in Denver is visiting me. [I have several sisters, and the one who is visiting is the one who lives in Denver.]
>
> We climbed a mountain that is over 15,000 feet high. [There are many mountains, so the identification of a rare characteristic of this mountain is essential.]

As in the preceding examples about the sisters, sometimes only the omission or the use of commas indicates whether a modifier is restrictive or nonrestrictive and thus signals the writer's exact meaning. That is, only the presence or the absence of the commas in those examples reveals whether the writer's only sister is visiting and she happens to live in Denver or the particular sister who lives in Denver is visiting, not the one who lives, say, in Miami.

The placement of a comma often has consequences and can actually reverse the meaning of a sentence. The two example sentences that follow illustrate such a reversal. In the first sentence, the one without the comma, the committee that oversees the budget opposes only a certain kind of spending. In the sentence with the comma, the committee opposes spending of any kind because all spending would increase the deficit.

> The committee that oversees the budget opposes spending which would increase the deficit.
>
> The committee that oversees the budget opposes spending, which would increase the budget.

Although writers have traditionally used *that* at the beginning of restrictive clauses, *which* has become acceptable if, as in the following example, it does not cause confusion. Grammar checkers, however, do not recognize this option and will instruct you to change *which* to *that*.

I like to drive a car *which* has fast acceleration and nimble handling.

(2) Commas set off supplemental appositives.

Appositives can supply supplemental, nonessential (nonrestrictive) details about nouns or pronouns, or they can limit the meaning of nouns or pronouns by indicating which one is meant (restrictive).

Even Milo Papadupolos**, my friend,** let me down. [Knowing more than one person with this name is unlikely; therefore, identifying Milo as a friend is not essential.]

Even **my friend** Milo Papadupolos let me down. [Presumably the writer has more than one friend, so the identification is essential here.]

Abbreviations of titles or degrees after names are treated as supplemental appositives.

Was the letter from Frances Evans**,** Ph.D.**,** or from F. H. Evans**,** M.D.?

Increasingly, however, *Jr., Sr., II,* and *III* are being treated as part of the name rather than as appositives, and hence the comma after the name is occasionally omitted. (See also chapter **39**.)

William Homer Barton**,** Jr.   OR   William Homer Barton Jr.

Exercise 4

Set off nonessential clauses, phrases, and appositives with commas.

1. Maine Coons long-haired cats with bushy tails have adapted to a harsh climate.
2. These animals which are extremely gentle despite their large size often weigh twenty pounds.
3. Most Maine Coons have exceptionally high intelligence for cats which enables them to recognize language and even to open doors.
4. Unlike most cats Maine Coons will play fetch with their owners.
5. According to a legend later proven to be false Maine Coons developed from interbreeding between wildcats and domestic cats.

31e | Commas set off parenthetical elements.

Parenthetical elements are nonessential words or phrases.

> Witches'-broom fungus and black pod rot, **however,** threaten the world's chocolate supply.
>
> An airline ticket, **for example,** can be delivered electronically.

When they cause little or no pause in reading, expressions such as *also, too, of course, perhaps, at least, therefore,* and *likewise* need not be set off by commas.

> My awareness of the absurd has therefore grown in recent years.

(1) Commas set off contrasted elements.

Commas separate sentence elements in which such words as *never* and *unlike* express contrast.

> A planet, **unlike** a star, reflects rather than generates light.

In sentences in which contrasted elements are introduced by *not* and *but,* some writers put a comma before *but* and others do not. Generally, the comma before *but* emphasizes the contrast.

> I disagree with people, but I base my opinion on facts, not on emotion.
>
> Automatic aircraft are flown, not by humans but by computers.

(2) Commas set off geographical names and items in dates and addresses.

See also **39b.**

> **Nashville, Tennessee,** is the largest country-and-western music center in the United States.
>
> Martha left for Peru on **Wednesday, February 12, 2003,** and returned on March 12.

OR

Martha left for Peru on **Wednesday, 12 February 2003,** and returned on 12 March. [The comma is omitted when the date precedes rather than follows the month.]

I had to write to **Ms. Melanie Hobson, 2873 Central Avenue, Orange Park, FL 32065.** [There is no comma between the state abbreviation and the ZIP code.]

(3) Commas set off mild interjections and terms of direct address.

A direct address, also called a **vocative,** is a word or phrase that speaks directly to some person, group, or thing.

Ah, that's what they mean by a firm mattress. [interjection]

Now is the time, **my friend,** to stop smoking. [vocative]

(4) Commas set off absolute phrases.

An **absolute phrase** is a part of a sentence that is not grammatically connected to any other part.

Their income being what it is, I don't expect them to fly home for Christmas.

She was staring at the stranger, **her heart pounding louder and louder.**

31f | Commas are occasionally needed for ease in reading.

Some commas are necessary to prevent misreading. Without the commas, the following sentences would confuse readers, if only temporarily.

Still, air is often polluted by diesel motors. [COMPARE Still air is often polluted . . . .]

The week after, I saw him at the supermarket. [COMPARE I saw him at the supermarket . . . the week after.]

In 2003, 600 building permits were issued. [COMPARE In the first quarter of 2003 600 . . . .]

Sometimes a comma replaces a clearly understood word or group of words.

Scholars often see the humor in mistakes, pedants never.

Exercise 5

Explain the reason for each comma used in the following sentences.

1. Alvar Nuñez Cabeza de Vaca, unlike most other Spanish conquistadors, came to perceive Native Americans as equals.
2. On February 15, 1527, Cabeza de Vaca was appointed to an expedition headed for the mainland of North America.
3. The expedition landed near present-day Tampa Bay, Florida, sometime in March 1528.
4. Devastated by misfortune, the expedition dwindled rapidly; Cabeza de Vaca and three other members, however, survived.
5. His endurance now tested, Cabeza de Vaca lived as a trader and healer among Native Americans of the Rio Grande Basin, learning from them and eventually speaking on their behalf to the Spanish crown.

Exercise 6

For humorous effect, the writer of the following paragraph deliberately omits commas. Identify where commas might be inserted to make reading easier. Compare your version with someone else's and comment on any differences you find.

[1]The commas are the most useful and usable of all the stops. [2]It is highly important to put them in place as you go along. [3]If you try to come back after doing a paragraph and stick them in the various spots that tempt you you will discover that they tend to swarm like minnows into all sorts of crevices whose existence you hadn't realized and before you know it the whole long sentence becomes immobilized and lashed up squirming in commas. [4]Better to use them sparingly, and with affection precisely when the need for one arises, nicely, by itself.

—**LEWIS THOMAS,** *The Medusa and the Snail*

31g | Unnecessary or misplaced commas send false signals.

Although a comma ordinarily signals a pause, not every pause calls for a comma. As you read the following sentence aloud, you may pause naturally at several places, but no commas are necessary.

> Heroic deeds done by ordinary people inspire others to act in ways that are not only moral but courageous.

(1) A comma does not separate a subject and its verb or a verb and its object.

Although speakers often pause after the subject or before the object of a sentence, such a pause should not be reflected by a comma.

> Rain at frequent intervals⊙can produce mosquitoes. [separation of subject (*rain*) and verb (*produce*)]
>
> The accountant said⊙that I couldn't deduct my trip. [separation of verb (*said*) and direct object (a noun clause, *that I couldn't . . .*)]

(2) Commas do not follow coordinating conjunctions, and they immediately precede them only when the conjunctions link independent clauses.

It is incorrect to use a comma after a coordinating conjunction (*and, but, for, nor, or, so,* or *yet*). Writers also sometimes put an unnecessary comma before a coordinating conjunction that does not link independent clauses. (See also chapter 17 and 31a.)

> We worked very hard on her campaign for state representative but⊙the incumbent was too strong in the northern counties. [separation of coordinating conjunction (*but*) and subject of the clause (*the incumbent*)]
>
> He parked the car⊙and closed the garage door. [separation of compound verbs (*parked* and *closed*)]

(3) Commas set off words and short phrases only if they are clearly parenthetical.

Parenthetical words and phrases are those that are nonessential—such as asides or interpolations. (See also 31e.)

Zoe was born⊙ in Chicago in 1985. [The phrase *in Chicago* modifies *born* and is an integral part of the sentence.]

Perhaps⊙ the thermostat is not set correctly. [*Perhaps* is not a parenthetical element.]

(4) Commas do not set off restrictive (essential) clauses, phrases, or appositives.

A restrictive clause, phrase, or appositive is essential to the meaning of the sentence. (See also **31d.**)

Everyone⊙ who has a mortgage ⊙ is required to have fire insurance. [The clause beginning with *who* is essential; people who do not have mortgages are not required to have fire insurance.]

The spectators watched two skaters⊙ dressed in identical black uniforms⊙ battle for the puck. [The skaters dressed in identical black uniforms were being watched, not any skaters dressed in uniforms of another color.]

(5) A comma does not precede the first item of a series or follow the last (including the last of a series of coordinate adjectives).

She was supposed to eat lots of green vegetables, such as⊙ broccoli, peas, and green beans. [No comma is needed before the first noun of the series (*broccoli*).]

Lamont is the most attractive, intelligent, and pleasant⊙ friend I have. [No comma is needed after the last adjective in the series (*pleasant*).]

E x e r c i s e 7

Explain the use of each comma in the following paragraph.

[1]Contrails, which are essentially artificial clouds, form when moisture in the air condenses around particles in jet exhaust. [2]Like ordinary clouds, contrails block incoming sunlight and trap heat radiated from Earth's surface. [3]This process reduces daytime highs and increases nighttime lows, narrowing the temperature range. [4]Multiple contrails can cluster together and obscure an area as large as Iowa, Illinois, and Missouri combined, magnifying the effect. [5]Although they may not alter the overall climate, contrails could still have environmental consequences. —LAURA CARSTEN, "Climate on the Wing"

The Semicolon

The semicolon may be the most rhetorical of the punctuation marks because it clarifies the relationship the writer wants the reader to make between ideas in a sentence. A stronger mark of punctuation than the comma, the semicolon connects grammatically equal elements such as two independent clauses (see **17b(1)**) and separates grammatically equal elements that contain internal commas. Two related independent clauses can be linked by a semicolon, connected by a comma and one of the co-ordinating conjunctions (*and, but, for, nor, or, so,* or *yet*), or punctuated as separate sentences. The method you choose depends to a large extent on your conscious rhetorical decision as well as on your sense of the way your ideas are connected.

This chapter will help you understand that semicolons

- link closely related independent clauses (**32a**),
- separate parts of a sentence containing internal commas (**32b**), but
- do not connect independent clauses with phrases or dependent clauses (**32c**).

Mary said she was hungry; Hugh thought she wanted to go out to dinner. [linking closely related clauses]

Watching silly, sentimental, dull soap operas; eating junk food like french fries, cheeseburgers, and milkshakes; and just doing nothing are my favorite ways to relax. [separating parts containing internal commas]

32a | **A semicolon connects independent clauses not linked by a coordinating conjunction.**

The semicolon can be a valuable resource for writers who sense that two "sentences" are so closely related that they belong in a single sentence but do not lend themselves to being joined by a coordinating conjunction.

Sometimes, a conjunctive adverb such as *however* or *therefore* (see **19c**) accompanies the semicolon and further establishes the exact relationship between the ideas.

Beyond the Rule

THE HISTORY OF THE SEMICOLON

The term *semicolon* comes from a Greek word, *kolon,* which meant "a unit of meaning," similar to a modern sentence. For more information on the history of the semicolon, visit www.harbrace.com.

1. **INDEPENDENT CLAUSE**	**.**	**INDEPENDENT CLAUSE**
Many Web sites are interesting	**.**	Some are not accurate.
2. **INDEPENDENT CLAUSE**	**, (and OR but)**	**INDEPENDENT CLAUSE**
Many Web sites are interesting	**, but**	some are not accurate.
3. **INDEPENDENT CLAUSE**	**; (however OR therefore),**	**INDEPENDENT CLAUSE**
Many Web sites are interesting	**; however,**	some are not accurate.
4. **INDEPENDENT CLAUSE**	**;**	**INDEPENDENT CLAUSE**
Many Web sites are interesting	**;**	some are not accurate.

If you read the sentences in the box aloud, you can probably hear different intonations for them. For instance, when you read the two sentences in the first pattern, your voice probably drops as you come to the end of the first one. That drop signifies the end of one statement and the beginning of another. When you read the second sentence pattern, your voice does not drop as much at the comma as it did at the period, and it rises when you say "but." That rise indicates that there is still some separation between the two ideas. When you read the third pattern, you probably keep your voice level as you say "interesting" but drop it as you say "however." That drop indicates that more is to come and that it will be related to what you have already said. When you read the last pattern, your voice maintains the same level when you say "interesting" and when you say "some." That lack of change in intonation indicates that the two ideas are closely related. These patterns also apply in sentences that combine different kinds of clauses (compound-complex sentences). (See 17c(4) and 32b.)

> Researchers now think that language functions as a kind of index for memories; events that occurred before we acquired language apparently aren't indexed, and so we cannot retrieve those memories at will.

A semicolon (instead of the usual comma) sometimes comes before a coordinating conjunction when a writer wants to emphasize the contrast between the two ideas being joined. (See also 31a.)

> Regular exercise is good for the body; but such exercise alone does not make us healthy.

Occasionally, a comma separates short, very closely related main clauses.

> Victory was ours, the war was over.

A semicolon comes before a transitional word or phrase or a conjunctive adverb (such as *for example, however, on the contrary,* or *therefore*) that occurs between independent clauses. (See 19c, especially the list on page 523.)

> Some glaciers are melting; **for example,** the Athabascan glacier has retreated a thousand feet in the last fifty years.

A comma can be omitted after a conjunctive adverb or a transitional expression if the adverb is essential to the sentence or if the comma is not needed to prevent misreading.

> Like jazz, hip-hop is a uniquely American form of music; indeed it can be said that both forms are fundamentally African American.

When the second independent clause explains or expands the first, a colon is sometimes substituted for the semicolon. Either is acceptable. (See 35d(1).)

32b | **Semicolons separate elements that themselves contain commas.**

When a series of phrases or clauses contain commas, semicolons indicate where each element ends and the next begins.

To survive, mountain lions need a large range area; a steady supply of deer, skunks, raccoons, foxes, and opossums; and plenty of room to mate and raise litters.

Exercise 1

Revise the following sentences, using semicolons to separate independent clauses and elements that contain internal commas.

1. Homelessness used to be typical only of the hardcore unemployed, but it is becoming more frequent among the working poor, some of whom earn the minimum hourly wage of $5.15, and few of whom can ever expect to earn the $14 hourly wage that would enable them to pay for a two-bedroom apartment.
2. The last time the minimum wage was raised was in 1997, however, housing costs went up an average of about 20 percent in one year, which means they could have doubled since the last time the minimum wage was increased.
3. In some homeless families, even though both adults work full-time, their pay is low, they often cannot afford even the least expensive housing, and they require state assistance, a form of welfare, to provide minimum shelter in a motel room for their children.
4. Such families are very crowded, living four, five, or six to a room, rarely having more than two double beds, a chair, and perhaps a roll-away bed, and lacking a place to keep the children's toys and school books.
5. These families eat at soup kitchens, they have no money for anything other than rent and basic clothing.

32c | Semicolons do not connect sentence elements that are grammatically unequal, such as phrases and clauses.

Semicolons do not connect clauses with phrases. (See 17a–b.)

We consulted Alinka Kibukian,́ the local meteorologist.

Needing them to provide summer shade,́ we planted two of the largest trees we could afford.

Do not use a semicolon to connect an independent clause with a dependent clause.

I learned that he would not graduate this term; which really surprised me.

I really should trade this car in; although I can still drive it.

Exercise 2

Replace any semicolon used between grammatically unequal sentence elements with the appropriate punctuation mark. Do not change properly used semicolons.

1. Every morning I take vitamins; a multivitamin and sometimes extra vitamin C.
2. I used to believe that I could get my vitamins from a balanced diet; then I found out that diet may not provide enough of some vitamins, such as folate.
3. By eating a balanced diet, getting plenty of exercise, and keeping stress to a minimum; I thought I would stay healthy.
4. New research suggests that multivitamins are beneficial; when our diets don't provide all the recommended amounts of every vitamin every day; our health can suffer.
5. Although taking one multivitamin tablet a day is a healthy habit; we don't need to buy the most potent or most expensive vitamins available.

Exercise 3

Find or compose one sentence to illustrate each of the following uses of the semicolon.

1. To link two related independent clauses
2. To connect a sentence element containing at least one dependent clause and one independent clause with another independent clause
3. To create a sharp division between two independent clauses
4. To separate clauses in a sentence containing a conjunctive adverb such as *however* or *therefore*
5. To separate elements that contain commas

33 The Apostrophe

Apostrophes serve a number of purposes. For example, you can use them to show that someone owns something (*my neighbor's television*), that someone has a specific relationship with someone else (*my neighbor's children*), or that someone has produced or created something (*my neighbor's recipe*). Apostrophes are also used in contractions (*can't, don't*) and in certain plural forms (*B.A.'s, M.D.'s*).

This chapter will help you use apostrophes to

- indicate ownership and other relationships (**33a**),
- mark omissions of letters or numbers (**33b**), and
- form certain plurals (**33c**).

33a | Apostrophes indicate ownership and other relationships.

An apostrophe most commonly indicates ownership or origin.

Fumi's computer, Dr. Smith's office, the photographer's camera [ownership]

Einstein's ideas, the student's decision, Murphy's Law [origin]

An apostrophe indicates other relationships as well. For example, you use an apostrophe to show how people are related or what physical or psychological traits they possess.

Linda's sister, my roommate's teacher, the employee's supervisor [human relationships]

Mona Lisa's smile, the author's ego, the team's determination [physical or psychological traits]

An apostrophe also indicates traits or features of animals, plants, objects, and abstract nouns.

the dog's ears, the tree's branches, the chair's legs, tyranny's influence

Words used to identify certain tools, buildings, events, and other things also include apostrophes.

tailor's scissors, driver's license, bachelor's degree
St. John's Cathedral, Parkinson's disease, Valentine's Day

You can also use an apostrophe with some forms of measurement.

a day's wages, an hour's delay, five dollars' worth of chocolates

A noun usually follows a word with an apostrophe. However, occasionally, the noun is omitted when it is understood from the context.

Is this Ana's or LaShonda's? [COMPARE Is this Ana's book or LaShonda's book?]

 In many cases, you can use either a word with an apostrophe and an *s* or a prepositional phrase beginning with *of.*

Louise Erdrich's novels, the novels **of** Louise Erdrich
the plane's arrival, the arrival **of** the plane

However, the apostrophe is more commonly used with nouns referring to people, and the prepositional phrase is used with most nouns referring to location.

my **uncle's** workshop, **Jan's** car, the **student's** paper [nouns referring to people]

the **end of** the movie, the **middle of** the day, the **front of** the building [nouns referring to location]

(1) Most singular nouns, indefinite pronouns, abbreviations, and acronyms require -'s to form the possessive case.

the dean's office   Parrish's paintings   Yeats's poems

anyone's computer   someone's birthday

Walter Bryan Jr.'s letter [To avoid confusion, no comma precedes *Jr.'s* here, although *Jr.* is sometimes set off by commas; see **31d**.]

the NFL's reputation   OPEC's price increase

For information on indefinite pronouns, see **21a**; for information on abbreviations and acronyms, see chapter **39**.

Unlike the possessive forms of nouns and indefinite pronouns, possessive pronouns *(my, mine, our, ours, your, yours, his, her, hers, its, their, theirs,* and *whose)* are not written with apostrophes (see **21b**).

Japanese democracy differs from **ours.**

The committee concluded **its** discussion.

 Be careful not to confuse possessive pronouns with contractions. Whenever you write a contraction, you should be able to substitute the complete words for it without changing the meaning.

Possessive Pronoun	Contraction
Its motor is small.	**It's** [it is] a small motor.
The board made **its** plan.	**It's** [it is] the board's plan.
Whose turn is it?	**Who's** [who is] representing us?

To form the possessive of most singular proper nouns, you add an apostrophe and an *s: Iowa's governor.* When a singular proper noun already ends in *-s,* though, you need to consult the publication guide for the discipline in which you are writing. To avoid confusing singular and plural forms, the *MLA Handbook for Writers of Research Papers* recommends always using *-'s,* as in *Illinois's legislature, Dickens's novels, Ms. Jones's address,* and *Descartes's reasoning. The Chicago Manual of Style,* however, notes some exceptions to this rule. An apostrophe without an *s* is used with a name ending in a syllable pronounced "eez" and with a singular noun ending in *-s: Sophocles' poetry, Physics' contribution.*

(2) Plural nouns ending in -s require only an apostrophe for the possessive form.

the boys' game   the babies' toys   the Joneses' house

Plural nouns that do not end in -s need both an apostrophe and an s.

men's lives   women's health   children's projects

The addition of an apostrophe does not make a noun plural. To make most nouns plural, add -s or -es. Add an apostrophe only to signal ownership, origin, relationships, and so on.

    protesters
The ~~protesters'~~ met in front of the conference center.

Likewise, to form the plural of a family name, use -s or -es, not an apostrophe.

    Johnsons
The ~~Johnson's~~ participated in the study. [COMPARE The Johnsons' participation in the study was crucial.]

              Jameses
The trophy was given to the ~~James's~~. [COMPARE The Jameses' trophy is on display in the lobby.]

(3) To show joint ownership or collaboration, add -'s or an apostrophe to the second noun only.

the carpenter and the **plumber's** decision [They made the decision collaboratively.]

Olga and **Nadia's** stocks [They jointly own more than one stock.]

the Becks and the **Lopezes'** cabin [They own one cabin jointly.]

(4) To show separate ownership or individual contributions, add -'s or an apostrophe to each noun.

the **carpenter's** and the **plumber's** proposals [They each made a proposal.]

Olga's and **Nadia's** apartments [They have different apartments.]

the **Becks'** and the **Lopezes'** cars [Each family owns a car.]

(5) Add -'s to the last word of compound nouns.

my brother-in-**law** 's friends, the attorney **general**'s statements [singular]

my brothers-in-**law** 's friends, the attorneys **general**'s statements [plural]

To avoid awkward constructions such as the last two, writers often re-phrase them using a prepositional phrase beginning with *of: the state-ments of the attorneys general.*

(6) Add -'s or an apostrophe to nouns that come before gerunds.

Lucy's **having** to be there seemed unnecessary. [gerund]

The family appreciated the lawyers' **handling** of the matter. [gerund]

Sometimes you may find it difficult to distinguish between a gerund and a participle (see **17a(3)**).

Our successful completion of the project depends on Terry's **providing** the illustrations. [gerund]

I remember my brother **telling** me the same joke last year. [participle]

Notice the difference in meaning. In the sentence containing a gerund, the emphasis is on the action; in the sentence containing a participle, the emphasis is on the person.

 When a gerund appears after a noun ending with -'*s* or with just an apostrophe, that noun is usually the subject of the gerund phrase.

Lucy has to be there → Lucy's having to be there

The **lawyers** handled the matter → The lawyers' handling of the matter

The gerund phrase may serve as the subject or object in the sentence (see **16c** and **17a(3)**).

subject
Lucy's having to be there seemed unnecessary.

object
The family appreciated **the lawyers' handling of the matter.**

(7) Follow an organization's preference for its name or the name of a product; follow local conventions for a geographical location.

Consumers Union   Actors' Equity   Shoppers Choice   Taster's Choice
Devil's Island   Devils Tower   Devil Mountain

Exercise 1

Following the pattern of the examples, change the modifier after each noun to a possessive form that precedes the noun.

EXAMPLES

proposals made by the committee   *the committee's proposals*
poems written by Keats   *Keats's poems*

1. the day named after St. Patrick
2. a leave of absence for six months
3. the position taken by HMOs
4. the report given by the eyewitness
5. the generosity characteristic of the Halvorsons
6. an article coauthored by Gloria and Alan
7. the weights of the children
8. the spying done by the neighbors
9. the restaurants in New Orleans
10. coffee roasted by Starbucks

33b | Apostrophes mark omissions in contractions, numbers, and words mimicking speech.

do not → don't
they will → they'll
class of 2006 → class of '06
you all → y'all
singing → singin'

Contractions are not always appropriate for formal contexts. Your audience may expect you to use full words instead (for example, *cannot* instead of *can't* and *will not* instead of *won't*).

A grammar checker will often flag problems with possessives, marking them as "possible" errors but not telling you whether the apostrophe goes before the *s* or after it, or whether you need an *s* at all. A grammar checker is usually right, however, about missing apostrophes in contractions such as *can't* and *don't*. See **Using a Grammar Checker** on page 468.

33c | **An apostrophe is not required in plurals of uppercase letters, numbers, abbreviations, and words referred to as words.**

Although an apostrophe was used in the past to form the plurals of uppercase letters, numbers, abbreviations, and words used as words, it is now used only rarely. These plurals are generally formed by simply adding *-s*.

the four *S*s   1990s   fours and fives   YWCAs   three *and*s

Apostrophes are used, however, with lowercase letters and with abbreviations that include two internal periods or a combination of uppercase and lowercase letters: *x*'s and *o*'s, B.A.'s, Ph.D.'s.

The MLA differs from this style in recommending the use of apostrophes for the plurals of uppercase letters (*A*'s *and B*'s).

E x e r c i s e   2

Insert apostrophes where needed in the following sentences. Be prepared to explain why they are necessary.

1. Whose responsibility is it to see whether its working?
2. Hansons book was published in the early 1920s.
3. They hired a rock n roll band for their wedding dance.
4. NPRs fund drive begins this weekend.

5. Youll have to include the ISBNs of the books youre going to purchase.
6. Only three of the proposals are still being considered: yours, ours, and the Wilbers.
7. Few students enrolled during the academic year 98–99.
8. There cant be more *x*s than there are *y*s.
9. The students formed groups of twos and threes.
10. The M.D.s disagreed on the patients prognosis.

Exercise 3

Add the apostrophes that are missing from the following paragraph.

[1]In his book *A Day in the Life: The Music and Artistry of the Beatles,* Mark Hertsgaard describes what he found in the archives of Londons Abbey Road Studios. [2]Although the Beatles released barely eleven hours worth of music in their eight-year studio career, the archives contain over four hundred hours of recordings from the 1960s, including a master tape of each song put out by EMI Records. [3]Also found in the archives are the working tapes that reveal each songs evolution. [4]For instance, to Hertsgaard, the first run-through of the song "A Day in the Life" sounds more like a folk ballad than the art song it became. [5]Used as the title of the book, this song is notable in other regards as well. [6]Hertsgaard shows how it reveals the collaboration of John Lennon and Paul McCartney. [7]Though the song could be called Johns because he came up with the narrative and its melody, it was Paul who made it a complete composition by providing the middle passage. [8]Yet perhaps the song is most significant because of its message. [9]When the British Broadcasting Corporation (BBC) accused the Beatles of promoting drugs and refused to play the recording, Paul McCartney responded to the BBCs ban by saying that the groups purpose was to turn people on "to the truth" rather than to drugs. [10]According to Hertsgaard, in "A Day in the Life," the Beatles were expressing their belief that the world could be released from the hold of power and greed: it could be rejuvenated.

34 Quotation Marks

Quotation marks are always used in pairs. The first pair indicates the beginning of the quotation, and the second indicates the end. This chapter will help you use quotation marks

- with direct quotations (**34a**),
- with titles of short works (**34b**),
- for words used ironically (**34c**), and
- in combination with other punctuation (**34d**).

34a | Quotation marks set off direct quotations.

Double quotation marks set off direct quotations, including those in dialogue, but not indirect ones. Single quotation marks enclose a quotation within a quotation.

(1) Double quotation marks enclose words that are direct quotations.

"Like branding steers or embalming the dead," writes David Sedaris, "teaching was a profession I had never seriously considered."
[Quotation marks enclose only the quotation, not any expression such as *she said* or *he replied*. Place the period inside the quotation marks.]

In direct quotations, reproduce all quoted material exactly as it appears in the original, including capitalization and punctuation. (See **10d**.) To learn how to set off long quotations as indented blocks, see pages 171, 314–315, and 344–345.

(2) Quotation marks are not used for paraphrases or for indirect quotations.

David Sedaris claims that he never wanted to become a teacher any more than he wanted to become a cowboy or mortician. [To paraphrase is to restate someone else's words in words of your own while accurately conveying that person's idea. See **10d(3)**.]

Dr. Schurman said that we wouldn't have class tomorrow. [An indirect quotation is a kind of paraphrase associated primarily with spoken language.]

(3) Single quotation marks enclose quotations within quotations.

"We have been going together for two years, and now all of a sudden she says, 'Let's just be friends,' " Derek complained. [The comma appears inside the quotation within a quotation; the period goes at the end of the sentence. (When a direct quotation appears within an indented block quotation, use double quotation marks.)]

 British English and some other languages reverse the positions of single and double quotation marks; they also sometimes place punctuation outside quotation marks. For college and professional writing within the United States, follow the American English convention. (See also **34d**.)

| **British and other usage** | In class, we compared Wordsworth's 'Upon Westminster Bridge' with Blake's 'London'. |
| **American English** | In class, we compared Wordsworth's "Upon Westminster Bridge" with Blake's "London." |

(4) Dialogue is enclosed in quotation marks.

Dialogue is directly quoted conversation. When quoting a dialogue, write what each person says, no matter how short, giving a separate paragraph to each speaker, and changing paragraphs whenever the speaker changes. Expressions such as *he said,* as well as closely related bits of narrative, can be included in the same paragraph as a direct quotation.

> Jack Maggs listened only fitfully, for he was more concerned with Mercy Larkin, and the mischief he imagined in those sleepy eyes.
>
> "He wants us now," cried Percy Buckle, pushing away his buttered toast.
>
> "I cannot go now, Sir."
>
> "Yes you can, Sir," winked Mr. Buckle. "I would not miss this for the world."
>
> "You're coming with me, Sir?"
>
> Mr. Buckle stood, slurping down his tea. "Wild horses couldn't stop me." Mercy Larkin made a hand signal Jack Maggs did not understand.
>
> —PETER CARY, *Jack Maggs*

When quoting more than one paragraph by a single speaker, put quotation marks at the beginning of each new paragraph. However, use only one set of closing quotation marks, at the end of the last paragraph.

(5) Thoughts are enclosed in quotation marks.

Quotation marks set off thoughts reported directly within a narrative.

> "I want to bake that cake again," I thought.

Quotation marks do not set off thoughts presented as ideas within an essay or other written text.

> I think that evening classes would attract students who work during the day.

(6) Short excerpts of poetry included within a sentence are enclosed in quotation marks.

When quoting fewer than four lines of poetry, enclose them in quotation marks and use a slash (see 35i) to indicate the line division.

> After watching a whale swim playfully, the speaker in "Visitation" concludes, "What did you think, that joy / was some slight thing?"

To learn how to treat longer quotations of poetry, see page 418.

34b | Quotation marks enclose the titles of short works, such as stories, essays, poems, and songs.

Lon Otto's *Cover Me* contains such wonderful stories as "Winners" and "How I Got Rid of That Stump." [short stories]

Annie Dillard's "Living Like Weasels" is frequently included in anthologies for college writing courses. [essay]

Did you read William Gibson's "Disneyland with the Death Penalty" when it appeared in *Wired?* [article in a periodical]

After opening *A History of God* by discussing the origins of Judaism, Christianity, and Islam, Karen Armstrong focuses on medieval religious thinking in "The God of the Philosophers." [chapter in a book]

"Big Black Car," by Lynn Emanuel, showed me how a good poem can make the ordinary seem extraordinary. [short poem; see 38a for titles of long poems]

I always want to laugh when I hear "Big Girls Don't Cry." [song]

Coral Browne starred in "An Englishman Abroad," part of the *Great Performances* series. [episode in a television series]

Use double quotation marks around the title of a short work that appears within a longer italicized (or underlined) title. Use single quotation marks for a shorter title within a longer title that is enclosed in double quotation marks.

Interpretations of "A Good Man Is Hard to Find" [long work discussing a short story by Flannery O'Connor]

"Irony in 'The Sick Rose' " [short work discussing a poem by William Blake]

34c | Quotation marks are sometimes used around a word or phrase to convey an ironic tone.

Writers sometimes use quotation marks to indicate that they are using a word or phrase ironically.

His "gourmet" dinner turned out to be processed turkey and instant mashed potatoes. [COMPARE His so-called gourmet dinner turned out to be processed turkey and instant mashed potatoes. The use of *so-called* eliminates the need for quotation marks.]

In this case, *gourmet* is given an ironic emphasis by the quotation marks. If you emphasize a questionable word choice, however, readers might wonder why you did not substitute another word or phrase.

He is too much of a "wimp" to be a good leader. [COMPARE He is too indecisive to be a good leader.]

Similarly, putting a cliché (see **29b**) in quotation marks gives it emphasis. Readers could conclude that you lacked the imagination to substitute a fresh expression for the hackneyed one.

34d | **Placement of other punctuation marks relative to quotation marks depends on the context.**

(1) Commas and periods are placed inside quotation marks.

Commas go inside closing quotation marks. Periods go inside closing quotation marks if the quotation ends the sentence.

"Amanda," she said, "we need to talk." [commas and period inside the quotation marks]

Jason admitted, "I didn't finish 'Sonny's Blues.' " [period inside the closing quotation marks, both single and double]

The period goes at the end of the sentence if other words follow the end of the quotation.

"I don't know why my CD player doesn't work," she said. [comma inside the closing quotation marks and period at the end of the sentence]

The period goes after a parenthetical citation when it follows a quotation that ends a sentence. For example, in MLA-style documentation, the page number in parentheses directly follows a quotation, unless it is a block quotation. (See page 314.)

In *A Natural History of Love,* Diane Ackerman writes, "Love is a demanding sport involving all the muscle groups, including the brain" (86). [The period ending the sentence follows the parenthetical citation.]

(2) Semicolons and colons are placed outside quotation marks.

Semicolons and colons always go outside the quotation marks.

> She spoke of "the gothic tale"; I immediately thought of "The
> Dunwich Horror": H. P. Lovecraft's masterpiece is the epitome of
> "gothic."

(3) Question marks, exclamation points, and dashes are placed outside quotation marks unless they are part of the quotation.

When a question mark, an exclamation point, or a dash is part of the quoted material, it goes *inside* the quotation marks. When it is not, it goes *outside* the quotation marks. When a quotation containing one of these marks ends a sentence you have written, do not add an additional end punctuation mark either inside or outside the quotation marks.

Inside the Quotation Marks

Pilate asked, "What is truth?"

Gordon shouted "Congratulations!"

"Achievement—success!—" states Heather Evans, "has become a national obsession."

Why do children keep asking "Why?" [Use one question mark inside the quotation marks when a question ends with a quoted question.]

Outside the Quotation Marks

Who wrote "The Figure a Sentence Makes"?

Stop playing "Dancing Queen"!

She exclaimed, "I'm surprised at you!"—understandable under the circumstances.

E x e r c i s e   1

Write a page of correctly punctuated dialogue between two friends who are disagreeing about a song or a story.

Insert quotation marks where they are needed in the following sentences. Do not alter sentences that are written correctly.

1. Have you read Ian Buruma's essay The Joys and Perils of Victimhood?

2. Buruma writes, The only way a new generation can be identified with the suffering of previous generations is for that suffering to be publicly acknowledged, over and over again.

3. When my reading group met to talk about this essay, I started our discussion by noting that the word *victim* is defined in my dictionary as anyone who is oppressed or mistreated.

4. So how can we tell who the real victims are? asked Claudia.

5. Cahit responded, I think that both the Israelis and the Palestinians are victims of violence.

6. Yes, agreed Claudia, I worry especially about the women and children in that part of the world. I wish I could say to them, Do not give up hope!

7. According to Tony, the situation in the Middle East would improve if people could learn to live and let live.

8. Using the events of September 11, 2001, as an example, Kyle argued that victims can be of any race, nationality, religion, or gender.

9. Rachel agreed but added that victims can be of different ages as well, pointing out that child abuse is a growing concern.

10. I see many victims of abuse when I volunteer at the Center for the Family, Mai explained, but we must be careful not to confuse abuse with discipline.

The Period and Other Punctuation Marks

Periods, question marks, exclamation points, colons, dashes, parentheses, brackets, ellipsis points, and slashes help clarify writing, usually by conveying tone and speech inflections. (For use of the hyphen, see 36f.) Notice how the punctuation marks in the sentences below signal meaning and intonation.

What a beautiful view! Mountains inspire awe. Don't you feel it?

Maia Weinstock reviews Michael Corballis's *From Hand to Mouth: The Origins of Language* (2002), saying that Corballis developed a new theory of how language began: A complex sign language "developed 2 million years ago . . . [H]umans made the transition to speech just 50,000 years ago."

Emily Dickinson—a much admired American poet—penned the lines "I found the phrase to every thought / I ever had, but one."

This chapter will help you understand how to use

- the end punctuation marks (the period (35a), the question mark (35b), and the exclamation point (35c)),
- the colon (35d),
- the dash (35e),
- parentheses (35f),
- brackets (35g),
- ellipsis points (35h), and
- the slash (35i).

To accommodate computerized typesetting, both CMS and the APA style manual call for only one space to follow a period, question mark, exclamation point, colon, ending parenthesis or bracket, and each of the

(Continued on page 722)

(Continued from page 721)

periods in ellipsis points. No spaces precede or follow a hyphen or dash. The MLA style manual uses only one space after ending punctuation marks but permits two if used consistently.

35a | Periods punctuate sentences and abbreviations.

Rhetorically and grammatically, the period indicates completion.

(1) A period marks the end of a declarative sentence or a mildly imperative one.

Global warming is a serious problem. [declarative sentence]

Respect the environment. [mildly imperative sentence COMPARE Watch out!]

"Be careful," he warned. [declarative sentence with a quotation containing an imperative]

She asks whether global warming really exists. [declarative sentence containing an indirect question]

"Does global warming really exist?" she asked. [declarative sentence containing a direct quotation that happens to be a question]

"It's a huge problem!" he shouted. [declarative sentence with a quotation containing an exclamation]

(2) A period follows an indirect question.

Indirect questions are phrased as statements, and therefore they end with periods.

They want to know what Ruth is doing. [COMPARE What is Ruth doing? (See **35b**.)]

(3) Periods follow some abbreviations.

Dr. Jr. a.m. p.m. vs. etc. et al.

Periods are not used with some other abbreviations (for example, *MVP,* *mph,* and *FM*). (See chapter **39**.) If you do not know whether an abbreviation uses a period, check a dictionary. Dictionaries often list options, such as *USA* or *U.S.A.* and *CST* or *C.S.T.*

Only one period follows an abbreviation that ends a sentence.

> The study was performed by Ben Werthman et al.

35b | A question mark follows a direct (but not an indirect) question.

Rhetorically, the question mark indicates uncertainty. A request is also sometimes stated as a question and is followed by a question mark: *Would you pass the salt?*

> What in the world is Shahri doing? [direct question]
>
> Did you hear them ask, "What is Shahri doing?" [A direct question quoted within a direct question is followed by one question mark inside the closing quotation marks. See **34d**.]
>
> What is Shahri doing? thinking? hoping? [A series of questions having the same subject and verb can be treated as elliptical; that is, only the first item needs to include both the subject and the verb.]

Declarative sentences sometimes contain direct questions.

> He asked, "Did David recommend a good mortgage company?" [Put a question mark inside the quotation marks when it concludes a direct question. See **34d(3)**.]
>
> When the question Why don't you invest in the stock market? comes up, we answer that we live on a budget. [A question mark follows the embedded question, which begins with a capital letter but is not enclosed in quotation marks. The comma follows the introductory clause (see **31b**).]

A question mark inside parentheses shows that the writer is not sure whether the preceding word, figure, or date is correct.

> Chaucer was born in 1340 (?) and died in 1400.

Do not punctuate an indirect question with a question mark. (See **35a(2)**.)

Indirect questions are written as declarative sentences. The subject and verb are not inverted as they would be in the related direct question.

We do not know when ~~will~~ the meeting ᵂⁱˡˡ end.

35c │ An exclamation point shows strong feeling.

Although the exclamation point can mark the end of a sentence—the same grammatical function as the other two end punctuation marks—its primary use is rhetorical, to create emphasis.

Wow! Amazing! That was the best movie I've ever seen!

When an exclamation point at the end of a sentence designates that sentence as emphatic, most writers replace the exclamation point with a period and rewrite the sentence to show the emphasis in other ways. When a direct quotation ends with an exclamation point, no comma or period is placed immediately after it.

"Get off the road!" he yelled.
He yelled, "Get off the road!"

Use the exclamation point sparingly. Overuse diminishes its value, and emphasis can be achieved in better ways (see chapter 26). A comma is preferred after mild interjections, and a period works better after mildly exclamatory expressions and mild imperatives.

Somebody give me a pencil, please.
How moving that final scene was.

E x e r c i s e   1

Compose and punctuate brief sentences of the following types.

1. a declarative sentence containing a quoted exclamation
2. a mild imperative

3. a direct question
4. a declarative sentence containing an indirect question
5. a declarative sentence containing a direct question

35d A colon calls attention to what follows, and it also separates figures in time references, parts of scriptural references, and titles from subtitles.

A colon generally signals that what follows is important. An independent clause precedes a colon. Leave only one space after a colon.

Beyond the Rule

STYLISTIC USES OF THE COLON

For information about stylistic uses of the colon, visit www.harbrace.com.

(1) A colon directs attention to an explanation or summary, a series, or a quotation.

I am always seeking the answer to the eternal question: How can we be joined to another person—spouse, parent, child—yet still remain ourselves?

A colon can introduce a second independent clause that explains or expands the first.

For I had no brain tumor, no eyestrain, no high blood pressure, nothing wrong with me at all: I simply had migraine headaches, and migraine headaches were, as everyone who did not have them knew, imaginary. —JOAN DIDION

They were concerned mainly about speed: Not only did they want a very fast computer, but they also had to have a very fast Internet connection.

Style manuals are fairly consistent on whether the first word following a colon is capitalized (see **37d**). All style manuals agree that after a colon you should capitalize the first letter of a rule or principle or of a quoted sentence. APA requires a capital letter when a complete sentence follows a colon. When other material follows a colon, MLA, CMS, and APA all recommend the use of a lowercase letter.

> I was finally confronted with what I had dreaded for months: The ultimate, balloon payment on my car loan was due. [complete sentence]
>
> I was finally confronted with what I had dreaded for months: the due date for that ultimate, balloon payment on my car loan. [phrase]

A colon is not used between a verb and its complement, between a verb and its object, between a preposition and its object, or after *such as.*

> The winners were: Asa, Vanna, and Jack.
>
> Many vegetarians do not eat dairy products, such as: butter and cheese.

A colon may introduce a list.

> There were three winners: Asa, Vanna, and Jack.
>
> OR   The winners were as follows: Asa, Vanna, and Jack.
>
> BUT   The winners included Asa, Vanna, and Jack.

(2) A colon separates titles from subtitles as well as figures in time references and in citations of scripture.

> I just read *Women's Ways of Knowing: The Development of Self, Voice, and Mind.*
>
> We are to be there by 11:30 A.M.

Many writers use a colon in scriptural references.

> He quoted from Psalms 3:5.

However, MLA recommends periods (Psalms 3.5), and recent biblical scholarship follows this practice as well.

(3) Colons have specialized uses in business correspondence.

A colon follows the salutation of a business letter and any notations.

> Dear Dr. Horner: Dear Maxine: enc:

A colon introduces the headings in a memo.

To: From: Subject: Date:

(4) The colon is also used in bibliographical entries.

(See chapters 10–11.)

Exercise 2

Insert colons where they are needed in the following sentences.

1. Before we discuss marketing, let's outline the behavior of consumers Consumer behavior is the process individuals go through as they select, buy, or use products or services to satisfy their needs and desires.
2. The process consists of six stages recognizing a need or desire, finding information, evaluating options, deciding to purchase, purchasing, and assessing purchases.
3. Many consumers rely on one popular publication for product information *Consumer Reports.*
4. When evaluating alternatives, a consumer uses criteria; for example, a house hunter might use some of the following criteria price, location, size, age, style, and landscaping design.
5. The postpurchase assessment has one of two results satisfaction or dissatisfaction with the product or service.

35e | A dash marks a break in thought, sets off a parenthetical element for emphasis or clarity, or follows an introductory list or series.

You can use your keyboard to form a dash by typing two hyphens with no spaces between, before, or after the hyphens. Most word-processing programs can be set to convert these hyphens automatically to an em dash (—).

Dashes signal a specific meaning, so use them purposefully rather than as easy or automatic substitutes for commas, semicolons, or colons.

(1) A dash marks a sudden break in thought, an abrupt change in tone, or a faltering in speech.

I was awed by the almost superhuman effort Stonehenge represents—but who wouldn't be?

I know who she is, Mrs.—Mrs.—Mrs. Somebody—the Mayor of Gilpin—or Springtown.

(2) A dash sets off a parenthetical element for emphasis or (if it contains commas) for clarity.

In many smaller cities of this nation, cable television operators—with the connivance of local government—have a virtual monopoly.

The trail down into the Grand Canyon—steep, narrow, winding, and lacking in guard rails—is treacherous.

(3) A dash occurs after an introductory list or series.

The main part of the following sentence sums up the meaning of the list.

Eager, determined to succeed, and scared to death—all of these describe my emotions the first day on the job.

35f | **Parentheses set off nonessential matter and enclose numerals or letters used for lists.**

Use parentheses to set off information that mainly illustrates or supplements the main part of the sentence or that is nonessential (parenthetical).

I accepted his explanation (up to a point) and set out to enjoy the evening. [an explanatory parenthetical expression]

In general, a sound argument contains (1) a clear statement of its point placed near the beginning and (2) a refutation of opposing positions, usually right after the point statement. [In long sentences especially, parenthetical enumeration highlights the points.]

The Search for Extraterrestrial Intelligence (SETI) uses the Very Large Array (VLA) outside Sicorro, New Mexico, to scan the sky. [first-time use of an acronym; see **39e** and the **Glossary of Terms**]

In the next example, an entire sentence is parenthetical.

> If we refuse to talk "like a lady," we are ridiculed and criticized for being unfeminine. ("She thinks like a man" is, at best, a left-handed compliment.) —ROBIN LAKOFF

Use parentheses sparingly; the elements they enclose should still read smoothly in the sentence as a whole.

Beyond the Rule

PARENTHETICAL RHETORIC

Although dashes and parentheses are both used to set off parenthetical material within sentences, their use is almost entirely rhetorical. They express different degrees of emphasis and are seldom used for any other purpose.

- Dashes set off parenthetical elements sharply and usually emphasize them.
- Parentheses usually deemphasize the elements they enclose.
- Commas also separate elements, usually without emphasizing them.

To see how a sentence can be punctuated in each of these ways, visit www.harbrace.com.

| 35g | Square brackets set off additions or alterations to quoted matter and replace parentheses within parentheses. |

Parker Pilgrim has written, "If he [Leonard Aaron] ever disapproved of any of his children's friends, he never let them know about it." [An unclear pronoun reference is explained by the bracketed addition.]

Not every expert agrees. (See, for example, Katie Hafner and Matthew Lyon's *Where Wizards Stay Up Late* [New York: Simon, 1996].) [Brackets replace parentheses within parentheses.]

[I]f the network was ever going to become more than a test bed . . . , word of its potential had to spread. —**KATIE HAFNER AND MATTHEW LYON**

[In CMS style, the brackets indicate that the capital *I* was a lowercase letter in the original. To avoid the awkwardness of this usage of brackets, construct the sentence so that it does not begin with the quotation: Hafner and Lyon note that "if the network . . . ."]

Another kind of brackets, angle brackets ($<$ $>$), often enclose Web addresses so that punctuation in the sentence is not confused with the dot(s) in the URL: <http://www.harbrace.com>.

35h	Ellipsis points indicate an omission from a quoted passage or a reflective pause or hesitation.

(1) Ellipsis points mark an omission within a quoted passage.

Whenever you omit anything from material you quote, make sure your omission does not change the meaning of the original. Replace the omitted material with **ellipsis points**—three equally spaced periods.

Omission within a quoted sentence

Original

A satire is supposed to make fun of whatever it is attacking. But there is no humor in *Natural Born Killers*. It is a relentlessly bloody story designed to shock us and to further numb us to the senselessness of reckless murder. The film wasn't made with the intent of stimulating morally depraved young people to commit similar crimes, but such a result can hardly be a surprise. —**JOHN GRISHAM**, "Unnatural Killers"

Noting that *Natural Born Killers* "wasn't made with the intent of stimulating . . . similar crimes," John Grisham points out that copycat behavior has, nevertheless, been one result.

Omission at the beginning or end of a quoted sentence   If the initial part of a quoted sentence is omitted, neither ellipsis points nor a capital letter is used at the beginning of the quotation, whether it is run into the text or set off in a block (see 10d(2)).

> John Grisham points out that "satire is supposed to make fun of whatever it is attacking." [The first word of the sentence has been omitted.]

An omission that coincides with the end of the sentence requires an end punctuation mark (a period, a question mark, or an exclamation point) in addition to the ellipsis points. Put a space after the last word quoted and before the three spaced periods. Place the end punctuation mark after the ellipsis points. If the quoted material is followed by a parenthetical source or page reference, the period comes after the second parenthesis.

> John Grisham points out that the film "is a relentlessly bloody story designed to shock us . . . ." OR "shock us . . ." (2). [MLA style]

Omission of a sentence or more   Omission of a sentence or more (even a paragraph or more) within a quoted passage is indicated by a period before the ellipsis points. A comma preceding the ellipses indicates the omission of part of one sentence and part or all of another.

Original

Cacao doesn't flower, as most plants do, at the tips of its outer and uppermost branches. Instead, its sweet white buds hang from the trunk and along a few fat branches, popping out of patches of bark called cushions, which form where leaves drop off. They're tiny, these flowers. Yet once pollinated by midges, no-see-ums that flit in the leafy detritus below, they'll make pulp-filled pods almost the size of rugby balls. The big, colorful, exuberant pods flop around the tree's trunk and dangle from its branches in a shameless display of ripeness—low-hanging fruit for forest animals that eat the juicy, satin-white pulp inside and disperse its bitter-tasting seeds, the magic beans.

—PATRICIA GADSBY, "Endangered Chocolate"

Cacao flowers "hang from the trunk and along a few fat branches, popping out of patches of bark called cushions, which form where leaves drop off. . . . The big, colorful, exuberant pods flop around the tree's trunk and dangle from its branches in a shameless display of ripeness." [Two sentences have been omitted from the original, and a sentence comes before and after the period and ellipsis points.]

Patricia Gadsby says of cacao flowers that, although "tiny, . . . once pollinated . . . they'll make pulp-filled pods almost the size of rugby balls."

[Three words have been omitted from the first sentence and eleven from the second. The first set of ellipsis points links the sentences.]

To avoid excessive use of ellipses, you can also recast a sentence.

> Although cacao flowers are small, as Patricia Gadsby notes, "once pollinated . . . they'll make pulp-filled pods almost the size of rugby balls."

You can also paraphrase a passage rather than editing it heavily. (See **10d(3)**.)

To indicate the omission of a full line or more in quoted poetry, use spaced periods covering the length of either the line above it or the omitted line.

> The yellow fog that rubs its back upon the window-panes,
> . . . .
> Curled once about the house, and fell asleep.
>
> —**T. S. ELIOT**, "The Love Song of J. Alfred Prufrock"

(2) Ellipsis points can occasionally mark a reflective pause or a hesitation.

> Keith saw four menacing youths coming toward him . . . and ran. [Alternatively, you could use a dash to indicate the pause in this sentence.]

35i | The slash is used to mark line divisions in quoted poetry and between terms to indicate that either term is applicable.

There are no spaces before and after a slash used between terms, but a space is inserted before and after a slash used between lines of poetry.

> Wallace Stevens refers to the listener who, "nothing himself, beholds **/** Nothing that is not there and the nothing that is."

Extensive use of the slash to indicate that either of two terms is applicable (as in *and/or* and *he/she*) can make writing choppy. You might want to use *or* instead of the slash.

When two terms combine to modify a noun, link the terms with a hyphen: *East-West differences.* (See **36f**.)

Exercise 3

Add appropriate dashes, parentheses, slashes, and brackets to the following sentences. Be ready to explain the reason for every mark you add.

1. Researchers in an exciting field (Artificial Intelligence AI) are working on devices to assist the elderly.
2. One such device is Pearl a robotic nurse that helps around the house.
3. Another application is cooking software that checks for missing and or incorrect ingredients.
4. Researchers are even investigating Global Positioning Systems GPS as a way to track Alzheimer patients' daily routines.
5. The actual cost of such devices expensive now but more affordable later is yet to be determined.

Exercise 4

Punctuate the following sentences with appropriate end marks, commas, colons, dashes, parentheses, and ellipsis points. Do not use unnecessary punctuation. Give a justification for each mark you add, especially where more than one type of mark (for example, commas, dashes, or parentheses) is acceptable.

1. Many small country towns are very similar a truck stop a gas station a crowded diner and three bars
2. If you don't want to miss pure Americana as you roar down the interstate, you'd better shout "whoa"
3. Why do we never see these quaint examples of pure Americana when we travel around the country on the interstates
4. The simple life, a nonexistent crime rate, and down-home values these are some of the advantages these little towns offer
5. Rolling across America on one of the big interstates I-20, I-40, I-70, I-80, or I-90 you are likely to pass within a few miles of a number of these towns

6. These towns almost certainly will have a regional or perhaps an ethnic flavor Hispanic in the southwest Scandinavian in the north

7. When I visit one of these out-of-the-way places, I always have a sense of well really a feeling of safety

8. I think a town like that might be the very best place to live in the whole world

9. There's one thing I can tell you Small town life is not boring

10. My one big question however is what do you do to earn a living there

Mechanics

36 Spelling, the Spell Checker, and Hyphenation

This chapter will help you

- use a spell checker (**36a**),
- spell words according to pronunciation (**36b**),
- spell words that sound alike (**36c**),
- use affixes (prefixes and suffixes) correctly (**36d**),
- deal with *ei* and *ie* (**36e**), and
- use hyphenation to link and divide words (**36f**).

People often decide whether you are intelligent or well informed based on how well you write and, in particular, how well you spell. With this in mind, writers routinely use spell checkers. But you don't always have access to a spell checker. For instance, there are times when you will be writing papers or essay exams in class (see chapter 4). You want to spell correctly on these assignments so that your teacher gets a good impression of your ability and rewards your work accordingly. Employers or supervisors may also evaluate your competence by your ability to spell correctly in job-related writing. And you need to spell correctly to find what you're looking for when you search the Web. For these reasons, a basic knowledge of spelling is always important.

Beyond the Rule

SHAPING UP YOUR SPELLING

Typically, misspellings result from carelessness, lack of shape recognition, confusion of words that sound alike, or a learning disability. If you're a poor speller who is serious about improving, visit www.harbrace.com to learn about resources available to you.

If you have trouble with spelling, use a dictionary. Be alert for restrictive labels. Dictionaries may list two unlabeled ways to spell a word—for example, *fulfill* and *fulfil*. In such cases, either form is correct, although the first option listed is sometimes more commonly used. Whatever spelling you choose, use it consistently.

36a | Spell checkers can be valuable tools.

The spell checker is a wonderful invention, but it doesn't relieve you of the responsibility for correct spelling. It can catch many errors, but it will not alert you to words you may have confused, such as *principal* and *principle,* because it cannot know which meaning you intend.

THE TRUTH ABOUT SPELL CHECKERS

A spell checker finds errors by checking the words in a document against the words in its dictionary. When it finds a word that does not match any words in its dictionary, it flags that word as misspelled. Thus, a spell checker will usually catch

- misspellings of common words,
- misspellings of irregular words,
- words in which a vowel changes when a suffix is added,
- a letter dropped or added when a prefix is added, and
- obvious typographical errors, such as *tge* for *the*.

However, a spell checker cannot determine whether a correctly spelled word is used incorrectly (for example, *there* in place of *their*), and it cannot determine whether a word that is not in its dictionary is incorrectly spelled. Therefore, you should keep in mind that a spell checker generally will *not* catch

- typographical errors that make correctly spelled words (such as *was* for *saw*),
- misuses of correctly spelled words that result from mistaking words not stressed in speech (such as *could of* or *would of* for *could have* or *would have*),

(Continued on page 738)

(Continued from page 737)

- words that are correctly spelled but incorrectly used (such as *affect* for *effect*), and misuses of some homophones (words that sound alike, such as *course* and *coarse*).

Although a spell checker may flag some commonly misused words, it may provide erroneous advice by suggesting incorrect alternative words. In addition, if a spell checker finds a word that is not in its dictionary, it may offer no alternatives at all. Therefore, you should always carefully evaluate any choices provided by a spell checker. You can also try the following strategies to help you use a spell checker effectively for avoiding, finding, and correcting spelling errors:

- Keep a separate file of words you tend to misspell. When you are preparing to edit a document, use the Search and Replace feature of your word processor to find and correct any misspellings of those words.

- If a spell checker regularly flags a word (or a name) that is not in its dictionary but is spelled correctly, you can give it a command to add that word or name to its dictionary. When you run the spell checker in the future, it will be able to check for that word or name.

It is also best to reject any offers your spell checker may make to correct all instances of a particular error. When used carefully, a spell checker can help you proofread your documents efficiently. Getting to know what the spell checker can and cannot do is the best way to use it effectively. And you should always proofread your writing yourself, never relying on a spell checker to locate all of the spelling errors.

36b | Spelling does not necessarily reflect pronunciation.

Many words in English are not spelled the way they are pronounced, so pronunciation is not a reliable guide to correct spelling. Sometimes, people skip over an unstressed syllable, as when *February* is pronounced "Febwary," or they slide over a sound that is hard to articulate, as when *library* is pronounced "libary." Other times, people add a sound—for instance, when they pronounce *athlete* as "athalete." And people also switch sounds around, as in "irrevelant" for *irrelevant*. Such mispronunciations can lead to misspellings. As an aid to remembering, it is sometimes helpful to consider the spelling of the root word—for example, the root word for *irrelevant* is *relevant*. You can also practice the correct spelling of a word by pronouncing it the way it is spelled.

TIPS FOR SPELLERS

Fixing Pronunciation Problems

- Check for unstressed syllables.
- Consider the spelling of the root word.
- Consider alternative pronunciations as spelling clues.

Beyond the Rule

WHEN PRONUNCIATION IS UNRELIABLE

For a list of words that are usually not pronounced the way they are spelled, visit www.harbrace.com.

The words *have, and,* and *than* are often not stressed in speech and are thus misspelled. A spell checker will not catch these misspellings.

I would ~~of~~ rather had fish ~~then~~ soup ~~an~~ salad.
$\qquad$ have $\qquad$ than $\qquad$ and

36c | **The meanings of words that sound alike are determined by their spelling.**

Pairs of words such as *forth* and *fourth* or *sole* and *soul* are **homophones:** They sound alike but have different meanings and spellings. A spell checker will not tell you if you have used the wrong word for your context.

Some words that have different meanings sound exactly alike (*break/brake*), others sound alike in certain dialects (*horse/hoarse*), and still others are only similar in sound, especially in rapid speech (*believe/belief*). The spell checker cannot identify words that are correctly spelled but incorrectly used. If you are unsure about the difference in meaning between any pair of words, consult a dictionary. A number of frequently confused words are listed with explanations in this handbook's **Glossary of Usage**.

Single words and two-word phrases that consist of the same letters but have different meanings can also be troublesome. Following are some examples.

He wore **everyday** clothes.	He wears them **every day.**
They don't fight **anymore.**	I can't eat **any more.**

Other examples are *awhile/a while, everybody/every body, everyone/every one, maybe/may be,* and *nobody/no body.*

A lot and *all right* are still spelled as two words. *Alot* is always considered incorrect; *alright* is considered incorrect except in newspapers and magazines. (See the **Glossary of Usage.**)

Singular nouns ending in *-nce* and plural nouns ending in *-nts* are easily confused.

Assistance is available.	I have two **assistants.**
My **patience** is frayed.	Some **patients** waited for hours.

Contractions and possessive pronouns are often confused. In contractions, an apostrophe indicates an omitted letter (or letters). In possessive pronouns, there is no apostrophe. (See **21b** and **33a.**)

TIPS FOR SPELLERS

Fixing Problems with Homophones

- Distinguish between possessives and contractions (*your* versus *you're*).
- Distinguish between single words and two-word phrases (*maybe* versus *may be*).
- Distinguish between the endings *-nce* and *-nts* (*instance* versus *instants*).
- Distinguish between other words that sound alike (*accept* versus *except*).

Contraction	Possessive
It's my turn next.	Each group waits **its** turn.
You're next.	**Your** turn is next.
There's no difference.	**Theirs** is no different.

36d | Prefixes change a word's meaning; suffixes may change its spelling.

A **prefix** is added to the beginning of a base word, called the **root**.

necessary, **un**necessary   moral, **im**moral

No letter is added or dropped when a prefix is added: *grand + daughter*. Adding a **suffix** to the end of a base word often changes the spelling.

beauty, beaut**iful**   describe, descri**ption**   BUT   resist, resist**ance**

Although spellings of words with suffixes are irregular, they follow certain conventions. Misspellings that result from adding prefixes or suffixes are usually detected by a spell checker.

(1) Dropping or retaining a final *e* depends on whether the suffix begins with a vowel.

- If a suffix begins with a vowel, the final *e* of the base word is dropped: bride, brid**al**; come, com**ing**; combine, combin**ation**; prime, prim**ary**.
- If a suffix begins with a consonant, the final *e* of the base word is retained: entire, entire**ly**; rude, rude**ness**; place, place**ment**; sure, sure**ly**. Some exceptions are *argument, awful, duly, ninth, truly,* and *wholly.*
- To keep the /s/ sound in *ce* or the /j/ sound in *ge*, retain the final *e* before *-able* or *–ous:* courage**ous**, manage**able**, notice**able**.

(2) A final consonant is usually doubled when a suffix begins with a vowel.

Double the final consonant before a suffix beginning with a vowel if (1) the consonant ends a one-syllable word or a stressed syllable or

(2) the consonant is preceded by a single vowel. If the suffix does not begin with a vowel, the consonant is not doubled.

drop, dro**pp**ing BUT droop, droo**p**ing
admit, admi**tt**ed BUT picket, picke**t**ed

(3) A final *y* is changed or retained depending on whether the suffix begins with a vowel.

Change a final *y* to *i* before adding a suffix—except *-ing*.

defy: def**ies**, def**ied**, def**iance** BUT def**ying**
modify: modif**ies**, modif**ied**, modif**ier** BUT modif**ying**

Most verbs ending in *y* preceded by a vowel do not change the *y* before adding *-s* or *-ed: stay, stays, stayed*. Similarly, some nouns, such as *joy* and *day*, retain the *y* when *-s* is added. The following spelling irregularities are especially troublesome: *lays, laid; pays, paid; says, said*.

(4) A final *l* is retained when *-ly* is added.

cool, coo**lly** formal, forma**lly** real, rea**lly** usual, usua**lly**

(5) The plural of nouns is formed by adding *-s* or *-es* to the singular.

Nouns do not use an apostrophe to form a plural. The apostrophe shows possession. (See chapter 33.)

scientist**s** sister**s**-in-law [chief word pluralized]
toy**s** the Smith**s** [proper name]

- For nouns ending in *f* or *fe*, change the ending to *ve* before adding *-s* when the sound of the plural changes from *f* to *v: thief, thie**ves**; life, li**ves** BUT roof, roof**s***.
- For nouns ending in *s, z, ch, sh*, or *x*, add *-es* when the plural adds another syllable: *box, box**es***; *peach, peach**es***; *the Rodriguez**es***.
- For nouns ending in *y* preceded by a consonant, add *-es* after changing the *y* to *i: company, compan**ies**; ninety, ninet**ies**; territory, territor**ies***.
- Although usage varies, most nouns ending in *o* preceded by a consonant add *-es*. Some can add *-s* or *-es: mottos, mottoes; zeros, zeroes*.
- Certain irregular nouns do not add *-s* or *-es* to form the plural: *woman, women; goose, geese; sheep, sheep; child, child**ren***.

TIPS FOR SPELLERS

Fixing Problems with Affixes

- Recognize prefixes *(moral/immoral)*.
- Recognize suffixes:
    dropping a final *e (bride/bridal)*
    doubling a final consonant *(drop/dropping)*
    changing *y* to *i (defy/defies)*
    retaining a final *l (real/really)*
    forming plurals *(toy/toys, box/boxes, man/men, criterion/criteria)*

Beyond the Rule

WORDS BORROWED FROM OTHER LANGUAGES

Words borrowed from Latin or Greek generally form their plurals as they did in the original language. If you aren't sure about how to make any word plural, look in a dictionary.

Singular	criterion	alumnus, -a	analysis	datum	species
Plural	criteria	alumni, -ae	analyses	data	species

Some words are spelled differently in Great Britain and the United States. Because American readers might find British usage inappropriate or confusing, use the American form.

American	theater	fertilize	color	connection
British	theatre	fertilise	colour	connexion

For further information, visit www.harbrace.com.

Exercise 1

Supply plural forms (including any optional spellings) for the following words. If a word is not covered by the rules, use a dictionary.

1. half
2. woman
3. potato
4. theory
5. radius
6. speech

7. genius	10. leaf	13. hero
8. passerby	11. phenomenon	14. Kelly
9. halo	12. bush	15. church

36e | *Ei* and *ie* are often confused.

When the sound of the letters is /ē/ (as in *me*), write *ie* except after *c*, where you should write *ei*:

chief, priest, yield BUT conceit, perceive, receive [after *c*]

When the sound is other than /ē/, you should usually write *ei*:

eight, foreign, heir, rein, their, weight

Some exceptions are *either, neither, friend, species,* and *weird.*

36f | Hyphens can link or divide words.

Hyphens not only link, or make a compound of, two or more words that function as a single word, but also divide words at the ends of lines.

Grammar checkers can identify many compound words and suggest a correct spelling, such as *double-space* instead of *doublespace*. Grammar checkers can also alert you to missing hyphens in most fractions (*one-fourth*) and compound numbers (*twenty-seven*) but not to those that are part of a compound noun (*ex-*) or adjective (*quasi-*) or are used to avoid ambiguity (*recover* versus *re-cover*).

(1) Hyphens sometimes link two or more words that form a compound functioning as a single word.

| Nouns | We planted forget-me-nots and Johnny-jump-ups. |
| Verbs | I double-checked. He hard-boiled the egg. |

Some compounds are listed in the dictionary with hyphens (*eye-opener, cross-examine*), others are written as two words (*eye chart, cross fire*), and still others are written as one word (*eyewitness, crossbreed*). When in doubt, consult a dictionary.

- Do not confuse the hyphen with the dash, which is keyboarded as a double hyphen with no spaces before and after. (See **35e**.)
- Use a hyphen to link two or more words serving as a single adjective before a noun: *self-imposed* exile, a *well-built* house [COMPARE a house that is well built].
- In a series of compound adjectives, a space may follow the hyphen in every item except the last one: *first- and second-degree burns.*
- Omit the hyphen after an adverb ending in *-ly* (*quickly frozen foods*), in names of chemical compounds (*sodium chloride solution*), and in a modifier using a letter or numeral as the second element (*group C homes, type IV virus*).
- Hyphenate to avoid ambiguity or an awkward combination of letters or syllables between a prefix and a base word: *anti-intellectual, de-emphasize, re-sign the petition* [COMPARE *resign the position*].
- In addition, hyphenate between a prefix and a capital letter and between a noun and the suffix *-elect: anti-American, President-elect.* Otherwise, do not hyphenate with prefixes or suffixes.

Exercise 2

Convert the following word groups using the pattern of the examples.

EXAMPLES

a movie lasting two hours   *a two-hour movie*

colors used with water   *watercolors*

1. an antique sofa covered in velvet
2. a brush for teeth
3. diplomats who solve problems
4. cereal in the shape of an *O*
5. a house twenty years old
6. a garage for three cars
7. a holiday lasting four days
8. a light used at night
9. a highway with four lanes
10. lightbulbs costing ten dollars

(2) Hyphens break words at the ends of lines.

If you must divide a word at the end of a line, use a hyphen to separate it between syllables.

In dictionaries, dots usually divide entries into syllables: **re·al·ly, pre·fer, pref·er·ence, sell·ing, set·ting.** But not every division between syllables is an appropriate place for dividing a word. Following are some general guidelines.

- Do not divide abbreviations, first and middle initials, capitalized acronyms, or one-syllable words.

  p.m. [NOT p.-m.]   USAF [NOT US-AF]

  through [NOT thr-ough]   UNESCO [NOT UNES-CO]

- Do not put only the first or last letter of a word at the beginning or end of a line or the last two letters of a word at the beginning of a line, even if they form a syllable.

omit	able	boa	dated	doesn't	safely	gravel	taxis
~~o·mit~~	~~a·ble~~	~~bo·a~~	~~dat·ed~~	~~does·n't~~	~~safe·ly~~	~~grav·el~~	~~tax·is~~

- Divide hyphenated words only at the hyphen.

  mass-|produce   father-|in-law OR father-in-|law

- Divide words between consonants, except when the division does not reflect pronunciation.

  pic-|nic   dis-|cuss   thun-|der   set-|ting   plan-|ning

  [COMPARE the pronunciation of *co-|bra* with that of *sell-|ing,* in which the base word already has a double consonant.]

Beyond the Rule

OTHER HYPHENS

In MLA style, three hyphens in a list of works cited indicate that the author is the same as in the previous entry. (See 11a.) For an example, visit www.harbrace.com.

Exercise 3

List five cues that help you remember certain difficult spellings. Share your list with classmates.

Exercise 4

Edit the following paragraph to correct misspellings and the usage of hyphens.

[1]My friend and I recently watched a videotape of *First-Knight* that she had recieved for her birthday; its a movie that is principly located in the make believe city of Camelot. [2]Of course, we had all heard the story of Lancelot and Guinevere, definately too of the most famous lovers in all of fiction, and there trouble relationship with King Arthur. [3]Despite this fact, we liked the movie alot because it successfully communicated the various phenomena associated with the conflict between love and loyalty. [4]One scene in which this conflict is most readly apparent occurs after Guinevere marries Arthur. [5]When her former home is attacked, Guinevere becomes concerned for her families safety and, not surprisingly, both men come to her rescue: Arthur, because Guinevere is his wife and because he loves her; and Lancelot, because Arthur is his king and because he also loves Guinevere. [6]In fact, all of the issues concerning love and loyalty portrayed in the movie's storyline are timeless ones and will be as importent in the twenty first century as they were in the eighth. [7]Nevertheless, although the filmmaker did a good job of teling the story, some of my friends didn't like the fact that the costumes worn by the acters and actresses were historicly inaccerate.

37 Capitals

Capital letters designate such things as names, peoples and their languages, geographical names, and certain organizations. Different styles for capitalization have been popular in the past, and no doubt others will be popular in the future.

This chapter will help you

- capitalize proper names (**37a**),
- use capitals for titles of persons (**37b**),
- capitalize words in titles of works (**37c**),
- capitalize the first word of directly quoted speech (**37d**), and
- avoid unnecessary capitalization (**37e**).

Rhetorically, capitalization contributes to clarity when it marks the beginning of a sentence; writers also capitalize proper nouns to establish a courteous relationship with the persons or entities they are writing about.

When you are uncertain whether to capitalize a particular word, look it up in a good, recent dictionary (see **28e**). Dictionaries list not only words and abbreviations that begin with capitals but also acronyms that use full capitals. (Acronyms are words made from the first letters of the words in a term or from syllables of a term. See **37a(10)** and **39e**.)

Tom Cruise   California   Rev.   Italians   Federal Express   EPA

A recent dictionary is also useful when the capitalization of a word depends on a particular meaning in context.

mosaic pictures   BUT   Mosaic law
on earth   BUT   the planet Earth

A style manual for the discipline in which you are writing is another useful guide for capitalization. (See pages 283–284.)

When you can choose whether or not to capitalize a word, it is important to follow one style consistently.

Beyond the Rule

UPPERCASE

Capital letters are often referred to as *uppercase* and noncapital letters as *lowercase* in reference to the parts of the typecase in which they were stored when type was set by hand. For more information, visit www.harbrace.com.

 When you type a final draft, you may notice that the AutoCorrect function of your word-processing program capitalizes letters that you want in lowercase form. For instance, it may capitalize items in a list that you intend to be part of a series completing a sentence—like those in the list at the beginning of this chapter. It's a good idea to turn off any automatic style or formatting function of a word processor.

37a | **Proper names are capitalized and so, usually, are their abbreviations and acronyms.**

As you study the following examples, notice that common nouns like *college, company, park,* and *street* are capitalized only when they are essential parts of proper names.

(1) Names and nicknames of persons or things and trade names are capitalized.

Zora Neale Hurston	Flight 224	Honda Accord
John Paul II	Academy Award	USS *Cole*
Skylab	Nike	Microsoft Windows

(2) Names of peoples and their languages are capitalized.

African Americans	Latinos	English	Swahili
Asians	Poles	Korean	Urdu
Eskimos	Sikhs	Spanish	Arabic

Blacks, Whites OR blacks, whites [Whichever you choose, be consistent.]

(3) Names of geographical features and of bridges, monuments, and buildings are capitalized.

Arctic Circle	Havana	Golden Gate Bridge
China	Iowa	Empire State Building
Ellis Island	Lincoln Memorial	Seventh Street
Grand Canyon	Mississippi River	Yellowstone National Park

When referring to two or more geographical features, however, do not capitalize the generic term: *Lincoln and Jefferson memorials, Yellowstone and Grand Canyon national parks.*

(4) Names of organizations, government agencies, institutions, and companies are capitalized.

B'nai B'rith	National Endowment for the Humanities
Congress of Racial Equality	Howard University
Phi Beta Kappa	New England Patriots
Internal Revenue Service	Ford Motor Company

When used as common nouns, *service, company,* and *university* are not capitalized.

(5) Names for days of the week, months, and holidays are capitalized.

| Wednesday | Fourth of July |
| August | Labor Day |

The names of the seasons—spring, summer, fall, winter—are not capitalized unless followed by a year: *Spring 2004.*

(6) Designations for historical documents, periods, events, and movements are capitalized.

Declaration of Independence   Gulf War   Renaissance

Impressionism   Stone Age   World Series

(7) Names of religions, their adherents, holy days, titles of holy books, and words denoting the Supreme Being are capitalized.

Buddhism, Christianity, Islam, Judaism

Buddhist, Christian, Muslim, Jew

Bodhi Day, Easter, Ramadan, Yom Kippur

Sutras, Bible, Koran, Talmud BUT biblical, talmudic

Buddha, God, Allah, Yahweh

Some writers always capitalize pronouns referring to the Supreme Being (except *who, whom, whose*). Others capitalize such pronouns only when capitalization is needed to prevent ambiguity, as in "The Lord commanded the prophet to warn His people."

(8) Personifications are capitalized.

Then, into the room walked Beauty. [COMPARE Her beauty stunned everyone.]

Her heart belonged to Envy. [COMPARE She frequently experienced envy.]

(See also 29a(4).)

(9) Words derived from proper names are capitalized.

Americanize [verb]   Orwellian [adjective]   Marxism [noun]

When a proper name becomes the name of a general class of objects or ideas, it is no longer capitalized.

zipper [originally a capitalized trademark]

blarney [derived from the Blarney Stone, said to impart skill in flattery to those who kiss it]

A word derived from a brand name, such as Xerox, Kodak, Polaroid, or Kleenex, should be capitalized. Because the corporations that own these brand names object to their use for generic purposes, use *photocopy, camera, instant snapshot,* or *tissue* instead. If you are not sure whether a proper name or derivative has come to stand for a general class, look in a dictionary. Many such words can be either capitalized or not.

French windows OR french windows

Roman numeral OR roman numeral

Beyond the Rule

CAPITALIZATION STYLE

Most American style books recommend that initial letters of words derived from proper names not be capitalized. *The Chicago Manual of Style,* however, suggests that you make your own choice, but do so consistently. *Merriam-Webster's Collegiate Dictionary* comments that such words are often capitalized, but it shows most of them in lowercase. For more information on capitalization styles, visit www.harbrace.com.

(10) Abbreviations and acronyms often appear in capitals.

These forms are derived from the initial letters of capitalized word groups:

AMEX, AT&T, CBS, CST, JFK, NFL, OPEC, UNESCO, YMCA

(See also **35a(3)** and chapter **39**.)

37b | Titles that precede the name of a person are capitalized but not those that follow it or stand alone.

Governor Peter Dunn	Peter Dunn, the governor
Captain Machado	Machado, our captain
Uncle Roy	Roy, my uncle
President Lincoln	the president of the United States

Words denoting family relationships are capitalized only when the words substitute for proper names.

Tell Mother I'll write soon. [COMPARE My mother wants me to write.]

> ### 37c | The first, last, and all major words in titles of works are capitalized.

All words in titles and subtitles of literary and artistic works are capitalized, except articles (*a, an,* and *the*), coordinating conjunctions (*and, but, for, nor, or, so,* and *yet*), prepositions (see the list on page 490), and the infinitive marker *to* (unless it is the first or last word in the title). (See also **34b** and **38a**.) APA style requires capitalizing any word that has four or more letters, including prepositions (except in references entries, where only the first word, the first word after a colon or a dash, and proper nouns or adjectives are capitalized). (See **11c**.)

The Scarlet Letter
From Here to Eternity

"How to Be a Leader"
"What This World Is Coming To"

Southwestern Pottery from Anasazi to Zuni [MLA and CMS]
Southwestern Pottery From Anasazi to Zuni [APA]

MLA, APA, and CMS recommend capitalizing all words of any hyphenated compound in a title, except for articles, coordinating conjunctions, and prepositions.

"The Building of the H-Bomb" [noun]
"The Arab-Israeli Dilemma" [proper adjective]
"Stop-and-Go Signals" [lowercase the coordinating conjunction]

Single-word compounds (*undercover, decommission*) in titles follow the normal rules of capitalization. However, if misreading could occur (as with *Un-ionized* or *Re-cover*), MLA and APA capitalize both elements if the second element begins with a capital letter (*Pre-Columbian*) or if the compound contains a doubled letter that could be hard to read (*Anti-Intellectual*). CMS capitalizes only those words that are proper nouns or adjectives.

"Colonial Anti-Independence Poetry" [MLA]

"Anti-Independence Behavior in Adolescents" [APA]

"Anti-independence Activities of Delaware's Tories" BUT "Pre-Columbian Artifacts in Peruvian Museums" [CMS]

> **37d** | The first word of every sentence (or any unit written as a sentence) and of any directly quoted speech is capitalized.

Procrastination is one of my specialties.

Experienced cooks are usually ready to try something new. (You can learn from them.) [parenthetical sentence]

Oh, really! Not right now. [units written as sentences]

Beth got out of the car and shouted, "Home at last!" [directly quoted speech]

"Stop dieting," he says, "and start exercising." OR "Stop dieting," he says. "And start exercising." [directly quoted speech in a single sentence and directly quoted speech in separate sentences]

I have only one rule: Pay attention. [independent clause following a colon; see **35d**]

A series of questions following an introductory element is usually capitalized when the intent is to draw attention to the questions. Otherwise, such questions may begin with lowercase letters.

How do we distinguish the legal codes for families? For individuals? For genetic research?

Are interest rates on car loans down to six percent? five? three?

For the treatment of directly quoted written material, see chapter 34.

> **37e** | Unnecessary capitals are distracting.

(1) Capitalizing common nouns can distract your readers.

Do not confuse a common noun with a proper noun naming a specific entity. A common noun preceded by the indefinite article *a* or *an* or by a modifier such as *every* or *several* is not capitalized.

a speech course in theater and television [COMPARE Speech 324: Theater and Television]

a university, my high school [COMPARE University of Michigan, Hickman High School]

However, always capitalize proper nouns, even when they are preceded by *a* or *an* or by a modifier such as *every* or *several*. In such cases, capitalized nouns name one or more members of a class.

a St. Bernard   every Virginian   several Canadians

(2) Using capitalization to indicate emphasis requires caution.

Occasionally, a common noun is capitalized for emphasis.

The motivation of many politicians is Power.

If you use capitals for emphasis, do so sparingly; overuse will weaken the effect. For other ways to achieve emphasis, see chapter 26.

STYLE SHEET FOR CAPITALIZATION

Capitals	No Capitals
the West [geographical region]	driving west [compass point]
Southerners [a group of people]	the southern plains
a Chihuahua [a breed of dog named after a state in Mexico]	a poodle [a breed of dog]
Washington State University [a specific institution]	a state university
German, Italian, Japanese [specific languages]	a language course
Revolutionary War [a specific war]	an eighteenth-century war
the U.S. Army OR US Army [a national army]	a peacetime army [an army of any nation]
Declaration of Independence [title of a document]	a declaration of independence
the PTA [OR the P.T.A.]	an organization for parents and teachers
May [specific month]	spring [general season]
Memorial Day [specific day]	a holiday

(Continued on page 756)

(Continued from page 755)

two Democratic candidates [refers to a political party]	democratic procedures [refers to a form of government]
a Ford tractor [brand name]	a farm tractor
Parkinson's disease [a disease named for a person]	flu, asthma, leukemia
Dr. Katherine Kadohata [a person's title]	every doctor, my doctor

Exercise 1

Write a sentence using each of the following words correctly.

1. president
2. President
3. company
4. Company
5. north
6. North
7. street
8. Street
9. republican
10. Republican
11. mountains
12. Mountains

Exercise 2

Insert capitals wherever needed.

¹when i went back to school after being in the navy, i began to see why i had had problems in school three years earlier. ²as a first-year student, i was delighted to be out from under my parents' supervision, and i spent more time and money at the college inn's perpetual party than i did studying german and zoology. ³roger gibson, my roommate that year, was from denver, colorado, and he drove a very fast pontiac firebird. ⁴we had some wonderful friday nights in that car when we should have been studying. ⁵when i flunked out in june, i joined the navy. ⁶basic training was a real eye-opener. ⁷lieutenant davis, my commanding officer, helped me understand how to use self-discipline. ⁸as i neared the end of my military service, i consulted a copy of *peterson's guide to colleges and universities.* ⁹i applied to laughlin state university because they offered two things that were important to me: a major in game theory and a cooperative education program. ¹⁰cooperative education allows me to apply some of my work experience for credit and to earn money to supplement the scholarship i get from the department of defense—often called the g.i. bill.

Italics

When you use italics, you let readers know that you are using a word or a group of words in a special way. For example, the following sentence is ambiguous.

> The linguistics students discussed the word stress.

Does this sentence mean that the students discussed a particular word or that they discussed an accent pattern? By italicizing *stress,* the writer indicates that it was the word, not the accent pattern, that the students discussed.

> The linguistics students discussed the word *stress.*

This chapter will help you use italics for

- the titles of separate works (**38a**),
- foreign words (**38b**),
- the names of legal cases (**38c**),
- the names of ships, submarines, aircraft, spacecraft, and satellites (**38d**),
- words, letters, or figures used as such or as statistical symbols or variables in algebraic expressions (**38e**), and
- emphasis of words (**38f**).

Word-processing programs make it easy to use italics. In handwritten or typewritten documents, you can indicate italics by underlining.

> Richard Russo's novel *Empire Falls* won a Pulitzer Prize.
> Richard Russo's novel <u>Empire Falls</u> won a Pulitzer Prize.

Although the use of italics instead of underlining is widely accepted in business writing, conventions for academic writing vary. The MLA recommends underlining, but the APA and the CMS prefer italics. If in doubt, follow the convention your audience expects. Remember, though, that in email and on Web pages, an underlined word or phrase often indicates a hyperlink. If you are unable to format your email or other electronic text with italics or underlining, use an underscore before and after words you would normally italicize.

Richard Russo's novel _Empire Falls_ won a Pulitzer Prize.

38a | Italics indicate titles of separate works.

A **separate work** is one published (or produced) as a whole rather than as part of a larger work. A newspaper, for example, is a separate work, but an editorial in a newspaper is not. Different conventions are used for indicating the title of the newspaper and the title of the editorial. (See 34a and 37c.) These conventions help readers realize the nature of a work and the relationship of one work to another.

Helen Keller's "Three Days to See" originally appeared in the *Atlantic Monthly.* [an essay in a magazine]

The titles of the following kinds of separate works are italicized.

Books	*The Bluest Eye*	*The God of Small Things*
Magazines	*Wired*	*National Geographic*
Newspapers	*USA Today*	*Wall Street Journal*
Plays, films, videotapes	*Death of a Salesman*	*A Beautiful Mind*
Television and radio shows	*Friends*	*A Prairie Home Companion*
Recordings	*A Day without Rain*	*Great Verdi Overtures*
Works of art	*American Gothic*	*David*
Long poems	*Paradise Lost*	*The Divine Comedy*
Pamphlets	*Saving Energy*	*Tips for Gardeners*
Comic strips	*Peanuts*	*Doonesbury*

When you include an italicized title in a sentence, switch to non-italic type to indicate that another title of a separate work is embedded within it.

The class read various selections from *Twentieth Century Interpretations of* Paradise Lost. [COMPARE We studied various interpretations of *Paradise Lost* last quarter.]

Titles are not italicized when they stand alone, for example, on a title page, a book cover, or a newspaper masthead. The title of a paper or report (unless it is also the title of a separate work) should not be italicized. (See also 37c.)

Neither italics nor quotation marks are necessary for titles of major historical documents or religious texts.

The Bill of Rights contains the first ten amendments to the U.S. Constitution.

The Bible, which is a sacred text just as the Koran or the Torah is, begins with the Book of Genesis.

According to the guidelines in the *MLA Handbook for Writers of Research Papers* and those in *The Chicago Manual of Style,* an initial *the* in a newspaper or periodical title is not italicized. It is not capitalized either, unless it begins a sentence.

The story was leaked to a journalist at the *New York Times.*

Also recommended is the omission of an article (*a, an,* or *the*) at the beginning of such a title when it would make a sentence awkward.

The report will appear in Thursday's ~~the~~ *Wall Street Journal.*

38b | Italics indicate foreign words.

The answer came in alphabetical order: *afar, esh, mayim, ruach:* earth, fire, water, wraith.   —CYNTHIA OZICK

Side by side, hunched low in the light rain, the two outcasts dip up *tsampa,* the roasted maize or barley meal, ground to powder and cooked as porridge or in tea, that is subsistence food in the Himalaya.

—PETER MATTHIESSEN

The Latin words used to classify plants and animals according to genus and species are also italicized.

Homo sapiens   *Rosa setigera*

Countless words borrowed from other languages have become part of English and are therefore not italicized. The more familiar a word becomes, the less likely it is to be italicized.

bayou (Choctaw)   karate (Japanese)   spaghetti (Italian)
cliché (French)   arroyo (Spanish)   curriculum vitae (Latin)

38c | **Italics identify the names of legal cases.**

Miranda v. Arizona   *Roe v. Wade*

The abbreviation *v.* (for "versus") may appear in either italic or nonitalic type, as long as the style is used consistently. Italics are also used for the shortened name of a well-known legal case.

According to the *Miranda* decision, suspects must be informed of their right to remain silent and their right to legal advice.

Italics are not used to refer to a case by other than its official name.

All the major networks covered the O. J. Simpson trial.

38d | **Italics identify the names of specific ships, submarines, aircraft, spacecraft, and satellites.**

USS *Enterprise*   USS *Hawkbill*   *Enola Gay*   *Atlantis*   *Aqua*

The names of trains and the trade names of aircraft are not italicized.

Orient Express   Boeing 747   Concorde

38e | **Italics indicate words, letters, or figures referred to as such or used as statistical symbols or as variables in algebraic expressions.**

The *p* in *ptarmigan* is silent.
The *8* on the sign has faded, and the *5* has disappeared.
The Pythagorean theorem is expressed as $a^2 + b^2 = c^2$.

According to the APA style manual, volume numbers in reference lists are italicized (see **11c**): *Memory & Cognition, 3,* 635–647.

When you think a sentence may be misunderstood, you can italicize words that you want readers to stress.

> These *are* the right files. [The italicized word receives more stress than it normally would.]

Italics can also emphasize emotional content.

> We have to go *now.* [The italicized word signals urgency.]

If overused, italics will lose their impact. Instead of italicizing (or underlining) words, try substituting more specific or forceful words (see chapters **26** and **29**) or varying sentence structures (chapter **27**).

Exercise 1

Identify all words that should be italicized in the following sentences. Explain why italics are necessary in each case.

1. Information about museum collections and exhibits can be found in art books, online museum Web sites, and special sections of magazines and newspapers such as Smithsonian Magazine and the New York Times.
2. The Web site for the Metropolitan Museum of Art has pictures of Anthony Caro's sculpture Odalisque and Charles Demuth's painting The Figure 5 in Gold.
3. The title page of William Blake's Songs of Innocence is included in Masterpieces of the Metropolitan Museum of Art.
4. This book includes a photograph of a beautiful script used in the Koran; the script is known as the maghribi, or Western, style.
5. The large Tyrannosaurus rex discovered by Sue Hendrickson in South Dakota is on display at the Field Museum.

6. The International Museum of Cartoon Art provides information about the designers of such comic strips as *Blondie, Peanuts, Mutt and Jeff,* and *Li'l Abner.*

7. *The Great Train Robbery, It Happened One Night,* and *Grand Illusion* are in the collection at the Celeste Bartos Film Preservation Center.

8. In 1998, the Songwriters Hall of Fame honored John Williams, who has written music for such movies as *Jaws, Star Wars,* and *E.T.*

9. The Smithsonian Institution's National Air and Space Museum houses an impressive collection of aircraft and spacecraft, including *Spirit of St. Louis* and *Gemini 4.*

10. The digital collection listed on the Web site Experience Music Project includes music from the albums *Fresh Cream* and *Bluesbreakers with Eric Clapton.*

Abbreviations, Acronyms, and Numbers

Abbreviations, acronyms, and numbers facilitate effective communication in both academic papers (see chapters 7 and 11–14) and business documents (chapter 15).

Abbreviations usually contain periods. Acronyms do not. An abbreviation is a shortened version of a word or phrase: *assn.* (association), *dept.* (department), *B.C.E.* (before the common era). An acronym is formed by combining the initial letters and/or syllables of a series of words: *AIDS* (**a**cquired **i**mmune **d**eficiency **s**yndrome), *sonar* (**so**und **na**vigation **r**anging).

This chapter will help you learn

- how and when to abbreviate (39a–d),
- when to explain an acronym (39e), and
- whether to spell out a number or use numerals (39f–g).

39a Abbreviations appear before or after proper names.

Designations such as *Ms., Mr., Mrs., Dr.,* and *Prof.* appear before proper names because they are a way of addressing people.

Ms. Gretel Lopez	Mrs. Adrienne Marcus	St. Peter
Mr. Julio Rodriguez	Dr. Thomas Redshaw	Prof. Robert Yagelski
Capt. Margaret Hoffner	Sen. Edward Kennedy	Rev. Kevin Burns

Designations such as *Jr., Sr., III,* and *M.D.* appear after proper names because they provide information about the individuals' status and are not a form of address.

Samuel Levy, Jr.	Deborah Hvidsten, M.D.	Henry VIII
Mark Ngo, Sr.	Erika C. Schuerer, Ph.D.	Putman Amory III

Avoid redundant designations.

> Dr. Carol Ballou OR Carol Ballou, M.D.
> [NOT Dr. Carol Ballou, M.D.]

Most abbreviations form plurals by adding *-s* alone, without an apostrophe: *Drs. Ballou and Hvidsten.* Exceptions are made when adding *-s* would create a different abbreviation, such as for *Mr.* and *Mrs.* When this is the case, consult a dictionary.

39b | **Abbreviations are used for addresses in correspondence.**

Although words such as *Street, Avenue, Road, Company,* and *Corporation* are usually written out when they appear in sentences, they are abbreviated when used in the address on an envelope. Similarly, the names of states are also abbreviated when they are part of an address.

Sentence Derson Manufacturing Company is located on Madison Street in Watertown, Minnesota.

Address Derson Manufacturing Co.
200 Madison St.
Watertown, MN 55388

When addressing correspondence within the United States, use the abbreviations designated by the U.S. Postal Service for the names of the states. (No period follows these abbreviations.) Spell out state names and words like *Company* and *Street* on the inside address of a business letter. Use abbreviations in the salutation.

Beyond the Rule

POSTAL ABBREVIATIONS

The abbreviations of states' names required for U.S. mail facilitate efficient delivery and always consist of two characters. Connecticut, for example, is CT, not Conn. For a list of these abbreviations, visit www.harbrace.com.

39c | Abbreviations are used in bibliographies and other citations of research sources.

The *MLA Handbook for Writers of Research Papers*, the *Publication Manual of the American Psychological Association*, and *The Chicago Manual of Style* all provide lists of abbreviations for writers to use when citing research sources in bibliographies, footnotes, and endnotes. (See also chapter 11.) Common abbreviations include the following (not all citation styles accept all of these abbreviations).

Bibliographies and Notes

anon.	Anonymous
Assn.	Association
biog.	biography, biographer, biographical
bk.	book
bull.	bulletin
c.	circa, about (for example, *c. 1920*)
col., cols.	column, columns
cont.	contents OR continues, continued
et al.	*et alii* ("and others")
fig.	figure
fwd.	foreword, foreword by
gen. ed.	general editor
illus.	illustrated by, illustrator, illustration
inc., Inc.	including; incorporated, Incorporated
intl.	international
introd.	introduction, introduction by
ms., mss.	manuscript, manuscripts
natl.	national
n.d.	no date
n.p.	no page number
no., nos.	number, numbers
p., pp.	page, pages
P, Pr.	Press
pref.	preface
pt., pts.	part, parts
rept.	report, reported by
trans.	translation, translated by
U, Univ.	University

(Continued on page 766)

(Continued from page 765)

Computer Terms

CD	compact disc
CD-ROM	compact disc read-only memory
DVD	digital video disc
FTP	File Transfer Protocol
HTML	HyperText Markup Language
http	hypertext transfer protocol
MB	megabyte
MOO	Multiuser domain, Object-Oriented
URL	Uniform Resource Locator
WWW, www	World Wide Web

Divisions of Government

Cong.	Congress
dept.	department
div.	division
govt.	government
GPO	Government Printing Office
HR	House of Representatives

Months

Jan.	January
Feb.	February
Mar.	March
Apr.	April
Aug.	August
Sept.	September
Oct.	October
Nov.	November
Dec.	December

For abbreviations of Latin terms used in writing, see **39d(6)**.

39d | Although abbreviations are usually too informal for use in sentences, some are acceptable substitutes for words.

When writing sentences, use abbreviations if they have become so familiar that readers can read them aloud easily. This is the case when abbreviations are used in place names, such as *St.* for Saint (as in *St. Louis*) or *Mt.* for mount or mountain (as in *Mt. Hood*). Similarly, titles of address (see **39a**) can be used in sentences. Other examples follow.

(1) Words that are abbreviated for special purposes are usually written out when they appear within sentences.

For ease of reading, the names of months, days of the week, and units of measurement are usually written out, not abbreviated, when they are included in sentences, as are words such as *Street* and *Corporation* (see **39b**).

> On a Tuesday in September, we drove ninety-nine miles to San Francisco, California, where we stayed in a hotel on Market Street.

Similarly, words such as *volume, chapter,* and *page* are written out within sentences, even though they are abbreviated in bibliographies and other citations of research sources (see **39c**).

> I read the introductory chapter and pages 82–89 in the first volume of the committee's report.

(2) A *clipped form* is a word shortened from a longer word.

Because it functions as a word, a **clipped form** does not end with a period. Some clipped forms—such as *rep* (for representative), *exec* (for executive), and *info* (for information)—are too informal for use in college writing. Others—such as *exam, lab,* and *math*—have become acceptable because they have been used so frequently that they no longer seem like abbreviations.

(3) Abbreviations designate time periods and zones.

> 82 BC [OR BCE] for before Christ [OR before the common era]
>
> AD 95 [OR 95 CE] for *anno Domini*, in the year of our Lord [OR the common era]
>
> 7:40 a.m. for *ante meridiem*, before noon
>
> 4:52 EST for Eastern Standard Time

Words designating units of time, such as *minute* and *month,* are written out when they appear in sentences. They can be abbreviated in tables or charts.

> sec.   min.   hr.   wk.   mo.   yr.

(4) The abbreviation for the United States (U.S. or US) should be used only as an adjective.

the U.S. Navy, the US economy [COMPARE The United States continues to enjoy a strong economy.]

In MLA style (see **11a**), use US rather than U.S. (The MLA recommends omitting periods in abbreviations made up of all capital letters, with the exception of initials used for personal names; see, however, **39d(5)**.)

(5) Some individuals are widely known by their initials.

JFK   LBJ   E. B. White   B. B. King

In most cases, however, first and last names should be written out in full.

Phyllis D. Miller

(6) Some abbreviations stand for expressions in Latin.

Certain abbreviations for Latin expressions are common in academic writing.

cf. [compare]   et al. [and others]   i.e. [that is]
e.g. [for example]   etc. [and so forth]   vs. OR v. [versus]

39e | **Acronyms are usually spelled out the first time they are used.**

Some acronyms have been used so frequently that they are likely to be recognized without explanation.

NASA   NATO   UNICEF

The ability to identify a particular acronym will vary from one audience to another. Some readers know that NAFTA stands for the North American Free Trade Agreement; others may not. By spelling out acronyms the first time you use them, you are being courteous and clear.

The Federal Emergency Management Administration (FEMA) was criticized . . . .

When you use an abbreviation, an acronym, or a number, you sometimes need an indefinite article. Choose *a* or *an* based on the pronunciation: Use *a* before a consonant sound and *an* before a vowel sound.

A picture of **a UN** delegation is on the front page of today's newspaper. [*UN* is pronounced as two letters.]

I have **an IBM** computer. [*IBM* is pronounced as three letters.]

The reporter interviewed **a NASA** engineer. [*NASA* is pronounced as one word.]

My friend drives **a 1964** Mustang. [*1964* is pronounced "nineteen sixty-four."]

Exercise 1

Place a check mark next to those forms that are appropriate for use within the sentences of a college essay. Correct those that are not.

1. after 8 p.m.
2. 457 *anno Domini*
3. on St. Clair Ave.
4. two blocks from Water Street
5. in Nov.
6. in the second mo. of the yr.
7. in Calif.
8. at the UN
9. Mr. Robert Lyons
10. for a prof.

39f | Depending on their use, numbers are treated in different ways.

When writing for general purposes, spell out numbers from one through one hundred (*nine employees, nineteen employees, ninety-one employees*). If one of these numbers is followed by a word such as *hundred, thousand,* or *million,* it should also be spelled out (*nine hundred years, ninety-one million years*). Use a numeral for any other number, unless it begins a sentence.

The register recorded 164 names.

One hundred sixty-four names were recorded in the register. [Notice that *and* is not used in numbers greater than one hundred. NOT One hundred and sixty-four names . . . .]

In a discussion of related items involving both single- and double- or triple-digit numbers, use figures for all numbers.

Only 5 of the 134 delegates attended the final meeting.

In scientific or technical writing, use numerals before symbols, measurement words, and abbreviations (*24%, 3 inches* or *3″, 30 cubic centimeters* or *30 cc*).

Style manuals differ in their treatment of numbers. The general guidelines given here are from *The Chicago Manual of Style*. Consult your instructor or supervisor or a manual for the specific discipline to be sure that you are following the appropriate conventions.

39g | Some numbers follow special conventions.

(1) Specific times of day can be expressed in either numbers or words.

4 p.m. OR four o'clock in the afternoon

9:30 a.m. OR half-past nine in the morning OR nine-thirty in the morning [Notice the use of hyphens.]

(2) Dates are usually indicated by both numbers and words.

May 20, 1976 OR 20 May 1976 [NOT May 20th, 1976]

the fourth of December OR December 4

the fifties OR the 1950s

the fourteenth century OR the 14th century

in 1362

from 1999 to 2003 OR 1999–2003 [Use an en dash, not a hyphen, in number ranges.]

Many cultures invert the numbers for the month and the day: *14/2/2003* or *14 February 2003*. In American practice, the month generally precedes the day: *2/14/2003* or *February 14, 2003*.

(3) Addresses require the use of numbers.

25 Arrow Drive, Apartment 1, Columbia, MO 78209
OR 25 Arrow Dr., Apt. 1, Columbia, MO 78209

21 Second Street

459 East 35 Street OR 459 East 35th Street

(4) Identification numbers are indicated with figures.

Channel 10   Edward III   Interstate 40   Room 311

(5) Pages and divisions of books and plays are indicated with figures.

page 15   chapter 8   part 2   in act 2, scene 1 OR in Act II, Scene I

(6) Decimals and percentages are expressed numerically.

a 2.5 average   12 percent   0.853 metric ton

(7) Large fractional numbers can be expressed with either figures or words or both.

5.2 million inhabitants   4.2 billion years

(8) Numbers can be stated in two ways.

The lawyer's fee will exceed two million dollars.

OR

The lawyer's fee will exceed $2,000,000.

Cultures differ in their use of the period and the comma with numbers. In American usage, a decimal point (period) indicates a number or part of a number that is smaller than one, and a comma divides larger numbers into units of three digits (thousands).

10,000 (ten thousand)   7.65 (seven and sixty-five one-hundredths)

In some other cultures, the decimal and the comma are reversed.

10.000 (ten thousand)   7,65 (seven and sixty-five one-hundredths)

E x e r c i s e   2

Edit the following sentences to correct the usage of abbreviations and numbers.

1. A Natl. Historic Landmark, Hoover Dam is located about 30 miles s.e. of Las. Vegas, Nev.

2. The dam is named after Herbert Hoover, the 31st pres. of the U.S.

3. It is administered by the U.S. Dept. of the Interior.

4. Built by the fed. gov. between nineteen thirty-three and 1935, this dam is still considered one of the greatest achievements in the history of civ. engineering.

5. Construction of the dam became possible after several states in the Southwest (namely, AZ, CA, CO, NV, NM, UT, and WY) agreed on a plan to share water from the river.

6. The concrete used in the dam would have built a highway 16 ft. wide, stretching all the way from San Francisco to NYC.

7. 3,500 men worked on the dam during an average month of construction; this work translated into a monthly payroll of $500,000.

8. Spanning the Colorado River, Hoover Dam created Lake Mead— a reservoir covering 247 sq. miles.

9. A popular tourist attraction, Hoover Dam was closed to the public after terrorists attacked the U.S. on 9/11/01.

10. Today, certain pts. on the dam remain closed to the public as part of the effort to improve U.S. security.

GLOSSARY OF USAGE

The term *usage* refers to the ways words are used in specific contexts. As you know from speaking and writing every day, the words you choose depend on your audience and your purpose. For example, you might use *guys* when you are at lunch with your friends but choose *people, classmates, employees,* or another more formal or precise word when you are writing a report. By learning about usage in this glossary, you will increase your ability to use words effectively. Many of the entries are context-specific; others distinguish between words that sound or look similar. Frequently confused words are defined in terms of their meanings (see the entry for *cite*) or their parts of speech (see the entry for *advice*).

The definitions and guidelines in this glossary will help you write clear and precise prose. Nonetheless, you should be aware that usage judgments may mask misunderstanding and prejudice. The idea of a standard potentially carries with it the assumption that any word not considered standard is inferior. Words labeled *nonstandard* are commonly condemned, even though they may be words some people have grown up hearing and using. A better way to discuss usage is to label what is conventional, or accepted practice, for a specific context. Thus, words commonly used in one context may not be appropriate in another. The words you use with your friends, for instance, likely differ from those you choose for a letter of application. This glossary uses the following labels to characterize usage.

Conventional	Words or phrases listed in dictionaries without special usage labels; generally considered appropriate in academic and professional writing.
Conversational	Words or phrases that dictionaries label *informal, slang,* or *colloquial*; although often used in informal speech and writing, not generally appropriate for formal writing assignments.
Unconventional	Words or phrases not generally considered appropriate in academic or professional writing and often labeled *nonstandard* in dictionaries; best avoided in formal contexts.

Because usage changes over time, attempts to redefine words are made every few years. However, agreement on usage occurs slowly, often after a period of debate. In this glossary, entries are marked ∗ when new usages have been reported by dictionary editors but may not yet be accepted by everyone. To choose between traditional and recent usage rules, you must consider your audience and your purpose (see chapter 1).

Beyond the Rule

ESTABLISHING USAGE RULES

To learn how usage definitions and rules are established, visit www.harbrace.com.

 Grammar checkers may identify some common usage errors (such as *its* instead of *it's*), but they will not find more subtle problems. Grammar checkers also rarely distinguish between words that are spelled similarly but have different meanings. For example, a grammar checker found nothing wrong with the following sentence, even though *capitol* is used incorrectly: *The capitol of Minnesota is St. Paul.* Grammar checkers can help you with some usage problems, but you should never rely on them. See Using a Grammar Checker on page 468.

a, an Use *a* before a consonant sound: **a** house, **a** U-turn, **a** one-term president. Use *an* before a vowel sound: **an** egg, **an** M.D., **an** hour. For the differences between *a* or *an* and *the,* see 23e.

a lot of *A lot of* is conversational for *many, much,* or *a great deal of:* They do not have ~~a lot of~~ much time. *A lot* is sometimes misspelled as *alot.*

a while, awhile *A while* means "a period of time." It is often used with the prepositions *after, for,* and *in:* We rested for **a while.** *Awhile* means "a short time." It is not used after a preposition: We rested **awhile.**

accept, except The verb *accept* means "to receive": I **accept** your apology. The verb *except* means "to exclude": The policy was to have everyone wait in line, but mothers and small children were **excepted.** The preposition *except* means "other than": All **except** Joe will attend the conference.

adapt, adopt *Adapt* means "to adjust" or "to change for a purpose": We will **adapt** to the new conditions. The author will **adapt** his short story for television. *Adopt* means "to take as one's own": The company will **adopt** a new policy.

adverse, averse *Adverse* means "unfavorable": That policy will have **adverse** effects. Usually followed by *to, averse* means "reluctant" or "opposed": I am not **averse** to making a few changes.

advice, advise *Advice* is a noun: They asked their attorney for **advice**. *Advise* is a verb: The attorney **advised** us to save all relevant documents.

affect, effect *Affect* is a verb that means "to influence" or "to touch the emotions": The lobbyist's pleas did not **affect** the politician's decision. The news of the accident deeply **affected** us. The noun *effect* means "a result": The **effect** of his decision on the staff's morale was positive and long lasting. When used as a verb, *effect* means "to produce" or "to cause": The activists believed that they could **effect** real political change.

* **aggravate** *Aggravate* means "to intensify or make worse": Lack of union representation **aggravated** the workers' discontent. Traditionally, *aggravate* was not synonymous with *annoy* or *irritate:* They were ~~aggravated~~ annoyed by the new stringent regulations. Current dictionaries consider this usage standard but conversational.

agree on, agree to, agree with *Agree on* means "to be in accord with others about something": We **agreed on** a date for the conference. *Agree to* means "to accept something" or "to consent to do something": The customer **agreed to** our terms. The negotiators **agreed to** conclude talks by midnight. *Agree with* means "to share an opinion with someone" or "to approve of something": I **agree with** you on this issue. No one **agreed with** his position.

ain't Unconventional unless used in dialogue or for humorous effect.

all The indefinite pronoun *all* is plural when it refers to people or things that can be counted: **All** were present. It is singular when it refers to things that cannot be counted: **All** is forgiven.

all ready, already *All ready* means "completely prepared": The rooms are **all ready** for the conference. *Already* means "by or before the time specified": She has **already** taken her final exams.

* **all right** *All right* means "acceptable." The students asked whether it was **all right** to use dictionaries during the exam. *Alright* is not yet a generally accepted spelling of *all right,* although it is becoming more common in journalistic writing.

all together, altogether *All together* means "as a group": The cast reviewed the script **all together**. *Altogether* means "wholly, thoroughly": That game is **altogether** too difficult.

allude, elude *Allude* means "to refer to indirectly": The professor **alluded** to a medieval text. *Elude* means "to evade" or "to escape from": For the moment his name **eludes** me.

allusion, illusion An *allusion* is a casual or indirect reference: The **allusion** was to Shakespeare's *Twelfth Night*. An *illusion* is a false idea or an unreal image: His idea of college is an **illusion.**

alot See **a lot of.**

already See **all ready, already.**

alright See **all right.**

altogether See **all together, altogether.**

a.m., p.m. Use these abbreviations only with figures: The show will begin at 7:00 **p.m.** [COMPARE The show will begin at seven *in the evening.*]

* **among, between** To follow traditional usage, use *among* with three or more entities (a group): The snorklers swam **among** the fish. Use *between* when referring to only two entities: The rivalry **between** the two teams is intense. Current dictionaries also note the possibility of using *between* to refer to more than two entities, especially when these entities are considered distinct: We have strengthened the lines of communication **between** the various departments.

amoral, immoral *Amoral* means "neither moral nor immoral" or "not caring about right or wrong": Complaining that U.S. schools are **amoral,** the senator proposed the addition of prayer time. *Immoral* means "not moral": Some philosophers consider war **immoral.**

amount of, number of Use *amount of* before nouns that cannot be counted: The **amount of** rain that fell last year was insufficient. Use *number of* with nouns that can be counted: The **number of** students attending college has increased.

an See **a, an.**

and etc. See **etc.**

and/or This combination denotes three options: one, the other, or both. These options can also be presented separately with *or:* The student's application should be signed by a parent **and/or** a teacher. The student's application should be signed by a parent, a teacher, **or** both.

* **angry at, angry with** Both *at* and *with* are commonly used after *angry,* although according to traditional guidelines, *with* should be used when a person is the cause of the anger: She was **angry with** me because I was late.

another, other, the other *Another* is followed by a singular noun: **another** book. *Other* is followed by a plural noun: **other** books. *The other* is followed by either a singular or a plural noun: **the other book, the other books.**

ante-, anti- *Ante-* is a prefix meaning "before" or "earlier": They waited in the **anteroom.** *Anti-* is a prefix meaning "against": **Antiwar** riots broke out across the country.

* **anxious, eager** *Anxious* means "worried" or "nervous": They are **anxious** about the strike. *Eager* means "keenly interested": They are **eager** to see the strike end. Dictionary editors report ample evidence of *anxious* being used to mean "eager," but this usage is still considered conversational.

anymore, any more *Anymore* meaning "any longer" or "now" most frequently occurs in negative sentences: Sarah doesn't work here **anymore.** Its use in positive sentences is considered conversational; *now* is generally used instead: All he ever does **anymore** now is watch television. As two words, *any more* appears with *not* to mean "no more": We do not have **any more** time.

anyone, any one *Anyone* means "any person at all": We did not know **anyone.** *Any one* refers to one of a group: **Any one** of the options is better than the current situation.

anyplace, everyplace, someplace According to traditional usage, each of these words should be written as two words (*any place, every place, some place*). Alternatively, *-where* can be used instead of *-place* (*anywhere, everywhere, somewhere*).

anyways, anywheres Unconventional; use *anyway* and *anywhere:* We decided to go **anyways.**

as Conversational when used after such verbs as *know, say,* and *see.* Use *that, if,* or *whether* instead: I do not know **as** whether my application is complete. Also considered conversational is the use of *as* instead of *who, which,* or *that:* Many of the performers **as** who have appeared on our program will be giving a concert this evening.

as, because The use of *as* to signal a cause may be vague; if it is, use *because* instead: **As** Because we were running out of water, we decided to turn around.

* **as, like** According to traditional usage, *as* begins either a phrase or a clause; *like* begins only a phrase: My brother drives too fast, just **like** as my father did. Current dictionaries note the informal use of *like* to begin clauses, especially after verbs such as *look, feel,* and *sound.*

* **as to** Traditionally, *as to* was considered imprecise: We were certain **as to** about the time. But current dictionaries recognize this two-word preposition as standard.

assure, ensure, insure *Assure* means "to state with confidence, alleviating any doubt": The flight attendant **assured** us that our flight would arrive on time. *Ensure* and *insure* are usually interchangeable to mean "make certain," but only *insure* means "to protect against loss": The editor **ensured** [OR **insured**] that the reporter's facts were accurate. Physicians must **insure** themselves against malpractice suits.

at this point in time Wordy for "at this time," "at this point," "now," or "then": At this point in time, no one had even heard of computers.

averse See **adverse, averse.**

awful, awfully Conversational when used to mean "very."

awhile See **a while, awhile.**

back up, backup Besides "to move in a reverse direction," the verb *back up* means "to make an archival copy of work on a computer": Did you remember to **back up** your files? *Backup* is a noun that refers to such a copy: I forgot to make a **backup** of that file.

bad Unconventional as an adverb; use *badly* instead. The team played **badly** yesterday. However, the adjective *bad* can be used after sensory verbs such as *feel, look,* and *smell:* I feel **bad** that I forgot to return your book yesterday. See 20a.

because *Because* may appear at the beginning of a sentence as long as it begins a dependent clause: **Because** the road was under construction, we had to take a detour. See also **as, because.**

being as, being that Unconventional; use *because* instead. Being as Because the road was closed, traffic was diverted to another route.

* **beside, besides** According to traditional usage, these two words have different meanings. *Beside* means "next to": The president sat **beside** the prime minister. *Besides* means "in addition to" or "other than": She has written many articles **besides** those on political reform. Current dictionaries report that professional writers regularly use *beside* to convey this meaning, as long as there is no risk of ambiguity.

better, had better *Better* is conversational. Use *had better* instead: We better had better finish the report by five o'clock.

between See **among, between.**

biannual, biennial *Biannual* means "twice in one year": An equinox is a **biannual** event. *Biennial* means "every two years": **Biennial** meetings last longer than annual meetings because they do not occur as frequently.

breath, breathe *Breath* is a noun: Take a deep **breath.** *Breathe* is a verb: **Breathe** deeply.

* bring, take Both words describe the same action but from different standpoints. *Bring* indicates movement toward the speaker: She **brought** me some flowers. *Take* implies movement away from the speaker: He **took** my overdue books to the library. Dictionaries report that this distinction is frequently blurred, especially when the speaker's standpoint is not relevant: He **brought** [OR **took**] her some flowers.

bunch Conversational to refer to a group: A **bunch** group of students participated in the experiment.

busted Unconventional. Use *broken* instead: Every day he walked past a **busted** broken vending machine on his way to class.

but that, but what Conversational after expressions of doubt such as *no doubt* or *did not know*. Use *that* instead: I do not doubt **but what** that they are correct.

* can, may According to traditional definitions, *can* refers to ability, and *may* refers to permission: You **can** [are able to] drive seventy miles an hour, but you **may** not [are not permitted to] exceed the speed limit. Current dictionaries report that in contemporary usage *can* and *may* are used interchangeably to denote possibility or permission, although *may* is used more frequently in formal contexts.

can't hardly, can't scarcely Unconventional. Use *can hardly* or *can scarcely:* The students **can't hardly** wait for summer vacation.

capital, capitol A *capital* is a governing city; it also means "funds." The **capital** of Minnesota is St. Paul. An anonymous donor provided the **capital** for the project. As a modifier, *capital* means "chief" or "principal": This year's election is of **capital** importance. It may also refer to the death penalty: **Capital** punishment is legal in some states. A *capitol* is a statehouse; the *Capitol* is the U.S. congressional building in Washington, D.C.

censor, censure, sensor As a verb, *censor* means "to remove or suppress because of immoral or otherwise objectionable ideas": Do you think a ratings board should **censor** films that have too much sex and violence? As a noun, *censor* refers to a person who is authorized to remove material considered objectionable: The **censor** recommended that the book be banned. The verb *censure* means "to blame or criticize"; the noun *censure* is an expression of disapproval or blame. The Senate **censured** Joseph McCarthy. He received a **censure** from the Senate. A *sensor* is a device that responds to a stimulus: The **sensor** detects changes in light.

center around Conversational for "to center on" or "to revolve around": The discussion **centered around** on the public's response to tax reform initiatives.

chair, chairman, chairperson As gender-neutral terms, *chairperson* and *chair* are preferred to *chairman*. See **28d(1)**.

cite, site, sight *Cite* means "to mention": Be sure to **cite** your sources. *Site* is a location: The president visited the **site** for the new library. As a verb, *site* also means "to situate": The builder **sited** the factory near the freeway. *Sight* means "to see": The crew **sighted** land. *Sight* also refers to a view: What an incredible **sight!**

climactic, climatic *Climactic* refers to a climax, or high point: The actors rehearsed the **climactic** scene. *Climatic* refers to the *climate:* Many environmentalists are worried about the recent **climatic** changes.

coarse, course *Coarse* refers to roughness: The jacket was made of **coarse** linen. *Course* refers to a route: Our **course** to the island was indirect. *Course* may also refer to a plan of study: I want to take a **course** in nutrition.

compare to, compare with *Compare to* means "to regard as similar," and *compare with* means "to examine to discover similarities or differences": She **compared** her mind **to** a dusty attic. The student **compared** the first draft **with** the second.

complement, complementary, compliment, complimentary *Complement* means "to complete" or "to balance": Their personalities **complement** each other. They have **complementary** personalities. *Compliment* means "to express praise": The professor **complimented** the students on their first drafts. Her remarks were **complimentary**. *Complimentary* may also mean "provided free of charge": We received **complimentary** tickets.

✻ **compose, comprise** *Compose* means "to make up": That collection **is composed** of medieval manuscripts. *Comprise* means "to consist of": The anthology **comprises** many famous essays. Dictionary editors have noted the increasing use of *comprise* to mean "to compose."

conscience, conscious, consciousness *Conscience* means "the sense of right and wrong": He examined his **conscience** before deciding whether to join the protest. *Conscious* means "awake": After an hour, the patient was fully **conscious.** After an hour, the patient regained **consciousness.** *Conscious* may also mean "aware": We were **conscious** of the possible consequences.

✻ **consensus of opinion** According to traditional usage, *of opinion* is redundant: The **consensus of opinion** was that binge drinking was adversely affecting nondrinkers as well. However, dictionary editors have questioned whether *consensus of opinion* is indeed redundant because there may also be a consensus of values or a consensus of practice.

consequently, subsequently *Consequently* means "as a result of": The surgeon made a serious mistake; **consequently,** both he and the hospital were being sued. *Subsequently* means "following": The negotiators met for several days and **subsequently** signed the treaty.

* **contact** Traditionally, this word was considered imprecise in academic writing for *telephone, see, write,* and other similar verbs: In case of an emergency, whom should we ~~contact~~ call? *Contact* is now often used to mean "communicate with."

continual, continually, continuous, continuously *Continual* means "constantly recurring": **Continual** interruptions kept us from completing the project. Telephone calls **continually** interrupted us. *Continuous* means "uninterrupted": The job applicant had a record of ten years' **continuous** employment. The job applicant worked **continuously** from 1992 to 2002.

* **convince, persuade** *Convince* means "to make someone believe something": His passionate speech **convinced** us that school reform was necessary. *Persuade* means "to motivate someone to act": She **persuaded** us to stop smoking. Dictionary editors note that many speakers now use *convince* as a synonym for *persuade.*

could care less Unconventional to express complete lack of concern. *Couldn't care less* is used in informal contexts.

could of See **of.**

council, counsel A *council* is an advisory or decision-making group: The student **council** supported the new safety regulations. A *counsel* is a legal adviser: The defense **counsel** conferred with the judge. As a verb, *counsel* means "to give advice": The new psychologist **counsels** people with eating disorders.

criteria, criterion *Criteria* is a plural noun meaning "a set of standards for judgment": The teachers explained the **criteria** for the assignment. The singular form is *criterion:* Their judgment was based on only one **criterion.**

* **data** *Data* is the plural form of *datum,* which means "piece of information" or "fact": When the **data are** complete, we will know the true cost. However, current dictionaries also note that *data* is frequently used as a mass entity (like the word *furniture*), appearing with a singular verb.

desert, dessert *Desert* can mean "a barren land": Gila monsters live in the **deserts** of the Southwest. When the second part of this word is stressed, *desert* refers to what is deserved; its plural form is frequently used: The villains received their just **deserts.** As a verb, *desert* means "to leave": I thought my friends had **deserted** me. *Dessert* refers to something sweet eaten at the end of a meal: They ordered apple pie for **dessert.**

device, devise *Device* is a noun: She invented a **device** that measures extremely small quantitites of liquid. *Devise* is a verb: We **devised** a plan that distributed the work equally.

dialogue Many readers consider the use of *dialogue* as a verb to be an example of unnecessary jargon. Use *discuss* or *exchange views* instead: The committee chair and several community members ~~dialogued about~~ discussed the issues.

differ from, differ with *Differ from* means "to be different": A bull snake **differs from** a rattlesnake in a number of ways. *Differ with* means "to disagree": Senator Brown has **differed with** Senator Owen on several issues.

different from, different than *Different from* is generally used with nouns, pronouns, noun phrases, and noun clauses: This school was **different from** most others. The school was **different from** what we had expected. *Different than* is used with adverbial clauses; *than* is the conjunction: We are no **different than** they are.

discreet, discrete, discretion *Discreet* means "showing good judgment or self-restraint": His friends complained openly, but his comments were quite **discreet.** *Discretion* is related to *discreet:* **Discretion** is the better part of valor. *Discrete* means "distinct": The participants in the study came from three **discrete** groups.

disinterested, uninterested *Disinterested* means "impartial": A **disinterested** observer will give a fair opinion. *Uninterested* means "lacking interest": She sleepily acknowledged that she was **uninterested** in the outcome of the game.

distinct, distinctive *Distinct* means "easily distinguishable or perceived": Each proposal has **distinct** advantages. *Distinctive* means "characteristic" or "serving to distinguish": We studied the **distinctive** features of hawks.

don't Use *doesn't* instead of *don't* with *he, she,* and *it:* It **don't** doesn't make sense.

drug Unconventional; use *dragged* instead of *drug:* The settlers must have **drug** dragged these large stones from the river.

* **due to** Traditionally, *due to* was not synonymous with *because of:* ~~Due to~~ Because of holiday traffic, we arrived an hour late. However, dictionary editors now consider this usage of *due to* acceptable, noting that it is widespread.

dyeing, dying *Dyeing* comes from *dye,* meaning "to color something, usually by soaking it": As a sign of solidarity, the students are **dyeing** their shirts the same color. *Dying* refers to the loss of life: Because of the drought, the plants are **dying.**

eager See **anxious, eager.**

effect See **affect, effect.**

e.g. Abbreviation of the Latin phrase *exempli gratia,* meaning "for example." Use only within parentheses: Some herbs are highly aromatic (**e.g.,** rosemary and sage). Otherwise, replace *e.g.* with the English equivalent, *for example* or *for instance:* The nonsmoking campaign has won many battles; **e.g.** for ex-

ample, few airlines allow smoking on their aircraft. Do not confuse *e.g.* with *i.e.,* meaning "that is."

elicit, illicit *Elicit* means "to draw forth": He is **eliciting** contributions for a new playground. *Illicit* means "unlawful": The newspaper reported their **illicit** mishandling of public funds.

elude See **allude, elude.**

emigrate from, immigrate to To *emigrate* is to leave one's own country: My ancestors **emigrated from** Ireland. To *immigrate* is to arrive in a different country to settle: The Ulster Scots **immigrated to** the southern United States.

eminent, imminent *Eminent* means "distinguished": An **eminent** scholar in physics will be giving a public lecture tomorrow. *Imminent* means "about to happen": The merger of the two companies is **imminent.**

ensure See **assure, ensure, insure.**

enthused Conversational. Use *enthusiastic* instead. Most students are ~~enthused~~ enthusiastic about the construction of a new student union.

especially, specially *Especially* emphasizes a characteristic or quality: Some people are **especially** sensitive to the sun. *Especially* also means "particularly": Wildflowers are abundant in this area, **especially** during April and May. *Specially* means "for a particular purpose" or "specifically": The classroom was **specially** designed for music students.

-ess This suffix has sexist connotations. Use *poet, author, actor,* and *waiter* or *server* instead of *poetess, authoress, actress,* and *waitress.* See **28d(1).**

etc. Abbreviation of the Latin phrase *et cetera,* meaning "and others of the same kind." Use only within parentheses: Be sure to bring appropriate camping gear (tent, sleeping bag, mess kit, **etc.**). Because *and* is part of the meaning of *etc.,* avoid using *and* with *etc.:* Many special events take place during orientation, including barbecues, games, and concerts~~, etc.~~

eventually, ultimately *Eventually* refers to some future time: She has made so many valuable contributions that I am sure she will **eventually** become the store supervisor. *Ultimately* refers to the final outcome after a series of events: The course was difficult but **ultimately** worthwhile.

everyday, every day *Everyday* means "routine" or "ordinary": These are **everyday** problems. *Every day* means "each day": I read the newspaper **every day.**

everyone, every one *Everyone* means "all": **Everyone** should attend. *Every one* refers to each person or item in a group: **Every one** of you should attend.

everyplace See **anyplace, everyplace, someplace.**

except See **accept, except.**

expect Conversational; use *think* or *believe* instead: I ~~expect~~ believe the answer is clear.

explicit, implicit *Explicit* means "expressed clearly and directly": Given his **explicit** directions, we knew how to proceed. *Implicit* means "implied or expressed indirectly": I mistakenly understood his silence to be his **implicit** approval of the project.

farther, further Generally, *farther* refers to geographic distance: We will have to drive **farther** tomorrow. *Further* refers to additional time or some other abstract noun: If you need **further** assistance, please let me know.

* **feel** Traditionally, *feel* was not synonymous with "think" or "believe": I ~~feel~~ think that more should be done to protect local habitat. Dictionary editors now consider such a use of *feel* to be a standard alternative.

female, male *Woman, man, girl,* and *boy* are the conventional words used to refer to gender. I interviewed two ~~females~~ women and three ~~males~~ men in my class. According to APA guidelines, *female* and *male* may be used when the age range within a group is broad: Most of the groups consisted of five **males** and five **females.** In addition, *male* and *female* may be used as modifiers when information about gender is relevant.

fewer, less *Fewer* occurs before nouns that can be counted: **fewer** technicians, **fewer** pencils. *Less* occurs before nouns that cannot be counted or before abstract nouns: **less** milk, **less** support. *Less than* may be used with measurements of time or distance: **less than** three months, **less than** twenty miles.

* **first, firstly; second, secondly** Many college instructors prefer the use of *first* and *second*. However, dictionary editors state that *firstly* and *secondly* are also well-established forms.

flunk Given the forcefulness of this term, *fail* is preferred in most contexts. She ~~flunked~~ failed the test by a slim margin.

foreword, forward A *foreword* is a preface: The **foreword** to the book provided useful background information. *Forward* refers to a frontward direction: To get a closer look, we moved **forward** slowly.

former, latter Used together, *former* refers to the first of two; *latter* to the second of two. John and Ian are both English; the **former** is from Manchester, and the **latter** is from Birmingham.

fun Conversational when used as an adjective: The children had ~~a fun time.~~

further See **farther, further.**

get Considered conversational in many common expressions: The weather ~~got better~~ improved overnight. I did not know what he ~~was getting at~~ meant.

go, goes Unconventional for *say(s), respond(s),* and other similar words: My friends say I'm strange, and I ~~go~~ reply, "You're right!"

good, well *Good* is an adjective, not an adverb. Use *well* instead: He pitched ~~good~~ well last night. *Good* in the sense of "in good health" may be used interchangeably with *well*: I feel **good** [OR **well**] this morning.

good and Conversational to mean "very" or "quite": They were ~~good and~~ quite angry about the tax increase.

had better See **better, had better.**

had ought to, hadn't ought to Unconventional. Omit *had,* or use *should not:* We ~~had~~ ought to apologize. We ~~hadn't ought to~~ should not have accused him in public.

a half a, a half an Unconventional; use *half of a/an, half a/an,* or *a half:* You should be able to complete the questionnaire in **a half ~~an~~** hour.

hanged, hung *Hanged* means "to put to death by hanging": The prisoner was **hanged** at dawn. For all other meanings, use *hung:* He **hung** the picture above his desk.

hardly Unconventional when combined with a negative word such as *not.* Depending on the intended meaning, either omit *hardly* or omit the negative word: The drivers could**n't hardly** see the road.

has got, have got Conversational; omit *got:* I **have ~~got~~** a meeting tomorrow.

he Unconventional to refer to people in general or a person whose gender is unknown. Use *he or she.* See **28d(1).**

he/she, his/her As a solution to the problem of sexist language, these combinations are not universally accepted. Consider using *he or she* and *his or her.* See **28d(1).**

herself, himself, myself, yourself Unconventional as subjects in a sentence. Joe and **myself** I will lead the discussion. See **21a.**

hisself Unconventional for *himself.*

hopefully Conversational to mean "I hope": ~~Hopefully,~~ I hope the game will not be canceled.

hung See **hanged, hung.**

idea, ideal An *idea* is a thought: The writer's main **idea** was stated in the first paragraph. An *ideal* is a model of perfection or a standard: The politician told her audience of her democratic **ideals.**

i.e. Abbreviation of the Latin phrase *id est,* meaning "that is." Use only within parentheses: All participants in the study ran the same distance (**i.e.,** six kilometers). Otherwise, replace *i.e.* with the English equivalent, *that is:* Assistance was offered to those who would have difficulty boarding, ~~i.e.~~ **that is,** the elderly, the disabled, and parents with small children. Do not confuse *i.e.* with *e.g.,* meaning "for example."

* **if, whether** Use *if* to mean "in the event that": The ceremony will be held indoors **if** it rains. *Whether* suggests alternatives: She doesn't know **whether** the ceremony will be held outdoors. Dictionary editors report that this usage is changing, noting that the use of *if* to refer to alternatives rarely causes confusion.

illicit See **elicit, illicit.**

illusion See **allusion, illusion.**

immigrate See **emigrate from, immigrate to.**

imminent See **eminent, imminent.**

immoral See **amoral, immoral.**

* **impact** Though it is commonly used as a verb in business writing, many college teachers still use *impact* as a noun only: The new tax ~~impacts~~ **affects** everyone.

implicit See **explicit, implicit.**

imply, infer *Imply* means "suggest without actually stating": Though he never mentioned the statistics, he **implied** that they were questionable. *Infer* means "draw a conclusion based on evidence": Given the tone of his voice, I **inferred** that he found the work substandard.

incredible, incredulous *Incredible* means "incapable of being believed": The tale of their journey was **incredible.** *Incredulous* means "disbelieving": We responded to the story with **incredulous** smirks.

individual *Individual* is used to distinguish a person from a group: An **individual** is easily influenced by the group. Otherwise, use *person* or *someone:* We notified ~~an individual~~ **someone** in the payroll office.

ingenious, ingenuous *Ingenious* means "creative or shrewd": This **ingenious** design will provide inexpensive energy. *Ingenuous* means "innocent or unworldly": Though considered **ingenuous** by most of her acquaintances, she understood clearly the causes of injustice.

in regards to Unconventional; see **regard, regarding, regards.**

inside of, outside of Drop *of* when unnecessary: Security guards stood **outside of** the front door. **Inside of** a year, everyone had moved away.

insure See **assure, ensure, insure.**

irregardless Unconventional; use *regardless* instead.

* **is because, is when, is where** Traditionally, only noun clauses followed the verb *be*. Clauses beginning with *because, when,* and *where* were thought to be adverbial clauses and were thus not used: The reason the project succeeded was **because** ~~that~~ it had ample funding. An essay test ~~is when~~ requires students ~~to~~ write paragraph-long answers. An armature is ~~where you have~~ a piece of soft iron connecting the poles of a magnet. Most dictionary editors would object to the examples above but would judge acceptable examples in which the subject and the subject complement are clearly related: Midnight **is when** the bells will ring. See **23d.**

its, it's *Its* indicates possession: The committee forwarded **its** recommendation. *It's* is a contraction of *it is:* **It's** a beautiful day.

-ize Some readers object to using this ending to create new verbs: *enronize.* Some of these new verbs, however, have already entered into common usage: *computerize.*

kind, sort, type When referring to one, use *this* or *that:* **This kind** [OR **sort** OR **type**] of argument is unacceptable. When referring to more than one, use *these* or *those:* **These kinds** [OR **sorts** OR **types**] of arguments are unacceptable.

kind of a, sort of a The word *a* is unnecessary: This **kind of** ~~a~~ book sells well. *Kind of* and *sort of* are not conventionally used to mean "somewhat": The report was ~~kind of~~ somewhat difficult to read.

later, latter *Later* means "after a specific time" or "a time after now": The concert ended **later** than we had expected. *Latter* refers to the second of two items: Of the two versions described, I prefer the **latter.**

lay, lie *Lay* (*laid, laying*) means "put" or "place": The public **laid** the blame on the current administration. *Lie* (*lay, lain, lying*) means "rest" or "recline": I had just **lain** down when the alarm went off. *Lay* takes an object (to **lay** something), while *lie* does not. These verbs may be confused because the present tense of *lay* and the past tense of *lie* are spelled the same way.

lead, led As a noun, *lead* means "a kind of metal": The paint had **lead** in it. As a verb, *lead* means "to conduct": The guide will **lead** a tour of the ruins this morning. *Led* is the past tense of the verb *lead:* He **led** the country from 1949 to 1960.

learn Unconventional to mean "teach." My mother ~~learned~~ taught me everything I know about local herbs.

* **leave** Unconventional to mean "let": ~~Leave~~ Let the paint dry overnight. *Let* and *leave* are interchangeable in the expression *let/leave alone,* meaning "to refrain from disturbing."

led See **lead, led.**

less, less than See **fewer, less.**

liable *Liable* generally means "likely" in an undesirable sense: If they invest money in that stock, they are **liable** to lose money. With her brains, she is ~~liable~~ **likely** to achieve success easily.

lie See **lay, lie.**

like See **as, like.**

literally Conversational when used to emphasize the meaning of another word: I was ~~literally~~ **nearly** frozen after I finished shoveling the sidewalk. *Literally* is conventionally used to indicate that an expression is not being used figuratively: My friend **literally** climbs the walls after work; his fellow rock climbers join him at the local gym.

* **loan** According to traditional definitions, *lend,* not *loan,* should be used to mean "to give temporarily": My friend will ~~loan~~ **lend** me her notes. However, dictionary editors report that the use of *loan* to mean "lend" in the financial sense is now considered standard: Banks **loan** money for mortgages.

lose, loose *Lose* is a verb: She does not **lose** her patience often. *Loose* is chiefly used as an adjective: A few of the tiles are **loose.**

lots, lots of Conversational for *many* or *much:* He has ~~lots of~~ **many** friends. We have ~~lots~~ **much** to do before the end of the quarter.

male See **female, male.**

mankind Considered sexist because it excludes women: All ~~mankind~~ **humanity** will benefit from this new discovery.

many, much *Many* is used with nouns that can be counted: **many** stores, too **many** assignments. *Much* is used with nouns that cannot be counted: **much** courage, not **much** time.

may See **can, may.**

may of, might of See **of.**

maybe, may be *Maybe* is an adverb: **Maybe** the negotiators will succeed this time. *May* and *be* are verbs: The rumor **may be** true.

* **media, medium** According to traditional definitions, *media* is a plural word: The **media** have sometimes created the news in addition to reporting it. The singular form is *medium:* The newspaper is one **medium** that people seem to trust. Dictionary editors note the frequent use of *media* as a collective noun taking a singular verb, but this usage is still considered conversational.

might could Conversational for "might be able to": The director **might could** ~~be able to~~ review your application next week.

morale, moral *Morale* refers to a mood or spirit: **Morale** was high. *Moral* refers to ethical conduct: The government had a **moral** duty to help the victims. *Moral* may also mean "the lesson of a story": The **moral** of the story is that to live well one must treat others well.

most Unconventional to mean "almost": We watch the news ~~most~~ almost every day.

much See **many, much.**

myself See **herself, himself, myself, yourself.**

neither . . . or Conventionally, *nor,* not *or,* follows *neither:* The book is **neither** as funny ~~or~~ nor as original as critics have reported.

not . . . no/none/nothing The use of multiple negative words is unconventional: I did **not** want ~~nothing~~ anything else. Multiple negation may be used for special effect.

nothing like, nowhere near Unconventional; use *not nearly* instead: Her new book is ~~nowhere near~~ not nearly as mysterious as her previous novel.

nowheres Unconventional; use *nowhere* instead: We met for two hours, but our discussion went **nowheres.**

number of When the expression *a number of* is used, the reference is plural: **A number of** positions **are** open. When *the number of* is used, the reference is singular: **The number of** possibilities **is** limited. Make sure that the verb agrees with the subject. See also **amount of, number of.**

of Often mistaken for the sound of the unstressed *have:* They must ~~of~~ have [OR could **have**, might **have**, may **have**, should **have**, would **have**] gone home.

off of Conversational; omit *of:* He walked **off** ~~of~~ the field.

OK, O.K., okay All three are acceptable spellings, but the usage of this expression is considered conversational. Choose a more specific word instead: All the passengers were ~~okay~~ uninjured.

on account of Conversational; use *because* or *because of:* The singer canceled her engagement ~~on account of~~ because of a sore throat.

on the other hand Use *however,* or make sure that the sentence or independent clause beginning with this transitional phrase is preceded by one starting with *on the one hand.*

other See **another, other, the other.**

ought See **had ought to, hadn't ought to.**

owing to the fact that Considered wordy; use *because* instead: ~~Owing to the fact that~~ Because more people came to the concert than were expected, the stage crew set up extra chairs in the aisles.

parameter Often considered an example of unnecessary jargon: We discussed the ~~parameters~~ characteristics of cross-cultural conflict.

passed, past *Passed* is the past tense of the verb *pass:* Everyone **passed** the test. *Past* means "beyond a time or location": The band marched **past** the bleachers.

people, persons In academic writing, *people* is preferred to *persons:* The reporter interviewed the ~~persons~~ people involved in the accident. *Persons* is occasionally used when emphasis is given to the individuals in a group: The person or **persons** who committed the crime will be prosecuted.

per In ordinary contexts, use *a* or *an:* You should drink eight glasses of water ~~per~~ a day.

percent, percentage *Percent* (also spelled *per cent*) is used with a specific number: **Sixty percent** of the students attended the ceremony. *Percentage* refers to an unspecified portion: The **percentage** of high school graduates attending college has increased in recent years.

perspective, prospective *Perspective* means "point of view": We discussed the issue from various **perspectives.** *Prospective* means "likely to become": **Prospective** elementary teachers visited nearby classrooms last Friday.

persuade See **convince, persuade.**

phenomena Plural of *phenomenon:* Natural **phenomena** were given scientific explanations.

plenty Conversational when used to mean "quite" or "sufficient": It was **plenty** ~~quite~~ humid the day we left. To mean "an adequate amount," *plenty* is followed by *of:* We have **plenty** of time.

plus *Plus* joins nouns or noun phrases to make a sentence seem like an equation: Her endless curiosity **plus** her boundless energy makes her the perfect camp counselor. Note that a singular form of the verb is required (i.e., *makes*). *Plus* is not used to join clauses: I telephoned ~~plus~~ and I sent flowers.

p.m. (P.M., P.M.) See **a.m., p.m.**

practicable, practical *Practicable* means "able to be put into practice": His plan was too complicated to be **practicable.** *Practical* means "sensible" or "useful": He read a self-help book for some **practical** advice on giving speeches.

precede, proceed To *precede* is to "go ahead of": A moment of silence **preceded** the applause. To *proceed* is to "go forward": After stopping for a short rest, we **proceeded** to our destination.

prejudice, prejudiced *Prejudice* is a noun: They were unaware of their **prejudice.** *Prejudiced* is an adjective: She accused me of being **prejudiced.**

pretty *Pretty* is used to mean "attractive" but not to mean "rather" or "somewhat": We were ~~**pretty**~~ rather tired after the trek to the summit.

* **previous to, prior to** Traditionally, these words were considered pretentious: ~~**Prior to**~~ Before our meeting, please study the reports. Dictionary editors now regard them as acceptable.

principal, principle As a noun, *principal* means "chief official": The **principal** greeted the students every day. It also means "capital": The loan's **principal** was still quite high. As an adjective, *principal* means "main": Tourism is the country's **principal** source of income. The noun *principle* refers to a rule, standard, or belief: She explained the three **principles** supporting the theory.

prior to See **previous to, prior to.**

proceed See **precede, proceed.**

prospective See **perspective.**

quotation, quote In academic writing, *quotation,* rather than *quote,* refers to a repeated or copied sentence or passage: She began her speech with a ~~**quote**~~ quotation from *Othello. Quote* expresses an action: My friend sometimes **quotes** lines from television commercials.

raise, rise *Raise* (*raised, raising*) means "to lift or cause to move upward, to bring up or increase": Retailers **raised** prices. *Rise* (*rose, risen, rising*) means "to get up" or "to ascend": The cost of living **rose** sharply. *Raise* takes an object (*raise* [something]); *rise* does not.

rarely ever Conversational; omit *ever:* He **rarely** ~~**ever**~~ goes to the library.

real, really *Really* rather than *real* is used to mean "very": He is from a ~~**real**~~ really small town. To ensure this word's effectiveness, use it sparingly.

reason is because See **is because, is when, is where.**

* **reason why** Traditionally, this combination was considered redundant: No one explained **the reason ~~why~~** the negotiations failed. [OR No one explained ~~**the reason why**~~ the negotiations failed.] However, dictionary editors report its use by highly regarded writers.

regard, regarding, regards These forms are used in the following expressions: *in regard to, with regard to, as regards,* and *regarding* [NOT *in regards to, with regards to,* or *as regarding*].

* **relation, relationship** According to traditional definitions, *relation* is used to link abstractions: We studied the **relation** between language and social change. *Relationship* is used to link people: The **relationship** between the two friends grew strong. However, dictionary editors now label as standard the use of *relationship* to connect abstractions.

respectfully, respectively *Respectfully* means "showing respect": The children learned to treat one another **respectfully.** *Respectively* means "in the order designated": We discussed the issue with the chair, the dean, and the provost, **respectively.**

rise See **raise, rise.**

sensor See **censor, censure, sensor.**

sensual, sensuous *Sensual* refers to gratification of the physical senses, often those associated with sexual pleasure: Frequently found in this music are **sensual** dance rhythms. *Sensuous* refers to gratification of the senses in response to art, music, nature, and so on: **Sensuous** landscape paintings lined the walls of the gallery.

shall, will Traditionally, *shall* was used with *I* or *we* to express future tense, and *will* was used with the other personal pronouns, but *shall* has almost disappeared in contemporary American English. *Shall* is still used in legal writing to indicate an obligation.

should of See **of.**

sight See **cite, site, sight.**

sit, set *Sit* means "to be seated": Jonathon **sat** in the front row. *Set* means "to place something": The research assistant **set** the chemicals on the counter. *Set* takes an object (*set* [something]). *Sit* does not.

site See **cite, site, sight.**

so *So* intensifies another word when it is used with *that:* They were **so** lonely **that** they planned a trip home. Instead of using *so* alone, find a precise modifier: She was ~~so~~ intensely focused on her career.

some Conversational when used to mean "remarkable" or "memorable": She was ~~some~~ a remarkable athlete.

someplace See **anyplace, everyplace, someplace.**

sometime, sometimes, some time *Sometime* means "at an unspecified time": They will meet **sometime** next month. *Sometimes* means "at times": **Sometimes** laws are unfair. *Some time* means "a span of time": They agreed to allow **some time** to pass before voting on the measure.

sort See **kind, sort, type.**

sort of a See **kind of a, sort of a.**

specially See **especially, specially.**

stationary, stationery *Stationary* means "in a fixed position": Traffic was **stationary** for an hour. *Stationery* means "writing paper and envelopes": The director ordered new department **stationery.**

subsequently See **consequently, subsequently.**

supposed to, used to Be sure to include the frequently unsounded *d* at the end of the verb form: We are **supposed** to leave at 9:30 A.M. We **used** to leave earlier.

sure Conversational when used to mean "certainly" or "undoubtedly": That play was **sure** certainly amusing.

sure and Conversational; use *sure to* instead: Be **sure and** to have the oil checked.

take See **bring, take.**

than, then *Than* is used in comparisons: The tape recorder is smaller **than** the radio. *Then* refers to a time sequence: Go straight ahead for three blocks; **then** turn left.

* **that, which** *Which* occurs in nonessential (nonrestrictive) clauses: Myanmar, **which** borders Thailand, was formerly called Burma. Both *that* and *which* occur in essential (restrictive) clauses, although traditionally only *that* was considered acceptable: I am looking for an atlas **that** [OR **which**] includes demographic information. (For more information on essential and nonessential clauses, see **31d** and **31g**.)

* **that, which, who** In essential (restrictive) clauses, *who* and *that* refer to people. We want to hire someone **who** [OR **that**] has had experience programming. Traditionally, only *who* was used to refer to people. *That,* as well as *which,* refers to things: He proposed a design **that** [OR **which**] will take advantage of solar energy.

their, there, they're *Their* is the possessive form of *they:* They will give **their** presentation tomorrow. *There* refers to location: I lived **there** for six years. *There* is also used as an expletive (see **30a**): **There is no explanation for the phenomenon.** *They're* is a contraction of *they are:* **They're** leaving in the morning.

theirself, theirselves Unconventional; use *themselves.* The students finished the project by **theirself** themselves.

them Unconventional to mean "those" or "these": I need **them** those books for my research.

then See **than, then.**

these kind, these sort, these type, those kind See **kind, sort, type.**

they Unconventional to indicate possession: They built ~~they~~ their house near a forest.

this here, that there, these here, them there *Here* and *there* are unconventional in these combinations: **This ~~here~~** number should be moved to the next column in the table.

thru *Through* is preferred in academic and professional writing: We drove ~~thru~~ through the whole state of South Dakota in one day.

thusly Unconventional; use *thus, in this way,* or *as follows* instead: He accompanied his father on archeological digs and ~~thusly~~ discovered his interest in ancient cultures.

time period Readers are likely to consider this combination redundant; use one word or the other, but not both: During this **time period,** the economy was strong.

to, too, two *To* is used in the infinitive form of a verb: She wanted **to** become an actress. *To* is also used as a preposition, usually indicating direction: They walked **to** the memorial. *Too* means "also": I voted for her **too.** *Too* also means "excessively": They are **too** busy this year. *Two* is a number: She studied abroad for **two** years.

toward, towards Although both are acceptable, *toward* is preferred in American English.

track, tract *Track* may refer to a mark left by someone or something: Deer **tracks** covered the lawn. *Track* may also refer to a course of action: You are on the right **track.** In addition, *track* may refer to awareness: I lost **track** of the time. *Tract* refers to a large area: They sold a **tract** of land near the river. *Tract* also refers to a short article expressing a strong opinion: His **tract** on radical environmentalism was published in the local paper.

try and Conversational for *try to:* The staff will **try ~~and~~ to** finish the project by Friday.

type See **kind, sort, type.**

ultimately See **eventually, ultimately.**

uninterested See **disinterested, uninterested.**

* **unique** Traditionally, *unique* meant "one of a kind" and thus was not preceded by a qualifier such as *more, most, quite,* or *very:* Her prose style is ~~quite~~ **unique.** However, dictionary editors note that *unique* is also widely used to mean "extraordinary."

usage, use *Use* is generally preferred to *usage* in nontechnical contexts: He designed the furniture for practical **usage** use.

use, utilize In most contexts, *use* is preferred to *utilize:* We **utilized** used a special dye in the experiment. However, *utilize* may suggest an effort to employ something for a purpose: We discussed how to **utilize** the new equipment we had been given.

used to See **supposed to, used to.**

very To ensure this word's effectiveness, use it sparingly. Whenever possible, choose a stronger adjective or adverb: She was **very satisfied** delighted with her new digital camera.

wait for, wait on *Wait for* means "to await": She refused to **wait on** for him. *Wait on* means "to serve": I **waited on** customers for seven years.

waive, wave *Waive* means "to give up": He **waived** his right to speak to an attorney. *Waive* also means "to refrain from enforcing": We **waived** the requirement because of her high recommendations. *Wave* means "to use a hand gesture to signal a person:" The police officer **waved** us on.

ways Conversational when referring to distance; use *way* instead: It's a long **ways** way from home.

weather, whether *Weather* refers to meteorological conditions: According to the **weather** report, it is going to snow today. *Whether* introduces alternatives: We should decide **whether** to respond.

well See **good, well.**

where Conversational for *that:* I saw on TV **where** that she had been elected.

where ... at, where ... to Conversational; omit *at* and *to:* **Where** is the library **at? Where** are you moving **to?**

whether See **if, whether.** See also **weather, whether.**

which See **that, which.** See also **that, which, who.**

who See **that, which, who.**

* **who, whom** *Who* is used as the subject or subject complement in a clause: We have decided to hire Marian Wright, **whom** who I believe is currently finishing her degree in business administration. [*Who* is the subject in *who is currently finishing her degree in business administration.*] *Whom* is used as an object: Jeff Kruger, **who** whom we hired in 2001, is now our top sales representative. [*Whom* is the object in *whom we hired.*] Dictionary editors note that in conversation *who* is commonly used as an object as long as it does not follow a preposition. See **21c.**

whose, who's *Whose* indicates possession: **Whose** book is this? The book was written by a young Mexican-American woman **whose** family still lives in Chiapas. *Who's* is the contraction of *who is:* **Who's** going to run in the election?

will See **shall, will.**

-wise College teachers may object to the use of this ending to create new words: *computerwise, businesswise.*

with regards to Unconventional; see **regard, regarding, regards.**

would of See **of.**

your, you're *Your* is the possessive of *you:* Let's meet in **your** office. *You're* is a contraction of *you are:* **You're** gaining strength.

yourself See **herself, himself, myself, yourself.**

GLOSSARY OF TERMS

This glossary provides brief definitions of frequently used terms. Consult the index for references to terms not listed here.

@ The "at" sign, used in email addresses to link the user name and the Internet location: <swebb@twu.edu>.

absolute phrase A sentencelike structure containing a subject and its modifiers (usually participial phrases or prepositional phrases). Unlike a sentence, an absolute phrase has no verb marked for person, number, or tense: *The ceremony finally over,* the graduates tossed their mortarboards in the air. See **17a(6)**, **27b(4)**, and **31e(4)**.

abstract A summary of the main points of a piece of writing, usually placed at the very beginning of the work. See **11d**.

abstract word A word that expresses a quality, concept, or emotion that cannot be perceived through the senses: *truth, justice, joy, future.* See **29a(3)**. COMPARE **concrete word.**

acronym A word formed by combining the initial letters or syllables of a series of words and pronounced as a word rather than as a series of letters: *OPEC* for *O*rganization of *P*etroleum *E*xporting *C*ountries. See **33a(1)**, **37a(10)**, and **39e**.

active voice See **voice.**

adjectival clause A dependent clause, sometimes called a *relative clause,* that modifies a noun or a pronoun. An adjectival clause may be essential (restrictive) or nonessential (nonrestrictive). See **17b(2)**, **20e**, and **31d**.

adjectival phrase A phrase that modifies a noun or pronoun. See **16c(3)** and **17a**.

adjective A word that modifies a noun or a pronoun. Adjectives typically end in suffixes such as *-al, -able, -ant, -ative, -ic, -ish, -less, -ous,* and *-y.* See **20a** and **20c**. Coordinate adjectives are two or more adjectives modifying the same noun and separated by a comma: a *brisk, cold* walk. See **31c(2)**.

adverb A word that modifies a verb, an adjective, an adverb, or a verbal. Adverbs commonly end in *-ly.* Some adverbs modify entire sentences: *Perhaps* the meeting could be postponed. See **20b–c**.

adverbial clause A dependent clause that modifies a verb, an adjective, or an adverb. See **17b(2)**, **27b(1)**, and **31b**.

adverbial particle A word such as *across, away, down, for, in, off, out, up,* or *with* that combines with a main verb to form a phrasal verb: *write down, look up.* See **22a(3)**.

adverbial phrase Phrase used as an adverb, usually indicating time, place, cause, or purpose. See **17a** and **24a**.

agreement The correspondence in number and person of a subject and a verb (see **22e**) or the correspondence in number and gender of a pronoun and its antecedent (see **21d**).

analogy Reference to something familiar (and often concrete) to explain something unfamiliar (and often abstract), or a direct comparison of certain features of two things that are in most ways dissimilar. See **2e(5)**.

analysis A separation of a whole into its parts. For example, a literary work may be separated into such elements as setting, plot, and character. See **2e(4)** and **13d**.

angle brackets Symbols (< >) used to indicate that an email address or a URL is to be understood as a single unit, without any internal spaces.

antecedent A word or group of words referred to by a pronoun. See **21d–e**.

APA Abbreviation for *American Psychological Association.* See **11c–d**.

appeal The means of persuasion in argumentative writing, relying on reason, authority, or emotion. See **7f**.

appositive A noun or noun phrase that identifies, describes, or explains an adjacent pronoun, noun, or noun phrase. Appositives may be essential (restrictive) or nonessential (nonrestrictive). See **16c(4)**, **17a(5)**, **24a**, **27b(4)**, **27c(3)**, and **31d**.

argument A kind of writing that uses various rhetorical strategies and appeals to convince the reader of the truth or falsity of an assertion or thesis. See chapter **7**.

article A word used to signal a noun. *The* is a definite article; *a* and *an* are indefinite articles. See **23e**.

asynchronous communication Online communication in which a period of time elapses between the sending and the receiving of a message. Internet newsgroups and electronic mailing lists are examples of asynchronous discussion groups. See **5c**. COMPARE **synchronous communication.**

attributive tag Short phrases that identify the source of a quotation: *according to Jones, Jones claims.* See **19d**.

auxiliary verb, auxiliary A verb that combines with a main verb. *Be, do,* and *have* are auxiliary verbs when they are used with main verbs. Also called *helping verbs.* Modal auxiliaries include *could, should,* and *may* and are used for such purposes as expressing doubt, obligation, and permission. See **17a(2)** and **22a**.

backing According to the Toulmin model, the support offered for a warrant. See 7h(3).

balanced sentence A sentence in which similar elements express contrasting or similar ideas. See 26g.

bibliography A list of books, articles, essays, or other sources, usually on a particular subject.

bookmark To save on a browser the address of a Web site. The saved addresses appear on a pulldown menu.

Boolean operators Words used to broaden or narrow electronic database searches. These include *or, and, not,* and *near.* Also called *logical operators.* See 8d(3).

brainstorming Generating ideas about a writing topic by listing ideas as they come to mind. See 2a(1).

browser Software that finds and displays Web pages. Most browsers can display images as well as text.

bulletin board An electronic message center where users with common interests post and read messages.

case The form of a noun or pronoun that indicates the relationship of the noun or pronoun to other words in a sentence. Pronouns can be subjects or subject complements (*subjective case*), objects (*objective case*), or markers of possession and other relations (*possessive case*). See 21b.

cause or consequence A relationship between results (*consequences*) and the reasons for them (*causes*). See 2e(4).

chat rooms Locations on the Internet where people can have online conversations.

chronological order The arrangement of events in the order of their occurrence. See 2e(1) and 3c(3).

citation Notation of a source used in a paper. See chapter 11.

claim A statement that a writer wants readers to accept. Also called a *proposition.* See 7d and 7h.

classification The placement of something into a category. Often used with division. See 2e(6).

clause A sequence of related words forming an independent unit (*independent clause*) or an embedded unit (*dependent clause* used as an adverb, adjective, or noun). A clause has both a subject and a predicate. See 17b and chapter 24.

cliché An expression that has lost its power to interest readers because of overuse. See **29b**.

clipped form A word that is a shortened form of another word: *bike* for *bicycle*. See **39d(2)**.

clustering A way to explore a writing topic by grouping related ideas and using circles and lines to indicate their relationships. See **2a(1)**.

CMS Abbreviation for *The Chicago Manual of Style*. See **11e**.

coherence The principle that ideas in a paragraph or an essay should be clearly connected, one sentence leading to the next, each idea evolving from the previous one. See **3c(3)**.

collaborative writing A method of writing involving the cooperative effort of two or more writers.

collective noun A noun that refers to a group: *team, faculty, committee*. See **22e(7)**.

colloquial A label for any word or phrase that is characteristic of informal speech. *Tummy* and *belly* are colloquial words; *stomach* is used in formal contexts. See **28c(2)** and **28e(1)**.

comma fault See **comma splice**.

comma splice A punctuation error in which two independent clauses are joined by a comma only. Sometimes called a *comma fault*. See chapter **19**.

common noun A noun referring to any or all members of a class or group (*woman, city, holiday*) rather than to specific members (*Susan, Reno, New Year's Day*). COMPARE **proper noun**. See **37e(1)**.

comparative degree See **degree of comparison**.

comparison Examination of similarities. See **2e(5)**.

complement A word or words used to complete the meaning of a verb. A *subject complement* is a word or phrase that follows a linking verb and renames or describes the subject. An *object complement* is a word or phrase that renames or describes a direct object when it follows such verbs as *make, paint, elect*, and *consider*. See **16c** and **20a**.

complete predicate See **predicate**.

complete subject See **subject**.

complex sentence A sentence containing one independent clause and at least one dependent clause. See **17c(3)**, **24a–b**, and **27c(1)**.

compound-complex sentence A sentence containing at least two independent clauses and one or more dependent clauses. See **17c(4)**.

compound predicate Predicate that has two parts joined by a connecting word such as *and, or,* or *but: Clara Barton nursed the injured during the Civil War* and *later founded the American Red Cross.* See 16a and 27c(2).

compound sentence A sentence containing at least two independent clauses and no dependent clauses. See 17c(2), 31a, and 32a.

compound subject Subject that has two parts joined by a connecting word such as *and, or,* or *but: Students and faculty* are discussing the issue of grade inflation. See 16a and 22e.

compound word Two or more words functioning as a single word: *ice cream, double-check.* See 36f.

concession Agreement with an opponent on certain points of an argument. See 7e(2) and 7g(3).

concrete word A word referring to what is experienced through the senses: *cologne, sunset, onions, thorns.* See 29a(3). COMPARE **abstract word.**

conditional clause An adverbial clause, usually beginning with *if,* that expresses a condition: *If it rains,* the outdoor concert will be postponed.

conjugation A set or table of verb forms that indicate tense, person, number, voice, and mood. See chapter 22.

conjunction A word used to connect other words, phrases, clauses, or sentences. Coordinating conjunctions (*and, but, or, nor, for, so,* and *yet*) connect and relate words and word groups of equal grammatical rank. When a coordinating conjunction links clauses, it appears at the beginning of the second clause. See 17b(3), 24a–b, and 31a. A subordinating conjunction such as *although, if,* and *when* begins a dependent clause and connects it to an independent clause. See 17b(3) and 24a–b. COMPARE **conjunctive adverb.**

conjunctive adverb A word such as *however, therefore,* and *nevertheless* that connects one independent clause to another. See 17b(3), 19c, and 32a. COMPARE **conjunction.**

connotation The suggested or implied meaning of a word, usually described as positive or negative. See 29a(2). COMPARE **denotation.**

consequence See **cause.**

consonant A speech sound such as /b/ or /f/ produced by a partial or complete obstruction of the air stream by the speech organs; also, a letter of the alphabet corresponding to a consonant sound. See 23e and 36d. COMPARE **vowel.**

context The circumstances surrounding the composition of a piece of writing: time, place, writer, audience, and medium. See 1b and 1e. Also, the surrounding information that helps give a particular word, sentence, or paragraph its meaning; for example, *cabinet* means "a group of leaders" in a paragraph about politics and "a place for storage" in a paragraph about kitchens. See **1d.**

contraction A word formed by combining two words and adding an apostrophe to replace the omitted letter or letters: *aren't, don't.* Contractions are used primarily in spoken or informal written language. See **33b.**

contrast Examination of differences. See **2e(5).**

controlling idea See **main idea.**

convention, conventional Language or behavior that follows the customs of a community such as the academic, medical, or business community.

coordinate adjective See **adjective.**

coordinating conjunction See **conjunction.**

coordination The use of grammatically equivalent constructions to link or balance ideas. See **24b(2).**

correlative conjunctions, correlatives Two-part connecting words such as *either . . . or* and *not only . . . but also.* See **17b(3)** and **25d.**

COS Abbreviation for *The Columbia Guide to Online Style.* See **11i.**

count nouns Nouns naming things that can be counted (*word, student, remark*). See **17a(1).** COMPARE **noncount nouns.**

credibility Believability. To be trusted, writers must appear credible to their audiences. See **1b–c, 7f,** and **9a–b.**

critical reading The ability to distinguish between fact and opinion, to recognize the importance of evidence and logic, to evaluate for credibility, and to avoid common fallacies. See chapters **1** and **7.**

CSE/CBE Abbreviation for *Council of Science Editors/Council of Biology Editors.* See **11g.**

cumulative sentence A sentence in which the subject and predicate come first, followed by modifiers: *She slept soundly, undisturbed by the noise of the party next door.* See **26b.** COMPARE **periodic sentence.**

dangling modifier A word or phrase that does not clearly modify another word or word group in the sentence. See **20f.** COMPARE **misplaced modifier.**

dangling participial phrase A verbal phrase that does not clearly modify another word or word group in the sentence. See **20f.**

database An organized collection of related information, usually in electronic form. A full-text database contains the complete, or nearly complete, text of articles. An abstract database contains summaries of articles. A bibliographic database contains limited information such as the subjects, titles, and authors of articles. See **8d**.

deductive reasoning A form of logical reasoning in which a conclusion is formed after relating a specific fact (minor premise) to a generalization (major premise). See **3c(1)**, **7h(2)**, and **12b**. COMPARE **inductive reasoning.**

degree of comparison The relative quality, quantity, or manner indicated by the form of an adjective or adverb: positive (*fast*), comparative (*faster*), or superlative (*fastest*). See **20c**.

demonstratives Four words (*this, that, these, those*) that distinguish one individual, thing, event, or idea from another. Demonstratives may occur with or without nouns: *This* [demonstrative determiner] *law* will go into effect in two years. *This* [demonstrative pronoun] will go into effect in two years.

denotation The direct or literal meaning of a word. See **29a(1)**. COMPARE **connotation.**

dependent clause See **clause.**

determiner A word that signals the approach of a noun. A determiner may be an article, a demonstrative, or a quantifier: *a reason, this reason, three reasons.* Sometimes possessives (*my, your, his, her, its, our,* and *their*) are called determiners.

development The elaboration of an idea through organized discussion supported by examples, details, and other information. See **2d**.

dialect A variety of language characteristic of a region, ethnic background, or social class. Dialects are distinguished by vocabulary, pronunciation, and syntax. See **28c**.

dial-up access The use of a modem and a telephone line to connect a computer to a network.

diction A writer's or speaker's choice of words. See chapters **28–30**.

direct address See **vocative.**

direct object See **object.**

direct quotation See **quotation.**

discussion list See **electronic mailing list.**

division Breaking a topic down into its constituent parts and showing the relationships among the parts. See **2e(6)**.

documentation The provision of sources cited in a research paper according to a given style, such as MLA or APA. See chapter **11**.

domain name Part of an Internet address that follows the host name, after a period: *cwu.edu.* The Internet is organized into seven domains: commerce (**.com**), education (**.edu**), government (**.gov**), military (**.mil**), network management (**.net**), nonprofit organizations (**.org**), and the designations for other countries (**.de** for Germany, **.uk** for the United Kingdom, and so on).

double-entry notebook A journal in which each entry has two distinct parts: summary and response. See **1d(3)**.

double negative The use of two negative words in one sentence. See **20g**.

download Transferring files from the Internet to a computer and saving them.

draft, drafting A working version of a piece of writing. The process of putting ideas into writing so that they can be revised and edited. See **1a** and chapter **2**.

editing Reviewing a draft to improve the clarity, effectiveness, and variety of sentences. See **1a** and **3f**.

electronic index An electronic database used to find the titles and authors of articles. Some electronic indexes include abstracts and full texts as well. See **8d(3)**.

electronic mailing list A list of subscribers who discuss or share information about a specific subject by sending email messages that are automatically distributed to the email addresses of all the other subscribers. Also referred to as a *Listserv,* a *discussion list,* or an *email list.* See **5c(1)**.

ellipsis points Three spaced periods that indicate either a pause or material omitted from a direct quotation. See **35h**.

elliptical clause A clause missing one or more words that are assumed to be understood. See **17b(2)** and **20f**.

elliptical construction The omission of an element essential to the grammar but not to the intended meaning: *Repairs will be made whenever (they are) necessary.* See **30d**.

emoticon A small icon that is made up of punctuation characters and shows how a sender wants part or all of an email message to be interpreted. For example, the emoticon :-) indicates a joke; it looks like a smiling face turned sideways.

emphasis Special weight or importance given to a word, sentence, or paragraph by any of a variety of techniques. See chapter **26**.

emphatic order Arranging information according to order of importance. See **3c(3)**.

empirical evidence Facts that can be tested or measured. See **12b**.

enthymeme A syllogism with an unstated premise or conclusion. See **7h(2).**

essential element A word or word group that modifies another word or word group, providing information that is essential for identification. Essential elements are not set off by commas, parentheses, or dashes: The woman *who witnessed the accident* was called to testify. Also called a *restrictive element.* COMPARE **nonessential element.**

ethos One of the three classical appeals; the demonstration of the writer's trustworthy character, good intentions, and substantial knowledge of a subject. Also called an *ethical appeal.* See **7f(1).** See also **logos** and **pathos.**

etymology The origin and historical development of a word. See **28e(4).**

euphemism An indirect, polite expression used instead of a direct one that the writer or speaker thinks may be offensive to someone. See **29b.**

evaluation Placement of value or rank on a specific claim or on an entire piece of writing. See chapter **9** and **13d.**

evidence Information supporting a generalization. Common types of evidence are facts, statistics, examples, testimony, sensory details, and logical inferences.

exigence The circumstance compelling one to write. See **1b** and **1e(4).**

expletive A word signaling a structural change in a sentence, usually used so that new or important information is given at the end of the sentence: *There were over four thousand runners in the marathon.* See **16c(1)** and **22e(4).**

expository writing Writing with the purpose of clarifying, explaining, or evaluating a subject in order to inform or instruct the reader. See **1e(1)** and **10a.**

expressive writing Writing that emphasizes the writer's own feelings and reactions to a topic. See **1e(1).**

fallacy A false argument based on faulty reasoning. See **7i.**

faulty predication A sentence error in which the predicate does not logically belong with the given subject. See **23d** and **29e.**

figurative language The use of words in an imaginative rather than in a literal sense. See **29a(4).**

figures of speech Use of language that describes things in novel ways or makes unexpected comparisons. Sometimes called *figurative language.* Metaphor, irony, and hyperbole are common figures of speech. See **29a(4).**

file A stored collection of electronic documents.

first person See **person.**

flaming Heated, confrontational exchanges via email. See **5c(1).**

focus The portion of a larger subject that will receive the writer's concentrated attention. See **2a**.

forum See **newsgroup**.

fragment A group of words that begins with a capital letter and ends with a period but that lacks a subject, a predicate, or both. See chapter **18**.

freeware Software available free of charge, usually by downloading it from the Internet; however, the user should be aware of the potential for downloading files infected with a computer virus.

freewriting A method of finding a writing topic by composing for a specified length of time without stopping to reflect, reread, or correct. See **2a(1)**.

ftp Abbreviation for *file transfer protocol*. The guidelines that establish the format in which files can be transmitted from computer to computer. See **11a(3)**.

fused sentence Two or more sentences run together, without the punctuation required to identify them as separate sentences. Also called a *run-on sentence*. See chapter **19**.

gender The grammatical label that distinguishes nouns or pronouns as masculine, feminine, or neuter. In English, grammatical gender usually corresponds to natural gender. *Gender* also describes how people see themselves, or are seen by others, as either male or female. See **21d** and **28d**.

generalization In argument, a conclusion drawn from facts, other evidence, or both. *Overgeneralization* refers to any statement that is too broad, indefinite, or sweeping in scope. See **7h**.

genre A literary category identified by its own conventions. Drama and poetry are common genres. See **13a**.

gerund A verbal that ends in *-ing* and functions as a noun: *Snowboarding* is a popular winter sport. See **17a(3)**, **21c(6)**, and **33a(6)**.

gerund phrase A verbal phrase that employs the *-ing* form of a verb and functions as a noun: Some students prefer *studying in the library.* See **17a(3)**.

grammar A system of rules for describing how words and sentences are structured.

helping verb See **auxiliary verb**.

home page The introductory page for a Web site.

homophones Words that have the same sound and sometimes the same spelling but differ in meaning: *their, there,* and *they're* or *capital* meaning "funds" and *capital* meaning "the top of a pillar." See **36c**.

hot link See **hyperlink**.

HTML Abbreviation for *HyperText Markup Language,* the system of codes that enables Web browsers to display Web pages.

hyperlink Embedded in a document and usually highlighted by color and underlining, a hyperlink is a Web address that allows users to move between Web pages or sites. Also called *hot link* or *link.* See chapter **5** and **8c**.

hypertext Text, encoded in HTML, that allows users to move to various parts of a Web document or to other Web documents. See chapter **5**.

hypothesis A tentative assumption that is tested in an experiment. See **12b** and **14a**.

idiom A language-specific expression whose meaning often cannot be derived from its elements. *Burning the midnight oil* means "staying up late studying." See **29c**.

imperative mood See **mood.**

inclusive language Language that includes all people and does not insult or ignore anyone based on age, ability, race, religion, class, gender, or sexual orientation. See **28d**.

indefinite article See **article.**

indefinite pronouns Pronouns such as *everyone* and *anything* that do not refer to specific individuals, objects, events, and so on. See **21d(1)** and **22e(6)**.

independent clause See **clause.**

indicative mood See **mood.**

indirect object See **object.**

indirect question A sentence that includes an embedded question, punctuated with a period instead of a question mark: My friends asked me *why I left the party early.* See **35b**.

indirect quotation See **quotation.**

inductive reasoning The reasoning process that begins with facts or observations and moves to general principles that account for those facts or observations. See **3c(1)**, **7h**, and **12b**. COMPARE **deductive reasoning.**

infinitive A verbal that consists of the base form of the verb, usually preceded by the infinitive marker *to.* An infinitive is used chiefly as a noun, less frequently as an adjective or adverb: My father likes *to golf.* See **17a(3)**.

infinitive phrase A verbal phrase that contains the infinitive form of a verb: They volunteered *to work at the local hospital.* See **17(a)3**.

inflection A change in the form of a word that indicates a grammatical feature such as number, person, tense, or degree. For example, *-ed* added to a verb indicates the past tense, and -er indicates the comparative degree of adjectives and adverbs.

intensifier See **qualifier.**

intensive pronoun See **reflexive pronoun.**

interjection A word expressing a simple exclamation: *Hey! Oops!* When used in sentences, mild interjections are set off by commas: *Oh,* excuse me. See **31e(3)** and **35c.**

Internet An international network of computers linked through telephone and fiber-optic lines. The Internet provides access to email and the World Wide Web, among other things. See **8c.**

interpretation Explanation of meaning or significance. See **13c–d.**

intransitive verb A verb that does not take an object: Everyone *laughed.* See **16d** and **22c.** COMPARE **transitive verb.**

invention Using strategies to generate ideas for writing. See **2a** and **2e.**

inversion A change in the usual subject-verb order of a sentence: *Are you* ready? See **26f.**

IRC Abbreviation for *Internet relay chat.* See **chat rooms.**

irony A deliberate inconsistency between what is stated and what is meant. See **34c.**

irregular verb A verb that does not take -ed to form both the past tense and the past participle. See **22a(2).** COMPARE **regular verb.**

ISP Abbreviation for *Internet service provider,* a service that connects subscribers to the Internet.

jargon Technical language appropriate as a shortcut to communication, used when an audience is knowledgeable about the topic and the terms. See **28c.**

journal A notebook in which a writer records personal responses, thoughts, and experiences. See **1d(3)** and **2a(1).** Also, a special-interest periodical (such as *Rhetoric Review* or *Environmental Legislation*). See **8d(3)** and **11a(3).**

keywords Specific words used with a search tool (such as Google) to find information on a research topic. See **8c.**

library research report A report that integrates a large number of sources on a specific topic. Each source is summarized and critiqued. See **14b.**

link See **hyperlink.**

linking verb A verb that relates a subject to a subject complement. Examples of linking verbs are *be, become, seem, appear, feel, look, taste, smell,* and *sound.* See **16c(3)**, **21b(1)**, and **22c**.

Listserv See **electronic mailing list**.

literary theory A scholarly explanation of the assumptions and values influencing the interpretation of a literary work. See **13c**.

literature review A report on current knowledge about a topic, including a critique of this knowledge and suggestions for additional research. See **14c**.

logical operators See **Boolean operators**.

logos One of the three classical appeals; the use of language to show clear reasoning. Also called a *logical appeal.* See **7f(1)**. See also **ethos** and **pathos**.

main clause Also called *independent clause.* See **clause**.

main idea The most important idea in a paragraph or an essay; all other ideas relate to it. See **2b** and **3c**. See also **topic sentence** and **thesis**.

mechanics Language conventions, other than punctuation, that ensure clarity of meaning; guidelines for using capital letters, abbreviations, numbers, italics, and so on. See chapters **37–39**.

microtheme A short response to an open-ended question that demonstrates an understanding of scientific principles. See **14c**.

misplaced modifier A descriptive or qualifying word or phrase placed in a position that confuses the reader: I read about a wildfire that was out of control *in yesterday's paper.* [The modifier belongs before *I* or after *read.*] See **20e**.

mixed construction A confusing sentence that is the result of an unintentional shift from one grammatical pattern to another: When police appeared who were supposed to calm the crowds showed up, most people had already gone home. [The sentence should be written with either *appeared* or *showed up,* not with both.] See **23c**.

mixed metaphor A construction that includes parts of two or more metaphors: Her *fiery* personality *dampened* our hopes of a compromise. See **23c**.

MLA Abbreviation for *Modern Language Association.* See **11a–b**.

modal auxiliary See **auxiliary verb**.

modifier A word or word group that describes, limits, or qualifies another. See chapter **20** and **21e(2)**.

MOO Acronym for *Multi-user dimension, Object-Oriented;* a text-based online space where many people can communicate simultaneously. See **5c(2)**.

mood A set of verb forms or inflections used to indicate how a speaker or writer regards an assertion: as a fact (*indicative mood*); as a command or instruction (*imperative mood*); or as a wish, hypothesis, recommendation, or condition contrary to fact (*subjunctive mood*). See **22d**.

MUD Acronym for *Multi-User Dimension;* a text-based online forum in which participants interact in real time. See **5c(2)**. See also **synchronous communication.**

netiquette Word formed from *Internet* and *etiquette* to name a set of guidelines for writing email messages and Listserv postings and for online behavior in general. See **5c(3)**.

newsgroup An online discussion group that is accessible to anyone and allows users to post messages about a specific topic. Also called a *forum.* See **5c(1)**.

nominalization Formation of a noun by adding a suffix to a verb or an adjective: *require, requirement; sad, sadness.*

nominative case Also called *subjective case.* See **case.**

noncount nouns Nouns naming things that cannot be counted (*architecture, water*). See **17a(1)**. COMPARE **count nouns.**

nonessential element A word or word group that modifies another word or word group but does not provide essential information for identification. Nonessential elements are set off by commas, parentheses, or dashes: Carol Murphy, *president of the university,* plans to meet with alumni representatives. Also called *nonrestrictive element.* See **31d**. COMPARE **essential element.**

nonrestrictive element See **nonessential element.**

nonstandard, nonstandardized Speech forms that are not considered conventional in many academic and professional settings. See **28e**.

noun A word that names a person, place, thing, idea, animal, quality, event, and so on: *Alanis, America, desk, justice, dog, strength, departure.* Plural nouns usually end in *-s* or *-es.* Singular possessive nouns usually end in *-'s;* plural possessive nouns usually end in *-s'.* See also **common noun, proper noun, count noun, noncount noun,** and **collective noun.**

noun clause A dependent clause used as a noun. See **17b(2)**.

noun phrase A noun and its modifiers. See **16b**.

number The property of a word that indicates whether it refers to one (*singular*) or to more than one (*plural*). Number is reflected in the word's form: *river/rivers, this/those, he sees/they see.* See **21d, 22b,** and **22e**.

object A noun, pronoun, noun phrase, or noun clause that follows a preposition or a transitive verb or verbal. A direct object names the person or thing that receives the action of the verb: I sent the *package*. An indirect object usually indicates to whom the action was directed or for whom the action was performed: I sent *you* the package. See **16c(2)**. The object of a preposition follows a preposition: I sent the package to *you*. See **17a(4)**.

object complement See **complement.**

object of a preposition See **object.**

objective case Also called *accusative case*. See **case.**

online Connected to or having access to the Internet.

online catalog A computerized database that includes information on all the holdings of a particular library. See **8d(1)**.

overgeneralization See **generalization.**

parallelism The repetition of a grammatical element or structure. See chapter **25**.

paraphrase A restatement of another writer's ideas in words that differ from those in the original passage. A paraphrase is about the same length as the original passage. See **10d(3)**.

parenthetical citation Source information placed between parentheses. See chapter **11**.

parenthetical element Any word, phrase, or clause that adds detail to a sentence or any sentence that adds detail to a paragraph but is not essential for understanding the core meaning. Commas, dashes, or parentheses separate these elements from the rest of the sentence or paragraph. See **31e**, **31g(3)**, and **35e–f.**

participial phrase A verbal phrase that includes a participle: The stagehand *carrying the trunk* fell over the threshold. See **17a(3)** and **20f**. See also **participle** and **phrase.**

participle A verb form that may function as part of a verb phrase (was *thinking*, had *determined*) or as a modifier (a *determined* effort; the couple, *thinking* about their past). A present participle is formed by adding *-ing* to the base form of a verb. A past participle is usually formed by adding *-ed* to the base form of a verb (*walked, passed*); however, many verbs have irregular past-participle forms (*written, bought, gone*). See **17a(3)**, **21c(6)**, and **22a.**

particle See **adverbial particle.**

parts of speech The classes into which words may be grouped according to their forms and grammatical relationships. The traditional parts of speech are verbs, nouns, pronouns, adjectives, adverbs, prepositions, conjunctions, and interjections.

passive voice See **voice.**

password A personal code that allows a user to access an Internet service account, an informational Web site, a special-topic forum, and so on. Passwords are intended to provide security against unauthorized access.

past participle See **participle.**

pathos One of the three classical appeals; the use of language to stir the feelings of an audience. Also called an *emotional appeal* or a *pathetic appeal.* See **7f(1).** See also **ethos** and **logos.**

pentad A set of five dramatic aspects used to explore a subject: the act, the actor, the scene, the agency, and the purpose. See **2a(1).**

perfect tenses See **tense.**

periodic sentence A sentence beginning with modifiers and ending with an independent clause: Hot, tired, yet optimistic as they neared the end of the day, the archeologists continued looking for evidence of an ancient house site. See **26b.** COMPARE **cumulative sentence.**

person The property of nouns, pronouns, and their corresponding verbs that distinguishes the speaker or writer (first person), the individuals addressed (second person), and the individuals or things referred to (third person). See **21a(1), 22b,** and **22e.**

personal pronoun A pronoun that refers to a specific person, place, thing, and so on. Pronoun forms correspond to three cases: subjective, objective, and possessive. See **21a(1).**

phrasal verb A grammatical unit consisting of a verb and an adverbial particle such as *after, in, up, off,* or *out: fill in, sort out.* See **22a(3).**

phrase A sequence of grammatically related words that functions as a unit in a sentence but lacks a subject, a predicate, or both: *in front of the stage.* See **17a.**

plagiarism The use of another writer's words or ideas without acknowledging the source. See **10e.**

plural See **number.**

point of view The vantage point from which a topic is viewed; also, the stance a writer takes: objective or impartial (third person), directive (second person), or personal (first person).

positive See **degree of comparison.**

possessive case See **case.**

predicate The part of a sentence that expresses what a subject is, does, or experiences. The complete predicate consists of the main verb, its auxiliaries, and any complements and modifiers. The simple predicate consists of only the main verb and any accompanying auxiliaries. See **16a–b**. COMPARE **subject.**

predication Stating or expressing something about the subject. See **16a** and **23d.**

prefix A small meaningful unit, usually consisting of a syllable or two, added to the beginning of a word to form a new one. Common prefixes include *re-,* meaning "again" (*review*), *pre-,* meaning "before" (*preview*), and *un-,* meaning "not" *(unbelievable).* See **36d.**

premise An assumption or a proposition on which an argument or explanation is based. In logic, premises are either major (general) or minor (specific); when combined correctly, they lead to a conclusion. See **7h.** See also **syllogism.**

preposition A word such as *at, in, by,* or *of* that relates a pronoun, noun, noun phrase, or noun clause to other words in the sentence. See **17a(4).**

prepositional phrase A preposition with its object and any modifiers: *at* the nearby airport, *by* the sea. See **17a(4).**

present participle See **participle.**

preview To skim a piece of writing for the main ideas. See **1a** and **1c.**

prewriting The initial stage of the writing process, concerned primarily with finding good topics and focusing ideas. See **1a** and **2a.**

primary source A source that provides firsthand information. See **8a.** COMPARE **secondary source.**

pronoun A word that takes the position of a noun, a noun phrase, or a noun clause and functions as that word or word group does: *it, that, he, them, mine.* See chapter **21.**

proofreading Checking the final draft of a paper to eliminate typographic, spelling, punctuation, and documentation errors. See **3g.**

proper adjective An adjective that is derived from the name of a person or place: *Marxist* theories. See **37a.**

proper noun The name of a specific person, place, organization, and so on: *Dr. Pimomo, Fargo, National Education Association.* Proper nouns are capitalized. See **37a.** COMPARE **common noun.**

proposition See **claim.**

purpose A writer's reason for writing. See **1b** and **1e.**

qualifier A word that intensifies or moderates the meaning of an adverb or adjective: *quite* pleased, *somewhat* reluctant. Words that intensify are sometimes called *intensifiers*.

qualitative data Evidence based on observations, interviews, and similar methods of data collection. See **12b**.

quantitative data Evidence that is reportable in numerical form. See **12b**.

quotation A *direct quotation* is the exact repetition of someone's spoken or written words. Also called *direct discourse*. An *indirect quotation* is a report of someone's written or spoken words not stated in the exact words of the writer or speaker. See **10d**, **34a**, and **37d**.

reciprocal pronoun One of two compound pronouns—*each other* or *one another*—expressing an interchangeable or mutual action or relationship: The two roommates helped *each other* complete the assignment. The members disagreed with *one another*.

redundancy Needless repetition. See **30a(1)**.

reflexive pronoun A pronoun that ends in *-self* or *-selves* (*myself* or *themselves*) and refers to a preceding noun or pronoun in the sentence: He added a picture of *himself* to his Web page. When used to provide emphasis, such a pronoun is called an *intensive pronoun:* The president *herself* awarded the scholarships.

refutation A strategy for addressing opposing points of view by discussing those views and explaining why they are unsatisfactory. See **7e(2)** and **7g(3)**.

regular verb A verb whose past tense and past participle are formed in the same way: by adding *-ed*, or sometimes *-d* or *-t*, to the base form. See **22a(1)**.

relative clause See **adjectival clause**.

relative pronoun A noun substitute (*who, whom, that, which,* or *whose*) used to introduce an adjectival clause, sometimes called a *relative clause*. See **17b(2)** and **21a(2)**.

restrictive element See **essential element**.

revision Changes made to an early draft that improve its focus, content, or organization. See **1a** and **3a–e**.

rhetoric The art of using language effectively, which involves the writer's purpose, the audience, the discovery and exploration of a subject, the arrangement and organization of ideas, the style and tone in which they are expressed, and the form in which they are delivered. See chapters **1**, **2**, and **7**.

rhetorical methods Strategies for developing and organizing ideas within a paragraph or an essay. See **2e**.

rhetorical situation The relationship among the writer, the audience, the text, and the context. See **1b** and **1d–e**.

Rogerian argument An approach to argumentation that is based on the work of psychologist Carl R. Rogers and that emphasizes the importance of withholding judgment of others' ideas until they are fully understood. See **7f(2)**.

run-on sentence See **fused sentence**.

scientific method A method used by scientists to collect and evaluate data. It includes observation, prediction, experimentation, and analysis. See chapter **14**.

search engine A Web-based program or Web site that enables users to search the Internet for documents. Sometimes called a *search tool.* See **8c**.

search tool See **search engine**.

secondary source A source that analyzes or interprets firsthand information. See **8a**. COMPARE **primary source**.

sentence fragment See **fragment**.

sentence modifier A modifier related to a whole sentence, not to a specific word or word group within it: *All things considered,* the committee acted appropriately when it approved the amendment to the bylaws.

sexist language Language that arbitrarily excludes one sex or that arbitrarily assigns stereotypical roles to one sex. See **28d(1)**. COMPARE **inclusive language**.

simple tenses See **tense**.

singular See **number**.

slang The casual vocabulary of specific groups or cultures, usually considered inappropriate for academic and professional writing but occasionally effective if the writer carefully considers purpose and audience. See **28c**.

slash The mark (/) used to separate lines of poetry or parts of an Internet address. See **35i**.

spatial order The ordering of details according to how they are encountered as the observer's eye moves vertically, horizontally, from far to near, and so forth. See **3c(3)**.

split infinitive The separation of the two parts of an infinitive form by at least one word: *to completely cover.* See **17a(3)**.

Standardized English The style of writing expected in most academic and business settings.

style An author's choice and arrangement of words, sentence structures, and ideas. See chapters **23–30.**

subject The general area addressed in a piece of writing. See **2a.** COMPARE **topic.** Also, the pronoun, noun, or noun phrase that carries out the action or assumes the state described in the predicate of a sentence. Usually preceding the predicate, the complete subject includes the main noun or pronoun and all determiners and modifiers. A simple subject consists of only the main noun or pronoun. See **16a.** COMPARE **predicate.**

subject complement See **complement.**

subjective case See **case.**

subjunctive mood See **mood.**

subordinating conjunction See **conjunction.**

subordination The connection of a structure, usually a dependent clause, to an independent clause: *Even though customers were satisfied with the product,* the company wanted to improve it. See chapter **24.**

suffix A small meaningful unit, usually consisting of a single syllable, added to the end of a word either to form a new word or to indicate a grammatical property such as number or degree: talk*s,* talk*ed,* fast*er,* fast*est.* See **36d.**

superlative See **degree of comparison.**

syllabus A concise summary of the main points of a course. See **1f(1).**

syllogism Method for deductive reasoning consisting of two premises and a conclusion. See **7h(2).** See also **premise.**

symbol A word or phrase that refers to an object, which in turn represents a concept or other abstraction. See **13b(6).**

synchronous communication Online communication in which messages are exchanged in real time; that is, the receiver of the message sees it on the computer screen right after the sender completes it. Internet chat rooms and MUDs are examples of synchronous discussion groups. See **5c.** COMPARE **asynchronous communication.**

synonym A word that has a meaning similar to that of another word; *daybreak* is a synonym for *dawn.* See **28f.**

syntax Sentence structure; the grammatical arrangement of words, phrases, and clauses.

synthesis Collecting and connecting information on a topic; usually involves summary, analysis, and interpretation.

tag question A question attached to the end of a related statement and set off by a comma: She came back, *didn't she?*

tense The form of a verb that indicates when and for how long an action or state occurs. Generally, simple tenses are used to report past, future, and habitual present actions (*I wrote, I will write, I write everyday*). Progressive tenses indicate uncompleted actions (*I was writing, I will be writing, I am writing*). Perfect tenses indicate actions performed prior to another time (*I had written, I will have written, I have written*). See 22b.

theme The main idea of a literary work. See 13b(1) and 13b(7).

thesis The central point or main idea of an essay. See 2b.

tone The writer's attitude toward the subject and the audience, usually conveyed through word choice and sentence structure. See 3a(3), 3b, and 13b(3).

topic The specific, narrowed main idea of an essay. See 2a. COMPARE **subject.**

topic sentence A statement of the main idea of a paragraph. See 3c(1).

Toulmin model A system of argumentation developed by philosopher Stephen Toulmin in which *argument* is defined as a logical progression, from data (evidence or reasons) to a claim (a debatable statement), based on a warrant (the underlying assumption connecting the two). See 7h(3).

transitions Words, phrases, sentences, or paragraphs that relate ideas by linking sentences, paragraphs, or larger segments of writing. See 3d.

transitive verb A verb that takes an object. The researchers *reported* their findings. See 16d and 22c. COMPARE **intransitive verb.**

truth In deductive reasoning, premises thought to be accurate, correct, realistic, and so on. See 7h(2). COMPARE **validity.**

Uniform Resource Locator See **URL.**

unity A quality of writing in which all the elements contribute to the development of a single idea or thesis. A paragraph is unified when each sentence contributes to the development of a central thought. See 3c(2) and chapter 23.

URL Abbreviation for *Uniform Resource Locator,* which identifies an Internet address, including the domain name and often a specific file to be accessed. For example, the URL for the Harbrace Web site includes the indicator that it is on the World Wide Web (http://www), the domain name (harbrace), and the domain (<u>com</u>), all separated by periods: <u>http://www.harbrace.com</u>. A slash precedes a subpage in the URL for a Web site. For example, <u>http://owl.english.purdue.edu/lab/index.html</u> indicates the subpage on which Purdue's Online Writing Lab posts an index of general information. See **8c.**

Usenet A worldwide online bulletin board system that contains thousands of newsgroups on a wide variety of topics.

user name The element of an email address that identifies a user to an Internet service provider.

validity In deductive reasoning, the accurate relationship between premises and a conclusion. See **7h(2).** COMPARE **truth.**

verb A word denoting action, occurrence, or existence (state of being). See **16b** and chapter **22.**

verb phrase A main verb and any auxiliaries. See **17a(2)** and **22a(4).**

verbal A verb form functioning as a noun, an adjective, or an adverb. See **17a(3).** See also **gerund, infinitive,** and **participle.**

vocative Set off by commas, the name of or the descriptive term for the person or persons being addressed. See **16c(4)** and **31e(3).**

voice A property of a verb that indicates the relationship between the verb and its subject. The *active voice* is used to show that the subject performs the action expressed by the verb; the *passive voice* is used to show that the subject receives the action. See **22c** and **26d.**

vowel A speech sound such as /o/ produced with little obstruction of the air stream by the speech organs. A vowel is represented in writing by the letters *a, e, i, o, u,* and sometimes *y.* See **23e** and **36d.** COMPARE **consonant.**

warrant According to the Toulmin model, the underlying assumption connecting a claim and data. See **7h(3).**

Web page See **World Wide Web.**

Web site See **World Wide Web.**

word order The arrangement of words in sentences.

World Wide Web (WWW) A system of Internet servers that store documents formatted in a special computer language (HTML). These documents are called *Web pages,* and a location containing several such pages is called a *Web site.* See chapters **5** and **6.**

writing process The various activities that writers perform: planning, drafting, revising, editing, and proofreading. See **1a** and chapters **2–3.**

Credits

English as a World Language Index

Entries in this index identify topics of interest to multilingual readers and writers. Numbers and letters in color refer to chapters and sections in the handbook; other numbers refer to pages.

Index

Numbers and letters in color refer to chapters and sections in the handbook; other numbers refer to pages.

(cont.)

(*con.*

(cont.)